THE MAGIC YEARS

Selma H. Fraiberg

THE MAGIC YEARS

**UNDERSTANDING AND HANDLING
THE PROBLEMS OF EARLY CHILDHOOD**

New York

CHARLES SCRIBNER'S SONS

Selections from the following sections were first published in *Parents' Magazine:* "The Missionaries Arrive" (under the title "Taming the Toddler,") "Travel and Perspectives" (under the title "Don't Cage That Crawler") and "Laughing Tiger." © copyright 1958, 1959 by Selma H. Fraiberg.

TO

My Husband and My Daughter

CONTENTS

PREFACE

THE magic years are the years of early childhood. By "magic" I do not mean that the child lives in an enchanted world where all the deepest longings are satisfied. It is only in the minds of adults that childhood is a paradise, a time of innocence and serene joy. The memory of a Golden Age is a delusion for, ironically, none of us remembers this time at all. At best we carry with us a few dusty memories, a handful of blurred and distorted pictures which often cannot even tell us why they should be remembered. This first period of childhood, roughly the first five years of life, is submerged like a buried city, and when we come back to these times with our children we are strangers and we cannot easily find our way.

These are "magic" years because the child in his early years is a magician—in the psychological sense. His earliest conception of the world is a magical one; he believes that his actions and his thoughts can bring about events. Later he extends this magic system and finds human attributes in natural phenomena and sees human or supra-human causes for natural events or for ordinary occurrences in his life. Gradually during these first years the child acquires knowledge of an objective world and is able to free his observations and his conclusions from the distortions of primitive thought.

But a magic world is an unstable world, at times a spooky world, and as the child gropes his way toward reason and an objective world he must wrestle with the dangerous creatures of his imagination and the real and imagined dangers of the outer world, and periodically we are confronted with his inexplicable fears or baffling behavior. Many of the problems presented by the child in these early years are, quite simply, disorders created by a primitive mental system that has not yet been subdued and put into its place by rational thought processes.

This book tells the story of personality development during the first five years of life and describes and discusses some of the typical problems that emerge with each developmental stage. I have tried to make this a practical book and for illustration have drawn extensively from the questions and problems that parents of normal children have brought to me over a period of years. But, as every parent knows, there are no short answers to the riddles posed by children even in the pre-school years. There are no household hints, directions before using, or universal antidotes to be prescribed in the rearing of a child. It is the quality of our understanding, often the intuitive understanding of a parent who is in intimate rapport with his child, that provides us with the right method at critical moments. But the inner life of a very young child is often inaccessible to us. Because we cannot remember this time of life, we cannot easily enter his world and adult intuition and imagination often fail before the problems presented by the pre-school child.

So it seemed to me that for a book of this sort to be really practical it must do more than describe typical problems and suggest methods of handling. It must also give insight into the mental life of the pre-school child and derive principles of child-rearing from the facts of development as well as the expectations of our culture. For these reasons, I chose to organize this book around developmental stages and to relate problems and methods specifically to a developmental period. It was convenient to divide early childhood into three periods, the first period covering the first eighteen months, the second covering the period eighteen months to three years, and the third covering the ages three to six. The book treats each period as a separate section with an introductory chapter or two describing personality development, followed by one or more chapters dealing with practical problems of child-rearing.

If we understand the process of child development, we see that each developmental phase brings with it characteristic problems. The parents' methods of helping the child must take into account the child's own development and his mental equipment at any given stage. This means that there is very little point in speaking categorically about "childhood anxieties" or "discipline problems in childhood." The anxieties of the two year old are not the same as the anxieties of the five year old. Even if the same crocodile hides under the bed of one small boy between the ages of two and five, the crocodile of the two year old is not the same beast as the crocodile of the five year old—from the psychological point of view. He's had a chance to grow with the boy and is a lot more complex after three years under the bed than he was the day he first moved in. Furthermore, what you do about the crocodile when the boy is two is not the same as what you do about him when the boy is five. The two year old doesn't talk very well, yet. And the two year old creates other difficulties for us because he is thoroughly convinced that there *is* a crocodile under the bed. The five year old, on the other hand, can discuss the crocodile problem and has the further advantage that he doesn't really believe the crocodile is there. Therefore, a practical book for parents needs to approach the crocodile problem from the point of view of the two year old and again from the point of view of the five year old.

Similarly in the case of "discipline" we do different things in teaching self-control to the two year old and to the five year old. And if we want our discipline to be effective, we need to know what a two year old is like, what possibilities he has for control of impulse, and what a five year old is like and what equipment he has for cooperating with our discipline. It's useful to know, then, that a five year old has, or should have, the beginnings of a conscience and real possibility for self-control and that our discipline can make use of this conscience for teaching.

It is just as useful to know that the two year old does not yet have internal controls and that our discipline must take into consideration a still inadequate control system yet must also build toward conscience. Obviously, then, the methods we employ in discipline of the two year old will be different from those used with the five year old. So we see again that we cannot speak of "discipline" without relating principles and methods to the developmental stage.

The suggestion for this book came from Helen Steers Burgess, who manages the extraordinary feat of keeping both ears to the ground in the fields of parent education and clinical child research, and who is editorial adviser to Scribners in these areas. As editor and parent educator, she had the impression that the clinical researchers were making large advances in understanding the psychology of the infant and the young child, that much of the psychoanalytic research and thinking in the area of ego development had enormous implications for child-rearing, but very little of this material was easily accessible to parents. She thought that parents might be interested in a book in which some of the problems of child-rearing were examined in the light of current thinking and research. This was the beginning of a most congenial collaboration between editor and author, and the book that emerged was the product of many editorial sessions and many more revisions than either of us can remember. If this book has succeeded in being a practical book for parents, much of the credit must go to Mrs. Burgess.

Although the responsibility for the ideas in this book is my own, I should like to record here my debt to certain scholars in the field. The writings of Anna Freud on ego psychology and her studies in early child development have illuminated the world of childhood for workers in the most varied professions and have been for me my introduction and most valuable guide to the "magic" years. The work of René Spitz in the psychology of infancy is in the foreground or background of large sections of this book, particularly in Chapters II, IV and IX. The writings of Heinz Hartmann and the late Ernst Kris in the field of psycho-analytic ego psychology have profoundly influenced my own thinking and I have extracted from their writings certain ideas that seemed to have practical value in child-rearing. Jean Piaget's investigations into the child's construction of reality provided part of the background out of which I wrote the story of mental development in infancy. Yet it should be made clear that while these writers have influenced my own thinking and that of others in the field, I have not attempted to represent the theories of any one of them (unless explicitly stated in the text) and I have assumed responsibility for collating a number of studies on the same subject and choosing among disparate or uncongenial views in discussing a single topic.

My husband, Louis, has given expert help and advice through-out the preparation of this manuscript and, above all, lent his gift of clarity whenever I needed it, which seemed to be very often. This book owes much to the final authority of his pencil and to his generous and enthusiastic support of this project from the beginning. My mother, Dora Horwitz, has given valuable as-sistance to me throughout the writing of this book and undertook the labor of deciphering and typing large parts of the original manuscript. I am grateful to her and to Florence Jordan for painstaking work in transcription and for many good suggestions that came from their first reading of this material.

SELMA H. FRAIBERG

PART I

Introduction

1. All About Witches, Ogres, Tigers, and Mental Health

A FABLE

There once was a boy named Frankie who was going to be the very model of a modern, scientifically reared child. His mother and his father consulted the writings of experts, subscribed to lecture series and educated themselves in all the rites and practices of child rearing sacred to these times. They knew how children develop fears and neurotic symptoms in early childhood and with the best intentions in the world they set out to rear a child who would be free—oh, as free as any child can be in this world of ours—of anxiety and neurotic tendencies.

So Frankie was breast-fed and weaned and toilet-trained at the proper ages and in the proper manner. A baby sister was provided for him at a period in his development best calculated to avoid trauma. It goes without saying that he was prepared for the new baby by approved techniques. His sex education was candid and thorough.

The probable sources of fear were located and systematically decontaminated in the program devised by Frankie's parents. Nursery rhymes and fairy tales were edited and revised; mice and their tails were never parted and ogres dined on Cheerios instead of human flesh. Witches and evil-doers practiced harmless forms of sorcery and were easily reformed by a light sentence or a mild rebuke. No one died in the fairy-tale world and no one died in Frankie's world. When Frankie's parakeet was stricken by a fatal disease, the corpse was removed and a successor installed before Frankie awakened from his afternoon nap. With all

*these precautions Frankie's parents found it difficult to explain
why Frankie should have any fears. But he did.*

*At the age of two when many children are afraid of disappear-
ing down the bath-tub drain, Frankie (quite independently and
without the influence of wayward companions) developed a fear
of going down the bath-tub drain.*

*In spite of all the careful preparations for the new baby, he
was not enthusiastic about her arrival and occupied himself with
the most unfilial plots for her disposal. Among the more humane
proposals he offered was that the baby should be taken back to
the dime store. (And you know how thorough his sex education
had been!)*

*And that wasn't all. At an age when other children waken from
bad dreams, Frankie also wakened from bad dreams. Incompre-
hensibly (for you know how ogres were reformed in Frankie's
nursery) Frankie was pursued in his bad dreams by a giant who
would eat him up!*

*And that wasn't all. In spite of the merciful treatment ac-
corded to witches in Frankie's education, Frankie disposed of
evil-doers in his own way when he made up stories. He got rid
of witches in his stories by having their heads chopped off.*

What is the point of this modern fable? What does it prove?
Doesn't it matter how we rear a child? Are the shibboleths of
modern child rearing a delusion of the scientist? Should we
abandon our beliefs about feeding, toilet-training, sex education
as matters of no consequence in promoting mental health?

Parental wisdom and understanding in the conduct of feeding,
toilet-training, sex education, discipline, serve the child's mental
health by promoting his love and confidence in his parents and
by strengthening his own equipment in regulating his body needs
and impulses. But the most ideal early training does not eliminate
all anxiety or remove the hazards that exist everywhere in the
child's world and in the very process of development itself.

We should not be shocked—for there is no way in which children can be reared without experiencing anxiety. Each stage in human development has its own hazards, its own dangers. We will find, further, that we do not always serve the child's mental health by vigilantly policing his environment for bogies, ogres and dead parakeets. We cannot avoid many of these fears. Nor do we need to. We do not, of course, deliberately expose a child to frightening experiences and we do not give substance to the idea of bogies by behaving like bogies ourselves, but when bogies, ogres and dead parakeets present themselves, it is usually best to deal with them in the open and to help the child deal with them on the same basis.

We are apt to confuse two things. Anxiety is not in itself a neurosis. Frankie, of our fable, is not to be regarded as neurotic —not on the basis of this evidence. Is he afraid of the bath-tub drain? Many two year olds share this fear. It is not necessarily an ominous sign. Has he bad dreams about a giant? Nearly all pre-school children have anxiety dreams of this type occasionally. Doesn't he like his baby sister in spite of the expert preparation? Preparation for a new baby is essential and makes things easier, but no amount of preliminary explanation can adequately prepare a child for that *real* baby and the *real* experience of sharing parental love.

It is not the bath-tub drain, the dream about the giant or the unpropitious arrival of a sibling that creates a neurosis. The future mental health of the child does not depend upon the presence or absence of ogres in his fantasy life, or on such fine points as the diets of ogres—perhaps not even on the number and frequency of appearance of ogres. *It depends upon the child's solution of the ogre problem.*

It is the way in which the child manages his irrational fears that determines their effect upon his personality development. If a fear of bogies and burglars and wild animals invades a child's life, if a child feels helpless and defenseless before his imagined dangers and develops an attitude of fearful submission to life as a result, then the solution is not a good one and some effects upon his future mental health can be anticipated. If a child behaves as if he were threatened by real and imaginary dangers on all sides and must be on guard and ready for attack, then his personality may be marked by traits of over-aggressiveness and defiance, and we must regard his solution as a poor one, too. But normally the child overcomes his irrational fears. And here is the most fascinating question of all: How does he do it? For the child is equipped with the means for overcoming his fears. Even in the second year he possesses a marvellously complex mental system which provides the means for anticipating danger, assessing danger, defending against danger and overcoming danger. Whether this equipment can be successfully employed by the child in overcoming his fears will depend, of course, on the parents who, in a sense, teach him to use his equipment. This means that if we understand the nature of the developing child and those parts of his personality that work for solution and resolution toward mental health, we are in the best position to assist him in developing his inner resources for dealing with fears.

WHAT IS MENTAL HEALTH?

IN RECENT years we have come to look upon mental health as if it were nothing more than the product of a special dietary regime, one that should include the proper proportions of love and security, constructive toys, wholesome companions, candid sex instruction, emotional outlets and controls, all put together in a balanced and healthful menu. Inevitably, this picture of a well-balanced mental diet evokes another picture, of the boiled vegetable plate from the dietician's kitchen, which nourishes but does not stimulate the appetite. The product of such a mental diet could just as easily grow up to be a well-adjusted bore.

Therefore, it seems proper in this discussion of mental health to restore the word "mental" to an honored position, to put the "mental" back into "mental health." For those qualities that distinguish one personality from another are mental qualities, and the condition which we speak of as mental health is not just the product of a nourishing mental diet—however important this may be—but the work of a complex mental system acting upon experience, reacting to experience, adapting, storing, integrating, in a continuous effort to maintain a balance between inner needs and outer demands.

Mental health depends upon an equilibrium between body needs, drives, and the demands of the outer world, but this equilibrium must not be conceived as a static one. The process of regulating drives, appetites, wishes, purely egocentric desires in accordance with social demands, takes place in the higher centers of the mind. It is that part of the personality that stands in closest relationship to consciousness and to reality which performs this vital function. It is the conscious ego that takes over these regulating and mediating functions, and it does this work for all of the waking hours of a human life.

We should not err by regarding personal satisfaction, "happiness," as the criterion for mental health. Mental health must be judged not only by the relative harmony that prevails within the human ego, but by the requirements of a civilized people for the attainment of the highest social values. If a child is "free of neurotic symptoms" but values his freedom from fear so highly that he will never in his lifetime risk himself for an idea or a principle, then this mental health does not serve human welfare. If he is "secure" but never aspires to anything but personal security, then this security cannot be valued in itself. If he is "well adjusted to the group" but secures his adjustment through uncritical acceptance of and compliance with the ideas of others, then this adjustment does not serve a democratic society. If he "adjusts well in school" but furnishes his mind with commonplace ideas and facts and nourishes this mind with the cheap fantasies of comic books, then what civilization can value the "adjustment" of this child?

The highest order of mental health must include the freedom of a man to employ his intelligence for the solution of human problems, his own and those of his society. This freedom of the intellect requires that the higher mental processes of reason and judgment should be removed as far as possible from magic, self-gratification and egocentric motives. The education of a child toward mental health must include training of the intellect. A child's emotional well-being is as much dependent upon the fullest use of his intellectual capacity as upon the satisfaction of basic body needs.

The highest order of mental health must include a solid and integrated value system, an organization within the personality that is both conscience and ideal self, with roots so deeply imbedded in the structure of personality that it cannot be violated or corrupted. We cannot speak of mental health in a personality where such an ethical system does not exist. If we employ such loose criteria as "personal satisfaction" or "adjustment to the group" for evaluating mental health, a delinquent may conceivably achieve the highest degree of personal satisfaction in the pursuit of his own objectives, and his adjustment to the group— the delinquent group—is as nicely worked out as you could imagine.

Theoretically, then, mental health depends upon the maintenance of a balance within the personality between the basic human urges and egocentric wishes on the one hand and the demands of conscience and society on the other hand. Under ordinary circumstances we are not aware of these two forces within our personality. But in times of conflict an impulse or a wish arises which conflicts with the standards of conscience or which for other reasons cannot be gratified in reality. In such instances we are aware of conflict and the ego takes over the role of judge or mediator between these two opposing forces. A healthy ego behaves like a reasonable and fair-minded judge and works to find solutions that satisfy both parties to the dispute. It allows direct satisfaction when this does not conflict with conscience or social requirements and flexibly permits indirect satisfactions when judgment rules otherwise. If a man finds himself with aggressive feelings toward a tyrannical boss, feelings which cannot be expressed directly without serious consequences, the ego, if it is a healthy ego, can employ the energy of the forbidden impulses for constructive actions which ultimately can lead to solution. At the very least it can offer the solace of day-dreams in which the boss is effectively put in his place. A less healthy ego, failing at mediation, helpless in the face of such conflict, may abandon its position and allow the conflict to find neurotic solutions.

A neurosis is a poor solution to conflict, or, more correctly, not a solution at all but a bad compromise. Underground, the conflict persists in a disguised form and, since the real conflict is not resolved, a neurosis perpetuates itself in a series of attempted compromises—neurotic symptoms. On the surface a neurosis resembles a cold war between two nations where strong demands are made by both sides and temporary compromises are achieved in order to avoid war. But since the basic issues are never dealt with, fresh grievances and demands are constantly in the making and more and more compromises and bad bargains are required to keep the conflict from breaking out into the open. The analogy of a cold war suggests another parallel. If each of the nations in conflict must be constantly prepared for the possibility of open warfare, it must expend larger and larger amounts of its wealth for defense purposes, leaving less and less of the national income for investment in other vital areas of national welfare. Eventually, so much of the national income and the energy of its people is tied up in defense that very little of either is available for the pursuit of healthy human goals. Here, a neurosis affords an exact parallel. For a neurosis engages a large amount of the energy of a human personality in order to prevent the outbreak of conflict. Energy which should be employed for the vital interests of the personality and the expansion of the personality must be diverted in large quantities for defense purposes. The result is impoverishment of the ego, a serious restriction of human functioning.

Whenever the underground conflict within the personality threatens to break out in the open, anxiety is created by the anticipation of danger. Anxiety then sets the whole process of neurotic defense and compromise into action once again, in the self-perpetuating process we have described. It would be correct to say that anxiety generates the neurotic process, but we must not deduce from this that anxiety is in itself a pathological manifestation. Anxiety need not produce a neurosis. In fact, anxiety may serve the widest variety of useful and healthy adaptations in the human personality.

WHAT IS ANXIETY?

In normal human development, dangers, real or imaginary, present themselves in various forms. If the ego did not acquire the means to deal with danger it would be reduced to chronic helplessness and panic. The instinctive reaction to danger is anxiety. In the beginning of life the infant behaves as if any unexpected event were a danger. We say he is "shocked" by a sudden loud noise, or sudden exposure to strong light. Later, when his attachment to his mother increases, he reacts to her disappearance from sight with anxiety, something still close to a shock reaction. There are large numbers of such circumstances that produce anxiety in an infant. Yet if the infant continued to react to all such events with terror and helplessness, he could scarcely survive in our world.

But soon we discover that the number of such "dangers" diminishes. Ordinary repetition of these experiences helps the infant overcome the sense of danger, and the "shock" reaction diminishes to something that is often not much more than a slight startle, or surprise. Meanwhile another means is developing within him for meeting "danger." (I use quotes because these are dangers to him, though not to us as adults.) He learns to *antici-pate* "danger" and prepare for it. And he prepares for "danger" by means *of anxiety!* His mother leaves him at nap-time or bed-time. In an earlier stage of development the infant reacted to her leaving with some manifestation of anxiety, an anxiety of surprise or shock following her disappearance. Now, at this later stage he produces a kind of anxiety, crying, protesting, when he ap-proaches his bed, or even his room. He anticipates the feared event and prepares for it by producing anxiety before the event takes place. This anticipatory anxiety is actually a help to him in managing the painful separation from his mother. We have some reason to believe that separation from his mother is less painful when he can anticipate it in this manner than it was in the earlier phase when each separation was like a surprise or shock. We think this is so because throughout all human development the effects of danger are less when the ego can prepare for it by pro-ducing anticipatory anxiety.

From this we immediately recognize that anxiety is not a pathological condition in itself but a necessary and normal physiological and mental preparation for danger. In fact, the *absence* of anticipatory anxiety may under certain circumstances invite neurosis! The man who succumbs to shock on the battle field is a man, who, for one reason or another, has not developed the necessary anticipatory anxiety which would have prepared him for danger and averted a traumatic neurosis. Anxiety is nec-essary for the survival of the individual under certain circum-stances. Failure to apprehend danger and to prepare for it may have disastrous results. We will find, further, that anxiety can serve the highest aims of man. The anxiety of performing artists before going on the stage may actually bring forth the highest abilities of the artist when the performance begins.

Anxiety serves social purposes. It is one of the motives in the acquisition of conscience. It is fear of disapproval from loved persons as well as the desire to be loved which brings about con-science in the child. It is fear of criticism from one's own conscience that brings about moral conduct. It was anxiety before danger of extinction which first bound human groups together for mutual security. We could go on endlessly with a catalogue of human inventions and human institutions to demonstrate how danger and the need to defend against danger provided the motive for the highest attainments of civilized man.

But we know that anxiety does not always serve useful ends for the individual or society. The inability to cope with danger may result in a sense of helplessness and inadequacy, in reactions of flight, in neurotic symptoms, or in anti-social behavior. Only in such cases can we speak of anxiety as pathological, but it would be more correct to say that the solution or attempted solution was a pathological one.

So we return to our aims in promoting the mental health of children. We need to understand the nature of the fears which appear in childhood and we need to examine the means by which children normally overcome the dangers, real and imaginary, which accompany each stage of development.

FIRST: A HUMAN PROTECTOR AGAINST DANGER.

LONG before the child develops his inner resources for overcoming dangers he is dependent upon his parents to satisfy his needs, to relieve him of tension, to anticipate danger and to remove the source of a disturbance. This is the situation of the infant. To the infant and very young child the parents are very powerful beings, magical creatures who divine secret wishes, satisfy the deepest longings, and perform miraculous feats.

We cannot remember this time of life, and if we try to recapture the feelings of earliest childhood we can only find something analogous in fairy tales. The genies who are summoned in fairy tales and bring forth tables heaped with delicacies, the fairies who grant the most extravagant wishes, the magic beasts who transport a child to far-off lands, the companion lion who overcomes all enemies, the kings and queens who command power over life, give us imaginative reconstructions of the small child's world.

We know that the infant and very small child need to feel that they can count on these powerful beings to relieve tension and alleviate fears. And we know that the child's later ability to tolerate tension and actively deal with anxiety situations will be determined in good part by the experiences of early years. During the period of infancy, of biological helplessness, we make very few demands upon the child and do everything possible to reduce tension and satisfy all needs. Gradually, as the child develops, he acquires means of his own to deal with increasingly complex situations. The parent gradually relinquishes his function as insulator and protector. But we know that even the most independent children will need to call upon the protection of parents at times of unusual stress. And the child, even when he can do without the protecting parent in times of ordinary stress, still carries within him the image of the strong and powerful parent to reassure himself. "If a burglar came into our house, my father would kill him dead." The protective function of the parent is so vital in early childhood that even children who are exposed to abnormal dangers may not develop acute anxiety if the parents are present. It is now well known that in war-time Britain the children who remained with their parents even during bombing attacks were able to tolerate anxiety better than the children who were separated from their parents and evacuated to protected zones.

But even the most loving and dedicated parents soon discover that in a child's world a good fairy is easily transformed into a witch, the friendly lion turns into a ferocious beast, the benevolent king becomes a monster and the paradise of early childhood is periodically invaded by dark and sinister creatures. These night creatures of the child's inner world are not so easily traced to real persons and real events in a child's life. While we are enormously flattered to recognize ourselves in a child's fantasy life as a good fairy, a genie, or a wise old king, we cannot help feeling indignant at the suggestion that we can also be represented as a witch, a bogey, or a monster. After all, we have never eaten or threatened to eat small boys and girls, we are not distillers of magic potions, we are not ferocious in anger, we do not order dreadful punishments for minor (or major) crimes. It is also true, to be fair about it, that we do not have magic wands, cannot be summoned from a bottle or a lamp to grant wishes, and do not wear a crown, but we are less inclined to argue about these distortions of parenthood.

How is it then that a beloved parent will be transformed, in the child's eyes, into a monster? If we look closely into the life of the small child we find that such transformations take place chiefly in those instances when we are compelled to interfere with the child's pleasure, when we interrupt a pleasurable activity or deny a wish, when we frustrate the child's wishes or appetites in some way. Then mother becomes the worstest, the baddest, the meanest mother in the world for the duration of a small child's rage. Now it is conceivable that if we never interfered with a child's pleasure seeking, granted all wishes, opposed nothing, we might never experience these negative reactions of the child, but the product of such child-rearing would not be a civilized child. We are required to interfere with the child's pleasure not only for practical reasons which are presented daily in the course of rearing a child—health, safety, the requirements of the family— but in order to bring about the evolution of a civilized man and woman. The child begins life as a pleasure-seeking animal; his infantile personality is organized around his own appetites and his own body. In the course of his rearing the goal of exclusive pleasure seeking must be modified drastically, the fundamental urges must be subject to the dictates of conscience and society, must be capable of postponement and in some instances of renunciation completely.

So there are no ways in which a child can avoid anxiety. If we banished all the witches and ogres from his bed-time stories and policed his daily life for every conceivable source of danger, he would still succeed in constructing his own imaginary monsters out of the conflicts of his young life. We do not need to be alarmed about the presence of fears in the small child's life if the child has the means to overcome them.

THE EGO DEFENDS AGAINST DANGER.

VERY early in life we can observe how each child reacts and adapts to experience in ways which are *specific for him.* We suspect that these tendencies are partly innate, for even our observations of new-born infants in a nursery will show how each infant will react in a specific and individual way to a sudden sound, or any strong stimulus, or to a frustration, like withdrawal of the nipple. But these tendencies are also capable of a high degree of modification as the child develops, as they come under the influence of environment and the higher and more complex mental processes.

So we will find that not only does each child react to danger in ways which are specific for him, but he will *defend* against danger, protect himself, in ways which are specific for him. Every human being is equipped mentally, as well as physiologically for defense against danger, for handling his own anxiety. The parent who understands his own child and his tendencies supports the positive tendencies in his child for meeting danger and overcoming his fears.

This means that as the child develops into a more complex person we cannot rely upon prescriptions and generalizations for helping him adapt, or in helping him overcome fears. We need to examine those healthy adaptive tendencies already at work within his personality and cooperate with them if we are to achieve our aims. All of this gives support to the parent who listens to professional advice or the advice of friends and says, "But that wouldn't work with my Susie!" It can very well be that a method or an approach which works with one child will have no effect upon another, if the method is not geared to the personality needs of the second child.

But now let's put aside theoretical considerations for the moment. Let's just look at a few very young children and see what we mean by "adaptive mechanisms" or "defenses" and how we can put them to work for us in early childhood training and personality development.

"LAUGHING TIGER."

LET ME introduce you to Laughing Tiger. I first met him myself when my niece Jannie was about two years eight months old. One afternoon as I entered the door of her grandparents' house, I found my niece just about to leave with her granduncle. Jan did not greet me; if anything, she looked a little annoyed at my entrance, like the actress who is interrupted during rehearsal by a clumsy stage-hand who blunders on stage. Still ignoring me, Jan pulled on white cotton gloves and clasped her patent purse in her hand in a fine imitation of a lady leaving for an afternoon engagement. Suddenly she turned and frowned at something behind her. "No!" she said firmly. "No, Laughing Tiger. You *cannot* come with us for an ice-cream cone. You stay right there. But Jannie can come with us. Come along Jannie!" And she stepped out the door with her uncle, swinging her purse grandly.

I thought I saw a shabby and wistful beast slink across the hall and disappear in the shadows. When I composed myself I found the child's grandmother and said, "*Who* is Laughing Tiger?" "He is the latest one," said grandmother. We understood each other. There had been a steady influx of imaginary companions in this household and an even greater number in the child's own. There were chairs which were sacred to Jane and Tommy, places reserved at the table for rabbits, dogs, and bears, and the very substantial and real child who directed this menagerie often did not answer to her own name. I noticed now that the child's grand-mother looked a little distraught, and I realized with sympathy that she must have had Laughing Tiger under foot for most of the afternoon.

"Why *Laughing* Tiger," I asked.

"He doesn't roar. He never scares children. He doesn't bite. He just laughs."

"Why couldn't he go for an ice-cream cone?"

"He has to learn to mind. He can't have everything his own way. . . . Anyway that's the way it was explained to me."

At dinner that evening my niece did not take notice of me until I was about to sit down. "Watch out!" she cried. I rose quickly, suspecting a tack. "You were sitting on Laughing Tiger!" she said sternly. "I'm sorry. Now will you please ask him to get out of my chair." "You can go now, Laughing Tiger," said Jan. And this docile and obedient beast got up from the table and left the company without a murmur.

Laughing Tiger remained with us for several months. As far as I was ever able to tell he led a solemn and uneventful life, with hardly anything to laugh about. He never demonstrated the ferocity of his species and gave no cause for alarm during his residence. He endured all the civilizing teachings of his mistress without rebelling or having a nervous breakdown. He obeyed all commands even when they were silly and contrary to his own interests. He was an irreproachable guest at the dinner table and a bulky but unobtrusive passenger in the family car. A few months after Jannie's third birthday he disap-peared, and nobody missed him.

Now the time has come to ask, "Who *was* Laughing Tiger?" If we go way back to the beginning we find that Laughing Tiger was the direct descendant of the savage and ferocious beasts who disturb the sleep of small children. It is not a coin-cidence that Laughing Tiger sprang into existence at a time when Jannie was very much afraid of animals who could bite and might even eat up a little girl. Even the more harmless dogs of the neighborhood occasionally scared her. At such times she must have felt very small and helpless before the imagined danger. Now if you are very little and helpless before dangers, imaginary or real, there are not too many solutions handy, good solutions anyway. You could, for example, stay close to mother or daddy at all times and let them protect you. Some children do go through such clinging periods and are afraid to leave a parent's side. But that's not a good solution. Or you could avoid going outside because of the danger of an encounter with a wild beast, or you could avoid going to sleep in order not to encounter dream animals. Any of these solutions are poor solutions because they are based on avoidance, and the child is not using his own resources to deal with his imaginary dangers. (Instead he is increasing his dependency upon his parents.)

Now there is one place where you can meet a ferocious beast on your own terms and leave victorious. That place is the imagination. It is a matter of individual taste and preference whether the beast should be slain, maimed, banished or reformed, but no one needs to feel helpless in the presence of imaginary beasts when the imagination offers such solutions.

Jan chose reform as her approach to the problem of ferocious animals. No one could suspect the terrible ancestry of Laughing Tiger once he set eyes on this bashful and cowardly beast. All of the dangerous attributes of tigers underwent a transformation in this new creation. Teeth? This tiger doesn't bare his teeth in a savage snarl; he laughs (hollowly, we think). Scare children? *He* is the one who is scared. Wild and uncontrolled? One word from his mistress and this hulk shrinks into his corner. Ferocious appetite? Well, if he exhibits good manners, he *may* have an ice-cream cone.

Now we suspect a parallel development here. The transformation of a tiger into an obedient and quiescent beast is probably a caricature of the civilizing process which the little girl is undergoing. The rewards and deprivations, the absurd demands which are made upon Laughing Tiger make as little sense to us as we view this comedy as the whims and wishes of the grown-up world make to a little girl. So we suspect that the reformed tiger is also a caricature of a little girl, and the original attributes of a tiger, its uncontrolled, impulsive and ferocious qualities represent those tendencies within the child which are undergoing a transformation. We notice, too, that Laughing Tiger's mistress is more severe and demanding than the persons who have undertaken the civilizing of the little girl Jan, and we confirm the psychological truth that the most zealous crusaders against vice are the reformed criminals; the strength of the original impulse is given over to the opposing wish.

But let's get back to imagination and its solutions for childhood problems. Jan's imaginary tiger gives her a kind of control over a danger which earlier had left her helpless and anxious. The little boy who stalks tigers and bears with his home-made Tommy-gun and his own sound effects, is coming to terms with the Tiger problem in his own way. (I have the impression that little boys are inclined to take direct action on the tiger problem, while the work of reforming tigers is left to the other sex which has long demonstrated its taste and talent for this approach.) Another very satisfactory approach to the tiger problem is to become a tiger. A very large number of small children have worked their way out of the most devilish encounters, outnumbered by ferocious animals on all sides, by disguising themselves as tigers and by out-roaring and out-threatening the enemy, causing consternation, disintegration and flight in his ranks.

Under ordinary circumstances, these practical experiences with invisible tigers, fought on home territory under the dining table, in the clothes closet, behind the couch, have a very good effect upon the mental health of children. Laughing Tiger was a very important factor in the eventual dissolution of Jan's animal fears. When he first made his appearance there was a noticeable improvement in this area. When he finally disappeared (and he was not replaced by any other animal), the fear of animals had largely subsided and it was evident that Jan no longer needed him. If we watch closely, we will see how the imaginary companions and enemies fade away at about the same time that the fear dissolves, which means that the child who has overcome his tigers in his play has learned to master his fear.

This is the general pattern in normal development. But now let's examine those conditions under which the fear does not disappear. As long as the danger is a fantasied danger, as long as the angry tiger keeps his place—in the zoo behind bars, in pretend games behind the couch—he can be dealt with as an imaginary tiger in imaginary games. Now, although it is most unlikely that a small boy or girl will ever encounter a real tiger under his bed, if he feels that someone whom he loves is a "dangerous" person and if he has some cause to fear this person, he will have much more difficulty in dealing with his fear, for this fear is at least partly real. The child who has cause to fear the real anger of a parent, especially in the extreme cases where a child has known rage, physical attack or violent threats from a parent—such a child cannot overcome his fears through imaginative play because his fears are real. In extreme cases, and especially in the case of delinquents, a world view is formed on the basis of these early real and unmastered dangers, a view in which the world is populated with dangerous persons against whom the child must constantly defend himself.

But these are extreme cases. They only serve to illustrate that whenever reality reinforces a child's fantasied dangers, the child will have more difficulty in overcoming them. This is why, on principle, we avoid any methods of handling a child which could reinforce his fantasies of danger. So, while parents may not regard a spanking as a physical attack or an assault on a child's body, the child may regard it as such, and experience it as a confirmation of his fears that grown-ups under certain circumstances can really hurt you. And sometimes, unavoidably, circumstances may confirm a child's internal fears. A tonsillectomy may be medically indicated. It can be disturbing to a small child because his fears of losing a part of his body are given some justification in this experience where something is removed from him. We cannot always avoid the situation in which a child's fears are confirmed in some way in reality but where it is within our control, as in the realm of everyday parent-child relationships and methods of handling, we try not to behave in such a way that a child need feel a real danger.

There are other conditions, too, under which childhood fears may not be overcome through the ordinary means at a child's disposal. Now it is one thing to *pretend* that you are a powerful being who can tame tigers and lions or scare them into submission, to *pretend* that the clothes closet is a jungle with wild beasts lurking within, to turn the nursery into a theater for the performance of this drama, and quite another thing to carry this drama within you, to make it part of your personality and to turn the world into a theater for the performance of this drama. Yet this can happen, too, and we need to take a look at this kind of development.

The child who tries to overcome his fear of tigers by becoming a tiger in his *play* is employing a perfectly healthy approach to the tiger problem. A child who stalks his parlor tigers with home-made weapons is conducting an honorable fight against his imaginary fears. But there are some children whose fears are so intense and so real to them that the sense of danger permeates all aspects of living, and the defense against danger becomes part of their personality equipment—and then we may have difficulties. Many problems of later childhood which we lump together under the heading "behavior disorder" can only be understood as elaborate defenses against imagined danger. The child who indiscriminately attacks other children in his neighborhood or in school feels impelled to attack by a fantasy in which he is in danger of attack and must attack first in self-defense. He will use the slightest gesture or harmlessly derogatory phrase used by another child to signify a hostile intention on the part of that child, and he will attack as if he were in great danger. He is so certain of the danger that if we talk to him about his attack afterward he will insist, with conviction, that the other guy was going to beat him up and he *had* to do it.

But what is this? This is not very far removed from the fantasy of our nursery tiger hunter who sees ferocious beasts in the clothes closet and under the couch and who must attack with his trusty Tommy-gun before the beast attacks him. But there is this important difference. Our nursery hunter keeps his tigers in their place. They don't roam the streets and imperil good citizens. They aren't real. Almost any two and a half year old will admit, if pressed, that there isn't really a tiger under the couch. And he very sensibly deals with his imaginary tigers by means of the imagination. It's a pretend fight with a pretend tiger. But our older child who attacks other children because of his fantasied fear of attack, has let his tigers get out of the parlor, so to speak. They have invaded his real world. They will cause much trouble there and they can't be brought under control as nicely as the parlor tigers can. When these "tough guys," the aggressive and belligerent youngsters, reveal themselves in clinical treatment we find the most fantastic fears as the motive force behind their behavior. When our therapy relieves them of these fears, the aggressive behavior subsides.

In the light of all this we can see that the imaginative play of children serves mental health by keeping the boundaries between fantasy and reality. If the rules of the game are adhered to, if the imaginary beasts are kept in their place and brought under control in the parlor, there is less likelihood that they will invade the real world.

There is great misunderstanding today about the place of fantasy in the small child's life. Imaginary companions have fallen into ill repute among many educators and parents. Jan's "Laughing Tiger" would be hastily exiled in many households. The notion has got around that imaginary companions are evidence of "insecurity," "withdrawal" and a latent neurosis. The imaginary companion is supposed to be a poor substitute for real companions and it is felt that the unfortunate child who possesses them should be strongly encouraged to abandon them in favor of real friends. Now, of course, if a child of any age abandons the real world and cannot form human ties, if a child is unable to establish meaningful relationships with persons and prefers his imaginary people, we have some cause for concern. But we must not confuse the neurotic uses of imagination with the healthy, and the child who employs his imagination and the people of his imagination to solve his problems is a child who is working for his own mental health. He can maintain his human ties and his good contact with reality while he maintains his imaginary world. Moreover, it can be demonstrated that the child's contact with the real world is *strengthened* by his periodic excursions into fantasy. It becomes easier to tolerate the frustrations of the real world and to accede to the demands of reality if one can restore himself at intervals in a world where the deepest wishes can achieve imaginary gratification.

But play is only one of the means by which the child attempts to overcome his fears. The child discovers, at a very early age, that his intelligence and his ability to acquire knowledge will also help him combat his fears. This brings us to another story and the illustration of another approach to the universal problems and fears of early childhood.

AN INFANT SCIENTIST.

MANY years ago I knew a small boy named Tony who showed an early preference for a particular means of overcoming fears. He did not care for imaginative play and he probably would have found no pleasure in hunting tigers or reforming them or drawing pictures of them. This was not his way. I do not recall that he was even particularly afraid of wild animals. His fears were more generalized. He was afraid of the strange, the unfamiliar, the unknown—common enough fears at all stages of development—and his approach was mainly an investigative one. If he could find out how something worked, if he could locate the causes for events, he felt himself in control and lost his fear.

At the age of two he showed no interest in conventional toys. His dearest toy was a pocket-sized screw driver which he carried with him everywhere. He displayed such dexterity with this screw driver that he succeeded in turning his home into a man-trap before he was able to talk. Unhinged cupboard doors collapsed upon touch or swung crazily from one out-of-reach hinge. Chairs and tables listed perilously or skated out from under while a lost caster or wheel rusted in the sand-pile.

Like many other children around the age of two, Tony was afraid of the vacuum cleaner and its deafening roar. Some children overcome their fear by learning to control the switch, to put themselves in command of the noise. Others, with a preference for play-acting, may transform themselves into vacuum cleaners and prowl around the floor making ear-splitting noises. But Tony was not the play-acting type and it was not enough for him to know that the switch on the vacuum cleaner controlled the noise. He had to find the noise. A number of investigations were conducted over a period of time. Tiny screws and wheels were removed and lost in this frantic research; and finally this limping monster issued its dying croak and succumbed without giving up its secret.

It was not enough for Tony to know that the electric wall outlets controlled light and that it was dangerous to fool with such things. Warnings only served to increase his need to locate the source of danger and find out "why." With his handy pocket screw driver he imperiled himself again and again by removing the plates from the wall outlets, and when his parents put a stop to this research, his fury was terrible to behold.

In spite of the fact that much of this research was unrewarding and in no way encouraged by the family, this pocket-sized scientist pursued his investigations with undiminished energy. As he grew older the mortality rate on electrical appliances grew less. He was no longer satisfied to take things apart to see how they worked; he wanted to reassemble them and make them work again. The same urgency and drive which earlier had gone into the investigation of mechanical process was now seen in the process of building and recreating.

When Tony was four, you could no longer say that his drive to investigate was motivated primarily by a need to master anxiety (as it was at the age of two). Investigation, discovery, reconstruction, were pleasures in themselves. When he was four and he occasionally removed the motor from his mother's washing machine, he was not motivated by an infantile wish to discover the source of the noise (as in the early investigation of the vacuum cleaner). At four he needed a more powerful motor for an invention he was working on, one that unfortunately was never brought to the final stages because of the unwillingness of a mother to sacrifice the family linen and hygiene to scientific progress.

We can see that a sublimation which may have originated in the process of overcoming childhood fears can become independent, finally, of the original motive. As in Tony's investigations we can see how it becomes an activity that serves a variety of purposes having nothing to do with its original aims. But it can also be demonstrated that such a healthy sublimation can be brought into service as a defense against anxiety when the need arises again. Tony's story provides us with a very good example:

When Tony was four he had an emergency appendectomy and was hospitalized for a two-week period. There could be no preparation for the hospitalization or for surgery, and we must assume that this was a frightening experience for a little boy. During his convalescence at the hospital relatives and friends brought him many toys, of course. But Tony at four, like Tony at two, did not care much for toys. When an aunt asked him what he would most like to have as a present he said unhesitatingly, "An old alarm clock that doesn't work." His aunt and other relatives presented him with their old alarm clocks. And Tony occupied himself during convalescence with the repair of old alarm clocks. They worked too!

This interests us. In the first place the dismantling and reassembling of an alarm clock is a very advanced mechanical task for a four year old. But also the degree to which this activity absorbed the four-year-old boy suggests that it had very great importance to him. We can suspect that the repair of the broken alarm clocks was connected with the recent surgery and the child's anxiety at that critical time. For the child, in great pain and unprepared for the emergency hospitalization and surgery, only knew that something was wrong and that the doctor would make him better, "fix him up," so to speak. Like all small children he must have felt terrified and helpless when he left his mother and was wheeled into the operating room to have "something" taken out that was hurting him. Now in his convalescence he was overcoming the painful effects of this experience. And what did he do? He took apart the alarm clocks and made them work again, just as the doctor fixed him and made him work again. He performed an operation on the alarm clocks and succeeded in making them well again. In this way he employed a well-established sublimation, mechanical investigation and construction, to overcome a frightening experience, and it proved to be very successful.

It is worth mentioning that anxiety may have played another role in the repair of the alarm clocks. Until this point Tony had never succeeded in reassembling an alarm clock. This is an advanced mechanical skill that is ordinarily beyond the scope of a four year old. His earlier trials had resulted in dismantled clocks and a formidable array of tiny screws and wheels and springs that baffled reconstruction. It is possible that anxiety after surgery provided such a powerful motive to "fix something," "to make something work" that the little boy could go beyond himself and accomplish something that had never been possible before.

In the years that followed Tony pursued his scientific interests. He continued to imperil his family with his basement inventions. Small explosions unsettled the family from time to time. His long-suffering mother grew accustomed to a washing machine that missed its motor and many times the family washing stagnated until the boy inventor came home from school. In the school years his interest in scientific subjects dwarfed all others. He never had any doubt that he would grow up to be a scientist. It only remained to choose an area in science. This decision was made in college and Tony today is a physicist.

IMAGINATION, THE INTELLECT AND MENTAL HEALTH.

FROM these examples we can see how the child in the earliest years begins to reveal characteristic ways of dealing with life problems. His creative and intellectual activities have wider aims than pleasure; they also serve to help him overcome the common fears and problems of childhood. Later, these tendencies are strengthened and may even become the basis of vocational choice, as in the case of Tony.

When we understand the importance of imagination and intellect for mental health we can draw certain inferences for child rearing. What we do to promote the creative and intellectual problem solving abilities of the child will also promote the child's mental health, that is, if we also take care not to make excessive or unreasonable demands upon the child. In encouraging the child's tendencies we need, also, to be sure that they are his tendencies and not our own. Suppose Jan's parents had found her play-acting tedious or discouraged it as a "retreat" into fantasy. And suppose her father, an engineer, had tried to induce her to solve her problems through a purely investigatory approach like Tony's. It might not have worked at all because this child's tendencies were not like those of Tony. Her intelligence, which was very good, was not of the same type. Presented with the problem of a roaring vacuum cleaner she would not have cared in the least about the mechanical aspects of its noise making. If her father had tried to show her where the noise came from, she would have been bored. But if someone were to invite her to play vacuum cleaner and had allowed her to crawl all over the floor roaring threateningly, she might have liked that just fine. As for Tony, the opposite conditions prevailed. He did not care about toys and did not customarily recreate events through imaginative play. If his parents had found his scientific investigations intolerable (which they very nearly were, at times) and had tried to shift his interests to conventional toys and imaginative play they might have had small success and would have deprived Tony of his own best measures for overcoming the problems and fears of early childhood. And the world would have lost a good scientist.

A critical friend speaks up: "You praise the human faculties of reason, imagination and conscience as factors that promote mental health. It would be easy to argue that the most rational of all men can be neurotic, that artists and other highly imaginative people are often quite screwy and that those who have acquired the strictest consciences may be the most susceptible to emotional disturbances. The history of the race also makes a sour comment on your views. For as man has advanced culturally and his celebrated faculties of reason, imagination and conscience have moved apace, we find him more and more disposed toward mental illness. And at this very moment in history his victorious reason, his science, offers him the means of destroying himself and the planet he inhabits and neither reason nor imagination nor conscience has yet produced an idea that may prevent him from doing so."

And I say: "If you want to play this cynical game I can go further. Only man is susceptible to neurosis. All these frustration experiments with animals in laboratories have produced nothing like a human neurosis. The chimpanzee, the dog, the mouse produce anxiety when the human experimenters expose them to danger situations. They may, indeed, become immobilized and helpless with repeated frustration, or they may produce muscular spasms that can be likened to human tics, or they may become stuporous in a way that resembles catatonia in the human. But they do not acquire neuroses. For the human neurosis is characterized by anxiety attached to ideas and the animal is incapable of having an idea. The human neurosis is the product of a conflict between drives and conscience and an animal does not own a conscience. The cynic can conclude from this scientific demonstration that man can avoid neurosis by returning to the trees."

But let's go back to the beginning of this argument. If reason, imagination and conscience do not, as you say, prevent a rational man, a creative man and a moral man from acquiring a neurosis, this does not constitute an indictment of the highest human faculties. While the chimpanzee possesses none of these faculties and lives in harmony with his nature we do not aspire to his mode of living, and he provides no models for human conduct. The two aspects of man's nature, the biological and the mental, are in conflict from the earliest period of life, and the harmony of man must be established in accordance with man's nature and not the nature of the chimpanzee. It is not the mental aspect of man that creates neurosis but the failure, at times of extreme stress, of the higher mental processes in bringing the primitive aspect of man under its control. It is as absurd to blame the higher mental faculties for man's neuroses as to blame the heart, the lungs or the digestive tract because they subject man to disease. Like these vital organs, the higher mental faculties work for health and the harmony of the whole person and normally carry on a valiant fight against disease and disharmony.

It has been fashionable in the past two generations to speak of the "costs" of civilization, the "tolls" exacted by civilization in mental disturbance. This has led to the mistaken view that we should abandon some of our civilized aims in order to reduce the costs to the individual. Because excessive guilt was found to be a factor in the etiology of neurosis, it was assumed erroneously, that a child should be reared without producing any guilt feelings in him. Because thwarted aggression was also a factor in neurotic symptom formation, it was mistakenly believed that aggression in the child should never be thwarted. Because repressed urges were regularly found in the analysis of neurotic symptoms, a philosophy of child rearing sprang up which sought to prevent "repressions" from taking place.

Freud, indeed, spoke of "the costs" of civilization and regarded neurosis as part of the price we pay for civilization, but he never said that this price was too high to pay for civilization and he never meant that we should abandon our civilized aims. He, himself, was the most civilized of men and bore the heritage of his civilization with pride and a deep sense of his own obligation to serve its highest aims. He valued morality for its own sake and for himself. The essence of his theory of neurosis is that biological man and moral man are essentially in conflict and that under certain circumstances this conflict may produce a neurosis. (Under happier circumstances this same conflict may produce the highest cultural achievements.) The essence of his psychoanalytic therapy was the restoration of harmony between the biological self and the moral self, and he would have regarded it as a bad therapy indeed if the moral side of man were not strengthened in this process. *Never* did Freud subscribe to the theory attributed to him that liberation of forbidden impulses would cure man of his mental ills. The permission of analytic therapy is the permission to *speak* of the dangerous and forbidden thoughts; it is not the permission to *act* them. The process enables the patient to bring the forbidden impulses under the control of the higher mental processes of reason and judgment, a process which automatically strengthens the moral side of man by partially freeing it from its primitive and irrational sources.

The question remains for us as it was for Freud: Can we progress toward a higher civilization, a higher morality without exacting a greater price from the human ego than it can pay? If we understand that neurosis need not be the price for moral achievement, that human drives can be controlled without imperiling the human psyche, then, hopefully, our growing knowledge of human psychology may lead the way to a new achievement in civilization. It may lead also to the further evolution of the moral side of man, a progress which is momentarily in jeopardy because of the degree of human suffering and loss of vitality that has accompanied our limping pace from the Stone Age to the Second World War.

But we are speaking of children and child-rearing here. Our aims are very modest ones. We are speaking about a single child in whom the hopes of his parents and our culture are embodied. Our knowledge of the child has expanded most hopefully in the past fifty years. We do not know and we cannot say how this knowledge will serve the moral evolution of man in the centuries to come. Our problem is to find out how a child who is to be reared in our culture today can achieve the necessary harmony between his drives and his conscience and between his ego and his society, serving the best interests of his society without succumbing to illness.

But, in fact, we do not yet know all the necessary answers to such vital questions. The problems of child-rearing which we will deal with in these pages can only be dealt with on the level of our present knowledge, a psychology of the child which is large but incomplete in vital areas. If we are willing to accept the limitations of a young science and to proceed with very modest aims and expectations in applying this knowledge to child-rearing, we can justify the existence of such a book as this one. We will try to bring together some of the more important discoveries in child development and child psychology to see in what way our present knowledge can promote the mental health of children.

PART II

The First Eighteen Months

2. "Shake Off Slumber, and Beware . . ."

THE NEW-BORN.

PERIODICALLY in his long sleep the new-born baby is aroused by hunger or discomfort and his unfocused milky eyes rest upon an object. In this momentary fixing of his eyes his face takes on a look of concentration and intelligence. He looks absorbed and meditative. We stand around him, the marvelling parents, grandparents, assorted relatives and friends, and someone leans over him and says, "What are you thinking about? Come on and tell us!" The blurry baby eyes rest briefly on the face bending over it, a ghost of a smile appears, then the ancient, tiny face grows blank and inscrutable, silent as the Sphinx to its supplicants.

The psychologist, too, has trouble in getting this fellow to reveal his inner life. He is the most uncooperative of all subjects. His close-mouthed attitude toward the researcher is responsible for a great deal of scientific dissension in the field of early infancy and for extraordinary flights of scientific imagination as well. In any case, the subject of these investigations does not engage in controversy and some of the most extravagant and daring theories of the inner life of infancy have never been disproved. Neither have they been proved.

We are probably on safe ground with the infant if we begin with few assumptions and work with the meager information that can be gained through direct observation. We see very little in the first two months that we can call "mental." In these early weeks the infant functions very largely on the basis of need and satisfaction. His hunger is a ravenous hunger, the tensions it produces are intolerable, and the satisfaction of this hunger is imperative.

He operates on an instinctive basis, the mouth rooting for the nipple when hunger is intense, but not "recognizing" the bottle or breast on sight when it is presented. His inability to recognize objects at this stage tells us that the function of memory is not yet established.

If we can imagine this world or reconstruct it, we can only find analogies in the world of the dream. Dim objects swim into view, then recede and melt into nothingness. A human face hovers over him like a ghostly mask, then dissolves. Events in his life have no connections. Even the satisfaction of his hunger has not yet been connected with the face of his mother, not to mention the person of his mother.

Our parental indignation is aroused at this. What do the scientists know! Oh, we could give dozens of examples of the way in which little Joe recognized his mother at four weeks! It's hard *not* to believe that when he smiles after nursing he isn't expressing his appreciation to his mother. It's hard not to believe that when he howls he's not expressing indignation at his mother's ineptness.

We are called upon to bear witness. Here is little Joe at four weeks. His mama is late in bringing his bottle to him. When she enters his room, she sees the very picture of an apoplectic gentleman diner, uttering incoherent noises, clenching his fists and denouncing the management of this place. Watching him, we do have an uneasy feeling that he has every intention of taking his business elsewhere.

"Don't tell me," says his mama, "that that baby wasn't mad at me!"

But he is not mad *at* his mother. Although he has met his mother on a number of occasions he has a poor memory for faces—at four weeks. What we see is simply an instinctive reaction evoked by hunger. He can't be mad at his mother because he hasn't yet learned that there is a person outside of himself who satisfies his needs. He's not complaining to the management because he doesn't know that the management is responsible for this meal. He experiences hunger, and something is put into his mouth that brings satisfaction. If we can risk an analogy, his meal comes to him like those bottomless jugs and pitchers of the fairy tales, always brimming over with an intoxicating liquor, always magically on hand when need arises, or the magic syllable is uttered. And the disappointing truth is that at this stage he does not reflect upon the source of supply any more than you or I think about a utility company when we turn on a tap to get water or press a switch to bring light.

Our antipathy to science is renewed. "Why then, I might just not need to be around for a couple of months," says the mother of Joe. "We could just have a device for feeding and changing diapers, a Brave New World nursery."

"No!" And this protest comes from the scientists. This brings all the psychologists in all the branches and schools of psychology to speak in one voice. They may disagree on many points as scientists; they may be hostile to each other's theories. But the importance of the mother to the infant from the first days of life is a point that is hardly disputed by any of them.

For these first weeks are not entirely a time of darkness and primeval chaos. An invisible web is spun around the child and his mother that emanates from the mother and through which the most subtle impressions are transmitted to the child. And while the infant doesn't "know" his mother, can't recognize her on sight, he is receiving an infinite number of impressions through physical contact with her that gradually lead to the formation of his image of her.

There is no visual memory yet, but the physical intimacy of mother and child is already producing reactions which will lead to the association of mother with pleasure, satisfaction and protection. The mother's presence, even in the early weeks, often produces a magical calming when the baby is fretful. The father, or other persons in the family, may also achieve the same effect. The point is that even if the mother is not yet discriminated from other persons, some association is established in which human contact represents satisfaction and protection. Part of this reaction is undoubtedly instinctive, part of it already represents a kind of "learning" through the repetition of pleasurable and comforting experiences with the mother and other persons.

In the earliest weeks we can see how physical contact with the mother or father represents protection to the baby. An excessively loud noise or any other strong stimulus that might create a startle reaction and crying in the baby if he is alone in his crib will have a very mild effect upon him if he happens to be in his mother's or father's arms. We will notice that even physical discomfort or pain will be tolerated if the baby is in physical contact with one of his parents. The shot in the doctor's office seems to have less shock effect if the baby is in his mother's arms instead of on the examining table when the injection is given. The discomforts of milder digestive upsets of the early weeks can be endured much better, as everyone knows, if the baby is held.

These are simple demonstrations of the ways in which the parent serves as protector and is instinctively felt as a protector before an infant can even identify a human face. The nervous system of the infant is not yet "cushioned" to absorb stimuli of excessive strength, and the parent's body takes over the absent function by cushioning against shock. We even suspect that the later stability in the nervous system in receiving and reacting to strong stimuli is not an independent neurological development but is connected with mothering and the satisfactions and sense of protection which the mother provides the child. Babies deprived of maternal care are demonstrably more irritable, more easily shocked throughout their infancy than babies who have known mothering.

But the parent is more than protector, of course, during those early weeks. Many exciting things are taking place within the child-parent relationship that are silent and invisible, like the process of germination. We know that they are taking place because visible signs of this process will appear in a predictable manner at the end of the second month of life. At this time the baby responds to the sight of a human face with a smile! This is a very special smile. It is not a reflex action, it is not a smile of satiation; it's a response smile, a smile that is elicited when a human face presents itself.

"WHY DOES THE BABY SMILE?"

THE response smile which occurs around two months is a significant milestone in the baby's development. Scientists have been much slower to grasp the significance of this event than a baby's parents. This is the occasion for great excitement. The news is transmitted to grandparents and all interested relatives. No trumpets are blown, no formal holidays proclaimed, but everyone concerned seems to understand that this smile is very special.

Now no parent cares in the least *why* the baby smiles, or why the psychologists think he smiles, and you might wish to skip the next few paragraphs except that I hope you don't. Why the baby smiles is a matter of some significance in understanding the early phases of human attachment in the infant.

First of all, let's remember that this response smile has had antecedents. Even in the early weeks we will notice that satisfaction in the course of nursing or at the end of the nursing period will cause the mouth to relax in a little smile of contentment. This early smile of satisfaction is an instinctive reaction and is not yet a response to a human face.

Now let's watch this baby as he nurses. If he is not too sleepy his eyes fix solemnly on the face of his mother. We have learned experimentally that he does not take in the whole face before him, only the upper part of the face, the eyes and forehead. Through repetition of the experience of nursing and its regular accompaniment, the human face, an association between nursing and the human face will be established. But more than this, the pleasure, the satisfactions of nursing become associated with the human face. Repetition of this pleasurable experience gradually traces an image of the face on the surface of the memory apparatus and the foundations of memory are established. When the mental image is firmly established the visual image of the human face is "recognized" (very crudely), that is, the sight of the human face evokes the mental image and it is "remembered." Now comes the turning point. This is not just a memory based on pictures, but a memory derived from image plus pleasure, the association established through nursing. The baby's response to the sight of the human face is now seen as a response of pleasure. He smiles at the sight of the human face. The little smile which had originated as an instinctive reaction to satisfaction in nursing is now produced occasionally, then more and more, at the sight of the face, as if the face evokes the memory of satisfaction and pleasure. The baby has made his first human connections.

We should not be disappointed to learn that the baby does not yet discriminate his mother's face from other human faces. "How can they prove *that?*" we'd like to know. "That smile certainly *looks* very special." We know this from two sets of observations. For many weeks after the response smile has been established, almost any human face that presents itself to the baby can elicit the smile. (Ironically, a mask representing the eyes and forehead of the human face can be presented to the baby of this age and this, too, will bring forth a pleasure response.) We may not find this so convincing a proof. How do we know this isn't just a sociable little guy who likes his mother *and* the rest of the human race? And maybe his response to the mask only proves that he has a sense of humor. Perhaps the second set of observations will be more convincing. Psychologists place the positive identification and differentiation of the mother's face around eight months because of certain responses of the infant which are familiar to all of us. He no longer smiles at any face that swims into view. On the contrary, let your jolliest uncle approach with beaming face and twenty keys on a chain to dangle before his eyes and he may be greeted by a quizzical look, an uncomprehending stare or—worse for family relations—a howl! Now let mother or father come over to offer reassurances to the baby and apologies to the uncle, and upon seeing these two faces, the baby relaxes, wriggles and smiles. He may study these three sets of faces for a few minutes and, finally satisfied that the familiar faces are re-established, he turns to the unfamiliar face and permits his uncle to jingle keys and make comical faces for which he may later be rewarded with a smile. Or let Grandma who is a frequent, but not constant visitor, offer to take over a bottle feeding. He is hungry, shows eagerness for the bottle, but when he takes in the face that is not mother's he looks dismayed, the face puckers and he howls in protest. "He never did *that* before!" says his grandmother. And it is true that several weeks ago when grandma had taken over a feeding he had polished off his bottle with as much zest as when his mother fed him.

This reaction to the strange face, the not-mother face, is the first positive evidence that he differentiates his mother's face from others. (We should not fail to mention that if father has had close contact with the baby and if there are sisters and brothers, these faces will be differentiated, too. We use "mother" as a convenient reference point and with the understanding that for the period of infancy she will be the primary love object.) The reaction to being fed by grandma shows us, too, that pleasure in eating is no longer simply a matter of biological need and satisfaction, but is bound to the person of his mother. He has finally linked this face, this person, with the satisfaction of his needs and regards her as the source of satisfaction. The pleasure and satisfaction given him through feeding and caring for him are now transferred to her image, and the sight of her face, her presence, will bring forth such crowing and joyful noises, and the disappearance of her face such disappointment that we can say that he loves his mother as a person.

That has a curious sound! "Loves his mother as a person." Obviously, since she is a person how else could he love her? And if we say that we mean "loves her as a person outside himself," that sounds just as foolish to our adult ears. Of course, she is a person outside himself. We know that! But the baby did not. He learned this slowly, awkwardly, in the course of the first months of life. For during the early months the infant doesn't differentiate between his body and other bodies, or between mental images and perceptions, between inner and outer. Everything is undifferentiated oneness, the oneness being centered in the baby himself.

At the time that the baby discovers that his mother is a person outside himself a tremendous amount of learning has taken place. In order to achieve something that seems commonplace to us he had to engage in hundreds of experiments over a period of months. He had to assemble hundreds of pieces in a vast and intricate jig-saw puzzle in order to establish a crude picture of the person-mother and a crude image of his own body. We can reconstruct these experiments largely through observation.

THE JIG-SAW PUZZLE WORLD.

THE two-month-old baby has hardly roused himself from the long night of his first weeks in this world when he is confronted with some of the most profound problems of the race. We invite him to study the nature of reality, to differentiate between inner and outer experience, to discriminate self and not-self and to establish useful criteria for each of these categories. A project of such magnitude in academic research would require extensive laboratory equipment and personnel; to be fair about it, it has taken just that to reconstruct the experiments of the infant. And there are few grown and fully accredited scientists who can equal the infant for zeal and energy in sorting out the raw data in this project. His equipment is limited to his sensory organs, his hands, his mouth and a primitive memory apparatus.

At two months, as we have seen, he recognizes an object that *we* know to be a human face and we know to be an object outside himself. But to the baby this is just an image, an image incidentally that he can't differentiate from the mental image, the picture in memory. But this face is one piece in the jig-saw puzzle—a key piece, we think. Then gradually in the weeks to come the association of breast or bottle, of hands, voice, a multitude of pleasurable sense experiences begin to cluster around this face and to form the crude image of a person.

Meantime the infant is conducting a series of complicated experiments in sensory discrimination. We must remember that in the early months he does not discriminate between his body and other bodies. When he clutches the finger of his mother or his father he doesn't see it as someone else's finger and his behavior indicates that he treats it exactly the same as he does his own finger. It takes him some time, in fact, to recognize his own hand at sight and to acquire even a rudimentary feeling that this is part of his own body. In the first group of experiments he discovers that the object that passes occasionally in front of his eyes (which *we* know to be his hand) is the same as the object that he introduces into his mouth. It now becomes one object with visual and taste qualities that he can identify. In another experimental series he discovers that the sensations that accompany the introduction of *this* object into his mouth are different from those experienced when he takes a nipple in his mouth, or a toy, or his mother's or father's finger. In still another related experiment he brings his two hands before his face and fingers them and gradually through thousands of repetitions discovers that there are special feelings that accompany these contacts between his own hands that are not like those experienced when he touches objects that we know to be outside his own body. To us, this seems to be a commonplace observation. Of course, contact with your own body and parts of your own body elicit different sensations from contact with objects outside. But for the infant this has to be discovered. He doesn't differentiate between his body and outside objects until he discovers these differences in sensation. Gradually he sorts out the data into two main categories which eventually become "me" feelings and "other" feelings.

One more major step must be taken before he is ready to respond to persons as objects outside himself. He has to distinguish between two sets of nearly identical pictures that obscure his tests of reality, of inner and outer experience. Let's use the picture of mother, as an example. One picture arises from without—the picture presented by perception when mother actually appears to the baby. The other picture arises from within—the picture produced by memory. It seems very strange to us, but in the early stages of mental functioning, the infant cannot easily differentiate between his mental image and the picture presented by the real object. He has to learn this. He is hungry, let us say, and hunger produces automatically the mental picture of its satisfaction. An image of the breast, or the bottle, or the associated human face, arises immediately. This is analogous to our own mental processes. If we are very hungry, the mental picture of a particularly desired food will be produced by memory. But we know that the fragrant stew served up by memory is not the same as the dish that appears on the table, that it is not real. We were not born with this knowledge. We learned it back in the dark ages of infancy. How is this learned? After hundreds of repetitions, the infant gradually discovers that a mental image of his meal does not lead to satisfaction. An imagining of the breast or the bottle leaves him hungry. A real breast, a real bottle, leads to satisfaction. Here are the first intimations of reality, the establishment of first principles.

Well, then, where does all this lead?

When this part of the jig-saw puzzle is put together (somewhere in the middle of the first year), when the infant begins to differentiate himself from an outer world, he has made the crucial step in personality development. He has discovered a self, the center of personality, and a person outside of himself to whom he is bound through ties of love. We do not need scientific confirmation for the discovery that every parent makes for himself at this point. "Why he's becoming a person!"

ON BECOMING A PERSON.

AT THIS point we can officially welcome the infant into the human fraternity. He enters this world in a manner entirely fitting for a civilized person—through love of another person, for he discovers himself and he discovers the world outside himself through his mother. All this talk about an infant researcher should not obscure the central point: It is the mother, the primary source of satisfactions in early infancy, who represents "the world" and it is through the attachment to mother that he discovers himself and the world outside. All the infant investigations we have described have proceeded from a central point: the relationship of child and mother. In the twilight world of the early weeks, a world of shifting, transient forms and sensations, one form became fixed and stable through constant association with pleasure and satisfaction—the human face. The repetition of *this* human face and the pleasure and satisfaction associated with it allow this face to become discriminated from other faces, and recognition of the mother takes place. The infant's contact with his mother's body and his own body makes it possible for him to differentiate sensations and to acquire the beginnings of self feelings. The differentiation of the mental image of mother and the perception of mother created the first intimations of reality. And the discovery of separateness, of a self and person outside of the self who is the source of satisfaction, makes possible the first love relationship, the love of the child for its mother.

This is not a biological metamorphosis, a developmental process that unfolds as structures become differentiated. These achievements, covering roughly the first nine months of life, are the achievements of the human family. Infants in institutions who are deprived of maternal care or a satisfactory substitute for maternal care do not make these discoveries. They remain in the primitive state of need gratification. Their mental processes are greatly retarded when compared to those of infants who receive normal maternal care. They indicate only the most sluggish interest in humans or objects around them. Since the outer world has no human representative who is consistently associated with satisfaction, pleasure and protection, there is no attraction to the world outside, and the mental position of earliest infancy, based on the body and its needs, remains the mental position in later development—unless maternal care is later provided.

The discovery by the normal baby of his separateness from his mother is the result of a gradual process. We are actually describing only the first phase in this process which takes place around the middle of the first year. It will be two more years before this process reaches the stage of personal identity, expressed in the first shaky and uncertain "I." But even in this first phase of infancy, the differentiation of the infant's body from his mother's body, the beginning recognition of a mother who exists outside one's self, reveals itself through a change in the baby's relationship to his mother.

The baby who protested when grandma attempted to give him his bottle was revealing this change. A few weeks ago, we recall, he had been perfectly willing for grandma or someone else to feed him. This means that the satisfaction of his needs was more important to him at that stage than *who* satisfied his needs. Now all this changes. He wants mother to feed him because her presence is a satisfaction and a pleasure in itself. His response to her no longer depends exclusively upon his body needs and their satisfaction. Now there is a very great qualitative difference between the love of this second stage and the response of the infant to his mother in the earlier stage. It is a difference that we recognize in love relationships in later years, too. If one partner loves another partner for the material advantages provided by the other partner we say this is not "true love." We put a higher value on love which is independent of material advantage, a love for the person himself. And while we cannot say in infancy that the child's love for his mother is independent of need gratification, we can see that the infant has made a large stride forward in this second phase of attachment when mother's person and her presence become satisfactions in themselves.

So it is at this point in the infant's development that we find ourselves saying, "Why, he's becoming a person—a real person!" He has changed, no doubt of it. From the moment that he begins to love a person whom he recognizes as outside himself, we have the impression that he is becoming humanized; he begins to acquire a personality of his own. He offers his own proof that civilization begins with love.

Like the beginnings of all "real love" the first stages of the infant's new attachment to his mother is an exclusive and proprietary love. The baby protests when his mother leaves him. Naptime and bed-time bring the most anguished cries. We have already seen that strangers may distress him during this phase. All of these disturbances are the result of love. His mother has become so important to him that her presence means satisfaction and her absence creates anxiety in him. For in the early stages of this attachment of the baby to his mother, the disappearance or absence of the mother is experienced as loss. The infant has not yet learned that when mother goes away she comes back. He behaves at such times as if mother were gone forever and his world is empty of meaning.

There is another parallel to be found in the experience of love in later life. In the early, very intense stages of love, the absence of a loved person is experienced like the loss of part of one's self. "I have no existence without you!" "I feel that I am not alive." "I am not a whole person!" This feeling that the loved person gives meaning to existence and intensifies the self feelings has its counterpart in the infant's experience in his early attachment to his mother. His mother is the link to the external world. When he loses her, even briefly, he is confused, disoriented, as if he had lost his connection with his new found world and with it his own newly discovered self feelings. When his mother returns he becomes "a person" again, he has regained his world and found himself once more.

So if we ask, "When does the child first experience anxiety in relation to the outer world?" the answer will be "When he first learns to love." Here is a riddle for the poets! Once again we have a demonstration of the fact that the very process of development creates problems for the child, produces anxiety. Some babies may exhibit mild anxiety at this stage, others a more intense kind. But some anxiety at separation from the mother is one of the inevitable consequences of the early stages of the child's attachment to loved persons. This anxiety will be largely overcome in the next few months.

The pocket-sized scientist is already at work on the problem. We assume he has a reliable set of parents who can give substantial proof that disappearance is followed by return. The other steps to solution of this problem will be undertaken in further research. The eight-month-old baby has to develop a concept! In the simplest terms, he has to find out what happens to an object when it disappears. The problem, to put it briefly, is this: The baby under nine months doesn't seem to have the slightest notion that an object has an independent existence, that it exists whether he sees it or not. This goes for human objects—his parents, members of his household—and it applies to his bottle, his toys, the furniture—in short, any object in his limited world. When the object disappears from view it ceases to exist. The baby does not imagine that it is *some* place, that it exists whether or not he sees it.

Are we doubtful? Let's follow some simple tests.

THE CASE OF THE VANISHING OBJECT.

HAVE you a six- or seven-month-old baby who snatches the glasses off your nose? If you do, you hardly need this piece of advice. Remove the glasses when the baby reaches for them, slip them in a pocket or behind a sofa pillow (and don't forget where *you* hid them!). Don't trouble to be sneaky about it, let the baby see you hide them. He will not go in search of them. He will stare at the place he last saw them—on your nose—then lose interest in the problem. He does not search for the glasses because he cannot imagine that they have an existence when he does not see them.

When the baby is around nine months old, don't rely on the old tricks. If he sees you remove your glasses and slip them behind a sofa pillow he will move the pillow and pounce on your glasses. He has learned that an object can be hidden from sight, yet can still exist! He can follow its movements in your hand to the place of hiding and actively search for it there. This is a tremendous step in learning and one that is likely to be overlooked by the parents whose glasses, earrings, pipes, fountain pens and key-cases are now not only lifted from their persons, but defy safekeeping. Parents who have babies in this stage of development are little interested in the theoretical aspects of the problem as posed here, but a theory can always bring some practical benefits. We still have some tricks up our sleeve. Let's try this: Let the baby see you slip your glasses behind the pillow. Let him find them, persuade him to give them to you, then hide the glasses under a second pillow. Now he is confused. He will search for the glasses under the *first* pillow, in the first hiding place, but he will not search for them in the second hiding place. This means that the baby can conceive of the glasses having an existence when hidden, but only in one place, the first hiding place where his search had earlier been successful. When the baby does not find the glasses under the first pillow, he continues to search for them there, but it does not occur to him to search for them in the second hiding place or anywhere else. An object can still vanish. In a few weeks he will extend his search from the first hiding place to the second one and he is on his way to the discovery that an object can be moved from place to place and still have a permanent existence.

If you are still wearing glasses while your child is between one year and eighteen months continue these hiding experiments with an old key-case and manage your glasses problem as best you can. (This book does not claim to be definitive or authoritative on all points.) During the first half of the second year the baby is really pretty good at following an object from your hand to two successive hiding places, *if* he can follow your movements with his eyes. This means that you still have one trick up your sleeve but it's practically your last chance to be one up on the child in these games. Try this: Put your key-case in a purse and close it. Let the baby see you do it and let him find it. This is old stuff to him now. Now persuade the baby to give the key-case back to you. Put it back into the purse and move the purse with its concealed key-case behind a sofa pillow. Remove the key-case slyly, taking care that this operation is concealed from the eagle eye of your child, and slip the key-case behind the pillow. Bring the empty purse back into view. Now ask your child to find the key-case. He will examine the empty purse, search for the missing key-case in its emptiness. He will look confused and puzzled, but it will not occur to him to search for the key-case behind the pillow although he had followed your movements originally to that place. He does not search for the key-case there or any other place because he has not *seen* you remove it. In other words he cannot yet imagine the object existing *some* place if he has lost track of its movements through his eyes.

But now he's almost ready for the final step in this process. Try your disappearing key-case trick for a few days and he's pretty certain to catch on. A few more experiments and he will fill in the visual gap with an imaginative reconstruction. He will establish the fact that a key-case can leave a purse without his perception of the process, but a key-case has a substantial existence some place and he will search for it in a fairly systematic way. He will find it and confirm for himself that an object has an existence independent of his perception of it. Your days as a magician are numbered and the child's era of magical belief is on the wane. This is an intellectual giant-step for the child in the second half of his second year and in a later chapter we will see how this emerging concept of an objective world opens up all the possibilities of rational thought processes. But we had started this story of the disappearing objects with another idea in mind.

We must remember that a child who lives in a world of vanishing objects perceives his human world on the same basis. It is not only glasses and key-cases and Teddy bears that have no existence when he cannot perceive them. Mothers and fathers, loved persons, are subjected to the same primitive reasoning. They appear and disappear in a ghostly fashion, like dream people. And, unlike the furniture of the objective world, these human love objects are necessary for the child's existence and his inner harmony. Until one has proof of the permanence of these loved persons, certainty that they have a substantial existence independent of one's perception of them, there will be disturbing feelings at times when these loved persons are absent. This does *not* mean that the child between the ages of six months and eighteen months lives in a state of constant anxiety. And it does *not* mean that parents must be constantly with a baby to give him reassurance. There are healthy mechanisms at work within the child's personality to reassure him. He can even make excellent use of his magic thinking during this period to assure himself that disappearance is followed by return; a loved person goes away and comes back. But since this magic belief doesn't always work—mother won't *always* be there when he needs her, can't always magically appear with a bottle when hunger is imperative, will sometimes be out for the evening when the baby wakens— the magical theory of disappearance and return will frequently break down. At such times anxiety—a mild anxiety or a very strong anxiety—will appear.

Unless this anxiety is very severe and pervasive, really disturbs the healthy functioning and development of the child, we do not need to be alarmed. It diminishes normally in the course of the child's development. And here is the practical application of the theory we have been discussing: As the child gradually constructs an objective world—a stable and coherent world in which appearance and disappearance, comings and goings, are subject to their own physical laws—he acquires an intellectual control over his environment that helps him to overcome his anxiety at separation. When you know that a mother and a father are substantial persons who cannot evaporate, who may be hidden from the eyes like the objects in the games we described and yet exist, the temporary absence of loved persons can be managed with far less anxiety.

TRAVEL AND PERSPECTIVES.

LET no one imagine from this lengthy description of babies and objects, that the nine- to eighteen-month-old baby worked on his concept of the permanence of objects from the repose of an arm chair. For this whole period of discoveries in the outside world is paralleled by a tremendous progress in motility.

In the last quarter of the first year the baby is no longer an observer of the passing scene. He is in it. Travel changes one's perspective. A chair, for example, is an object of one dimension when viewed by a six-month-old baby propped up on the sofa, or by an eight-month-old baby doing push-ups on a rug. It's even very likely that the child of this age confronted at various times with different perspectives of the same chair would see not one chair, but several chairs, corresponding to each perspective. It's when you start to get around under your own steam that you discover what a chair really is. Parents who want a fresh point of view on their furniture are advised to drop down on all fours and accompany the nine or ten month old on his rounds. It is probably many years since you last studied the underside of a dining room chair. The ten month old will study this marvel with as much concentration and reverence as a tourist in the Cathedral of Chartres. Upon leaving the underside of the chair he pauses to wrestle with one of the legs, gets the feel of its roundness and its slipperiness and sinks his two front teeth into it in order to sample flavor and texture. In a number of circle tours around the chair at various times in the days and weeks to come he discovers that the various profiles he has been meeting are the several faces of one object, the object we call a chair.

Every object in his environment must be constructed in this way until its various aspects are united into a whole. The study of a cup will occupy him for weeks, for countless mealtimes, while the function of the cup as perceived by his mother will hardly interest him at all. To drink milk from the cup will be the least absorbing activity in connection with the cup while he is conducting his research on the nature of a cup. He examines the outer surface of the cup, explores the inner surface, discovers its hollowness, bangs it on the tray for its sound effects. Rivers of milk, orange-juice, and water cascade from cup to tray to kitchen floor adding joy to the experiment. His mother, engaged in unceasing labor with sponges and mops, can hardly be blamed if she does not encourage these experiments, but she is never consulted. He is an expert at dislodging the cup in her hand and seizing it for his own purposes; he is outraged at her interference with his experiments. Before he concludes these experiments he has discovered every property of a cup that can be extracted through his study and experimentation (including breakage) and then settles down to a utilitarian view of a cup which gratifies his mother.

We can multiply such studies in the nature of objects to include nearly everything accessible to him. It is a colossal undertaking, a feat of learning of such magnitude in such a brief time that we have no analogies in later life which compare in scale. The traveler analogy we started out with is a very slight and inadequate one. For the discovery of a new country or a new city in later life does not really approximate the discovery of a world in which the very nature of objects must be constructed.

The world he discovers is a vast and intricate jig-saw puzzle, thousands of pieces scrambled together in crazy juxtaposition. Piece by piece he assembles the fragments into whole objects and the objects into groups until he emerges with a fairly coherent picture of the tiny piece of world he inhabits. At eighteen months he has even begun to give names to some of these objects. This learning of the first eighteen months is a prodigious intellectual feat. No wonder every parent thinks his baby is a genius. He is!

And like all geniuses this baby works indefatigably at his discoveries. He is intoxicated with his new-found world; he devours it with every sense organ. He marvels at the bit of dust he picks up in his fingers. A piece of cellophane, a scrap of foil, a satin ribbon will fill him with rapture. He revels in the kitchen cupboards, pursues the hidden treasures of drawers, waste-baskets and garbage cans. This urge for discovery is like an insatiable hunger that drives him on and on relentlessly. He is drunk with fatigue, but he cannot stop. The hunger for sensory experience is as intense and all-consuming as the belly hunger of the first months of life. But this baby, navigating toward his first birthday, or charging ahead into the second year, has almost forgotten his belly. He can do without your nourishing custards, your little jars of puréed vegetables and strained liver. He refuels briefly, bangs on the tray of the high-chair for release, and is off again on his grand tour.

What drives him on? What is the source of this energy? A most exciting new psychological development, no doubt, but what mother has time or energy to contemplate it? For the mother of this dynamo has grown lean and hollow-eyed as she pursues him all over the map. And just at the point that she feels *she* needs two naps a day, this indefatigable globe trotter makes it very clear that *he* is not interested in any naps, thank you, he just has too much work to do. The mother of this child will naturally be little interested in these developments from a psychological point of view and will be heartily excused if she prefers to skip the next few lines, or even abandon the whole project and turn to a book of science fiction.

Nevertheless, it *is* an exciting development, a marvelous transformation in energy and goals. Energy that once was centered exclusively on the satisfaction of body needs is now released in part for the pursuit of goals outside the body in the objective world. The hunger that once was exclusively body hunger has been transformed into a voracious appetite for the world. Love that centered first in the mother who satisfied body needs has expanded and ramified to embrace the ever-widening horizons of his world. The baby is in love with the world he has discovered through his mother's love, and he behaves like those intoxicated lovers in songs and verse who find that the whole world has been transformed through love and the most common objects are infused with beauty.

This analogy may strike us as somewhat extravagant, but it is not a bad one at all and has a sober, scientific backing. For babies who are deprived of maternal care, babies of sterile institutions, are not attracted to objects; they do not find pleasure and excitement in discovery. They possess the same sensory organs as other babies, they learn to sit up, to crawl, to walk. But since human objects have given them no pleasure, there is no pleasure in the world outside their bodies. Such babies remain, for an alarmingly long time (and sometimes permanently) on the psychological level of the young infant. The body and the body needs remain the center of existence for them. It appears, then, that the miraculous achievement of the normal infant, the movement away from body-centeredness to object relationships is not just the product of biological maturation but the achievement of the human family through ties of love.

LOCOMOTION AND THE SOLITARY SELF.

IF WE look closely at two lines of development in the last quarter of the first year we find a paradox. Around the same time that the baby demonstrates his strong attachment to his mother, at that period during which he can hardly bear to be separated from her, he is already beginning to leave her! He is starting to crawl, and with the beginnings of independent locomotion the ties to the mother's body are loosened. After a few weeks spent in straightening out mechanical problems (many babies start off in reverse gear and nearly all of them find their bellies touching bottom), this baby cuts his moorings and goes steaming off for new worlds, leaving his mother with an empty lap.

But how can we account for the paradox? He moves toward the mother and away from the mother in the same period of development! And if the ties to mother are so strong, if anxiety at separation is so pronounced during this phase, why should he not remain in the safety and close intimacy of his mother's arms? Why should he go off for reckless adventure, to be trapped in the dark cave under the sofa, to be assaulted by capricious lamps and obstinate tables? If you or I should go off to explore strange territory and find ourselves slugged by unseen villains at every turn, we'd prudently retire to our homeland, after which the most persuasive travel agent could not lure us through his front door. But this adventurer is stopped by nothing. He pauses briefly for first-aid after a collision that raises an egg-sized lump on his head, he allows his mother to stanch the flow of blood from his nose, he is cheered by a kiss and a few moments in his mother's lap, and then he is off again to risk another duel with the lamp, another skirmish with the temperamental chair.

You don't have to encourage him. You don't have to offer him any incentives to lure him on to new achievements. This is a self-starting, self-perpetuating mechanism. I once watched an eight-month-old girl for three weeks as she subdued an obstinate tea-cart. She could climb on to the lower shelf of the cart, but the cart perversely moved when she did. After days of futile trials, she finally learned to tackle the tea cart from the back which rested on wooden gliders instead of from the front which rested on wheels. Now she was on it. But how to get out? It was too large a drop to climb out of the cart and her pride was hurt if she was helped out of the cart. She usually fell on her face through any of her own methods of debarkation. But several times a day she set out for the cart, solemn and determined. As she started to climb on to the lower shelf she whimpered very softly, already anticipating, we felt, the danger of getting out and the inevitable fall on her face. Her parents tried to discourage her, to distract her to other activities. It was too painful for grown-ups to watch. But if anyone interfered she protested loudly. She *had* to do it. And finally at the end of three weeks she discovered a technique for backing out of the cart, reversing the getting-in method. When she achieved this, she crowed with delight and then for days practiced getting in and getting out until she had mastered it expertly. From this point she moved on to more daring ascents, climbing a few steps of the staircase, then a few more, and a few more, till the staircase became a bore. She tackled chairs, any kind of chair, undismayed by those that teetered and collapsed on her. The urge to climb, the urge upward, was so powerful that no obstacle, no accident could deter her.

All this activity is leading to the establishment of the upright posture. The crawling baby learns to pull himself up to a standing position and begins to maintain this position for longer and longer periods. It will be many weeks before the baby stands alone briefly, many more weeks before he takes his first independent steps. It all unfolds as inevitably as an evolutionary process. But consider the hazards that attend each phase of this process, the bumps, the spills, the perilous falls. When we consider it, the child's achievement of the upright posture is truly heroic.

What impels him? A powerful drive that urges him upward, the legacy of those remote ancestors who cleverly learned to balance themselves on their hind legs in order to put the front paws to work. It is a biological urge that is largely independent of environmental influence. Curiously enough, even the unattached babies of poor institutions seem to learn to sit up, to crawl, to stand and to walk at approximately the same ages that family-reared babies do, while we recall that in other developmental areas that are dependent upon strong human ties for incentive, these institutional babies were severely retarded. And this striving for the upright posture is so powerful that it impels the child forward even when he repeatedly experiences dangers and body injuries and the surrender of maternal protection that necessarily accompanies each of these stages in independent locomotion. In fact we should observe that the means for overcoming the anxiety are identical with the means for producing it. It is through repetition of the experience of crawling, climbing, standing upright, walking, that the hazards are finally overcome and the successful achievement of these goals gradually diminishes the anxiety.

As the child moves toward the upright posture his personality undergoes a change. The average overworked mother is not aware of a personality change as such but of certain difficulties in maintaining the old routines. Changing the baby's diapers which used to be a one-two-three operation has turned into a performance that ideally requires two assistants. First, you catch your baby. Then you put him on his back to change him. He protests loudly. Unpin the wet diaper and sing his favorite little ditty with two diaper pins in your mouth. In a moment your baby has wriggled free, made an expert turn and is sitting upright grinning at you or crawling off in another direction. Repeat step one. Give him a toy to hold, and work fast, because there he is, *up* again!

What's happened? A few weeks ago he found your singing enchanting and it took this or very little else to keep him quiet on his back for the thirty seconds required to change a diaper. But now the moment his spine makes contact with an under-surface, a hidden spring is released and up pops the baby!

It has to do with establishing the upright posture. He can't tolerate being flat on his back and passive, and is impelled by the most irresistible urge to upright himself, the same urge that sends him climbing and pulling himself up, over and over all day to the point of exhaustion. It is an inner necessity, having more to do with defiance of gravity than defiance of the mother.

We can test this in other areas, too. Not so long ago he went peacefully off to his naps or his night's sleep, dozing off in his mother's arms before he reached the bed. But now, however groggy he may be, he is likely to protest furiously at the moment he is put down in his crib, and he summons all his reserves of energy to upright himself, pulling himself up at the bars of the crib the instant after you have put him down. Now admittedly this is not a clear-cut example since the baby at this stage also hates naps and bed-times because they mean separation from loved persons and all the pleasures of his new-found world. But there is this other element, too, and one that recurs so frequently in one context or another during this phase of motor development that it is worth considering apart from other factors for the moment: Motor activity is so vital to the child of this age that interference, restriction of this activity even through another biological process, sleep, is intolerable to him.

We must remember, too, that the child experiences a certain amount of anxiety in connection with these adventures in locomotion and that activity, in itself, is one of the means by which he masters motor skills and masters anxiety as well. His behavior is not unlike ours, as adults, when we begin to learn a new sport, like skiing, that involves a certain amount of risk. The novice skier may feel the full measure of his anxiety when he gets his skis off and mentally reviews his hazardous first attempts. He feels impelled to get back on his skis, to go over his lesson, repeat it again and again until he has mastered the technique and mastered the danger. At night he cannot fall asleep. He is skiing in bed, and his muscles go through all the motions involuntarily as the events of the day are mentally repeated.

The baby mastering the skills that lead to establishment of the upright posture behaves in much the same way as the novice skier. He feels compelled to repeat the activity hundreds of times until he has mastered the skill and mastered his anxiety. He often reveals that he is having difficulty in "unwinding" when we put him to bed for his nap or for the night, and if you peek into his room while he is settling down for sleep (or unsettling down for sleep), you may see him, groggy and cross-eyed with fatigue, still climbing and pulling himself upright, collapsing momentarily with weariness, then exerting himself for another climb. He repeats this over and over until finally he cannot lift himself even once more and succumbs to sleep. One set of parents discovered their eight-month-old daughter climbing in her sleep on several occasions during this mastery period. At eleven or twelve at night they could hear soft sounds in the baby's room and upon entering would find the baby standing in her crib, dazed and dimly conscious, too sleepy to protest when she was put down in her bed again. When the art of standing was perfected, the baby gave up practicing in her sleep.

The first time the baby stands unsupported and the first wobbly, independent steps are milestones in personality development as well as in motor development. To stand unsupported, to take that first step is a brave and lonely thing to do. For it is not a fear of falling, as such, that creates apprehension in the child of this age. He takes these little spills and bumps with good grace. But it is the fear of loss of support that looms big at this stage. Until this point he has employed contact with another human body or a stable piece of furniture for his exercises in standing or taking steps. We notice toward the end of the supported period that the baby is actually using only token support, the lightest touch of his mother's or father's hand serves as "support" while actually he is employing his own body fully for balance. But he is not yet ready to let go of the symbolic contact with mother's body, the supporting human hand. When he does let go for that first step it is usually for another visible or known means of support, another pair of hands, a nearby chair or table. And when he *really* lets go, many weeks later, and takes a half dozen or so steps on his own, he often retains symbolic contact in a comical way. I know one small girl who bravely toddled forth clasping her own hands together, hanging on to her *own* hand. You will notice in the period preceding and immediately following walking the baby likes to have an object in one or both hands to hang on to.

So independent standing and walking represent, truly, a cutting of the moorings to the mother's body. There must be a solemn and terrible aloneness that comes over the child as he takes those first independent steps. All this is lost to memory and we can only reconstruct it through analogies in later life. It must be like the first dive from a diving board, or the first time alone at the wheel of a car. There is the awful sense of aloneness, of time standing still, that follows the spring from the board or in leaving the curb in command of the wheel. In such moments there is a heightened awareness of self, a feeling of being absolutely alone in an empty world that is exalting and terrifying. To the child who takes his first steps and finds himself walking alone, this moment must bring the first sharp sense of the uniqueness and separateness of his body and his person, the discovery of the solitary self.

The discovery of independent locomotion and the discovery of a new self usher in a new phase in personality development. The toddler is quite giddy with his new achievements. He behaves as if he had invented this new mode of locomotion (which in a restricted sense is true) and he is quite in love with himself for being so clever. From dawn to dusk he marches around in an ecstatic, drunken dance, which ends only when he collapses with fatigue. He can no longer be contained within the four walls of his house and the fenced-in yard is like a prison to him. Given practically unlimited space he staggers joyfully with open arms toward the end of the horizon. Given half a chance he might make it.

THE MISSIONARIES ARRIVE.

THIS idyllic picture of life in the second year needs some correction. The portrait of a joyful savage winging his way through an island paradise does not take into account certain influences of civilization that interfere with at least some of the joys.

The missionaries have arrived. They come bearing culture to the joyful savage. They smuggled themselves in as infatuated parents, of course. They nurtured him, made themselves indispensable to him, lured him into discovery of their fascinating world, and after a decent interval they come forth with salesmen's smiles to promote higher civilization.

Somewhere between eight and fifteen months they sell him on the novelty and greater convenience of a cup over the breast or bottle. By the time he himself has come to regard the cup as a mark of good breeding and taste the missionaries have lost interest in the cup and are promoting the hygiene and etiquette of potty chairs and toilets which, he is assured, will elevate him into still higher strata of culture. In the meantime, the missionaries are on hand to interfere with a rapidly growing list of simple pleasures. They urge him to part with treasures he discovers in his travels, the rusty bolts, charred corn-cobs and dried up apple-cores that are so difficult to find unless you know where to look for them. They send unsolicited rescue parties to prevent him from scaling marvellous heights, from sloshing through inky puddles, or pursuing the elusive tail of the family dog. They are forever on hand with a clean diaper, a pile of fresh clothes and hypocritical smiles to induce him to leave whatever it is he is doing for whatever it is they want him to be doing, and it's certain to be a bore. They are there to interfere with the joys of emptying garbage cans and waste-baskets. And, of course, they bring in proposals of naps and bed-time at the most unfortunate moments and for reasons that are clear only to them.

Now, admittedly, such interference is necessary in order to bring culture to a fellow who obviously needs it. But from the baby's point of view most of this culture stuff makes no sense at all. He only knows that certain vital interests are being interfered with, and since his missionaries and he do not even speak the same language, the confusion will not be cleared up for some time.

The baby resists these interferences with his own investigations and creative interests. This earns him the reputation of being "negative" and permits us to speak of the second year as "a negativistic phase." This is not entirely fair to the toddler who lacks the means for stating his case. If he had a good lawyer he could easily demonstrate that most of the negating comes from the side of the culture bearers and his "negativism" is essentially a negation of their negation.

But while we are being fair about it, we have to look at the side of the culture bearers, too. It is necessary that the baby give up the breast or bottle for the cup, and that he learn to use the potty and acquire control over elimination. It is necessary for hygienic reasons to get him to part with many of his treasures. It is dangerous for him to climb bookshelves and ladders. It is inconvenient to clean the kitchen floor of garbage several times a day. It is necessary to take a groggy baby up to his bed even if he thinks he could keep going for several more hours.

Somehow these educational objectives must be achieved, but it is no longer so easy to find the educational means. Not so long ago, even in the last quarter of the first year, he was quite willing to trade with us. He would cheerfully part with the rusty bolt if you gave him a spoon to play with, or put a little block in his hand. Since few objects were valued for themselves, almost any object could substitute for any other object. But also during the same period he was still so closely bound to the body and person of his mother that her aims and his aims were not sharply differentiated. He could fall in easily with her movements, like a dancing partner who is guided by subtle kinesthetic cues.

But in the second year the child who has gained a large degree of physical independence from his mother and who is increasingly aware of his own separate body and personality is a child who can no longer be a passive partner. He has his own rhythm, his own style, and often he seems to value his difference from his mother, his off-beat steps, as if they themselves were the signs of his individuality and uniqueness. To do just the opposite of what mother wants strikes him as being the very essence of his individuality. It's as if he establishes his independence, his separateness from his mother, by being opposite. (Many years later, in adolescence, he will do the same thing. He will declare his adolescent independence by opposing, on principle, any views upheld by his parents or members of their generation.)

So the toddler, with only a few words at his command, has come upon "no" as a priceless addition to his vocabulary. He says "no" with splendid authority to almost any question addressed to him. Very often it is a "no" pronounced in the best of spirits and doesn't even signal an intention. It may even preface an opposite intention. He loves his bath. "Tony, would you like to have your bath now?" "No!" Cheerfully. (But he has already started to climb the stairs.) Marjorie can hardly wait to get outdoors in the morning. "Margie, shall we go 'bye now?" "No!" (And she has started toward the door.) What is this? A confusion of meaning? Not at all. They know the meaning of "no" quite well. It's a political gesture, a matter of maintaining party differences while voting with the opposition on certain issues. It can be paraphrased in the language of the *Congressional Record*. "I wish to state at the outset that in casting my vote for the amendment on the bath and the amendment to go outdoors, I am not influenced by the powerful interest groups that are behind both these amendments, but I am only exercising my duty to serve the best interests of the people, in which case I am obliged to vote 'yes' to the amendment on the bath and 'yes' to the amendment on going outdoors because they are both in the best interests of the people and I am in favor of baths and outdoor life." It's a matter of keeping the record clear.

But let's not get the impression that this toddler spends the better part of his day being negative. The trouble with a term like "negativistic phase" is that it distorts the whole picture of development. The chief characteristic of the second year is not negativism but a powerful striving to become a person and to establish permanent bonds with the world of reality. We must remember when we speak of the "negativism" of the toddler that this is also the child who is intoxicated with the discoveries of the second year, a joyful child who is firmly bound to his parents and his new-found world through ties of love. The so-called negativism is one of the aspects of this development, but under ordinary circumstances it does not become anarchy. It's a kind of declaration of independence, but there is no intention to unseat the government.

We can run into serious trouble in the second year if we look upon this behavior as a nursery revolution and march in with full power for quelling a major revolt. If we turn every instance of pants changing, treasure hunting, napping, puddle wading and garbage distribution into a governmental crisis we can easily bring on fierce defiance, tantrums, and all the fireworks of revolt in the nursery. But the fireworks are *not* necessarily part of the picture of the second year. These are not the inevitable accompaniments of negativism in the second year. A full-scale rebellion of this sort is a reaction to too much pressure or forceful methods of control from the outside.

With better understanding of the second year we can look upon the negativism as a declaration of independence but one that need not alarm the government in power, or call for a special session of congress, or new legislation or a show of force. The citizen can be allowed to protest the matter of the changing of his pants (they are his pants anyway) and the government can exercise its prerogatives in the matter of pants changing without bringing on a crisis. When the citizen is small and wriggly, is illiterate and indeed cannot even speak his native language, it takes ingenuity and patience to accomplish this, but if we do not handle this as conspiracy against the government, he will finally acquire the desirable attitude that changing his pants is an ordinary event and one that will not deprive him of his human rights. So we do not squash the new found spirit of independence, but we direct its pursuit along other lines, encouraging it where it can be useful in personality growth and exercising reasonable restraint and prohibition where it is not. If we err and regard this negativistic phase as a revolution that imperils the government instead of a passing developmental phase we may find ourselves engaged in a struggle with a baby which can be prolonged for years, one that frequently produces a child who behaves as though his integrity as a person is in danger if he submits to the smallest demands of his parents.

AT EIGHTEEN MONTHS.

THE middle of the second year is a milestone in child development. It is just about this point, sometimes sooner, often later, that the child begins to acquire language, and language marks the beginning of a new era. With language the child is able to move from a primitive system of thought (picture thinking) to a second and higher mode of thought in which word symbols predominate. It is this second system that is employed later for the complicated mental acrobatics of logical or ordered thinking. In a later chapter we will discuss some of the implications of language for child development.

So it is convenient in our story to pause at this point somewhere in the middle of the second year and to take stock:

We began with a baby in the first month of life, not yet roused out of the long sleep that follows birth, an infant whose brief contact with the world about him was caused by urgent body tensions and the need for satisfaction. He possessed sensory organs but no sensory discrimination. His mind was very nearly an immaculate blank, not yet able to preserve images and reproduce them, that is, the function of memory had not yet emerged. His world was a chaos of undifferentiated sensation from which he slipped gratefully into the nothingness of sleep.

At eighteen months this baby is travelling extensively and has acquired a small but useful vocabulary (just enough to get a meal and bargain with the natives). He has encountered some of the fundamental problems of the human race—the nature of reality, of subjective and objective experience, causality, the vicissitudes of love, and has made promising studies in each of these areas. We could easily forgive him if these first encounters with our world should create a desire to go back to sleep twenty hours a day. But this fellow upsets all notions about human inertia by forging ahead like a locomotive right into the densities of human activity. Sleep?

Now having seduced him into the sensory pleasures of this world and caused him to embrace it with his whole being, let us try to take it away from him and put him back into darkness. Sleep? But look he can't keep his eyes open! He's drunk with fatigue. He howls with indignation at the extended hands, rouses himself with a mighty exertion from near collapse to protest to these villains who take away his bright and beautiful world. From his crib, in the darkened room he denounces these monster parents, then pleads for commutation of sentence in eloquent noises. He fights valiantly, begins to fail—then succumbs to his enemy, Sleep.

3. "Civilization and Its Discontents"

BUT now what are the practical uses of these researches in child development? The parent who has spent the night with a howling infant may have little appreciation for the interesting theories which I have presented here. There are so many practical problems in the rearing of an infant, so many real demands upon the parent. Is there any use in knowing that an infant at one stage experiences the world in one way and at another stage in another way? Do we need to know these fine points in infant development in order to be good parents? Well, strictly speaking, no. Good parents will manage with or without a knowledge of the theory of child development. But with such knowledge I believe that the job of rearing a child can be made easier. The unease, the uncertainty and anxiety which is experienced by even the best of parents when presented with a child's incomprehensible behavior can be alleviated at least in part by such knowledge. Further—and now we are very practical—it is this knowledge which can guide the parent in handling the difficult situations, in helping the child overcome the typical problems of each stage of development.

Let's begin with an illustration, one of the practical problems which may emerge in the first three months of life. On behalf of the sleepless parents let's take an affliction of early infancy which creates very practical problems for parents. We can describe the problem in this way: The infant cries fitfully for hours. He may doze off after a lusty meal and wake up an hour later whimpering, crying fretfully, then screaming. If his mother holds him he may subside for a while, but soon the howling begins again. He is not ill. He does not have colic. We'll assume for purposes of this illustration that a physician has examined the child and finds no medical problem. What is this then? "He must be hungry," his mother says, but doubtfully, recalling a prodigious meal. He is offered another feeding, but after a short time it's clear this isn't what he wanted at all. But if he isn't hungry, why does he make those sucking motions with his mouth, and why does he seem to want something in his mouth?

We need to have a theory. Let's try an old one, first. "He is spoiled and he just wants attention. He is using crying as a weapon against his parents, as a means of getting his own way." Now this theory is based on the premise that an under-three-month-old infant has the mental equipment to carry out a plot against his parents, that he takes pleasure in disturbing their sleep and in exercising his tyranny over them. In order to carry out such a diabolical scheme the infant would have to have (1) an idea (2) a perception of events in an objective world (3) at least a rudimentary ability to see causal relations. Our knowledge of the mental equipment of the under-three-month-old infant will not support this theory. He can't yet have an idea that his behavior can influence events in an objective world since he has neither ideas nor a perception of self in relation to an objective world.

Let's try another theory which takes into account the needs and the equipment of the infant of this age. At this stage his behavior is still motivated by urgent biological needs. Any disturbance which he manifests will be produced by pain or discomfort originating in a body organ. Either organic illness or an unsatisfied body need will produce pain or discomfort in the infant of this age. Since we have ruled out organic disturbance as a primary cause in this disturbance, we need to examine the problem as an unsatisfied body urge. Since we have also ruled out hunger as a factor, we need to look further. But the patient won't talk.

We observe his behavior during these crying sessions. In the moments that he is not crying the mouth makes urgent sucking motions and sometimes the hand will find its way into the mouth to be vigorously sucked. This suggests the possibility that the unsatisfied need which we are searching for is connected with sucking. But how can that be? Haven't we established the fact that this infant has been fed and is not hungry? True. But we also know that sucking is experienced by the infant as a need which is independent of hunger. It is largely satisfied through nursing, especially in the breast-fed infant who has to work hard for his meal, but a large number of babies are left, even after feeding, with still unsatisfied sucking needs and this is experienced as an unbearable tension in the mouth. It is this tension which produces the disturbance we have described. Since this need is very specific we find that walking the baby, offering him more food, any of the usual means of comfort, will have little or no effect.

If we are right, if this distress is unsatisfied sucking need, then the provision of additional sucking should alleviate the discomfort. In the last few years a few very perceptive pediatricians began to try the old-fashioned pacifier with the infants who showed all these signs of unsatisfied sucking need. In all but a very small percentage of cases this disturbance, which had long baffled parents and pediatricians, cleared up in a short time!

But isn't there a danger that a pacifier might be habit-forming? Dr. Spock who has furthered the cause of the pacifier as a specific measure for this specific need has shown that it is rarely "habit forming" and, as a matter of fact, most babies on whom it has been tried, begin to lose interest in the pacifier when the intense sucking needs begin to subside. I have observed that around three or four months there is diminished interest in the pacifier in those babies who used it and this corresponds to our observations that the sucking need also begins to lose its urgent and imperative quality around this stage. At the point where the baby himself begins to lose interest in the pacifier it's probably a good idea to withdraw it gradually and see if he can't manage without it. If he still seems to need it, one can restore it to him temporarily.

I think we might only run into difficulties in the use of a pacifier if we continue to use it in later months, quite literally as a pacifier, that is to keep the baby quiet. In the last half of the first year it is unlikely that the baby needs additional sucking from a pacifier. Its continued use, then, may be due to other causes. Perhaps a busy mother has found it too easy to quiet the baby by putting the pacifier in his mouth. Here there is a chance that the baby will become attached to the pacifier as a kind of all-purpose soother and we don't want to encourage this tendency.

The problem of unsatisfied sucking need and the use of the pacifier for supplementary sucking is a good demonstration of the relationship of theory to practice. As long as the cause of this infant disturbance was unknown or misconstrued, we could find no workable solutions. If we operate on the old theory that the infant is a cunning fellow who plots the overthrow of his parents behind the bars of his crib, then our methods of handling this disturbance will be based on principles of counter revolution. As a matter of fact that is just about what happened in the nurseries of thirty years ago. Well-intentioned parents, confronted with a screaming infant who was neither hungry, wet nor sick, maintained a siege on the other side of the nursery door, heroically resisting the onslaught from within, each parent holding the other back from the weakness of surrender, for the rebel's character was in danger if they gave an inch, and the question of Who Was To Be Master of This House was being settled this night.

Today we wince at these memories of an earlier child training. This victory over a three-month-old infant seems shabby and pointless to our modern views. And while the infant of this age does not consciously hold grudges, the urgent drives of this period are not diverted by an act of will on the part of parents. If satisfaction is denied them, the tension increases and will be discharged through crying, fretfulness, disturbances of eating, elimination, or sleep. In the end the drives are victorious in early infancy. There was no victory over them in the "let them cry it out" nursery of the '20's; the drives avenged themselves in the increase in those disturbances of infancy which derive from unsatisfied urges. There was no "discipline" achieved then or now for the tiny infant because he has no equipment to cooperate with us in the management of his drives.

FEEDING AND FEEDING THEORIES.

PERHAPS you remember our attempts in the '20's and '30's to discipline the infant stomach. The by-the-clock feeding schedules of this era were derived from a psychological theory that character formation begins from the day of birth, and orderly habits of feeding were expected to lay the foundations for a firm character. The four-hour-feeding schedule was based upon the observation that the average baby will waken for feedings *about* every four hours during the first months. The statistically average baby with a built-in Swiss Movement probably did not suffer much from this scientific caprice unless he frivolously changed over from Standard to Daylight Saving Time, or Eastern to Central, in which case he was in trouble, too. But the Independent, the Radical, whose stomach contracted under another time system or with no time system to speak of, fell into bad times during this era. The task of disciplining this unruly fellow, of getting the stomach to contract with the average, became a career for conscientious parents of that time. A good mother of the period closed her ears to the noise, set her teeth, and waited until the kitchen clock registered hunger. The consequence of "giving in" to such eccentric appetites in infants was set forth in stern addresses to parents in home magazines. This was known as coddling and was destined to lead to malformations of character.

The proponents of these theories were able to testify that in time most babies, regardless of personal idiosyncracies, were won over to Standard Time, i.e., the four-hour schedule. This might appear to be a tribute to the plasticity of human beings, but the facts are that most babies, without benefit of the clock or the caprices of psychology, arrive at something like a four-hour schedule after the first two or three months. This is a matter that has to do with the size of the baby at birth, the growth needs of a particular baby and a number of other factors, but all our contemporary evidence seems to show that it cannot be masterminded by an adult with a clock.

Our experiment in getting babies' stomachs to contract at orderly intervals produced some unforeseen consequences. A struggle over food was set up in the earliest months of infancy and very often the battle over food was waged over the family dinner table for years afterward. Eating problems were high on the list of complaints to pediatricians and child guidance clinics in the '20's and '30's. The thwarted instincts got their revenge.

Today's baby is fed when he shows signs of hunger, and if this seems trite to the contemporary reader, let me remind him that twenty years were devoted to the reform of infant stomachs before we emerged with this cliché. Today's baby, with his unreconstructed stomach, shows every sign of flourishing under this regime. His relationship with his mother is more harmonious than that of the clock baby because his mother satisfies his hunger. And since food and the obtaining of food creates no struggle between him and his mother, feeding problems have dropped way down on the list of complaints to pediatricians and guidance clinics.

"How do we know," says a cautious mother, "that today's theory is a better theory? These theories begin to resemble women's fashions. How do we know that clock feeding won't come back next year along with a change in the hem line?"

Parents have a right to be skeptical when they survey the eccentric turns of child-rearing practices in the past twenty-five years. But what makes a good theory? A theory is not, after all, a fashion. A scientific theory derives from observation. It is a valid theory when it passes rigid tests in use. The theories of infant feeding we described in use in the '20's were poor theories because they were not derived from a large body of observation. They were poor theories, also, in that they made assumptions regarding the physical and mental equipment of an infant that could not have been verified through infant observation. All available information then, as well as now, shows that the infant in the early months has no mental processes that could enable him to postpone satisfaction of his hunger or suppress his appetite. The infant's hunger is imperative, the drive for satisfaction is urgent, biologically reinforced to insure survival. To withhold satisfaction of this hunger is to oppose the most necessary and impelling drives of the infant. With this information we could predict from an arm-chair—no need for large-scale experimentation—that withholding of satisfaction would produce reactions of extreme helplessness and distress in an infant and produce conflict between him and his mother.

We think today's theories of infant feeding are better theories because they take into strict account the nature of the infant and the kind of equipment he brings into the world. We think they are better theories because they have held up well in the test. The methods derived from our present-day theories promote a harmonious infant-mother relationship. They have substantially reduced the incidence of serious feeding disturbances in children.

Our present-day methods of infant feeding are not really new at all, of course. They are practically as old as the human race. All that is new is the empirical evidence that has been built up to give scientific support to the methods. Fashions in feeding infants? Unless we should choose to ignore an enormous body of scientific information on infant development—or unless a new breed of infants appears on the face of the earth, there is probably not much chance that these methods will be drastically revised.

But why do we go to so much trouble to discuss old and new theories of infant rearing? It's a roundabout way of arriving at a point which is really the point of this book. A method of child-rearing is not—or should not be—a whim, a fashion or a shibboleth. It should derive from an understanding of the developing child, of his physical and mental equipment at any given stage and, therefore, his readiness at any given stage to adapt, to learn, to regulate his behavior according to parental expectations.

If we follow these principles, we can see that there is not *a* method of child rearing but a method for this particular child at this particular stage in his development. From this we can see that a method that is indicated for one stage of development may be completely unsuited for another stage of development. For example, the principle underlying our care of the infant in the first months is one of total gratification of need. But if we apply this principle to the rearing of the two year old or the still older child we would be rearing a self-centered, extremely dependent, ill-mannered child. The difference clearly is in the equipment of the infant and equipment of the older child. We satisfy, as far as possible, all needs of the tiny infant because he is completely dependent and has no means for controlling his own urges. But as the child's physical and mental equipment matures he is able more and more to take over the regulation of his own body needs and to control his impulses. As his readiness for self-control gradually reveals itself, we increase our expectations for him and alter our methods accordingly.

A very large number of the problems that appear in infancy and childhood appear at the juncture points of new developmental phases. As we saw in the preceding chapter, each of the major phases of development in infancy brings forth new problems for the child and for his parents. The emergence of a strong love bond between the baby and his mother produces a period of anxiety at separation in the child. The onset of independent locomotion, the striving for the upright posture, produces its own anxieties and typical behavior problems whenever body activity is interfered with. Body independence in the second year and the emerging sense of an independent self bring forth a period of negativism. The cultural demands of weaning and toilet training in the second year create their own problems for the pleasure-loving child who is now expected more and more to meet externally imposed demands.

Each child reacts in his own way to the problems presented by new phases of development. There may be transitory disturbances of eating or sleeping or disorders of behavior that accompany any of these phases. For these reasons it no longer makes sense to speak of "feeding problems" or "sleep problems" or "negative behavior" as if they were distinct categories, but to speak of "problems of development" and to search for the meaning of feeding and sleep disturbances or behavior disorders in the developmental phase which has produced them. If we employ this approach we will find that these disturbances have special significance for each developmental phase and we are in a much better position to understand them and to find methods of dealing with them.

DISTURBANCES CONNECTED WITH SEPARATION ANXIETY.

WE HAVE already seen in our earlier discussion how the baby in the third quarter of the first year commonly reacts to separation from his mother with some anxiety. Babies vary a great deal in their reactions. This anxiety may be very mild or it may be fairly severe. Typically, we see something like this: The baby protests when mother leaves him, if only for a short time. He complains if she occupies herself with tasks in another room. He doesn't want other persons to take care of him. He objects to bed-time, nap-time, the inevitable times of separation.

The developmental problem, as we have seen, is connected with the baby's strong attachment to his mother and his primitive fear that when she disappears she is lost to him. When he can't see her, she has ceased to exist in this primitive thinking. It's very clear that what this baby needs is a concept; he needs to know that his mother has a permanent and substantial existence independent of his perception of her. But this concept will not emerge for a few months yet and in the meantime the baby has a problem and his parents have a problem.

Now, of course, the baby doesn't just mope around for a few months until the concept emerges. He is actively investigating problems of disappearance and return in the extensive experiments of this period. We would find the spirit of scientific inquiry admirable in this pocket-size scientist if he didn't choose to employ his parents as the chief subjects in these experiments on disappearance and return. We would also find it easier if he confined his studies to the daylight hours. However fruitful for his science, it is very hard on parents to give demonstrations of the permanence of their existence at 2:00 a.m. They have enough trouble proving they're alive to themselves at that hour!

So there are a number of practical problems for parents as well as the baby during this period. How shall we deal with these reactions to separation? How can we help the baby overcome these problems? Should mother remain with him constantly to reassure him? Even if this were practical, what would it achieve? The baby might not experience anxiety, but he would not learn to develop his own means for overcoming the fear of separation. What shall we do, then?

Experienced mothers have learned that they do not need to rush in to offer comfort and reassurance for every cry or protest which comes from the infant, especially the baby of this age. In the last quarter of the first year and in the second year we find that the infant can tolerate small amounts of discomfort and anxiety without being reduced to helplessness or panic. Frequently, at this age, the protesting and complaining at minor frustrations or at mother's leaving him for a while, will die down after a short time without requiring reassurance. Even at bedtime the ritual protests and indignant noises of the older infant may not require a visit. If we wait a bit the sounds subside without reassurance from us. But if the crying of the infant is of another kind, if we sense unusual anxiety or terror, we know that he is in real need of us and we go to him to offer comfort and reassurance.

Let's see if we can find a principle here which can guide us. We understand that the older infant finds it painful to be separated from beloved persons. We grant him the right to protest. At the same time this pain, this discomfort, is something he can learn to tolerate *if it is not excessive*. We need to help him manage small amounts of discomfort and frustration. If we are too quick to offer our reassuring presence, he doesn't need to develop his own tolerance. How do we know how much he can tolerate? By testing a bit the limits of his tolerance become known to us. The point at which protesting and complaining crying turns into an urgent or terrified summons is the point where most of us would feel he needs us and we would go to him. This is real anxiety and he needs our reassurance. But we need not regard all crying of the older infant and young child as being of the same order. At this age, in contrast to the period of early infancy, the baby can manage small amounts of anxiety or discomfort by himself. We only need to judge his *real* need for parental reassurance and give it.

The night waking that commonly occurs during this phase also requires good judgment in handling. The baby who wakens with anxious cries should, of course, be reassured by mother or father. Often it is sufficient for him to hear the voice of a parent, to be patted gently, in order to return to sleep. As far as possible we should try to reassure the child in his own bed. Picking him up, rocking him, is usually not necessary and seems indicated only when the baby is unusually distressed by anxiety or illness. In the common, not very severe types of night waking we encounter at this age we should not find it necessary to walk with the child, visit, produce toys, get drinks of water and in other ways create diversions and entertainment for him. We find if we offer special satisfactions and pleasures to the child who wakens at night that we provide another motive for waking, quite apart from the need for reassurance—the motive of pleasure gain. The outstanding example of this is found in those cases where a mother, yielding to her own fatigue, takes the baby into her own bed. This solution is such a satisfactory one from the baby's point of view that he can practically be depended upon to waken regularly for a repeat performance. It's not a good solution for the parents and from the point of view of the baby's mental health it is not a good solution either. We are much better off if we do not get into such situations.

But what about the baby who has severe anxiety at bed-time, wakens several times a night in great fright and shows signs of extreme fear whenever he is briefly separated from his mother during the day? Here we are dealing with something else. The methods which normally are helpful to babies in overcoming separation fears may have very limited usefulness. We need to go in search of causes first of all.

What kinds of things might produce severe and excessive reactions to separation? It may be that some experience connected with separation from mother has caused the child to feel in danger if mother is away. A fairly uncomplicated example comes to mind. When Carol was eight months old, she developed a sleep disturbance that was unusually severe. She wakened screaming around eleven each night and in spite of her parents' efforts to console her and reassure her, she could not be persuaded to go back to sleep for hours. Her terror was very real and she clung to her mother desperately, in dread of her bed and the possibility of mother's leaving her. The sleep disturbance had started when she wakened one night when her parents were out and a stranger, an unfamiliar baby sitter, came into the room. At the sight of the strange face, the baby began to scream in terror. The sitter presumably did everything she could to reassure Carol, but Carol's terrified crying continued for hours, actually until the parents returned home. From that night on and for several weeks to come Carol wakened regularly at night, repeating the heart-breaking cries, the tense wakefulness, even though her parents were there to give proof that they had not gone away.

Why did this event make such an impression on the baby? "It's funny," said her parents. "She never seemed to mind before if she wakened and saw a baby sitter instead of us. We haven't always been able to get the same sitter. We just didn't expect anything like this." To understand this event we need to fill in the gaps through our understanding of infant development. Carol's reaction to the stranger now, in contrast to her earlier reaction, "she never seemed to mind before," tells us of her altered relationship to her mother, a characteristic of her age. We know that the attachment to the mother is especially strong at this stage of development and a strange face may disturb the child at this age even when encountered in the day-time. The reaction to the strange face, as we have seen, is an indication of the discrimination of the mother as a person and the recognition of her as the person who gives satisfactions and protection. The stranger's face that appears when mother's face is expected produces anxiety because it symbolizes the absence or loss of the mother. Ordinarily, in such circumstances, the child's anxiety disappears as soon as he becomes aware of mother's presence. But when Carol wakened that night and saw the stranger's face, mother did not appear to relieve the anxiety and this experience made a very strong impression on the baby.

But why should Carol continue to waken at night after this event? And why isn't she reassured after seeing her parents and able to go back to sleep? Here, again, since the baby cannot tell us, we need to fall back on a theoretical explanation. We have good reason to believe that babies of Carol's age, even perhaps younger, have dreams of a fairly simple type. One type of dream which is fairly common in the whole period of early childhood is the anxiety dream in which a frightening experience in waking life is repeated over and over. The dreaming child, re-experiencing the anxiety, will typically waken with frightened cries which are both a reaction to the dream and a summons to the parents.

It is very probable that Carol's regular waking with great anxiety following the experience with the sitter was caused by an anxiety dream in which the event was repeated, the strange face appeared in the dream and recreated the original anxiety.

And why doesn't she go back to sleep after mother and father appear to reassure her and demonstrate that everything is all right? Why does she remain tense and wakeful as if dreading the return to bed and to sleep? Very possibly because if she goes back to the bed and falls asleep that stranger's face will come back to frighten her! For Carol doesn't know that she dreams. Until well into the third year she may not know that she dreams. In infancy and early childhood the events of the dream are taken as real events and we know how even the two year old who has some language and can tell us what frightened him will feel convinced that there really *was* a tiger in his bed.

We can't explain any of this to Carol. She has no language yet. She doesn't discriminate between dream and reality. Her anxiety is causing her great distress. Her parents' attempts to reassure her have not had much effect on the night waking. What can we do? We need to find some means of helping Carol overcome her anxiety, but what means do we have for helping a pre-verbal child?

Let's look for cues in normal child development. How does the baby normally overcome his anxiety at separation? Babies who do not suffer with excessive anxiety seem to develop their own methods of overcoming such fears. We observe that they approach the problem on the basis of "disappearance and return." A mother, for example, "disappears" but regularly returns. The baby at this stage probably sees this as a magical disappearance and return since, we must remember, he doesn't yet have the concept of a substantial or permanent object that exists whether he sees it or not. But this magic suffices for ordinary purposes. The magic explanation can break down under certain experiences. If mother "disappears" and does not return, especially if the baby is anxious or has special need for her, and if a familiar person cannot substitute for her in her absence, then the magic formula is of no use and the baby, without other means for reassuring himself, experiences strong anxiety.

But let's continue our observations of the normal infant of this age as he investigates the problem of disappearance and return. What is his favorite game during this phase of development? Peek-a-boo and all the variations of this game will occupy the baby interminably. He will play the game by pulling a diaper or his bib over his face, then pull it off with cries of delight. He will play hiding games with any cooperative adult, watching them disappear with a solemn expression on his face, greeting their return with joyful screams. He can keep up such games much longer than you can.

What is the pleasure in these games? If the disappearance and return of loved persons is such a problem to him, why should the baby turn all this into a boisterous game? The game serves several purposes. First, by *repeating* disappearance and return under conditions that he can control (the missing person can *always* be discovered again with brief waiting) he is helping himself to overcome his anxiety in connection with this problem. Second, the game allows him to turn a situation that would, in reality, be painful, into a pleasurable experience.

Now let's make a parallel observation with Carol. She also *repeats* the experience of mother's disappearance in her night-time waking. She repeats the original anxiety as well. There is even a similarity in the mechanism involved in Carol's repetition and the kind of repetition we see in the games of normal infants. Carol, too, is repeating this frightening experience in order to overcome its effects. (If you or I should have a frightening experience, a burglary, for example, we would find ourselves repeating the event through talking about it for several days to anyone who cares to listen. This verbal repetition would help us overcome the bad effects of the experience.) But Carol has no language; she can only repeat the experience through primitive mechanisms, as in the anxiety dream.

So here, finally, is the way in which our knowledge of normal child development provides the clue to handling Carol's sleep disturbance. Theoretically, if we can help Carol employ repetition of disappearance and return in the game that serves all normal babies in overcoming separation anxiety, she might be able to work out her problem in the daytime instead of the nighttime. Repetition through the game might replace repetition through the dream. Furthermore, since the game of disappearance and return can be controlled and the dream and the nightwaking cannot be brought under control so easily, it offers a much better opportunity for mastery than the dream.

This piece of theory became the basis for the measures that were recommended in helping Carol overcome her anxiety. Carol was given every opportunity to play "going away" and "coming back" through the nursery games we have described. Mama would hide her face; mama's face would return. Mama would disappear around the corner; mama would come back. In this way play substituted for language. The game said "Mama always comes back" at this stage of development where language explanations were not possible. The game afforded Carol a measure of control over disappearance and return, for she could always "bring back" her mother. And, of course, the game allowed Carol to work out the problem in her waking hours so that gradually the sleep disturbance disappeared.

From the standpoint of prevention of such a sleep disturbance as Carol's we can see that it is not advisable to bring unfamiliar persons in for baby care if we can help it. After the early months, that is, as soon as the baby clearly discriminates his mother's face and reacts to strange faces, the baby needs to know the person who is going to substitute for his mother, if only for a few hours of care. To waken at night and not find a mother may be unpleasant and may bring some tears, but it need not be a shocking and frightening experience unless the person who appears is a stranger.

ACTIVITY BRINGS PROBLEMS, TOO.

As SOON as the baby moves from passive dependence upon his mother into active use of his body for pursuit of his own objectives, a new set of problems emerges. A large number of these problems originate in the conflicting interest of a baby and his family. For example, the baby's interest in self-feeding in the last quarter of the first year, a laudatory thing in itself, is not entirely in the best interests of his mother. Puréed vegetables, which have not yet reached the stage of color styling in the most advanced commercial baby firms, produce a startling decorative effect upon the walls and ceilings of today's kitchen, painted in the light and cheerful colors that have not yet been color-styled to coordinate with puréed vegetables. Then there is the baby himself, with misfired cereal in his hair, applesauce glistening in his eyes, a beard of spinach, and a small lunch under each chin, all the while harboring another three-course meal and beverages under the façade of his plastic apron. Furthermore, the baby *likes* his lunch in his hair and is not at all concerned about the applesauce in his eyes, and any mother can tell you that it will be easier to mop up the kitchen floor and get the puréed vegetables off the ceiling than to persuade the baby to allow his mother to approach him with a face-cloth. Therefore, it is understandable that at this stage of development the baby's drive toward activity, self-help and independence—all splendid and admirable signs in themselves—come into conflict with his mother's interests. She's glad, of course, that he's developing so well and beginning to show his independence—but it was so much neater when mama did the feeding.

How do problems get started? Here's a short story of a short-lived feeding disturbance, one that showed some promise of becoming a more complicated problem before the trouble was spotted:

Paul was a husky nine month old whose appetite from the day

he was born was so lusty that the problem was getting enough food into him at a fast enough rate. He loved his bottle and every variety of solid food he encountered. Meal times were festive occasions with the baby crooning over his favorite dishes and carrying on a line of chatter with his mother in rollicking good spirits. In brief, he was the last baby in the world you would expect to develop a feeding disturbance. But one day when he was nine months old he went on a food strike, and the strike lasted three very unpleasant days.

What had happened? His appetite seemed good enough. But soon after the meal started Paul would begin fussing, tossing himself about in the high chair, pushing away the spoon extended by his mother, batting the cup out of his mother's hand, wailing, complaining—obviously quite mad about something. Was it teething? Well, we'll keep it in mind as a possibility. Had mother started weaning to the cup? No. But it's another important point to keep in mind in understanding feeding disturbances at this age, for weaning can sometimes bring on a revolt through eating disturbances if a baby feels that too much is being expected of him too fast.

It might have been teething, it might have been a great number of things, but after three days of this baffling food strike Paul's parents made a discovery. Paul's father took over a feeding when mother was occupied with dinner preparations and Paul ate heartily and well! Paul's mother stopped what she was doing and watched. "Then it must have something to do with me!" she thought. "I am doing something. But what?" She watched—all the while feeling the implied criticism of herself, and feeling herself a failure as a mother—and this is what she saw: Paul grabbed the spoon from Papa and plastered his face with strained carrots. Papa seemed quite unconcerned. Paul snatched the cup of milk, lifted it clumsily to his face, up-turned the cup and a river of milk cascaded to the floor. Paul's father dodged the avalanche neatly, but his attitude was still serene. Paul's mother winced and moved swiftly for the mop. At the end of this meal Paul's face was a morbid green and orange. His hair was sticky and spikey with applesauce, the floor was blotched for an area of five feet, Paul was happy (he still managed to get a considerable quantity inside of him) and papa was unruffled.

Paul's mother, being a fair-minded woman, saw herself in the same situation. This is what she saw: She saw herself, expertly substituting an extra spoon when Paul would snatch hers. (It works with some babies, maybe with all babies up to a certain stage of development, but after that point the baby wants the fun of actively feeding himself and he *wants* to handle his food and enjoys the messiness.) She saw herself expertly catching the cup, before it turned upside down, and moving it out of reach. (But at this stage of development a baby is fascinated by the cup, wants to bring the cup to his mouth, wants to play with it, wants to see how the river of milk flows out of the cup.) But, of course, it's much neater if mama does the feeding. So mama was engaged in a silent contest with the baby. The baby wanted to be active and to play with his food; mama understandably, but unwisely, was preventing this.

This feeding disturbance was easily remedied. Paul's mother began to allow as much freedom in self-feeding as Paul required. She allowed him to handle spoons and cups to his heart's content. (She wisely put only a little milk in the bottom of the cup he was experimenting with—and increased the amount as skill in drinking improved.) She learned to regard a baby plastered with his lunch and a floor covered with debris with equanimity. She became inventive in giving him foods in forms that he could easily handle with his fingers—hard cooked egg, soft-cooked whole carrots—mashed potatoes, stewed fruits, and so forth. The food strike ended the moment mama caught on. From this point on Paul and his mother were back in their old harmony.

But what about manners? How will a child learn to develop manners if he is permitted to mess and slop his food? He learns remarkably well, we find. The pleasure in messing with food subsides after a while. Meantime the child is learning to use a spoon and a cup, and after an awkward interval the pleasure in handling these tools replaces the primitive pleasure in messing. Paul, for example, was feeding himself practically without assistance at something under one year. He used his fingers or a spoon and handled his cup himself at this stage. At fifteen months he used the spoon and a small fork for most of his self-feeding without any awkwardness. Nearly all babies who are encouraged in their early efforts at self-feeding develop skills in handling eating tools at a surprisingly early stage. The use of tools is modeled after the use of fingers and the skills in finger feeding gradually become transferred to the use of tools.

In the story of Paul we can see how easy it is to fall into a contest with a baby and how thwarted activity can lead to revolt in the baby which may take some unexpected forms of expression. It is possible that if Paul's mother had not recognized the problem in the food strike that this minor eating disturbance might have progressed and become something more serious.

Activity brings other problems, other conflicts of interest between a baby and his family. Activity for the baby means handling objects, the ash-trays, table ornaments, books, the precious toys of older brothers and sisters. Granted that the word "no" has a place in child rearing, the parent who utters "no, no" to a small child hundreds of times a day will soon find either that he is not heard any longer, or that his baby regards "no, no" as a charming game, or that his baby begins to produce little tantrums.

If we can take a cue from principles of child development, we see that a certain amount of active handling of objects is absolutely necessary for the child in discovering and learning about the world around him. He also needs to learn that some activities are not allowed, but here we need to employ wisdom. To teach a baby not to handle mama's precious table ornaments would require such an expenditure of energy, would involve so many contests in the course of baby's day, that the question can be properly raised, "Is it worth it?" Precious and breakable objects are best put out of reach for a few months while the child is learning about objects. We can encourage his learning about objects through allowing him to play with pots and pans and kitchen implements. We can keep some old books on a lower shelf for the baby to play with. (Pulling books out of the shelves loses its fascination after a while if it doesn't become a game with mama and papa, and within a few months it will be even easier to handle this when the baby likes picture books and can be given a shelf of his own.)

In other words, we avoid getting into contests with the baby and we reserve the "no, no" for the occasions during the day when it is really needed.

"But isn't all this terribly permissive? Doesn't a child need to learn self-control?" Yes, of course a child needs to learn self-control. But we're speaking of a baby who doesn't have the means for self-control yet. He only knows that some acts bring parental disapproval. He is not capable of imposing prohibitions upon himself. The desire to look, to touch, to handle is as urgent for him as hunger and as necessary for his intellectual growth as the books we will give him later on. There is only one way to teach an active baby or toddler not to be curious about objects and not to handle them, and this is to use fear, and if we use such severe punishments, a child will avoid forbidden objects and he will also lose his curiosity, with serious consequences for his intellectual development.

We must also remember that this discovery of the world of objects is the phase that precedes language development. Touching, handling, experiencing objects, is the indispensable preliminary to naming objects. A child does not learn the name of an object until he has had physical contact with it, "knows" it. We can find an easy parallel in our own word use even in adult life. We will have difficulty in remembering proper names unless we have had some personal experience, some human contact with the person whose name we have heard. The baby must know the object through his senses before he is ready to learn the name for an object.

As I write this I think of a little girl, Barbara, who had been brought to see me at the age of four because she could not talk. Her vocabulary was not larger than that of an eighteen-month-old child, that is, she had about a dozen words. There was some question, therefore, of serious mental retardation, but there were also some indications in non-verbal tests that this child might have a higher intelligence.

When Barbara entered my playroom she ran around in a giddy and distracted fashion, pointing at every object that attracted her attention and crying shrilly, "NO! NO! NO!" She could not even be encouraged to handle objects and recoiled each time I offered her a toy or one of the desk objects she admired.

For many reasons, none of them simple, Barbara had never made normal contact with objects. The grandmother who cared for Barbara while mother worked had severely restricted the child's contacts with objects through stern prohibitions and punishments. Fear of the grandmother and anxiety during mother's absence had created a disturbance in the child's relationship to human objects as well.

In order to help Barbara, we had to provide the four-year-old girl with the experiences she had missed in the second year. We had to restore a mama to a little girl, we had to build human ties which had been broken in the second year, and we had to open up the world of objects to this child, to allow her to touch, to handle, to experience objects as the necessary, the indispensable phase that leads to language. Within a year the four-year-old who could not talk had acquired a vocabulary that placed her almost within the normal range for her age.

Barbara's story is not at all typical, of course. I only cite it here to show how extremes of restriction in early childhood, rigid prohibitions against the handling and experiencing of objects can lead to a crippling of intellectual functioning and, in Barbara's case, an inability to develop speech.

So, if we can find a principle to guide us in the handling of the child between nine and eighteen months, we can see that we need to allow enough opportunity for handling and investigation of objects to further intellectual development and just enough restriction required for family harmony and for the safety of the child.

This principle is applicable, too, to the handling of the activity needs connected with motor development. We have already seen how the child has powerful drives to achieve the upright posture and how mastery of crawling, climbing, standing, walking is achieved through thousands of repetitions of each of the component acts of this process. The child's need for activity is felt as strongly as any other biological urge. During the period of mastery the desire for unrestricted motor activity is an essential need. Now clearly there need to be some restrictions for the safety of a child who is quite without judgment during a good part of this period. He will imperil himself dozens of times during a day and we will have to remove an outraged baby from the rocking chair that is about to catapult him, or the chest of drawers from which he is about to take off. He will be mad at us for rescuing him from a danger that is not at all clear to him, but rescue him we must.

On the other hand, if we restrict a large part of his activity either through our own exaggerated anxiety or because his activity is a great trouble to us, we will run into another group of problems. If we follow him around in great fear that he will bump his head under the table, if we are turned to jelly every time he takes a flop, he will certainly feel our anxiety, and his own self-confidence will suffer as a consequence. We will also run into trouble with an active, creeping child if we restrict him to a play-pen, or keep him in a play-pen when he shows signs of rebellion at this confinement. It is understandable that it serves the convenience of a busy mother with more than one child to have the baby in a place where she can easily keep her eye on him, or leave him safely for a short time, but if we want to avoid a nursery revolution we should use good judgment here, recognizing the need of a child for activity and space and providing it within the practical limitations of the house plan and mother's own needs. When the play-pen has outlived its usefulness and becomes a prison to an active child it will serve no purpose to persuade the baby to remain in it.

When the baby begins to walk we need to keep in mind the same principles. Restricted space creates more problems with a toddler than most of us realize. Apartment dwellers and the owners of small, efficient homes will justly greet this remark with a cynical retort. What *can* you do, after all, if the space has already been restricted by a diabolical architect? But if we recognize the toddler's need for active mastery of his new-found motor skills, we can apply a little ingenuity in room arrangement to create space without hazards for a small child and greatly reduce the conflict between child and parents. Outdoor play space is a necessity for this age and if there is no yard adjacent to the home the city's parks or tot-lots will provide a decent substitute and it will be well worth the trouble to a busy mother if time can be arranged each day for outdoor activity. In short, body activity is a vital need for this age, and too many restrictions on motility create irritability, temper outbursts and conflicts between baby and family which require much time to undo and are often easily avoided through practical approaches to the child's needs.

INTRODUCTION TO BOWEL TRAINING.

IF WE ask, "When is the best time to begin toilet training?" we can find some clues through a knowledge of child development. In order for a child to cooperate in his toilet training he must be able to control the sphincter muscles, he must have the ability to postpone the urge to defecate, and he must be able to give a signal to be taken to the bathroom, or to get there under his own steam. In normal child development all of these conditions may not be present until fifteen to eighteen months, or later.

It is possible to get an eight- or nine-month-old baby with

regular movements to sit on a potty after breakfast until he produces a b.m., but the baby at this age is not a partner in his training. His successes are due to his mother's knowledge of his elimination pattern, and his willingness to sit on the potty chair can be attributed to the fact that, if he is not yet actively crawling, there is not much else he can do but sit—and a potty chair is as good a seat as any. Usually, we find that the baby whose training started out on this basis will show a marked disinclination to use of the potty after he begins to get around on his own and has any choice in the matter and for several months following the first independent locomotion he may not be any more cooperative about the use of a potty than a child who has never had the pleasure of making its acquaintance. It's hard to say whether there are any advantages in beginning the training of the child before he is able to participate in the process, to cooperate actively in his own training.

Even at a later stage of development, let us say in the second year, when we are able to engage the child's cooperation in the process of toilet training, we are impressed with the difficulties he encounters in understanding these new demands and in cooperating with them. First of all, although it is perfectly plain to us that the use of a potty is a respectable and civilized way of disposing of the body's products, from the child's point of view it makes very little sense at the beginning. Let's look at it first from his standpoint.

His mother first "introduces" him to the potty, sometimes to the toilet with a little seat. The word "introduces" is a euphemism since at thirteen or fourteen months he is not pleased to make its acquaintance and little cares whether he meets it again. But he loves his mommy and for reasons which he cannot divine she would like him to sit on the little chair with the hole or the big toilet with the little seat with the hole. So he does. It's a bore and there are lots of other things he'd rather do, but he good naturedly agrees to sit on the hole. One day, partly by clever design and quickness on his mother's part, largely by accident, he produces a b.m. in the pot or on the toilet. His mother's face registers delight and surprise and she makes approving sounds and little cries of "good" and "big-boy." He is not sure just what he has done to bring forth such a demonstration from his mother but now he finds out. In the bottom of the pot rests an object, one that is familiar to him from another context, let us say, and which is apparently the cause of this accolade. He joins in the congratulatory noises just to be sociable, but it is not yet clear to him just how this object got there and why it has created such joy in his mother.

Since he doesn't know how he achieved this miracle he is unable to repeat it voluntarily. But in the weeks and months to come mother's anticipation and other accidental successes combine to produce an association between defecation and the potty. He also comes to know that he made this object, that it came from him. But this presents a problem in itself. He regards this b.m. as part of his body. We say that's ridiculous and how could he imagine that a body's waste product was part of the body? But he doesn't know that and we could never explain it to him at this age, either. No, the best he can do in explaining this phenomenon with the type of thinking he has at his disposal is this: it is like an appendage to the body, it is part of his body and as part of himself he values this product. He has already learned that his mother values it, too. And since he produces his b.m.'s on the potty to please his mother, he comes to regard this act in the same way that an older child regards a gift to a loved person.

Now in order to engage the cooperation of the second-year child in this education for cleanliness we become partners with him in a fraud. We behave as if these productions on the potty are objects of value; we accept this gift of love with demonstrations of approval—after which we indifferently flush it down the toilet! From the point of view of the child in the second year this is one of life's great mysteries. When he values an object he wants to keep it and see it. This goes for beloved persons, beloved toys, cherished objects. The fate of his gift, its disappearance into the cavern of noisy rushing waters, strikes him as a strange way to accept and dispose of an offering of such value.

The toilet itself adds to the madness and mystery of this operation, in the eyes of the second-year child. Whatever *we* may think of the convenience and efficiency of indoor plumbing, the small child has his own ideas. This vitreous monster with its yawning jaws does not invite friendship or confidence at this age. The most superficial observation will reveal that it swallows up objects with a mighty roar, causes them to disappear in its secret depths, then rises again thirstily for its next victim which might be—just anyone.

I recall a little boy who had never been persuaded to use the toilet and who came to me at the age of four because "he couldn't be trained." He was still soiling and wetting his pants. He was a perfectly intelligent child who understood very well what was expected of him and he had long ago learned that everybody else used the toilet, all big boys and girls and their mommies and daddies. His parents thought he was being stubborn and defiant and that he was soiling his pants out of revenge. I suppose this was true to a certain extent. But when he got to know me and to trust me he confided to me that "there is a lobster in the toilet that's gonna eat me up." This baffled me until I asked a few careful questions and learned that he meant "there is a *monster* in the toilet" and then I understood him very well. He was very glad to tell me about the monster who lived in the toilet. He had been trying to explain this to people for years, but they wouldn't believe him. The monster lived in the toilet and made noises like a lion. "Gr-r-r, I'm gonna eat you up!" My patient demonstrated this to me, sneaking out of a closet stealthily, creeping up behind me, and roaring mightily "Gr-r-r-, I'm a lobster, I'm gonna eat you up!" "Now be scared!" he whispered fiercely.

Now considering the situation, my patient was behaving with understandable caution. If there is a monster in the toilet, it's much smarter to make your do-do's in your pants, risking censure, disgrace, or anything that comes. But is this nonsense? Is this little boy pulling my leg with this lobster stuff? Do kids really believe that? I can only say that after going into the matter of monsters in the toilet in several fruitful discussions my patient began to use the toilet for the first time in his life and the monster descended to the psychic depths from which he had emerged.

But this is very unusual. Most children of four have long ago established toilet habits and they would probably be a little cynical if they heard my patient's theory. But before the age of reason most other children, too, have entertained such fantastic theories about the toilet. The reason we capture this theory in our four year old is that he never overcame this fear which normally should have subsided in the third year. And because he never overcame it he was able to put into words at the age of four what our little children in the second year can only express in behavior or by means of a limited vocabulary.

If we understand the process of toilet training from the point of view of the pre-verbal child with his primitive thinking we can help the child accept his training and cooperate with it, we can understand his difficulties and not increase them, and we can avoid some serious problems which can emerge from the training period. We can easily understand, for example, why training on the potty will be more acceptable than training on the toilet. On the potty the child can sit with his feet on the ground which reassures him against the fear of falling. On the potty he doesn't have to have direct contact with the noisy machine that makes things disappear. The size of the potty chair is "right" for him; the big toilet is as high as his waist and even with a little toilet seat, it's very high up. It's conceivable that many adults would endure constipation rather than sit on a toilet in a bathroom scaled for giants in which the seat is level with the adult waist. Even if you know you can't fall in, you might decide that, after all, this is something that can wait.

Let's return to a problem that we posed at the very beginning of this discussion, the problem of engaging the cooperation of an active and busy toddler in an educational project that doesn't interest him in the least at the beginning. The important thing to remember is that no normally active child in the second year will submit to a method of training in which he is compelled to sit on a potty until he produces. It will require considerable parental pressure to get an active toddler to sit there for more than a few minutes, and such pressure or insistence will inevitably create rebellion and an inability to produce on the potty. Furthermore the method of regularly placing a child on the potty does not in itself induce a bowel movement, of course, and "works" as a method only in those cases where a child regularly tends to have his movements at a certain time, shortly after breakfast, for example. For those children who do not have their bowel movements at regular times (very possibly these children are in the majority in the second year) this procedure will probably lead to an impasse between child and mother. From the child's point of view this sitting on the potty seems completely foolish.

Another method commonly employed in training is "catching" the child at the point he shows signs of beginning a movement and leading him off to the potty chair. If this method is employed it requires considerable tact on the part of the mother. We need to remember that we are interrupting a natural function, or asking at the very least for a postponement, and if we rush in at this point and whisk the baby off to the potty in a frenzy of activity, the baby will react with anxiety to the experience and the whole problem of achieving sphincter control will be burdened by the child's apprehension about getting to the potty on time.

Whatever method we use we want to avoid pressure, contests of will, anxiety about getting to the potty, and shame about failure. We want to find ways in which we can enlist the child's interest and cooperation in achieving bowel and bladder control. If we look upon this process as education that continues for months and if we take advantage of the child's own readiness to participate in this process, we can patiently win the child's interest and participation in his achievement.

In the beginning stages, when we see him having a b.m., it's probably a good idea to comment on it matter of factly, using a word to identify the act, a word or sound that the child himself can use later on to signal his wish to go to the potty. "Danny's having a b.m." (or any nursery term or sound you wish). Just commenting on this regularly when we notice him having a b.m. will indicate our interest in the process and begin to attract his attention to a process that he has taken for granted throughout. We don't need to do another thing for a little while. After many repetitions a toddler—being a toddler—will begin to draw our attention to the process, knowing that it interests us. (He would do the same thing if we commented or showed our interest regularly in any kind of performance of his—his attempts to use a spoon, or his clapping his hands to music. Soon he would invite our attention to his performance by using a sound or signal to attract us.) So, with his bowel movement, one fine day, if we do not notice or comment, he will make a sound, or use the word we have been using, or in some other way tell us he is having a b.m., and now we have got him to tell us or signal us when he realizes he is having a movement or is about to have one.

Around this point, when we have a signal, it seems right to begin to establish a connection between having a b.m. and a place to have a b.m. It may be fairly easy to suggest that he sit down on the potty chair when he is having his b.m. and to lead him to it. It may not even matter the first few times if we don't take down his pants. We just want him to associate the b.m. with the potty chair and to learn to get there, to sit down and to have it. But anyway one lucky day the child tells us or signals us that he is having or is about to have a b.m., we lead him to the potty chair, get his pants down, and to his great interest and surprise the b.m. goes into the pot. We are pleased, he is interested and pleased that we are pleased, and the first step in training has been completed.

And now will he regularly take himself off to the pot when the urge is felt? Far from it, of course. The next day he may forget about it, or give his signal too late, or just prefer to have his b.m. in the old familiar way. He may not produce another b.m. in the pot for days—or weeks. Meantime we encourage and remind him, approving his successes and not troubling ourselves or him with his failures and eventually, usually after several months, the successes are more frequent than the lapses and finally success is fairly regular.

Well, then, what motives have we employed in getting the child's cooperation in training? Why should a little toddler cooperate in a process that makes so little sense to him at the start? First of all—and most obvious—is his pleasure in having pleased his mother. He recognizes very early that his success in using the potty is met with her approval. This doesn't mean, of course, that his mother needs to put on a large demonstration for his successes or to react to each production as if it were a work of art. It's quite enough to show our honest approval and pleasure in his efforts and his success and, in fact, we can run into trouble by overpraising this accomplishment. If a child feels that his b.m. is so highly prized and valuable he may understandably be reluctant to part with it. But the second important motive in the child's cooperation with bowel training is his own pleasure in accomplishment. He, himself, comes to look upon his success in using the potty as an achievement. He is interested in his b.m. at this stage of his development and appears to take some pride in its production. Since he is quite without embarrassment about his body products, he wants to touch his stool at the beginning of training and we need tactfully to divert him from this without creating a fuss or creating deep shame in him. And since he values his stool as a production of his own body, we also need to appreciate his feelings in our disposing of his b.m. To praise him for his achievement, his "gift," and then hastily flush it down the toilet certainly baffles a child at the beginning of his training. It may make it a little easier for him at the beginning if we allow the stool to remain in the pot while he is in the bathroom. At a later stage when the regular disappearance of his b.m. interests him but doesn't much trouble him, he may like flushing it away himself.

All this is achieved very gradually in the course of the second year and part of the third year. Even after the child knows how to use the potty and gives a signal he will alternate cooperative periods with uncooperative periods, or a "yes" day for the potty and a "no" day. He is not being spiteful or mean in doing this; it's just part of difficult learning. But if we engage in a struggle with the child and turn the toilet training into a duel with two strong-willed opponents we may get outright defiance. And since it's his b.m. and he is the one who ultimately controls the time and place for evacuation, guess who wins most of the time. My friend, The Lobster, with his usual facility for putting the mental processes of the second year into four-year-old language sized up this situation candidly. "*I'm* the boss of my do-do's, not my mother!" he said.

If we do not understand how difficult it is for a small child to master this first lesson in postponement and control of an urge, we can easily become impatient. Many parents do not know that *normally* the process of toilet training, including bladder control, can take many months and we can expect occasional relapses until well into the fourth year. When we hear of a child under eighteen months who is "completely trained overnight" or "in a few days" we can immediately be suspicious. In order to get a small child to acquire control in a very short time, so much pressure must be exerted upon him that we can be certain we will pay a price either in terms of the permanence of this training or in problems in another area. For it probably means that this child learned control quickly through fear of consequences and that the necessity to retain control in order to avoid the dangerous consequences will require such an exertion on his part that problems in this or other areas commonly develop.

SOME DISTURBANCES CONNECTED WITH BOWEL TRAINING.

WE WILL observe in the most normal children that as soon as we begin to make demands upon the child for controlling a body urge some tensions will arise, some anxieties may appear. It is often very puzzling to parents to see a child develop some type of problem behavior around the time toilet training is begun, or is under way, and to find no very clear connection between the behavior and the attitude toward toilet training. If a child develops temper tantrums at this period and also shows an aversion to using the toilet or potty, it's not at all difficult to see the connection, and understanding parents will very sensibly go easy on the toilet training for a while. But here is Patty at seventeen months who is the most cooperative child these days, sits on her potty, is pleased with her successes and behaves in every way like a child who is progressing nicely in her training. But lately Patty has been very difficult at bed-time and has begun to waken two or three times a night. When did this begin? Around fourteen months. When did toilet training begin? Around fourteen months. Could there be any connection? But how could there be when she's such a lamb about her training? Any other little problems? Well, she's fussy about getting her dress dirty, not terribly fussy, you know, but we have remarked on that. Oh, yes, and she's afraid of the maid. We've had her since Patty was five months old, but lately Patty just won't let her take care of her. "Does the maid have anything to do with the toileting?" "Oh, yes, if I'm out she may take over." "Is Patty upset when she has an accident in her pants?" "Yes, at times. She'll cling to me and ask to be held. I always tell her it's all right. I've never scolded her for accidents or made her feel ashamed." "Could the maid have scolded or made shaming remarks?" "I never thought of that. . . ." Little by little we try to piece together the story. Patty, it seems, is trying too hard to achieve her toilet training. Her reactions of shame for accidents and her fussiness about getting her dress dirty are a bit excessive for a child of her age who is learning bowel control. She goes willingly to the toilet because she loves her mommy and wants to please her, but the effort to maintain control is too much for her and she has become afraid of losing control, of having accidents. We suspect that this is also why she is afraid to go to sleep at night. When she is asleep she might lose control, have an accident. Understanding this, working on the theory that there is a relationship between the toilet training and this new set of problems, we propose that we relax the toilet training and our expectations of Patty at this point and see what happens. To everyone's satisfaction and relief Patty's anxiety diminishes in the next week or two, the fussiness about dirt is no longer manifest and the sleeping problem goes back to normal proportions with just the right amount of reluctance to go to sleep that we expect of a healthy child who loves her world, but no longer the anxiety, bordering on terror which had accompanied going to sleep.

In other instances we will see a child who is cooperative in his training, showing little resistance to the process, but who is now very uncooperative, negative and defiant about all manner of other things in his daily routine. Here again, we may find that the child has become obedient with regard to his training out of a wish to obtain mother's approval, or out of a fear of mother's disapproval, and the negative and defiant feelings are removed to another area and expressed in ways that are far removed from the toilet experience. Among the eating disturbances in the second year we have found a number of instances in which a refusal to eat or fussiness in eating coincided with the onset of toilet training. Here, again, the negativism which was the suppressed attitude toward the training process was removed to another area and expressed in regard to food.

Does all this sound very strange and implausible? Are these effects of toilet training just another group of theories which we have concocted to explain some problems of the second year which could be explained more simply? There is a very simple test for these theories when the child is so young that cause and effect are in a close relationship. Whenever we suspect that a relationship exists between a new disturbance of behavior or a manifestation of anxiety and new demands which are being made upon a small child, we propose as a test that we give up the new requirement for a short time and observe the effects (as we did with Patty). In the case of toilet training, when we find that a new disturbance has appeared coincidentally with the requirements for use of the potty, we may suggest that the mother put aside her encouragement of the training or her expectations for the child for a few days or a week or two. It is very impressive to see in a large number of these cases, how the eating disturbance, the temper tantrums, or the sleep disturbance subside when the training is temporarily given up. This would indicate that in these cases a relationship did exist between the training and the new experience. In other cases, where the simple test does not bring about the same result or an improvement in the situation, we can infer other or more complex motives for the disturbance. In those instances in which a disturbance cleared up through temporarily putting aside the training it was usually enough to wait a few weeks until the child was able to resume his training with less anxiety, then to pursue a much more relaxed type of training. Often it is quite sufficient to recognize these symptoms as signs of tension around toilet training and, still continuing encouragement of the training, relax our expectations for the child, go more slowly, give more reassurance.

PREVENTION OF DISORDERS THROUGH EARLY DETECTION.

By RECOGNIZING the signs of disturbance at an early stage we can often apply such simple remedies and prevent a minor disturbance of childhood from becoming a more serious one. We ask ourselves, "What new requirement have we introduced into the child's life or what new problems is he facing in his normal growth and development?" We may find that the child who has just given up the bottle and is very proud of his new achievement ("he didn't seem to mind at all"), has unaccountably developed food fads and fussiness at meal times. Or we may find that a child who has just learned to walk and is giddy with his own achievement ("no fear at all, he'd climb to the top of the bookcase if we let him!") has taken to waking several times a night. Now, of course, we do not need to give back the bottle in the first case and we cannot stop the second child from walking when he is ready for it. But it is very useful to establish the connection if we can because it can help us understand the meaning of a puzzling piece of behavior and our handling of this behavior can be guided by this understanding. If we know that the period of food fads is related to giving up the bottle we will not be upset by the fussiness over food and we will put aside the temptation to coax at meal times or otherwise put pressure on the child. This could lead to perpetuation of meal-time fussiness. If we are patient, and the child is otherwise not under great pressure, we may find the food fussiness gradually disappearing in the course of a few weeks.

Similarly if we know that walking is a big step forward in independence for the small child and that he sometimes feels a little scared at the achievement of so much independence, we will not be alarmed at the night waking and our handling of the problem will be determined by our insight. We will give a certain amount of reassurance at night without giving so much attention and cuddling that we provide an additional motive for waking. We will keep an eye on the day-time behavior, supporting independence without putting any additional pressure on the child for more independence and allowing him, at times when he seems to want it, to be a little baby. If this problem is specifically related to the achievement of a new step in development, walking, it will disappear after a while with mastery of this new skill.

PART III

Eighteen Months to Three Years

4. In Brobdingnag

THE MAGICIAN.

THE magician is seated in his high chair and looks upon the world with favor. He is at the height of his powers. If he closes his eyes, he causes the world to disappear. If he opens his eyes, he causes the world to come back. If there is harmony within him, the world is harmonious. If rage shatters his inner harmony, the unity of the world is shattered. If desire arises within him, he utters the magic syllables that cause the desired object to appear. His wishes, his thoughts, his gestures, his noises command the universe.

The magician stands midway between two worlds, but the world he commands at eighteen months is already waiting to take away his magic, and he himself has begun to make certain observations which cast doubt upon his powers. Somewhere around the end of the first year he began to discover that he was not the initiator of all activity, that causes for certain events existed outside of himself, quite independent of his needs and his wishes, but now, in the middle of the second year, the magician makes a discovery which will slowly lead him to his downfall. The magician will be undone by his own magic. For when he ascends to the heights of word-magic, when he discovers he can command with a word, he will be lured into a new world, he will commit himself unknowingly to new laws of thinking, the principles of this second world which oppose magic by means of the word.

Magic belongs to the first system of thought, the pre-verbal world. What we call rational thought processes can only come about through the development of language and the second system of thought is built on words and the manipulation of words.

The few words which the magician commands at eighteen months do not yet serve higher mental processes. They serve his wants, his immediate needs, and he acquires them in much the same way that the untutored adult acquires a foreign language by first learning the words for his needs—in what we call "restaurant French." If the child in the second year learns "mama," "cookie," "bye-bye," "car," it is because he wants mama, wants a cookie, wants to go bye-bye, wants to go in the car. He learns the names of certain objects which are desirable to him. But he does not yet have rational or orderly thought processes, he has neither the vocabulary nor the concepts to construct an organized and coherent view of the world or events around him. So the first stages of language development are still closer to the primitive system of thought than they are to the secondary thought processes. They serve magic, not reason. And the child's view of the world is still dominated by his primitive thinking. He is still a magician.

The sources of a magician's powers are always of interest to his audience, and this seems to be an excellent time to inquire into the mental processes of a practicing magician who came by his secrets legitimately and who performs without hokum. This fellow in the high chair believes in his work.

He discovered his powers accidentally, very early in the first year of his life when tensions within his body magically produced an object, a breast or a bottle, which relieved tension. We are inclined to argue with him right there. This is not magic. These tensions we know perfectly well gave rise to certain manifestations which were recognized by a person outside himself who then ministered to his needs. But the magician could not have known this. He could only connect need and satisfaction in a primitive cause-and-effect relationship. Later when he began to differentiate his body from other bodies the primitive cause-and-effect (need brings satisfaction), moved one step further to "need brings a *person* who gives satisfaction." We notice that his body and his needs bring about a desired event in this pre-thinking stage.

As his world enlarges he sees all objects, all events as the result of his own activity. The rattle does not have the property of making a noise; *he* makes the noise by manipulating the rattle. The Teddy bear does not occupy a certain space outside himself; the Teddy bear is "there" only if he sees it. The existence of all things in the outer world is known to him only through his sense organs; objects have no independent existence. In this way all objects outside himself appear to him as connected with his own actions. We say that he is egocentric because he is the center of his world and he conceives objects and events outside of himself as the consequence of his activity, of his grasping, his seeing, his hearing. In this sense he is the cause of all things.

In the first half of the second year, as we have already seen, he has made some observations which lead him to the correct conclusion that objects outside himself can exist independently of his perception of them and he is able imaginatively to reconstruct their movements in space. This is a great advance from the earlier view in which objects were merely extensions of his own ego and his own activity, but his psychological position still remains egocentered; he is still a mover and cause of things because he must command objects and events for his own needs and his own purposes. In a word—a word which is not yet part of the magician's vocabulary—he is omnipotent.

Like all magicians he believes that his wishes, his thoughts, his words are the instruments of his magic powers. In this way we *Implication* see how these later developments in thinking are still modeled after the simple "need brings satisfaction" of the earliest months of life. Long after reason has deprived the magician of his magic, and for all the days of his life, the belief that wishes can bring about real events will persist in a secret part of the self.

Whatever a magician believes, the truth of the matter is that he derives his power from his audience. The career of a magician ends in the moment that his audience disbelieves his magic. So there must always be a magician and there must always be believers in order for magic to take place. The career of our high-chair magician is blighted almost from the start by a clique of unbelievers, who consider it their duty to rise up and protest, to give argument, present proof and to offer their prosaic selves and their own hard-earned wisdom as a substitute for this enchanted world. They are formidable opponents, for their power is infinitely greater than that of the high-chair magician. They are the source of love, they minister to the body needs of the high-chair magician. They are absolutely indispensable, and the proof of their indispensability is regularly seen in the failure of the magician's career.

The unbelievers, the rationalists, the parents and educators, consider it their duty and their right to oppose magic with Truth, to fight magic with Reason, to put magic to the test of Reality. They are missionaries who are ordained to bring an alien and higher culture to the savage in order that he may free his imagination for more advanced modes of thought, and free his activity and his cultural achievements from the slavery of body needs. For as long as the primitive mind is dominated by the urgency of needs and the urgency of their satisfaction, mental activity will be restricted to the satisfaction and means of satisfaction of body urges.

We have seen that magic thinking is the earliest mental activity, the mental process which accompanies the need-satisfaction principle of early development. In psychoanalytic terms, the functioning of the child in the early months and years is dominated by the Pleasure Principle, that is, a striving for satisfaction. Mental processes develop in this early period in the service of body needs. (Recall that one of the earliest forms of thought according to our construction was the picture, the mental image of a satisfaction, the breast or bottle, which was activated by sensations of hunger.) Now in order for mental processes to progress to the higher modes of thought, orderly thinking, logic, and abstraction, thinking must be freed from magic and freed from its earlier dependence upon body needs and their satisfaction. Here, the parents, the representatives of Reality, become the missionaries of a higher culture. They must educate the child to a coherent and rational view of the world and to do this they must, in effect, oppose magic thinking and the instinctual strivings which have satisfaction as their only goal. This is a job that demands the greatest intuitive knowledge and skill on the part of parents. Our technical language has a phrase for the governing principle of the second mode of thought. We call it the Reality Principle which means, of course, that the higher form of thinking is governed by the principles of reality instead of the earlier principle of pleasure.

The work of a missionary is not immediately rewarded. Anyone who sets out to convert a Pleasure Principle into a Reality Principle whether on a Pacific Island or in an American suburb must know the forces which resist his efforts. The missionary converts through love; his teachings cannot have effect unless he can compensate by an offer of love for what he must take away. His censorship will fall on deaf ears unless fear of loss of love will act upon the primitive mentality like a brake. The missionary cannot be a zealot. If he meets the force of primitive resistance with the force of his ideas in a collision of minds, the missionary will lose. In some parts of the Pacific the missionary will lose his vocation, or worse. In an American family the worst that can happen is that he will lose his influence.

Above all, in the early stages of conversion, the missionary must be content if the primitive mind takes in half the truth. If the primitive accepts the truth of the new religion, but keeps his old idols under the bed, the missionary must not deplore or threaten or lose his wits. If he is wise he will assign a place where the old idols, the old beliefs, and the old magic can still reside and even serve a benevolent purpose. The conversion of a primitive in an American suburb should make allowances for the sacrifice to new principles. It should leave a place in the mind where the banished dreams can be eternally renewed, where magic and omnipotence can be practiced harmlessly, where wishes bring about their own satisfaction. All that we ask is allegiance to the Reality Principle, and consignment of magic to certain regions of the mind. We grant the right of a deposed magician to practice the sorcery of the day-dream and we provide an island in our world of reality where he can command the creatures of his imagination through play.

ABRACADABRA.

LANGUAGE originates in magic. The first "words" of a baby are not words at all, but magic incantations, sounds uttered for pleasure and employed indiscriminately to bring about a desired event. Sometime in the last quarter of the first year the baby makes the sounds "mama" or "dada." The baby is surprised and pleased at the excitement he creates in his parents and can easily be induced to repeat this performance dozens of times a day. Unfortunately, he doesn't know who or what "mama" is. He will look right into your eyes and say "mama" and you melt at the lovely sound, and he will look right into his father's eyes and say "mama" and his father, embarrassed, corrects him. He will pursue the dog's tail chanting "mama," and he will reach for a cookie yelling "mama" and he will lie in his crib murmuring "mamama-mamamamama"—and he hasn't a thought in his head for M-O-T-H-E-R and the million things she gave him. He doesn't connect the word and the person at this point.

But he has discovered, or will discover shortly, that the syllable "mama," repeated several times if necessary, will magically cause the appearance of the invaluable woman who ministers to all needs and guards him against all evil. He doesn't know just how this happens, but he attributes this to his own magic powers. Like all magicians, he does not inquire into the nature of his gifts.

This formula, he discovers, can be extended to cover a number of situations. When he wants the cookie on the table he utters the magic syllables "mama." He is not addressing the cookie as "mama" even as he is not addressing his own mother as "mama."

"Mama," here, can be translated as "abracadabra," magic utterance to bring about a desired event, cookie in the mouth. Now since his mother speaks English-as-she-is-spoken, she interprets this chant addressed to the cookie as the equivalent of "Mama, I want a cookie" and will negotiate a meeting of baby and cookie which has the effect of extending the magic of the word "mama" to bring about almost any desirable event. The baby is quick to discover, too, that in times of stress, or when calamities like naps and bed-time befall him, the magic syllables "mama" will cause his mother to appear.

In the course of many months the syllables "mama" gradually come to designate the person "Mama." Through thousands of repetitions in varied circumstances the baby discovers that the magic word brings about a specific event, the appearance of his mother. It does not bring his father to him, though the syllables "dada" usually will. It does not induce the dog to allow his tail to be pulled. It does not cause the cookie to come down from the table to be eaten by him. And finally the syllables "mama" become identified with the person who answers, who is summoned by these sounds. The word and the object are now one.

As soon as objects acquire names, a higher form of word magic is established. When, for example, the word "mama" is finally identified with the person "Mama" the magician discovers that the word can evoke a mental image of Mama even when it does not summon the real Mama to his side. By having the word "Mama," he is able to give permanence and stability to the mental image of mother and can imaginatively recreate her when he needs her. "What's so special about that?" one may wonder. Well, let's look at this phenomenon in action.

Susie, like every healthy child in the second year, goes off to bed with bitter protests. Goodnights are said and Susie is left in her bed. Soon after her parents leave, the protesting noises cease and a cheerful monologue commences. "Mama-dada Cocolodolodolobyemamamamabye Cocococococodadada-

dadadadagar. Hiyadoodee. Mumumumumumumumumumum."
Translation: "Mama, Daddy, Coco (dog), stroller, g'bye, Mama,
g'bye, Coco, Daddy, Car. Hiya, Susie. Mamamamamamama."
This speech and variations of it continue for fifteen or twenty
minutes until Susie falls asleep. It is carried on in splendid
rolling cadences exactly like the cadences of English and, what
is most interesting, Susie is talking to herself and is not making
any attempt to communicate directly with all the persons and
objects named. Note, too, that this whole performance is conducted in the best of spirits and that the terrible grief of going
to bed has quickly subsided.

This is word magic, again, but word magic of a special kind.
In the moment before Susie is put to bed there is the terrible
pain of leaving her beautiful world and its beloved persons and
objects. In the darkness she recreates her lost world, brings back
the absent people and objects by uttering their names! She is
like the sorcerer who conjures ghosts by calling their names.

This bed-time soliloquy is so commonplace that few parents
will marvel at it, but if we examine its meaning we will find
that this is one of the early triumphs of language. These few
words, the names of objects, are capable of substituting for the
objects themselves, a mental experience substitutes for a real
experience, and by doing so a painful emotion, anxiety, is overcome. This is a good example of the way in which language
gives the human being the possibility of control over his circumstances and over his instinctual reactions.

Here is a further example. It is spring and Susie is enchanted
by the flowers in her own garden and in the front yard borders
that she sees on her walks. She is allowed to pick the flowers
in her own garden, but the parents cannot give her permission
to pick flowers in the front yards of neighbors. She cries briefly
when her father or mother prevent her from picking the neighbors' flowers. "Fars! Fars!" (flowers), she says in a voice full
of longing. "Aren't they pretty!" her father says, and they admire
the flowers for a few moments and walk on. Within a few days

Susie no longer insists upon picking flowers in the neighbors' front yards. Instead, she stops on her walks, bends over a flower bed and says, "Fars! Pitty!" (pretty) and looks up at her mother or father to share the experience. "Very pretty, very nice!" they say, making conversation. "Pitty, Nize!" Susie says. She seems entirely satisfied with this and resumes her walk. At her next encounter with neighbors' flowers she repeats this performance exactly.

What has made it possible for Susie to forego the pleasure of picking the flowers and possessing them for herself? Word magic, again. The words "far" (flower), "pitty," "nize" substitute for the object. Instead of making physical contact with the flowers through touching them she makes contact through words, naming the flower, admiring it. Instead of picking the flowers to make them her own, she employs words to designate the object and possesses the flowers by possessing the symbol, the word.

In this example words substitute for an act. And this leads us into a discussion of one of the most important functions of language. Words substitute for human acts and the uniquely human achievements of control of body urges, delay, postponement and even renunciation of gratification are very largely due to the higher mental processes that are made possible by language. The human possibility of consciously inhibiting an action and renouncing, if only temporarily, an expected satisfaction, is largely dependent upon the human faculties of judgment and reasoning, functions which are inconceivable without language.

We take our language equipment so much for granted that it may be difficult to see at first glance how language becomes a means for control of body impulses. Let's consider, for a moment, the case of our non-verbal four-year-old beagle who understands only a few words like "walk," "down," "no," "stay here," and doesn't always choose to understand these. Each night he is confronted with a crisis that demands a simple piece of reasoning and a renunciation of an immediate gratification for the attainment of a more desirable goal that would be in his grasp within a split second. Here is the dilemma: At the end of the evening Brandy is bribed with a biscuit to leave his favorite piece of furniture and descend the basement stairs to his own bed. He is a sociable dog who hates to leave good company and a good chair for solitude and a doggy mattress in the furnace room. One of us will move toward the basement stairs with a biscuit in hand while Brandy follows with a moody look on his face. At the top of the stairs he stops and sits down. He will not budge at this point. Now his master or his mistress (there never were more foolish names for such as we are) will descend the stairs, biscuit in hand, whistling, chirping and making other conventional noises to which dogs are said to respond. Brandy sits like an ornamental lion at the top of the stairs. At this point, each night, we think we are lost. It's a breathless moment. Will he rise above instinct at last? Will he renounce Dog Yummies and his enslavement to his appetite and by this single gesture rise like a rocket to some new elevation in the evolutionary scale? And if he does what will become of us? If we cannot influence him through his appetites and his devotion to us, nothing will prevent him from asserting himself as the rightful owner of our house (a point that had long been disputed anyway) and we might easily find ourselves at the top of the stairs each night, staring moodily into the darkness.

So we wait at the bottom of the stairs. It's a good game. We secretly would like to see him win, at least once. The beagle looks mournfully at the biscuit in his master's hand. His tail wags uncertainly. On his poor, sad, hound's face you can almost read the dilemma. He dimly recognizes that a trap is in store for him. He doesn't want to go downstairs, but he does want the biscuit. A few minutes pass. Suddenly, unable to withstand the longing another moment, Brandy descends the stairs in pursuit of his biscuit and is easily led to his bed. A few minutes later when we are back upstairs, we may hear pathetic little mewling noises from the regions below. Brandy, having eaten his biscuit, remembers finally why he hadn't wanted to go downstairs in the first place.

The events as described here have gone on nearly every night for four years. The sequence is practically unvarying. Why hasn't Brandy caught on after hundreds of repetitions that if he can forego the satisfaction of a Dog Yummy he can avoid being led downstairs and will gain the greater satisfaction of luxury and companionship upstairs? Well, to put it bluntly, he can't keep two ideas in his head at the same time. Properly speaking, he doesn't even have an idea. At best, he has pictures in his head. But the real biscuit dangling in front of his eyes has no trouble competing with the mental picture of a solitary bed in the furnace room. He cannot see connections between these events except in the most rudimentary sense. The two events of a biscuit in his master's hand and what we see as its sequel, the solitary bed, would appear to him as two separate events; he would not see one *causing* the other. He hesitates at the top of the stairs *not* because he can imaginatively reconstruct the sequence of events to follow, but because his sensory memory prompts him to anticipate something unpleasant connected with the taking of the biscuit. But he couldn't tell himself why.

In order to link these two events in a meaningful way he would need words. If he could translate the whole experience from biscuit to solitary bed in a practical symbol system he would be able to construct mentally the sequence of events without going through the action. He would need to have the equivalent symbols for our conditional sentence, "*If* I take the biscuit, I'll wind up in the doggone furnace room." He could then negate the impulse through the symbolic equivalent, "Who wants the lousy biscuit anyway?" He could then march back to his favorite piece of furniture and sneer at his family, and by this single act of renunciation he would rise above his species. But he has no language. Without language he is obliged to go through the *actions* of this nightly ritual, from biscuit to solitary bed, because he cannot symbolically reconstruct it and draw inferences from the parts of the experience.

But why should we go to so much trouble to examine the mental limitations of an animal? Because, of course, the absence of language restricts the possibility of an animal's rising above his instinctual nature. In the absence of language the mental processes of reasoning and judgment cannot exist and the animal cannot make choices that are independent of instinctual need or instinctual conduct. All those qualities that we call human derive from the possibility within every human being of acquiring control over the instinctual self and of modifying his character and his circumstances through an intelligence that has a large degree of independence from the primary human drives. We have excellent reasons to believe that these uniquely human achievements are not alone the product of a superior mental apparatus, but that the apparatus itself acquires the possibility of controlling this vast and intricate organization of the human personality through language!

All this has tremendous importance to us in discussing methods of child-rearing. Soon after the child begins to acquire some language we find the whole job of child-rearing made easier. It is not only because we have improved communication between parents and child—although this is very important—but the child himself begins to acquire control over impulse through words. (The example of Susie and the flowers.) The child also begins to feel that words give him control over external events. We are always amused to find that when the child acquires the word "bye-bye," he begins to take the departures of his parents with more grace. It's as if the word gives him command of the situation. He behaves comically as if he controlled the comings and goings of people through his incantation "bye-bye." When he acquires the words "g'night" or "night-night," he even feels a little better about going off to bed. Again he behaves as if the words give him control over the situation, as if no one is obliging him to go to bed, as if he controls his own exits and entrances by means of the magic utterance.

We will also find, as the child begins to acquire language, that he can sometimes control his own impulses or avoid danger situations by uttering the parental prohibition to himself. A child with only a few words will be able to check certain impulses if he has the necessary words in his limited vocabulary. He may reach out his hand to touch the stove, say "hot" to himself and withdraw his hand. Only a few weeks ago before he had the word "hot" he had to have the parental admonition "hot" to check his impulse. Now, in possession of the word, he can check his own impulse. Something similar can be observed in the use of the word "no," although every parent can testify this does not become a reliable self-prohibition for a long time. But we will see something like this: A toddler, not knowing that he is observed, will march over to an electric wall outlet which he knows to be "out of bounds." The impulse to fiddle with the plugged-in lamp cord comes over him. "No, no, no," he mumbles to himself, all the while tugging at the lamp cord. At this stage the prohibition does not check the act. But gradually we will see that his "no, no" acquires more and more reliability and will serve at times as a self-imposed admonition that effectively checks the impulse.

In other words, language makes it possible for a child to incorporate his parents' verbal prohibitions, to make them part of himself. By acquiring the verbal form of the prohibition, he can incorporate it and employ it for self-control. We don't speak of a conscience yet in the child who is just acquiring language, but we can see very clearly how language plays an indispensable role in the formation of conscience. In fact, the moral achievement of man, the whole complex of factors that go into the organization of conscience is very largely based upon language.

A VOYAGE TO BROBDINGNAG.

"I NOW intend to give the reader a short Description of this Country as far as I have travelled in it . . . ," says Gulliver. It is strange and marvellous to know that each of us has travelled in Brobdingnag and none of us can remember that country inhabited by a race of giants. Sometimes in a dream, more rarely in the experience of the uncanny in waking life, a memory returns and for a moment we find a link with this forgotten period of our life. For the experiences of the first three years of life are almost entirely lost to us, and when we attempt to enter into a small child's world, we come as foreigners who have forgotten the landscape and no longer speak the native tongue.

We have good reason to believe that memories of early childhood do not persist in consciousness because of the absence or fragmentary character of language covering this period. Words serve as fixatives for mental images. Memories which have no word labels attached to them are stored away in a kind of attic clutter. Who remembers the contents of the barrel in the attic when the careless housewife has neglected to pin a label on it naming its contents? Even at the end of the second year of life when word tags exist for a number of objects in the child's life, these words are discrete and do not yet bind together the parts of an experience or organize them in a way that can produce a coherent memory.

The mingled wonder and terror of a Gulliver in the country of giants strikes deep into memory and there are moments in the Voyage to Brobdingnag when we experience something of the quality of this land. But something is absent. Gulliver's voyage is coherent; his narrative is connected and has meaning. The quality of the small child's Brobdingnag is the quality of a world viewed with primitive mental faculties, a world in the second and third year of life which is still in large part disordered and incoherent, a world which the child explains to himself by means of magic thought.

When the child has acquired some language, we get some extraordinary glimpses of this fantastic world:

When my friend David was two and a half years old, he was being prepared for a trip to Europe with his parents. He was a very bright child, talked well for his age and seemed to take in everything his parents had to say with interest and enthusiasm. The whole family would fly to Europe (David knew what an airplane was), they would see many unusual things, they would go swimming, go on trains, meet some of David's friends there. The preparation story was carried on with just the right amount of emphasis for a couple of weeks before the trip. But after a while David's parents noticed that he stopped asking questions about "Yurp" and even seemed depressed when he heard his parents talk about it. The parents tried to find out what was troubling him. He was most reluctant to talk about it. Then one day, David came out with his secret in an agonizing confession. "I can't go to Yurp!" he said, and the tears came very fast. "I don't know how to fly, yet!"

To understand this complex reaction we need to understand a number of things in David's world view. First of all, he didn't know how to fly, "yet," which means that he expected that his all-powerful parents would know how to fly to "Yurp," but that this was one of a number of advanced skills which he hadn't mastered yet. Second is the point of confusion about the airplane. He had entirely missed the point that the family would fly *in* an airplane. But he had seen an airplane? Yes, he had seen airplanes in the sky—like birds only they make a noise—but the concept of plane as a vehicle, a plane having people inside was not something he could obtain through watching an airplane in the sky. None of us can remember now whether he had had the experience of seeing a plane loading passengers on the ground at the airport, an experience which theoretically could have helped in constructing the new concept, but it might not have made a bit of difference. He would probably not have been able to connect the big plane on the ground with the little plane in the sky, even if he had watched the whole process of take-off. This sequence, which we see as a connected series of actions, one that presents a moving picture to our eyes, would be seen by a two year old as a series of disconnected actions, and because of changes in perspective and size of the plane as it moves through the sequence of its actions, the meaning of the series of observations would not be grasped by a child of David's age.

But the most interesting point of all in David's story is this: Here is a little boy who speaks our language so well that we can confidently discuss European trips and travel plans with him, but we discover that, after all, we are not speaking the same language. In the fantastic world of a two year old all things are possible, and a mother, a father and a little boy will assemble on their front lawn one morning, flap their arms and take off for a continent across the sea. Unfortunately, the parents do not notice that the little boy has not learned how to fly "yet," and the little boy stays rooted to the ground while his parents wing their way to "Yurp," quite unmindful of the fact that a member of the party is still grounded. All this from the common verb form "to fly" which is accepted literally by a small boy who believes all things are possible in this astonishing world.

It is only fair to admit that the concrete and literal meaning of the word will endure forever, and even in later years it returns to us in unexpected moments to assault our reason. Last night I fell asleep with some thoughts about language and meaning inspired by David's story. Early this morning I was wakened by the ringing telephone and groped my way in half-sleep to answer it. A little voice said, "I just found out that the brownies are flying up today and I can't come for my appointment." Years of professional discipline have insulated me completely against the macabre, the occult and the fermentations of troubled minds. I asked the voice to repeat its message and was not relieved to hear it restated distinctly. I asked no further questions lest I betray the possibility that my own mind had come unhinged and summoned all the professional poise at my disposal to change Amy's appointment time, presumably to an hour that would not conflict with her levitation or the antics of brownies.

Afterward I sat down in a chair and mulled over this message. Several minutes passed before I could get rid of the persistent image of a ten-year-old girl who could not keep her appointment with a child therapist because of a mid-air convocation of brownies. By this time, however, I had no difficulty in understanding the message. "Flying up" I recalled (by straining my memory) was the unfortunate whimsy employed by the Girl Scouts of America to denote the elevation of a lower-class Brownie to an upper class Scout. Amy was a Brownie. Amy was "flying-up" today. When my husband came into the room I said carefully, "I have just had a telephone call. The brownies are flying up today and Amy cannot keep her appointment." This had a splendid effect. He was momentarily shaken but quickly recovered, thinking he had misunderstood. When I explained to him, he was all sympathy. He is an English teacher.

Before any of my readers pass judgment upon my mental competence I should explain this lapse. The effect of this mysterious message was due to the fact that in sleep states or states bordering on sleep our mental processes regress to primitive modes of thought. "To fly-up" came to me literally, pictorially, just as it did to David with his two year old's mode of thinking. In dreams, themselves, language is represented largely through pictures. For example, if Amy should have a dream about her promotion in the Brownies it is conceivable that the dream would represent this idea through a picture of "flying-up" in the same way that her words evoked a mental image of "flying-up" to me in my sleepy state.

In childhood, the ambiguities of language are a great trouble. Do you remember "The Secret Life of James Thurber" and the sinister events of that childhood in Columbus, Ohio? In Columbus there were businessmen who were tied up in their offices (invariably at five o'clock), gagged and bound to their chairs, but miraculously able to reach a telephone. There was the man who left town under a cloud, Mrs. Huston who was terribly cut up when her daughter died on the operating table, and an alarming creature named Mrs. Johnson who was all ears when she heard the news about Betty.

I recall the story of a two-year-old girl who developed a morbid fear of ants. She cried out in terror when she saw one because, she said, the ants would eat her up. Her parents were completely baffled because the same little girl would cheerfully put her fist in the mouth of any big dog who came up to greet her and never accused even the most ferocious animal in the zoo of a wish to eat her up. It was weeks before the matter was cleared up. The child's grandmother remembered that one day when she opened the kitchen cupboard she discovered some ants. Mimi, the two year old, was in the kitchen when grandmother threw up her hands in alarm and said to the cook, "Those ants are here again. They will eat *everything* up!"

In the marvellous world of the two year old, if there are ants that will eat *everything* up, they will eat up a little girl, too. Problems of relative size do not enter into the matter. Grandma, herself, seemed horrified by the prospect and the housewifely commotion in the kitchen over the appearance of the ants must have struck the little girl as an entirely suitable reaction to the prospect of being devoured by ants.

In the small child's Brobdingnag all things are possible. Healthy, good-sized boys and girls around the age of two years are said to disappear down bath-tub drains. Impossible, you say. Very well, so you say. But just to be on the safe side, the two year old intimates, he'd rather not take a bath today.

Well-equipped modern households in Brobdingnag keep a

monster in their closets. When hooked up to an electrical wall outlet it inflates with a deafening roar and sucks everything in its path into its chromium-plated jaw. "It's nothing, dear. Only a vacuum cleaner!" *Only* a vacuum cleaner. Dear Lady, I can only hope that one morning you will rise from your bed and encounter a roaring iron monster twice your size, steadily eating a path toward you, its monster guts shrieking with the labor of unspeakable digestion. I can only hope, Madam, that you will ignore the sales talk and take to your heels.

The panda's eye has fallen out. An empty socket and the first glimpse of the cotton entrails that pull out easily now in an urgent, sickening search. And suddenly the panda is a flaccid sack and horror spreads over you. The panda is no more. He is a nothing, and for the first time the thought comes over you that *you* could lose your stuffing and become a nothing. "Never mind, dear. Don't cry so. We can get another panda." "NO! NO! NO!" And no words can be found in this new tongue, the English language, to tell of the dreadful secret tugged from the bowels of the panda.

So the world of the two year old is still at times a spooky twilight world that is closer to the world of the dream than the world of reality. As in a dream, a little boy in a respectable and prosaic middle-class family encounters a mechanical monster in his living room that pursues him with eager jaws and terrible noises from its belly. As in a dream, a little girl splashing with joyful abandon in a porcelain bath tub observes the water sucked thirstily down the drain and sees herself suddenly, horribly, sucked down the drain into the void. It is in dreams that we encounter the ants that can devour one little girl and her grandmother and the cook as well. Dream people may take off for "Yurp" by poising themselves on the front lawn, flapping their arms and ascending without effort.

In time, these monsters, these man-eating ants, devouring drain pipes and flying humans will be relegated to the attic, so many useless acquisitions, not easily disposed of, but happily forgotten. They will rarely emerge in broad daylight in the after-years of reason. They become the attic debris, the useless, forgotten, dusty souvenirs that turn up in dreams bringing with them, astonishingly, the same horror, awe, grief and helplessness of the original experience.

The dreamer wakens and the merciful thought comes to him, "It's only a dream!" The sense of reality rolls over him like a tide and gives him back the safe years of distance from these dark and terrible events. But the child who lives mid-way between the world of magic and the world of reality does not see that one world excludes the other: The two worlds exist side by side; reason is not affronted by the appearance of a monster in the living room or cannibal ants in the cozy kitchen. The sense of reality is not yet strong enough to judge and exclude certain phenomena from the picture of the real world.

MAGIC AND SCIENCE.

WHY DWELL on this one-sided view of the two and three year old as magician? It would be just as fair to call him a scientist, an experimenter, a researcher and these things are just what a magician is not!

The case for the scientist is very strong. Given the physical boundaries of his world, we have to grant the toddler a remarkable ability to make observations and to search indefatigably for causes. No subject is too commonplace for his study. He analyzes the contents of waste-baskets, garbage cans, clothes closets, kitchen cupboards and drawers with a zeal and energy that would do credit to a whole archeological expedition. In fact, when he has completed these excavations it is impossible to believe that so much debris could be dug up by one small investigator, working in solitude with no other aid but his bare hands. "What's inside?" is the burning question that leads him to perform rare forms of surgery on Teddy bears, dolls and other stuffed toys which now lie about the house in various stages of mutilation. "To make it work!" is the driving need behind the endless play with electric switches, knobs on radios and television sets, locks on doors. And he is a remarkable observer. He puts us to shame, at times, by his ability to see details which we do not. *He* is the one who will notice that the elf in his picture book is not wearing the feather in his cap that he had worn in all earlier pictures. It is he who discovers that we have omitted a detail in our retelling of a familiar story. It is he who recognizes that the mysterious fragment of the picture puzzle is a shoe, while father with his advanced university degrees is under the impression that the manufacturer had slipped in part of another puzzle by mistake.

We give this junior scientist a high score on all these points: He is a meticulous observer, a zealous investigator and a cataloguer. There is only one thing wrong with his science—the conclusions!

He discovers that if he turns the knob on the television set certain pictures appear. He repeats the experiment several hundred times so we cannot suspect him of drawing inferences from an inadequate number of trials and we can't speak a word against the statistical method employed here. On the basis of this perfectly valid research procedure he is able to conclude and confirm each time that it is *he* who makes the little people come out of the box by turning the switch!

He is a scientist, but he is still a magician. We feel drawn to his defense. After all, this two year old cannot draw upon a knowledge of electronics to explain the phenomena of television! All very true. It is only worth pointing out that even at this stage of development when he seeks causes for phenomena which cannot be accounted for in his limited practical experience, he resorts to magic thinking. Moreover he tends to explain all unfamiliar or otherwise unexplainable events in his world as caused by human activity, his own or someone else's activity. Piaget tells the charming story of his eighteen-

month-old daughter who observed that Papa made clouds with
his pipe and also observed that there were mists, over the
mountains and clouds in the skies. In her way of calling attention to these groups of observations it was clear that she
believed that it was Papa who made the mists and the clouds
with his pipe.

So we need to say that the science of the toddler is unreliable because his theories of causality are still rooted in magic.
The belief that human activity is the cause of all things, is only
an extension of the child's infantile, egocentric belief that he or
his activity is the cause of all things. When a scientist makes
observations he must be able to exclude his subjective reactions and to discover the independent laws which govern the
subject or phenomena under scrutiny. But when the small child
hears thunder he may think that a man in the sky is angry.
When he studies a tree he is troubled to find that it has arms
but no legs. He finds human or animal forms in the clouds,
on the sands of the beach, in the shadows at dusk, as if the
nature of the objective world must first be sought in terms of
a human body and its functions. So much of his early learning
is derived from observations of his own body and its functions
that when he extends learning outward to the objective world
he must apply these first-found laws (as he sees them) to
phenomena outside of himself. This leads, of course, to some
very strange conclusions in this infant science.

Let's consider the observations of a two and a half year old
whose mother is pregnant. (Question: "Do they really notice
at this age?" Answer: Does the little boy who notices that the
elf in his picture book is not wearing the feather in his cap,
really *not* notice that his mommy is very fat?) So our small
friend, we assume, has made the observation that mommy has
a fat tummy and in a few weeks before mother is due to deliver he is told about the baby in mommy's tummy. He may
not even ask how the baby got in there. He has his own theory!
We may find the theory being worked out in the days that

follow. He announces at breakfast one morning that he is going to eat *all* his cereal and *all* his bananas and *all* his milk and he will have a baby grow in his tummy, too. This theory may even get to be quite troublesome in a few days. He may, like one little fellow, I know, refuse to go to the bathroom out of solicitous feelings for the baby he's making in his tummy. We may find that our friend will defend his theory very strongly, but in the end, of course, he will need to give it up for the one we give him. He will learn that a baby is not made through eating something, and that only mommies can have a baby grown inside of them. But we should not be surprised to find that long after the little child has learned the facts as we give them to him he may hold on to his earlier theories.

But we wanted to make another point here. How did the two and a half year old arrive at a theory of making a baby through eating? We can readily see how he developed this theory through observations of his own body and its functions. How does something get inside of one? Through eating. And if you keep it inside of you and don't let it out, it will grow into a baby!

We should also consider what the small child imagines the inside of his body to be like. When we grown-ups picture the insides of our bodies, anatomical drawings flash into our minds and we place the body organs according to our anatomical knowledge. The child, until a surprisingly late age, even eight or nine, imagines his body as a hollow organ, encased in skin. It is all "stomach" in his imagination, a big hollow tube which is filled with food at intervals and emptied of food at other intervals. It is interesting to ask a six or seven year old to draw what he thinks he looks like inside and to see the drawing of an undifferentiated cavern into which the child may, upon re-flection, insert a "heart" in some out-of-the-way place. If you ask a question, "Where is the stomach?" the child will usually point to the interior of his drawing, indicating all of it. And since the child, at an early age, has discovered that if his skin is scratched or cut, blood will appear, he visualizes the interior of his body as a kind of reservoir in which blood, food and wastes are somehow contained.

Now the more conscious the child becomes of himself as a person, an "I," the more he values this body which encloses and contains his personality. His "wholeness" as a personality, his psychic integrity, seems to be closely bound up with the completeness and integrity of the body. It is interesting that in the third year as the concept of "I" emerges, the child often goes through a stage of fussiness about scratches, cuts and bruises which earlier might have resulted in a brief display of tears and not much more. This is also the Band-Aid stage and everyone knows that if he wants to create good will in a two year old, a box of Band-Aids is a most treasured gift and the donor will be long remembered. The two year old plasters Band-Aids on the most inperceptible scratches, or even purely imaginary ones. He feels immediately restored after a trifling hurt if we paste a Band-Aid on him. The two year old feels "whole" again when his scratch is covered by the Band-Aid; it's as if a leak in the container, the body, is sealed up and his completeness as a personality is re-established by this magic act. We can suspect a certain kinship between this idea and the fear of primitive people that the spirit or the soul may escape the confines of the body.

But the child does not value his body only because it is the container for his personality. Long before it becomes inhabited by an "I," before the person within him becomes conscious of his identity and uniqueness, the body has become the object of awareness through sensations of tension and pleasurable release of tension. And the body as a source of pleasure makes its own claims upon its owner, draws attention to itself and its specific organs, and becomes valued because it is an organ of pleasure.

In the early phases of child development specific organs become the focus of awareness because of the greater amounts of tension and pleasure which accompany their functions. If we ask in which organ pleasure is concentrated in the infant, we must all agree this is the mouth. Later, in the second year, the child becomes aware of the sensations of tension and relief which accompany evacuation and we are able to see how the anus achieves importance for a short period of time as a focus of body tensions and satisfactions. From the earliest months of life the child discovers sensations in the genital organs, but we see that the genitals do not achieve importance as a focus of pleasurable sensations until the third year and later. At this time we begin to see an increase in interest in the genitals and more frequent handling of them. From the third year on the genitals assume greater importance to the child because they have become organs of special pleasure.

There are two main reasons, then, why the child values his body. It is the source of his self-feelings, the physical and substantial "I," and it is the source of pleasure. And if we ask why in the third year the child should show greater concern for his body, its safety and its intactness, we can see how this concern is in direct proportion to the increase in self-awareness and the valuation of the body as "self" and as an organ of pleasure. I do not wish to ignore the reality that fear of injury to the body is basically fear of physical pain, but this alone could not account for the increase in fears of body damage in the third year, nor would it account for the ideas which accompany these fears.

The child's primitive thinking plays an important part in the fantasies about body damage which we encounter in small children. We have said that the child's image of his own body enters into his conception of phenomena in the external world. He gives body forms and functions to all manner of things as he observes and studies objects and events outside of him. In the same way his image of his own body is the model for his conception of all human or animal bodies when he is very small. If he is a boy he imagines that all people are made the way he is made. Everyone in the world must have a head, two arms, two legs and a penis. If she is a girl, she has formed her conception of the human body on the basis of observations on her own body. So we can say that the child has no clear concept of "boy" or "girl," maleness or femaleness, until the time that he makes his first observations on the genital differences between himself and a creature unlike himself. What he sees in these first encounters is a matter of considerable interest to us, for he observes and, like the little boy who learned about his mother's pregnancy, he explains what he has seen by means of primitive thinking!

From direct observations of small children we know that these first observations of genital differences produce reactions of surprise or shock. (Something similar, perhaps not as strong, will be experienced by a grown person if he has a sudden encounter with a maimed or crippled person.) The child who has not conceived of human bodies as being different from his own reacts to this discovery according to his own sex. If he is a little boy observing a little girl he sees that something is "missing" on her. If she is a little girl she sees that the little boy has something that she doesn't have, that something is "missing" on her. When the child tries to explain these observations to himself he can only come up with primitive theories. "Somebody must have taken it away." "It must have been cut off." The little boy may regard the little girl as mutilated. Fears that some similar catastrophe may befall his penis may be expressed by him. The little girl may react as if she had really been injured, really had something taken away from her.

So we see that the first discoveries of maleness and femaleness, and of one's own sex, are made under circumstances which are unavoidably disturbing and painful and give rise to infantile fantasies of body damage and mutilation. If a child should carry over these feelings into later stages of development we can see how the boy's attitude toward his own masculinity and the girl's feelings about her own femininity might be disturbed. But normally the child overcomes these feelings and develops appropriate feelings of pride and pleasure in being a boy, in being a girl. He achieves this in several ways. First, his primitive theories give way when tested against reality. Further observations lead the child to conclude that there are two different kinds of bodies and he is able to classify himself. His fears regarding body damage will slowly give way before the realization that nobody in the world will inflict damage on his body. And his parents will give him the necessary information which will correct his own primitive theories. He will learn that nothing was taken away from the little girl and that nothing will be taken away from him, that they were both made the way they are from the very beginning. He will also learn that he is made just like his father, that the little girl is made just like her mother, and in this way the child begins to take pride in his own sex because he is made just like a beloved parent.

This education takes a long time. We find that even in the next stage of development, the three to five stage, that some elements of the primitive theory of sexual differences will survive, even if not fully conscious. And long after the child has no use for these primitive theories and knows they are nonsense, they may come back to plague him from time to time, in a nightmare, in a distorted fantasy. But later he *knows* they are not real and this knowledge equips him to deal with such frightening thoughts.

"I"

AT THE beginning "I" is a shaky and uncertain term in the child's vocabulary. The concepts "I" and "you," which are still a little fuzzy, give rise to scrambled pronouns in the child's speech. I remember Lawrie at the age of two and a half, the "I-want-to-do-it-myself stage. "NoNO NoNoNo!" he protested to mother who wanted to help him dress. "I do it yourself! I do it yourself!"

And this first "I" is an "I" seeking satisfaction, an "I" of wants. Often it is linked like a Siamese twin to a verb expressing desire, "Iwanna." The "Iwannas" of this age stretch for miles between dawn and dusk every day. "Iwanna" is a chant, a magic incantation, which by simple repetition is believed to bring about a desired object or event. "Horsie!" Lawrie screams in ecstasy as the car passes a farm. His parents hold their breath. Then it cames. "I wanna horsie. I wanna horsie. I wanna horsie." This chant continues until a farmer and a tractor come into view. A new joy seizes Lawrie. "Tractor. Tractor. I wanna Tractor!" An interurban bus appears. "Bus, Daddy, bus! I wanna bus!" "What else do you want?" says his mama. "I wanna big truck. I wanna farmer. I wanna Daddy's car. I wanna store . . ." He goes on compiling a list which is too long to print. Then he falls asleep exhausted.

But, mercifully, the two year old who is a creature of strong desires and urgent demands is also developing in another direction. He is more and more willing to accept substitutes for his unattainable wishes, to give up the real satisfaction of a wish for an imagined satisfaction. If he cannot have a horse he can invent a horse with a piece of rope for a halter and a cooperative relative or a piece of furniture. Or better still, if he can't have a horse, he can *be* a horse with a rope tied around his middle. He will also accept a toy horse or a rocking horse as a satisfactory substitute.

And here we begin to see how the insatiable "I" of the early stages of growth, the "I" that is linked to biological principles of tension and relief of tension, desire and immediate fulfillment begins its gradual transformation into an "I" that restricts its appetites in accord with the demands of reality. "I," the ego in psychological terms, becomes a mediator between the two strong forces which control human activity. On the one hand, are the biological forces, the urges which arise out of body needs and demand satisfaction. On the other hand, are the forces of reality, physical and social, which restrict the possibilities of gratification. When the demands of biology are counterbalanced by the demands of reality a conflict is set up within the ego. It becomes the job of a special part of the ego, the judging and reasoning part, to find a solution to the conflict and to satisfy the demands of the two opposing forces. The solution is usually a compromise in which the ego as mediator gives something to both parties to the quarrel, very much as a judge settles a dispute between claimants with equal rights by giving part satisfaction to each party and asking each party to surrender some of his claims.

The analogy of a court dispute presided over by a fair-minded judge is a better one for later stages of ego development than the early stages we are describing. If we employ the analogy at all for the ego of the two to three year old we might say that the lower courts are most susceptible to corruption and it is here that we are most likely to find bribery, prejudice and downright knavery in the settling of disputes. Consider the following cases:

Case 1. Thirty-month-old Julia finds herself alone in the kitchen while her mother is on the telephone. A bowl of eggs is on the table. An urge is experienced by Julia to make scrambled eggs. She reaches for the eggs, but now the claims of reality are experienced with equal strength. Her mother would not approve. The resulting conflict within the ego is experienced as "I want" and "No, you mustn't" and the case for both sides is presented and a decision arrived at within the moment. When Julia's mother returns to the kitchen, she finds her daughter cheerfully plopping eggs on the linoleum and scolding herself sharply for each plop, "NoNoNo. Mustn't dood it. NoNoNo. *Mustn't* dood it!"

In this case we see that the claims of both sides of the conflict have been fairly heard in the lower courts and a victory was achieved by each side. The judge in this case has probably been guilty of accepting bribes from both sides, but if we accuse him of corrupt practice, he would argue warmly that he had been scrupulously fair in dealing with the claims of both disputants.

Case 2. Two-year-old Tommy doesn't care for the potty chair. It's all right for some people—his Teddy bear sits there all day sometimes—but he himself prefers diapers. Diapers are not for big boys? Very well, then, they're not. He likes it that way. But not entirely. He would like to please his mother. And sometimes just before he feels the urge for a b.m. he struggles with the problem. To go or not to go. To do it in his pants or do it on the potty. To keep it or to give it up. To satisfy himself or to satisfy the demands of reality. One day he marches into the bathroom in a businesslike way and closes the door. A little while later he excitedly calls his mother. His mother arrives expectantly and in good spirits. Tommy is sitting on the potty chair with a triumphant smile on his face. His pants are still on, he has made a b.m. in his diapers, *but he is sitting on the potty*. His ego has worked out a brilliant compromise, giving satisfaction to the claims of both parties. He does not understand why his mother looks so confused.

In this case the judge has collaborated with one of the claimants in the case to perpetrate a fraud on the other. However, if the judge were to be accused of corrupt practice, he would argue that it was impossible to be fair to both sides in these disputes over property, and Reality which wins most judgments in these cases should be satisfied with a token payment. Big corporations shouldn't take advantage of the small businessman. The property in this case is not worth much anyway.

Case 3. (A majority of these cases in the lower courts have to do with elimination.) Thirty-two-month-old Sally, completely toilet trained—well, almost—wears ruffled panties as a badge of merit, a certificate of confidence, and is vain of her new achievement. She is playing outdoors with her friend Margie, same age, with a less reliable bladder which keeps her in plastic pants. Sally feels the urge to urinate but hates to take the time out to go into the house. There is momentary conflict between the urge to urinate and the requirements of reality. The conflict is short-lived. When Sally's mother appears a little while later she finds her daughter with wet pants. Mother comments on this mildly, but Sally is deeply regretful that she has not lived up to the honor of ruffled silk panties. Now eyeing the incontinent Margie in plastic pants, she sings out an accusation. "Bad dirl, Margie!" she says. "Margie wet my pants!"

Here we see a more complex operation of corruption in the lower courts. The ego consents to the urge, the judge goes to sleep, and when reality comes back to represent its case the judge dismisses the evidence and cooperates with the delinquent to manufacture a case against an innocent party.

Fortunately, in all these instances of corruption in the lower courts there is no need to despair for the human race. We can even regard these as very favorable signs of development! For in each case in which we see this conniving and bribery, these slick compromises, one important fact stands out: This two-year-old ego is taking into account the demands of reality even while it employs these stratagems to get around it. When Julia plops the eggs on the floor and scolds herself for doing it, she is taking the first wobbly steps in self-control. The criticism comes *after* the act in the first steps; soon it will come before the act and prevent it, inhibit it. You will notice the same mechanism at work whenever we begin to teach the very young child to control an urge. The child who begins his toilet training will typically give the signal to go to the potty *after* he has made the b.m. in his diapers. This is a sign of progress and we can now count on the fact that within a short time he will begin to give the signal before defecation occurs. When Tommy works out his compromise in the bathroom in which he sits on the potty but makes the b.m. in his pants, he is making the first steps in use of the potty and indicating his *wish* to please his mother. Soon he will begin to use the potty. When Sally puts the blame for her wet pants on her friend Margie, she is telling us that wet pants have become unacceptable to her and she is on the way to establishment of better control.

We cannot speak of anything like a conscience at this age. Even when the child of this age acquires some control over his urges and his impulses we can't properly use the word conscience. At this age children are capable of guilt feelings over misbehavior, but the guilt feelings do not emerge until the act is discovered. It's when mother comes into the kitchen and finds scrambled eggs on the linoleum that Julia feels ashamed at her lapse. An older child, one who possesses a conscience, will be troubled with self-reproaches and feelings of shame for his naughtiness, even if he is not discovered. The older child, then, has taken the voice of criticism, the voice of authority into his ego where it functions as the voice of conscience. But our two year olds and our three year olds experience guilt feelings only when they feel or anticipate disapproval from the outside. In doing this, they have taken the first steps toward the goal of conscience, but there is a long way ahead before the policeman outside becomes the policeman inside.

"He should know better!" "I've told him over and over!" Parents of two year olds find it baffling to own a child who understands everything, who gives the most promising signs of a brilliant future in the White House or the Princeton Institute for Advanced Study, but who exhibits the most distressing signs of mental deficiency in certain areas. It is very difficult to explain how this two and a half year old can put together a ten-piece puzzle after being shown how just *once*, but he can't learn to keep his hands off daddy's phonograph records after several hundred repetitions of the word "no."

Now the difference between these two types of learning is this: In the first instance, in learning to put a puzzle together, a simple wish and its fulfillment are combined in the act of putting the puzzle together. "I make the horsie!" Here the native intelligence of the child encounters no obstacles beyond those presented by the problem itself. In the second instance a wish (to play with Daddy's records) must be blocked in order for learning to take place, that is, the child can only learn *not* to play with daddy's records by opposing his own wish. In all instances, and throughout life to a certain extent, learning which requires the negation of a wish, the blocking of an impulse, will be the most difficult type of learning. It is necessary in civilized society that such learning take place, but the difficulties encountered must be appreciated by us when we begin the education of the child in self-control. For in such instances education opposes biology. The drives which are part of the biological equipment of the human personality have no goal but their own satisfaction.

Education requires that the child control his drives, which in a certain sense means opposing himself. Control of the drives in some instances may require only postponement of the satisfaction, in others the ability to accept part gratification, in still others substitute gratifications and in special instances the blocking of drive satisfaction through special mechanism of defense. Each of these measures is a fascinating study in itself.

What does it mean at the age of two to postpone a satisfaction? A story comes to mind. When our friend Jan ("Laughing Tiger") was two and a half she had an extraordinary love of sweet things. When her meal came to a close, and it was time for dessert to come around she became excited and banged on her high-chair tray with a spoon. "Dzert! Dzert!" The clamor at times was deafening. This kind of display which can be funny at times can lose its enchantment for even a doting mother when the family meal needs watching, and a baby is waiting to be fed, and a husband is due home any moment. This time the dessert was ice-cream and Jannie's mother had to go downstairs to the freezer to get it. The shrill sounds of "Dzert!" and the banging spoon got under mother's skin tonight. "Oh, Jannie, have a little patience!" she said irritably, and left to go down to the freezer. When the mother returned to the kitchen she started with alarm when she saw Jannie. The child seemed to be having a convulsion. She was sitting rigidly in her high-chair, her fists clenched, her eyes fixed, her face beet-red, and she seemed not to be breathing. The mother dropped everything and ran to the child. "Jannie! What's the matter?" she cried. Jannie exhaled and relaxed her fists. "I'm having patience!" she said.

This is what "having patience" can mean to a two year old. The postponement of an urgent wish requires such an exertion that the child has to summon all his reserves of energy to oppose the wish. Usually the child of this age cannot summon enough opposition to his own urges when they are very strong and this makes Two a very difficult age for the family.

Everyone complains about the two year old. His parents complain about his wilfulness, his stubbornness. His older sister complains about his poor group integration. "He won't share. He wants everything for himself!" If there is a younger brother or sister, an infant, he adds his lamentations to this chorus. In the rare moments when this two year old is not to be heard or seen, when welcome silence descends upon the household, the intuitive mother tenses herself in expectation of a shriek of pain which will certainly come in a moment from the direction of the baby's room. Everyone complains. But the family dog does not complain. When the two year old comes after him with joyful cries, this sensible beast takes off to his sanctuary under the couch.

But miraculously, out of these ominous beginnings, a civilized child begins to emerge. For we have painted a dark picture, the two year old, as his worrying parents see him. There is another side of the two year old, which holds the real promise for the future.

He loves, deeply, tenderly, extravagantly and he holds the love of his parents more dearly than anything in the world. To be fair about it, he also loves himself very, very much and this conflict between self-love and love of others is the source of much of his difficulty at this age. But when put to the test, it is love for his parents which wins out. When he has displeased them he is disconsolate and even his self-love is dimin-

ished when he feels the displeasure of his parents. He wants to
be good in order to earn their love and approval; he wants to
be good so that he can love himself. (This is what we mean,
later, by self-esteem). He begins his progress as a social being
by adopting the attitude of his parents toward his unacceptable impulses. He comes to dislike them, too. And the first
progress in dealing with his unacceptable impulses is revealed
in a way that we would not immediately recognize as progress. He casts them out of himself and attributes them to
persons or objects outside.

He acquires a number of companions, imaginary ones, who
personify his Vices like characters in a morality play. (The
Virtues he keeps to himself. Charity, Good Works, Truth, Al-
truism, all dwell in harmony within him.) Hate, Selfishness,
Uncleanliness, Envy and a host of other evils are cast out like
devils and forced to obtain other hosts.

"I don't like Gerald. *Gerald bites!*" Stevie reports at the
dinner table. "Who's Gerald?" says his mother, puzzled. "Gerald
is my friend," says Stevie. "Where does he live?" says Mama,
not catching on. "In the basement," says Stevie. "Does *Stevie*
bite when he gets mad?" his father asks shrewdly. "Oh, no.
Not Stevie!" says the boy named Stevie. "Stevie is a good boy."
And adds loyally, "Stevie is my friend."

In this way Gerald comes to live in the house and can be
counted on to complicate family living. When Daddy's pipes
are broken, no one is more indignant than the two-year-old
son who is under suspicion. "Gerald, did you break my daddy's
pipes?" he demands to know. Gerald can offer nothing in his
defense and it's plain as the nose on Gerald's face that only he
could have committed this crime. When Gerald is not the per-
petrator of a dozen crimes a day, he is the sly fellow who gets
other people to carry out his evil plans. When circumstantial
evidence points to Stevie as the person who tossed his sister's
dolly into the toilet, he cries out despairingly, "Gerald made me
do it!" Occasionally the devil is invited to come back home.
Steel yourself for a bad day when Stevie comes down to

breakfast one morning in a savage mood and refuses to answer to his own name. "Stevie, do you want orange juice or pine-apple juice?" "I'm not Stevie," comes the ominous reply. "Don't want any joos." "Stevie, would you like. . . . ?" "My name isn't Stevie. I'm Gerald!" And Gerald immediately makes his presence known in a memorable display of temper at the family breakfast table.

Now to appreciate the function of Gerald we should not dismiss him simply as a scapegoat. He is that, of course, but most important is the fact that he represents the beginning of self-criticism, the beginning opposition of Stevie to his own unacceptable impulses. The first step in that direction is casting them out. What's good about that? we say. Why call that a step in the civilizing process when everyone knows that it is the most primitive way of dealing with one's impulses? And that's true, too. If we encounter this mechanism in adults, or even in older children, we do not think highly of the personality organization of such a person. We complain about persons who do not recognize their own faults but criticize them in others. No one, even in maturity, is ever completely free of this primitive tendency, but we certainly don't value it as a civilized trait. Why call this progress for Stevie?

We have said that casting out is the first step for Stevie in setting up opposition to his own unacceptable tendencies. Now when you and I wrestle with our temptations we recognize that the temptation comes from within, that the evil is in us and we oppose the unwelcome impulse by marshalling the forces of conscience. If a conflict between impulse and the prohibitions of conscience comes about we feel it as an internal conflict, a struggle within ourselves between two forces which originate within our own personality. Most important, for our purposes here, we recognize the bad impulse as our own. We don't like it but we can't disown it either. But the child of Stevie's age behaves as if the bad impulse were not his own, as if it originated outside of him, in fact existed in another person.

Now Stevie knows that Gerald has no existence, that he is an invention, but by creating Gerald he achieves several important gains for himself. First of all, and most obvious, he attempts to avoid criticism from his parents for his own misdeeds and his own unacceptable impulses. "Gerald did it." Second and equally important he can maintain his self-love; for if he acknowledged that a bad impulse was his own, that a naughty boy lived right inside him, *was* himself, he could not love himself and this would be unbearable. (We adults react in a similar way when we discover and acknowledge a disagreeable tendency within ourselves. Our self-esteem falls to zero, we cannot love ourselves until we have found a way of disposing of this unacceptable trait. The feeling of desolation which accompanies this discovery is also unbearable to us. We feel, we say, as if we have lost our last friend. And so we have when we cannot even love ourselves.)

A third function of Gerald is in line with the historic purposes of devils; it is the function of a devil to present himself in any form of his choosing in order to be licked. It is very difficult for man to wrestle with his vices in their abstract forms. In the history of civilization it was apparently a very long time before man recognized that the devils and spirits who plagued him and tempted him were the personifications of tendencies within his own nature. It's much easier to do battle with an opponent outside the self than an opponent within. The trouble with carrying on a fight with yourself is that if you win, you lose, and if you lose, you win. A devil offers himself as an objective opponent and the merit of a victory over a devil is that it is indisputable.

The devil was undoubtedly created at the dawn of civilization, cast out of the soul of a barbarian who became the first civilized man by opposing his own nature. So the casting out of Gerald is a momentous event in the young life of Stevie. It means that he feels a division in his own personality between the forces which we call drives and urges and the forces which we call reason and judgment, that part of the personality which develops largely under the influence of environment. The opposition between these two parts of the personality will depend upon the degree to which the rational side can bring under control the biological side. In Stevie's first struggles he repeats the experience of that remote ancestor who cast out his devil; he makes Gerald an objective opponent with whom he can more easily do battle.

What kind of battle? We flip back a page or two to locate Gerald in this narrative and we see no signs of a fight between Stevie and his devil. They seem to get along rather well, a good pair who suit each other's purposes. There is even some solid evidence that Gerald wins easily when there is any disagreement between the two. Anyone who has wrestled with devils must confess a similar experience in the first stages. What is important, in fact, *is the way Stevie talks to his devil!*

Am I joking? Not at all. "Gerald, did you break my daddy's pipes?" Stevie asks with indignation. Very well, insincere indignation, perhaps, but since the whole case is phony we can hardly expect a more convincing rebuke. No, what is important is that he addresses Gerald in the manner and tone of a parent rebuking a child for his naughtiness, that he has borrowed the attitude of his parents toward naughtiness, behaves like a parent toward a part of himself, represented as Gerald. It is comical, ludicrous, we can hardly take it seriously as a step in personality growth, and yet it is indubitably a sign that the faculty of self-criticism is emerging which eventually enables the child to control his own impulses. In clinical jargon we say that he has begun to identify himself with his parents and their standards, their prohibitions. Real identification with parental standards has not, of course, taken place as yet. There is a long way ahead for the two year old before he will be able to take these standards into himself, make them part of his personality, and employ them for self-control. For many months to come he will need to depend upon controls from the outside to restrict his own behavior. He will try to be "good" not to please himself, but to please his parents whom he loves. He will inhibit a naughty impulse not because he himself cannot allow it but because he anticipates the criticism, the disapproval of his parents. There is no conscience yet; only the preliminary stages of conscience building.

A fourth function of Gerald is to put himself out of business, for while he serves a purpose during a certain phase of development, it is very evident that he is not the kind of fellow you want for a permanent boarder. Somewhere along the line Gerald has to move back to his place of origin. Stevie has to take responsibility for his Gerald, to acknowledge that however disagreeable it is to have disharmony within the ego, to struggle with one's own naughty impulses, the fact is that Gerald does not exist outside of the personality, that Gerald and Stevie are one, or, as the child might see it, two parts of himself. This step is taken in the natural course of events as a consequence of the parental attitude toward Gerald, for no parent allows the fiction of Gerald to obscure the real issues. The parent insists that it was Stevie who broke Daddy's pipes. The parent does not accept a fictional devil who prompted Stevie to toss his sister's doll into the toilet. The parent does not believe that the little boy in a tantrum at the breakfast table is a mythical Gerald. The fiction of Gerald is confronted with all the forces of reality and diminishes with each failure to overcome them. Gradually Gerald loses his function and Stevie reluctantly accepts temptation and naughty impulses as tendencies which originate within himself. Gerald is heard from less and less. One day you say to Stevie, "Say, whatever happened to Gerald? I haven't heard about him for a long time." "Who's Gerald?" says Stevie. He is genuinely puzzled.

5. Education Toward Reality

WE HAVE established the fact that the two year old does not have a conscience. This leads us to a subject of the greatest interest to the parents of the small child. How does he get one? Now one of the difficulties in discussing "a stage in development" is the corollary "he will outgrow it," which is sometimes popularly understood to mean a metamorphosis, a spontaneous emergence of a new stage in the life cycle, in analogy with the caterpillar and the butterfly. Unfortunately, the human child does not metamorphosize and if we wait patiently for the miracle to appear and do not take a hand in the process of social development and conscience we will find that this pleasure-loving fellow is perfectly content to leave matters as they are.

We must be careful not to confuse two types of development in the child. Physical development follows a definite and predictable path toward maturation. For example, a child who learns to crawl will certainly outgrow this mode of locomotion and proceed toward walking. This kind of maturation follows inherited tendencies in the human and has a certain degree of independence from teaching. But social development, the acquisition of standards of behavior, the restriction of impulses and urges, will not develop without teaching. The little child will not acquire control over his impulses unless we require him to. He has no incentives of his own, no inherited tendencies "to be good," "to be unselfish," to control his appetites and his temper. His parents provide the incentives. Much later in his development the child will call these incentives his own.

146

Now in speaking of "conscience building" in the small child we need to face the fact ruefully that even under the best educational program the two year old will reach his third birthday with greatly improved self-control, but no conscience in the strict meaning of the term! By this we mean that his self-control is still dependent upon factors outside himself, namely, the approval or disapproval of his parents. A conscience, in the proper sense of the word, consists of standards and prohibitions which have been taken over by the personality and which govern behavior from within. Such an internal system of standards will usually not require outside controls to support it. When one has a conscience he forbids himself to do certain things, checks his impulses, experiences guilt reactions for transgressions, without the need for a "policeman" outside. Such a conscience does not emerge in the child until the fifth or sixth year. It will not become a stable part of his personality until the ninth or tenth year. It will not become completely independent of outside authority until the child becomes independent of his parents in the last phase of adolescence.

Then why should we speak of conscience building in a discussion of two year olds? Because we have learned that the *patterns* of parental control which are established in the earliest years of life serve as the patterns for self-control in later years, that is, they become the patterns of conscience. In this way we can speak of conscience *building* in the early years of life before a conscience has appeared.

We understand, then, that control over impulse in the period between eighteen months and three years is still largely dependent upon external factors. Julia's impulse to make scrambled eggs on the kitchen floor could be easily negated if her mother were in the same room when the urge came upon her. In the absence of anything like a conscience there is no self-restraint imposed upon the impulse to smash eggs. At best, a well-behaved two year old might conjure up the image of a disapproving mama and, in anticipation of this disapproval might abandon the scrambled eggs project before it got started. But no prompting of conscience enters into this.

So if we ask, "What means does the two year old have to control his behavior?" we give first place on the list to his parents. It is his love for his parents and the value he places on parental approval or disapproval that largely influence his conduct. This sounds so banal as to be unworthy of mention and yet it needs to be reiterated and it needs to be thoroughly understood. Obviously, if a child does not care whether we approve or disapprove his acts, he has no motive to control his behavior and will simply do whatever pleases him.

"Unfair!" comes a reproachful chorus of parents of two year olds. "We've said no, no, no, in ten thousand ways every day for months and he still won't keep away from his father's phonograph records, he still plays around with the electric wall socket, and what's more he *grins* at us while he's doing it. Isn't *that* parental disapproval? Or what's wrong with us?"

The protesting parents need an apology and an explanation. When the two year old persists in repeating all the acts that have met with parental disapproval, it doesn't necessarily bring discredit upon the parents and the quality of their love for him or his love for them. As we have seen, he is still a fellow of strong urges and inadequate equipment for controlling his urges. Until language development can come to his aid in controlling impulse there will be many months of tedious repetitions of the same prohibitions and a cumulative effect that is so slow that the average parent hardly notices it. Even so, you will see the two year old hesitate before repeating his favorite gambit and you will notice a guilty look creep over his face every now and then when he is reproached by his parents, signs that he is aware of the parental attitude and is reacting to it. And when, some welcome month in the second year, he does begin to show some ability to control his urges, it is because the wish to gain parental approval has finally proved stronger than his wish to pursue the unacceptable behavior.

So there is really no need to change our original statement. Ultimately the victory over certain urges in this young child is achieved through the wish to please the parents. It is giving up one satisfaction, the gratification of the personal wish, for the greater satisfaction and reward of parental approval. We only need this corollary for the very young child: It takes much time, many repetitions of the same type of incident, before the small child is able to sacrifice his own pleasure-seeking for the gain of another satisfaction, parental approval.

In the preceding chapter we observed that the two year old has special difficulties in learning control whenever he must *oppose* his own wish. A perfectly intelligent two year old who understands a fair amount of English, who can perform fairly complicated intellectual feats, does not "understand" the word "no." This difficulty, we have seen, is not an intellectual disability and not "just plain stubbornness." His wishes are very powerful and he hasn't yet acquired the means to say "no" to himself. So this is the time when the unwary parent can find himself in a contest with a toddler. When the simple prohibition doesn't work, the parent may resort to stronger methods. The parent who doesn't believe in slapping hands or spanking may find himself doing just this. Then a new cycle is created where an angry and rebellious two year old finds a second motive for performing the forbidden act, retaliation. There is real danger that such a contest may lead to stronger and stronger demands on both sides with serious impairment of the child-parent relationship. But if the parent is to be effective in teaching control he must not permit his relationship with the child to deteriorate into a state of war. Then all teaching is blocked.

"But you can't reason with him at this age! What *can* you do?" And it is true that before the age of reason, and before language development eases our communication with the small child, we feel restricted in our means of influence. While we can all agree that a firm and positive "no," and a manifestation of parental disapproval have a place in discipline, we must not look upon prohibitions as the only means of educating for self-control. We find that the child who does not yet have language at his command, the child under two and a half, will be able to cooperate with our education if we go easy on the "blocking" techniques, the outright prohibitions, the "no's" and go heavy on "substitution" techniques, that is the redirection of certain impulses and the offering of substitute satisfactions.

We mean that the child who is not yet ready to block his own impulses effectively may be ready to accept new directions for his impulses and new or substitute goals. In the case of the two year old and the phonograph records it will be easier (but not easy) to provide an acceptable substitute for the forbidden objects, another direction for the strong desire to look and to handle, than to keep up the chant of "no, no, no." (It would be still easier to get the phonograph records out of the way, but we'll assume for the time being that this is not practical or possible.) *Before* we get into a "no, no, no" contest with the two year old, we may find it useful to have an old album of records, ready for discard, which we can give him each time the urge to take down Daddy's records is manifest. These are the "Daddy's records" he can play with; look we keep them here for Jonny, and Jonny can play with these but not with the other records. We suspect that the fact that these are Daddy's records has a special meaning for Jonny. He loves Daddy and in wanting something that belongs to Daddy, he is expressing his positive feelings for Daddy. Therefore a substitute object might need to be a Daddy object to be acceptable.

"All this," says the parent looking me straight in the eye, "is easier said than done! Did *you* ever try to get a two year old to change his mind about something he wanted—to accept a substitute?" Sure. It's hard work! It takes patient repetition and teaching. But the chances are good that something will come of this teaching, and the chances are not very good at this age that a long day of "no, no, no's" will bring anything but a bad case of nerves to mother and child. Also, I want to repeat that it is easier to employ such a substitution technique *before* a no, no, no contest sets in. Once daddy's phonograph records become a prize in the contest, the substitute becomes more difficult to accept.

Of course, since we know how necessary it is for the toddler to touch and handle everything he sees, it is obvious that we can avoid a lot of unnecessary conflict by getting precious and breakable objects out of the way for a few months. Some parents protest this advice. "I don't want my living room denuded. He has to learn to respect property sometime, why not now?" It's very true that he will have to learn this sometime. Why not now? He doesn't have enough control yet, and we don't have good communication through language yet. Teaching him "not to touch" at this stage of beginning self-control is arduous and exhausting. In a few months, perhaps in the last half of the third year, we may find him ready to meet us half way in such control because his ability to control his own impulses will have progressed. We must remember that we are already making important demands upon him for self-control in terms of toilet training, in managing his aggressions, in sacrificing self-interest for the interests of others, and we may find that some educational problems can be postponed in the interest of the child and the harmony of the family. Respect for an ash-tray or a Venetian figurine is not the most important objective in our heavy educational program during the early months of the third year.

But we do not want to depart from the problem we are investigating. We are interested in the problem of teaching beginning control through redirection, substitution of goals. Aside from phonograph records and coffee-table ornaments the two year old presents us with some practical and serious educational problems which cannot be put away in cupboards. A good many such problems center around "aggression."

Let's consider the problem presented by a young friend of mine a while back. When Lawrie was twenty-eight months old a baby sister arrived. Lawrie had been prepared for the baby and he knew that the baby was inside his Mommy and would come out one day. We are in favor of preparation stories of new and important events, but we must admit that no child can be prepared for the *reality* of a new baby, no child can anticipate or imagine his new life with a real baby in the family. Moreover, there is one element in the getting of a new baby which we tend to overlook. Mother *leaves* Lawrie to go to the hospital and it is the first time he has ever experienced such a long separation from his mother. The sense of loss and desertion is felt more strongly than rivalry with a mythical sister during that week without mother. When mother does return with a new baby, the feeling of abandonment joins forces with the feelings toward a rival to produce a particularly vehement reaction. It's as if mother had actually abandoned him to find another child to love.

Lawrie tried hard during the first weeks. He imitated the grown-ups who cooed and clucked at the baby. He "helped" take care of her. But the conflict between love and hate was hardly to be endured at times. When he hugged the baby and murmured endearments, the conflicting urge resulted in a too strenuous hug. At times aggression got the upper hand and he pinched the baby or slapped her, or came after her menacingly with a stick or a block.

Now very clearly we can't allow Lawrie or any child to attack an infant. We are sympathetic with his feelings, but we have to prevent him from hurting the baby. Lawrie's parents were firm with him about this. They told him they could not allow him to hurt the baby and showed their disapproval at such times. This was necessary, of course. But now matters became more complicated. Lawrie made heroic efforts to control himself with the baby (not always with success) but now the efforts to control himself produced temper tantrums "over nothing" dozens of times a day. The little boy who had been so cheerful and good natured a few weeks ago was now stormy and negativistic and his parents foresaw difficulties ahead if they could not help him now. Lawrie's parents did everything possible to reassure him of their love for him. This was helpful, but the inner rage was not diminished. There were strong feelings which needed to be expressed, but the only way in which this small child could express them was in action, because *he could not express them in words.* Yet we could not, of course, permit him to attack the baby.

So here is our dilemma with the child of Lawrie's age. We cannot allow him to express his aggression against his sister through physical attack and the vocabulary of the twenty-eight-month-old child is inadequate for expression through words.

If Lawrie were older, if he had enough words at his command, we could say, "I can't let you hurt the baby, but when you feel so angry at her you can tell me about it." And we would help the child put his feelings of jealousy into words. An older child— even a three year old—could say, "You like her better than me," or "I want her to go back. Don't want no baby sister." An older child might be able to put his destructive feelings into words: "I wish she was an ant. Then I could step on her!" In these ways and many others the child relieves himself of his feelings through putting his injured feeling and his hostile wishes into words. Through expressing his feelings in words he diminishes the need for jealous and destructive acts toward the baby; the words are a substitute for acts, and verbal expression will usually afford the child enough relief so that he can inhibit the hostile actions toward the baby.

But what shall we do for Lawrie who can't yet speak well enough to put his feelings into words? If he cannot be permitted to express these feelings through words, is there another kind of substitute for the forbidden acts that will allow him to discharge his feelings without directing them toward the baby?

Lawrie's parents were friends of mine and around this time we talked over means of helping him out. I proposed that we obtain a plastic, inflated dummy called Puncho and provide Lawrie with a substitute target for his aggression. We would tell Lawrie that he could hit Puncho when he got mad, but we could not let him hit the baby. So Puncho was purchased from the nearest drugstore and was installed in haste and high hopes by Lawrie's parents. In fairy tales about child psychologists and parents this is where the story should end with successful resolution and harmony restored. Let's see what really happened.

On the following day Lawrie's mother called me. "Something went wrong in your book!" she informed me with the unabashed criticism that comes easily to all my friends and relatives. (Parents who consult me professionally are always certain that something is wrong with *them* if my advice does not work.) "What happened?" I said. "Lawrie doesn't *want* to hit Puncho. He says Puncho is his friend. He hugs Puncho and he wants to take him to bed. Now we've got this plastic gorilla right smack in the middle of the living room taking up the only floor space that isn't already taken up by the piano and the couch and Lawrie's truck fleet. But never mind that. What does it say in the book? What do we do now?"

We carefully reconsidered the whole situation. After all, Lawrie's attitude was very sensible. He had no grievances against Puncho. Puncho hadn't done anything to him. And he did have real grievances against Karen. It would be difficult to get him to transfer his feelings of enmity from a real rival to a plastic dummy whom he regarded as a friend. The one thing we could count on, however, is that friendship is very unstable at Lawrie's age and if Puncho could stick around for a while, love might cool and the antagonistic feelings which are always on tap might direct themselves to Puncho after all. So we decided to give Puncho a fair trial for a week, maybe longer. Each time Lawrie tried to hit the baby we would repeat the explanation that if he was mad he could hit Puncho, but he could not hit the baby.

It was almost two weeks before Puncho replaced Karen as a target for Lawrie's aggression. Within a few more weeks Puncho's physical condition was almost beyond the point of salvage. But by that time it didn't matter. Puncho rendered useful services for an interim period of adjustment. Lawrie's attacks upon Karen ceased, his temper tantrums diminished and the normal amount of rivalry and resentment that remained toward Karen was entirely manageable and under control.

Now this may seem like an extraordinary amount of space to devote to a story about a small boy's not-extraordinary hostility toward a new baby and the means by which he was helped to overcome it. But I think Lawrie's story helps us in establishing a principle for the handling of aggression in the early stages of teaching control. Lawrie is required to inhibit his aggression toward his sister, but in making this demand of Lawrie, we recognize the strength of the feelings and the inadequate means of control at his age and choose a method of handling which permits some expression of the urge in an acceptable way toward a substitute target.

We see how certain other means of handling this problem can produce additional problems at this age. When Lawrie was first required to stop his attacks upon his sister the aggression which could find no expression in an act was discharged in another undesirable way, temper tantrums. I have known other children who produced different types of problems under similar circumstances. A little girl who was spanked repeatedly for her attacks against a baby brother became a model child who showed no signs of aggression at all after a while, but she developed a serious sleep disturbance and a number of fears which caused her to cling to her mother all day. Another little girl who was taught to substitute loving acts for hostile acts against her little sister developed a pattern of displaying exaggerated love for anyone toward whom she felt hostile, and acquired a symptom through which the suppressed anger could be discharged, bed-wetting.

From these examples it can be seen that a two year old can be taught to curb his aggressions completely if the parents employ strong enough methods, but the achievement of such control at an early age may be bought at a price which few parents today would be willing to pay. The slow *education* for control demands much more parental time and patience at the beginning, but the child who learns control in this way will be the child who acquires healthy self-discipline later. While it is tedious to teach a Lawrie to express his aggressive feelings toward a plastic dummy instead of his sister, it is actually far more tedious to put up with temper tantrums a dozen times a day, to be up several times a night with an anxious child, or to change the bed-linen of an enuretic child for several years to come. The thwarted instincts have a way of avenging themselves if we do not give them partial satisfaction while we are in the process of modifying them.

While we are on the subject of plastic dummies and substitute targets for aggression, let's pause to take a critical view of the handling of aggression in young children. *The method employed for the handling of Lawrie's aggression is only suitable for the pre-verbal child or the child who does not yet have adequate command of language.* It is a primitive educational tactic and we should rarely find it necessary to employ such methods with the four and five year old. It would be hard to think of any occasion when it would be desirable with a school-age child. As soon as the child begins to acquire language we begin to educate away from simple discharge of aggression, we gradually increase our demands upon him to put his feelings into words, to handle his conflicts through words, to achieve control over impulse through language. Whatever need the older child has for simple, physical discharge of aggression is adequately met through games and play. We do not expect that his family life or neighborhood life should be conducted on the basis of simple tension discharge, i.e., "I'm mad at you, so I sock you," or "I'm mad at you so I'll have a tempter tantrum right here and now."

Our educational work becomes easier with language. We can begin to put the improved language ability to work for us in control. When the child discharges his feelings in an outburst of temper, we look down disapprovingly on such a baby way of making his wants or feelings known. "You're a big boy and you can talk!" we say to him. "You can *tell* me what you want." We encourage expression in language, approve him for his efforts to employ words instead of a primitive discharge of feeling. And

in subtle and sometimes outspoken ways we take care to see that
the outburst of temper is not rewarded, gains nothing for him,
whereas verbal expression gives him a fair hearing and the
chance whenever possible that he can obtain his wish. Of
course, we do not see an automatic end to temper outbursts
with the acquisition of improved language ability and we grant
the child lapses in control, but we are educating away from the
primitive mode of expression to a higher mode with the expectation that in the years that follow more and more control will be
exerted by the higher thought processes to replace the simple
and primitive tension-discharge mechanisms which the very
small child must employ.

We need to emphasize this process because there is a tendency
in our more lenient child-training of today to permit the child
to remain on the tension-discharge level longer than he needs to.
We are indulgent toward the temper outburst, the physical
attack, the scream and the demand for immediate satisfaction
or attention way past the time that the child can be expected to
have the means for control. It is not unusual today to find even
six, seven and eight year olds, otherwise perfectly normal kids,
who are still operating on a primitive discharge basis only because nothing more has ever been required of them!

Parents are understandably confused about just how much
control can be expected of a child at any given age, and since
there are dangers in making too strong demands for control
before a child is ready for it, many parents have preferred to
err in the other direction. But there are also dangers in expecting
too little of a child. For the child whose impulsiveness is in-
dulged, who retains his primitive-discharge mechanisms, is not
only an ill-behaved child but a child whose intellectual development is slowed down. No matter how well he is endowed in-
tellectually, if direct action and immediate gratification are the
guiding principles of his behavior, there will be less incentive
to develop the higher mental processes, to reason, to employ
the imagination creatively, to sublimate. In short, if we do not

require the child to replace direct action gradually with the higher modes of mental activity, the child will be naturally inclined to remain on the primitive level of discharge because it is easier.

Can we find a principle in child development that can guide us in our expectations for the child so that our demands for control can be attuned to the child's readiness? Clearly, before language and thought can substitute for action we need to be more indulgent of the child's need to discharge feelings through physical means. This means that up to the middle of the third year, with wide variations for normal development at either end of the third year, the mental processes are not sufficiently well developed to serve control and that therefore we can't expect too much from the child. This doesn't mean that we aren't at work on developing controls, showing our approval for good behavior and disapproval for misdemeanors and destructive acts, but we know the child doesn't have the means for control that come with the development of mental processes and we are not surprised by his lapses. Gradually, as the mental processes develop, and we can follow this through language development, we find more and more readiness to substitute words and thoughts for action and we increase our expectations for the child, asking him to employ words and thoughts to a larger and still larger extent in dealing with his impulses. But we must remember that months and years go into this education and though we can expect improved control by the end of the third year, this is still a pleasure-loving little fellow and lapses in control will be frequent, and we are not surprised. We are teachers. We hold up standards to the child, often a little beyond what he can actually achieve, but we know how difficult this learning is and we accept the lapses, the regressions and the plateaus when they inevitably occur.

WEAK SPOTS IN THE CONTROL SYSTEM.

So WE begin to see something like a control system when language takes over the job of engineering the mental machinery, allowing certain impulses to go through, redirecting others along alternative routes, blocking still others at dangerous intersections. Unfortunately, a highly organized control system will not be perfected by the child for several years and the mechanical problems in operating the early model, two-year-old mental apparatus, create many vexing problems for the child. Consider, for example, the inefficiency of this early model control system. The two and a half year old who has to say, "No, no, mustn't dood it" to himself whenever a wayward impulse seizes him, has to expend enormous amounts of energy to stop himself. He has to tell himself what to do with an impulse each time he needs to manage it. This becomes tiresome, probably as tiresome for the two year old as for his parents in the parallel situation of telling him what to do. So a good deal of the time the young child either neglects to send himself signals or signals too late. But compare this "hand-operated" apparatus with the late model automatic system that takes over later. At five or six a large part of this system is completely automatic. A signal is flashed, a response is made, and the impulse is stopped or discharged without any conscious thought directing it! Unless the apparatus comes up against a problem for which a fresh solution must be found, it can handle a vast number of decisions without bringing them up for conference at all. Under ordinary circumstances a six year old confronted with a bowl of eggs on the kitchen table does not experience either the impulse to smash them or the self-prohibition against smashing them. If the mischievous impulse arises, it is checked before it becomes fully conscious. And so it goes for hundreds of decisions in the course of the day. An automatic signal system takes over a large part of the management of impulses in the older child where the two year old is obligated to struggle laboriously with such impulses on a conscious level.

So the two year old's inefficient control system is full of mechanical flaws and is subject to many disorders. The signals get mixed, the signals may never be sent at all, and sometimes the two year old finds the whole business of running this switchboard too complicated and attributes the failures in connections to diabolical agents outside of himself, like Stevie's "Gerald." But we will also find that many of the anxieties of this stage of development can be attributed to weaknesses in the control system. A little child who is trying hard to manage his impulses is subjected to the tensions of opposing wishes and may acquire strange and inexplicable fears in his attempts to resolve conflict. In such instances the control system appears to be making more demands upon the child than he is ready to make. So the mechanical difficulties in this early control system run the gamut from low efficiency to exaggerated severity and we may even find the whole gamut demonstrated in the behavior of one child.

How does a stable control system emerge from this early disorder? Let's follow our friend Stevie for a little while. We recall that in the early stages of his attempts to overcome certain impulses he renounced them and attributed them to a mythical Gerald who was then criticized freely by Stevie for these traits and blamed for Stevie's own lapses in control. We saw this as a first step in self-criticism. But we also saw this as the small child's difficulty in reconciling opposing tendencies within himself and in taking responsibility for his own impulses. Eventually a Stevie must come to terms with his Gerald, to acknowledge that the naughty impulses arise within himself, are part of himself and can be controlled by him.

But in some instances we will see a child who has great difficulty in achieving this reconciliation of the two parts of himself, who persists even in later stages of development in projecting his own naughtiness onto others or in other ways denying responsibility for his acts to the point that we might regard as unusual even for childhood. For we expect to see even in the two year old some signs that he can accept responsibility for his own acts, and signs that he feels remorse or guilt for his wrong-doing. If we see a child of five or six or older who employs such mechanisms extensively to evade responsibility for his own acts and who therefore experiences no personal guilt, we have to assume that something has interfered with normal development. We put a different interpretation upon the behavior of the five or six year old than we do on the behavior of the two year old. In the case of the older child we see that an important step in ego development has not yet taken place. We can assume that a sequence of developmental steps was broken at a certain point. Most often we find that the point at which development was disturbed was the critical second and third year.

But what might interfere with normal progress in personality development at this stage? How is it that a child might fail to make the necessary step forward in ego development which is evidenced by the ability to take responsibility for his own acts? Either one of two conditions might interfere with normal progress in this area of ego development.

On the one hand, we can see how an attitude of over-indulgence on the part of the parents could bring about the situation where a child feels no personal responsibility for his acts. If parents are uncritical or do not expect the child to take responsibility for his acts, there will be no motive, of course, for the child to do so. If the child feels that he loses nothing in his parents' estimation of him by following his own impulses, there is no reason why this pleasure-loving two year old should restrict his own behavior or be critical of it himself.

Paradoxically, an over-strict, too severe attitude on the part of the parents toward a small child's behavior can produce a similar, but not identical picture. If a child feels that his naughtiness will bring about severe punishment, or total and devastating rejection of him as a person, he may go through step one in this specific process of development by casting out his naughty self, but he may have great difficulty in moving on to step two, accepting his naughtiness as part of himself, taking responsibility for his own acts and discovering the means for controlling them. In other words, such a child would have two motives for leaving his naughtiness "outside." First, fear of the extreme punishment; second, loss of self-love by admitting that the naughty child is part of himself. On the surface, this child who is defending against extreme anxiety will resemble our first example, the child who has been over-indulged. Our second child, too, may be a "behavior problem" at the age of five, six or older. He will lack the means for effective self-control; he will deny personal responsibility for his acts and show no appropriate guilt feelings for his misbehavior. But the underlying mechanism for this behavior will be more complex than that of our first example.

When we see how either extreme of parental handling can produce difficulties in personality development, can prevent the normal and necessary steps in self-control from emerging, we naturally find ourselves with many questions on the whole problem of discipline, on the teaching of self-control to young children. So far as theoretical considerations are concerned in this discussion, we can draw one important inference at this point: A discipline which is extremely lenient or a discipline which is extremely harsh can disturb the process of conscience-building and produce a similar result—a child with ineffective controls.

In these two examples we have seen a failure in control of the drives. But now let's consider some other consequences of the child's early struggles with his urges. If we follow a normal child's development from eighteen months to the age of three, we will see that certain strivings, certain impulses, have already undergone some alterations. Some of these have vanished so completely that we cannot find a trace of their original form when the child reaches the age of three. Some have persisted but have changed their mode of expression.

The second group are, of course, easiest to identify. When two-year-old Carol occupies herself for hours making mud-pies, it takes no special psychological divination to find the older, infantile pleasure which has been altered in this play. Carol may even tell you with the characteristic candor of her age that she is making b.m.'s or Kakas. What has changed is the goal of the old pleasure. The eighteen-month-old Carol who was fascinated by her b.m.'s and even enjoyed playing with them until she discovered that the civilized world frowned on such pleasures, is now the two-and-a-half-year-old Carol who accepts and upholds this civilized view and takes pleasure in a substitute activity which the civilized world sanctions. The substitute activity is far enough removed from the original pleasure so that Carol would feel ashamed of an impulse to play with b.m.'s, but no shame attaches itself to this play with mud.

In those instances where we can provide new goals or substitute activities for the infantile strivings which must be given up we achieve our best success in training. It is not easy for the little child to give up the infantile form of his strivings either, but in the end he can accept the change of goal since some form of gratification is provided for the urge. So we see how even the strong aggressive tendencies of small children can be diverted from an original goal to a substitute. We can't let Lawrie strike the baby, we say. "If you're mad you can hit Teddy bear, or Puncho, but you can't hurt the baby." Lawrie will not be happy about finding a substitute goal for his aggression (the original one is so much more responsive), but it is easier for him to change the goal than transform the urge, or inhibit it entirely at this point in his development, and he can go along with us on this score.

But now let's return to an earlier point. Certain urges, we have said, seem to disappear in the course of early development. If we look for them we can't find a trace of them in their original form. This is a very different case from the two we have just cited. Carol's pleasure in dirtiness and messing is still recognizable as such even when she has changed its goal. Lawrie's aggressive striking out is still aggression even when he finds a substitute object. But what happened to Steve's biting of people between two years and three years? "Does it matter?" says his mother wincing at the memory. "He gave it up, mercifully." We are all grateful to Stevie for overcoming this unfortunate tendency and I am not suggesting in any way that Stevie's psyche was damaged by giving up biting of people or that his parents should reproach themselves for their natural reluctance to gratify their child's cannibalistic urges. But just the same, what happened to it? And what happened to the *idea* behind the biting of people, the idea that one can eat up another person?

The biting of people had to be given up along with the idea that one's fellow humans can be incorporated through eating and made part of oneself. (By the way, this is not altogether a destructive idea. While some children will bite in a rage they will also bite out of love, in much the same spirit as a child might say, "I love you so much I could eat you up!") So Stevie's biting is prohibited emphatically by his parents. "I don't like that! I can't let you do that! That hurts!" Stevie is required to control his impulse toward biting people. In the process of acquiring control, he shows his own criticism of his biting by creating Gerald, the naughty boy who bites people. But when he finally begins to relinquish his biting, to control successfully his urge to bite, something happens which might be easily overlooked by us, or mistakenly interpreted.

He is a perfectly healthy little boy with no more fears and worries than any other youngsters his age, but one night he awakens screaming for Mommy and Daddy. "Ginger bited me!" he wails. Ginger is the little cocker spaniel next door. Stevie had been playing with him that afternoon. Mother had been there the whole time. Ginger had not bitten Stevie. "No, darling, Ginger didn't bite you!" says Mama, comforting him. "He did. He bited me on my foot." Stevie has wakened from a dream. But like other two and a half year olds, he doesn't know that he has dreamed. He takes the events of the dream like real events. It takes a little time to comfort Stevie and get him back to sleep.

Next morning when Ginger comes over to Stevie's yard, Stevie cries out for his mother. Again he cries out, "Ginger bited me. He bited me!" It takes much patience to help Stevie over his fear of Ginger. And even later when these two become friends again, the old fear might return from time to time.

Meantime Stevie continues to grow and astonish his parents with his precocity and his achievements in self-control and reasonableness—and nobody notices that *Stevie is no longer biting people!*

So if we ask, "What happened to the urge to bite people?" we have to say "it disappeared." Stevie stopped biting people. But it is not only in fairy tales that evil spirits are commanded to disappear and reappear later in unrecognizable forms. Here, the fairy tale only imitates the mental processes themselves. For Stevie's dream in which the dog "bited" him was a visitation in disguise from the same evil which Stevie had cast out. The dog who bites Stevie represented Stevie's urge to bite people which is prohibited not only by the parents but now by Stevie himself. The *wish* to bite, which is denied satisfaction in waking life, becomes the motive for a dream in which the wish again seeks satisfaction in disguise. It would be correct to say that Stevie's fear of the dog in the dream was fear of his own wish to bite as well as his fear of being bitten.

We notice some very important differences between the early efforts to handle the wish to bite and these later ones. In the casting out of Gerald the wish to bite was projected on to Gerald. Stevie "got rid of" the bad wish by simply giving it to someone else. He did not himself give up his biting or the wish to bite. He only said Gerald did it. In this later stage of development he recognizes the wish as his own, not Gerald's (Gerald vanished a while back) and he, himself, tries to oppose it and prevent it from obtaining satisfaction. But now the dream makes use of the same primitive mechanism by transferring the wish to bite onto another object, a very appropriate one, a dog. And then we observe something new has been added. The fear is that the dog will bite *Stevie!* Gerald, that reliable conspirator of a few months ago, never once bit or threatened to bite Stevie. Only other people. So we see now how the overcoming of the wish to bite is accompanied by a new development in which the wish is projected upon an outside object, the dog, and is now experienced as boomeranging on the little boy who originally had the wish. What does this mean? Does it mean that someone has threatened Stevie with retaliation for his biting? Does it mean that he has had the experience of being bitten by a dog? Curiously enough, this mechanism can be observed even if the child has not been threatened or had the experience of being bitten. It works this way:

The wish to bite which originated in Stevie is projected upon an outside object, the dog, and as the result of the projection is no longer experienced by Stevie as an inner wish of his own. This is an unconscious mental process which has resulted in the partial repression of the forbidden wish. But complete repression of such a wish cannot take place and the impulse to bite someone will continue to arise. Now each time it arises Stevie does not experience it as an inner wish but as an outer wish, not as something which originates in him but as something which originates in the dog. By the same mechanism, the danger which Stevie feels in connection with this wish is also removed to the outside. Each time the impulse to bite arises within Stevie it is experienced as something outside which threatens him.

Do we need to be alarmed at this new development? No. We have all seen normal children who go through phases which are very similar to this. It helps to know why the child of a certain age develops certain types of fears, and later we'll speak of the parents' role in helping the child overcome these fears. Normally, Stevie's fear of Ginger will subside after a while, at the time that Stevie achieves better success in dealing with his own impulses and doesn't have to be afraid of them. The fear may return again when Stevie is three or four and has to deal with certain other impulses which overwhelm him, but normally we can expect it to subside again when he has successfully overcome them.

If we look at some other common fears of Stevie's age, we can see a similar mechanism at work. Peter, who loves the zoo and has never reacted to the roaring lions with much anxiety, now clings to his Daddy when the lions roar. He thinks the lion is angry when he roars. Peter, these days, is doing his two-and-a-half-year-old best to bring his own aggression under control and we can see why the lion is disturbing to him. Sally has a fear of rain for a few weeks in the second year and this baffles the family. Why doesn't she like the rain. "It's vet!" she explains sensibly. "Of course, the rain is wet," says her mama. But that isn't what Sally means. She has been trying, trying too hard perhaps, to have dry nights and when she wakes up wet, she is irritable and disappointed. "Vet!" she complains. So her fear of rain ("It's vet!") is her fear that she will wet herself. We could go on to catalogue a large number of fears of children this age which are the results of the child's early efforts to bring his own impulses under control. In these instances the child's fear is essentially a fear of his own impulses which are transferred to objects or phenomena outside himself. In each case, normally the fear will subside when the child has learned to control successfully the particular impulse which is disturbing him.

But now shouldn't we mention that there are times when these "typical" fears move over the borderline and provide us with some cause for concern? I would say, as an example, that if Stevie's fear of dogs should spread and interfere with other normal functions of his age, we should give it special consideration. If his fear of dogs should become so intense that he is afraid to leave the house, afraid to leave mother's side most of the day, we should say that something is at work in this problem which requires our serious attention. If Peter should overcome his aggression so completely and so thoroughly that he becomes a passive and absolutely obedient little boy, we need to be concerned. If Sally's fear of wetting herself becomes so severe that she is afraid to go to sleep because she might lose control, afraid to play with water in the sand-box, afraid to take her bath if the avoidance of water and wetness takes on such large proportions, we can no longer consider such reactions within the range of normal development. In each of these instances the child's fears are restricting his normal activities, they have spread into other areas, and the child does not give us signs that he is acquiring his own means for overcoming them. In such instances we usually wish to get professional counsel.

HELPING THE CHILD OVERCOME HIS FEARS.

NORMALLY the child overcomes his small-sized anxieties with the help of his parents. Some of the measures we employ are as old as the human race and hardly need to be catalogued here. Simple parental reassurance subdues some of the garden variety of fears of this age. This happens because parents are endowed with magical powers by children of this age and can banish dangers by uttering a few words or offering the protection of their arms.

But sometimes we find that parental reassurance has practically no effect on the child's fear and yet the fear itself is not a very large one, not in any sense pathological. Let's take Sally's fear of rain. "But the rain won't hurt you, Sally," her parents say over and over. Yet Sally is not relieved. "Vet! Vet!" she insists. Since reassurance has no effect we need to find out a little more about this fear. It is the "vet"ness of the rain that troubles Sally and we have already suggested that her own "vet"ness is what is troubling her. She is also troubled when she wakes up to find herself "vet." She has been trying very hard to wake up dry, and her reaction to the "vet"ness of the rain is identical with her reaction to wetting herself. This suggests that mother may be putting a little too much pressure on Sally for keeping dry and that Sally is trying too hard to achieve control and reacting too strongly to her occasional lapses. We suggest that her mother relax her attitude toward the failures to keep dry and give reassurances to Sally about her occasional wetting. Moderate praise for the successes and a cheerful acceptance of the lapses will make it much easier for her to achieve control and will relieve her of the sense of pressure and anxiety. This works. The fears about rain disappear, the anxiety about her own wetting subsides, and Sally is free to move at her own pace to the goal of dry nights.

Peter's fear of the roaring lions at the zoo begins to extend itself into other areas a few weeks later when he is near two and a half. His parents notice that he quickly leaves the room when the vacuum cleaner begins to roar, that he hastily leaves the bathroom when the toilet flushes and he closes his fairy tale books and walks away when he encounters pictures of lions. But also—and this is much more troubling to his parents—he has begun to avoid his father and is easily moved to tears whenever his father reproves him for even minor offenses. One day when his father scolds him for leaving the back yard without permission, Peter runs off to his room in tears. "Don't like Daddy when he roars!" Peter sobs when his mother comes into the room. So it is Daddy's roaring, too, that Peter fears and perhaps this accounts for the fear of roaring noises that had been so prominent for several weeks.

"But do I *roar?*" said Peter's father when he was given this report by the mother. In all fairness, Peter's father probably did not "roar" when he scolded Peter, but to a little boy the booming bass voice of an angry father must have sounded like a roaring lion. Peter seemed afraid of his father's anger, yet his father had never hurt him or threatened him in any way. How can we account for this? Peter's father had, in fact, been putting too much pressure on Peter for good behavior. Peter's dawdling, his obstinacy, his occasional outbursts of temper were exactly the combination of two-year-old traits that could set off a brisk and efficient businessman at home. Peter's father was essentially a kindly man, but since he was unaccustomed to the ways of small children, these traits appeared to him as dangerous portents for the future. So when Peter was obstinate, his father was severe. When Peter displayed his temper, his father displayed his own. This means that in the hour or two a day that Peter saw his father the lion roared a great deal.

Now since this lion was really a harmless lion and would never hurt a little boy, why was Peter so afraid of father's anger? This exaggerated fear derived from two sources. On one side was the child's love of his father and his anxiety when he experienced the overwhelming disapproval of his father. On the other side was Peter's fear of his own impulses. When he, Peter, got angry *he* wanted to hurt someone, *he* felt as if he could not control his anger, and *he* "roared" like a lion himself. So it would also be true, as we suggested in the earlier comments on Peter and the roaring lions at the zoo, that he was afraid of his own anger which he could not always control. But then, in the next step in this process fear of his own anger and fear of father's anger fuse and the quality of the small child's fury is attributed to the father's anger. Peter then behaves as if his father would do something destructive to him when he is angry which is what Peter would like to do to others when he is angry.

We will find that as Peter achieves better control over his impulses he will be less inclined to attribute dangerous motives to others. When he tames the lion in himself, he will be less afraid of his father. But in the meantime the relationship between Peter and his father has become seriously disturbed and father is in a very unfavorable position for helping Peter learn self-control. Such fear of a parent is not a good motive for learning self-control.

What we need to do at this point, obviously, is to build the positive relationship between father and son and give it stability so that when father is obliged to be critical the child can absorb criticism without feeling devastated, and can employ his love for his father as the chief motive for modifying his behavior. This means, too, that Peter's father needs to modify his own role in relation to Peter. He will have more influence over Peter if the few hours they spend together during the week can afford both of them a chance to get to know each other. A papa who appears briefly in a small child's life between the hours of six and seven and spends a good part of this hour criticizing and scolding lends himself easily to the fantasy of a roaring lion because the human and loving side of the father is not in evidence long enough to correct the fantasy.

In general, Peter's father will find that his son will achieve a better self-control—and achieve it sooner—if father can bring his expectations for good conduct down to standards that are really possible for a two year old. The small child who finds that no matter how hard he tries he cannot achieve the standards set by an exacting and critical parent will either give up in despair or develop tremendous anxiety in connection with control—a danger which we already see in Peter's behavior. It is obvious, too, that a father who frequently loses his own temper cannot easily offer his behavior as a model for a little boy who needs to control his own. One of the strongest motives in achieving standards of conduct is the desire of the child to emulate a beloved parent.

The real Peter's father was, in fact, a sensitive man who had no wish to be a formidable person in his child's eyes and was deeply troubled by Peter's reactions. Like so many well-intentioned parents, he found himself in a tangle with his child without knowing why, and out of helplessness and a vague feeling that his parental authority was being challenged he found himself growing sterner, more exacting and finally losing his temper much too often.

It was not at all difficult to restore harmony between this father and small son and to relieve Peter of his exaggerated fears. With better understanding of the whole situation Peter's father relaxed and allowed himself to enjoy the relationship with a little boy. Peter's father had not understood earlier how important a

father can be in the life of such a young child. As a new relationship developed between Peter and his father and their hours
together were spent in pleasant companionship, Peter's fear of
his father diminished rapidly and along with this the fear of
noises and of lions subsided dramatically. Love and admiration
of the father now served as incentives for self-control and Peter
began to make normal progress in control of his impulses.

Many of the fears of early childhood do not reveal themselves
in open and recognizable forms at all. They present themselves in
disguise and we may have much difficulty in recognizing certain
types of behavior as manifestations of anxiety. This one for
example:

Nancy, twenty-one months old, has always loved her bath and
now, suddenly she begins to protest and stiffen as soon as mother
puts her in the tub. If mother is insistent, even gently insistent,
Nancy has a tantrum. Bathtime has become nerve wracking for
mother and she is rapidly losing patience with this nonsense.
The stubbornness and defiance in Nancy's behavior provokes
mother to sharpness and sternness, which in turn brings forth
more defiance from Nancy and soon the two are engaged in a
contest.

What is this? Is it just another manifestation of the negativism of this age? Does she just enjoy being dirty? Is she
"testing out" her mother? "A good spanking will cure her of
that," says a visiting great-aunt who happens to be present during one of these bath-time scenes. And Nancy's mother, almost
at her wit's end, wonders if she hasn't been too soft about this
whole business. It isn't at all clear, of course, just what a spanking would "cure" Nancy of, and this is the trouble with all such
advice by the advocates of spanking. It is an action which, under
all circumstances, is unrelated to the facts of the case. In this
circumstance it would mean that since nobody knows why
Nancy is reacting the way she is, we will employ a meaningless
punishment for a meaningless piece of behavior.

Let's try another approach and let the great-aunts go off in a huff to complain to all other great-aunts that there is nothing that would do today's child so much good as a good spanking. Let's consider what defiance can mean. Defiance can mean many things. A two year old who doesn't want to go to bed can become defiant and his defiance may only signify his resentment at giving up the pleasures of play. A two and a half year old found playing with scissors may become defiant when his mother takes them away, and again the defiance may mean only a reaction to deprivation of an interesting play thing. In either of these cases the parent can handle the defiance by acting firmly but tactfully, and the chances are very good that the child will accept the necessary interference with a pleasure. But now let's look at another type of defiance. You are two and you are afraid that the big dog next door will chew you to pieces and your father says, "Oh, come on. Let's go over to see the nice doggie and pat him. *He* won't bite!" And your father starts to lead you by the hand—and you rebel. You may cry, protest, pull away, and if father grows more insistent you may scream and throw a little tantrum. *This* defiance is defiance toward the adult who wants to lead you into an imagined danger.

In any of these examples it is not difficult to recognize which defiance signifies resistance to interruption of a pleasurable experience and which defiance represents defense against anxiety. But when we are confronted with Nancy's defiance of her mother at bath-time the issues are not so clear. It doesn't seem to be connected with interruption of a pleasure and, furthermore, the bath had been until recently one of the great pleasures in Nancy's life. It isn't obviously associated with fear. A bathtub doesn't bite. There hasn't even been an accident in the bath that might lend validity to a fear. Nancy doesn't talk well enough to tell us why she avoids the bath. How can we find out the meaning of this behavior?

Usually in early childhood there is a close enough connection between an event and a child's reactions so that we can search our memories and come up with some clues. As soon as Nancy's mother gave up the notion that Nancy's behavior toward the bath was simply two-year-old obstinacy, she remembered something that had not appeared to be very important at the time but had preceded by a day or so the onset of the bath rebellion. Nancy had been reluctant to get out of the tub on that occasion and her mother started to let the water out of the tub. Nancy had not seemed to notice the water level slowly dropping but toward the end she watched with rapt attention as the last of the bath water was sucked down the drain. Suddenly she stood up in the tub and demanded urgently to get out. It was after this event that Nancy became fussy about taking her bath. Then the mother recalled that for several weeks preceding this event Nancy had asked repeatedly to watch the toilet flush and on one occasion had even tossed her Teddy bear in the toilet bowl. He was rescued just in time by Nancy's mother.

From these isolated and seemingly not very important events we can draw a conclusion that seems preposterous to an adult. Nancy's avoidance of the bath which follows her observation of the disappearance of water down the bath drain and her observation that objects disappear down the toilet, suggests that Nancy is afraid that she, too, could disappear down a drain. The grown-up, even an older child, will dismiss this as nonsense. We *know* that a child cannot go down that little hole. How do we know this? We have a concept of relative size. We know the approximate boundaries and size of our bodies and the relationship of a drain-hole diameter to the size of our own bodies. But Nancy at twenty-one months does not know this. She will need to carry on a series of experiments for a long time before she acquires knowledge of the amount of space which her body occupies.

There is another reason why such fears of losing oneself, of vanishing into nothingness, should become so prominent among children of Nancy's age. The emerging self-sense, the sense of identity is closely bound up with the body concept. While no child has ever had the experience of having his body disappear, he has experienced the disappearance of his conscious ego in sleep or states bordering on sleep. It is disturbing to the child who has newly found his identity to lose it, to see it disappear as consciousness dissolves in the moment before falling asleep. We have already suggested that this is one of the reasons why so many children of this age fight off sleep. We can see the application of these ideas to Nancy's fear of vanishing down a drain. It is the fear of losing one's self, of dissolving into noth-ingness.

"All very interesting," says Nancy's mother. "But in the mean-time what do we do? Do we give up baths until Nancy acquires a concept of her body size or overcomes her fear of loss of identity? And since Nancy doesn't talk very well, yet, just how could we explain anything to her anyway?"

Now, of course, we don't want to wait until Nancy learns about relative size before giving her a bath! She still needs to have her bath and unless the anxiety is very strong we would continue to bathe her in the tub. But our knowledge that she is afraid will make a difference in our handling. We will not behave as if she were being "just stubborn" and we must show her who is boss. We'll be specially gentle and reassuring and do everything possible to make the bath pleasant and encour-age her to play in the tub. It will be easier for a time if we allow the water to remain in the tub while Nancy is in the bath and even for a while after she is out of the tub.

Her concern with the flushing toilet suggests that there may be some anxiety connected with toilet training that needs to be taken into account too. We recall from an earlier discussion of toilet training that children during the training period com-monly react with some anxiety to the disappearance of their stools. Some reassurances in this area and relaxation of any pressures in toilet training might ease the anxieties about drains, too.

Above all, we may find that play will provide many possibili-ties for Nancy in overcoming her fear. We can find a kind of water play which Nancy herself can control. Perhaps she will find it fun to give her rubber toys a bath in the wash basin. Here she can manipulate the drain if she likes and let the water in and out without involving her own person, but other objects instead. We can demonstrate, or she can find out herself, that her toys will not disappear down the drain. In this way the situation which has created anxiety in Nancy can be reproduced without repeating the danger to herself. Also, Nancy becomes active in this game in the wash basin; she does to her toys what she has had done to her, and the activity in itself becomes a means for overcoming a dreaded situation in which Nancy had felt helpless and afraid. We will also use every other opportunity which presents itself in the course of Nancy's day to demonstrate to her and let her find out herself something about the relationship of her body size to other objects. In all these ways we can help her overcome her fear.

Now of course, if we didn't know about the meaning of Nancy's bathtub rebellion I can't say that Nancy would be destined for neurosis either. She'd probably overcome it herself in time. But in the meantime, if we do not understand this behavior as a manifestation of fear, our handling of the situation can go awry; we might strengthen the fear by putting pressure on a scared child, by forcing her into a situation that she construes to be dangerous, or by turning the situation into a contest of wills. Then we might run into trouble—no, not necessarily a neurosis—but increased difficulties, more defiance and temper outbursts which spill over into other areas of the child's life. Also, it is very likely that abhorrence of the bath and struggles centering about bathing could continue for many years to come. So, if we understand the meaning of a piece of behavior, we can find the techniques for handling it, we can ease the child's tensions and our own and repair a situation that may lead at least to unpleasant consequences for the present and the future.

PART IV

Three Years to Six

6. A Shift in the Center
of the Universe

TOWARD THE AGE OF REASON.

"In *my* experience," Roger would say when he was delivering an opinion. He was six. He had opinions about chemistry, astronomy, governmental affairs, human behavior and life in the Ice Age. Some of his views were right and some were wrong. He liked to preface them all with a thoughtful and considered, "In *my* experience." Once when he caught me suppressing a smile at his "experience" he looked up at me reproachfully and I was ashamed.

Well, why not? I said to myself later. What's so funny about that, after all? In his experience, in his six years, he has acquired a knowledge of the objective world and a grasp of physical causality that surpasses in many ways the knowledge of the common man of a century ago. His science is slight, uncertain and distorted in parts, but it demands objective proof and it is in many ways freer from the contamination of magical thinking than the mind of the average man of a century ago.

He does not believe in witches or ghosts. Why? "'Cause I never saw one." He explains: "A long, long time ago when I was little I used to think that there were, but I prob'ly only thought that because I read about them in stories, or maybe because I had dreams about them." If I remember correctly, the last witch was tried in this country about a century ago and in those days the average man listened to the testimony of his dreams in a way that Roger would simply sneer at. "Where do dreams come from, Roger?" I asked once. "Well," he said in his careful considered way, "if you asked me that a few years ago when I was little, I would have said they came from another land. But I know now that they come from up here" (tapping his forehead). "Roger, if a little kid asked you what a dream was, how would you explain it to him?" "Wel-l-l, I'd tell him it was like thinking in your sleep, only it's a different kind of thinking." Few men knew this a half century ago.

He wants proof for everything. Roger says: "How do you know if something is true if you don't see it?" And another time: "Is it *real* if you can't see it? Like a cell. You can't see it with your eyes. Then is it *real?*" I give him a small microscope for Christmas. He views a section of onion tissue under the microscope and sees a cell for the first time. He is enraptured. He turns to hug me, then says in an awed voice, "Then is it more *real* when I see it now with the microscope than when I saw the onion skin just plain with my eyes?"

When he was four he worried about his "bad thoughts." He thought of killing people, of being a robber, of setting fires. And sometimes his thoughts became so real to him that he was afraid that he might really do something terrible and the bad wishes were exchanged for fears in which terrible punishments awaited him. But listen to Roger at the age of five. He comes in one day with the news that two boys set fire to a new house in construction across the street from his house. He says soberly: "You know, I think those boys have worser problems than I have!" He explains. "'Cause if you only *think* about doing something like that it can't hurt anyone. But if you *do* it then you can really hurt someone." So he has learned at last that thoughts and actions are not the same, that his thoughts could not magically produce effects!

But there are shadowy areas in Roger's thinking where the old ideas and the new combine in a kind of pseudo-science. "Could a person fall out of the world?" he asks me one day. (He is close to six. He knows that the earth is a sphere. He has studied the globe.) He continues. "I mean if a person got to the edge of the globe, couldn't he fall down, down, down?" It is clear that his older idea of a flat earth, and the old fear of falling over the edge of a flat world, has been transferred to his improved concept of a spherical earth. He cannot get rid of this idea even after I explain it to him. Then he says, "You know sometimes I dream I'm falling down, down, down, and then I wake up." So now we can see why he hangs on to the old idea even with his improved science. In the dream it is *as if* he were falling "out of the world" and the sensory experiences which accompany this dream are so real to him that he cannot get rid of the primitive notion even though he knows better.

In certain other areas of knowledge this bright six year old betrays confusion. His mother has given him quite adequate information on sexual matters, but he has difficulty in remembering certain vital points in this instruction even when mother, at his request, goes over his questions again and again. He says, "Now *where* does the baby come out of the mother? I forgot again." "Where do you think?" "Well, I keep thinking it's the head. But I *know* that's not right."

Now this is a curious lapse in a bright six year old, a fellow who has mastered more difficult problems—in his experience. Here's the trouble. A scientist of any age can only work with the data available to him. He can obtain confirmation of hypotheses through observation and testing within the limits of his equipment. Roger has been informed in his sex education that "a special passageway," "an opening" exists in ladies and girls and that the baby comes out of this opening when it is ready. Now this mysterious "special passageway" cannot be seen. Given any of the means of observation open to a small boy or girl, there is no way of confirming the existence of this place. Roger had seen baby girls diapered. He did not see "a special passage-way." On at least one occasion he persuaded a little girl friend to further the cause of science by allowing him to peek. The experiment provided no additional information and ended in humiliation, for the mother of his small friend arrived on the scene and put an end to research with exclamations and sounds of outrage. Roger was forced to conclude that if this special passageway existed (and sometimes he was inclined to doubt it), it must be a secret passageway with a concealed door, like Ali Baba's cave, one that reveals its mysteries only to those who command the secret words. (Of course, there is a certain amount of truth in this!)

So Roger's investigations come to an inconclusive end. The existence of a "special passageway" cannot be proved but must be accepted on faith. And because it doesn't make sense to him, it is just this fact that keeps dropping out of the story of the birth of a baby. And because a little girl's mother was outraged at his curiosity, he feels that there is something dangerous about this mysterious place. Anxiety adds another motive to forgetting. So he can't remember, after repeated answers to his question, where the baby comes out of the mother. "I keep thinking it's the head, but I *know* that's not right." Why the head, we wonder. By what fantastic exercise of the imagination could a baby come out of the head? Well, from the point of view of a six year old it makes just as much sense as the explanation we have given him and it has the advantage of being far removed anatomically from that other place that a certain little girl's mother disapproves of in the strongest terms.

We can see that Roger's science is well advanced for his age but whenever he is confronted by facts that cannot be confirmed he falls back on primitive thinking. Whenever his thinking is governed by a strong emotion he may distort objective fact. But on the whole we have the impression that magic has resigned. It is no longer the party in power. It engages in obstructionist activity; it sometimes gains the floor and takes over. It will never be thoroughly routed but nearly always it succumbs to the stronger forces of reason.

And this naturally brings us to a comparison of "I" the magician and "I" the reasoner.

OF MICE AND MEN.

"Does a mouse know it's a mouse?" Roger asked me when he was five. "What do you mean?" I asked. "Well, like I know I'm *me*. Does a mouse know he's a mouse." I was cagey. "Tell me what you think," I said. "Well, I think a mouse doesn't know it's a mouse, but I don't know why I know that." Roger thought some more. "Well, a dog is smarter than a mouse. Does a dog know it's a dog?" He looked doubtful.

Roger was on the right track. He knew that knowledge about one's self and knowledge of personal identity were somehow connected with intelligence and he knew that human intelligence was of a different order from animal intelligence, but he couldn't pursue these ideas to their conclusion. But a dog does not know it is a dog; a mouse does not know it is a mouse; and even among the higher primates we will find that the most advanced chimpanzee does not know he is a chimpanzee. Elaborate experiments have been performed which show that certain mental feats of young chimps can be equated with the mental achievements of human children, but so far no test has turned up a chimpanzee that can give evidence at the age of five years as Roger has: "I know I'm me." For this reason the chimpanzee, however precocious he may be, has no future. He will not improve himself or his species and he may never do anything more clever than discover that an experimenter has removed one or more of five bananas from his cage, which will credit him with the ability to "count."

For the fundamental quality of human intelligence derives from this knowledge of a self which is separate and distinct from an objective world. Our infant magician of an earlier chapter had no means of acquiring knowledge of causes and events in the outside world as long as he considered his actions and his thoughts as the cause of all things. A child who believes, as the toddler does, that he has caused the little men and women to come out of the television set, will not be able to acquire even the most elementary concept of the instrument known as television or the means by which these images are transmitted. A child who believes that a clap of thunder is like his own anger cannot yet make discoveries about the natural causes of thunder. A child who doesn't know that his self is separate from other persons and their selves will confuse his motives and the motives of others and attribute his thoughts to other people (as we see in the early toddler period) so that his knowledge of the world of people is distorted. On the other hand, a child who doesn't yet know that in spite of his separate and distinct self he is similar to other human beings will not yet possess the basis for social intelligence which requires each of us to put ourselves in the place of others, to identify with others in order to live as members of a society.

When Roger was three he once threw a suburban nursery school into disorder by proclaiming that he was God and he could *make* Susie and Peter and Margie and Alan and everybody else do just what he wanted. Yes, and Miss Barrett and Miss Patterson, too. He was in a terrible temper and the small fry in this nursery regarded this wrathful prophet among them with awe and apprehension. Nobody believed him, of course, but no one rose to denounce the false prophet either. There is just enough magic and belief in omnipotence lurking in the mind of the three year old so that claims of extraordinary powers may not be entirely discredited. And what had set Roger off this day? No one remembers. Probably someone had refused to give up a swing, or a trike. It doesn't matter.

Roger didn't believe he was God either, we presume. But behind this outburst was a day-dream, a wish to be all powerful, to compel others to do his bidding, to have a world of *his* making. "What would you do if you were God?" I once asked him. "Then, I'd be my own boss," he said cheerfully. His aspirations in this realm turned out to be very close to those of an overworked and underpaid clerk in a department store who consoled himself at night with dreams of glory in which a stroke of fortune put him in the boss's job. "If I was God, then I wouldn't have to go to bed. And I wouldn't have to get up in the morning and get on the bus and go to nursery school. And then I would live in a little house all by myself." All these, we have to concede, are modest desires. On the other hand, we found upon further exploration of this day-dream that Roger would not hesitate to use any divine powers that came with this office, if he were hard pressed to do it. He had a little list—they never will be missed—of black-hearted and irretrievably lost sinners (most of whom had not yet achieved their fifth birthdays) and a dossier on each. Michael: He stole my gun. Barbara: She throws sand in the sand pile. Sheila: She spits and calls me names. The punishments which this stern providence might be called to mete out were regarded by Roger as entirely just and merited by the crimes. Michael? Well, he might have to be electrocuted—unless he gave back the gun, of course. Barbara would get germs in her throat so that she might get sick and die. But no mercy for the spitting, name-calling Sheila. She would get runned over, and if she didn't die, a robber would break into her house and kill her dead.

We have the uneasy feeling in listening to all this that we are witnessing the birth of another dictator. The autobiographical accounts of dictators will always reveal some such childhood day-dream as the inspiration for their careers. But mercifully most of these day-dreams do not survive the nursery and I had almost forgotten about this one until one day, when Roger was six, he visited me with a new program to discuss.

The six-year-old Roger, you remember, was the scientist, the cautious reasoner. His ideas and plans were still grand in their conception but, as he himself pointed out, they *could* happen. Well, on this day when Roger was well past his sixth birthday, he nourished himself on a whole sack of potato chips while he unfolded a new plan to me.

"Say. Is there any place left in America for another city?" he wanted to know.

"Oh, yes."

"But isn't it all *owned* by somebody?"

"No. The government still owns thousands and thousands of acres of land that anybody could buy for a small amount of money if he developed it."

"Does this land have *lots* of trees on it?"

"Yes, lots."

"Oh, boy! 'Cause I want lots of trees!"

"What for?"

"I need a lot of land for this idea. It's . . . well . . . it's like a city, only bigger. Maybe the size of Detroit, only bigger."

"You mean you want to build your own city?"

"That's right."

"How come?"

"I don't like the world. It's too small. There isn't enough room to do all the things I want to do. So if I had my own city I could do whatever I wanted to do."

"What does that mean?" I said suspiciously. "And what would you be there?"

"Well, I couldn't be king, of course, because there aren't kings anymore." (A note of sadness in his voice.) "But I'd sort of be in charge because I was the one who made the city."

"I see. Now if this is the place where you could do everything you wanted, explain what that means. Suppose you didn't like somebody, for example. Could you just beat up on him then?"

"Well, no. You see only the people I liked would be let in to this city."

"I see. But what does it mean, then, that you can do anything you like. Would you have laws?"

"Oh, yes. We'd have speed limits and things like that. Like the laws in America but not so strict. We wouldn't punish people hard for speeding."

"What about more serious things. What about stealing, for

example? If somebody in your city saw something he wanted could he just take it. Could he do whatever he wants to do like that?"

"Oh, no. You don't understand. In my city everything belongs to everyone else. Everyone has the same things. So you wouldn't *need* to steal."

"Where did you get that idea? Did you ever hear of some place like that?"

"No. I thought it up myself." (I doubted this but could never check on it.)

"Tell me more. Supposing someone was invited into this city because you liked him and he was nice at first and then it turned out he was bad. What would you do?"

Roger made an eloquent gesture with his thumb. "Out," he said briefly. "Have to leave the city."

"What else about the city? Describe it to me."

"Well, it would have a big wall around it. . . ." He is thoughtful for a moment. "But what would I need a wall for? I could just have signs around it so not everybody could be let in."

In Roger's six-year-old Utopia we have no trouble at all in tracing some of the elements of the old "I am God" fantasies of nursery school days. His longing for a world which he can control, his wish to be powerful, were the motives in both the nursery fantasy and the six-year-old Utopia. But the little dictator of the nursery has been transformed in this citizen-in-charge of The City; his dominion has been reduced from the world to an area only slightly larger than Detroit; and the ideas which govern Roger's Utopia are within the scope of reality while the God fantasies were crude productions of an infant mentality still governed by magic and a belief in omnipotence.

The society envisioned by the six-year-old Roger is governed by an ethic that is flexible within certain limits and strict at the outer limits. It is reasonable, just, non-authoritarian. It accepts without question the need for government and laws. (Roger's three-year-old Utopia was custom built for his own desires

There were no laws, no governing principles.) There are penalties in Roger's City for breaking the law, but the penalties are just. "We wouldn't punish people hard for speeding." Roger's Utopia comes to grips with the problem of evil in a manner that astonishes us in a six-year-old boy. He recognizes that stealing, for example, is connected with greed, envy, unsatisfied longing and proposes a society in which "everyone has the same things. So you wouldn't need to steal." It doesn't matter whether Roger has heard about such societies or invented the idea himself, as he thought. What does matter is that he sought prevention and remedies for human ills through the machinery of society itself. In the three-year-old day-dream the only solution he found to human frailty was mighty retaliation which wiped the offender off the earth. Even the irretrievably lost in Roger's society, the citizen who turned out bad, does not merit a death penalty as did the small sinner of the three-year-old society. He is ostracized. Presumably he is sent back to Detroit.

The differences between the God fantasy at three and the Utopia at six are not simply the differences in intellectual equipment of three and six. The differences must be credited to the civilizing process that takes place between three and six. Only someone who believes that he is the center of the universe, that his wishes and his desires could magically produce effects, will evolve a fantasy of being God. This corresponds to Roger's mental state at the age of three (though ordinarily most three year olds have begun to move away from this extreme egocentric position). But in three years the civilizing process has moved Roger from the center of the universe to a modest place in human society. It has not deprived him of ambition and has not caused him to give up all self-interest, but it has pressed ambition and self-interest into the service of others as well as himself and has restricted the possibilities of ambition (even in imagination) in accordance with reality. While Roger's Utopia is improbable, it is not impossible. While the motive for the day-dream is egocentric, it is also social.

This leads us to consider the transformations of self-love that are achieved between the time of the God fantasy and Utopian fantasy. The day-dream at three only served to nourish self-love. The extent, the magnificence, of this self-love is revealed simply in the fact that other people are not even included in Roger's universe except for purposes of extermination. He wants to live alone in a little house of his own. But in the Utopia of the six year old, Roger will share the good life of his society, and the necessity for a life with other people is implicit in the fantasy. A good portion of the love that has been invested in himself at three has been transferred to others. Since he gives others what he desires for himself, we can say that he has learned to love others as he loves himself, although perhaps this is too grand a statement to make about such a little boy.

We could say that Roger has developed "social sensitivity," that is, an awareness of himself in relation to others and an appreciation of the feelings and the rights of other humans. But how did he acquire this? To use Roger's mouse as an example, a mouse does not govern his relationship to other mice by an appreciation of their feelings. Apart from deficiencies in intelligence in the mouse, the absence of sensitivity to the feelings of other mice can probably be attributed to the fact that the mouse does not know he is a mouse. He has no awareness of himself, he has no possibilities of self-observation; he doesn't know that he has "feelings," however limited these may be in the case of a mouse. Since the qualities of his own "mouseness" are not known to him, he has no possibility of recognizing the "mouseness" of other mice. So the social relationships of mice, and of higher animals, too, are governed by instinct and, to a limited degree, economic necessity, but we can find no parallel among animals for the society of humans which derives from a special quality in human intelligence, the ability imaginatively to put oneself in the place of others. Roger knows how other people feel because he knows how he would feel under similar circumstances, that is to say he can *identify* with others. We take this factor of identification so much for granted in the conduct of our human relationships that we need to look at it with fresh eyes in our study of child development in order to see how the child acquires this capacity.

We recall that Roger demonstrated no capacity for "feeling himself into" the situation of others in his three-year-old daydream or, for that matter in his three-year-old behavior. Most three year olds are only on the threshold of this type of identification. If, for example, we are called upon to deal with a malicious act on the part of one three year old toward another, and if we should say, "How would *you* feel if someone did that to you?" we are likely to find the subject of our sermon quite unmoved. At that moment he simply doesn't care how the other guy feels, and his imagination does not carry him into the personality of his victim. Nothing matters but his own feelings, and we see how the egocentricity of the child of this age is still so great that he can't easily take this step outside of himself.

At three years and four we can even see how the child sometimes finds pleasure in cruel acts. I was watching my four-year-old neighbor, Marcia, one afternoon a few years ago. A caterpillar crawled cautiously along the sidewalk and Marcia, the most charming and sweet-tempered of little girls, moved toward it with a sinister smile on her baby face. Then with a sudden movement, she lifted her foot and squashed the caterpillar, juicily, under her shoe. Afterwards she inspected the smashed remains with interest and undiminished pleasure. Yet only two years later, when Marcia and I would walk together in the park, the sight of a mangled worm or a dead bird would fill her with horror and disgust. It made her sick, she said, to see something dead. It made her feel like crying. If it was dead, it could never come alive again.

Somehow in these two years Marcia had lost her pleasure in destructive acts. She had also discovered that death was final, that a lost life was irretrievable, and that life, even the life of a caterpillar, was a precious thing. In her child's way she did not put a higher value on the life of a human being than the life of an insect. She believed that the worm and the bird had a consciousness like human consciousnesses, that they loved mothers and fathers, brothers and sisters, and through a brutal act had lost life. *She had put herself imaginatively in the place of the worm and suffered through identification.*

If I now say that Marcia was becoming civilized, I do not mean, of course, that mourning for dead insects is a civilized trait but that the capacity to put oneself in the place of another living creature, to extend one's ego beyond the ego's own boundaries, is the unique quality of man's intelligence and is the indispensable quality in the morality of man. We will see that this capacity for identification reveals itself more significantly in Marcia's relationships with people. Her understanding of "how another person feels" becomes an important factor in governing her behavior, in restricting aggressive and destructive acts and words. This capacity for identification is implicit in our concept of the civilized person.

But we should also ask, "What happened to the pleasure in destruction which we observed in the four-year-old girl and the caterpillar?" This has disappeared and in its place has come disgust, moral revulsion. Sadistic pleasure has been turned into its opposite, pain, unpleasure, specifically, in this instance, revulsion. In fact, if we were to remind Marcia that once she enjoyed squashing caterpillars, she might not believe us. She would not remember at all! In that case it would be correct to say that pleasure in destruction, sadistic pleasure, had undergone repression.

Repression? But isn't that bad? Isn't it possible that this repressed sadism will create a neurosis? It is possible—but not necessary. We have already mentioned that repression, in itself, does not create a neurosis. And this brings us to a further point. *It is necessary* in a civilized society, that sadism, pleasure in inflicting pain, undergo repression. *An attitude of disgust and re-*

Identification + moral dev. (Nts interrelatedness of cog + affective aspects...)

192   A SHIFT IN THE CENTER OF THE UNIVERSE

vulsion toward the destruction of human beings or human works is necessary for the preservation of human values.

From the story of Roger and the story of Marcia we see very clearly that those qualities that we call human empathy, identification, love that transcends love of self, the high valuation of life itself, and the moral revulsion against acts, and even ideas, that seek destruction—all of these qualities are not innate in human nature but are the products of family education in the earliest years.

It would be unnecessary to say this if it were not for the fact that today a great misunderstanding has arisen in child rearing. In the belief that children "go through phases" (which they do), many parents adopt an attitude of Spartan endurance for the span of "the phase" in the expectation that spontaneous growth or evolution will take place at its conclusion. While it is true that each phase has its own characteristics, the progress through successive phases of development is largely influenced by the child's environment.

If Marcia's pleasure in destruction had not encountered censure from the parents whom she loved, there would be no reason for her to give it up. We know that some children do not surrender pleasure in destruction, and their moral development is disturbed as a consequence. But not only censure is required for the giving up of sadistic pleasure. For the child discovers that he achieves the greater pleasure of parental love and approval as a consequence of giving up destructive activity. He discovers, further, that in taking over the parental attitude toward such unacceptable behavior he becomes more like the parent, he can identify with his parents.

In brief, the child's "humanization" is a two-way process of identification. He acquires the capacity to extend himself beyond the boundaries of his own ego, to occupy imaginatively the egos of other human beings and hence "to know how others feel" and this constitutes one side of the process we call "identification." But he also has the capacity to take other egos into his, to incorporate the personality, or certain aspects of the personality of another person, to make certain qualities of that personality his own. In the case of moral development, the judgments, standards, values of beloved persons are taken over by the child, made part of his own personality. We call this identification, too.

"WHO AM I?" "WHERE DID I COME FROM?"

AN ANIMAL that knows who it is, one that has a sense of his own identity, is a discontented creature, doomed to create new problems for himself for the duration of his stay on this planet. Since neither the mouse nor the chimp knows what he is, he is spared all the vexing problems that follow this discovery. But as soon as the human animal who asked himself this question emerged, he plunged himself and his descendants into an eternity of doubt and brooding, speculation and truth-seeking that has goaded him through the centuries as relentlessly as hunger or sexual longing. The chimp that does not know that he exists is not driven to discover his origins and is spared the tragic necessity of contemplating his own end. And even if the animal experimenters succeed in teaching a chimp to count one hundred bananas or to play chess, the chimp will develop no science and he will exhibit no appreciation of beauty, for the greatest part of man's wisdom may be traced back to the eternal questions of beginnings and endings, the quest to give meaning to his existence, to life itself.

But what has all this to do with the mental and emotional development of children? Bear with me. There's a good analogy to be made.

Ultimately, all of man's knowledge must derive from investigations of himself. When man first attempted to explain natural phenomena, he did so by attributing human qualities, his own qualities, to the phenomena observed. The wind was the breath of an unseen superhuman, or god. Thunder was the wrath and vengeance of a giant spirit. He found human forms in the trees and clouds and human attributes in the changing seasons, the new day, the night. He was obliged to explain the natural world by means of the observations he had made upon his own body and his own nature. Even this was an intellectual achievement for man, for only man is capable of making observations upon himself. The greater intellectual feat was not achieved for thousands of centuries, when man was able to find the independent laws that govern the world of nature and detach his observations from self-observation.

But in the beginning man's intellectual curiosity was strongly impelled by the urge to divine his own nature. It was in this way that man achieved his intellectual powers and simultaneously, by the same process, a victory over his biological nature. He was able to submit his body and his urges to control by the intellect, which opened the way to all the achievements that we call human. In brief, self-observation led to self-control. The observing part of the self, which we call the "ego," acquired more and more power over the biological self and borrowed some of the energy of the drives themselves for greater intellectual activity.

In all these respects the human child recapitulates the history of his race. The child's first discoveries of "I" are made through his own body. In an earlier chapter we saw how the infant acquired the first differentiation of inner and outer, of "self" and "not-self" through experiencing his own body. The sensations of touching himself, of tasting his own fingers, of seeing his own hands pass before his eyes—all these and many other sensations were gradually organized into a primitive concept of "self." Later, in the second and third year, the concept of "I" made its uncertain entrance on the scene, and the child with his newly acquired speech made a further differentiation of self and not-self through the word "I." During the same period we saw how the child, like the primitive, tried to "explain" natural phenom-

ena by finding analogies between his own body and its functions and his own emotions. During this same busy period of
development another milestone occurred. Observations upon his
own body and chance observations of other human bodies produced the discovery of "maleness" and "femaleness." The concept of "I" was now strengthened by the fact of sexual difference
("I am a boy," "I am a girl") and solidified by the knowledge,
"I am a boy made just like father" or "I am a girl made just like
mother," so that identification with the parent of his own sex
consolidates the "I" feelings at this stage.

It is very much worth mentioning at this point that how a
child feels about himself, how he values himself, will also be
tied up with his feelings about his own body. Since the child
values his body products, considers them part of his body, he
acquires some of his "good" and "bad" feelings about himself
through these early attitudes toward his body and body products. The child who feels that his b.m.'s or his urine is bad,
disgusting or shameful will incorporate some of these attitudes
toward his own body in his ego and may struggle with feelings
that he, as a person, is disgusting or unworthy. The child who
discovers that his genitals give him good feelings but arouse
disgust or horror in a loved person, mother or father, may come
to feel that such feelings are bad, that his body is bad and that
he, as a person, is bad. Also, since the child's feelings toward
his own masculinity or femininity are linked to his attitude toward his sex-organs, the child who finds his body disgusting
may find the fact of his own sex disgusting, too. All of these
things have led to principles of sex education today that take
into account the early attitudes toward the body as the foundation for sound personality organization.

Somewhere around the age of three or four, when the sense
of "I" has achieved some degree of organization, when the child
knows "who" he is, his intelligence is strained by a new set of
problems. He has begun to learn that everything has a cause
and he wants to know the "because" of everything. He wants to

know how things are made. And the most fascinating problem of all is how he was made and where he came from.

"Where was I before I was born?" Sally asks her mama when she is five.

"Don't you remember?" says Mama. "I told you."

"Oh, I don't mean *that!*" says Sally crossly. "I mean *before* I grew inside you."

"Well," says Mama lamely, "you were a tiny, tiny egg."

"I don't mean *that.* I mean *before* I was a tiny, tiny egg."

"Well, you were—well, you see, you were nothing."

"Nothing!" Sally is horrified. "How could I be *nothing!*"

Of all the strange explanations Sally had been given regarding her origins, this one was the most fantastic. How could she have been a nothing? She cannot imagine that once she had not existed, just as she cannot imagine an end to this existence. The imagination of the grown man and woman fails before this problem, too. When the poet wants to summon the idea of personal death in its most tragic and awesome sense he finds it in the idea of "not being." "When I have fears that I may cease to be. . . ," says Keats. "To be or not to be. . . ," says Shakespeare. The extinction of one's own personality is the essence of the horror of death. When the child acquires the full sense of himself as a person, the idea of "not being" enters his thoughts in two ways, from the side of Beginnings ("Where was I before I was born?") and from the side of Endings ("What happens when you die?"). He asks numerous questions. We give him answers. He repeats his questions over and over, we observe, as if the explanations we have given him are not satisfactory. If we go into the matter with him we will find that his ideas of how he came to be are a curious blend of the facts we have given him and the theories he has arrived at on his own. The truth of the matter is that he doesn't quite believe us!

"A tiny, tiny egg. . . ," we tell him.

"How tiny?"

"Oh, so tiny you can hardly see it." (Maybe we make a pencil dot on a sheet of blank paper to illustrate it.)

He is skeptical. Even the stork story makes more sense than this to a four or five year old. Maybe an ant could come from such a tiny, tiny egg, but not he. He revises this fact in his own theory and you will usually find that the egg has grown to the size of a hen's egg or an ostrich egg, which certainly makes a lot more sense than the ant egg you've described to him.

"The daddy plants a seed. . . ." At least two generations of parents have been grateful for this circumlocution introduced by books on sex education. In this way, it appears, we have introduced the agricultural fallacy into the large collection of fallacies which the child brings to sexual knowledge without any help from us. I recall a certain literal-minded fellow of six who was led into minor delinquency by the hopes engendered in him by this piece of information. He stole a package of cucumber seeds from the dime store and planted them (package and all) under a telephone pole "so's me and Polly can have a baby next summer."

Things are really not much better if the parents offer the additional piece of information that "the daddy plants a seed in the mommy." The agricultural analogy has given rise to some surprising theories among the best-educated children on just how that seed gets planted. Children reared on the agricultural explanation have offered to me various remote-control theories on how the seed gets into the mama. One boy of six figured out that it flew into the mother, a perfectly sensible theory when you follow his thinking. He argued strongly and effectively for the air-borne theory, citing pollination as the analogy in the plant world. Other children attribute the feat of planting the seed to advancements in modern medical science. The doctor is frequently cited as the mediator in this process. Obviously, such a complicated and delicate process as getting the seed out of the father and planting it in the mother demands the highest medical skill and should not be left to amateurs.

Since I am always interested in these theories of children, I ask them to explain it to me and they are usually glad to do so. Billy, who is six, is not quite sure what the doctor does, but he thinks the doctor does a little operation on the father to get the seed out and then he plants it in the mother "in the right place." "And where is that?" "That's the $64,000 question!" says Billy, and bows out gracefully. Marcia's theory is not so complicated. "First the doctor gets the seed out of the father." "How does he do that?" "How should I know? Then he makes it into a kind of pill and the mother swallows it." Marcia owns a father cat and a mother cat and has had three or four litters of kittens in her home. "How did Mike and Betsy get their kittens?" "Oh, *they* mated! You aughta know that!" "And they didn't need a doctor?" "No, of course not. Cats and dogs don't go to doctors. They just mate. But people can't do *that!*"

Very well, then, the agricultural analogies have their pitfalls. What happens if you just give the human facts to children at the appropriate age, without disguising papa as the sower of seeds and mama as the good earth or an apple blossom? Well, that can be done, too. There are simple explanations that can be given the average five or six year old when he asks. But the trouble with the straight story is that it is more fantastic to the mind of the small child than his own theories. Over a period of several weeks I helped a small patient of six figure out just how this seed got into the mother. When we were all through and he drew the correct conclusion he was incredulous. "Well," he said loyally, "maybe some parents do that but not mine!"

But is that reaction explained by the fact that my patient had a neurosis? Did someone give him a sense of shame about sexual matters? No, it turns out to be not so simple. Perfectly normal children react in the same way when they are first confronted with these facts. They may not deny it outright as my patient did, but they tend to deny it in other ways, most commonly by forgetting these facts soon after learning them.

For children, even the children of the most enlightened parents, have difficulty in grasping the idea that their parents have a sexual life. And even when they have the facts of procreation better straightened out—in the school years—they do not grasp the fact that the parents may have a sexual life for any other purpose than making a baby. The idea that this act may be an act of love and of pleasure is alien to his child's viewpoint. No matter how expertly we have presented the material, he may still look upon coitus as an aggressive act, even a painful act, having nothing in his own experience or imagination to correct this idea. Indeed the most common analogy that the child can find in his own experience for the penetration of a human body is the experience of "getting a shot" in the doctor's office. Since the child cannot conceive of this act as "making love," he looks upon it only as a means of getting a baby and does not understand that his parents may perform such an act for pleasure. Here again I am reminded of a story. The mother of a six year old was answering some of her daughter's questions about the new baby (the third child) that was expected in two months. Katie said, "Mother, can some mothers and daddies try to have a baby and not get one?" "That's right," said her mother. "Gee, aren't we lucky in our family," Katie said. "Everytime you and daddy tried we got a baby!" Her mother decided not to go into the matter.

In our conscientious efforts to help the child understand the process of making a baby, we have resorted to anatomical drawings, photographs of sperm and ova under high power magnification, all the graphic devices that might conceivably clarify this difficult process to the child. The educational method is valid, but we soon discover that these illustrations create their own variety of confusion.

Let me tell you a little bit more about Billy. You remember it was he who offered the theory that the doctor does a little operation on the father to get the seed out and then plants it in the mother "in the right place." "But why an operation, Billy?" "'Cause there's no other way of getting it out," he said sadly. "Why is that?" "'Cause the seed is so big." "So big? How big?" "Oh, about as big as a marble." "As big as a marble? How do you know that?" "I saw the picture. It was in my book." Now he was getting very indignant because I seemed not to agree with his theory and was apparently disputing the facts of A Book. (Children are very pious about the facts they learn from books even at this age.) "Please draw me a picture of what you saw in your book, Billy." And Billy obliged. He drew "a seed" about the size of a marble with a little tail on it and I recognized it as the drawing of a sperm under high-power magnification. But now this was equally baffling because Billy was a smart little fellow who understood the principle of magnification and knew, after I questioned him, that the sperm itself could not be seen except under the microscope and that the picture in the book was an enlargement. Well, then, how had he gotten the notion? I think because the picture of the sperm under high power magnification had more reality to him than a sperm that was so tiny that it couldn't be seen. He could believe in the sperm as big as a marble, but he could not believe in the invisible one.

When you've just come up from magic and have learned not to believe without evidence, when you have discredited witches because you never *saw* one, sneered at fairies because you never *saw* one, the process of procreation as described by the adults in the child's world strains the child's new-found reality sense to its utmost. There is the sperm that can't be seen. The egg that can't be seen. The special opening in girls and women that can't be seen. And the mysterious process of sexual union that cannot, of course, be seen or even imagined well by the child. So we must not be surprised that the child who "knows everything," according to his parents, understands very little of it.

If we are able to test a child's understanding of the facts we have given him, we will find, just as we did in some of the examples used here, that the child has superimposed the new information we have given him upon his old, personal theories and the result is a curious mixture of fact and fantasy that is uniquely the child's own. Here is Mike, for example, who at four "knew everything" according to his parents. When Mike first asked questions of his mother she read him a book (one actually more suitable for older children) and Mike listened attentively, asked to have some portions of the book reread to him occasionally and showed the same quick grasp of new material that he would have revealed after his parents read him children's books on astronomy or the life of primitive man. When I knew him he could recite the story of a baby by rote from "sperm meets egg" to "the baby comes out of special passageway." But when I had occasion to ask him a few questions, I found that "the sperm meets the egg in the mother's stomach" having found its way through the mother's mouth in some mysterious fashion, and that "the special passageway" wasn't so special after all. He wasn't sure if it were the place where the wee-wee comes out or where the b.m. comes out, but it was one or the other! He also offered me a novel theory that I have never encountered before. "Did you know," he said solemnly, "that some of the mother's eggs *never* get to be babies because the daddy eats them up?" I asked him to explain this to me. "It says so in my book!" he insisted. I could get nothing more from him on this subject and later consulted the book myself to see what Mike had heard and what was distorted. In his book I found this sentence: "Although fish lay millions of eggs, few of these will become baby fish because the father or other animals eat them up!"

In later discussions with Mike I found out that he had not actually misheard this passage; he simply attributed the fate of fish eggs to the fate of human eggs. He had not been able to account for the fact that a mother has more eggs than she has babies and this detail from his book fitted nicely into his macabre theory. To Mike the notion of a father eating up the eggs seemed no more fantastic than some of the other things he heard about in this book. But notice something else. He had taken all the important facts of procreation, memorized them, and still came out with a theory based upon eating and elimination. His private theories, before parental enlightenment, were typical theories of a small child derived from observations on his own body functioning. How would something get into "a stomach"? By eating, of course. How would it get out? By elimination, of course. All of this makes more sense to a little boy of Mike's age han the facts presented by the book or by his parents. But he las a proper respect for the book and for any information given lim by respected authorities like his parents, so he works out a compromise in his mind which nicely accommodates his private theories and the newly learned facts.

All this strikes us as a disappointing appraisal of the results of sex instruction. Does this mean that we should abandon sex instruction or return to stork and cabbage stories? We need not be discouraged. We do not give up other forms of education because the child has difficulty in grasping facts and principles. But it is necessary to understand the sexual theories of a small child in order to give sex instruction. If we fully appreciate the difficulties of little children in grasping sex information, our techniques of sex instruction will be modified accordingly. Problems of timing information, methods of presentation, can all be derived from an understanding of the child's mental processes at a particular stage of development.

In a later chapter we will go into the problems and methods of sex education in greater detail.

ABOUT THE OEDIPUS COMPLEX.

"WHEN I grow up," says Jimmy at the dinner table, "I'm gonna marry Mama."

"Jimmy's nuts!" says the sensible voice of eight-year-old Jane. "You can't marry Mama and anyway what would happen to Daddy?" Exasperating, logical female! Who cares about your good reasons and your dull good sense! There's an answer for that, too. "He'll be old," says the dreamer, through a mouthful of string-beans. "And he'll be dead." Then, awed by the enormity of his words, the dreamer adds hastily, "But he might not be dead, and maybe I'll marry Marcia instead."

It's absurd, of course. It's another one of the impossible day-dreams of childhood. If Jimmy announces at the dinner table that he has decided to marry Mama when he grows up, is that so different from a number of other plans that originate in the fertile imagination of this four year old? He is also going to be a bus driver when he grows up. Last week he was going to be a garbage man. And recently he made reservations for the first trip to the moon. (Five years before Sputnik!) (He had kindly offered advance reservations to other members of his family and was surprised by the lack of interest and foresight they revealed.) And now he proposes to marry Mama when he grows up.

If this is a childhood day-dream why do we attach more significance to it than any other day-dream? Well, first of all, because the child himself attaches great importance to it. The love expressed in this childhood fantasy is deeply felt. The wish to replace the father in the small boy's fantasy has a parallel in the little girl's fantasy of replacing the mother. In the case of both sexes the wish is strong enough to create a period of conflict in the child, for the very nature of the wish implies rivalry with the parent of his own sex and aggressive wishes toward that parent. But this love of early childhood creates the impossible situation in which the rival parent is also the object of love. When Jimmy imagines his father's death and his replacement of his father, he comes face to face with a powerful contradictory feeling. He also loves his father very much and the thought of his father's death fills him with horror. We do not normally encounter such difficulties in the love experience of later life.

This love attachment in early childhood to the parent of the opposite sex and its many ramifications in the conflict with the rival parent—the aggression, the guilt feelings and the form of its resolution—was given the name "Oedipus complex" by

Freud. It was discovered, as everyone knows, through Freud's self-analysis and through the analysis of neurotic patients. Later, direct observations of small children showed unmistakably that all normal children go through such a phase in their development and that it need not, of course, result in neurosis. The Oedipus complex is not, in itself, pathological or pathogenic. Normally, its conflicts are resolved, and—what is also interesting—will usually not even be remembered.

We need to remind ourselves that this impossible day-dream is probably as old as the human race, and for thousands of years before it was discovered and investigated psychoanalytically little children had dreamed the impossible day-dream, experienced its conflicting passions and finally renounced it without anyone being the wiser. There are millions of parents today who have never heard of the Oedipus complex and wouldn't recognize it if they saw it in their children, and most of these parents are successfully rearing their children without this information. For the truth of the matter is whether we know about an Oedipus complex or don't know about it the outcome for the child remains the same. It's a day-dream without any possibility of fulfillment, now or ever. It is a dream of love that must end in disappointment and renunciation for all children. It ends in renunciation of the impossible wishes and, normally, in the resolution of the conflicts engendered by them. The rivalries subside and the personality reintegrates in the most promising fashion. For we find that the rivalry with the parent of own sex is finally overcome by the strength of the positive ties. The child around the age of six reveals a strengthened identification with the parent who had so recently been his rival. It's as if the child says, "Since I cannot take my father's place, be my father, I will be *like* him," and now begins to model himself after his father. Normally, this is the outcome for all boys, with a parallel process of identification with the mother in the case of girls.

But in a study of child development we need to give an important place to the role of the Oedipus complex in emotional development of the three to five year old. Parental understanding can be a great aid in helping the child to successful resolution of the conflicts of this age. (And there has been so much misunderstanding among enlightened parents on the meaning of the oedipal phase and "correct" or "incorrect" parental attitudes that there is much need for clarification.) Furthermore, certain disturbances of this period can only be understood when we view them as disturbances in the love relationships of the child to his parents which are centered in oedipal strivings.

At first glance, these disturbances seem to have no apparent connection with the oedipal conflicts. For let no one imagine that the child between three and five acts out a drama of love and rivalry within his family in explicit terms. Nor should we imagine that everything he does in this period of development is somehow connected with the Oedipus complex. He is developing in many other directions and he has many other things to think about during these years. But there are certain typical disturbances for this age that are connected with oedipal conflicts although we might not immediately guess these connections from the various disguises they assume.

Let's follow the story of Jimmy a little further and see how some of the apparently inexplicable behavior and fears of a child of this age can be connected with oedipal conflicts:

Jimmy was uncomfortable after he exposed his day-dream at the dinner table, though only the cynical Jane had addressed herself to the topic. He didn't really wish his father to grow old and die; he loved him very much. And there is enough magic in the thinking of the four year old to cause Jimmy great discomfort after he uttered this thought. Suppose the bad thought should come true? Suppose his father should die?

Jimmy spent the rest of the evening in dark moodiness and irritability. He seemed to be having one of his difficult times. At bedtime he wanted Daddy to read him a story. No, he didn't want *that* story. This one, then? No. Oh, he didn't want a story at all. What did he want? Well, records. Would Daddy play records for him? No, not this one—that one. No, not that one—this one. But what *did* he want then? And he cried that everyone was mean to him and he hated this old house and he would go to live at Allen's house and never, never come back and then in a cold fury he struck out at his father. The baffled parents didn't know what to make of this behavior. Finally, his father said that he had had enough of this and Jimmy was to go to his room until he calmed down and there would be no story and no records for tonight. Ah, this was what Jimmy seemed to be waiting for! "You're mean. You're the meanest father in the whole world and I wish you was dead!" And he stomped off to his room, slamming the door behind him.

"What on earth got into that child tonight?" his parents asked each other. And by this time everyone had forgotten the dinner table conversation. After all who can keep all these things in mind in the course of a busy day? And who would have connected this temperamental behavior with the conversation at the dinner table even if he had remembered it?

Certainly there are no obvious connections when we first follow these bed-time events. But let's see if we can make some sense out of the sequence of events. At dinner Jimmy confides his day-dream about marrying mama after his father's death and then, guilty and troubled, hastily tried to take back his words. Later during story time, usually one of the pleasantest times with his father, he is irritable and whiny. Nothing satisfies him. He wants this; no he doesn't. He can't make up his mind about the simplest decision and wavers back and forth in exasperatirg fashion. Here we suspect that Jimmy can't make up his mind about something a lot more important than the choice of a story or phonograph record. It's really the "do I want?" or "don't I want?" that occupied him at the dinner table. "Do I want my Daddy to be dead?" "Don't I want him to be dead?" The indecision that belongs to this terrible problem is transferred to the relatively unimportant problem of a choice in story and records.

Then, although his father is patient with him in this yes-no-yes period of the story hour, Jimmy's own frustration mounts and becomes intolerable. Now he screams out his accusation that everyone is mean to him, that he hates this old house and will go to live at a friend's house and never, never come back. What nonsense is this? If we take this only as a reaction to the problem of choosing a story or a phonograph record the whole business is merely ludicrous. First of all, his father had not been mean to him and had been the model of patience throughout this yes-no scene, and second, why leave home over the problem of choosing a story? Again, none of this makes sense unless we know the play-within-the-play. For the inner drama has to do with Jimmy's conflict in relation to his parents, a wanting and not wanting his mother, a wanting and not wanting to get rid of his father. Jimmy does not know why he is so upset about the stories and the records and his parents don't know either. The announcement that he will leave home has nothing to do really with the story hour and nothing to do with his father's attitude about the stories. It is part of the unconscious dialogue; it belongs to the play within the play. Perhaps it is like saying, "There is *no* solution to such a problem; it would be better to find another family."

But there is something else, too. He is goading his father, trying his father's patience to the extreme. Unconsciously, he wants his father to get angry, to put a stop to this. And, of course, his father does reach the limits of his patience and becomes stern and tells Jimmy to go to his room. And now, as if this were just what Jimmy wanted, he cries out that Daddy is mean and he wishes he were dead. It's as if Jimmy were asking for punishment for his bad wishes and, at the same time uses the occasion of the punishment to justify his angry feelings toward his father and with it to justify the bad wish, for now he says in his fury, "I wish you was dead!"

There is a last episode in this story of Jimmy's day that should be told:

That night Jimmy wakened from a terrible dream and cried

out for his Daddy. A tiger broke out of his cage in the zoo and came through the window of the living room and chased Jimmy through the house. Jimmy ran up to his room and slammed the door. The tiger tried to crash down the door to kill Jimmy and Jimmy was trying to hold the door closed and he screamed and screamed for Daddy and nobody came and he was afraid that Daddy was dead. And then he woke up.

There was nothing that Jimmy's father could do except comfort the child and reassure him, of course. But since we are interested in finding connections between certain fears and the oedipal conflicts of this age, let's see if we can understand some aspects of Jimmy's anxiety dream.

In the dream Jimmy is being chased by an enraged tiger who wants to kill him. In reality, on the evening of the dream, an enraged little boy had told his father he wished he were dead and had stalked off to his room in a temper. So the anger of the little boy is transformed in the dream into the anger of a tiger, the dangerous wish to have someone dead boomerangs and the little boy is in danger of his life. But in the dream we notice, too, that Jimmy's anger and his bad wishes are attributed to the tiger who pursues him and we suspect that the tiger also stands for the father who, in a small boy's imagination will punish him for his bad wishes, do to him what he wished to do to the father. And the little boy who, in real life, ran up to his room and slammed the door in anger, is a little boy in the dream who escapes to his room with a tiger in pursuit and slams the door to keep the tiger out. The little boy who had announced his independence at eight in the evening, the boy who did not need his father, is a little boy in the dream who screams for his daddy's protection and help in the dream. For Jimmy is afraid of his bad wishes and wants to be protected from his own bad impulses. He loves his father dearly and in the dream when he called for Daddy and Daddy didn't come, he was *afraid* that Daddy was dead, that the bad wish had come true.

So we see how the dream represents the punishment for the

bad wishes, how all the bad thoughts and the events of the day are reversed and the punishment appears as exact retribution for the bad wishes.

From the story of Jimmy we can see how an oedipal conflict reveals itself in occasional distortions of conduct (as in the bedtime scene over the books and records), in excessive guilt feelings, in occasional bad dreams, in various manifestations that would not immediately be recognized as belonging to the Oedipus complex. In fact, we are much more likely to see oedipal feelings masked in a puzzling piece of behavior or an anxiety than to hear the child outspokenly profess his love for his mother and his wish to replace his father. There are likely to be few instances of the kind of proposal Jimmy made at the dinner table during the whole period known as the oedipal phase. This is because these ideas evoke guilt feelings in the child and they are already in a state of partial repression in the very young child.

Somewhere in the fifth or sixth year—perhaps a little later— the impossible day-dream begins to fade and is finally banished to the subterranean depths where the ghosts of all discarded day-dreams lie. It may never be remembered. It need not be remembered at all. It is only necessary that the impossible aims of this day-dream be renounced without disturbing the love ties between a child and his parents and without crippling the capacity for love in later years.

7. Education for Love

THE MEANING OF SEX EDUCATION.

FROM all we have said so far about sex instruction, we can see that the giving of facts about procreation is only a small part of the job of sex education. It is an important part, but we no longer believe that we can assign it such an all-embracing significance as did the early proponents of sex instruction. For in the early days of the movement for sex education we believed that frankness and honesty about sexual matters would, *in themselves*, prevent later disturbances in sexual functioning. We now know that sexual satisfaction in adult life depends upon a large number of factors, some of which are bound up in sex instruction in early childhood and all of which can be condensed in the following summary statement: Fulfillment in adult sexual experience depends upon the degree to which a man has confidence and pleasure in his masculinity and a woman has satisfaction and pleasure in her femininity and the degree to which both a man and a woman have given up their childhood attachments to parents and possess the means of loving completely a person of the opposite sex.

This means that sex education in the broadest sense must educate the child for the fulfillment of his sexual role, to give optimum satisfaction in being a boy or in being a girl, and that the ties to parents must be strong enough and tender enough to ensure the possibility of a rich love life, yet not so strong or so all-consuming as to prevent the child from later forming new love attachments in mature love and marriage. This is a very large order, indeed!

If we assign sex instruction, the giving of facts, to its proper place in the light of this larger problem we would have to say something like this: Sex instruction *per se* is successful when-ever it has served the purpose of strengthening the child's satis-faction in his own sexual role and his destiny in this sexual role and when it has dealt with the facts of procreation, of anatomy, of sexual feelings in such a way that the child's guilt and anxiety are reduced and his confidence and love of his parents are deep-ened. This means that we should not be so troubled about the results of our sex instruction when we discover that the young child has not really understood our factual presentation and has even distorted these facts in his own thinking. We have plenty of time to straighten him out on the facts and we should com-fort ourselves with the knowledge that even with the best edu-cation the child cannot be completely educated because his child's body and his child's experience cannot provide him with the means for complete understanding.

But let's see how far even the most thorough sex instruction can go if the child's attitude toward his sexual role is unfavor-able. A little girl can learn everything we have to give about the mechanics of procreation and about the preparations in her own body for a future motherhood. But if being a girl is a dis-appointment, or even a loathesome state for her, if motherhood is only the crowning insult to the wretched state of femininity, what good will the lovely facts of why-you-are-made-the-way-you-are do for this disappointed and self-disparaging child? If a little boy is presented with all the facts of origins in the nicest, frankest way, but regards women as dangerous creatures and considers his own masculinity threatened by women, the knowl-edge that he will one day be a husband and father and perform a sexual act with a woman may be more disturbing than com-plete ignorance.

So the aim of sex education is not only to teach the facts, but to create in the child a group of desirable attitudes toward his own body, the fact of his own sex and his sexual role now and in the future. This means that sex education includes our parental attitude toward a child's masturbation and sex-play; it includes our handling of the oedipal attachments; and, finally, it includes our influence in shaping the child's identification with members of his own sex and satisfaction with his sexual role. The giving of sex information plays a part in education of the child in each of these areas, but it cannot be divorced from them; it is not a separate curriculum.

THE PARENTAL DILEMMA.*

EVERY enlightened parent today knows what *not* to do when confronted with a child's masturbation or sex-play. We must not create shame in the child. We do not threaten him. Every informed parent knows that excessive shame and anxiety in connection with the genitals can seriously disturb the child's personality development and may cripple his sexual functioning in adult life.

But the experts have not been so helpful to parents on the other side of the question: How do you act toward a child's sexual behavior in such a way that you neither give license to unlimited freedom nor create harmful attitudes in the child?

The dilemma of the modern parent is nicely capsuled in the following story: The mother of a six year old, Tommy, overheard her son when he invited his girl friend Polly up to his room to look at his picture card collection. The mother, wincing at this nursery version of a male gambit, heard them go upstairs and close the door. She recalled with discomfort that only a few weeks ago Polly's mother had found the two children engaged in toilet games in the back yard and had sent Tommy home with a stern warning. Tommy's mother wondered uncer-

* The substance of this section appeared originally in my article "Helping Children Develop Controls," *Child Study*, Winter 1954-55, published by the Child Study Association of America, to whom I am indebted for its use.

tainly what to do. After a discreet interval she went upstairs. She approached the door of Tommy's room, fumbling for the right words in such a moment. Her knowledge that ill-chosen words might be harmful in such a situation caused her to discard one idea after another. She was not even sure that in this day and age such interference was a parental prerogative. Finally she knocked and said, "May I come in?" Her son replied with something inaudible, and she opened the door. Tommy and Polly exhibited great poise considering that both were in partial undress. The mother, clutching for a neutral phrase, found herself saying, "Don't you children feel chilly?" And the answer, truthful as George Washington's, bounced back upon her: "No."

It is true that the mother's uncertain handling here led to an impasse, but no harm was done. It was probably better that Tommy's mother let him know that she knew about these games than to pretend ignorance. For in spite of the splendid aplomb which Tommy demonstrated when his mother came upon his secret games with Polly, he was ashamed and worried about these games, as his mother found out later. He was relieved to know that his mother knew about his secret and that, unlike Polly's mother, she did not think such things were shameful or bad. Tommy, like so many children, had almost arranged the situation so that mother would "find out."

At the same time, Tommy's mother needs to get something more than simple reassurance across to him, for he is at an age when he can be helped to understand that there are other ways in which he can satisfy his sexual curiosity than through games that little children play. I think it would have been possible for Tommy's mother to handle the incident in Tommy's room simply by asking to come in, quietly suggesting that the children get dressed and find something else to do, then talking with Tommy later and privately about the incident. Here the mother could get across the idea that it is natural for children to be curious about how a boy was made and how a girl was made but that Tommy would find that he could not get the answers to his questions by looking and playing games. He could ask Mother and Daddy all the questions he wanted to so they could help him figure it out. In this way Tommy would not be made to feel ashamed and frightened; on the contrary, he would be relieved. His normal and necessary curiosity would not be destroyed since other means for its satisfaction would be offered.

So much of what we do and say in relation to the sexual behavior of children depends upon the age of the child and type of sexual behavior. A type of behavior which is "normal" or "typical" for one stage of development is not appropriate for another. Our evaluation of the behavior and our methods of handling it will be different for different stages of development. Let us take an example:

If a three-year-old boy in nursery school finds it fascinating to observe how little girls urinate, we would consider this a normal expression of interest in sexual differences; that is, *normal for his age.* Our method of handling such interest in nursery school children is to allow natural observations during the toileting time. Normally, this type of interest subsides so that in school-age youngsters it will take the form of some giggling and joking about toilet functions, but a diminished interest in direct observation. But suppose our three year old cannot give up his fascination with looking and at the age of eight creates a problem in his summer camp by his insistent and repetitious peeking into the girls' lavatories. We would no longer consider this activity appropriate for his age, and we could assume that the persistence of this infantile form of sexual behavior was rooted in a personal problem.

If we applied the same methods of handling to the fascinated looking of the eight year old as we apply to such curiosity in the three year old we would offer no solutions to the eight year old's problems. For with the three year old we can operate on the assumption that normal opportunities to make observations will satisfy the need for looking, especially when this is combined with answers to the child's questions. But with the eight year old, looking does not satisfy the curiosity, as we can see from the persistence of this behavior. His looking is motivated more by anxiety than curiosity. It is as if he could not believe his eyes and must look again and again. We would be doing both the eight year old and his fellow campers a disservice if we were to treat these incidents in the same way that we would in nursery school; that is by providing opportunities for looking. The camp staff would be correct in not allowing this behavior, in placing realistic limits as kindly and firmly as possible. If we are to help the child with his problems, we must seek its meaning rather than try to provide outlets for its expression.

Similarly we recognize that masturbation means different things at different ages. Two and three year olds are sometimes very casual in the ways in which they handle themselves. In games or in quiet periods the hand may stray to the genital region and the child seems quite unconcerned about the presence of adults or other children. It is usually unnecessary to comment on this to very little children. As the child grows older he tends to restrict his occasional masturbation to moments when he is alone. We consider this a normal development which goes along with the child's growing social sense. We support this realization by the child that masturbation is a private affair not because it is shameful or bad, but because it is one of a number of things which are regarded as private acts. In a school-age child frequent and open masturbation or touching of the genitalia would not have the same meaning as the casual handling of the toddler. The persistence of this type of masturbation in the older child may indicate some unresolved anxieties which require our attention.

In fact, it is important to note that not all the things we call masturbation in childhood are properly speaking masturbation. The boy who hangs on to his penis or needs to touch it repeatedly throughout the day usually derives no pleasure from these acts. These are signs of anxiety. The child repeatedly touches his penis or holds on to it in order to reassure himself that the penis is all right. The child who handles his or her genitals openly at any age where this is no longer to be expected is performing a more complicated act than masturbation. He is calling attention to his masturbation, making a confession, inviting a reaction, sometimes inviting punishment or criticism as well. In all these cases parents would probably want advice on evaluating the behavior of the child and in handling it properly.

HOW FAR SHOULD THE CHILD'S CURIOSITY BE SATISFIED?*

IF A CHILD is curious about the way in which his mother's or father's body is made, should he be given opportunities to see the parent nude, to satisfy his curiosity directly by looking? In recent years many parents have attempted to meet the problem of the child's curiosity by permitting the child to observe them in dressing, to come into the bathroom, or to take showers with them. Yet our observations of children who have been reared in such permissive homes have shown that this freedom produces its own varieties of guilt and anxiety in a child; that, paradoxically, too much freedom produces a conflict closely resembling that which comes from too much restriction. These direct observations do not really satisfy the child's curiosity, for the sight of the nude body really explains nothing, but the child may experience this looking as secretly exciting (even when he appears not to notice) and then becomes ashamed of his own reactions.

Yet children are quite open in their curiosity about their parents and how grown-ups are made. Parents who want to be honest and natural and yet understandably to preserve their own

* A portion of this section appeared originally in my article "Helping Children Develop Controls," *Child Study*, Winter 1954-55, published by Child Study Association of America, to whom I am indebted for its use.

privacy may find themselves quite uncertain about the handling of some circumstances. I recall the concern of a father who once asked my opinion on the handling of a problem with his four-year-old daughter. She asked repeatedly to visit her father in the bathroom, showed her interest in her father's penis and recently had asked to touch it. Should he permit this? His wife felt that if this action satisfied the child's curiosity, it should be allowed. "But I don't mind telling you," the father said challengingly, "that I'd find this embarrassing." I realized that the father thought that modern psychology would support the view that this direct curiosity should be satisfied. He was really very much surprised and relieved when I told him that I didn't think it was necessary or good for his little daughter to satisfy her curiosity in this way.

But if we restrict the child's curiosity, if we interfere with these manifestations of sexuality, won't the child feel that there must be something secret and shameful about such things? There need not be, of course. If we are alarmed and shocked by this curiosity, if we make threats, we might certainly create unnecessary feelings of shame in the child. But suppose the father who sought my opinion were to say this to his daughter: "I know that all children are curious about how grown-ups are made. But grown-ups like to be alone sometimes, just as children do. If you want to know how grown-ups are made, you can *ask* me and you can ask Mommy and we'll explain it to you. So tell me what it is you want to know."

Such an answer would accomplish several things. We acknowledge the child's right to be curious. We have not said that her wish is dangerous or bad, but we have asked her to put her curiosity into words as a substitute for looking and examining. We have denied her the privilege of an intimacy with her father, but we have not denied her the right to be curious and to ask questions.

The same principle may be applied in the handling of sex-play between children. While we regard the examination games as a normal manifestation of sexual interest and curiosity in early childhood, we can be certain that the child will find few of the answers to his questions through exploration, and some of his discoveries may make him anxious and confused. The wise parent will try to help the child bring out his curiosity in questions and help him clarify some of his misunderstanding in discussion. Here, sex information can become the means for controlling direct sexual activity, for we need to consider that sexual behavior, like any other behavior, must have some reasonable limits placed upon it.

ON GIVING SEX INFORMATION.

WE HAVE seen that at the time the child asks his first questions, and for a long time afterwards, he already has his own notions, his private theories about procreation. These theories are based upon his own observations of body functioning which most commonly lead the child to draw analogies from eating and elimination. The facts we give him are beyond his experience, they appear to him as strange or even fantastic, and the educational achievement may be only one theory (ours) superimposed on other theories (his). The result is often further confusion.

It may be very helpful, then, to take the child's private theories into account *before* we introduce him to new facts. "Where does the baby come from, Mama?" "Tell me where *you* think it comes from, Danny." Or we can say, "You try to guess and then I'll help you figure it out." In this way we can deal with the child's theories first and help him look at them, too.

Debby who is four is taken to see her new baby cousin "just born."

"How did Aunt Margaret get Helen, Mommy?"

"Well how do you think, Debby?"

"She bought her at the dime store!" (Giggling.)

"Did you ever see babies at the dime store, Debby?"

"Nope!" (Still giggling.)

"Well, guess again. I'll help you figure it out."

Silence. "Jonny's mommy is fat!" (Debby knew that Jonny's family would be getting a new baby, but she had not asked questions of her mother. She tells us in this way, however, that she has made her own connections, and she is right, of course.)

"And why do you think Jonny's mommy is fat, Debby?"

"Cause she ate something too big!"

"Is that what you think?—Guess again."

"Jonny's gonna get a new baby. Jonny said so."

"Do you think that's why Jonny's mommy is so fat, Debby?"

"But *why* is she so fat, Mommy?" (Still not sure of her own conclusions.)

So Debby's mama explains that Jonny's mother has a baby growing inside of her, which Debby had already known or guessed. But she needed to have her mother say so. Debby really seems to have some other questions in mind, but she doesn't ask them just yet.

Now at this point Debby's mother offers no further information and waits. It would be easy to plunge into the whole story from "seed meets egg" to "the baby comes out of a special opening" and this is where we most frequently err in giving information to the child. These facts can have no meaning to the child until he has digested them piece by piece and until he has given up his own theories. So Debby's mama waits.

During the next few days Debby asks no further questions but may be seen engaged in private research. An old doll named Honey is disemboweled by Debby without yielding anatomical secrets or a stowaway baby. A wetting doll named Nancy is fed pieces of bread and apple and examined several times a day for hopeful signs. Debby herself has taken to posturing in front of a mirror and has perfected a slouch that throws her little belly forward in a fine imitation of pregnant women. Seeing his daughter in this remarkable posture alarmed papa one day.

"What's the matter, Debby?" he said. "Does something hurt you?" "I'm having a baby," she said gravely. "When you're a grown up lady you will have a baby," said her papa tactfully. "I want one *now*," says Debby a little defiantly. And later at the dinner table, picking away at her food, she says reflectively, "But what *do* the ladies eat to get the babies?"

Later at bedtime when she is alone with her, mother says, "Then you think that ladies need to eat something to get a baby?" "Sure." "What do you think that would be?" "Sump'm," says Debbie. "Sump'm big. Maybe a watermelon or a pumpkin." "But how could a lady eat a watermelon or a pumpkin and get a baby?" "Maybe she eats a little one and it grows and grows and gets to be big."

During this recital Debby's mother listens tactfully and by no means ridicules her daughter's theories. If we want children to share their thoughts with us we need to be specially careful not to make them feel foolish when they present their ideas. So Debby's mother says she is glad Debby gave her her ideas on this, and now would she like Mommy to explain? The mother, she says, does not eat something to make a baby, but grown-up ladies are specially made inside so they can make a baby. Then mother gives the information about a very little egg and how the baby starts from an egg. She is careful, too, to explain how the baby grows in a *special* place inside the mother. This place is *not* the place where our food goes. It is not a stomach. Debby may find this hard to grasp, but her mother wants to start out correctly by dissociating the place where the baby grows from the stomach in order gradually to educate Debby away from her food theories.

Debby wants to know if she, too, has a little egg in her and if she can make a baby if she wants to. Mother explains that when Debby is a grown-up lady she will have eggs and she can grow babies. But she will need to have a husband, too, because babies must have a father. Mother leaves it at that. She doesn't tell Debby about the father's role just yet unless Debby should specifically inquire. Most children do not ask questions about the father's role along with the first questions about how a baby grows inside the mother. Debby will have enough to absorb just from these few facts mother has given her this evening. And mother does not yet tell Debby how the baby gets out. She can count on the fact that Debby's curiosity will lead her to ask this question after a while. If we use the child's own questions as a guide there is rarely a danger of going too fast in sex education.

From time to time in the weeks that follow Debby asks her mother to explain again about the little egg and how it grows. She has trouble in remembering these details and once when mother asks her if she will explain to Mommy, Debby gives a careful recital of the facts with one major distortion. It appears that the mommy *eats* a little egg! (During this same period Debby had been fussy about her breakfast eggs and expressed concern about what happens to the little chick that is growing inside.) So the mother again must deal with Debby's eating theories and patiently go over this material again.

Several weeks pass. Jonnie's baby brother has arrived and his mother is home from the hospital. Debby says one day, while deep in thought, "Did it hurt Jonny's mama when they cut her open?" (No, Jonny's mother did not have a caesarian nor did Debby overhear any grown up talk on the subject. This was her own idea.) "Do you think they had to cut her open to get the baby out?" "That's what I think," says Debby candidly. "Can you think of any other ways in which a baby could come out?" "Maybe the mother pops," says Debby, and makes a terrible face, "like a balloon." (Now the mother understands another inexplicable happening of a few days ago. Debby had blown up a balloon and when it popped, she cried out in terror and could not be consoled for a long time.) Debby's mother says no, a mama does not have to have an operation and a mama does not pop. Does Debby have some other ideas. "Well, then," says Debby reluctantly, "it *must* come out from the b.m. place!" Debby's mother reminds her that the baby is not like food and it is not made by eating something. So if a baby grows in a special place in the mother, wouldn't it be a good idea for that place to have its own opening for the baby to come out? Debby looks surprised and doubtful. "Where's *that?*" she says suspiciously. Her mother picks up a doll. "If this were a real girl or lady, how many openings would she have down here?" "One for wee-wee and one for b.m.," says Debby promptly. "Show me where they are." Debby points. "That's right. But there is one more right here (showing Debby) and that's the place where the baby comes out." Debby wants to know if she has such a place. Her mother assures her that she does, but in a little girl it is a very little opening.

We can expect that Debby will puzzle over this information for a long time to come. There will be further questions, confusion, a reversion to earlier theories, and it is probably true that several years will pass before Debby really has these facts fully integrated. But the approach employed by Debby's parents has the best promise of bringing about eventual assimilation of this information. The information is given step by step and is linked to the child's questions. Information is not given until the child's own theories have been explored. In other words, we want to avoid building sex education over the child's distorted theories as far as it is possible to avoid it. Even when we have already given certain facts to the child it is well, when the next group of questions comes up, to ask the child first if he will explain what he understands.

It may be many months before Debby inquires about the father's role in procreation, or she may ask right away. At any rate, her questions will indicate to us her readiness for any new information. If we ourselves introduce sex information through a complicated story method in which all the facts are given at once, there is no chance for the child to absorb this difficult education, no chance to deal with her misconceptions first. We would actually only add to the confusion already present in the child's mind. However, there are exceptions to this principle that should be taken into account. If a child of school age has not asked about the father's role, for instance, we can assume that there is some reluctance to ask the necessary questions. He may already have been introduced to this fact through other children and has found the whole matter somewhat repugnant. In such a case it would be correct for parents to find a tactful way of opening up the subject and inviting the child's questions.

THE EDUCATIONAL ROLE OF THE PARENTS DURING THE OEDIPAL PHASE.

WE HAVE already seen that the love attachments of the oedipal phase are a normal part of child development during the years three to five or six. Normally, too, the child gives up the impossible day-dream of replacing a mother or father, and the conflicts that manifest themselves during this period subside.

We know that this childhood love and the resolution of its conflicts will influence the later attitudes toward love in adolescence and maturity. If the attachment of the boy to his mother or the girl to her father persists unchanged in later years there will be difficulty in exchanging the old love of childhood for the new love of maturity. Parents—including those who have never heard of an Oedipus complex—play a vital role in the resolution of these conflicts, and, to the credit of parents, most children relinquish the impossible day-dream, move on to the absorbing interests of the school years, grow into maturity and possess the necessary freedom from childhood attachments to find new loves. How is this done?

Reality (and this includes the parents who are certainly part of the child's reality) plays the decisive role. A little boy cannot have his mother all to himself now—or ever. A little girl cannot replace her mother in her father's affections now—or ever. A Jimmy cannot get rid of his father and have his father at the same time, and since he's really very fond of his father he relinquishes his futile day-dream in favor of another that offers real possibilities of satisfaction. He can become *like* his father. And one day he, too, will marry and have children.

But the child does not renounce his oedipal wishes without the aid of his parents. For whether parents know about an Oedipus complex or don't know about it, the parents represent reality and it is they who say in effect, "Such wishes cannot be realized now—or ever." There is no need for words, actually; parents get this across through their attitudes. Whether Jimmy's father knows why Jimmy is challenging his authority in the bed-time tirade or whether he doesn't know, he is obliged to deal with the behavior, and in sending Jimmy off to his room he is saying in effect, "I am your father and you are only a little boy. Whatever the reason for this uncontrolled behavior tonight, I don't care for it and I don't allow it."

It is the parental attitude, parental conduct, that says to a child that he cannot have his mother all to himself, that he cannot become a rival with his father for his mother's affections. All this gets across in hundreds of subtle ways.

From the early years Jimmy—all children—must realize that parents have a private life together, a special love for each other from which a child is excluded. Children are often resentful of this fact, but it is important that they be helped to accept it. We know how small children protest when mother and father go out for an evening or go off for a short holiday. Many parents actually feel guilty about even such necessary exclusion of a child from their private lives. Yet this is a necessary education for the child in understanding that the parents have a private relationship as well as the relationship they share with their children.

The parents' bedroom can become a symbol of such privacy and it is a sound principle to maintain this privacy from earliest childhood on. This means, of course, that the child does not sleep in his parents' room, but it also means that the child should not be taken into bed with his parents. Even when the child wakens from a bad dream and asks to stay with his parents, we will find it much wiser to comfort him in his own bed. For these reasons and others that we have already discussed, it it also well to exclude the child when parents are dressing or bathing or using the toilet.

But isn't this making too much fuss about the privacy of parents? Won't the child get the impression that his parents are being excessively secretive? We don't need to create this impression either, of course. A matter-of-fact statement of the principle of privacy, a principle established early and maintained throughout childhood is not too difficult to maintain in the family.

In these ways and many others we create the feeling in the child that his parents' relationship to each other and their love for each other must be respected. A child, dearly loved as he is, may not intrude upon this intimate relationship, cannot share the intimacies of his parents' lives, and cannot obtain the exclusive love of a parent. If the child has fantasies about marrying the parent of his choice, fantasies about a more intimate and exclusive love, the fantasy remains a fantasy, for we do nothing to encourage it, and without encouragement the fantasy will be given up.

But sometimes in a home where the relationship between the parents is disturbed, a parent disappointed in marital love may make a child his exclusive love interest. A mother may demonstrate tenderness for her son while she remains aloof from her husband. A father may be charmed by his small daughter and lavish gifts and attentions on her that the mother herself rarely receives. In such instances the childhood day-dream of having a special and intimate relationship with a parent, of excluding the rival parent, is given some substance in real life. The fantasy is nourished in part by the attitude of the parents, and the child may have more difficulty in giving up his fantasies than the child who has known from early days that his mother and father belong to each other and that the quality of their love for each other is different from the quality of their love for him.

For the same reasons we should not look upon the child's occasional demonstrations of coyness and flirtatiousness with a parent as something "cute." The little asides and jokes that grown-ups make at such times are well understood by children and are taken as signs of encouragement. We do not need to be amused or flattered by a child's demonstration of erotic feelings. The parental ego doesn't need this. Neither should we be shocked by such demonstrations, of course. But if we do not look upon this flirtatious behavior as amusing or entertaining, if our attitude is grown-up, fatherly and motherly, such behavior will soon be discontinued through lack of encouragement.

The child's rivalry with the parent of his own sex also requires firmness and tact. Sometimes, quite unconsciously, a father may react to his son's competitive feelings and jealousy as if the little boy really were a rival. In such instances we may see a father and small boy engaged in a long-drawn-out struggle for supremacy, each reacting to the other's challenge. Neither father nor son is conscious of one of the motives, the child's rivalry with his father for his mother, and the struggle takes place on a number of battlegrounds that the child himself sets up within the home: father's T.V. program or son's program; father's rights to a peaceful evening or the son's rights to play Superman in the living room; father's final word on the subject, or the little boy's final word. Sometimes the rivalry may even be more open and on the main issue; father's right to enjoy mother's company alone or a little boy's right to have mother alone, played out in a late evening drama with a little boy who refuses to go to bed, or once in bed refuses to stay there, making frequent appearances thereafter in the living room.

Now it becomes very clear that a father who has established his authority early in a child's life—an authority that is reasonable but firm and undisputed—will not be seriously challenged by a little boy's rivalry, and what is just as important, a little boy will not seriously challenge the authority of such a father. In other words, it is often the child who has successfully challenged the father's authority and rights from earliest childhood on, who will, during this stage of development, attempt to challenge seriously the father's rights to the mother. The child who has learned in countless small ways that he cannot "win" in a struggle with his father, that he is only a little boy, will find it easier to accept the fact that he cannot be victorious in this struggle over a loved person.

But let us take care to understand this. We do not mean, of course, that a child should be intimidated, that he should feel passive and helpless before the authority and position of his father. Though he needs to accept the authority of his father on vital issues, we grant him the right to his feelings and we grant him the right to express them within certain limits.

Shall we return to Jimmy for a moment? From Jimmy's terrible dream we know that he was very much afraid of the hostile wishes he had expressed to his father. If we interpret the dream and its ending correctly he was calling to his father to protect him from the terrible danger of the enraged tiger, that is, Jimmy himself. He was also afraid of dreadful punishment for his bad wishes and needed Daddy's protection against this imagined danger, too.

Somehow Jimmy's father wants to get the idea across to him that he need not be afraid that his father or someone else will punish him for his angry thoughts, that having bad wishes doesn't mean that the bad wishes will come true. Jimmy doesn't have to be afraid that his angry thought, "I wish you was dead," will make Daddy die. This is very important to get across to a child of Jimmy's age, for some primitive thinking still dominates certain areas of the child's life and many youngsters torture themselves with the fear that a terrible wish will be realized.

IDENTIFICATION.

THE WISH to replace a father or a mother must be given up and something else must take its place. A little boy cannot *be* his father, but he can be *like* his father. A little girl cannot take her mother's place in her father's affections, but by making herself *like* her mother, she achieves another kind of satisfaction. And so we find that the good solution to this conflict in love of early childhood is the best possible solution for the development of good patterns of sex identification. The healthy outcome of this early disappointment in love is a strengthening of masculinity in the boy and femininity in the girl.

How does this come about? We said earlier that the rivalry with a parent in early childhood is complicated by the fact that the rival is also the object of a child's love. If Jimmy did not love his father so deeply, his conflict over his bad wishes would not be so intense. In the end it is love that wins out, and the little boy gives up his day-dream and his hostile wishes against his father because the love for father is far stronger than the hate. And out of this love for father will come enduring qualities of masculinity. We expect that love of father will cause the child to emulate his father, to take the father as his model of masculinity.

But wait, we're going a bit fast here. Isn't it true that a child takes the parent of his own sex as a model much earlier in childhood? Margie is only thirty months old and she's a perfect small edition of her mama. She can't quite speak a decent sentence, but she has her mama's trick of sprinkling exclamation points throughout the most ordinary chatter. And even mama will admit that when Margie is pushed a little too far she has the same sweet stubbornness that mama herself will show in the same circumstances. When Arthur, not quite three, puts on a tie "just like daddy's" his voice goes down one octave. And keep your face straight when this little man drives his trike down the driveway and mutters curses at imaginary drivers who obstruct the road.

Then, of course, the roots of identification go deep into earliest childhood. These first imitations of a parent precede and lay the groundwork for a solid identification with that parent. In identification certain qualities of another person are taken over and made a permanent part of the personality. Identification can include a whole range of personality traits or attributes of another person which are taken over and made part of one's self. Just for the present we'll confine ourselves to one aspect of the process of identification, sex identification, in order to see how this process promotes healthy development in the child.

Integrity in a personality is achieved in a large measure by the acceptance of one's biological self, one's sex. Where the aims of the personality are in harmony with the biological fact of sex, we can expect the highest degree of stability within the whole personality. We need only a moment's reflection to confirm this. If a little girl accepts her girl's body and her feminine destiny, and if her aspirations for herself are in harmony with these biological facts, there will be no motives for those powerful conflicts which can sometimes produce neurosis. But if a little girl despises her girl's body, believes that girls are inferior beings in our culture and aspires to masculine goals for herself, the resulting disharmony between biological fact and ego goals will produce conflict in the personality.

If a little boy feels that masculinity is not valued in his world, or that the attainment of masculine goals is too dangerous, he may choose a course which makes no demands upon his masculinity, but again the disharmony between the biological fact of masculinity and the negation of that fact in the ego's strivings will set up a conflict within the personality. We must remember that the image of the self is derived first of all from the image of the body and that the maleness or femaleness of this body is an inescapable fact. Whoever tries to set up an image of himself that denies or negates these facts will find himself opposing his biological self in a struggle that constantly renews itself.

Yet every child, boy or girl, passes through a phase in development in which he or she "plays at" being the opposite sex. We are not alarmed when confronted with a delicious and utterly feminine little girl of three in bonnet and pinafore and starched petticoat who totes a Buck Rogers automatic in her innocent handbag. This little woman may also be found in an unguarded moment attempting to urinate like a boy, and in still less guarded moments berating her mama for getting her "borned" before she was finished. And if a little boy of the same age, who is otherwise pleased with himself and wants to grow up to be a truck driver, should announce that he is making a baby in his stomach, we are not horrified and we do not need to make an appointment for him at a child guidance clinic.

We would feel differently, however, if a school-age child should express strong opposition to the way in which he is made. For we expect that sometime before the seventh or eighth year a child will not only accept the biological facts of maleness and femaleness but, through identification with the parent of his own sex, derive pleasure from the fact.

ON BEING A GIRL.

THE little girl of three who berates her mama for getting her "borned" before she was finished will give up her masculine ambitions quite naturally in the years that come when she discovers that being a girl has special satisfactions for her. It helps, of course, to know that "someday" she will become a mama, too, and that she is made specially so that she can have babies grow inside her body. But that is "someday" and perhaps the greatest satisfaction for the little girl in being a girl is in being "just like mommy." A mother who has found satisfaction herself in being a woman will, of course, communicate this to her daughter without words. A father who is pleased at having a daughter, who values femininity for itself, will give great impetus to the process of feminine identification in his little girl by the fact that he loves his daughter and values her femininity. (The father who consciously or unconsciously is disappointed in having a daughter and who tries to make his daughter into a son, will certainly complicate the little girl's development for she will understand that to be really loved by her father she must behave like a son.)

But when we speak of "femininity" and the development of a feminine attitude in the little girl, let us be sure that we are speaking of attributes that really deserve to be called feminine. While a little girl's attitude toward pretty clothes is usually regarded as "feminine" (and may very well be just that), it is not in itself evidence of a feminine attitude. It may be as true of the nine-year-old girl and the twenty-nine-year-old girl as for the three-year-old girl that these feminine ornaments only conceal a masculine attitude, like the Buck Rogers automatic in the dainty handbag. Feminine attitudes must be adduced from other and more profound evidence. The harmony between a mother and daughter in a school-age child is a favorable sign of the girl's positive attitude toward femininity, that is, the positive feeling toward mother as the representative of femininity will usually indicate a good attitude on the part of the girl toward her own femininity. The absence of strong rivalry with boys, or aggressive attitudes towards boys and men, is a favorable indication of femininity in a school-age girl. Pleasure in feminine activities and association with other girls must also be counted highly as a sign of acceptance of femininity. The day-dreams and aspirations of the little girl also tell us the degree to which she has accepted her femininity.

But we understand that femininity (or masculinity) is not an absolute quality. Nor is the acceptance of femininity a sudden acquisition at the close of a developmental phase. There are many compromises within the personality between feminine and masculine goals which do not result in neurosis and which need not create conflict. The little girl who leaves her dolls to go out with the boys to chase Indians is not necessarily in danger of abandoning her femininity. (The most casual appraisal of our childhood friends will remind us how many tom-boys grew up to be excellent wives and mothers.) It is only when the personality of a girl is dominated by masculine tendencies and when femininity is repudiated that we need to feel some concern for the future development of the little girl.

I once knew a little girl who hated all things connected with girls and women and was very outspoken in her contempt of femininity. She competed with her little brother and with the boys in the neighborhood and tried to outdo them at their own games. She detested dresses, hair-ribbons, and girls' games and fought with her mother over any attempt to "make a lady" out of her. Her envy of boys and her depreciation of her own sex had originated at the time her own little brother was born. But this was not the decisive factor. A great many little girls will be presented with baby brothers sometime during their early years and they need not on this account repudiate their own femininity. What had happened then?

She had had all the normal feelings of jealousy toward the baby brother when he came into the family. Other little girls do, too. She felt that her parents preferred the baby because he was a boy. This may not have been true, but she felt it was. She then attempted to make herself as much like a boy as possible in the hope that her parents would love her better than the baby. This, too, is a very typical first reaction of little girls to the birth of a baby brother. But most little girls will overcome this disappointment and envy, and this little girl had not. The decisive factor, then, was not the birth of the baby brother but the inability, thereafter, to find satisfactions in being a girl. It was as if she could not believe that she could be loved as a girl.

Her parents had seen one aspect of the conflict clearly enough —the rivalry with the new baby—and had done all the things that understanding parents do to ease the painful feelings at this time. What they had not seen—and this is often difficult to detect—is that jealousy had profoundly disturbed her feelings about being a girl and that her repudiation of femininity did not alter with time but actually grew more extreme. The conflicts with mother, nursery-school teachers, the whole world of women, grew stronger as time went on. She rejected them as she rejected the feminine part of herself. To her father and other men in her family she presented herself as a rather engaging little tom-boy, inviting—and getting—the kind of games that men play with little boys, shadow-boxing, fencing, rough-and-tumble games.

So we can see how this child was offering herself as a little boy in the expectation that if she were a boy she might have greater value in the world. What she had needed from her parents was an additional kind of help when she reacted with such passionate envy to the birth of the baby brother. It was not enough to reassure her that she was loved and that the new baby had not taken love away from her. She needed to know, in addition, that she was loved *as a girl*. More than words, of course, she needed to feel that her parents found pleasure in her being a girl, in her femininity. She needed to know that she did not make herself more lovable to her father by behaving like a boy but that she was loved for herself as a little girl and loved for her feminine qualities. She needed her mother's help in finding pleasure in femininity, in discovering the special satisfactions in being a woman.

It is so easy for parents to be drawn into a child's conflicts as these parents were. A mother becomes understandably distressed by the tom-boy's sloppiness, her unkempt hair, her jeans, her cow-boy antics, and the urge to "make a lady out of her" is irresistible and leads repeatedly to conflicts over dress, manners, a hundred details in the ordinary routine of a day. But ladies are not made by wearing down their resistance to femininity. And it is so easy for a father to fall in with the tom-boy's romping and rough play which, after all, brings him closer to his own childhood than the incomprehensible girl games of a daughter. It is understandable that a father might not easily guess the motives behind such behavior and unconsciously fall in with the little girl's game of being a boy. But a little girl who finds that her tom-boy antics do, indeed, bring her closer to her father will have even less incentive to give them up in favor of feminine pursuits.

Obviously, the little tom-boy will not be coerced into "being a lady" by her mother nor will she herself abandon her pose as a boy if it brings satisfactions to her. What we need to do is to strengthen and promote the feminine side of the child, diminish the satisfactions gained through playing boy and eventually, without conflict over jeans, hair-do's and manners, the boy pose may be given up because being a girl has greater satisfactions.

The mother is, of course, the central figure in the girl's feminine development. It is through the mother that the girl acquires her standards of feminine behavior; it is through love of the mother and identification with her that the girl achieves a positive identification with her own sex.

All of this does not mean that a mother must exert herself in building a relationship with her daughter. There is no need for a mother to arrange special mother-daughter jaunts to restaurants, stores, theaters and such places. They are fine as occasional treats (if they really give pleasure to mother and daughter), but these planned recreational projects are not in themselves the things that build relationship and lead to identification. Identification is achieved through love and the wish to emulate a beloved person. This means that without self-conscious effort and planning, identification will take place as naturally as love through the everyday experiences of family living. We encourage and nurture the process, actually educate the child along the lines of identification, but this is not a formal course of instruction.

In recent years we have devoted ourselves to various artificial expedients for the education of the girl toward femininity. Homemaking, baby care, "family relations," "good grooming," even sex education have been moved out of the orbit of the mother-daughter relationship to become fields of study in the elementary school or merit badges in the Girl Scouts. Such formal instruction in the so-called arts of womanhood probably has little effect upon a girl's attitude toward her feminine role, but the alienation of these forms of feminine education from the family and from the central figure in the girl's feminine development, her mother, has the effect of devitalizing these aspects of femininity, creating symbols of femininity which have lost their vital connections with love, intimacy and the deeper motives that bring forth feminine identifications.

It is possible for a girl to cook, to know the correct technique for bathing a baby, to know how to apply make-up and style her hair and to possess a scientific sex education, and yet not be made more feminine by this instruction. It is easy to acquire the external signs of femininity. But it is only when the symbols of femininity are united with a genuinely feminine attitude that we can take them as positive signs of feminine development. This kind of femininity will never be achieved through classroom teaching or merit badges. This is the achievement of a mother.

ON BEING A BOY.

LET's consider the little boy and the establishment of masculine values in his personality. First of all what do we mean by masculinity? I once knew a little boy of six who maintained a reign of terror in his neighborhood beating up the little kids, attacking with sticks and rocks. At home he spent his leisure hours impersonating Superman in acrobatic descents from the top of the piano, or at other times in the role of Roy Rogers galloping wildly over the furniture. He was rough, he was tough, he was the strongest guy in the world. But at night he wet his bed.

His parents brought him to see me because they understood that his bed-wetting was a symptom of an inner conflict. When we got around to discussing the behavior of this child, I discovered that neither parent felt that his behavior was "a problem"! Papa, especially, was indignant at the complaints of neighbors. Little Pete, he said, was just a real boy and if the neighbors wanted a make a sissy out of him, they'd see if they'd get any cooperation from Pete's parents. A boy has to be tough. A boy has to take care of himself. He, papa, had taught Pete how to stand up for himself. . . .

But was this "toughness" of Pete's a sign of masculinity? Were the attacks on other children simply an excess of boyish exuberance? Were his Superman antics at home just a sign of high spirits, a greater amount of masculine drive? The truth of the matter is that Pete was a frightened little boy who attacked other children because he was afraid of being attacked. He lived in a fantasy world in which he was constantly in danger of attack. His Superman antics, his rough-and-tough cowboy play were part of his elaborate defense against imagined danger. *If* he were Superman, he wouldn't have to be afraid of anyone. *If* he were a tough guy, a cowboy hero, he would be able to fight off attackers; he could make them afraid of *him*. And at night, when he was asleep, the fears that he warded off by day through fighting and through playing Superman, returned to plague him. And in his sleep he was helpless and defenseless, and he wet his bed.

Granted that a boy in our culture needs to be able to "take care of himself" if he is threatened, and granted that "aggressivity" is a masculine trait, raw physical aggression is not in itself an index to masculinity. By the time a boy has reached the age of five or six, physical aggression should play a small part in his system of masculine values (and in ours). Games and play permit sublimated forms of aggression and the healthy child can make use of such activities to discharge his aggressive impulses with modified goals. Language development has reached a point where grievances can be expressed in words, and solutions to problems can be found through ideas and communication of ideas.

A little American boy has a number of other difficulties in acquiring his masculine values. In our culture women are, to a very large extent, the culture bearers. Mother is the educator of conscience, the teacher of standards of conduct, the teacher of moral values. Mother and school teachers take over a heavy share of the education for intellectual values. By tradition, in America, they have the job of teaching appreciation of literature, music, art, "the finer things of life." Now why women should have a mandate in this region of child education I cannot say, but it has an important effect upon the developing boy and serious cultural implications as well. Since the little boy acquires these values largely from women, he regards them as "feminine" and has difficulty in integrating them into his masculine personality. If a little boy has good manners, he is in danger of "being a sissy" in his own estimate and in the opinion of his peers. Why? Because the teaching of good manners is the job of the women in our culture and to acquire good manners is to be "like" a woman, or a girl. If a boy is studious and has intellectual pursuits, he also runs the risk of condemnation from his peers; his masculinity is questioned. If he plays a musical instrument, he must not play it too well or devote himself too arduously to music or he will invite the teasing and ridicule of his friends. If he should acquire a deep appreciation for literature or (may the Lord help him) poetry, he will do well to keep it to himself, like a secret vice, for if it is discovered he will lose his status as a male.

But what is this? Civilized conduct, manners, are not masculine or feminine. Mental activity is not masculine or feminine. Music, art, poetry have no gender. But if these activities and pursuits are fostered almost exclusively by women in a child's education, they acquire "femininity" by identification of the idea with the woman teacher.

But let's not confine ourselves to intellectual values. Our morality, in America, is also acquired through women to a large measure. The portrait of an American boy squirming under the moral tutelage of an American woman is at least as old as Huck Finn and Tom Sawyer. Now all children in all nations and for all times resist moral teaching, but when this education is largely given over to women, the male child acquires a divided attitude toward these teachings. Both Tom and Huck behaved as if their masculine principles were in danger if they submitted to Aunt Polly and the Widow Watson and resisted these teachings as strongly as they resisted a bath. Like the intellectual values which remain uncertainly "feminine" in the boy's personality, a morality that is acquired largely through a woman's teaching becomes "feminine" by identification. So to be "good," that is, reasonably well-behaved, considerate of the feelings of others, able to accept frustration and disappointment, comes darn close to "being a sissy" in our boy culture in America.

But it's not really that simple, either. For when women, the mothers and teachers take over the job of moral teaching, they have difficulty, being women, in understanding the nature of the male they are instructing. Having no experience in being a boy, they impose feminine standards of behavior upon the male. The greater energy and activity of the male puts him at a great disadvantage in the eyes of many mothers and female teachers who compare him unfavorably with the more docile and tractable little girl of the same age. Girls are regarded as less troublesome and better behaved—"good," in other words—and boys are regarded as restless, mischievous, willful, "not good," by some mamas and many teachers.

The standard for good behavior in the classroom is very often the girl standard. I think unhappily of a little six-year-old boy I know who came to visit me one day completely crushed by the day's events. At school he had been sent up to the principal for disturbing his class. (His high-spirited seat partner had poked him in the ribs and he had returned the poke in the honorable tradition of males.) His teacher, who had never been a boy, regarded this exchange of pokes as a border incident that verged on war and marshalled all the energy required to quell a major revolt to censure these boys for a breach of the classroom code. When my small friend protested and stated his case, she bristled, cracked out a reprimand and sent him off to the principal's office. There he was lectured by a dragon who did not trouble herself about the events that led to this crisis because she knew boys and could assume that they were trouble-makers, noise-makers, shufflers, whisperers, pokers and punchers. She concluded her lecture with a caustic allusion to family honor. The trouble-maker's *sister*, she said significantly, had been one of the very best students, and best *citizens* this school had ever known.

"Girls *never* get into trouble," my young friend said wistfully. "Sometimes I think it would be better to be a girl."

It seems that we are not very sure in our culture just what a boy should be like. On the one hand, we set before him the models of Abe Lincoln and George Washington and on the other hand the model of a gangster. On the one hand, we equate masculinity with toughness and violence and on the other hand we give the major part of his education to women who want him to be docile like a nice little girl.

I want to defend the little boy here, for he has a tough job finding his place in our society. But I also think we need to question some of the values that we have called "masculine." A boy is not more "masculine" because he can beat up every kid on the block, because he is tough, never cries and never shows his feelings about anything. But we need to recognize, too, that a boy is not a girl, that he cannot be bound to the code of women and girls, that his biological make-up disposes him toward greater activity and aggressiveness and that his educators must understand this. We can employ the active, aggressive components in the boy's biological equipment in an educational program that makes suitable allowance for direct discharge of energy in physical activity and indirect discharge through learning and creative activity (which make use of "aggressive" energy too). As part of our education we educate away from raw discharge of aggression, the bullying, the tantrum, the destructive and sadistic acts, but we employ these energies for other activities, sublimated activities, and we should never wish to eradicate these tendencies or reverse them so that a boy needs to become passive and feminine in order to win our approval.

As the father regains prestige in the American home we may hope to see less conflict in the American boy regarding his masculinity. For the father who takes an active part in his son's upbringing offers himself as a model that can be integrated into the child's personality. There is less resistance to the incorporation of male-inspired values into the masculine personality of the developing boy than in the case of the female-inspired values, and in the ideal situation there should be a harmony of values in the attitude of both parents. But it is not enough for father to be "a pal" to his son. Perhaps we have overstressed this side of the relationship of son and father altogether too much. There should be shared interests of course. There should be activities together, of course. But a father need not be a play-mate for his son and a father must reserve a good-sized place in his relationship to his son for the exercise of parental authority when the occasion demands it.

We have a hard time in our culture defining the role of the father in a democratic society. Very close to the early days of this republic an astute European observer like de Tocqueville recognized the changing pattern of family life in America which emerged spontaneously in a society that had overthrown the absolute rule of a king and abandoned the European pattern of the state. The American father, like the president and other elected leaders of this republic could be challenged and criticized. The sons of the republic did not bow down to any authority, though they accepted the principle of governmental authority expressing the will of the people.

In adapting the principle of democratic government to the family we run into some obvious difficulties. The child does not elect his parents and he is not a responsible and functioning citizen in the society of his family. His father cannot be guided by the popular will of an electorate or a governing body to whom he is responsible. He cannot be guided by the popular will of his children either, unless he is prepared to lose his sanity and his life's savings. If he is an earnest, democratic father, he may go in for family councils and such things, but this is likely to become a hoax in the name of democracy which any five year old can spot in a minute.

We need to rescue the American father from the unreasonable and false situation into which we have put him in the name of democracy. We will have no tyrants either, for authority does not mean tyranny. And authority of the kind I speak does not require physical force or the exercise of power for the sake of power. It is a reasonable and just authority (as authority must be in a democratic society) exercised confidently as the prerogative of a father, deriving its strength from the ties of love that bind a parent and child.

8. Education of Conscience

THE DAWN OF CONSCIENCE.

EARLIER we spoke of the "building" of conscience in the very young child. We established the fact that the two year old does not have a conscience in the proper sense of the word. He may know that certain acts are "right" or "wrong" because of the approval or disapproval of his parents. He may even feel ashamed when he is caught in some mischief. But he does not yet have a system of built-in controls which is what we mean by conscience. Whether he exercises control over some impulse may depend very simply on whether his mother is in the same room or not. Whether he feels ashamed of naughtiness may depend just as simply on whether the mischievous act is discovered or not, so that control is still largely dependent upon an outside agency, the parents.

But somewhere around the age of four or five we see signs of an internal government in the personality of the child. The parents have an agent working for them in the form of a conscience. The agent, being new on the job, is not always effective. He even appears to be easily corrupted at times. Often he seems asleep on duty and then, surprisingly, he rouses himself and becomes a perfect zealot, demanding more of this poor child than the parents themselves would. Parents will be surprised to find that the agent is at times far more severe than they are. Parents who are just and reasonable, who never utter severe threats, may find that their agent is tormenting their child and threatening cruel and barbarous punishments for bad thoughts or misdeeds. He induces some anxieties in the child during his early period of government. He is instrumental in creating bad dreams. In exceptional cases he may produce a neurosis. At times the parents have to step in to soften the influence of their agent. But even this can be a little difficult, for the agent is now not only the parents' but the child's own. Curiously enough, he derives his power and energy from the child's own impulses! How? In much the same way that the reformed criminal becomes the most zealous anti-vice crusader. The stronger the original impulse or wish, the stronger the anti-wish, the counter-force. This explains why the child in the first stages of overcoming his unacceptable impulses employs such severe counter-measures, creates his own bogies and fantasied punishments to subdue his "bad" wishes. Later, when his "bad" impulses have been brought under control he doesn't need the severe counter-measures either, and then we see a greater harmony in the whole personality.

What is a "good," that is an effective, conscience from the point of view of mental health? A good conscience in these terms is one that can regulate and control the primary human drives according to the requirements of society. It is the repository of moral values, of ideals and standards for behavior, and affords the individual the possibility of judging and criticizing himself. It is not an effective conscience in terms of mental health if it reigns as a tyrant within the ego, mercilessly forbidding and tormenting or accusing and punishing for the smallest transgressions. It is not an effective conscience if it is easily corrupted, if it is a watchman that goes to sleep on the job when the burglars break in, if it is a highly placed official who takes bribes from the opposition, if it is a bookkeeper who balances the accounts by falsifying the ledger on both sides. To be effective a conscience must uphold standards and enforce them without tyranny or deceit; it must produce guilt-feelings which are appropriate to the situation, and it must afford the basic drives a certain amount of direct satisfaction and a wide variety of indirect satisfactions.

In short, a good, or an effective conscience must behave like a good and effective parent!

If we are satisfied with this definition of an effective conscience, let's proceed to an examination of the methods of parental education that lead to its formation.

DISCIPLINE.

THE word discipline has fallen into ill repute. It had respectable origins in a Latin root which established its connections with learning and education. It still retains its connections with education in the dictionary: "training that develops self-control, character, or orderliness and efficiency," but common usage has corrupted the word so that "discipline" today is used synonymously with punishment, most particularly corporal punishment.

I am in favor of restoring the word "discipline" in its ancient and honorable sense. It is teaching, education, and when employed for child-rearing it should have the significance of education of character. In discussing methods of discipline we should then hew close to the real significance of this term and speak of those methods that instruct, make learning possible. For various reasons I do not regard corporal punishment as a means of education or as a method of developing self-control. Later I shall discuss this, too.

There are really no fancy tricks in the education of the child for self-control. All the clever stratagems, the household recipes for obtaining the cooperation of a child in the control of impulse boil down to one essential point: The child cooperates in his training because he wants parental love and approval and he feels parental disapproval as a temporary withdrawal of affection and esteem. Many parents may be shocked by this last statement. Shouldn't a child always feel loved "just the same" no matter what he has done? Let's examine this idea carefully because a misunderstanding of this principle has led to much confusion in our present-day education of the child. Of course, a child who is in fact unloved will have no incentives for healthy development and will develop serious personality disturbances. And a child who is made to feel worthless and degraded for his childhood offenses will come to believe in his own worthlessness and unlovability and out of this degradation of the self come the mental cripples and the outcasts of our society. But we are not speaking of the so-called rejected child and we are not speaking of a parental discipline that creates in a child the feeling of being utterly unloved and abandoned. The most wanted, most beloved child in the world will feel his parents' disapproval or criticism of him as withdrawal of their affection. And when he is restored to good favor he will experience this as a regaining of parental affection and approval. For this is the way in which the child is constituted. This is the way he experiences love.

There's a fine point in all this that we need to tackle. If a child feels that he is loved "just the same" when he kicks his father during a temper tantrum as those other times when his reasonable self is in command, what motive does he have to control his temper? If he loses nothing in his father's eyes by behaving in this way, why should he exert himself to establish self-control? And does his father really love him "just the same" in the moment that he nurses a bruised shin, or the moment after? One day a specimen of such a father may be produced but he doesn't yet exist and for purposes of rearing a child it's hard to imagine how the human race would profit by it. For the child needs to know that his parents do not feel "just the same" toward him under all circumstances or he will have no incentive to work for the ideals his parents set for him or to restrict his own behavior.

But we need to understand that there is a vast difference between this temporary withdrawal of affection, or favor, or approval on the part of a loving parent toward his child who has behaved badly and the absence of affection or love on the part of a parent who is obliged to deal with his child's impulsive behavior. If the fundamental love ties between parents and a child are absent or disturbed, the disapproval or criticism of a parent will have little effect except to confirm the child's feeling that he is unloved and that no matter what he does he will not gain parental love or lose it.

What happens, then, to the normal child with good affectionate ties to his parents when he experiences his parents' disapproval and criticism of him for an act of naughtiness? We have said that he experiences the parental disapproval as a temporary withdrawal of parental affection, that is, temporary for the short time he is "out of favor." Now, because of the close tie-up between the feelings of being loved and approved by parents and the feelings of self-love, the child also experiences a disturbance in his self-esteem. In other words, a fall from esteem in the eyes of the parents produces a drop in self-esteem. A number of emotional reactions now combine to produce the feeling which we call "guilt."

The experience of a sense of guilt for wrong-doing is necessary for the development of self-control. The guilt feelings will later serve as a warning signal which the child can produce himself when an impulse to repeat the naughty act comes over him. When the child can produce his own warning signals, independent of the actual presence of the adult, he is on the way to developing a conscience. Later, these warning signals can work almost automatically so that an impulse can be checked before the act is initiated and often without any conscious struggle.

We can see that guilt feelings are indispensable for the development of a conscience. And we have already seen that a properly functioning conscience must be able to produce guilt feelings in order to serve self-control. But this brings us to another disagreeable topic in modern methods of child-rearing. For "guilt" has become a bad word among many enlightened parents today. "Isn't it bad for a child to have guilt feelings?" they say. "Won't it make him neurotic?"

Here we need to establish the difference between the guilt feelings produced by a healthy personality and neurotic guilt feelings. It is essentially the difference between a reasonable conscience and a tyrannical conscience! We have said a healthy conscience can produce guilt feelings which are appropriate, which are merited by the act. A healthy personality makes use of these guilt feelings to prevent repetition of the unworthy or shameful act. But the neurotic conscience behaves like a gestapo headquarters within the personality, mercilessly tracking down dangerous or potentially dangerous ideas and every remote relative of these ideas, accusing, threatening, tormenting in an interminable inquisition to establish guilt for trivial offenses or crimes committed in dreams. Such guilt feelings have the effect of putting the whole personality under arrest and since the links to real events are finally lost in this unending tribunal and this farcical trial of a personality is largely unconscious, these guilt feelings can rarely be employed for constructive action or for enlarging the personality.

Let's define these differences more closely. A child who destroys his older brother's precious model airplane in a fit of temper needs to feel guilty about his act, and if he shows remorse and self-reproach afterward, we should regard these guilt feelings as appropriate to the situation. But here is another child who is afraid to throw a ball in a game, who is afraid to give an opinion that is contrary to another voiced opinion. He doesn't know why he is afraid to throw a ball and he doesn't know why he doesn't dare to disagree with anyone. In the course of psychotherapy we learn that he is afraid that if his aggression broke out he might really hurt someone, so his conscience, like a gestapo agent searches out every remote connection of the idea "aggression" and puts them under arrest. "To throw a ball" is regarded as an act of aggression. To voice a contrary opinion is an act of aggression. But the child does not know this. He only knows that he must not throw a ball and must not disagree, for if he should, he would feel guilty. Such guilt feelings as these are exaggerated out of all proportion to the circumstances of a ball game or ordinary discussions.

We need to make use of a child's guilt reactions in training for self-control, but the sensitive and wise parent knows he must never abuse the power of his child's love for him to create guilt of such strength that the child fears his normal impulses. And we should probably mention at the outset of this discussion that there are areas of child training where we do *not* want to create guilt feelings in a child. Clearly in toilet training we do not want to produce guilt feelings in the child for his lapses in control. We do not want the exploring toddler to feel guilty about his normal and necessary desire to touch and examine objects in his environment. We do not want the child to feel ashamed of touching his genitals or of his normal curiosity about sexual matters.

But the nursery-age child who has lost control of his temper and engages in a destructive act needs to feel some guilt for his behavior. The child who endangers the safety of another child by throwing stones or rocks needs to feel guilty about his uncontrolled and dangerous behavior. The child who insists upon having his own way and who employs every disagreeable means at his disposal to achieve his ends should feel some guilt at his babyish display. The child who has deliberately disobeyed his parents' safety rules on playing in the street also needs to feel some guilt about his behavior. The child who steals trinkets in the dime store, at an age when he would know the meaning of stealing, should also experience guilt for what he has done. The child who has lied to escape responsibility for a forbidden act needs to have some guilt for his moral evasion. In each of these instances and in hundreds of others of their kind, the child's guilt reactions, that is, his own moral repudiation of an act, will eventually serve to inhibit the impulse to repeat the act when the occasion for misconduct appears again.

In other words, the child needs to have some guilt feelings when he has performed a destructive act or has abandoned the accepted moral principles of his family and community, but in order to employ this guilt for constructive purposes, i.e., to inhibit the unacceptable behavior, the guilt feelings need to be appropriate to the situation and should not lead to self-punishing and self-torturing acts or thoughts that severely restrict the normal functions of the ego. It is enough for the child who throws stones at his enemy to feel sufficient guilt so that he stops throwing stones. He does not need to feel like a potential murderer and out of fear of his own aggressive impulses, repudiate all aggression like the little boy who could not even throw a ball. The corollary to this in parental training principles is: A child needs to feel our disapproval at certain times, but if our reaction is of such strength that the child feels worthless and despised for his offense, we have abused our power as parents and have created the possibility that exaggerated guilt feelings and self-hatred will play a part in this child's personality development. We want the child to develop enough guilt or remorse for his misconduct so that he can acquire the means for self-control, but there is no need to exaggerate the consequences of naughtiness and to develop excessive guilt feelings in order to develop such control.

Many parents feel troubled—guilty, in fact—at the thought of allowing a child to have guilt feelings. "Wouldn't it be better," a parent proposes, "to let the child feel that we are not criticizing or disapproving of *him*, but we are only criticizing his act?" Theoretically, such a child would not need to have guilt feelings to control his actions but would avoid the repetition of the criticized act because the act elicits parental disapproval. But how does this really work? Realistically, every child knows that when a piece of bad behavior has brought forth criticism from his parents *he* is out of favor, not his deed alone. When Julia makes scrambled eggs on the kitchen floor, we do not reproach the eggs for allowing themselves to be smashed, and we do not address our criticism to the act of egg-smashing as if it had been engineered by spirits. We address ourselves to Julia and our criticism is of her because she is responsible for smashing the eggs. All the fancy rhetoric does not change the fact that we disapprove of Julia in that moment. If we do not hold a child responsible for his own acts, if we treat the act as if it were divorced from the person, we only provide a ready-made system for evasion of responsibility. Since the child himself is all too ready to attribute his undesirable behavior to imaginary companions or supernatural causes that induced the eggs to smash themselves, we only perpetuate the child's own tendencies to disclaim his unwanted impulses and deeds. But sound education of the child must correct this tendency. A child must know that he causes his acts, that he is responsible for them, and it's difficult to see how a parental approach that separates doer from deed can educate conscience.

The product of such an education turned up in a *New Yorker* item while I was writing this.

OPPRESSED

THE SEVEN-YEAR-OLD SON OF A FRIEND OF OURS WAS RECENTLY REBUKED FOR MAKING DESIGNS IN CLAY UPON THE NEWLY PAINTED WALLS OF HIS PLAYROOM. "I'M GETTING SICK OF THIS," THE BOY COMPLAINED. "EVERYTHING I DO, YOU BLAME ON ME."

The sight of a remorseful child is felt as a personal reproach by many parents, today, who then follow a demonstration of disapproval to a mischievous child with a hasty and guilty hug and kiss. The situation where the child is supposed to have guilt feelings is curiously reversed in many homes where the parent develops guilt feelings instead. Now there are times when a parent can justifiably have guilt feelings about his own behavior toward a child—when he has over-reacted, made foolish threats, or unjustly criticized his child. But I am speaking of ordinary events in a family which require the parent to show disapproval or criticism of a child's misconduct, and even when such disapproval is justified by the child's behavior, we find parents who are made guilty by the manifestations of guilt feelings in the child.

Not long ago an intelligent and conscientious mother took issue with me on the matter of guilt feelings in child-training. She did not want her child to feel guilty about misbehavior. "I think it's far better to smack a child and get it over with. Clear the air. Then everyone feels better and it's done. When I was a child I much preferred my mother's spankings to my father's disapproval. All he had to do was look at me reproachfully and I felt miserable. With Mother you were naughty, you got a swift smack, and it was all over. All of us kids preferred Mother's smacks to Dad's way."

It's probably true that my friend as a child preferred her mother's swift smack to her father's reproach. But I think it is also true that many of the estimable qualities of conscience in this intelligent and deeply humane woman had come from father's reproach and owed little to mother's smacks. For father's reproach left the child with the feeling that she had not measured up to his good opinion of her and that she had allowed her own standards for herself to lapse. Father's reproach was matched by the little girl's self-reproach, accompanied by guilt feelings. We will grant that these feelings are uncomfortable, even painful, but they play a crucial role in conscience development. On the other hand, "Mother's smacks" left no residue of guilt feelings, no painful feelings to deal with within oneself. "I was naughty; I paid for it; now we are all square. The slate is clean." It clears the air, as our informant reported to us, but it leaves very little behind that can be used in the building of an effective conscience. Why is this? The discussion of this problem leads naturally into the larger area of the role of punishment in child-training.

re
spanking

THE PSYCHOLOGY OF PUNISHMENT.

THERE are, of course, many forms of punishment employed by parents in child-rearing. Punishment is often used synonymously with physical punishment, but when we speak of punishment here we are including many other categories. If a child is deprived of a privilege as a consequence for naughtiness, this is a punishment. If a child is sent up to his room for uncontrolled behavior, this, too, is a punishment. Any penalty, however mild, imposed by a parent upon his child is, of course, a punishment, and in this discussion we shall include all these categories and all gradations of punishment.

In theory, a punishment should "teach a lesson" or "correct." Therefore, in this study of the techniques of conscience-building, we should examine each of these methods in order to see what is learned by the child.

We might begin with spanking since it was this subject that led up to our consideration of punishments. In discussions with parents, I find this the most difficult of all subjects. At PTA meetings it is the subject that creates unrest and discomfort in the audience as every parent braces himself for anticipated criticism. For it appears that most parents spank their children sometimes, and nearly all the parents who spank their children feel guilty about it, and when the lecturer takes a position against spanking, all the parents who spank feel as if *they* are being spanked by the lecturer.

I don't believe in spanking parents, either. It is clear that I do not favor physical punishment for children and I intend to explain my views more fully, but for the moment let's just talk about parental feelings in the matter of spanking. Most parents, we find, do not have any convictions about spanking as a means of education and are embarrassed to find themselves employing a punishment that they can't really justify to themselves. Some parents, however, will defend spanking on the grounds that: "It's the only thing you can do at times," or "You've got to let them know you mean business," or "Sometimes they just ask for it," or "It clears the air," or "I was spanked when I was a kid and it never did me any harm." But we find that even the parents who justify spanking to themselves are defensive and embarrassed about it when you come right down to it. I suspect that deep in the memory of every parent are the feelings that had attended his own childhood spankings, the feelings of humiliation, of helplessness, of submission through fear. The parent who finds himself spanking his own child cannot dispel the ghosts of his own child-hood and uneasily reflects to himself that he is doing something to his child that had caused him the deepest resentment in his own early life.

But if we ask the question of any parent who spanks, "Does it work?" we will very likely get the answer, "Well, not really. But it works for a while anyway." For apart from all feelings on the subject, even its exponents cannot claim that this punishment teaches anything. At its worst, it is the only punishment that creates its own appetite, so to speak; it is self-perpetuating be-cause no learning takes place and the cycle of crime and punish-ment renews itself interminably.

So the "lessons" which a spanking are supposed to teach some-how fail to become integrated in the form of conscience. But wouldn't the memory of the punishment serve as a warning the next time the child is impelled to repeat his misdeed? It might, of course, but then the motive for controlling the naughty impulse is a motive that comes from the outside, a fear of external author-ity and a fear of punishment, and we will find that a conscience which functions on this basis is not a very reliable conscience. If fear of punishment from the outside, instead of the child's own guilt feelings, sets off the danger signal, there are a number of subterfuges open to the child. He may only need to assure him-self that he will not be found out in order to pursue his mischief. Or, calculating the pleasure-pain risks, he may decide to have his fun even if he has to pay for it later. But the child who is capable of developing guilt feelings when he considers doing something which is "bad," has a signal system within himself which will warn him and inhibit the act. Unlike the child whose control system is "outside," this child with a conscience does not need a policeman around in order to control his behavior. The child with a conscience has his policeman inside.

There are a number of other possibilities in learning which spanking provides, none of which are intended by parents. A child may learn how to avoid successfully any guilt feelings for bad behavior by setting up a cycle in which the punishment cancels the "crime" and the child, having paid for his mischief, is free to repeat the act another time without attendant guilt feelings. Some children have an elaborate accounting system which permits them to go into debt on the "sin" side of the ledger up to a certain amount and pay off periodically on the punishment side by getting themselves spanked. With the ledger balanced, such a child can make a fresh start and go into debt again. "Sometimes they just ask for it!" say the defenders of spanking. This, in itself, should serve as a warning to parents. The child who does everything possible to provoke a spanking is a child who is carrying a secret debt on the sin side of the ledger which the parent is invited to wipe out by means of a spanking. A spanking is just what this child does *not* need!

I recall a six-year-old boy named Freddie who stole coins from corner newspaper boxes, and occasionally relieved his schoolmates of their lunch money but who managed his thefts so adroitly that he was rarely discovered. When he was finally caught, he admitted to a large number of thefts in the preceding months and seemed quite untroubled about the whole business. His parents were as disturbed about his lack of guilt as they were about the thefts themselves. How had he managed these thefts without guilt feelings? During his periodic stealing forays he did not seem troubled or anxious at home. Instead he became more aggressive than usual, picking fights with his brother, provoking his father's anger through incessant petty and irritating tactics or through negative, obstinate behavior of one kind or another which finally culminated in a spanking—a longed-for spanking—we were able to see later. Only later, when the parents, upon my advice, gave up the spankings and employed other means of helping Freddie establish controls was this child able to experience guilt feelings for his misbehavior and finally to acquire the means for controlling his own behavior.

While Freddie may be considered a mild delinquent, it is worth mentioning that many non-delinquent children who are disciplined chiefly through spanking acquire the kind of bookkeeping approach to misconduct which we observed in Freddie. There are children, otherwise normal, who depend upon spankings to relieve their sense of guilt. "Every once in a while," says a father, "something gets into that little guy. He eggs me on, gets more and more stubborn about some unimportant thing, really just asking for it, and when I finally lose my temper and give him a swat, he calms down and then he's my best friend. It's the only thing that works with him when he gets in that mood." This father was defending spanking when he described this situation, one that sounds fairly familiar to us, by the way. But the child who provokes punishment in this way, quite obviously "asking for it," is the child who is using spanking to get rid of guilt feelings in another department of his ledger. The child may not know this—very probably he does not. All that he experiences is an irresistible urge to be punished. The spanking becomes part of a system and is required to balance the ledger. The parent who finds his child begging for punishment should not become a partner in the system. It would be much better to put a stop to this punishment-seeking by locating the causes. Often they are not real crimes like Freddie's but crimes of the imagination like Jimmy's. You remember how Jimmy provoked his father unmercifully for the whole evening that followed the expression of the awful thought that his father might die. Whatever the reason for "asking for punishment" the parent who cooperates with a spanking will only serve the system and not the moral education of his child.

Many grown men and women might feel impelled to argue strongly against the case I have set up. "I was spanked as a child," says a mother, "and I do not have an unreliable conscience as a result of spanking." As it happens, this mother is right, and yet her statement does not stand as a defense for spanking. For her conscience was acquired through a strong love for her parents and a desire to be loved and esteemed by them. The moral lessons were not achieved through the parental spankings as such but through the love relationship. Here we can assume the spankings did not damage the relationship of child and parents and did not lead to disturbances of conscience because of the strength of the fundamental ties. But we cannot credit the spankings with the achievement of conscience. We can conclude by saying that when the relationship between a child and his parents is fundamentally sound, a spanking may not be damaging to conscience development, but *it does not promote such development either.*

With all sympathy for the trials and harassments in the life of a parent, and with understanding of the sense of helplessness that may lead a good parent to spank or punish in ways that he does not believe in, I still feel that there are better and more successful means of teaching control. When parents understand these other measures, and can employ them in discipline, they find that they need not resort, through helplessness, to physical means of control.

But are all forms of punishment by parents to be put in the same category with spanking? No, I think there is a place for punishment in child-rearing. Some types of punishment can teach moral and social values and may be said to serve conscience education. Let's examine some of the punishments that are commonly used in child rearing and see how they work or do not work for building self-control.

It may be necessary at times for parents or teachers to deprive a child of a privilege following some demonstration of unacceptable behavior. Now the principle involved in such a punishment is not, or should not be, revenge or retaliation on the part of the educator. If this punishment is to teach then it must be set forth as a reasonable and logical consequence of misbehavior. Let's take a simple example: Margaret who is six is in one of her unreasonable moods. It's Sunday afternoon. She had wanted to go to the park with her parents and little sister, but rain is threatening and it seems best to stay home. Mother tries to get her occupied in drawing, then in sewing doll clothes, then in cutting and pasting pictures in her scrap-book. Any of these activities would normally have absorbed Margaret, but today nothing suits her. She grows more and more irritable and whiny. She taunts the baby and snatches toys from her. She tries to switch off the television set while her father is watching a program that interests him. She then tries to drown out the program through singing loudly and shrilly. When reproved, she becomes more whiny and more recalcitrant, invents fresh ways of annoying her parents and molesting the baby until the family living room has been turned into bedlam. Finally her father tells her severely that she will have to leave and go up to her room. When she thinks that she can control herself she can come down to join the family again.

Here the educational objective of the punishment is to demonstrate to Margaret that if she cannot control her behavior and must disturb the family she will have to be temporarily excluded from family activity. As a punishment it is a reasonable and logical consequence for the kind of conduct Margaret had demonstrated. It says in effect, "We cannot have you disturb the whole family with your negative and obstinate behavior (*whatever* the deeper meaning of this behavior can be) and you are asked to leave the room until you feel you can return as a reasonable member of the family, at which time you will be welcome to join us again." The logic will not be missed by Margaret at the age of six and the justice of the punishment should also be apparent to her, at least after she has calmed down.

But now suppose the father had altered this punishment in certain ways. Suppose he had said, "Now go up to your room and stay there until dinner time" (and let's suppose it is now three). In this case Margaret would be asked to stew in her room for three hours and during this time she would probably occupy herself with revenge fantasies instead of remorse for having behaved like an infant. In this instance no learning would have taken place through the punishment. We can easily find a principle in this: If the punishment is excessive, that is, exceeds a child's tolerance, it will have no beneficial effects and will only feed the child's sense of being unjustly treated and give rise to hostile and vengeful feelings. No child can profit from this kind of extreme exile. Even a half hour may be too long for most children to sustain a sense of guilt for having disturbed the family's peace or, for that matter even to retain the memory of the incidents that had led to banishment. But why put a time limit on this exile? Margaret's father's conditions are simple and leave some degree of control in the hands of Margaret. When *she* feels that she can control herself she can come back and join the family. This may mean five minutes in her room or fifteen or more, whatever is required by her personal cooling-off needs under the circumstances. When she has calmed down and regained her reasonable self and the ability to control herself, she is welcome to return.

Let's examine some of the other possibilities in the handling of this Sunday afternoon crisis. Suppose Margaret's parents attempted to reason with her during this demonstration, or suppose they tried to get to the bottom of things, tried to find out what was bothering her to get her to behave in this unreasonable fashion. It is certainly desirable, whenever possible, to locate causes and it is certainly desirable to appeal to reason. But the chances are that when a child is quite out of control there is not enough of his reasonable self available to clear up misunderstandings or to appraise the irrational behavior. Many well-intentioned parents feel obliged to pursue the appeal to reason with all odds against them and we have all witnessed the family drama in which a parent confronts a screaming or densely obstinate child with a logical examination of his position. The appeal to reason had better be postponed until the tantrum is over and reason has returned at least in part. In the case of Margaret, for example, there might be a good point in talking with her about her behavior *after* she has calmed down and she is in a position to look at herself. Such a talk, if it is not calculated by parents to "rub it in," or start an argument all over again, can also serve the education for self-control, for when the child can examine his irrational behavior by means of reason he has taken a step toward control of his irrational behavior.

Let's imagine other punishments which Margaret's father might have employed. Let's suppose Margaret was very proud of her new bike and her father, knowing how much she loved it, chose to penalize Margaret for her behavior by taking away biking privileges for a few days. In the heat of the moment many parents blindly grope for the privilege that is most prized by a child and use the deprivation of this privilege as the punishment. But on reflection we can see that deprivation of biking privileges has no logical connection with Margaret's behavior on Sunday afternoon; it appears to the child like a retaliatory act and not as the reasonable consequence of misconduct. There is nothing to be learned from such a punishment and it may only feed the child's sense of being unjustly treated and cause him to erase the memory of the events that had provoked the punishment. On the other hand, if Margaret had abused her biking privileges or her parents' safety rules, deprivation of the bike for a day or two or three would certainly make sense. The same criticism applies to the indiscriminate deprivation of television for any and all offenses, a favorite punishment these days. While many parents claim that it is a useful form of discipline in their families, its indiscriminate application teaches nothing and only serves as a weapon in the hands of parents. If we appreciate the principle of learning in discipline, then the withdrawal of television privileges should be reserved as far as possible for offenses and abuses that concern television viewing.

We find that all learning is made more effective through the establishment of logical connections between events and ideas. This is why a punishment to be effective, to teach, must also try to establish logical connections. At the age when the child's own reasoning ability takes ascendancy over magic thinking, the child himself wants to see logical connections between his acts and their consequences. When my friend Ann was five she took her kindergarten teacher sharply to task for a disciplinary action that ignored logic. For several days Ann's mother had noticed that her daughter, an enthusiastic painter, was not bringing home her paintings for the home bulletin board. When Ann was questioned about this she answered obliquely that she had not painted anything. After a few days Ann's mother found an occasion to talk with the kindergarten teacher when she called for Ann at school one afternoon. Ann, she was told, had not been painting for several days. Ann was being punished for talking during nap periods (!). Each day Ann had been warned that if she talked at nap time she would have to be deprived of the class painting period. Each day Ann had talked anyway. At this point Ann appeared and the teacher invited her to come over to discuss this matter. "Well," said Ann tartly, "I don't see any connection between talking at nap-time and painting." "Well, then," said her teacher, taken aback, "what would *you* do with a little girl who insisted upon talking during nap time?" "Well," said Ann, "if I had a little girl who talked during nap time, I'd ask her to take her nap someplace else or make her leave the room, but I don't see any connection between talking and painting!" It made much more sense to Ann that if she disturbed her neighbors at nap time she should be separated from them as a punishment. But to deprive her of her painting was not only illogical but unjust. Out of resentment and an outraged sense of justice she had pursued her talking at nap time even though she knew the punishment that awaited.

But there are also times when the logical punishment is *not* the best punishment or the correct punishment. Consider this punishment: When Nancy was seven she got her first public library card and trudged two miles once or twice a week to the nearest branch library to borrow books. She was a passionate reader and the trips to the library were the high points of her life. But she soon became careless about returning books, and library fines mounted up at times. Nancy's father finally became very angry about her lack of responsibility and after repeated warnings, took away her library card for a month. Now this was a "logical" punishment but a very poor one. First of all, it was excessive and extreme. For while carelessness and irresponsibility may require parental handling, failure to return library books is not a major crime and does not require the most extreme penalty. (For a book-loving child this is like being sent to Siberia.) On principle, *any* punishment of a month's duration is too long for a seven-year-old child. Second, the father was employing a punishment that ran counter to an educational objective. A child's pleasure in reading is one of the most promising signs in his early intellectual development. If we deprive Nancy of her reading and make this new-found world the battleground on which "responsibility" is to be won, and if arguments and contests of will and penalties and moral object lessons are all to be derived from this new world, we may find after a while that the pleasure in books diminishes and the two-mile trek to the library seems very long to this small girl. The "logical" punishment becomes absurd.

Most seven year olds are not able to take full responsibility for details like returning books. They need reminding. Keeping an eye on the library books of younger children (and sometimes older children) is one of the clerical chores that goes along with the job of parenthood. When children are a little older than Nancy and have an allowance that covers recreational items, we can expect them to pay their library fines out of their own funds and a more responsible attitude toward book borrowing is not so difficult to achieve. In the meantime the sums required for bailing out a seven or eight year old who has neglected to return a library book are really not very large. Even at the high estimate of fifty cents a month, where else can you get such a bargain?

There are other instances, too, when the logical punishment may be a poor one. Larry, at five, frequently acts up at the family dinner table. He may play with his food in a most unappetizing way, or sling peas at his brother, or make noises or clown, or in a dozen other ways make himself unwelcome at the table. On several occasions his father has ordered him to leave the table and has sent him upstairs without his dinner. Larry then stomps off in a rage and instead of learning a lesson from this drastic punishment, he sulks for several hours and plots revenge in his room. What's wrong with this punishment?

It's the deprivation of food that brings on the trouble. Food has a highly complex symbolic meaning to all of us. It reaches down to the psychological depths of personality. If we involve food in punishment we may touch off a kind of psychological chain reaction that produces more feeling than we would expect as the result of the immediate situation. Even if the child is not really very hungry at the time the punishment is administered, the symbolic meaning of deprivation of food will produce fury, will touch off fantasies in which the parents are monsters who will even let a child go hungry, and the whole episode produces such outrage that the intended lesson is lost.

If a child's behavior at the table is intolerable, as Larry's behavior was, he might be warned that if he cannot control himself he will be asked to have his dinner alone in another room, and if the behavior continues, the punishment should be carried out. This is a logical consequence of dinner table disturbance that does not carry with it the highly charged feelings of food deprivation. We are saying in effect, "If you cannot behave at the family table, we'd rather not have you with us tonight." In a way it is a more logical as well as more reasonable punishment than food deprivation, since it emphasizes the social aspect of family dining.

"But," says a mother, "I really don't think my five year old would care if he were to dine by himself!" In that case we need to look for something else. For, of course, if family dining is not regarded as a pleasure by a child, deprivation of it will not matter to him either. In this case the family had better examine the climate of the family dinner table. If the dinner table is the place where family tensions are discharged, if parents are tired and irritable and little interested in the talk of small children, if old conflicts about food, eating or not eating are revived at this time, then clowning and messing with food may be one of the ways in which a child discharges his tension. Here, punishment of the child is not the answer, but a correction of the situation that produces this behavior.

But now to return to principles in punishment: We have seen that the most effective punishments are those which teach through presenting logical consequences for misbehavior. At the same time, a punishment, however "logical" may fail to instruct if it is too severe, exceeds the child's tolerance, or negates other more important educational aims. A punishment, however mild in principle, may lose its effect completely if it is extended over a long period of time. Deprivation of biking privileges may be a mild punishment for disobeying safety rules, but if the child is young and the punishment extends for several days we may wind up with a hostile child and not a penitent one. If an eight or nine year old is asked to pay for a broken window out of his allowance of thirty-five cents a week, he will be in debt for so many weeks or months that he will not even remember after a while why a deduction is made from his allowance. A child who is out of favor with his parents for behaving badly, may feel guilty and remorseful for an hour afterwards, but if the coolness extends for many hours he will simply feel resentful.

And last, there are times when the greatest parental wisdom may lie in applying no punishment at all. Consider a situation like this one: Four-year-old George has been warned many times by his parents that he must not throw stones when he gets into fights with his friends. Then the inevitable accident occurs. In fighting with his friend Sam, a sharp stone strikes the other child right above the eye and George witnesses the horror of blood streaming down the child's face, a mother summoned by her screaming child, and his little friend carried off for an emergency trip to the hospital. It is a deep cut that requires stitches and George fully realizes that if the stone had cut a half inch lower Sam might have lost the sight of his eye. George is filled with horror and guilt at what he has done, and what he might have done. Should George be punished by his parents? There is no need to teach George a lesson on the danger of throwing stones.

[handwritten margin note: What about the need to feel punished? (see next pg)]

He has seen the tragic consequences. His own guilt feelings are punishment enough. Nor do we want to relieve his guilt feelings through a punishment administered by parents. It is much better that he be left with the full impact of his own guilt.

Having examined some of the methods of punishment and their place in conscience building, we return full circle to the point from which we started. In the last analysis, whether any method of discipline "works" will depend upon the fundamental relationship of a child to his parents. When a parent says, "But *nothing* seems to work with my child; he does as he pleases!" the answer does not lie in a fancier technique of discipline, but an examination of the parent-child relationship. If a parent finds himself overwhelmed with "discipline problems" with one or another of his children, it is well to sit down and consider what is going amiss, what is disturbing the relationship between child and parents. Sometimes it is a temporary disturbance in the relationship caused by the birth of a new baby, or a new step in development, or a new circumstance such as the beginning of nursery school or kindergarten. But if a child presents problems of discipline over a long period of time, parents need to reappraise the whole situation either by themselves or with outside counsel. Punishment is not the answer.

THE ACQUISITION OF MORAL VALUES.

THERE is another type of moral education that depends not so much upon the handling of overt behavior in children as other means of transmitting attitudes from parent to child. While children certainly acquire parental attitudes as the consequence of parental reactions to their overt behavior, a rather large educational job is done through the day-by-day assimilation of attitudes that comes simply through close association among human beings who love each other. The example of honesty in parents goes further toward the development of honesty in the child than mere disciplinary action for non-truth telling. Parental attitudes toward the weak, the crippled, the suffering will be incorporated more readily through assimilation than through the Sunday School donation or the contribution of pennies to a charitable drive. Parental revulsion against the murder of man or the murder of civilized values is a more eloquent teacher than the sermon.

Parents today appear to have much uncertainty about their roles as moral guides. Part of this uncertainty is a reaction against the fear techniques that were employed in moral teaching in former generations. Since today's parent does not wish to teach his child moral attitudes through threats or exaggerated horror or fearful warnings he seems afraid to show any moral reactions to his child as if he might then create excessive guilt feelings in the child. This means that many parents who have firm moral beliefs about lying, stealing, murder and destruction fail to transmit them to their children in a profound and meaningful way. Parents tolerate the moral lapses or even the absence of moral principles in their children way beyond the period when we can expect a child to have incorporated moral values in his own personality.

I recall a six year old who cheerfully admitted to me that he and his little friends pilfered things from the dime store. It was a kind of game they played. None of these children needed or even wanted the things they stole. I asked my small friend if his parents knew about his stealing. Yes, his mother had found out a couple of times when he had brought home some things. What had mother said? "She said it wasn't nice and I shouldn't do it again!" I had a mental picture of this mother, a very nice woman, incidentally, quite incapable of dishonest acts herself, bending over backward in this situation in order to be "an understanding mother," "a non-punitive mother" and really being quite ineffectual because she was afraid to transmit her own feelings about the situation. Later I talked with the mother. How had she felt when her child came home with these things he had stolen? "Frankly,

I felt horrible. I was disappointed in my child, disappointed in myself and it was all I could do to bring myself to talk with him about it." "Did you tell him how you felt about it and how disappointed you were in him?" "Oh, no!" said this mother, really quite proud of herself for being so objective and understanding. "After all stealing from the dime store is not so serious. Don't all children go through stages like that?"

Now, of course, stealing from a dime store is not a major crime. And probably every child has stolen at one time or another. And this child is not a delinquent or a child who is severely disturbed, so we do not need to attach special significance to his acts. But how is this child to acquire a moral attitude toward stealing that will successfully prevent him from pilfering if his parents do not reveal their own moral attitude toward stealing and in fact treat this act with the same degree of casual admonishment that they would treat a lapse in table manners? Of course, it would also be wrong to threaten a child, as parents did in other times, with police action, detention homes or hell-fire and cause a small culprit to feel that he was a dangerous criminal. We can teach moral attitudes without resorting to such cruel methods. It should be enough for a parent who has a strong relationship with his child to express his feelings about his child's stealing, to show his disappointment and his deep concern that his child should do such a thing, in brief, to get his own moral attitude across to his child in such a way that the child can feel it and make use of it in developing his own moral attitude toward stealing. This does not apply, of course, to the parent who has an ungovernable temper, or the parent who is convinced that a theft from the dime store augurs a criminal career for his child. Here, the moral anxiety of such parents had better not be expressed to a child in the terms that the parent feels them. But for most of us ordinary parents who have moral convictions without moral hysteria, it seems safe enough to get across to our children just how we and other civilized people do feel about such things.

Another aspect of parental uncertainty in moral education is seen in the attitude of parents toward the crime and horror fare that is provided by television, movies and comic books. Most parents deplore this stuff; some defend it as a harmless means of discharge of aggression. Very few parents who deplore, however, are willing to take a stand—really a moral stand—on their children's viewing and reading tastes. Now a child who is exposed to the education of these stories of murder, violence and sadism will acquire a set of values that are certainly at variance—to say the least—with those values that his parents desire for him. After witnessing a dozen or more screen murders in an afternoon and evening in his own living room, day after day for so and so many years, he cannot hold sacred the idea of a human life, nor can he regard the brutal ending of a life as a tragedy. At best he will acquire a spurious moral lesson intoned by the sponsor while a janitor sweeps the corpses off the stage: "Crime does not pay!" Now the moral principle behind the civilized view of taking a life is *not* that it "does not pay," i.e., "you'll get caught in the end." This is like the morality of the two year old, the child who has not yet acquired a conscience, who judges the "rightness" and "wrongness" of an act according to whether he gets caught or not. It is also the morality of the delinquent. But the civilized man abhors the idea of murder because he exalts the value of human life and because the destruction of another man's life would be morally impossible for him even if there were no possibility of discovery of the crime.

The child who is glutted on television and comic book fare will have a hard time discovering for himself that his society regards a human life as sacred. Who can hold a tragic view of death when the static of pistol shots assaults the ear from 4:00 p.m. to bed-time and the cheery voice of the sponsor rises over bloody screams and death rattles to bring the message of the hearty breakfast? The parental voice, if it is heard at all above this din, will have a tough time competing with the education of the screen.

But most often the parental voice is not heard at all. For although most parents detest these stories and their degradation of human beings and human values, they also tolerate them. While they hold their own values and live by them they do not raise objections to Johnny's other education and Johnny is afforded the privilege of most nice children in nice homes of being entertained and educated by gangsters, dope addicts, sadists and morons in his own living room. By this I do *not* mean that such programs are an education for delinquency. Delinquents are not made this way. But I do mean that human values are debased in these stories, and in the endless repetition of these stories and their themes, they undergo some debasement in the child's mind, too.

I'm tempted to follow these ideas a little further and cite an example. Some time ago on Lincoln's birthday, the story of Lincoln's last years was dramatized on television. I knew a number of children who had seen it and the reactions were various. Of course, Abraham Lincoln is not a culture hero for today's child. He led a dull life by the standards of modern youth. There were no feats of physical bravery, he killed neither bears nor Indians, and the deeds of moral courage of this shy and humble man impressed no child that I know. In fact, it seemed to me that the shyness and awkwardness of the man made him a particularly embarrassing kind of hero for a child today, for whom shyness is one of the deadly sins—being so ungroupy and leading so surely to unpopularity. Knowing all this, I was surprised at the enthusiasm I encountered in the children who reported they had seen Abraham Lincoln's story on television. After listening to these reports I began to understand.

You see, there was this guy named Booth and right out in the middle of a play he shot the President and escaped. This was the biggest murder story ever. A true story, too. The daring of this guy named Booth in shooting a president awed the most cynical and bored of television's crime-sated junior viewers. Of course the F.B.I. (!) hunted down this guy and caught him (a completely satisfactory end, demonstrating that even in Lincoln's day, way back in the time of the dinosaurs, crime did not pay and the F.B.I. always got its man). I asked one fellow, an eight year old, how he felt when the President was killed. "Well, that's the chance you have to take when you get to be President," he said philosophically. "That's why I wouldn't like to be President."

None of my young friends had viewed this play as a tragedy. No one reported sorrow or even a child's indignation at the murder of a great man. But these were not completely insensitive kids. How had they all missed the point of this drama? I had the impression they had viewed this play with a set of stereotypes acquired through years of education in "the crime story." The writers of television and movie murder scripts, the comic book writers, have neither the imagination nor the time to invest their murder victims with a personality or a significant life. For all practical purposes the victim is a corpse before he is murdered. Since his life has no significance for the audience, his death is of no consequence either. Of course, there is a side benefit to the audience in having a victim who is a cipher. If the victim has no significance for the audience, his murder can be "enjoyed" without complicating emotional reactions. A literary work has the opposite intention. If murder is dealt with as a literary theme, it succeeds as a work if it disturbs us, if it arouses complex emotional reactions on behalf of the victim and his murderer as well. In this way a literary work deepens our humanity. But our small friends had never been given the possibility of caring about the victim of a murder, of experiencing pain or sorrow or grief for the cruel death of a man, even if that man is a fiction. And because the children had never, or rarely, met this experience through the formula of the murder story, they were incapable of reacting to the tragedy of the murder of Lincoln.

Do I appear to dwell upon this point excessively? You see I regard the child's television and comic book world as part of his moral environment. Let me reiterate: I do *not* mean that this world causes a child to become immoral or delinquent, an impossible feat for a cheap story since moral education or the lack of it derives from more fundamental sources in the relationship of a child to his parents. I mean this: that the child who is exposed regularly, monotonously to the formula of the crime story, the meaningless life, the violent and meaningless death, a hunt, a capture, a sentence and an idiot moral lesson, will suffer a blunting of moral sensibility because this formula reduces human values to absurdity. It is superfluous to mention that the child's imagination likewise is dulled and flattened by the monotony and emptiness of these formula stories. But it is worth mentioning in this context because moral growth is also dependent upon the imagination. When a child's story world provides him with limitless possibilities of experience through the imagination, allows him to deepen his understanding of human nature and the human situation, his moral sense is deepened also. But the television and comic book story world restrict the imagination of the child and inhibit moral development by reducing human problems to a formula.

Let's not entertain the argument that fairy tales also employ simple formulas and add nothing to the child's understanding of human nature. The fairy-tale world is frankly an invented world and makes no attempt to represent reality or the human situation. The child accepts it on these terms and after the age of four or five does not draw any implications from this fantastic world for the conduct of people in the real world. A frankly fantastic world can be easily put in its place by the small child and enjoyed with complete abandonment because "it can't happen," "it's just pretend." But the television film, and comic book story attempts to make real, or realistically represent, an imaginary world, and even when it deals with completely fantastic happenings in outer space, for example, it employs devices to "make it real" and in this way makes it more difficult for the child to divorce these happenings from the real world.

For all these reasons I think we need to take the child's television, movie and comic book entertainment very seriously as educational influences. We need to consider what it means to a child who receives a moral education from his parents and is entertained in his own living room, with the consent of his parents, by a constant flow of visitors from the underworld and outer space whose views on society and human values would have been barely tolerated in a Neanderthal cave. We do not ordinarily invite such visitors into our living rooms and we do not regard murder and brutality as home entertainments. If we are earnest and moral parents, we have spent many years in building an attitude in our children toward raw aggression, violence and sadism. We have considered it necessary that our small children give up the primitive pleasure in destructive acts and acquire a civilized attitude of revulsion toward sadism. But when murder and violence are offered as an entertainment diet, how is the child helped to give up pleasure in the destructive act?

Many parents argue that such entertainment provides a harmless form of release of the child's aggressive impulses. This view derives from a mistaken notion of the role of aggression in personality development. While we grant that the child has aggressive impulses and aggressive fantasies even without the aid of the ready-made fantasy world of television and comic books, we do not have to provide a constant means of discharge of those impulses. As we have seen in earlier discussions, the raw discharge of aggression does not serve personality development and the personality that deals with aggression on the basis of impulse-discharge is operating on the simplest, most primitive basis. It is our job to modify these impulses in the child, to provide indirect satisfactions for aggressive impulses and socially valued goals for these tendencies. A certain amount of aggressive energy goes into learning, creative work, the attainment of personal goals, but when we examine these sublimated activities we see that the raw material "aggression" has undergone such modification in the service of these higher social aims that we can scarcely recognize them as "aggression." It can even be argued that the more we provide the child with primitive means of discharge of aggression, the *less likely* he is to seek modified and sublimated goals for his aggression.

At any rate, it would be difficult to argue that any child "needs" four or five hours a day of bloody entertainment for the satisfaction of his suppressed aggressive longings, and the consistently low level of this entertainment raises the question whether he "needs" any of this at all. The best we can say is that an occasional entertainment of this type may do no harm and will not have the stifling effect on imagination and values that comes with a steady diet.

If we take our children's education seriously, we must admit that there is something grotesque in the situation where we crusade for better schools, better teachers, libraries, and museums and turn over a good share of our children's education to the manufacturers of breakfast food. So it seems to me that parents who prefer their own brand of education can justifiably exercise the same supervision over this commercial education as they do over any other department of the child's education. Since parents have no voice in the commercial education of their children as they do in their own tax-supported institutions of learning, their supervision of television programs, radio, films and comic books necessarily becomes a form of censorship. This means that the parent goes to some trouble to acquaint himself with the subject matter of these programs and the content of comic books and permits or does not permit his child's viewing or reading on the basis of his judgment.

I know that many parents pale at the prospect of censorship and feel themselves quite unequal to the protests of their young. They flinch before the argument, "But Susie's mother lets her, and Jimmy can buy all the comic books he wants," and the wavering parent frequently submits on the basis, "After all why not?" and "Why should my child feel different?" To these parents who are able to withstand such arguments I offer consolation from clinical practice. I have never encountered a child who acquired a neurosis as the result of a parent's firm and tactful censorship and supervision of his viewing and reading habits. I have never seen a good relationship between parents and children damaged by the exercise of this parental prerogative. On the contrary, children who have a sound relationship to their parents usually regard supervision as a parental right. Furthermore, in the event that a child feels "different" from his neighbors because he has not had the privilege of viewing the machine-gunning of a bank clerk by a thug, or has not shared the excitement of a comic book portraying exotic forms of torture, I think the parent need not trouble himself. This difference can be endured. The brief unhappiness that follows the denial of the appetite for sadism is also an endurable sorrow. The child will bear no scars on his psyche and the human race may profit by it.

THE RIGHT TO FEEL.

EARLY one morning I received a telephone call from a friend—the mother of a five-year-old boy. "I'm calling from upstairs," she said in a low voice: "so Greg won't hear this." There was a pause. "Ernest died this morning! What shall I tell Greg?" "How terrible!" I said. "But who is Ernest?" "Ernest is Greg's hamster!" she said. "This will break his heart. I don't know how to tell him. Bill is going to stop off at the pet shop on his way home from work tonight and pick up a new hamster, but I just dread breaking the news to Greg. Please tell me what to say to him." "Why don't you tell him that his hamster died?" I said. "Died!" said my friend, shrinking at my crudity. "What I want to know is how I can break the news gently to him and spare him the pain of this whole experience! I thought I would tell him that Ernest went to heaven. Would it be all right to tell him that?" "Only if you're sure that Ernest went to heaven," I said in my best consulting-room voice. "Oh, stop!" my friend begged. "This is very serious. I don't mean the hamster. I mean this is Greg's first experience with death. I don't want him to be hurt."

"All right," I said. "Then what right do we have to deprive Greg of his feelings? Why isn't he entitled to his grief over the death of his pet? Why can't he cry and why can't he feel the full measure of pain that comes with the discovery that death is an end and that Ernest is no more?" "But he's only a child!" said my friend. "How can he possibly know what death means?" "But isn't this how he will know what death means? Do we ever know more about death than this—the reaction to the loss of someone loved?"

And so we argued, my friend wanting to prevent her son from feeling a loss and I defending Greg's human rights in feeling a loss. I think I finally convinced Greg's mother when I told her that Greg would be better able to endure the loss of his pet if we allowed him to realize the experience fully, to feel all he needed to feel.

In our efforts to protect children from painful emotions we may deprive them of their own best means of mastering painful experiences. Mourning, even if it is mourning for a dead hamster, is a necessary measure for overcoming the effects of loss. A child who is not allowed feelings of grief over a pet or a more significant loss is obliged to fall back on more primitive measures of defense, to deny the pain of loss, for example, and to feel nothing. If a child were consistently reared on this basis, deprived of the possibility of experiencing grief, he would become an impoverished person, without quality or depth in his emotional life. We need to respect a child's right to experience a loss fully and deeply. This means, too, that we do not bury the dead pet and rush to the pet store for a replacement. This is a devaluation of a child's love. It is like saying to him, "Don't feel badly; your love is not important; all hamsters, all dogs, all cats are replaceable, and you can love one as well as another." But if all loved things are readily replaceable what does a child learn about love or loss? The time for replacing the lost pet is when mourning has done its work and the child himself is ready to attach himself to a new animal.

Other stories come to mind which illustrate the problems of parents in dealing with the painful emotions of children. I once knew a little boy who was unable to cry and reacted to loss and to separations from loved persons with an inscrutable indifference, although he regularly produced allergic symptoms at such times. Often he spoke to me about his grandfather whom he had loved dearly and who died when my patient was five. He had many memories of his grandfather and spoke of him with much affection, but he had no memory of the grandfather's death or the year that followed his death. Neither was there any emotion attached to the idea of grandfather's death. But the death of the grandfather had been a great calamity in this child's family and the circumstances of the death were tragic in the extreme. Why was nothing of this remembered? And why was there no emotion attached to the loss of the grandfather or to death or separation from loved persons? All of this was exceedingly complex, but one very significant factor was the reaction of the child's mother at the time of the grandfather's death. Her own grief had been nearly unsupportable, but she was determined not to break down in the presence of the children: "It would make things harder for them." With heroic self-discipline she contained her feelings and presented a façade of her accustomed self to the children. With this I could understand my patient's strange reaction to death and loss. It was not "indifference" as it appeared on the surface, but an identification with his mother's outward behavior at the time of his grandfather's death. Since mother had not permitted her own grief to be revealed, the child behaved as if grief were an impermissible emotion. His suppressed longing to cry could only be satisfied by the symptomatic weeping that accompanied his allergy. It would have been much better for this child if his mother had not concealed her grief from him, for if he could have shared her grief in some way he would have received permission, as it were, to have his own feelings, and mourning for the loved grandfather would have helped him to overcome the shock of his death.

Many times, quite unconsciously, we cut off a child's feelings because they are so painful to us. I think now of Doug, a six year old, who had terrible anxiety dreams and wet his bed each night but presented a day-time picture of a cheerful, buoyant carefree little boy. He insisted that in the day-time he wasn't afraid of anything and never thought of scary things. He was actually being quite truthful, it turns out. Other children hate having their teeth drilled at the dentist's. Not Doug. He liked it. How come? "I always get a chocolate sundae afterward." "But even so, drilling hurts and don't you worry about that, Doug?" "Oh, no. I never think about how it's gonna hurt. I just think about the chocolate sundae." Other kids might worry about an appendectomy. But Doug didn't. "All I think about is all the presents I'll get when I'm in the hospital." Whenever unpleasant subjects appeared in our talks together he automatically switched to his Index of Pleasant Topics and began to talk about the baseball game he was going to tomorrow, the birthday party next Saturday or the new electric train he had just received. When I saw him once on the morning after a particularly terrifying dream that had kept him awake half the night, he could not bring himself to talk about the dream but spent the better part of an hour talking about his new bike.

Now, of course, if Doug were able to worry about the dentist and the appendectomy and other unpleasant events *before* they occurred, he would not be the sort of fellow who has recurrent anxiety dreams as his chief symptom. For some reason, we had to assume, he did not build up the anticipatory anxiety that would help him to meet crises. It was in the anxiety dreams that he experienced the anticipatory anxiety that was omitted in waking life. We learned that one of the important determinants in his unusual way of handling anxiety was his parents' way of helping him meet danger from the earliest days on.

They were good parents and devoted parents and Doug was their first child. Even when he was a baby they found themselves very upset by any of the usual manifestations of distress or pain or anxiety. Their impulse at such times was to step in quickly and offer a distraction or an amusement or something that would provide immediate solace. "Don't cry, dear. Look, look. See the pretty bird! Here are Daddy's keys to play with. Here's a cookie." Later the same principle was employed in the handling of many of Doug's fears or his encounters with unpleasant circumstances. He was educated not to cry or react to the shot in the doctor's office by the promise of surprises, something very pleasant, immediately afterwards. The educational principle was "Let's not think about the nasty shot. Let's just think about the nice surprise afterwards." Or a variation: "Let's not think how lonesome it will be when Mother and Daddy are on their trip. Let's just think about the presents and the surprises they will bring back."

Now it's probably true that nearly every parent has sometimes employed such tactics in helping a child meet an unpleasant experience, but in the case of Doug's parents this was truly an educational principle applied broadly and fairly consistently to the handling of every circumstance where anxiety might develop. His parents moved in so swiftly to prevent anxiety from developing that the child scarcely had a chance to become aware of it himself. He could not prepare for danger by developing anticipatory anxiety because this was not "allowable"; it was so painful to the parents. Gradually, as we see, he acquired the parents' method of handling his anxiety and made it his own. Everytime anticipatory anxiety might have emerged into consciousness he substituted a pleasant thought for the dreaded event or the danger. In this way both Doug and his parents were spared unpleasant feelings, but Doug was also deprived of an important means for preparing for danger, anticipatory anxiety. I do not want to oversimplify the problem of night terrors in a child, but *one* of the contributing factors in Doug's disturbance was the inability to prepare for danger, something which his parents had innocently and unknowingly deprived him of.

A half century ago the right of a child to feel anger toward parents and siblings would have been disputed. Curiously enough, as I write now about children's rights to have feelings, I cannot easily find an example of a child known to me now who has been denied the right to feel anger. It is strange that in the whole gamut of emotions, hostility has been singled out in recent years as the prerogative of the young and there is hardly a parent today who does not regard it as such. But the "right" to have a feeling is not the same as a license to inflict it on others, and in the matter of license we appear to have erred gravely in the education of today's child.

A child may have the right to feel angry and to give expression to his feelings—within certain limits. But should a child be permitted to strike his parents? When Jimmy of an earlier chapter* struck his father in a fit of temper, his father felt that he had had quite enough and sent Jimmy off to his room. Many modern parents would have felt more indulgent. After all, they would say, the child was very upset, he lost control, and maybe he got rid of a lot of pent-up feelings and felt much better afterwards. But I do not think that Jimmy felt relieved afterwards; on the contrary, we find that the child who strikes a parent is made more anxious afterwards. I think that Jimmy's father acted wisely. He did not retaliate with an act of aggression toward the child, but he firmly called a halt to this and said in effect, "I can't allow you to do this!" I do not know if Jimmy's father knew why he felt he had to put a stop to this behavior, but his instincts were right. For when a child loses control of himself to the extent of striking his parent, he is really very frightened to find that he cannot control his own aggression and he is relieved to have the parent step in and put the brakes on when he can't stop himself. We can see this in Jimmy's anxiety dream, too, for you remember that he called to his father to save him from the enraged tiger, that is, Jimmy himself.

The child's fear of loss of control is something that needs more widespread understanding among parents. It can even be an important motive in creating a neurosis. I recall a little seven year old who had a severe neurosis. Along with the neurotic symptoms he had rages of such intensity that often he wantonly

* See pp. 202, 205, 223, 227.

destroyed any objects within reach. He had a recurrent anxiety dream which he told me about. He was riding downhill on his bike at tremendous speed and when he tried to apply the brakes to stop himself nothing happened and he and his bike went sailing downhill toward destruction. This child was tremendously relieved when I helped him understand his dream and told him that I would be able to help him so that whenever he needed his brakes to work they would work for him, in other words, that I would help him achieve self-control.

Let's consider other limits of aggression within the home. If we can see good reasons for placing striking of parents out of bounds how about some of the verbal forms of aggression that we are so indulgent of today? Should we allow name-calling of parents and abusive language? I cannot imagine how it can serve the mental health of any child to be permitted such displays of uncontrolled verbal aggression. This is very close to physical assault and the child who is permitted such license in verbal attack is just as likely to suffer bad effects as the child who is permitted to hit his parents. Of course, we do not need to make the child feel that he is a black sinner and will be struck by a bolt of lightning for his name-calling. It should be enough for a parent to call a halt to this display, "That's enough. I don't care to hear any more of this. You're completely out of control and I don't like this one bit. When you've calmed down we'll discuss this business like two human beings." A child can be permitted to express his anger without resorting to savage name-calling. If he does so, if he loses control, he needs to know from his parents that he has overstepped the line. This doesn't go.

Let's consider, too, the limits of aggression in sibling situations. "Sibling rivalry" is regarded as another prerogative of today's child and the licensed hostility in this area sometimes reaches the point of barbarity. We find that physical attacks by siblings on each other are regarded by many parents as one of the natural accompaniments of family life. "Just as long as they don't murder each other," parents may say indulgently. Yet I can think of no good reason why children beyond the nursery age should settle their differences through jungle tactics, and even in the nursery years we should begin the education away from physical attack. I have known households where nine- and ten-year-old boys and girls were continuing a war that began the day a baby came home. The quarrels of these older children were like the quarrels of toddlers. "That's my chair! She's sitting in my chair!" Or, "He got a bigger piece of pie than I did!" Tears. Stamping of feet. A slap. Shrieks. A deadly battle is on.

But why should the nursery rivalries persist in unmodified form for eight years—or longer? Is it because the jealousies were more severe or because these children were never required to find solutions to their rivalries beyond those of the early years? I suspect that in most cases it was because these children were not required to give up the infantile forms of their rivalry. The right to have sibling rivalry is so firmly entrenched in the modern family that parents show a tendency in their own behavior to protect those rights. In the case of two big children engaged in battle over the rights to a chair it would not be unusual to find their parents solemnly presiding over the dispute, seriously listening to the claims on both sides and issuing a sober judgement giving property rights to one of the contestants. It then happens that the contestant whose case was thrown out of court accuses the judge of favoritism, reproaches his parents for not loving him and preferring his sister, and there follows a lengthy protestation of love from the parents and the quarrel and reproaches are renewed. It might have been more to the point if the parents had treated the whole matter as it deserved to be treated, as a piece of nonsense.

On the other hand, we find that many times parents do not step in to prevent their children from destroying each other through words or the subtler forms of sadism. In the name of sibling rivalry, children today are permitted extraordinary license in cruel name-calling and refined torments designed to undermine each other's personalities. Parents who would never themselves do anything to depreciate the masculinity of a young son may find that the older sister is making a career of it, devoting herself to the work of undermining his self-confidence through taunts, disparaging remarks, and cruel jokes. If we close our ears to all this ("After all brothers and sisters will fight, you know!") we do nothing to help the older sister overcome her aggressive feelings toward boys, and we are allowing her to damage the personality development of her younger brother.

It seems to me that we have to draw the line in sibling rivalry whenever rivalry goes out of bounds into destructive behavior of a physical or verbal kind. The principle needs to be this: *Whatever* the reasons for your feelings you will have to find civilized solutions.

What are the good and the healthy solutions to sibling rivalry? Not all sisters and brothers continue their rivalries for all the years of their lives. A good many of them develop strong and enduring ties of love, and the rivalries and petty jealousies are overcome by the stronger forces of love. Somewhere along the line of development the rivals must accept the impossibility of any of them obtaining the exclusive love of a parent. In coming to terms with this fact the hostilities die down and the rivals, who all have in common their love of the same set of parents, find themselves bound together through a common love. This has obvious implications for parents in handling sibling rivalry. It means that we educate the child to an acceptance of the impossibility of achieving the exclusive love of a parent, that we do not behave in any ways that encourage the rivalries, that we are not amused or flattered by the signs of jealousy and that we very clearly show our expectations that children beyond the nursery age can find solutions to their rivalries without resorting to infantile displays.

All of this brings us finally to another group of "rights" in the emotional development of the child. These rights have to do with love and the valuation of love. We grant that every child has the right to claim the love of his parents. But if a child is to grow in his capacity to love and to emerge as an adult capable of mature love, parents must be able to claim the love of their children—and to make claims upon this love! The parent who loves his child dearly but asks for nothing in return might qualify as a saint, but he will not qualify as a parent. For a child who can claim love without meeting any of the obligations of love will be a self-centered child and many such children have grown up in our time to become petulant lovers and sullen marriage partners because the promise of unconditional love has not been fulfilled. "I know I am selfish and I have a vile temper and I'm moody and a spendthrift, but you should love me in spite of my faults!" these spoiled children say to each other in marriage. And because they believe in their right to be loved—in spite of everything—they do not alter themselves to make themselves worthy of love, but change partners and renew the quest for unconditional love. It is a mistake to look upon these capricious lovers as incurable romantics. They are really in love with themselves. Even their most unattractive qualities are absorbed and forgiven in this self-love, and what they seek in a partner is someone who can love them as well as they love themselves. In all such cases we can conclude that something went wrong in the education for love. These were the children who never relinquished the self-love of the earliest years.

There are obligations in love even for little children. Love is given, but it is also earned. At every step of the way in development a child is obliged to give up territories in his self-love in order to earn parental love and approval. In order to sacrifice many of his private and egocentric wishes he must put a high valuation on parental love, which means that parents themselves need to look upon their love not only as "a right" but as a powerful incentive to the child to alter himself.

PART V

Conclusion

9. Toward the Future

ALL KINDS OF FORTUNES.

ONCE many years ago a six-year-old girl began her treatment with me. She was not at all sure just how this lady was going to cure her of her fears but she was a child of the Buck Rogers Age and she confidently awaited any miracles that I might choose to produce for her benefit. She soon let it be known among her close friends that she went to a Lady Fortune Teller who helped her with her problems, and her prestige rose so high that other little girls besieged their parents to be allowed to go to the Lady Fortune Teller. I did not notice a rise in new cases as a result, but this word of mouth advertising had a stimulating effect upon my Hallowe'en business that year, bringing to my door an unprecedented number of nervous ghosts, skeletons, and out-of-season Easter bunnies who snatched my alms and fled, giggling and screeching, into the frosty night.

I managed to straighten out this misunderstanding with my patient who was disappointed but stuck by me loyally. Some months later I had an occasion to ask her: "And do you still think I'm a fortune teller?" "No," she said sadly. "I know better now. You can tell fortunes backwards but not frontwards."

She was perfectly right, of course. To put it another way, the achievements of psychoanalysis permit us to reconstruct a child's history, to examine his personality in the light of this history, and to be able to say, "This is how this child's personality is made; this is why he is what he is." But neither psychoanalysis nor any other psychology can predict the further course of personality development, to say "with these data and

with our estimate of the child's personality at the age of three—
or the age of six—or the age of fifteen—we can now predict
the further evolution of his personality."

We have brought our story of child development up to the
age of six and we find ourselves in the absurd position of writing
the last chapter of a story that has just begun. For the child is
not finished at six; his personality is not fixed or frozen into
permanent form. The danger in writing about the first six years
of life is that we give rise to the suspicion that the personality
is irrevocably stamped in these years. There is in fact a popular
fallacy, something that might be called "Childhood as Destiny,"
a belief that the experiences of early childhood determine one's
fate and commit the personality to rigid patterns of behavior
and that thereafter nothing short of a psychoanalysis can modify
this edifice. But a child's destiny is not made at his mother's
breast; his destiny is not made on the potty chair. His fate is
not sealed by the arrival of a sibling, or a tonsillectomy, or the
death of a pet parakeet. We do not improve our understanding
of personality development by substituting a rigid determinism
for the three weird sisters who hovered over the cradles of
babies in mythology. Such arbitrary views arise from a misunderstanding of psychoanalytic theory, for while the experiences
of early childhood provide the foundations for personality development, there is no way of predicting in early childhood how
these experiences will influence personality development. This is
because the adaptive mechanisms in each child's personality are
at work very early in development, acting upon experience in
ways that are unique for this personality, and the product in
the personality depends ultimately upon the ego and the mode
of adaptation and not the experience itself.

So we cannot predict. We try. There are dedicated scientists
in psychology labs today who are tormented with the uncer-
tainties in the science of personality, and they measure and
compute these imponderables. But when everything is measured
and computed, they don't know whether any characteristic in a

single child will become fixed in the personality structure or whether it will be transformed in further development. Will a trait like over-aggressiveness in a four year old become permanent in the personality structure or will it be reversed in two years in the direction of passivity? Will it produce neurotic conflict or a severe conduct disorder or will it be brought under control through successful sublimations? No mathematical calculation can give the answer, no electronic brain can digest the data of one child's brief history and the infinite variables in his future development and come out with a valid prediction.

"But wait a moment!" someone must be thinking. "Don't you people employ prediction in your clinical practice? When you make a diagnostic study of a disturbed child and recommend the appropriate form of treatment, aren't you making a kind of prediction, a negative prediction anyway, on the basis that if this child does not receive treatment, his disturbance will interfere with his future development, or will become progressively worse, or will not lead to spontaneous recovery? And how do you know that?"

This is true. We do employ a kind of prediction in clinical practice. What's more, these predictions in the area of emotional disturbance made by good clinicians have a much greater reliability than predictions in the area of normal personality development. And this is why: A severe neurosis gives rigidity to the personality; it produces stereotyped reactions which are often quite independent of the objective situation and which are not modified by objective circumstances. Such a severe emotional disturbance has the effect of immobilizing the adaptive mechanisms in the ego so that they cannot work for fresh solutions to conflict and successful resolution of conflict. It is very clear, then, that if we are dealing with a personality that has lost its capacity for spontaneity and is obliged to produce stereotyped modes of behavior when confronted with the most various external events, this personality becomes highly predictable in those areas of functioning that are subjected to the illness.

If we contrast these conditions with those that obtain in normal child development, we can see why it is so difficult to predict the course of personality development. The normal child, even during periods of emotional disturbance, has the capacity to adapt and to change. His personality undergoes continual modification for all the years of childhood (and for that matter for all the mature years that follow, except that in maturity the main lines of personality development are fixed). As long as the ego retains its flexibility and is not committed to rigid or stereotyped modes of behavior we can never predict with any degree of accuracy the effects of future events upon this personality.

This leads us to another point. In clinical practice we are very good at finding out what went wrong in a child's development. We are able to put together the pieces of a child's history and establish which events or which attitudes of the parent have produced his emotional disturbance. We are not nearly so good in reconstructing the histories of children who do *not* develop emotional disturbances. There's a good reason for this. The child who does not develop an illness does not come to us for treatment, and the story of his development cannot be analyzed in detail. Only in recent years have psychoanalysts begun to study child development through observation of non-clinical cases, following presumably normal children from infancy to maturity. It will be several years before these data are compiled. In the meantime, we do not yet have the answers to some of the most fascinating problems in child development. We do not yet know, for example, why one child, exposed to a certain set of experiences which we regard as pathogenic, will develop a neurosis according to expectation and another child will overcome the effects with no serious or disabling effects in his personality development. Or let me put this more fairly: We think we know, and we have a good deal of scattered observation on the subject, but we do not have the same detailed observations on the mechanisms in personality that work for successful resolution as we do for the mechanisms that work for disease.

Consider this story: (It is one that comes immediately to mind from clinical experiences, but I could easily cite others.)

Many years ago in a clinic for disturbed children, the staff met to consider the case of a ten-year-old boy named Eddie. Eddie had been referred to the clinic by his school because of truancy. In spite of frequent absences, his school achievement was at least average, his attitude toward teachers and classmates was friendly and his conduct was irreproachable. Why did he skip school? He told us. Every now and then when his father was drunk Eddie needed to stay home to take care of him. And then, because there was no money for food he had to find odd jobs in the neighborhood for a little while until his father could go back to work. When his father was able to get work again, Eddie would go back to school.

His father was a brutal drunkard. His mother had been committed two years earlier to a state institution for mental defectives. Two older brothers and one sister were also in institutions for the feeble minded. The four oldest children in the family, now old enough to be out on their own, all had police records dating back to childhood. Eddie was the youngest. He was the only one still living at home. His intelligence was at least normal. He had a good scholastic record. He had never been involved in delinquent acts. He had no neurotic symptoms, but he was slightly obese. (We argued as clinicians whether we should speak of overeating as a neurotic symptom in a child for whom food could represent, very simply, survival. An academic point. Call it neurotic if you will. Still, how will you explain that a child reared in the most degraded and hopeless circumstances should arrive at the age of ten with nothing worse than a tendency toward obesity?)

How did this child survive? It is not remarkable that the others in this diseased home should have succumbed one by one, but how do you explain an Eddie? Better intelligence? Well, partly, but this is not insurance against neglect and corruption in the home. "A strong ego," we said, wincing at our cliché, for "a strong ego" is not given as part of the constitutional endowment. It can be demonstrated empirically that the ego which can withstand exceptional strain is the product of good nurture. No matter how good the basic equipment is in an infant it will not survive neglect or impoverishment in human ties.

So we had to assume that someone in this family of defective and incompetent and diseased people had given this boy adequate or more than adequate care and love. But who? The child had spoken affectionately of his mother, but we had not known how to estimate his ties to her. Each time our thoughts centered on this woman committed to an institution for low-grade mental defectives we remembered the seven other children in the family, the mentally deficient, delinquent, hopelessly incompetent children of a demonstratively incompetent mother, and we could not imagine how she could have succeeded as a mother with this child. Then was it the father who cared for this child? No, this was an even more improbable hypothesis. We knew more about the father than the mother. He was a brutal, silent, detached and empty man who seemed to have no human ties and no connections with any of his children. He had been dependent upon his wife in a simple and primitive way. She fed him and took care of him when he needed her care. Eddie, himself, without claiming any love for his father, took care of the man when he was drunk, scrounged for food and odd jobs to buy food, and did those things for his father that his mother did when she was still in the home. But this did not speak for a strong attachment between the father and the boy, and for the boy's part this solicitude for the father seemed to have less to do with ties to the father than ties to the mother, for the child was behaving like a mother to his father.

It was improbable, it was incredible, but we had to believe that this poor feeble-minded mother who had raised seven chil·

dren to disgrace the community had also raised one child who possessed at the age of ten some admirable human qualities. He was intelligent, he had meaningful human attachments, he had a conscience, he had astonishing resourcefulness, and a drive to survive that had overcome the most formidable obstacles of his home and community. We would never be able to find out how she had accomplished this, but this child was indisputably a child who had known good mothering. He was the baby of the family. Was it possible that this limited mother who had had yearly pregnancies from the first child on, had found the whole business of being a mother too confusing, too taxing, had succeeded better with the last baby because no new babies came along to tax her limited capacities? And because he was better endowed physically and mentally than any of the other babies, was he more responsive, more gratifying than the other babies? In some ways not known to us he must have been specially dear to this woman. Even a feeble-minded woman can have the capacity for love, and if life is not too confusing, if there are not too many demanding babies and too many hardships, such a woman can be a good mother, too.

So we do not know with certainty why Eddie turned out so well, but we know why the seven other children in this family turned out so badly. Moreover, if any of the seven older children had come to our clinic in early childhood we could have predicted delinquency, but if Eddie had been known to us in early childhood, we could not have predicted mental stability for him. If we had known him at four, we might have been able to say something like this: "This child has average intelligence; he reveals a strong ego development, which may serve him in overcoming some of the overwhelming handicaps of his home and his community, but the prognosis for normal development is poor as long as he remains in this pathological home." In other words we can lean on something we call "a strong ego" and those things that are included in the term "strong ego" have a high predictive value for mental health, but when even "a strong ego" is subjected to excessive strains over a period of years we cannot predict, especially in childhood, that it can retain its integrity or that it will not succumb to illness.

All of which confirms the sagacity of my seven-year-old patient who observed that we could not "tell fortunes frontwards." With a record in prognostication that is really not much better than that of other oracles you must wonder at our audacity in stating positively that Eddie had known good mothering. How could we be so sure of ourselves? Why should our "backwards fortune telling" invite your confidence when there are so many unknowns in this child's history? This is how we knew:

No matter how exceptional a child's mental equipment may be at birth there are certain factors in personality development that cannot be achieved without mothering, without strong and meaningful ties. An Eddie who gives evidence at the age of ten that he is capable of good human relationships, that he can come to grips with reality no matter how painful it may be, that he can learn satisfactorily in school, that he possesses a conscience which can resist even the extraordinary temptations of his home and community, is his own proof that he had known good mothering.

"But how can you *prove* that!" the reader objects. "How do you know that Eddie might not be an extraordinary individual with a powerful drive that enabled him to overcome the adversities of his environment? After all you can't possibly have experimental proof for these assumptions."

But we do. And this brings us to another part of the story.

LESSONS FROM THE LABORATORIES OF HUMAN ERROR AND DISASTER.

No MADMAN has ever set up an experiment in which infants and young children were deprived of human ties in order to study the effects upon personality development. But human

error and disaster have provided a kind of ghastly laboratory
for such studies. The abandoned babies raised in sterile nurseries, the unwanted babies and children shifted from home to
home, the motherless children of war, tyranny and atrocity
reared in institutions and concentration camps—all these have
provided the evidence. While many of these institutions provided for the physical needs of infants, most of them shared
this deficiency: The grouping of a number of babies and small
children under the supervision of a number of staff persons
could not create the conditions for attachment between a child
and an adult, and the human connections between children and
personnel in charge were weak, unstable and shifting.

Children who spent their infancy and formative years under
these conditions revealed the effects in an impoverishment of
the personality, as if a nutritional deficiency had affected the
early structures and devitalized parts of the personality. These
children who had never experienced love, who had never be-
longed to anyone, and were never attached to anyone except on
the most primitive basis of food and survival, were unable in
later years to bind themselves to other people, to love deeply,
to feel deeply, to experience tenderness, grief or shame to the
measure that gives dimension to the human personality.

The intellectual development of the unattached babies and
children was very slow. They acquired at a creeping pace those
things that children in families learn at a galloping pace. The
unattached babies were slow to acquire an interest in objects
around them, as if a world outside their bodies scarcely existed.
They were dull and apathetic babies, not through defective
equipment, but because no human being gave them pleasure in
the world outside their own bodies and beyond the satisfaction
of body needs. The unattached children were slow, appallingly
slow, to acquire language. Of course, we know that occasionally
a very bright child in a normal home may also be "a slow talker,"
but these children as a group were consistently slower than the
average in acquiring speech. If they remained in an institution

for the formative years and if the deprivations in human ties were never compensated for by institutional personnel, language development was consistently retarded and, in many instances, the language of these children revealed certain peculiarities. Language for the unattached child did not serve communication effectively. Like the early stages of infant speech development, the speech of these children was self-related, personal and often quite unintelligible to others. It was a language acquired without close human ties and the words had the detached, uncertain and ambiguous quality of the whole structure of relationships in the empty world of these children. Their later learning was severely retarded in all areas dependent upon language use. Intellectual functioning, in general, was retarded and the intellectual capacity of these children could only be guessed at through mental testing.

The unattached children were slow to acquire a sense of personal identity, of "I-ness" in the full sense of the term, and when "I" emerged as word and concept it was a late acquisition by the standards of family-reared children and retained the blurred and uncertain quality of a two year old's "I" far along the road of development, in some cases permanently. But why is this important? "I" is the integrating factor in personality development. The sense of personal identity is the concept that binds self-feelings and differentiation of one's own body, thoughts, subjective reactions from persons and objects outside. Infants are not born with this sense. In the early weeks they do not differentiate between their bodies and other bodies, between their mental pictures and real objects outside. The average child does not acquire the word and the concept "I" until the middle of the third year. When "I" emerges it brings with it a great improvement in the reality sense of the child, a sharpened differentiation of self and not-self, of inner and outer, subjective and objective, and a corresponding shift from the magic thinking that characterizes infancy to the rational thinking that characterizes higher mental processes. (Though the two and a half year old is still far from being rational!)

But the sense of personal identity is acquired through human ties. Before there can be differentiation of self and outer world, the outer world must have a representative. A child who lives in a world of insubstantial and shifting human objects and is unbound to any of these will have difficulty in forming a stable image of himself. And because human objects, the first "realities" are unsatisfying and impermanent, his reality sense is correspondingly poor. We mean by this that he has difficulty in differentiating between inner and outer, subjective states and reactions and objective conditions. This does not mean that he is mentally ill—which is a far more complex state—but it does mean that his personality is marked by tendencies to distort, to employ magic or wishful thinking far beyond the age at which we normally find primitive thought in children, and it means that he is slow to acquire knowledge about the world around him and a coherent, organized view of the tiny piece of earth that he inhabits. So these unattached children were unstable children, highly vulnerable to all manner of mental pathology, and in later life they contributed to the ranks of the mentally disordered to a frighteningly large degree.

We have said that the ability to control impulse, to triumph over body urges is one of the most distinguished achievements of man. We can learn from the unattached children that this achievement is dependent every step of the way on ties to the human educator. Where the human ties between child and educator are unstable and shifting, as in the institutions we have described, the child has the greatest difficulty in achieving the most elementary forms of self-control, and if he achieves them at all under such circumstances they often do not become reliable controls in later childhood, that is, they may fail to get "built-in" or integrated into the personality in the form of conscience. Even the first task in control of body urges, toilet training, could not be achieved by the unattached toddlers until a surprisingly late stage, and problems of elimination and control continued in a large number of cases into later childhood.

All learning of impulse control, especially control of aggressive impulses, was acquired with great difficulty by the unattached and neglected children of the poor institutions. Often, it appeared not to be achieved at all, and behavior problems verging on the pathological, sometimes grossly pathological, were, and are, the common diseases of such institutions. For a child normally acquires control over his impulses through his attachment to his parents, through his wish to please them and his wish to emulate them. In the absence of strong human ties the child finds himself without positive motives for control of impulse. The sterile institutions were obliged, like parents and parent substitutes, to teach control and to subdue aggressive behavior, but since ties of love usually did not exist between educator and child, control when it was achieved often had a terrible aspect. It was control achieved through fearful submission to authority (or the tyranny of the child group); it was based on survival needs, and like all controls based on fear alone, it either reduced a human being to helpless slavery or it created a passive face and a raging interior, a personality capable of extreme and unpredictable violence. It is possible that many of these institutions did not employ brutality in their handling of children. But the absence of positive human ties can brutalize a child as surely as repeated acts of sadism.

We have used the sterile institutions as the chilling example, the unpremeditated experiment, for the study of the effects of emotional deprivation on human development. It goes without saying that children can be reared in homes where the extreme mental or emotional disability of parents can deprive them of human ties. They can be subjected, like many children in foster homes, to constant changes in homes and families so that no positive ties can develop. In such instances the effect on personality development can be very similar to those we have observed in the sterile institutions.

"This is all very impressive," someone says, "but you have described bad institutions, pathological home situations. Surely, if these institutions were operated on mental hygiene principles, with professionally trained staff and if close human ties were offered these children, they should develop as well as or better than children in their own homes. Think of the advantages for babies and children of a professionally trained staff bringing the best of modern science to child-rearing. Now *that* would be an experiment!"

We have that, too. Disaster has provided every conceivable laboratory for the study of human nature. There are model institutions for children, among them one I shall use as an example, The Hampstead Nurseries.

LESSONS FROM A MODEL INSTITUTION.

THE Hampstead Nurseries were set up in England during World War II for the care of infants and children who were deprived of one or both parents or who, for other reasons, could not be cared for in their homes. Its directors were two world-renowned child analysts, Anna Freud and Dorothy Burlingham. These nurseries were staffed by carefully selected children's workers under professional supervision. Their policies and practices were derived from the best of contemporary knowledge of child development and child psychology. The ties between children and staff members were fostered with full understanding of the importance of relationship in personality development.

How did these babies and children fare? On the whole, the crippling effects of institutional life were eliminated in this program. These children fared better, by far, than the unattached children of sterile institutions. But in certain vital areas of development these children, reared under optimum institutional conditions, did not fare as well as the average child in a family!

In speech, for example, the average toddler tested at two

years in the Hampstead Nurseries was six months retarded as compared with the average child reared in his own home. Control of aggressive impulses was more difficult for the small children to achieve. These children were very late in achieving toilet training and the staff encountered more difficulties in obtaining the cooperation of the children in toileting than we normally encounter in a home. In general, in those areas of development which are dependent upon strong emotional ties to a parent or parent substitute, these babies and young children were retarded, in spite of the fact that this institution promoted the ties between children and adults!

It is worthwhile mentioning that later, when the Hampstead Nurseries grouped the infants and toddlers into small "families" with one or two adults serving as the exclusive "parents" for the artificial families, there was an improvement in the developmental achievements of these children. But an artificial family is not really a family, and the kindness and affection that a nurse may feel for her charges is not qualitatively the same as that of a parent who is bound to the child through the deepest, most permanent ties of love. An institutional nurse cannot bind herself to children who can never be her children, who will always belong to someone else. And inevitably nurses leave an institution and other nurses replace them, so that rarely will the child, even in a model institution, have a permanent mother substitute.

And the last vital point: Nurses cannot be father substitutes so that the vast range of human emotion which centers around two parents and the permanent ties to a family must be cut off for children even in this model institution. Further, since identification with parents is basic for the patterning of sexual roles and for the building of firm values and behavior ideals, the child reared in an artificial family will have greater difficulty in acquiring a stable, well-integrated character.

The conclusion to be drawn from this evidence is impressive: Here we have an institution which can bring professional skill and wisdom to the job of child-rearing, and in assessing its accomplishments it modestly takes a back seat to a statistically average family with an average baby. The lesson is very clear. All the wisdom in the world about child-rearing cannot, by itself, replace intimate human ties, family ties, as the center of human development. This should not surprise us. Neither was it a surprise to the two distinguished child analysts who directed the nursery. The significance of family ties in healthy child development had been an integral part of their science long before they undertook direction of a nursery. And these comparisons should not lead to false conclusions either. They should not be taken as a depreciation of child psychology, but as an appreciation of the family, the point of departure for all sound psychological thinking.

CAN WE INSURE AGAINST NEUROSIS?

WE SHOULD not conclude, either, that the child who has strong ties to his parents is insured against neurosis. We can only say that he will have the best possible measures within his personality to deal with conflict, which may then provide greater resistance to neurotic ills. But a neurosis is not necessarily an indictment of the parent-child relationship; a neurotic child is not necessarily an unloved child, or a rejected child. The child who has never known love and who has no human attachments does not develop a neurosis in the strict clinical meaning of the term. The unattached child is subject to other types of disorders. He might develop bizarre features in his personality, he might be subject to primitive fears and pathological distortions of reality, he might have uncontrollable urges that lead to delinquency or violence, but he would probably not acquire a neurosis because a neurosis involves moral conflicts and conflicts of love which could not exist in a child who had never known significant human attachments. The merit of a neurosis—if there is anything good to be said about it at all—is that it is a civilized disease. The child who suffers a disturbance in his love relationships or anxieties of conscience offers proof of his humanity even in illness. But the sickness of the unattached child is more terrible because it is less human; there is only a primitive ego engaged in a lonely and violent struggle for its own existence.

Indeed, it can be argued that the real threat to humanity does not lie in neurosis but in the diseases of the ego, the diseases of isolation, detachment and emotional sterility. These are the diseases that are produced in the early years by the absence of human ties or the destruction of human ties. In the absence of human ties those mental qualities that we call human will fail to develop or will be grafted upon a personality that cannot nourish them, so that at best they will be imitations of virtues, personality façades. The devastating effects of two world wars, revolution, tyranny and mass murder are seen in cruelest caricature in the thousands of hollow men who have come to live among us. The destruction of families and family ties has produced in frightening numbers an aberrant child and man who lives as a stranger in the human community. He is rootless, unbound, uncommitted, unloved and untouchable. He is sometimes a criminal, whether child or adult, and you have read that he commits acts of violence without motive and without remorse. He offers himself and the vacancy within him to be leased by other personalities—the gang leaders, mob-rulers, fascist leaders and the organizers of lunatic movements and societies. He performs useful services for them; he can perform brutal acts that might cause another criminal at least a twinge of conscience, he can risk his life when more prudent villains would stay home, and he can do these things because he values no man's life, not even his own. All that he asks in return is that he may borrow a personality or an idea to clothe his nakedness and give a reason, however perverse, for his existence in a meaningless world.

We have more reason to fear the hollow man than the poor neurotic who is tormented by his own conscience. As long as man is capable of moral conflicts—even if they lead to neurosis —there is hope for him. But what shall we do with a man who has no attachments? Who can breathe humanity into his emptiness?

The conclusions to be drawn from this long discussion are very simple ones. The best of our knowledge in contemporary psychology cannot tell us with scientific exactness how we shall prevent neuroses in childhood, but it can tell us exactly how a child becomes humanized. It also turns out that the humanizing process in child-rearing bears a certain relationship to the mental stability of children.

We have learned that those mental qualities which we call "human" are not part of the constitutional endowment of the infant, are not instinctive as are the characteristics of other animals, and will not be acquired simply through maturation. The quality of human love which transcends love of self is the product of the human family and the particular kind of attachments that are nurtured there. The quality of human intelligence which depends very largely on manipulation of symbols, especially language, is not simply the product of a superior mental and vocal apparatus; it is achieved through the earliest love attachments. Man's consciousness of himself as a being, the concept of "I," of personal identity—the very center of his humanness—is achieved through the early bonds of child and parent. The triumph of man over his instinctual nature, his willingness to restrict, inhibit, even to oppose his own urges when they conflict with higher goals for himself, is again the product of learning, an achievement through love in the early years of development. Conscience itself, the most civilizing of all achievements in human evolution, is not part of constitutional endowment, as any parent can testify, but the endowment of parental love and education.

If we read our evidence correctly, it appears that parents need not be paragons; they may be inexperienced, they may be permitted to err in the fashion of the species, to employ sometimes a wrong method or an unendorsed technique, and still have an excellent chance of rearing a healthy child if the bonds between parents and child are strong and provide the incentives for growth and development in the child. For the decisive factors in mental health are the capacities of the ego for dealing with conflict, the ability to tolerate frustration, to adapt, and to find solutions that bring harmony between inner needs and outer reality. These qualities of the ego are themselves the product of the child's bonds to his parents, the product of the humanizing process.

INDEX

Praise for Eric Tyson

"Eric Tyson is doing something important — namely, helping people at all income levels to take control of their financial futures. This book is a natural outgrowth of Tyson's vision that he has nurtured for years. Like Henry Ford, he wants to make something that was previously accessible only to the wealthy accessible to middle-income Americans."

> — James C. Collins, coauthor of the national bestseller *Built to Last;* former Lecturer in Business, Stanford Graduate School of Business

"*Personal Finance For Dummies* is the perfect book for people who feel guilty about inadequately managing their money but are intimidated by all of the publications out there. It's a painless way to learn how to take control."

> — National Public Radio's *Sound Money*

"Eric Tyson . . . seems the perfect writer for a *For Dummies* book. He doesn't tell you what to do or consider doing without explaining the why's and how's — and the booby traps to avoid — in plain English. . . . It will lead you through the thickets of your own finances as painlessly as I can imagine."

> — *Chicago Tribune*

"This book provides easy-to-understand personal financial information and advice for those without great wealth or knowledge in this area. Practitioners like Eric Tyson, who care about the well-being of middle-income people, are rare in today's society."

> — Joel Hyatt, founder of Hyatt Legal Services, one of the nation's largest general-practice personal legal service firms

"Worth getting. Scores of all-purpose money-management books reach bookstores every year, but only once every couple of years does a standout personal finance primer come along. *Personal Finance For Dummies,* by financial counselor and columnist Eric Tyson, provides detailed, action-oriented advice on everyday financial questions. . . . Tyson's style is readable and unintimidating."

> — Kristin Davis, *Kiplinger's Personal Finance* magazine

"This is a great book. It's understandable. Other financial books are too technical and this one really is different."

> — Business Radio Network

More Bestselling For Dummies Titles by Eric Tyson

Investing For Dummies®

A *Wall Street Journal* bestseller, this book walks you through how to build wealth in stocks, real estate, and small business as well as other investments.

Mutual Funds For Dummies®

This best-selling guide is now updated to include current fund and portfolio recommendations. Using the practical tips and techniques, you'll design a mutual fund investment plan suited to your income, lifestyle, and risk preferences.

Taxes For Dummies®

The complete, best-selling reference for completing your tax return and making tax-wise financial decisions year-round. Tyson coauthors this book with tax experts David Silverman and Margaret Munro.

Home Buying For Dummies®

America's #1 real estate book includes coverage of online resources in addition to sound financial advice from Eric Tyson and frontline real estate insights from industry veteran Ray Brown. Also available from America's best-selling real estate team of Tyson and Brown — *House Selling For Dummies* and *Mortgages For Dummies*.

Real Estate Investing For Dummies®

Real estate is a proven wealth-building investment, but many people don't know how to go about making and managing rental property investments. Real estate and property management expert Robert Griswold and Eric Tyson cover the gamut of property investment options, strategies, and techniques.

Small Business For Dummies®

Take control of your future and make the leap from employee to entrepreneur with this enterprising guide. From drafting a business plan to managing costs, you'll profit from expert advice and real-world examples that cover every aspect of building your own business. Tyson coauthors this book with fellow entrepreneur Jim Schell.

Personal Finance FOR DUMMIES® 5TH EDITION

by Eric Tyson, MBA

WILEY

Wiley Publishing, Inc.

Personal Finance For Dummies®, 5th Edition

Published by
Wiley Publishing, Inc.
111 River St.
Hoboken, NJ 07030-5774
www.wiley.com

WILEY

About the Author

Eric Tyson first became interested in money more than three decades ago. After his father was laid off during the 1973 recession and received some retirement money from Philco-Ford, Eric worked with his dad to make investing decisions with the money. A couple years later, Eric won his high school's science fair with a project on what influences the stock market. Dr. Martin Zweig, who provided some guidance, awarded Eric a one-year subscription to the *Zweig Forecast,* a famous investment newsletter. Of course, Eric's mom and dad share some credit with Martin for Eric's victory.

After toiling away for a number of years as a management consultant to Fortune 500 financial-service firms, Eric finally figured out how to pursue his dream. He took his inside knowledge of the banking, investment, and insurance industries and committed himself to making personal financial management accessible to all.

Today, Eric is an internationally acclaimed and bestselling personal finance book author, syndicated columnist, and speaker. He has worked with and taught people from all financial situations, so he knows the financial concerns and questions of real folks just like you. Despite being handicapped by an MBA from the Stanford Graduate School of Business and a B.S. in Economics and Biology from Yale University, Eric remains a master of "keeping it simple."

An accomplished personal finance writer, his "Investor's Guide" syndicated column, distributed by King Features, is read by millions nationally, and he was an award-winning columnist for the *San Francisco Examiner.* He is the author of five national bestselling financial books in the *For Dummies* series on personal finance, investing, mutual funds, home buying (coauthor), and taxes (coauthor). The prior edition of this book was awarded the Benjamin Franklin Award for best book of the year in the Business category.

His latest book, *Mind Over Money: Your Path to Wealth and Happiness* (CDS/Perseus), examines the problematic financial habits people engage in and provides proven strategies for overcoming them.

Eric's work has been featured and quoted in hundreds of local and national publications, including *Newsweek, The Wall Street Journal, Los Angeles Times, Chicago Tribune, Forbes, Kiplinger's Personal Finance* magazine, *Parenting, Money, Family Money,* and *Bottom Line/Personal;* on NBC's *Today Show,* ABC, CNBC, PBS *Nightly Business Report,* CNN, and FOX-TV; and on CBS national radio, NPR's *Sound Money,* Bloomberg Business Radio, and Business Radio Network.

Dedication

This book is hereby and irrevocably dedicated to my family and friends, as well as to my counseling clients and customers, who ultimately have taught me everything that I know about how to explain financial terms and strategies so that all of us may benefit.

Author's Acknowledgments

Being an entrepreneur involves endless challenges, and without the support and input of my good friends and mentors Peter Mazonson, Jim Collins, and my best friend and wife, Judy, I couldn't have accomplished what I have.

I hold many people accountable for my perverse and maniacal interest in figuring out the financial services industry and money matters, but most of the blame falls on my loving parents, Charles and Paulina, who taught me most of what I know that's been of use in the real world.

I'd also like to thank Michael Bloom, Chris Dominguez, Maggie McCall, David Ish, Paul Kozak, Chris Treadway, Sally St. Lawrence, K.T. Rabin, Will Hearst III, Ray Brown, Susan Wolf, Rich Caramella, Lisa Baker, Renn Vera, Maureen Taylor, Jerry Jacob, Robert Crum, Duc Nguyen, Maria Carmicino, and all the good folks at King Features for believing in and supporting my writing and teaching.

Many thanks to all the people who provided insightful comments on this edition and previous editions of this book, especially financial planner Sheryl Garrett, Bill Urban, Barton Francis, Mike van den Akker, Gretchen Morgenson, Craig Litman, Gerri Detweiler, Mark White, Alan Bush, Nancy Coolidge, and Chris Jensen.

And thanks to all the wonderful people at my publisher on the front line and behind the scenes, especially Kathy Cox and Alissa Schwipps.

Publisher's Acknowledgments

We're proud of this book; please send us your comments through our Dummies online registration form located at www.dummies.com/register/.

Some of the people who helped bring this book to market include the following:

Acquisitions, Editorial, and Media Development

Senior Project Editor: Alissa Schwipps

(Previous Edition: Marcia L. Johnson)

Acquisitions Editor: Kathy Cox

Assistant Editor: Courtney Allen

Copy Editor: Danielle Voirol

    (Previous Edition: Greg Pearson)

Editorial Program Coordinator: Hanna K. Scott

Technical Editor: Sheryl Garrett, CFP®

Senior Editorial Manager: Jennifer Ehrlich

Editorial Assistants: Erin Calligan, Nadine Bell, David Lutton

Cartoons: Rich Tennant (www.the5thwave.com)

Composition Services

Project Coordinator: Tera Knapp

Layout and Graphics: Andrea Dahl, Barbara Moore, Barry Offringa, Heather Ryan, Alicia B. South

Proofreaders: Laura Albert, Leeann Harney, Techbooks

Indexer: Techbooks

Publishing and Editorial for Consumer Dummies

    Diane Graves Steele, Vice President and Publisher, Consumer Dummies

    Joyce Pepple, Acquisitions Director, Consumer Dummies

    Kristin A. Cocks, Product Development Director, Consumer Dummies

    Michael Spring, Vice President and Publisher, Travel

    Kelly Regan, Editorial Director, Travel

Publishing for Technology Dummies

    Andy Cummings, Vice President and Publisher, Dummies Technology/General User

Composition Services

    Gerry Fahey, Vice President of Production Services

    Debbie Stailey, Director of Composition Services

Contents at a Glance

Table of Contents

Part IV: Insurance: Protecting What You've Got...........305

Chapter 15: Insurance: Getting What You Need at the Best Price ...307

Chapter 16: Insurance on You: Life, Disability, and Health 325

Introduction

*I*f your personal financial knowledge is limited, you're probably not at fault. Personal Finance 101 isn't offered in our schools — not in high school and not even in the best colleges and graduate programs. It should be. (Of course, if it were, I wouldn't be able to write fun and useful books such as this — or maybe they'd use this book in the course!)

People keep making the same common financial mistakes over and over — procrastinating and lack of planning, wasteful spending, falling prey to financial salespeople and pitches, failing to do sufficient research before making important financial decisions, and so on. This book can keep you from falling into the same traps and get you going on the best paths.

As unfair as it may seem, numerous pitfalls await you when you seek help for your financial problems. The world is filled with biased and bad financial advice. As a practicing financial counselor and now as a writer, I constantly see and hear about the consequences of poor advice. Of course, every profession has bad apples, but too many of the people calling themselves "financial planners" have conflicts of interest and an inadequate competence level.

All too often, financial advice ignores the big picture and focuses narrowly on investing. Because money is not an end in itself but a part of your whole life, this book helps connect your financial goals and challenges to the rest of your life. You need a broad understanding of personal finance to include all areas of your financial life: spending, taxes, saving and investing, insurance, and planning for major goals like education, buying a home, and retirement.

Even if you understand the financial basics, thinking about your finances in a holistic way can be difficult. Sometimes you're too close to the situation to be objective. Like the organization of your desk or home (or disorganization, as the case may be), your finances may reflect the history of your life more than they reflect a comprehensive plan for your future.

You're likely a busy person who doesn't have enough hours in the day to get things done. Thus, you want to know how to diagnose your financial situation efficiently (and painlessly) and determine what you should do next. Unfortunately, after figuring out which financial strategies make sense for you, choosing specific financial products in the marketplace can be a nightmare. You have literally thousands of investment, insurance, and loan options to choose from. Talk about information overload!

To complicate matters even more, you probably hear about most products through advertising that can be misleading, if not downright false. Of course, some ethical and outstanding firms advertise, but so do those that are more interested in converting your hard-earned income and savings into their profits. And they may not be here tomorrow when you need them.

You want to know the best places to go for your circumstances, so this book contains specific, tried-and-proven recommendations. I also suggest where to turn next if you need more information and help.

About This Book

You selected wisely in picking up a copy of *Personal Finance For Dummies,* 5th Edition! More than 1.5 million copies of prior editions of this book are in print, and as you can see from the quotes in the front of this edition, readers and reviewers alike were pleased with those editions. This book was also previously awarded the prestigious Benjamin Franklin Award for best book of the year in Business.

However, I never rest on my laurels. So the book you hold in your hands reflects more hard work and brings you the freshest material for addressing your personal financial quandaries.

Here are some of the major updates you may notice as you peruse the pages of this book:

- ✔ Coverage of new and revised tax laws and how to best take advantage of them

- ✔ The latest information on what's going on with Social Security and Medicare and what it means for how you should prepare for and live in retirement

- ✔ Updated investment recommendations — especially in the areas of mutual funds/other managed investments and real estate — throughout Part III

- ✔ Enhanced coverage of smart spending, which includes finding the best ways to shop online, minimizing bank fees and lousy service, coping with higher energy costs, eating healthy without spending a fortune, and spending wisely on technology

- ✔ Complete analysis of the new bankruptcy laws and the best ways to reduce and eliminate the financial plague of consumer debt

- ✔ Additional coverage of smart ways to use credit, understanding your credit scores, and how to improve them

- ✔ Expanded coverage of education savings options and education tax breaks and how they impact financial aid

- Revised recommendations for where to get the best insurance deals and expanded coverage on preparing for natural disasters

- Updated details on how to avoid identity theft and other scams

- Expanded and updated coverage of financial resources (especially online resources)

- The latest advice on how to simplify your financial life and pass on what you know to others you love

Aside from being packed with updated information, another great feature of this book is that you can read it from cover to cover if you want, or you can read each chapter and part without having to read what comes before, which is useful if you have better things to do with your free time. (Handy cross-references direct you to somewhere else in the book for more details on a particular subject.) This book also makes for great reading anywhere you may be sitting for a length of time (just not in an airplane lavatory, as I don't want you to annoy your fellow passengers with overstaying).

Conventions Used in This Book

To help you navigate the waters of this book, I've set up a few conventions:

- I use *italics* for emphasis and to highlight new words or terms that I define.

- I use **boldface** text to indicate the action part of numbered steps and to highlight key words or phrases in bulleted lists.

- I put all Web addresses in `monofont` for easy identification.

What You Don't Need to Read

I've written this book so you can find information easily and easily understand what you find. And although I'd like to believe that you want to pore over every last word between the two yellow and black covers, I actually make it easy for you to identify "skippable" material. This information is the stuff that, although interesting, isn't essential for you to know:

- **Text in sidebars:** The sidebars are the shaded boxes that appear here and there. They include helpful information and observations but aren't necessary reading.

- **Anything with a Technical Stuff icon attached:** This information is interesting but not critical to your understanding of the topic at hand.

Foolish Assumptions

In writing this book, I made some assumptions about you, dear reader:

- ✓ You want expert advice about important financial topics — such as getting out of high-interest consumer debt, planning for major goals, or investing — and you want answers quickly.

- ✓ Or perhaps you want a crash course in personal finance and are looking for a book you can read cover-to-cover to help solidify major financial concepts and get you thinking about your finances in a more comprehensive way.

- ✓ Or maybe you're just tired of picking up scattered piles of bills, receipts, and junk mail every time the kids chase the cat around the den, so you plan to use this book as a paperweight.

Seriously though, this book is basic enough to help a novice get his or her arms around thorny financial issues. But advanced readers will be challenged, as well, to think about their finances in a new way and identify areas for improvement. Check out the table of contents for a chapter-by-chapter rundown of what this book offers. You can also look up a specific topic in the index. Or you can turn a few pages and start at the beginning: Chapter 1.

How This Book Is Organized

This book is organized into six parts, with each covering a major area of your personal finances. The chapters within each part cover specific topics in detail. Here's a summary of what you can find in each part.

Part 1: Assessing Your Fitness and Setting Goals

This part explains how to diagnose your current financial health and explores common reasons for any missing links in your personal finance knowledge. We all have dreams and goals, so in this part, I also encourage you to think about your financial (and personal) aspirations and figure out how much you should be saving if you want to retire someday or accomplish other important goals.

Part II: Saving More, Spending Less

Most people don't have gobs of extra cash. Therefore, this part shows you how to figure out where all your dollars are going and tells you how to reduce your spending. Chapter 5 is devoted to helping you get out from under the burden of high-interest consumer debt (such as credit card debt). I also provide specifics for reducing your tax burden.

Part III: Building Wealth with Wise Investing

Earning and saving money is hard work, so you should be careful when it comes to investing what you've worked so hard to save (or waited so long to inherit!). In this part, I assist you with picking investments wisely and help you understand investment risks, returns, and a whole lot more. I explain all the major, and best, investment options. I recommend specific strategies and investments to use both inside and outside of tax-sheltered retirement accounts. I also discuss buying, selling, and investing in real estate, as well as other wealth-building investments.

Part IV: Insurance: Protecting What You've Got

Insurance is an important part of your financial life. Unfortunately, for most people, insurance is a thoroughly overwhelming and dreadfully boring topic. But perhaps I can pique your interest in this esoteric topic by telling you that you're probably paying more than you should for insurance and that you probably don't have the right coverage for your situation. This part tells you all you ever wanted to know (okay, fine — all you *never* wanted to know but probably should know anyway) about how to buy the right insurance at the best price.

Part V: Where to Go for More Help

As you build your financial knowledge, more questions and issues may arise. In this part, I discuss where to go and what to avoid when you seek financial information and advice. I also discuss hiring a financial planner as well as investigating resources in print, on the air, and online.

Part VI: The Part of Tens

The chapters in this part can help you manage major life changes and protect yourself from the increasingly common problem of identity theft.

Glossary

The world of money is filled with jargon, so you'll be happy to know that this book includes a comprehensive glossary of financial terms that are often tossed around but seldom explained.

Icons Used in This Book

The icons in this book help you find particular kinds of information that may be of use to you:

This nerdy looking guy appears beside discussions that aren't critical if you just want to understand basic concepts and get answers to your financial questions. You can safely ignore these sections, but reading them can help deepen and enhance your personal financial knowledge. This stuff can also come in handy if you're ever on a game show, or if you find yourself stuck on an elevator with a financial geek.

This target flags strategy recommendations for making the most of your money (for example, paying off your credit card debt with your lottery winnings).

This icon highlights the best financial products in the areas of investments, insurance, and so on. These products can help you implement my strategy recommendations.

This icon points out information that you'll definitely want to remember.

This icon marks things to avoid and points out common mistakes people make when managing their finances.

This icon alerts you to scams and scoundrels who prey on the unsuspecting.

This icon tells you when you should consider doing some additional research. Don't worry — I explain what to look for and what to look out for.

Where to Go from Here

This book is organized so you can go wherever you want to find complete information. Want advice on reducing your debt, for example? Head to Chapter 5. If you're interested in investing strategies, go to Part III for that. You can use the table of contents to find broad categories of information or the index to look up more specific things.

If you're not sure where you want to go, you may want to start with Part I. It gives you all the basic info you need to assess your financial situation and points to places where you can find more detailed information for improving it.

Part I
Assessing Your Fitness and Setting Goals

The 5th Wave   By Rich Tennant

"Isn't that our bookkeeper?"

In this part . . .

I discuss the concepts that underlie sensible personal financial management. You find out why you didn't know all these concepts before now (and whom to blame). Here, you undergo a (gentle) financial physical exam to diagnose your current economic health, and I show you how to identify where your hard-earned dollars are going. I also cover understanding and improving your credit report and scores and how to plan for and accomplish your financial goals.

Chapter 1

Improving Your Financial Literacy

- -

In This Chapter

▶ Looking at what your parents and others taught you about money

▶ Studying money management in schools

▶ Hitting the books (and other sources): Questioning reliability

▶ Overcoming real and imagined financial hurdles

- -

*U*nfortunately, most Americans don't know how to manage their personal finances because they were never taught how to do so. Their parents may have avoided discussing money in front of the kids, and nearly all our high schools and colleges lack even one course that teaches this vital, lifelong-needed skill.

Some people are fortunate enough to learn the financial keys to success at home, from knowledgeable friends, and from good books like this one. Others either never learn the keys to success, or they learn them the hard way — by making lots of costly mistakes. People who lack knowledge make more mistakes, and the more financial errors you commit, the more money passes through your hands and out of your life. In addition to the enormous financial costs, you experience the emotional toll of not feeling in control of your finances. Increased stress and anxiety go hand in hand with not mastering your money.

This chapter examines where people learn about finances and helps you decide whether your current knowledge is helping you or holding you back. You can find out how to improve your financial literacy and take responsibility for your finances, putting you in charge and reducing your anxiety about money. After all, you have more important things to worry about, like what's for dinner.

Talking Money at Home

I was fortunate in that my parents instilled in me the importance of personal financial management. Mom and Dad taught me a lot of things that have been invaluable throughout my life, and among those things were sound principles for earning, spending, and saving money. My parents had to know how to do these things, because they were raising a family of three children on (usually) one modest income. They knew the importance of making the most of what you have and of passing that vital skill on to your kids.

In many families, however, money is a taboo subject — parents don't level with their kids about the limitations, realities, and details of their budgets. Some parents I talk with believe that dealing with money is an adult issue and that kids should be insulated from it so that they can enjoy being kids. In many families, kids may hear about money *only* when disagreements and financial crises bubble to the surface. Thus begins the harmful cycle of children having negative associations with money and financial management.

In other cases, parents with the best of intentions pass on their bad money-management habits. You may have learned from a parent, for example, to buy things to cheer yourself up. Or you may have witnessed a family member mani-acally chasing get-rich-quick business and investment ideas. Now I'm not saying that you shouldn't listen to your parents. But in the area of personal finance, as in any other area, poor family advice and modeling can be problematic.

Think about where your parents learned about money management, and then consider whether they had the time, energy, or inclination to research choices before making their decisions. For example, if they didn't do enough research or had faulty information, your parents may mistakenly think that banks are the best places for investing money or that buying stocks is like going to Las Vegas. (You can find the best places for investing your money in Part III of this book.)

In still other cases, the parents have the right approach, but the kids go to the other extreme out of rebellion. For example, if your parents spent money carefully and thoughtfully and at times made you feel denied, you may tend to do the opposite, buying yourself gifts the moment any extra money comes your way.

Although you and I can't change what the educational system and your parents did or didn't teach you about personal finances, you now have the ability to find out what you need to know to manage your finances.

If you have children of your own, I'm sure you agree that kids really are amazing. Don't underestimate their potential or send them out into the world without the skills they need to be productive and happy adults. Buy them some good financial books when they head off to college or begin their first job.

Financial illiteracy: A costly situation

The lack of proficiency in personal financial management causes not only tremendous anxiety but also serious problems. Consider the following sobering statistics:

✔ Studies show that less than 20 percent of baby boomers are saving adequately for retirement and that one-quarter of the adults between the ages of 35 and 54 have not even *begun* to save for retirement.

✔ One out of every two marriages in America ends in divorce. Studies show that financial disagreement is one of the leading causes of marital discord. In a survey conducted by *Worth* magazine and the market research firm of Roper/Starch, couples admitted to fighting about money more than anything else (more than three times more often than they fight about their sex lives). And a staggering 57 percent of those surveyed agreed with the statement "In every marriage, money eventually becomes the most important concern."

✔ Less than 10 percent of American adults understand a 401(k) well enough to explain it to someone else. Fewer than one in four can explain what a municipal bond is.

✔ Only 8 percent of investors knew that there's not any agency or organization that "insures you against losing money as the result of fraud in your investment portfolio," according to a survey conducted by the Securities Investor Protection Corporation and the Investor Protection Trust.

✔ Nearly 80 percent of consumers do not know how the grace period on a credit card works. An even greater percentage doesn't understand that interest starts accumulating *immediately* for new purchases on credit cards with outstanding debts.

✔ Fifty-three percent of people who took a multiple choice investing quiz did not know that *total return* was the best measure of a mutual fund's performance.

Picking Up on Personal Finance in the Classroom

In schools, the main problem with personal finance education is the lack of classes, not that kids already know the information or that the skills are too complex for children to understand.

Nancy Donovan teaches personal finance to her fifth-grade math class as a way to illustrate how math can be used in the real world. "Students choose a career, find jobs, and figure out what their taxes and take-home paychecks will be. They also have to rent apartments and figure out a monthly budget," says Donovan. "Students like it, and parents have commented to me how surprised they are with how much financial knowledge their kids can handle." Donovan also has her students invest $10,000 (play money) and then track the investments' performance.

Urging schools to teach the basics of personal finance is just common sense. We should be teaching our children how to manage a household budget, the importance of saving money for future goals, and the consequences of over-spending. Unfortunately, few schools offer classes like Donovan's. In most cases, the financial basics aren't taught at all.

In the handful of schools that do offer a course remotely related to personal finance, the class is typically in economics (and an elective at that). "Archaic theory is being taught, and it doesn't do anything for the students as far as preparing them for the real world," says one high school principal I know. Having taken more than my fair share of economics courses in college, I understand the principal's concerns.

Some people argue that teaching children financial basics is the parents' job. However, this well-meant sentiment is what we're relying on now, and for all too many, it isn't working. In some families, financial illiteracy is passed on from generation to generation.

We must recognize that education takes place in the home, on the streets, and in the schools. Therefore, schools must bear some responsibility for teaching this skill. However, if you're raising children, remember that no one cares as much as you do or has as much ability to teach the important life skill of personal money management.

Identifying Unreliable Sources of Information

Some people are smart enough to realize that they're not financial geniuses. So they set out to take control of their finances by reading or consulting a financial advisor. Because the pitfalls are so numerous and the challenges so mighty when choosing an advisor, I devote Chapter 18 to the financial planning business and tell you what you need to know to avoid being fooled.

Reading is good. Reading is fundamental. But reading to find out how to manage your money can be dangerous if you're a novice. Misinformation can come from popular and seemingly reliable information sources, as I explain in the following sections.

Recognizing fake financial gurus

Before you take financial advice from anyone, examine his or her background, including professional work experience and education credentials. This is true whether you're getting advice from an advisor, writer, talk show host, or television financial reporter.

If you can't easily find such information, that's usually a red flag. People with something to hide or a lack of something redeeming to say about themselves usually don't promote their background.

Of course, just because someone seems to have a relatively impressive sounding background doesn't mean that she has your best interests in mind or has honestly presented her qualifications. *Forbes* magazine journalist William P. Barrett presented a sobering review of financial author Suze Orman's stated credentials and qualifications:

> "Besides books and other royalties, Orman's earned income has come mainly from selling insurance — which gets much more attention in her book than do stocks or bonds. . . . The jacket of her video says she has '18 years of experience at major Wall Street institutions.' In fact, she has 7. The 'nearly 1,000 new clients each year' touted on her publisher's Web site are simply fans making inquiries by mail."

When the *Forbes* piece came out, Orman's publicist tried to discredit it and made it sound as if the magazine had falsely criticized Orman. In response, the *San Francisco Chronicle,* which is the nearest major newspaper to Orman's hometown, picked up on the *Forbes* piece and ran a story of their own — written by Mark Veverka in his "Street Smarts" column — which substantiated the *Forbes* story.

Veverka went through the *Forbes* piece point by point and gave Orman's company and the public relations firm numerous opportunities to provide information contrary to the piece, but they did not. Here's some of what Veverka recounts from his contact with them:

> "If you want your side told, you have to return reporters' telephone calls. But alas, no callback.

> ". . . On Wednesday, December 6, Orman's publicist said a written response to the *Forbes* piece and the 'Street Smarts' column would be sent by facsimile to the *Chronicle* that day. However, no fax was ever sent. They blew me off. Twice.

> "In what was becoming an extraordinary effort to be fair, I placed more telephone calls over several days to Orman Financial and the publicist, asking for either an interview with Orman or an official response. If Orman didn't fudge about her years on Wall Street or didn't let her commodity-trading adviser license lapse, surely we could straighten all of this out, right?

> "Still, no answer. Nada. On December 17, I called yet again. Finally, literally on deadline, a woman who identified herself as Orman's 'consultant' called me to talk 'off the record' about the column. What she ended up doing was bashing the *Forbes* piece and my column but not for publication. More importantly, she offered no official retort to allegations made by veteran *Forbes* writer William Barrett. I have to say, it was an incredibly unprofessional attempt at spinning. And I've been spun by the worst of them."

Even then you can't always accept stated credentials and qualifications at face value, because some people lie. You can't sniff out liars by the way they look, their gender, or their age. You can, however, increase your chances of being tipped off by being skeptical. You can see a number of hucksters in the print publishing field for what they are by using common sense in reviewing some of their outrageous claims.

One formerly best-selling personal finance book (*Wealth Without Risk,* by Charles Givens) advises you to "Buy disability insurance only if you are in poor health or accident prone." Putting aside the minor detail that no insurance company (that's interested in making a profit) is going to issue you a disability policy after you fall into poor health, how do you know when you're going to be accident-prone? Because health problems and auto accidents cause many disabilities, you can't see disabilities coming unless your horoscope happens to warn you!

Some sources of advice, such as Wade Cook's investment seminars, lure you in by promising outrageous returns. The stock market has generated average annual returns of about 10 percent over the long term. However, Cook, a former taxi driver, promoted his seminars as an "alive, hands-on, do the deals, two-day intense course in making huge returns in the stock market. If you aren't getting 20% per month, or 300% annualized returns on your investments, you need to be there." (I guess I do, as does every investment manager and individual investor I know!)

Cook's get-rich-quick seminars, which cost more than $6,000, were so successful at attracting people that his company went public in the late 1990s and generated annual revenues of more than $100 million.

Cook's "techniques" included trading in and out of stocks and options on stocks after short holding periods of weeks, days, or even hours. His trading strategies can best be described as techniques that are based upon technical analysis — that is, charting a stock's price movements and volume history, and then making predictions based on those charts.

The perils of following an approach that advocates short-term trading with the allure of high profits are numerous:

- ✔ You're going to rack up enormous brokerage commissions.

- ✔ On occasions where your short-term trades produce a profit, you pay high ordinary income tax rates rather than the far lower capital gains rate for investments held more than 12 months.

- ✔ You're not going to make big profits — quite the reverse. If you stick with this approach, you'll underperform the market averages.

- ✔ You're going to make yourself a nervous wreck. This type of trading is gambling, not investing. Get sucked up in it, and you'll lose more than money — you may also lose the love and respect of your family and friends.

If Cook's followers were indeed earning the 300 percent annual returns his seminars claim to help you achieve, any investor starting with just $10,000 would vault to the top of the list of the world's wealthiest people (ahead of Bill Gates and Warren Buffett) in just 11 years!

Understanding how undeserving investment gurus get popular

You may be wondering how Givens and Cook became so popular despite the obvious flaws in their advice. Givens made the most of his talent for working the media and his great self-promotion through seminars. One of the problems with the mass media is that hucksters can get good publicity because many members of the media are themselves financially illiterate, and they love a good story. So charming hucksters get all sorts of free coverage, getting quoted in the press and invited to appear on a number of national television and radio programs.

Thousands of people went to seminars conducted by Givens, partly because of the credibility Givens built through media appearances. As has now been well documented by some of those same members of the media, many unsuspecting investors were sold commission-laden products, including risky limited partnerships, through his organization.

Consider the case of Helen Giszczak, a 69-year-old retired secretary. She invested nearly two-thirds of her modest life savings in limited partnerships, which she said were described to her by Givens's associates as "probably the most conservative investments we know of." But some of her limited partnerships ended up in bankruptcy, while the others lost much of their value.

Helen Giszczak appeared on the *Donahue* show with John Allen, an investment broker turned securities lawyer who helped her sue Givens's organization to get her money back. After a lengthy dialogue with Giszczak and Allen, Phil Donahue asked Helen how a smart person like her could get sucked in like that. She replied, "He was on your show and Oprah's. You gave him credibility. You gave him free advertising."

Wade Cook, on the other hand, promoted his seminars through infomercials and other advertising, including radio ads on respected news stations. The high stock market returns of the 1990s brought greed back into fashion. (My experience has been that you see more of this greed near market tops than you do near market bottoms.)

The attorneys general of numerous states sued Cook's company and sought millions of dollars in consumer refunds. The suits alleged that the company lied about its investment track record (not a big surprise — this company claimed that you'd make 300 percent per year in stocks!).

Cook's company settled the blizzard of state and Federal Trade Commission (FTC) lawsuits against his firm by agreeing to accurately disclose its trading record in future promotions and give refunds to customers who were misled by past inflated return claims.

According to a news report by *Bloomberg News,* Cook's firm disclosed that it lost a whopping 89 percent of its own money trading during the last reporting year. As Deb Bortner, director of the Washington State Securities Division and president of the North American Securities Administrators Association observed, "Either Wade is unable to follow his own system, which he claims is simple to follow, or the system doesn't work."

Don't assume that someone with something to sell, who is getting good press and running lots of ads, will take care of you. That "guru" may just be good at press relations and self-promotion. Certainly, talk shows and the media at large can and do provide useful information on a variety of topics, but bad eggs sometimes turn up. These bad eggs may not always smell bad upfront. In fact, they may hoodwink people for years before finally being exposed. Please review Part V for the details on resources you can trust and those that could cause you to go bust!

Pandering to advertisers

Thousands of publications and media outlets — newspapers, magazines, Web sites, radio, television, and so on — dole out personal financial advice and perspectives. Although many of these "service providers" collect revenue from subscribers, virtually all are dependent — in some cases, fully dependent (especially on the Internet, radio, and television) — on advertising dollars. Although advertising is a necessary part of capitalism, advertisers can taint and, in some cases, dictate the content of what you read, listen to, and view.

Consider this case from a nonfinancial publication — *Modern Bride* magazine. *Harper's* magazine got ahold of an apologetic letter (which it humorously entitled "To Love, Honor And Obey Our Advertisers") that *Bride's* fashion advertising director sent to the magazine's advertisers. Here's an excerpt of that letter:

> "*Bride's* recommends that its readers (your customers) negotiate price, borrow a slip or petticoat, and compare catalog shoe prices, and tells its readers that the groom's tuxedo may be free. It is difficult to understand why *Bride's* was compelled to publish this information. With 57 years of publishing experience and support to the bridal industry, *Bride's* could and should have been more sensitive to the retailers that it purports to serve. All of us in the bridal business must concentrate on projecting full-service bridal retailing in a positive light."

I don't find it difficult to understand why the writer of the criticized *Bride's* article suggested cost-saving strategies to its readers — she was trying to give them useful information and advice! Now, revealing letters like this one are hard to come by, so how can you, a consumer of financial information, separate the good publications from the advertiser-biased publications? After writing and working for a number of publications, and observing the workings of even more, I've developed some ideas on the subject.

Be sure to consider how dependent a publication or media outlet is on advertising. I find that "free" publications, radio, and television are the ones that most often create conflicts of interest by pandering to advertisers. (All three derive all their revenue from advertising.)

Much of what's on the Internet is advertiser-driven, as well. Many of the investing sites on the Internet offer advice about individual stocks. Interestingly, such sites derive much of their revenue from online brokerage firms seeking to recruit customers who are foolish enough to believe that selecting their own stocks is the best way to invest. (See Part III for more information about your investment options.)

As you read various publications, watch TV, or listen to the radio, note how consumer-oriented these media are. Do you get the feeling that they're looking out for your interests? For example, if lots of auto manufacturers advertise, does the media outlet ever tell you how to save money when shopping for a car or the importance of buying a car within your means? Or are they primarily creating an advertiser-friendly broadcast or publication?

Jumping over Real and Imaginary Hurdles to Financial Success

Perhaps you know that you should live within your means, buy and hold sound investments for the long term, and secure proper insurance coverage; however, you can't bring yourself to do these things. We all know how difficult it is to break habits that you've practiced for many years. The temptation to spend money lurks everywhere you turn. Ads show attractive and popular people enjoying the fruits of their labors — a new car, an exotic vacation, and a lavish home.

Maybe you felt deprived by your tightwad parents as a youngster, or maybe you're bored with life and you like the adventure of buying new things. If only you could hit it big on one or two investments, you think, you could get rich quick and do what you really want with your life. As for disasters and catastrophes, well, those things happen to other people, not to you. Besides, you'll probably have advance warning of pending problems, so you can prepare accordingly, right?

Your emotions and temptations can get the better of you. Certainly, part of successfully managing your finances involves coming to terms with your shortcomings and the consequences of your behaviors. If you don't, you may end up enslaved to a dead-end job so you can keep feeding your spending addiction. Or you may spend more time with your investments than you do with your family and friends. Or unexpected events can leave you reeling financially; disasters and catastrophes can happen to anyone at any time.

Discovering what (or who) is holding you back

A variety of personal and emotional hurdles can get in the way of making the best financial moves. As I discuss earlier in this chapter, a lack of financial knowledge (which stems from a lack of personal financial education) can stand in the way of making good decisions.

But I've seen some people caught in the psychological trap of blaming something else for their financial problems. For example, some people believe that all our adult problems can be traced back to childhood and how we were raised. Behaviors ranging from substance abuse and credit card addiction to sexual infidelity are supposedly caused by our roots.

I don't want to disregard the negative impact particular backgrounds can have on some people's tendency to make the wrong choices during their lives. Exploring your personal history can certainly yield clues to what makes you tick. That said, we are adults making choices and engaging in behaviors that affect ourselves as well as others. We shouldn't blame our parents for our own inability to plan for our financial futures, live within our means, and make sound investments.

Some people also tend to blame their financial shortcomings on not earning more income. Such people believe that if only they earned more, their financial (and personal) problems would melt away.

My experience working and speaking with people from diverse economic backgrounds has taught me that achieving financial success — and more importantly, personal happiness — has virtually nothing to do with how much income a person makes but rather with what she makes of what she does have. I know financially wealthy people who are emotionally poor even though they have all the material goods they want. Likewise, I know people who are quite happy, content, and emotionally wealthy even though they're struggling financially.

Americans — even those who have not had an "easy" life — should be able to come up with numerous things to be happy about and grateful for: a family who loves them; friends who laugh at their stupid jokes; the freedom to catch a movie or play or to read a good book; a great singing voice, sense of humor, or a full head of hair.

Developing good financial habits

After you understand the basic concepts and know where to buy the best financial products when you need them, you'll soon see that managing personal finances well is not much more difficult than other things you do regularly, like tying your shoelaces and getting to work each day.

Regardless of your income, you can make your dollars stretch further if you practice good financial habits and avoid mistakes. In fact, the lower your income, the more important it is that you make the most of your income and savings (because you don't have the luxury of falling back on your next fat paycheck to bail you out).

More and more industries are subject to global competition, so you need to be on your financial toes now more than ever. Job security is waning; layoffs and retraining for new jobs are increasing. Putting in 30 years for one company and retiring with the gold watch and lifetime pension are becoming as rare as never having problems with your computer.

Speaking of company pensions, odds are increasing that you work for an employer that has you save toward your own retirement instead of providing a pension for you. Not only do you need to save the money, you must also decide how to invest it. Chapter 11 can help you get a handle on investing in retirement accounts.

Personal finance involves much more than managing and investing money. It also includes making all the pieces of your financial life fit together; it means lifting yourself out of financial illiteracy. Like planning a vacation, managing your personal finances means forming a plan for making the best use of your limited time and dollars.

Intelligent personal financial strategies have little to do with your gender, ethnicity, or marital status. We all need to manage our finances wisely. Some aspects of financial management become more or less important at different points in your life, but for the most part, the principles remain the same for everyone.

Knowing the right answers isn't enough. You have to practice good financial habits just as you practice other good habits, such as brushing your teeth. Don't be overwhelmed. As you read this book, make a short list of your financial marching orders and then start working away. Throughout this book, I highlight ways you can overcome temptations and keep control of your money rather than let your emotions and money rule you. (I discuss common financial problems in Chapter 2.)

What you do with your money is a quite personal and confidential matter. In this book, I try to provide guidance that can keep you in sound financial health. You don't have to take it all — pick what works best for you and understand the pros and cons of your options. But from this day forward, please don't make the easily avoidable mistakes or overlook the sound strategies that I discuss throughout this book.

If you're young, congratulations for being so forward-thinking as to realize the immense value of investing in your personal financial education. You'll reap the rewards for decades to come. But even if you're not so young, you surely have many years to make the most of the money you currently have, the money you're going to earn, and even the money you may inherit!

Throughout your journey, I hope to challenge and even change the way you think about money and about making important personal financial decisions — and sometimes even about the meaning of life. No, I'm not a philosopher, but I do know that money — for better but more often for worse — is connected to many other parts of our lives.

Chapter 2

Measuring Your Financial Health

. . . .

In This Chapter

▶ Determining assets, liabilities, and your (financial) net worth

▶ Requesting (and fixing) your credit reports

▶ Making sense of your credit score

▶ Understanding bad debt, good debt, and too much debt

▶ Calculating your rate of savings

▶ Assessing your investment and insurance know-how

. . . .

*H*ow financially healthy are you? You may already know some or even all the bad news. Or perhaps things aren't quite as bad as they seem.

When was the last time you sat down surrounded by all your personal and financial documents and took stock of your overall financial situation, including reviewing your spending, savings, future goals, and insurance? If you're like most people, you've either never done this exercise or you did so a long time ago.

This chapter guides you through a *financial physical* to help you detect problems with your current financial health. But don't dwell on your "problems." View them for what they are — opportunities for improving your financial situation. In fact, the more areas for improvement you can identify, the greater the potential you may have to build real wealth and accomplish your financial and personal goals.

Avoiding Common Money Mistakes

Financial problems, like many medical problems, are best detected early (clean living doesn't hurt, either). Here are some common personal financial problems I've seen in my work as a financial counselor:

✔ **Not planning:** Human beings were born to procrastinate. That's why we have deadlines (like April 15) — and deadline extensions (need another six months to get that tax return done?). Unfortunately, you may have no explicit deadlines with your overall finances. You can allow your credit card debt to accumulate, or you can leave your savings sitting in lousy investments for years. You can pay higher taxes, leave gaps in your retirement and insurance coverage, and overpay for financial products. Of course, planning your finances isn't as much fun as planning a vacation, but doing the former can help you take more of the latter. See Chapter 4 for info on setting financial goals.

✔ **Overspending:** Simple arithmetic helps you determine that savings is the difference between what you earn and what you spend (assuming that you're not spending more than you're earning!). To increase your savings, you either have to work more (yuck!), increase your earning power through education or job advancement, get to know a wealthy family who wants to leave its fortune to you, or spend less. For most of us, especially over the short-term, the thrifty approach is the key to building savings and wealth. Check out Chapter 3 for a primer on figuring out where your money goes; Chapter 6 gives advice for reducing your spending.

✔ **Buying with consumer credit:** Even with the benefit of today's lower interest rates, carrying a balance month-to-month on your credit card or buying a car on credit means that even more of your future earnings are going to be earmarked for debt repayment. Buying on credit encourages you to spend more than you can really afford. Chapter 5 discusses debt and credit problems.

✔ **Delaying saving for retirement:** Most people say that they want to retire by their mid-60s or sooner. But in order to accomplish this goal, most people need to save a reasonable chunk (around 10 percent) of their incomes starting sooner rather than later. The longer you wait to start saving for retirement, the harder reaching your goal will be. And you'll pay much more in taxes to boot if you don't take advantage of the tax benefits of investing through particular retirement accounts. For information on planning for retirement, see Chapters 4 and 11.

✔ **Falling prey to financial sales pitches:** Great deals that can't wait for a little reflection or a second opinion are often disasters waiting to happen. A sucker may be born every minute, but a slick salesperson is pitching something every second! Steer clear of people who pressure you to make decisions, promise you high investment returns, and lack the proper training and experience to help you. For basic investment concepts and what kinds of investments to avoid, turn to Chapter 8.

✔ **Not doing your homework:** To get the best deal, shop around, read reviews, and get advice from objective third parties. You also need to check references and track records so that you don't hire incompetent, self-serving, or fraudulent financial advisors. (For more on hiring financial planners, see Chapter 18.) But with all the different financial products available, making informed financial decisions has become an overwhelming task. I do a lot of the homework for you with the recommendations in this book. I also explain what additional research you need to do and how to do it.

✔ **Making decisions based on emotion:** You're most vulnerable to making the wrong moves financially after a major life change (a job loss or divorce, for example) or when you feel pressure. Maybe your investments plunged in value. Or perhaps a recent divorce has you fearing that you won't be able to afford to retire when you planned, so you pour thousands of dollars into some newfangled financial product. Take your time and keep your emotions out of the picture. In Chapter 21, I discuss how to approach major life changes with an eye on determining what changes you may need to make to your financial picture.

✔ **Not separating the wheat from the chaff:** In any field in which you're not an expert, you run the danger of following the advice of someone who you think is an expert but really isn't. This book shows you how to separate the financial fluff from the financial facts. (Flip to Chapter 20 for info on how to evaluate financial advice in the mass media.) You are the person who is best able to manage your personal finances. Educate and trust yourself!

✔ **Exposing yourself to catastrophic risk:** You're vulnerable if you and your family don't have insurance to pay for financially devastating losses. People without a savings reserve and support network can end up homeless. Many people lack sufficient insurance coverage to replace their income. Don't wait for a tragedy to strike to find out whether you have the right insurance coverage. Check out Part IV for more on insurance.

✔ **Focusing too much on money:** Placing too much emphasis on making and saving money can warp your perspective on what's important in life. Money is not the first or even second priority in happy people's lives. Your health, relationships with family and friends, career satisfaction, and fulfilling interests should be more important.

Most problems can be fixed over time with changes in your behavior. (That's what the rest of the book is all about.)

Determining Your Financial Net Worth

Your financial net worth is an important barometer of your monetary health. Your net worth indicates your capacity to accomplish major financial goals, such as buying a home, retiring, and withstanding unexpected expenses or loss of income.

Your financial net worth has absolutely, positively *no* relationship to your worth as a human being. This is not a test. You don't have to compare your number with your neighbor's. Financial net worth is not the scorecard of life.

Your *net worth* is your financial assets minus your financial liabilities:

```
Financial Assets - Financial Liabilities = Net Worth
```

The following sections tell you how to determine those numbers.

Adding up your financial assets

A *financial asset* is real money or an investment you can convert to hard dollars that you can use to buy things now or in the future.

Financial assets generally include the money you have in bank accounts, stocks, bonds, and mutual fund accounts (see Part III, which deals with investments). Money that you have in retirement accounts (including those with your employer) and the value of any businesses or real estate that you own are also included.

I generally recommend that you exclude your personal residence when figuring your financial assets. Include your home only if you expect to someday sell it or otherwise live off the money you now have tied up in it (perhaps by taking out a reverse mortgage, which I discuss in Chapter 14). If you plan on someday tapping into the *equity* (the difference between the market value and any debt owed on the property), add that portion of the equity that you expect to use to your list of assets.

Assets can also include your future expected Social Security benefits and pension payments (if your employer has such a plan). These assets are usually quoted in dollars per month rather than in a lump sum value. I explain in a moment how to account for these monthly benefits when tallying your financial assets.

Consumer items — such as your car, clothing, stereo, and wine collection — do *not* count as financial assets. I know that adding these things to your assets makes your assets *look* larger (and some financial software packages and publications encourage you to list these items as assets), but you can't live off them unless you sell them.

Subtracting your financial liabilities

To arrive at your financial net worth, you must subtract your *financial liabilities* from your assets. Liabilities include loans and debts outstanding, such as credit card and auto loan debts. When figuring your liabilities, include money you borrowed from family and friends — unless you're not gonna pay it back! Include mortgage debt on your home as a liability *only* if you include the value of your home in your asset list. Be sure to also include debt owed on other real estate — no matter what (because you counted the value of investment real estate as an asset).

Crunching your numbers

Table 2-1 provides a place for you to figure your financial assets. Go ahead and write in the spaces provided, unless you plan to lend this book to someone and you don't want to put your money situation on display. *Note:* See Table 4-1 in Chapter 4 to estimate your Social Security benefits.

Table 2-1	Your Financial Assets
Account	*Value*
Savings and investment accounts (including retirement accounts):	
Example: Bank savings account	$5,000
_____	$_____
_____	$_____
_____	$_____
_____	$_____
_____	$_____
_____	$_____
Total =	$_____
Benefits earned that pay a monthly retirement income:	
Employer's pensions	$_____ / month
Social Security	$_____ / month
	× 240*
Total =	$_____
Total Financial Assets (add the two totals) =	$_____

* To convert benefits that will be paid to you monthly into a total dollar amount, and for purposes of simplification, assume that you will spend 20 years in retirement. (Ah, think of two decades of lollygagging around — vacationing, harassing the kids, spoiling the grandkids, starting another career, or maybe just living off the fat of the land.) As a shortcut, multiply the benefits that you'll collect monthly in retirement by 240 (12 months per year times 20 years). Inflation may reduce the value of your employer's pension if it doesn't contain a cost-of-living increase each year in the same way that Social Security does. Don't sweat this now — you can take care of it in the section on retirement planning in Chapter 4.

Now comes the potentially depressing part — figuring out your debts and loans in Table 2-2.

Table 2-2	Your Financial Liabilities
Loan	**Balance**
Example: Gouge 'Em Bank Credit Card	$4,000
_____	$_____
_____	$_____
_____	$_____
_____	$_____
_____	$_____
_____	$_____
Total Financial Liabilities =	$_____

Now you can subtract your liabilities from your assets to figure your net worth in Table 2-3.

Table 2-3	Your Net Worth
Find	*Write It Here*
Total Financial Assets (from Table 2-1)	$_____
Total Financial Liabilities (from Table 2-2)	−$_____
Net Worth =	$_____

Interpreting your net worth results

Your net worth is important and useful only to you and your unique situation and goals. What seems like a lot of money to a person with a simple lifestyle may seem like a pittance to a person with high expectations and a desire for an opulent lifestyle.

In Chapter 4, you can crunch some more numbers to determine your financial status more precisely for goals such as retirement planning. I also discuss saving toward other important goals in that chapter. In the meantime, if your net worth (excluding expected monthly retirement benefits such as those from Social Security and pensions) is negative or less than half your annual income, take notice. You have lots of company — in fact, you're with the majority of Americans. If you're in your 20s and you're just starting to work, a low net worth is less concerning.

Getting rid of your debts — the highest-interest ones first — is the most important thing. Then you need to build a safety reserve equal to three to six months of living expenses. You should definitely find out more about getting out of debt, reducing your spending, and developing tax-wise ways to save and invest your future earnings.

Examining Your Credit Score and Reports

You may not know it (or care), but you probably have a personal credit report and a credit score. Lenders examine your credit report and score before granting you a loan or credit line.

Understanding what your credit data includes and means

A credit report contains information such as

- **Personal identifying information:** Includes name, address, Social Security number, and so on
- **Record of credit accounts:** Details when each account was opened, latest balance, payment history, and so on
- **Bankruptcy filings:** If you've filed bankruptcy in recent years
- **Inquiries:** Lists who has pulled your credit report because you've applied for credit

Your *credit score,* which is not the same as your credit report, is a three-digit score based on the report. Lenders use your credit score as a predictor of your likelihood of defaulting on repaying your borrowings. As such, your credit score has a major impact on whether a lender is willing to extend you a particular loan and at what interest rate.

FICO is the leading credit score in the industry and was developed by Fair Isaac and Company. FICO scores range from a low of 300 to a high of 850. As with college entrance examinations such as the SAT, higher scores are better. The higher your credit score, the lower your predicted likelihood of defaulting on a loan (see Figure 2-1). The "rate of credit delinquency" refers to the percentage of consumers who will become 90 days late or later in repaying a creditor within the next two years. As you can see in the chart, consumers with low credit scores have dramatically higher rates of falling behind in their loans. Thus, low credit scorers are considered much riskier borrowers, and fewer lenders will be willing to offer you a given loan; those who do will charge you relatively high rates.

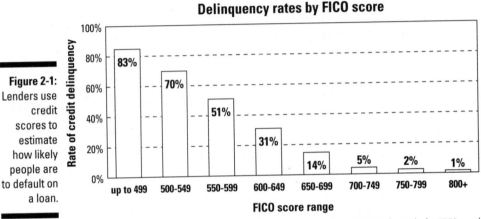

Delinquency rates by FICO score

Figure 2-1: Lenders use credit scores to estimate how likely people are to default on a loan.

Source: Fair Isaac Corporation (myFICO.com)

The median FICO score is around 710. According to Liz Weston, author of *Your Credit Score: How to Fix, Improve, and Protect the 3-digit Number that Shapes Your Financial Future* (Prentice Hall), you will generally qualify for the best lending rates if your credit score is 620 or higher. Credit scores below 620 are not considered good, and lenders consider these loans risky. With some types of loans (such as home equity loans), to qualify for the best rates, you may need a credit score of at least 760 or 780.

Obtaining your credit reports and score

Given the importance of your personal credit report, you may be pleased to know that you're entitled to receive a free copy of your credit report annually from each of the three credit bureaus (Equifax, Experian, and TransUnion).

If you visit www.annualcreditreport.com, you can view and print copies of your credit report information from each of the three credit agencies (alternatively, call 877-322-8228 and have your reports mailed to you). After entering some personal data at the Web site, check the box indicating that you want to obtain all three credit reports, as each report may have slightly different information. You'll then be directed to one of the three bureaus, and after you finish verifying that you are who you claim to be at that site, you can easily navigate back to annualcreditreport.com so you can continue to the next agency's site.

When you receive your reports, the best first step is to examine them for possible mistakes (more in a moment regarding fixing problems in your reports). I recently did that myself and found minor errors on two of the three reports. It took me two minutes to correct one of the errors (by submitting a request to that credit reporting agency's Web site), and it took about half an hour to get the other mistake fixed (a small doctor's bill was erroneously listed as unpaid and in collections).

You may be surprised to find that your credit reports do *not* include your credit score. The reason for this is quite simple: The 2003 law mandating that the three credit agencies provide a free credit report annually to each U.S. citizen who requests a copy did not mandate that they provide the credit score. Thus, if you wish to obtain your credit score, it's going to cost you.

You can request your credit score from Fair Isaac, but you'll get whacked $15 for every request (that can set you back $45 to see your FICO score for each credit bureau). Save your money. If you're going to purchase your credit score, you can do so for less from the individual credit bureaus — Equifax, for example, charges just $7.

If you do spring for your current credit score, be clear about what you're buying. You may not realize that you're agreeing to some sort of an ongoing credit monitoring service for say $50 to $100 per year.

Improving your credit reports and score

Instead of simply throwing money into buying your credit scores or paying for some ongoing monitoring service that you may not pay attention to anyway, take an interest in improving your credit standing and score. Working to boost your credit rating is especially worthwhile if you know that your credit report contains detrimental information.

Here are the most important actions that you can take to boost your attractiveness to lenders:

- ✔ **Get all three of your credit reports, and be sure each is accurate.** Correct errors (as I explain in the next section) and be especially sure to get accounts removed if they aren't yours and they show late payments or are in collection.

- ✔ **If your report includes late or missed payments more than seven years old, ask to have those removed.** Ditto for a bankruptcy more than ten years ago.

- ✔ **Pay all your bills on time.** To ensure on-time payments, sign up for automatic bill payment, which most companies (like phone and utility providers) enable you to use.

✔ **Be loyal if it doesn't cost you.** The older the age of loan accounts you have open, the better for your credit rating. Closing old accounts and opening a bunch of new ones generally lowers your credit score.

But don't be loyal if it costs you! For example, if you can refinance your mortgage and save some good money, by all means do so. The same logic applies if you're carrying credit card debt at a high interest rate and want to transfer that balance to a lower rate card. If your current credit card provider refuses to match a lower rate you find elsewhere, move your balance and save yourself some money (see Chapter 5 for details).

✔ **Limit your debt and debt accounts.** The more loans, especially consumer loans, that you hold and the higher the balances, the lower your credit score will be.

✔ **Work to pay down consumer revolving debt (such as on credit cards).** Please read Chapters 5 and 6 for suggestions.

Getting credit report errors corrected

If you obtain your credit report and find a boo-boo on it that you don't recognize as being your mistake or fault, do *not* assume that the information is correct. Credit reporting bureaus and the creditors who report credit information to these bureaus often make mistakes.

You hope and expect that, if a credit bureau has negative and incorrect information in your credit report and you bring the error to their attention, they will graciously and expeditiously fix the mistake. If you believe that, you're the world's greatest optimist; perhaps you also think you won't have to wait in line at the Department of Motor Vehicles, post office, or your local bank at noon on payday.

Odds are, you're going to have to fill out a form on a Web site, make some phone calls, or write a letter or two to fix the problems on your credit report. Here's how to correct most errors that aren't your fault:

✔ **If the credit problem is someone else's:** A surprising number of personal credit report glitches are the result of someone else's negative information getting on your credit report. If the bad information on your report is completely foreign-looking to you, tell the credit bureau and explain that you need more information because you don't recognize the creditor.

✔ **If the creditor made a mistake:** Creditors make mistakes, too. You need to write or call the creditor to get them to correct the erroneous information that they sent to the credit bureau. Phoning first usually works best. (The credit bureau should be able to tell you how to reach the creditor if you don't know how.) If necessary, follow up with a letter.

Whether you speak with a credit bureau or an actual lender, make notes of your conversations. If representatives say that they can fix the problem, get their names and extensions, and follow up with them if they don't deliver as promised. If you're ensnared in bureaucratic red tape, escalate the situation by speaking with a department manager. By law, bureaus are required to respond to a request to fix a credit error within 30 days — hold the bureau accountable!

Telling your side of the story

With a minor credit infraction, some lenders may simply ask for an explanation. Years ago, I had a credit report blemish that was the result of being away for several weeks and missing the payment due date for a couple small bills. When my proposed mortgage lender saw my late payments, the lender asked for a simple written explanation.

You and a creditor may not see eye to eye on a problem, and the creditor may refuse to budge. If that's the case, credit bureaus are required by law to allow you to add a 100-word explanation to your credit file.

Sidestepping "credit repair" firms

Online and in newspapers and magazines, you may see ads for credit repair companies that claim to fix your credit report problems. In the worst cases I've seen, these firms charge outrageous amounts of money and don't come close to fulfilling their marketing hype.

If you have legitimate glitches on your credit report, credit repair firms can't make the glitches disappear. Hope springs eternal, however — some people would like to believe that their credit problems can be fixed.

Remember — if your problems are fixable, you can fix them yourself, and you don't need to pay a company big bucks to do it.

Knowing the Difference between Bad Debt and Good Debt

Why do you borrow money? Usually, you borrow money because you don't have enough to buy something you want or need — like a college education. If you want to buy a four-year college education, you can easily spend $100,000, $150,000, or more. Not too many people have that kind of spare cash. So borrowing money to finance part of that cost enables you to buy the education.

How about a new car? A trip to your friendly local car dealer shows you that a new set of wheels will set you back $20,000+. Although more people may have the money to pay for that than, say, the college education, what if you don't? Should you finance the car the way you finance the education?

The auto dealers and bankers who are eager to make you an auto loan say that you deserve and can afford to drive a nice, new car, and they tell you to borrow away (or lease, which I don't love either — please see Chapter 6). I just say, "No! No! No!" Why do I disagree with the auto dealers and lenders? For starters, I'm not trying to sell you a car or loan from which I derive a profit! More importantly, there's a *big* difference between borrowing for something that represents a long-term investment and borrowing for short-term consumption.

If you spend, say, $1,500 on a vacation, the money is gone. Poof! You may have fond memories and even some Kodak moments, but you have no financial value to show for it. "But," you say, "vacations replenish my soul and make me more productive when I return. In fact, the vacation more than pays for itself!"

Great. I'm not saying that you shouldn't take a vacation. By all means, take one, two, three, or as many as you can afford yearly. But that's the point: *Take what you can afford.* If you have to borrow money in the form of an outstanding balance on your credit card for many months in order to take the vacation, you *can't afford* it.

Consuming your way to bad debt

I use the term *bad debt* to refer to debt incurred for consumption, because such debt is harmful to your long-term financial health.

You'll be able to take many more vacations during your lifetime if you save the cash in advance. If you get into the habit of borrowing and paying all that interest for vacations, cars, clothing, and other consumer items, you'll spend more of your future income paying back the debt and interest, leaving you with less money for your other goals.

The relatively high interest rates that banks and other lenders charge for bad (consumer) debt is one of the reasons you're less able to save money when using such debt. Not only does money borrowed through credit cards, auto loans, and other types of consumer loans carry a relatively high interest rate, but it also isn't tax-deductible.

I'm not saying that you should never borrow money and that all debt is bad. Good debt, such as that used to buy real estate and small businesses, is generally available at lower interest rates than bad debt and is usually tax-deductible. If well managed, these investments may also increase in value. Borrowing to pay for educational expenses can also make sense. Education is generally a good long-term investment, because it can increase your earning potential. And student loan interest is tax deductible subject to certain limitations (see Chapter 7).

The lure of easy credit

Many years ago, I worked as a management consultant and did a lot of work with companies in the financial services' industry, including some of the major credit card companies. Their game then, as it is now, was to push cards into the hands of as many people as possible who have a tendency and propensity to carry debt month to month at high interest rates. Their direct marketing campaigns are quite effective. Ditto for the auto manufacturers who successfully entice many people who can't really afford to spend $20,000, $30,000, or more on a brand new car to buy new autos financed with an auto loan or lease. And just as alcohol and cigarette makers target young people with their advertising, credit card companies are recruiting and grooming the next generation of overspenders on college campuses. Unbelievably, our highest institutions of learning receive large fees from credit card companies for being allowed to promote their cards on campuses!

As credit is widely available today, so too are suggestions for how to spend it. We're bombarded with ads 24/7 on radio, television, Web sites, the sides of buses and trains and the tops of taxicabs, people's clothing, and cars. If you wanted to go a day without advertising, you couldn't — you're surrounded!

Recognizing bad debt overload

Calculating how much debt you have relative to your annual income is a useful way to size up your debt load. Ignore, for now, good debt — the loans you may owe on real estate, a business, an education, and so on (I get to that in the next section). I'm focusing on bad debt, the higher-interest debt used to buy items that depreciate in value.

To calculate your bad debt danger ratio, divide your bad debt by your annual income. For example, suppose that you earn $40,000 per year. Between your credit cards and an auto loan, you have $20,000 of debt. In this case, your bad debt represents 50 percent of your annual income.

$$\frac{\text{bad debt}}{\text{annual income}} \quad = \quad \text{bad debt danger ratio}$$

The financially healthy amount of bad debt is zero. Not everyone agrees with me. One major U.S. credit card company says — in its "educational" materials, which it gives to schools to teach students about supposedly sound financial management — that carrying consumer debt amounting to 10 to 20 percent of your annual income is just fine.

When your bad debt danger ratio starts to push beyond 25 percent, it can spell real trouble. Such high levels of high-interest consumer debt on credit cards and auto loans grow like cancer. The growth of the debt can snowball and get out of control unless something significant intervenes. If you have consumer debt beyond 25 percent of your annual income, see Chapter 5 to find out how to get out of debt.

How much good debt is acceptable? The answer varies. The key question is: Are you able to save sufficiently to accomplish your goals? In the "Analyzing Your Savings" section, later in this chapter, I help you figure out how much you're actually saving, and in Chapter 4, I help you determine what you should save to accomplish your goals. (See Chapter 14 to find out how much mortgage debt is appropriate to take on when buying a home.)

Borrow money only for investments (good debt) — for purchasing things that retain and hopefully increase in value over the long term, such as an education, real estate, or your own business. Don't borrow money for consumption (bad debt) — for spending on things that decrease in value and eventually become financially worthless, such as cars, clothing, vacations, and so on.

Assessing good debt: Can you get too much?

As with good food, of course, you can get too much of a good thing! When you incur debt for investment purposes — to buy real estate, for small business, even your education — you hope to see a positive return on your invested dollars.

But some real estate investments don't work out. Some small businesses crash and burn and some educational degrees and programs don't help in the way that some hope that they could.

There's no magic formula for determining when you have too much "good debt." In extreme cases, I've seen entrepreneurs, for example, borrow up to their eyeballs to get a business off the ground. Sometimes this works and they end up financially rewarded, but in most cases, it doesn't.

Here are two important questions to ponder and discuss with your loved ones about the seemingly "good debt" you're taking on:

- ✔ Are you and your loved ones able to sleep well at night and function well during the day, free from great worry about how you're going to meet next month's expenses?
- ✔ Are you and your loved ones financially able to save what you'd like to work toward your goals (see Chapter 4)?

If you find your debt is too high, you may be able to use some of the debt-reduction strategies in Chapter 5.

Playing the credit card float

Given what I have to say about the vagaries of consumer debt, you may think that I'm always against using credit cards. Actually, I have credit cards, and I use them — but I pay my balance in full each month. Besides the convenience credit cards offer me — in not having to carry around extra cash and checks — I receive another benefit: I have free use of the bank's money extended to me through my credit card charges. (Some cards offer other benefits, such as frequent flyer miles. Also, purchases made on credit cards may be contested if the seller of the product or service doesn't stand behind what it sells.)

When you charge on a credit card that *does not* have an outstanding balance carried over from the prior month, you typically have several weeks (known as the *grace period*) from the date of the charge to the time when you must pay your bill. This is called *playing the float*. Had you paid for this purchase by cash or check, you would have had to shell out the money sooner.

If you have difficulty saving money, and plastic tends to burn holes through your budget, forget the float game. You're better off not using credit cards. The same applies to those who pay their bills in full but spend more because it's so easy to do so with a piece of plastic. (For info on alternatives to using credit cards, see Chapter 5.)

Analyzing Your Savings

How much money have you actually saved in the past year? By savings, I mean the amount of new money you added to your nest egg, stash, or whatever you like to call it.

Most people don't know or have only a vague idea of the rate at which they're saving money. The answer may sober, terrify, or pleasantly surprise you. In order to calculate your savings over the past year, you need to calculate your net worth as of today *and* as of one year ago.

The amount you actually saved over the past year is equal to the change in your net worth over the past year — in other words, your net worth today minus your net worth from one year ago. I know it may be a pain to find statements showing what your investments were worth a year ago, but bear with me; it's a useful exercise.

If you own your home, ignore this in the calculations. (You can consider the extra payments you make to pay off your mortgage principal faster as new savings.) And don't include personal property and consumer goods, such as your car, computer, clothing, and so on, with your assets.

When you have your net worth figures from both years, plug them into Step 1 of Table 2-4. If you're anticipating the exercise and are already subtracting your net worth of a year ago from what it is today in order to determine your rate of savings, your instincts are correct, but the exercise isn't quite that simple. You need to do a few more calculations in Step 2 of Table 2-4. Why? Well, counting the appreciation of the investments you've owned over the past year as savings wouldn't be fair. Suppose that you bought 100 shares of a stock a year ago at $17 per share, and now the value is at $34 per share. Your investment increased in value by $1,700 during the past year. Although you'd be the envy of your friends at the next party if you casually mentioned your investments, the $1,700 of increased value is not really savings. Instead, it represents appreciation on your investments, so you must remove this appreciation from the calculations. (Just so you know, I'm not unfairly penalizing you for your shrewd investments — you also get to add back the decline in value of your less-successful investments.)

Table 2-4		Your Savings Rate over the Past Year	
Step 1: Figuring your savings			
Today		*One Year Ago*	
Savings & investments	$_____	Savings & investments	$_____
– Loans & debts	$_____	– Loans & debts	$_____
= Net worth today	$_____	= Net worth 1 year ago	$_____
Step 2: Correcting for changes in value of investments you owned during the year			
Net worth today		$_____	
– Net worth 1 year ago		$_____	
– Appreciation of investments (over past year)		$_____	
+ Depreciation of investments (over past year)		$_____	
= Savings rate		$_____	

If all this calculating gives you a headache, you get stuck, or you just hate crunching numbers, try the intuitive, seat-of-the-pants approach: Save a regular portion of your monthly income. You can save it in a separate savings or retirement account.

How much do you save in a typical month? Get out the statements for accounts you contribute to or save money in monthly. It doesn't matter if you're saving money in a retirement account that you can't access — money is money.

Note: If you save, say, $200 per month for a few months, and then you spend it all on auto repairs, you're not really saving. If you contributed $3,000 to an individual retirement account (IRA), for example, but you depleted money that you had from long ago (in other words, it wasn't saved during the past year), you should not count the $3,000 IRA contribution as new savings.

You should be saving at least 5 to 10 percent of your annual income for longer-term financial goals such as retirement (Chapter 4 helps you to fine-tune your savings goals). If you're not, be sure to read Chapter 6 to find out how to reduce your spending and increase your savings.

Evaluating Your Investment Knowledge

Congratulations! If you stuck with me from the beginning of this chapter, you completed the hardest part of your financial physical. The physical is a whole lot easier from here on out!

Regardless of how much or how little money you have invested in banks, mutual funds, or other types of accounts, you want to invest your money in the wisest way possible. Knowing the rights and wrongs of investing is vital to your long-term financial well-being. Few people have so much extra money that they can afford major or frequent investing mistakes.

Answering "yes" or "no" to the following questions can help you determine how much time you need to spend with my Investing Crash Course in Part III, which focuses on investing. *Note:* The more "no" answers you reluctantly scribble, the more you need to find out about investing, and the faster you should turn to Part III.

_____ Do you understand the investments you currently hold?

_____ Is the money that you'd need to tap in the event of a short-term emergency in an investment where the principal does not fluctuate in value?

_____ Do you know what marginal income-tax bracket (combined federal and state) you're in, and do you factor that in when choosing investments?

_____ For money outside of retirement accounts, do you understand how these investments produce income and gains and whether these types of investments make the most sense from the standpoint of your tax situation?

_____ Do you have your money in different, diversified investments that aren't dependent on one or a few securities or one type of investment (that is, bonds, stocks, real estate, and so on)?

_____ Is the money that you're going to need for a major expenditure in the next few years invested in conservative investments rather than in riskier investments such as stocks or pork bellies?

_____ Is the money that you have earmarked for longer-term purposes (more than five years) invested to produce returns that are well ahead of inflation?

_____ If you currently invest in or plan to invest in individual stocks, do you understand how to evaluate a stock, including reviewing the company's balance sheet, income statement, competitive position, price-earnings ratio versus its peer group, and so on?

_____ If you work with a financial advisor, do you understand what that person is recommending that you do, are you comfortable with those actions and that advisor, and is that person compensated in a way that minimizes potential conflicts of interest in the strategies and investments he or she recommends?

Making and saving money is not a guarantee of financial success but rather a prerequisite. If you don't know how to choose sound investments that meet your needs, you'll likely end up throwing money away, which leads to the same end result as never having earned and saved it in the first place. Worse still, you won't be able to derive any enjoyment from spending the lost money on things that you perhaps need or want. Turn to Part III to discover the best ways to invest; otherwise, you may wind up spinning your wheels working and saving.

Assessing Your Insurance Savvy

In this section, you have to deal with the prickly subject of protecting your assets and yourself with _insurance_. (The following questions help you get started.) If you're like most people, reviewing your insurance policies and coverages is about as much fun as a root canal. Open wide!

_____ Do you understand the individual coverages, protection types, and amounts of each insurance policy you have?

_____ Does your current insurance protection make sense given your current financial situation (as opposed to your situation when you bought the policies)?

_____ If you wouldn't be able to make it financially without your income, do you have adequate long-term disability insurance coverage?

_____ If you have family members who are dependent on your continued income, do you have adequate life insurance coverage to replace your income should you die?

_____ Do you buy insurance through discount brokers, fee-for-service advisors, and companies that sell directly to the public (bypassing agents)?

_____ Do you carry enough liability insurance on your home, car (including umbrella/excess liability), and business to protect all your assets?

_____ Have you recently (in the last year or two) shopped around for the best price on your insurance policies?

_____ Do you know whether your insurance companies have good track records when it comes to paying claims and keeping customers satisfied?

That wasn't so bad, was it? If you answered "no" more than once or twice, don't feel bad — nine out of ten people make significant mistakes when buying insurance. Find your insurance salvation in Part IV. If you answered "yes" to all the preceding questions, you can spare yourself from reading Part IV, but bear in mind that many people need as much help in this area as they do in other aspects of personal finance.

Chapter 3

Determining Where Your Money Goes

In This Chapter

▶ Understanding why people overspend

▶ Assessing your spending

A s a financial counselor, I've worked with people who bring in tiny incomes, people who have incomes of hundreds of thousands of dollars or more, and everyone in between. At every income level, people fall into one of the following three categories:

✔ People who spend more than they earn (accumulating debt)

✔ People who spend all that they earn (saving nothing)

✔ People who save 2, 5, 10, or even 20 percent (or more!)

I've seen $40,000 earners who save 20 percent of their income ($8,000), $80,000 earners who save just 5 percent ($4,000), and people earning well into six figures annually who save nothing or accumulate debt.

Suppose that you currently earn $50,000 per year and spend all of it. You may wonder, "How can I save money?" Good question!

Rather than knock yourself out at a second job or hustle for that next promotion, you may want to try living below your income — in other words, spending less than you earn. (I know spending less than you earn is hard to imagine, but you can do it.) Consider that for every discontented person earning and spending $50,000 per year, someone else is out there making do on $45,000.

A great many people live on less than you make. If you spend as they do, you can save and invest the difference. In this chapter, I examine why people overspend and help you look at your own spending habits. When you know where your money goes, you can find ways to spend less and save more (see Chapter 6) so that someday, you, too, can live richly and achieve your life's goals.

Examining the Roots of Overspending

If you're like most people, you must live within your means in order to accomplish your financial goals. This requires spending less than you earn and then investing your "savings" intelligently (unless you plan on winning the lottery or gaining a large inheritance). To put yourself in a position that allows you to start saving, take a close look at your spending habits.

Many folks earn just enough to make ends meet. And some can't even do that; they simply spend more than they make. The result of such spending habits is, of course, an accumulation of debt: Witness the U.S. government and its over seven trillion dollars' worth of debt accumulation!

Most of the influences in society encourage you to spend; credit is so widely and easily available. Think about it: More often than not, you're referred to as a *consumer* in the media and in the hallowed halls of our government. You're not referred to as a person, a citizen, or a human being.

Here are some of the adversaries you're up against as you attempt to control your spending.

Access to credit

As you probably already know, spending money is easy. Thanks to innovations like ATMs and credit cards, your money is always available, 24/7. Every little outlet in the mall pitches its own credit card, and so do the gas stations across the street and the convenience stores down the road. It certainly won't surprise me when little kids down our street start taking credit cards at their lemonade stand. I can hear it now: "We take Visa, Mr. Tyson, but we don't take American Express."

Sometimes it may seem as though lenders are trying to give away money by making credit so easily available. But this free money is a dangerous illusion. When it comes to consumer debt (credit cards, auto loans, and the like), lenders aren't giving away anything except the opportunity for you to get in over your head, rack up high interest charges, and delay your progress toward your financial and personal goals.

Credit is most dangerous when you make consumption purchases you can't afford in the first place.

Misusing credit cards

The modern day bank credit card was invented by Bank of America near the end of the baby boom. The credit industry has been booming along with the boomers ever since.

If you pay your bill in full every month, credit cards offer a convenient way to buy things with an interest-free, short-term loan. But if you carry your debt over from month to month at high interest rates, credit cards encourage you to live beyond your means. Credit cards make it easy and tempting to spend money that you don't have.

You'll never pay off your credit card debt if you keep charging on your card and make only the minimum monthly payments. Interest continues to pile up on your outstanding debt. Paying only the minimum monthly payment could lead to your carrying high-interest debt on your card for decades (not just months or years)!

If you have a knack for charging up a storm and spending more than you should with those little pieces of plastic, only one solution exists: Get rid of your credit cards. Put scissors to the plastic. Go cold turkey. You can function without them. (See Chapter 5 for details on how to live without credit cards.)

Taking out car loans

Walking onto a car lot and going home with a new car that you could never afford if you had to pay cash is easy. The dealer gets you thinking in terms of monthly payments that sound small when compared to what that four-wheeler is *really* gonna cost you. Auto loans are easy for just about anyone to get (except maybe a recently paroled felon).

Suppose you're tired of driving around in your old clunker. The car is battle-scarred and boring, and you don't like to be seen in it. Plus, the car is likely to need more repairs in the months ahead. So off you go to your friendly local car dealer.

You start looking around at all the shiny, new cars, and then — like the feeling you experience when spotting a water fountain on a scorching hot day — there it is: the replacement for your old clunker. This new car is sleek and clean, and it has A/C, stereo, and power everything.

Before you can read the fine print on the sticker page on the side window, the salesperson moseys on up next to you. He gets you talking about how nice the car is, the weather, or anything but the sticker price of that car.

"How," you begin to think to yourself, "can this guy afford to spend time with me without knowing if I can afford this thing?" After a test drive and more talk about the car, the weather, and your love life (or lack thereof) comes your moment of truth.

The salesperson, it seems, doesn't care about how much money you have. Whether you have lots of money or very little doesn't matter. The car is only $399 a month!

"That price isn't bad," you think. Heck, you were expecting to hear that the car costs at least 25 grand. Before you know it, the dealer runs a credit report on you and has you sign a few papers, and minutes later you're driving home — the proud owner of a new car.

The dealer wants you to think in terms of monthly payments because the cost *sounds* so cheap: $399 for a car. But, of course, that's $399 per month, every month, for many, many months. You're gonna be payin' forever — after all, you just bought a car that cost a huge chunk (perhaps 100 percent or more) of your yearly take-home income!

But it gets worse. What does the total sticker price come to when interest charges are added in? (Even if interest charges are low, you may still be buying a car with a sticker price you can't afford.) And what about insurance, registration, and maintenance over the seven or so years that you'll own the car? Now you're probably up to more than a year's worth of your income. Ouch! (See Chapter 6 for information on how to spend what you can afford on a car.)

Bending to outside influences and agendas

You go out with some friends to dinner, a ballgame, or a show. Try to remember the last time one of you said, "Let's go someplace (or do something) cheaper. I can't afford to spend this much." On the one hand, you don't want to be a stick in the mud. But on the other hand, some of your friends have more money than you do — and the ones who don't may be running up debt fast.

Some people just have to see the latest hit movie, wear the latest designer clothes, or get the newest handheld personal digital assistant. They don't want to feel left out or behind the times.

When was the last time you heard someone say that he decided to forego a purchase because he was saving for retirement or a home purchase? It doesn't happen often, does it? Just dealing with the here-and-now and forgetting your long-term needs and goals is tempting. This mindset leads people to toil away for too many years in jobs they dislike.

Living for today has its virtues: Tomorrow *may* not come. But odds are good that it will. Will you still feel the same way about today's spending decisions tomorrow? Or will you feel guilty that you again failed to stick to your goals?

Your spending habits should be driven by your desires and plans, not those of others. If you haven't set any goals yet, you may not know how much you should be saving. Chapter 4 helps you kick-start the planning and saving process.

Spending to feel good

Life is full of stress, obligations, and demands. "I work hard," you say, "and darn it, I deserve to indulge!" Especially after your boss took the credit for your last great idea or blamed you for his last major screwup. So you buy something expensive or go to a fancy restaurant. Feel better? You won't when the bill arrives. And the more you spend, the less you save, and the longer you'll be stuck working for jerks like your boss!

Just as people can become addicted to alcohol, tobacco, television, and the Internet, some people also become addicted to the high they get from spending. Researchers can identify a number of psychological causes for spending addiction, with some relating to how your parents handled money and spending. (And you thought you'd identified all the problems you can blame on Mom and Dad!)

If your spending and debt problems are chronic, or even if you'd simply like to be a better consumer and saver, see Chapter 5 for more information.

Analyzing Your Spending

Brushing your teeth, eating a diverse diet including plenty of fruits and vegetables, and exercising regularly are good habits. Spending less than you earn and saving enough to meet your future financial objectives are the financial equivalents of these habits.

Despite relatively high incomes compared with the rest of the world, most Americans have a hard time saving a good percentage of their incomes. Why? Because we spend too much — often far more than necessary.

The first step to saving more of the income that you work so hard for is to figure out where that income typically gets spent. The spending analysis in the next section helps you determine where your income is going. You should do the spending analysis if any of the following apply to you:

- ✔ You aren't saving enough money to meet your financial goals. (If you're not sure whether this is the case, please see Chapter 4.)

- ✔ You feel as though your spending is out of control, or you don't really know where all your income goes.

✔ You're anticipating a significant life change (for example, marriage, leaving your job to start a business, having children, retiring, and so on).

If you're already a good saver, you may not need to complete the spending analysis. If you're saving enough to accomplish your goals, I don't see much value in continually tracking your spending. You've already established the good habit — saving. Tracking exactly where you spend your money month after month is *not* the good habit. As long as you're saving enough, I say, who cares where the leftover money is being spent?! (You may still benefit from perusing my smarter spending recommendations in Chapter 6.)

The immediate goal of a spending analysis is to figure out where you typically spend your money. The long-range goal is to establish a good habit: Maintaining a regular, automatic savings routine.

Notice the first four letters in the word *analysis.* (You may never have noticed, but I feel the need to bring it to your attention.) Knowing where your money is going each month is useful, and making changes in your spending behavior and cutting out the fat so you can save more money and meet your financial goals is terrific. However, you may make yourself and those around you miserable if you're anal-retentive about documenting precisely where you spend every single dollar and cent.

Saving what you need to achieve your goals is what matters most.

Tracking spending the low-tech way

Doing a spending analysis is a little bit like being a detective. Your goal is to reconstruct the crime of spending. You probably have some major clues at your fingertips or piled somewhere on the desk or table where you pay bills.

Unless you keep meticulous records that detail every dollar you spend, you won't have perfect information. Don't sweat it! A number of available sources should allow you to reconstruct where you've been spending the bulk of your money. To get started, get out your

✔ Recent pay stubs

✔ Tax returns

✔ Checkbook register or canceled checks (and monthly debit card transactions)

✔ Credit and charge card bills

Ideally, you want to assemble the documents needed to track one year's (12 months') spending. But if your spending patterns don't fluctuate greatly from month to month (or if your dog ate some of the old bills), you can reduce your data gathering to one six-month period, or to every second or third month for the past year. If you take a major vacation or spend a large amount on gifts during certain months of the year, make sure that you include these months in your analysis.

Purchases made with cash are the hardest to track because they don't leave a paper trail. Over the course of a week or perhaps even a month, you *could* keep a record of everything you buy with cash. Tracking cash can be an enlightening exercise, but it can also be a hassle. If you're lazy like I sometimes am or you lack the time and patience, try *estimating*. Think about a typical week or month — how often do you buy things with cash? For example, if you eat lunch out four days a week, paying around $6 a shot, that's about $100 a month. You may also want to try adding up all the cash withdrawals from your checking account statement and then working backwards to try to remember where you spent the cash.

Separate your expenditures into as many useful and detailed categories as possible. Table 3-1 gives you a suggested format; you can tailor it to fit your needs. Remember, if you lump too much of your spending into broad, meaningless categories like *Other,* you'll end up right back where you started — wondering where all the money went. (***Note:*** When completing the tax section in Table 3-1, report the total tax you paid for the year as tabulated on your annual income tax return — and take the total Social Security and Medicare taxes paid from your end-of-year pay stub — rather than the tax withheld or paid during the year.)

Tracking your spending on the computer

Software programs can assist you with paying bills and tracking your spending. The main advantage of using software is that you can continually track your spending as long as you keep entering the information. These software packages can even help speed up the check-writing process (after you figure out how to use them, which isn't always an easy thing to do).

But you don't need a computer and fancy software to pay your bills and figure out where you're spending money. Many people I know stop entering data after a few months. If tracking your spending is what you're after, you need to enter information from the bills you pay by check and the expenses you pay by credit card and cash. Like home exercise equipment and exotic kitchen appliances, such software often ends up in the consumer graveyard.

Paper, pencil, and a calculator work just fine for tracking your spending.

If you want to try computerizing your bill payments and expense tracking, I recommend the best software packages in Chapter 19.

Table 3-1	Detailing Your Spending	
Category	*Monthly Average ($)*	*Percent of Total Gross Income (%)*
Taxes, taxes, taxes (income)		_____
FICA (Social Security & Medicare)	_____	
Federal	_____	
State and local	_____	
The roof over your head		_____
Rent	_____	
Mortgage	_____	
Property taxes	_____	
Gas/electric/oil	_____	
Water/garbage	_____	
Phones	_____	
Cable TV & Internet	_____	
Gardener/housekeeper	_____	
Furniture/appliances	_____	
Maintenance/repairs	_____	
Food, glorious food		_____
Supermarket	_____	
Restaurants and take-out	_____	
Getting around		_____
Gasoline	_____	
Maintenance/repairs	_____	
State registration fees	_____	
Tolls and parking	_____	
Bus or subway fares	_____	
Style		_____
Clothing	_____	
Shoes	_____	

Category	Monthly Average ($)	Percent of Total Gross Income (%)
Jewelry (watches, earrings)	_____	
Dry cleaning	_____	
Debt repayments (excluding mortgage)		_____
Credit/charge cards	_____	
Auto loans	_____	
Student loans	_____	
Other	_____	
Fun stuff		_____
Entertainment (movies, concerts)	_____	
Vacation and travel	_____	
Gifts	_____	
Hobbies	_____	
Subscriptions/memberships	_____	
Pets	_____	
Other	_____	
Personal care		_____
Haircuts	_____	
Health club or gym	_____	
Makeup	_____	
Other	_____	
Personal business		_____
Accountant/attorney/financial advisor	_____	
Other	_____	
Health care		_____
Physicians and hospitals	_____	
Drugs	_____	
Dental and vision	_____	

(continued)

Table 3-1 *(continued)*

Category	Monthly Average ($)	Percent of Total Gross Income (%)
Therapy	_____	
Insurance		_____
Homeowner's/renter's	_____	
Auto	_____	
Health	_____	
Life	_____	
Disability	_____	
Umbrella liability	_____	
Educational expenses		_____
Tuition	_____	
Books	_____	
Supplies	_____	
Children		_____
Day care	_____	
Toys	_____	
Child support	_____	
Charitable donations	_____	_____
Other		_____
_____	_____	
_____	_____	
_____	_____	
_____	_____	
_____	_____	

TIP

Don't waste time on financial administration

Tom is the model of financial organization. His financial documents are neatly organized into color-coded folders. Every month, he enters all his spending information into his computer. He even carries a notebook to detail his cash spending so that every penny is accounted for.

Tom also balances his checkbook "to make sure that everything is in order." He can't remember the last time his bank made a mistake, but he knows someone who once found a $50 error.

If you spend seven hours per month balancing your checkbook and detailing all your spending (as Tom does), you may be wasting nearly two weeks' worth of time per year — the equivalent of two-thirds of your vacation time if you take three weeks annually.

Suppose that, every other year, you're "lucky" enough to find a $100 error the bank made in its favor. If you spend just three hours per month tracking your spending and balancing your checkbook to discover this glitch, you'll be spending 72 hours over two years to find a $100 mistake. Your hourly pay: a wafer-thin $1.39 per hour. You can make more flipping burgers at a burger joint. (***Note:*** If you make significant-sized deposits or withdrawals, make sure that you capture them on your statement.)

To add insult to injury, you may not have the desire and energy to do the more important stuff after working a full week and doing all your financial and other chores. Your big personal financial picture — establishing goals, choosing wise investments, securing proper insurance coverage — may continue to be shoved to the back burner. As a result, you may lose thousands of dollars annually. Over the course of your adult life, this amount could translate into tens or even hundreds of thousands of lost dollars.

Tom, for example, didn't know how much he should be saving to meet his retirement goals. He

didn't review his employer's benefit materials, so he didn't understand his insurance and retirement plan options. He knew that he paid a lot in taxes, but he wasn't sure how to reduce his taxes.

You want to make the most of your money. Unless you truly enjoy dealing with money, you need to prioritize the money activities you work on. Time is limited and life is short. Working harder on financial administration doesn't earn you bonus points. The more time you spend dealing with your personal finances, the less time you have available to gab with friends, watch a good movie, read a good novel, and do other things you really enjoy.

Don't get me wrong — nothing is inherently wrong with balancing your checkbook. In fact, if you regularly bounce checks because you don't know how low your balance is, the exercise may save you a lot in returned check fees. However, if you keep enough money in your checking account so that you don't have to worry about the balance reaching $0 or if you have overdraft protection, balancing your checkbook is probably a waste of time, even if your hourly wages aren't lofty. I haven't balanced mine in years (but please don't tell my bank — it might start making some "mistakes" and siphoning money out).

If you're busy, consider ways to reduce the amount of time you spend on mundane financial tasks like bill paying. Many companies, for example, allow you to pay your monthly bills electronically via your bank checking account or your credit card. (Don't use this option unless you pay your credit card bill in full each month.) The fewer bills you have to pay, the fewer separate checks and envelopes you must process each month. That translates into more free time and fewer paper cuts!

Chapter 4

Establishing and Achieving Goals

In my work as a financial counselor, I always asked new clients what their short- and long-term personal and financial goals were. Most people reported that reflecting on this question was incredibly valuable, because they hadn't considered it for a long time — if ever.

In this chapter, I help you dream about what you want to get out of life. Although my expertise is in personal finance, I wouldn't be doing my job if I didn't get you to consider your nonfinancial goals and how money fits into the rest of your life goals. So before I jump into how to establish and save toward common financial goals, I want to take a moment to discuss how you think about making and saving money, as well as how to best fit your financial goals into the rest of your life.

Creating Your Own Definition of "Wealth"

Pick up just about any major financial magazine or newspaper, or scan stories on the Internet, and you'll quickly see our culture's obsession with financial wealth. The more money financial executives, movie stars, or professional athletes have, the more publicity and attention they seem to get. In fact, many publications go as far as ranking those people who earn the most or have amassed the greatest wealth!

I'm frankly perplexed at why many of the most affluent and highest-income earners maintain workaholic schedules despite being married and having kids. From what I observe, our society seems to define "wealth" as fat paychecks; huge investment account balances; the ability to hire full-time employees to raise children; being too busy with a career to maintain friendships or take an interest in neighbors, community, or important social problems; and the freedom to be unfaithful and dump your spouse when you're no longer pleased with him or her.

Of course, you don't need to buy into any of these concepts. The following sections can help you gain some perspective.

Acknowledging what money can't buy

Recall the handful of best moments in your life. Odds are, these times don't include the time you bought a car or found a designer sweater that you liked. The old saying is true: The most enjoyable and precious things of value in your life can't be bought.

The following statement should go without saying, but I must say it, because too many people act as if it isn't so: Money can't buy happiness. It's tempting to think that if you could only make 20 percent more or twice as much money, you'd be happier because you'd have more money to travel, eat out, and buy that new car you've been eyeing, right? Not so. A great deal of thoughtful research suggests that little relationship exists between money and happiness.

"Wealth is like health: Although its absence can breed misery, having it is no guarantee of happiness," says psychology professor Dr. David G. Myers in his book *The Pursuit of Happiness: Discovering the Pathway to Fulfillment, Well-Being, and Enduring Personal Joy* (Harper).

Despite cheap air travel, VCRs, compact discs, microwaves, computers, voice mail, and all the other stuff that's supposed to make our lives easier and more enjoyable, Americans aren't any happier than they were four decades ago. According to research conducted by the National Opinion Research Center, the number of Americans who say they're "very happy" has dropped over the past two generations. These unexpected results occur even though incomes, after being adjusted for inflation, have more than doubled during that time.

As Dr. Myers observes in *The Pursuit of Happiness,* ". . . if anything, to judge by soaring rates of depression, the quintupling of the violent crime rate since 1960, the doubling of the divorce rate, and the tripling of the teen suicide rate, we're richer and less happy."

What's your relationship to money?

Over the years in my work as a financial counselor, I've come to find that how a person relates to and feels about money has a great impact on how good he is at managing his money and making important financial decisions. For example, knowing that you have a net worth of negative $13,200 because of credit card debt is useful, but it's probably not enough information for you to do something constructive about your problem. A logical next step would be to examine your current spending and take steps to reduce your debt load.

Although I cover practical solutions to common financial quandaries later in this book, I also discuss the more touchy-feely side of money. For example, some people who continually rack up consumer debt have a spending addiction. Other people who jump in and out of investments and follow them like a hawk have psychological obstacles that prevent them from holding onto investments.

And then you have those somewhat philosophical and psychological issues relating to money and the meaning of life. Saving more money and increasing your net worth isn't always the best approach. In my work, I've come across numerous people who attach too much significance to personal wealth accumulation and neglect important human relationships in their pursuit of more money. Some retirees have a hard time loosening the purse springs and actually spending some of the money they worked so hard to save for their golden years.

Balancing your financial goals with other important life goals is key to your happiness. What's the point, for example, of staying in a well-paying, admired profession if you don't care for the work and you're mainly doing it for the financial rewards? Life is too short and precious for you to squander away your days.

So as you read through the various chapters and sections of this book, please consider your higher life goals and purposes. What are your nonfinancial priorities (family, friends, causes), and how can you best accomplish your goals with the financial resources you do have? If you really want to examine your priorities and your relationship to money, I have a new book, *Mind over Money: Your Path to Wealth and Happiness* (CDS Books), which delves into how we feel about money, why we have the financial habits that we do, and how you can overcome those obstacles holding you back.

Managing the balancing act

Believe it or not, some people save too much. In my counseling practice, I saw plenty of people who fell into that category. If making and saving money is a good thing, then the more the better, right?

Well, take the admittedly extreme case of Anne Scheiber, who, on a modest income, started saving at a young age, allowing her money to compound in wealth-building investments such as stocks over many years. As a result, she was able to amass $20 million before she passed away at the age of 101.

Scheiber lived in a cramped studio apartment and never used her investments. She didn't even use the interest or dividends — she lived solely on her Social Security benefits and the small pension from her employer. Scheiber was extreme in her frugality and obsessed with her savings. As reported by James Glassman in the *Washington Post,* "She had few friends . . . she was an unhappy person, totally consumed by her securities accounts and her money."

Most people, myself included, wouldn't choose to live and save the way that Scheiber did. She saved for the sake of saving: no goal, no plan, no reward for herself. Saving should be a means to an end, not something that makes you *mean* to the end.

Even those who are saving for an ultimate goal can become consumed by their saving habits. I see some people pursuing higher-paying jobs and pinching pennies in order to retire early. But sometimes they make too many personal sacrifices today while chasing after some vision of their lives tomorrow. Others get consumed by work and then don't notice or understand why their family and friends feel neglected.

Another problem with seeking to amass wealth is that tomorrow may not come. Even if all goes according to plan, will you know how to be happy when you're not working if you spend your entire life making money? More importantly, who will be around to share your leisure time? One of the costs of an intense career is time spent away from friends and family. You may realize your goal of retiring early, but you may be putting off too much living today in expectation of living tomorrow. As Charles D'Orleans said in 1465, "It's very well to be thrifty, but don't amass a hoard of regrets."

Of course, at the other extreme are spendthrifts who live only for today. A friend of mine once said, "I'm not into delayed gratification. "Shop 'til you drop" seems to be the motto of this personality type. "Why save when I might not be here tomorrow?" reasons this type of person.

The danger of this approach is that tomorrow may come after all, and most people don't want to spend all their tomorrows working for a living. The earlier neglect of saving, however, may make it necessary for you to work when you're older. And if for some reason you can't work and you have little money to live on, much less live enjoyably, the situation can be tragic. The only difference between a person without any savings or access to credit and some homeless people is a few months of unemployment.

Making and saving money is like eating food. If you don't eat enough, you may suffer. If you eat too much, the overage may go to waste or make you overweight. The right amount, perhaps with some extra to spare, affords you a healthy, balanced, peaceful existence. Money should be treated with respect and acknowledged for what it is — a means to an end and a precious resource that shouldn't be thoughtlessly squandered and wasted.

As Dr. David Myers, whom I introduced earlier in this chapter, says: "Satisfaction isn't so much getting what you want as wanting what you have. There are two ways to be rich: one is to have great wealth, the other is to have few wants." Find ways to make the most of the money that does pass through your hands, and never lose sight of all that is far more important than money.

Prioritizing Your Savings Goals

Most people I know have financial goals. The rest of this chapter discusses the most common financial goals and how to work toward them. See whether any of the following reflect your ambitions:

- **Becoming part of the landed gentry:** Renting and dealing with landlords can be a financial and emotional drag, so most folks want to buy into the American dream and own some real estate — the most basic of which is your own home.

- **Retiring:** No, retiring does not imply sitting on a rocking chair watching the world go by while hoping that some long lost friend, your son's or daughter's family, or the neighborhood dog comes by to visit. Retiring is a catch-all term for discontinuing full-time work or perhaps not even working for pay at all.

- **Educating the kids:** No, all those diaper changes, late-night feedings, and trips to the zoo aren't enough to get Junior out of your house and into the real world as a productive, self-sufficient adult. You may want to help your children get a college education. Unfortunately, that can cost a truckload of dough.

- **Owning your own business:** Many employees want to face the challenges and rewards that come with being the boss. The primary reason that most people continue just to dream is that they lack the money to leave their primary job. Although many businesses don't require gobs of start-up cash, almost all require that you withstand a substantial reduction in your income during the early years.

Because each of us is different, we can have goals (other than those in the previous list) that are unique to our own situation. Accomplishing such goals almost always requires saving money. As one of my favorite Chinese proverbs says, "Do not wait until you are thirsty to dig a well." In other words, don't wait to save money until you're ready to accomplish a personal or financial goal!

Knowing what's most important to you

Unless you earn really big bucks or have a large family inheritance to fall back on, your personal and financial desires will probably outstrip your resources. Thus, you must prioritize your goals.

One of the biggest mistakes I see people make is rushing into financial decisions without considering what's really important to them. Because many of us get caught up in the responsibilities of our daily lives, we often don't have time for reflection.

As a result of my experience counseling and teaching people about better personal financial management, I can tell you that the folks who accomplish their goals aren't necessarily smarter or higher-income earners than those who don't. People who identify their goals and then work toward them, which often requires changing some habits, are the ones who accomplish their goals.

Valuing retirement accounts

Where possible, you should try to save and invest in accounts that offer you a tax advantage. This is precisely what retirement accounts offer you. These accounts — known by such enlightening acronyms and names as 401(k), 403(b), SEP-IRAs, Keoghs, and so on — offer tax breaks to people of all economic means. Consider the following advantages to investing in retirement accounts:

- ✔ **Contributions are usually tax-deductible.** By putting money in a retirement account, not only do you plan wisely for your future, but you also get an immediate financial reward: lower taxes — and lower taxes mean more money available for saving and investing. Retirement account contributions are generally not taxed at either the federal or state income tax level until withdrawal (but they're still subject to Social Security and Medicare taxes when earned). If you're paying, say, 35 percent between federal and state taxes (refer to Chapter 7 to determine your tax bracket), a $5,000 contribution to a retirement account lowers your taxes by $1,750.

- ✔ **Returns on your investment compound over time without taxation.** After you put money into a retirement account, any interest, dividends, and appreciation add to your account without being taxed. Of course, there's no such thing as a free lunch — these accounts don't allow for complete tax avoidance. Yet you can get a really great lunch at a discount: You get to defer taxes on all the accumulating gains and profits until you withdraw the money down the road. Thus, more money is working for you over a longer period of time. (The newer Roth IRA that I discuss in Chapter 11 offers no upfront tax breaks but does allow future tax-free withdrawal of investment earnings.)

In the early 2000s, the tax rates on stock dividends and for long-term capital gains (on investments held more than one year) were lowered. This created some concern that investing through retirement accounts may no longer be worthwhile because all investment earnings are taxed at the relatively high ordinary income tax rates when money is withdrawn from retirement accounts. By contrast, if you invest outside of retirement accounts, you pay a lower rate of tax on stock dividends and on the sale of an investment held for more than one year. I'll cut to the chase: The vast, vast majority of people are still much better off contributing to retirement accounts (for more info, please see Chapter 7).

✔ **In some company retirement accounts, companies match a portion of your own contributions.** Thus, in addition to tax breaks, you get free extra money courtesy of your employer!

Dealing with competing goals

Unless you enjoy paying higher taxes, why would you save money outside of retirement accounts, which shelter your money from taxation? The reason is that some financial goals are not easily achieved by saving in retirement accounts. Also, retirement accounts have caps on the amount you can contribute annually.

If you're accumulating money for a down payment on a home or to start or buy a business, for example, you'll probably need to save that money outside of a retirement account. Why? Because if you withdraw funds from retirement accounts before age 59½ and you're not retired, not only do you have to pay income taxes on the withdrawals, but you also generally have to pay *early withdrawal penalties* — 10 percent of the withdrawn amount in federal tax and whatever your state charges. (See the sidebar, "Avoiding retirement account early withdrawal penalties," for exceptions to this rule.)

Because you're constrained by your financial resources, you need to prioritize your goals. Before funding your retirement accounts and racking up those tax breaks, read on to consider your other goals.

Avoiding retirement account early withdrawal penalties

You can find ways to avoid the early withdrawal penalties that the tax gods normally apply.

Suppose that you read this book at a young age, develop sound financial habits early, and save enough to retire before age 59½. In this case, you can take money out of your retirement account without triggering penalties (which are normally 10 percent of the amount withdrawn for federal income tax plus whatever your state levies). The IRS allows you to withdraw money before 59½ if you do so in equal, annual installments based on your life expectancy. The IRS (this is slightly chilling) even has a little table that allows you to look up your life expectancy.

You can now also make penalty-free withdrawals from individual retirement accounts for either a first-time home purchase (limit of $10,000) or higher educational expenses for you, your spouse, your children, or your grandchildren.

The other conditions under which you can make penalty-free early withdrawals from retirement accounts are not as enjoyable: If you have major medical expenses (exceeding 7.5 percent of your income) or a disability, you may be exempt from the penalties under certain conditions.

If you get into a financial pinch while you're still employed, be aware that some company retirement plans allow you to borrow against your balance. This tactic is like loaning money to yourself — the interest payments go back into your account.

If you lose your job and withdraw retirement account money simply because you need it to live on, the penalties do apply. However, if you're not working and you're earning so little income that you need to raid your retirement account, you surely fall into a low tax bracket. The lower income taxes you pay (when compared to the taxes you would have paid on that money had you not sheltered it in a retirement account in the first place) should make up for most or all of the penalty.

Building Emergency Reserves

Because you don't know what the future holds, preparing for the unexpected is financially wise. Even if you're the lucky sort who sometimes finds $5 bills on street corners, you can't control the sometimes chaotic world in which we live.

Conventional wisdom says that you should have approximately six months of living expenses put away for an emergency. This particular amount may or may not be right for you, because it depends, of course, on how expensive the emergency is. Why six months, anyway? And where should you put it? Unfortunately, no hard and fast rules exist. How much of an emergency stash you need depends on your situation.

I recommend saving the following emergency amounts under differing circumstances (in Chapter 12, I recommend good places to invest this money):

- ✔ **Three months' living expenses:** Choose this option if you have other accounts, such as a 401(k), or family members and close friends whom you can tap for a short-term loan. This minimalist approach makes sense when you're trying to maximize investments elsewhere (for example, in retirement accounts) or you have stable sources of income (employment or otherwise).

- ✔ **Six months' living expenses:** This amount is appropriate if you don't have other places to turn for a loan or you have some instability in your employment situation or source of income.

- ✔ **Up to one year's living expenses:** Set aside this much if your income fluctuates wildly from year to year or if your profession involves a high risk of job loss; finding another job could take you a long time, and you don't have other places to turn for a loan.

In the event that your only current source of emergency funds is a high-interest credit card, you should first save at least three months' worth of living expenses in an accessible account before funding a retirement account or saving for other goals.

Saving to Buy a Home or Business

When you're starting out financially, deciding whether to save money to buy a home or to put money into a retirement account presents a dilemma. In the long run, owning your own home is a wise financial move. On the other hand, saving sooner for retirement makes achieving your goals easier.

Presuming both goals are important to you, you should be saving towards both buying a home *and* for retirement. If you're eager to own a home, you can throw all your savings toward achieving that goal and temporarily put your retirement savings on hold. Save for both purposes simultaneously if you're not in a rush.

You may be able to eat your cake and have it, too, if you work for an employer that allows borrowing against retirement account balances. You can save money in the retirement account and then borrow against it for the down payment of a home. Be careful, though. Retirement account loans typically must be paid back within a set number of years (check with your employer), or immediately if you quit or lose your job. As I mention earlier in this chapter, you're also allowed to make penalty-free withdrawals of up to $10,000 from individual retirement accounts toward a first-time home purchase.

When saving money for starting or buying a business, most people encounter the same dilemma they face when deciding to save to buy a house: If you fund your retirement accounts to the exclusion of earmarking money for your small-business dreams, your entrepreneurial aspirations may never become a reality. Generally, I advocate hedging your bets by saving money in your tax-sheltered retirement accounts as well as toward your business venture. As I discuss in Part III, an investment in your own small business can produce great rewards, so you may feel comfortable focusing your savings on your own business.

Funding Kids' Educational Expenses

Wanting to provide for your children's future is perfectly natural. But doing so before you've saved adequately toward your own goals can be a major financial mistake. The college financial-aid system effectively penalizes you for saving money outside of retirement accounts and penalizes you even more if the money's invested in the child's name.

This concept may sound selfish, but you need to take care of *your* future first. You should first take advantage of saving through your tax-sheltered retirement accounts before you set aside money in custodial savings accounts for your kids. This practice isn't selfish: Do you really want to have to leech off your kids when you're old and frail because you didn't save any money for yourself? (See Chapter 13 for a complete explanation of how to save for educational expenses.)

Saving for Big Purchases

If you want to buy a car, a canoe, or a plane ticket to France, do not, I repeat, do not buy such things with *consumer credit* (that is, carry debt month-to-month to finance the purchase on a credit card or auto loan). As I explain in Chapter 5, cars, boats, vacations, and the like are consumer items, not wealth-building investments, such as real estate or small businesses. A car begins to depreciate the moment you drive it off the sales lot. A plane ticket to France is worthless the moment you arrive back home. (I know your memories will be priceless, but they won't pay the bills.)

Paying for high-interest consumer debt can cripple your ability not only to save for long-term goals but also to make major purchases in the future. Interest on consumer debt is exorbitantly expensive — up to 18 percent for most credit cards. When contemplating the purchase of a consumer item on credit, add up the total interest you end up paying on your debt and call it the price of instant gratification.

Don't deny yourself gratification; just learn how to delay it. Get into the habit of saving for your larger consumer purchases to avoid paying for them over time with high-interest consumer credit. When saving up for a consumer purchase such as a car, a money market account or short-term bond fund (see Chapter 12) is a good place to store your short-term savings.

Preparing for Retirement

Many people toil away at work, dreaming about a future in which they can stop the daily commute and grind; get out from under that daily deluge of faxes, voice mails, and e-mails; and do what they want, when they want. People often assume that this magical day will arrive either on their next true day off or when they retire or win the lottery — whichever comes first.

I've never cared much for the term *retire*. This word seems to imply idleness or the end of usefulness to society. But if retirement means not having to work at a job (especially one you don't enjoy) and having financial flexibility and independence, then I'm all for it.

Being able to retire sooner rather than later is part of the American dream. But this idea has some obvious problems. First, you set yourself up for disappointment. If you want to retire by your mid-60s (when Social Security kicks in), you need to save enough money to support yourself for 20 years, maybe longer. Two decades is a long time to live off your savings. You're going to need a good-sized chunk of money — more than most people realize.

The earlier you hope to retire, the more money you need to set aside, and the sooner you have to start saving — unless you plan to work part-time in retirement to earn more income! See Chapter 5 for more details about how to save for retirement.

Many of the people I speak to say that they do want to retire, and most say "the sooner, the better." Yet more than half of Americans between the ages of 18 and 34, and a quarter of those ages 35 to 54, have not begun to save for retirement. When I asked one of my middle-aged counseling clients, who had saved little for retirement, when he would like to retire, he deadpanned, "Sometime before I die." If you're in this group (and even if you're not), determine where you stand financially regarding retirement. If you're like most working people, you need to increase your savings rate for retirement.

Don't neglect nonfinancial preparations for retirement

Investing your money is just one (and not even the most important) aspect of preparing for your retirement. In order to enjoy the lifestyle that your retirement savings will provide you, you need to invest energy into other areas of your life as well:

✔ Few things are more important than your health. Without your health, enjoying the good things in life can be hard. Unfortunately, many people aren't motivated to care about their health until after they discover problems. By then, it may be too late.

Although exercising regularly, eating a balanced and nutritious diet, and avoiding substance abuse can't guarantee you a healthful future, these good habits go a long way toward preventing many of the most common causes of death and debilitating disease. Regular medical exams also are important in detecting problems early.

✔ In addition to your physical health, be sure to invest in your psychological health. People live longer and have happier and healthier lives when they have a circle of family and friends around them for support.

Unfortunately, many people become more isolated and lose regular contact with business associates, friends, and family members as they grow older.

Happy retirees tend to stay active, getting involved in volunteer organizations and new social circles. They may travel to see old friends or younger relatives who may be too busy to visit them.

Treat retirement life like a bubbly, inviting hot tub set at 102 degrees. You want to ease yourself in nice and slow; jumping in hastily can take most of the pleasantness out of the experience. Abruptly leaving your job without a plan for spending all that free time is an invitation to boredom and depression. Everyone needs a sense of purpose and a sense of routine. Establishing hobbies, volunteer work, or a sideline business while gradually cutting back your regular work schedule can be a terrific way to ease into retirement.

Figuring what you need for retirement

If you hope to someday reduce the time you spend working or cease working altogether, you'll need sufficient savings to support yourself. Many people — particularly young people and those who don't work well with numbers — underestimate the amount of money needed to retire. To figure out how much you should save per month to achieve your retirement goals, you need to crunch a few numbers. (Don't worry — this number-crunching should be easier than doing your taxes.)

Luckily for you, you don't have to start cold. Studies show how people typically spend money before and during retirement. Most people need about 70 to 80 percent of their pre-retirement income throughout retirement to maintain their standard of living. For example, if your household earns

$50,000 per year before retirement, you're likely to need $35,000 to $40,000 (70 to 80 percent of $50,000) per year during retirement to live the way you're accustomed to living. The 70 to 80 percent is an average. Some people may need more simply because they have more time on their hands to spend their money. Others adjust their standard of living and live on less.

You, of course, are not average in any way — you're unique! So how do you figure out what you're going to need? The following three profiles provide a rough estimate of the percentage of your pre-retirement income you're going to need during retirement. Pick the one that most accurately describes your situation. If you fall between two descriptions, pick a percentage that fits in between the two.

To maintain your standard of living in retirement, you may need about

> ✔ **65 percent of your pre-retirement income if you**
>
> • Save a large amount (15 percent or more) of your annual earnings
>
> • Are a high-income earner
>
> • Will own your home free of debt by the time you retire
>
> • Do not anticipate leading a lifestyle in retirement that reflects your current high income
>
> If you're an especially high-income earner who lives well beneath your means, you may be able to do just fine with even less than 65 percent. Pick an annual dollar amount or percentage of your current income that will allow the kind of retirement lifestyle you desire.
>
> ✔ **75 percent of your pre-retirement income if you**
>
> • Save a reasonable amount (5 to 14 percent) of your annual earnings
>
> • Will still have some mortgage debt or a modest rent to pay by the time you retire
>
> • Anticipate having a standard of living in retirement that's comparable to what you have today
>
> ✔ **85 percent of your pre-retirement income if you**
>
> • Save little or none of your annual earnings (less than 5 percent)
>
> • Will have a relatively significant mortgage payment or sizeable rent to pay in retirement
>
> • Anticipate wanting or needing to maintain your current lifestyle throughout retirement

Of course, you can use a more precise approach to figure out how much you need per year in retirement. Be forewarned, though, that this more personalized method is far more time-consuming, and because you're making projections into an uncertain future, it may not be any more accurate than the simple method I just explained. If you're data-oriented, you may feel comfortable tackling this method: You need to figure out where you're spending your money today (worksheets are available in Chapter 3) and then work up some projections for your expected spending needs in retirement (the information in Chapter 19 may help you, as well).

Understanding retirement building blocks

Did you play with Lego blocks or Tinkertoys when you were a child? You start by building a foundation on the ground, and then you build up. Before you know it, you're creating bridges, castles, and panda bears. Although preparing financially for retirement isn't exactly like playing with blocks, the concept is the same: You need a basic foundation so that your necessary retirement reserves can grow.

If you've been working steadily, you may already have a good foundation, even if you haven't been actively saving toward retirement. In the pages ahead, I walk you through the probable components of your future retirement income and show you how to figure how much you should be saving to reach particular retirement goals.

Counting on Social Security

According to polls, nearly half of American adults under the age of 35, and more than a third of those between the ages of 35 and 49, think that Social Security benefits will not be available by the time they retire.

Contrary to widespread cynicism, Social Security should be available when you retire, no matter how old you are today. In fact, Social Security is one of the sacred cow political programs. Imagine what would happen to the group of politicians who voted not to pay any more benefits!

If you think that you can never retire because you don't have any money saved, I'm happy to inform you that you're probably wrong. You likely have some Social Security. But Social Security is generally not enough to live on comfortably.

Social Security is intended to provide you with a subsistence level of retirement income for the basic necessities: food, shelter, and clothing. Social Security is not intended to be your sole source of income. Some elderly are quite dependent upon Social Security: For 22 percent of the elderly, Social Security is their only income source; for two out of three Social Security recipients, their Social Security retirement check accounts for at least half of their total retirement income. Few working people could maintain their current lifestyles into retirement without supplementing Social Security with personal savings and company retirement plans.

How much will I get from Social Security?

Table 4-1 shows the approximate size of your expected monthly allowance from Social Security. The first column gives your average *yearly employment earnings* (in today's dollars) on which you pay Social Security taxes. The second column contains the approximate *monthly benefit amount* (in today's dollars) that you'll receive when eligible for full benefits.

Note: The benefit amounts in Table 4-1 are for an individual income earner. If you're married and one of you doesn't work for pay, the nonworking spouse collects 50 percent of what the working spouse collects. Working spouses are eligible for either individual benefits or half of their spouse's benefits — whichever amount is greater.

Table 4-1	Your Expected Social Security Benefits
Annual Earnings	*Approximate Monthly Benefit (Value in Today's Dollars)*
$10,000	$525
$20,000	$755
$30,000	$940
$40,000	$1,130
$50,000	$1,310
$60,000	$1,500
$70,000	$1,670
$80,000	$1,760
$90,000	$1,845
$100,000	$1,925
$120,000	$2,035
$150,000	$2,070

More Social Security details

When the Social Security system was created in the 1930s, its designers underestimated how long people would live in retirement. Thanks to scientific advances and improved medical care, life expectancies have risen substantially since that time. As a result, many of today's retirees get back far more than they paid into the system.

The age at which you can start collecting full benefits has increased, and it may increase again. In the "good old days" (prior to changes made in Social Security regulations in 1983), you could collect full Social Security payments at age 65, assuming you were eligible. This rule no longer holds true. If you were born before 1938, you're still eligible to collect full Social Security benefits at age 65. If you were born in 1960 or after, you have to wait until age 67 for full benefits. If you were born between 1938 and 1959, full benefits are payable to you at age 66 (plus or minus some number of months, depending on the year you were born).

These regulations may seem unfair, but they're necessary for updating the system to fit with the realities of our increased longevity, large federal budget deficits, and aging baby boomers. Without changes, the Social Security system may collapse, because it'll be fed by a relatively small number of workers while supporting large numbers of retirees.

In addition to paying for retirement-income checks for retirees, your Social Security taxes also help fund disability insurance for you, survivor income insurance for your financial dependents, and Medicare (the health insurance program for retirees).

The amount of Social Security benefits you receive in retirement depends on your average earnings during your working years. Don't worry about the fact that you probably earned a lot less many years ago. The Social Security benefits calculations increase your older earnings to account for the lower cost of living and wages in prior years.

How much work makes me eligible?

To be eligible to collect Social Security benefits, you need to have worked a minimum number of calendar quarters. If you were born after 1928, you need 40 quarters of work credits to qualify for Social Security retirement benefits.

If for some reason you work only the first half of a year or only during summer months, don't despair. You don't need to work part of every quarter to get a quarter's credit. You get credits based on the income you earn during the year. As of this writing, you get the full four quarters credited to your account if you earn $3,880 or more in a year. (Before 1978, folks got one quarter's credit for each actual calendar quarter in which they earned $50.) To get 40 quarters of coverage, you basically need to work (at least portions of) ten years.

To get credits, your income must be reported and you must pay taxes on it (including Social Security tax). In other words, you and those you employ encounter problems when you neglect to declare income or you pay people under the table: You may be cheating yourself, or others, out of valuable benefits.

To get a more precise handle on your Social Security benefits, call the Social Security Administration at 800-772-1213 and ask for Form 7004, which allows you to receive a record of your reported earnings and an estimate of your Social Security benefits. (You can also visit the Social Security Administration Web site at www.ssa.gov.) Or you can just wait by your mailbox — the government now annually mails a personal Social Security Statement that includes estimates of the benefits you and your family members may qualify for. (Check your earnings record, because occasional errors do arise and — surprise — they usually aren't in your favor.)

Planning your personal savings/investment strategy

Money you're saving toward retirement can include money under the mattress as well as money in a retirement account such as an individual retirement account (IRA), 401(k), or similar plan (see Chapter 11). You may have also earmarked investments in nonretirement accounts for your retirement.

Equity (the difference between the market value less any mortgage balances owed) in rental real estate can be counted toward your retirement, as well. Deciding whether to include the equity in your primary residence (your home) is trickier. If you don't want to count on using this money in retirement, don't include it when you tally your stash. You may want to count a portion of your home equity in your total assets for retirement. Many people sell their homes when they retire and move to a cheaper region of the country, move closer to family, or downsize to a more manageable household. And increasing numbers of older retirees are tapping their homes' equity through reverse mortgages (see Chapter 14 for information on mortgages).

Making the most of pensions

Pension plans are a benefit offered by some employers — mostly larger organizations and government agencies. Even if your current employer doesn't offer a pension, you may have earned pension benefits through a previous job.

The plans I'm referring to are known as *defined-benefit plans*. With these plans, you qualify for a monthly benefit amount to be paid to you in retirement based on your years of service for a specific employer.

Although each company's plan differs, all plans calculate and pay benefits based on a formula. A typical formula might credit you with 1.5 percent of your salary for each year of service (full-time employment). For example, if you work ten years, you earn a monthly retirement benefit worth 15 percent of your monthly salary.

Pension benefits can be quite valuable. In the better plans, employers put away the equivalent of 5 to 10 percent of your salary to pay your future pension. This money is in addition to your salary —you never see it in your paycheck, and it isn't taxed. The employer puts this money away in an account for your retirement.

To qualify for pension benefits, you don't have to stay with an employer long enough to receive the 25-year gold watch. Under current government regulations, employees must be fully *vested* (entitled to receive full benefits based on years of service upon reaching retirement age) after five years of full-time service.

Defined-benefit pension plans are becoming rarer for two major reasons:

✔ They're costly for employers to maintain. Many employees don't understand how these plans work and why they're so valuable, so companies don't get mileage out of their pension expenditures — employees don't see the money, so they don't appreciate the company's generosity.

✔ Most of the new jobs being generated in the U.S. economy are with small companies that typically don't offer these types of plans.

More employers offer plans like 401(k)s, in which employees elect to save money out of their own paychecks. Known as *defined-contribution plans,* these plans allow you to save toward your retirement at your own expense rather than at your employer's expense. (To encourage participation in defined-contribution plans, some employers "match" a portion of their employees' contributions.) More of the burden and responsibility of investing for retirement falls on your shoulders with 401(k) and similar plans, so it's important to understand how these plans work. Most people are ill-equipped to know how much to save and how to invest the money. The retirement planning worksheet in the next section should help get you started with figuring out the amount you need to save. (Part III shows you how to invest.)

Retirement planning worksheet

Now that you've toured the components of your future retirement income, take a shot at tallying where you stand in terms of retirement preparations.

Don't be afraid to do this exercise — it's not difficult, and you may find that you're not in such bad shape. I even explain how to catch up if you find that you're behind in saving for retirement.

Note: The following worksheet (Table 4-2) and the Growth Multiplier (Table 4-3) assume that you're going to retire at age 66 and that your investments will produce an annual rate of return that is 4 percent higher than the rate of inflation. (For example, if inflation averages 3 percent, this table assumes that you will earn 7 percent per year on your investments.)

Table 4-2	Retirement Planning Worksheet
Retirement Income or Needs	*Amount*
1. Annual retirement income needed in today's dollars (see earlier in this chapter)	$ _____ / year
2. Annual Social Security (see Table 4-1)	– $ _____ / year
3. Annual pension benefits (ask your benefits department); multiply by 60% if your pension won't increase with inflation during retirement	– $ _____ / year
4. Annual retirement income needed from personal savings (subtract lines 2 and 3 from line 1)	= $ _____ / year
5. Savings needed to retire at age 66 (multiply line 4 by 15)	$ _____
6. Value of current retirement savings	$ _____
7. Value of current retirement savings at retirement (multiply line 6 by Growth Multiplier in Table 4-3)	$ _____
8. Amount you still need to save (line 5 minus line 7)	$ _____
9. Amount you need to save per month (multiply line 8 by Savings Factor in Table 4-3)	$ _____ / month

To get a more precise handle on where you stand in terms of retirement planning (especially if you'd like to retire earlier than your mid-60s), call T. Rowe Price at 800-638-5660 and ask for the company's retirement planning booklets. You can also turn to Chapter 19, where I recommend retirement planning software and Web sites that can ease your number-crunching burdens.

Table 4-3	Growth Multiplier	
Your Current Age	*Growth Multiplier*	*Savings Factor*
26	4.8	0.001
28	4.4	0.001
30	4.1	0.001
32	3.8	0.001
34	3.5	0.001
36	3.2	0.001
38	3.0	0.002
40	2.8	0.002
42	2.6	0.002
44	2.4	0.002
46	2.2	0.003
48	2.0	0.003
50	1.9	0.004
52	1.7	0.005
54	1.6	0.006
56	1.5	0.007
58	1.4	0.009
60	1.3	0.013
62	1.2	0.020
64	1.1	0.041

Making up for lost time

If the amount you need to save per month to reach your retirement goals seems daunting, all is not lost. Remember: Winners never quit, and quitters never win. Here are my top recommendations for making up for lost time:

✔ **Question your spending.** You have two ways to boost your savings: Earn more money or cut your spending (or do both). Most people don't spend their money nearly as thoughtfully as they earn it. Refer to Chapter 6 for suggestions and strategies for reducing your spending.

✔ **Be more realistic about your retirement age.** If you extend the age at which you plan to retire, you get a double benefit: You're earning and saving money for more years, and you're spending your nest egg over fewer years. Of course, if your job is making you crazy, this option may not be too appealing. Try to find work that makes you happy, and consider working, at least part-time, during the early years typically considered the retirement years.

✔ **Use your home equity.** The prospect of tapping the cash in your home can be troubling. After getting together the down payment, you probably worked for many years to pay off that sucker. You're delighted not to have to mail a mortgage payment to the bank anymore. But what's the use of owning a house free of mortgage debt when you lack sufficient retirement reserves? All the money that's tied up in the house can be used to help increase your standard of living in retirement.

You have a number of ways to tap your home's equity. You can sell your home and either move to a lower-cost property or rent an apartment. Tax laws allow you to realize up to $250,000 in tax-free profit from the sale of your house ($500,000 if you're married). Another option is a *reverse mortgage,* in which you get a monthly income check as you build a loan balance against the value of your home. The loan is paid when your home is finally sold. (See Chapter 14 for more information about reverse mortgages.)

✔ **Get your investments growing.** The faster the rate at which your money grows and compounds, the less you need to save each year to reach your goals. Earning just a few extra percentage points per year on your investments can dramatically slash the amount you need to save. The younger you are, the more powerful the effect of compounding interest. For example, if you're in your mid-30s and your investments appreciate 6 percent per year (rather than 4 percent) faster than the rate of inflation, the amount you need to save each month to reach your retirement goals drops by about 40 percent! (See Part III, on investing.)

✔ **Turn a hobby into supplemental retirement income.** Even if you've earned a living in the same career over many decades, you have skills that are portable and can be put to profitable use. Pick something you enjoy and are good at, develop a business plan, and get smart about how to market your services and wares (check out the latest edition of *Small Business For Dummies* from Wiley Publishing, which I co-wrote with veteran entrepreneur Jim Schell). Remember, as people get busier, more specialized services are created to support their hectic lives. A demand for quality, homemade goods of all varieties also exists. Be creative! You never know — you may wind up profiled in a business publication!

✔ **Invest to gain tax-free and other free money.** By investing in a tax-wise fashion, you can boost the effective rate of return on your investments without taking on additional risk.

In addition to the tax benefits you gain from funding most types of retirement accounts in this chapter (see the earlier section, "Valuing retirement accounts"), some employers offer free matching money. Also, the government now offers tax credits (see Chapter 7) for low and moderate income earners who utilize retirement accounts.

As for money outside of tax-sheltered retirement accounts, if you're in a relatively high tax bracket, you may earn more by investing in tax-free investments and other vehicles that minimize highly taxed distributions.

✔ **Think about inheritances.** Although you should never count on an inheritance to support your retirement, you may inherit money someday. If you want to see what impact an inheritance has on your retirement calculations, add a conservative estimate of the amount you expect to inherit to your current total savings in Table 4-2.

Part II
Saving More, Spending Less

WHENEVER CARL USED HIS CREDIT CARD, THE RESULTS WERE ALWAYS DISASTROUS.

In this part . . .

I detail numerous ways to make your dollars go toward building up your savings rather than toward wasteful spending. Are you buried in debt with little to show for it? Well, it's never too late to start digging out. Here you find out how to reduce your debt burden. I also devote an entire chapter to discussing taxes and how to legally minimize them, because too much of your money may be going to Uncle Sam.

Chapter 5

Dealing with Debt

. . . .

In This Chapter

▶ Using your savings to lower your debt

▶ Getting out of debt when you don't have savings

▶ Understanding the pros and cons of filing bankruptcy

▶ Halting your spending and debting

. . . .

Accumulating *bad debt* (consumer debt) by buying things like new living room furniture or a new car that you really can't afford is like living on a diet of sugar and caffeine: a quick fix with little nutritional value. Borrowing on your credit card to afford an extravagantly expensive vacation is detrimental to your long-term financial health.

When debt is used for investing in your future, I call it *good debt* (see Chapter 2). Borrowing money to pay for an education, buy real estate, or invest in a small business is like eating fruits and vegetables for their vitamins. That's not to say that you can't get yourself into trouble when accumulating good debt. Just as you can gorge yourself on too much "good food," you can absolutely develop financial indigestion from too much good debt.

In this chapter, I mainly help you battle the increasing problem of consumer debt. Getting rid of your bad debts may be even more difficult than giving up the junk foods you love. But in the long run, you'll be glad you did; you'll be financially healthier and emotionally happier. And after you get rid of your high-cost consumer debts, make sure you practice the best way to avoid future credit problems: *Don't borrow with bad debt.*

Before you decide which debt reduction strategies make sense for you, you must first consider your overall financial situation (see Chapter 2) and assess your alternatives. (I discuss strategies for reducing your current spending — which help you free up more cash to pay down your debts — in the next chapter.)

Using Savings to Reduce Your Consumer Debt

Many people build a mental brick wall between their savings and investment accounts and their consumer debt accounts. By failing to view their finances holistically, they simply fall into the habit of looking at these accounts individually. The thought of putting a door in that big brick wall doesn't occur to them.

Understanding how you gain

If you have the savings to pay off consumer debt, like high-interest credit card and auto loans, do so. (Make sure you pay off the loans with the highest interest rates first.) Sure, you diminish your savings, but you also reduce your debts. Although your savings and investments may be earning decent returns, odds are good that the interest you're paying on your consumer debts is higher.

Paying off consumer loans on a credit card at, say, 12 percent is like finding an investment with a guaranteed return of 12 percent — *tax-free*. You would actually need to find an investment that yielded even more — around 18 percent — to net 12 percent after paying taxes in order to justify not paying off your 12 percent loans. The higher your tax bracket (see Chapter 7), the higher the return you need on your investments to justify keeping high-interest consumer debt.

Even if you think that you're an investment genius and you can earn more on your investments, swallow your ego and pay down your consumer debts anyway. In order to chase that higher potential return from investments, you need to take substantial risk. You *may* earn more investing in that hot stock tip or that bargain real estate located on a toxic waste site, but more than likely, you won't.

If you use your savings to pay down consumer debts, be careful to leave yourself enough of an emergency cushion. (In Chapter 4, I tell you how to determine how large of an emergency reserve you should have.) You want to be in a position to withstand an unexpected large expense or temporary loss of income. On the other hand, if you use savings to pay down credit card debt, you can run your credit card balances back up in a financial pinch (unless your card gets canceled), or you can turn to a family member or wealthy friend for a low-interest loan.

Discovering money to pay down consumer debts

Have you ever reached into the pocket of an old winter parka and found a rolled-up $20 bill you forgot you had? Stumbling across some forgotten funds is always a pleasant experience. But before you root through all your closets in search of stray cash to help you pay down that nagging credit card debt, check out some of these financial jacket pockets you may have overlooked:

- ✔ **Borrow against your cash value life insurance policy.** If you were approached by a life insurance agent, he or she probably sold you a cash value policy because it pays high commissions to insurance agents. Or perhaps your parents bought one of these policies for you when you were a child. Borrow against the cash value to pay down your debts. (*Note:* You may want to consider discontinuing your cash value policy altogether and simply withdraw the cash balance — see Chapter 16 for details.)

- ✔ **Sell investments held outside of retirement accounts.** Maybe you have some shares of stock or a Treasury bond gathering dust in your safety deposit box. Consider cashing in these investments to pay down your consumer loans. Just be sure to consider the tax consequences of selling these investments. If possible, sell only those investments that won't generate a big tax bill.

- ✔ **Borrow against the equity in your home.** If you're a homeowner, you may be able to tap into your home's *equity,* which is the difference between the property's market value and outstanding loan balance. You can generally borrow against real estate at a lower interest rate and get a tax deduction to boot. You must take care to ensure that you don't overborrow on your home and risk losing it to foreclosure.

- ✔ **Borrow against your employer's retirement account.** Check with your employer's benefits department to see whether you can borrow against your retirement account balance. The interest rate is usually reasonable. Be careful, though — if you leave your job (or if you're asked to leave), you may have to repay the loan within only 60 days. Also recognize that you'll miss out on investment returns on the money borrowed.

- ✔ **Borrow from friends and family.** They know you, love you, realize your shortcomings, and probably won't be as cold-hearted as some bankers. Money borrowed from family members can have strings attached, of course. Treating the obligation seriously is important. To avoid misunderstandings, write up a simple agreement listing the terms and conditions of the loan. Unless your family members are like the worst bankers I know, you'll probably get a fair interest rate, and your family will have the satisfaction of helping you out — just don't forget to pay them back.

Decreasing Debt When You Lack Savings

If you lack savings to throw at your consumer debts, not surprisingly, you have some work to do. If you're currently spending all your income (and more!), you need to figure out how you can decrease your spending (see Chapter 6 for lots of great ideas) and/or increase your income. In the meantime, you need to slow the growth of your debt.

Reducing your credit card's interest rate

Different credit cards charge different interest rates. So why pay 14, 16, or 18 percent (or more) when you can pay less? The credit card business has become quite competitive. Gone are the days where all banks charge 18 percent or more for VISA and MasterCard.

Until you get your debt paid off, slow the growth of your debt by reducing the interest rate you're paying. Here are sound ways to do that:

- ✔ **Apply for a lower-rate credit card.** If you're earning a decent income, you're not too burdened with debt, and you have a clean credit record, qualifying for lower-rate cards is relatively painless. Some persistence (and cleanup work) may be required if you have income and debt problems or nicks in your credit report. After you're approved for a new, lower-interest-rate card, you can simply transfer your outstanding balance from your higher-rate card.

  Among the banks with consistently low-interest-rate credit cards, I like 5Star Bank (800-776-2265), which offers a no-annual-fee card with a 7.9 percent interest rate. CardWeb.com's Web site has a credit card locator tool that you may find useful (www.cardweb.com/cardlocator/). In addition, the site presents monthly surveys of low-interest-rate and no-annual-fee cards (among others, including secured cards).

- ✔ **Call the bank(s) that issued your current high-interest-rate credit card(s) and say that you want to cancel your card(s) because you found a competitor that offers no annual fee and a lower interest rate.** Your bank may choose to match the terms of the "competitor" rather than lose you as a customer.

- ✔ **While you're paying down your credit card balance(s), stop making new charges on cards that have outstanding balances.** Many people don't realize that interest starts to accumulate *immediately* when they carry a balance. *You have no grace period* — the 20-odd days you normally have to pay your balance in full without incurring interest charges — if you carry a credit card balance month to month.

Understanding all credit card terms and conditions

Avoid getting lured into applying for a credit card that hypes an extremely low interest rate. One such card advertises a 1.9 percent rate, but you have to dig into the fine print for the rest of the story.

First, any card that offers such a low interest rate will honor that rate only for a short period of time — in this case, six months. After six months, the interest rate skyrockets to nearly 15 percent.

But wait, there's more: Make just one late payment or exceed your credit limit, and the company raises your interest rate to 19.8 percent (or even 24, 29 percent, or more) and slaps you with a $29 fee for each such infraction (some banks charge $39). If you want a cash advance on your card, you get socked with a fee equal to 3 percent of the amount advanced. (During the economic slowdown in the early 2000s, some banks were even advertising 0 percent interest rates — although that rate generally applied only to balances transferred from another card, and such cards were subject to all of the other vagaries discussed in this section.)

Now, I'm not saying that everyone should avoid this type of card. Such a card may make sense for you if you want to transfer an outstanding balance and then pay off that balance within a matter of months, cancel the card, and avoid getting socked with the high fees on the card.

If you hunt around for a low-interest-rate credit card, be sure to check out all the terms and conditions. Start by reviewing the uniform rates and terms disclosure, which details the myriad fees and conditions. Also, be sure that you understand how the future interest rate is determined on cards that charge variable interest rates.

Cutting up your credit cards

If you have a pattern of living beyond your means by buying on credit, get rid of the culprit — the credit card, that is. To kick the habit, a smoker needs to toss *all* the cigarettes, and an alcoholic needs to get rid of *all* the booze. Cut up *all* of your credit cards and call the issuers of the cards to cancel your accounts. And when you buy consumer items such as cars and furniture, do not apply for E-Z credit.

The world worked fine back in the years B.C. (Before Credit). Think about it: Just a couple generations ago, credit cards didn't even exist. People paid with cash and checks — imagine that! You *can* function without buying anything on a credit card. In certain cases, you may need a card as collateral — such as when renting a car. When you bring back the rental car, however, you can pay with cash or check. Leave the card at home in the back of your sock drawer or freezer, and pull (or thaw) it out only for the occasional car rental.

If you can trust yourself, keep a separate credit card *only* for new purchases that you know you can absolutely pay in full each month. No one needs three, five, or ten credit cards! You can live with one (and actually none), given the wide acceptance of most cards. Count 'em up, including retail store and gas cards, and get rid of 'em. Retailers such as department stores and gas stations just love to give you their cards. Not only do these cards charge outrageously high interest rates, but they also are not widely accepted like VISA and MasterCard. Virtually all retailers accept VISA and MasterCard. More credit lines mean more temptation to spend what you can't afford.

If you decide to keep one widely accepted credit card instead of getting rid of them all, be careful. You may be tempted to let debt accumulate and roll over for a month or two, starting up the whole horrible process of running up your consumer debt again. Rather than keeping one credit card, consider getting a debit card.

Discovering debit cards: The best of both worlds

Credit cards are the main reason today's consumers are buying more than they can afford. So logic says that one way you can keep your spending in check is to stop using your credit cards. But in a society that's used to the widely accepted VISA and MasterCard plastic for purchases, changing habits is hard. And you may be legitimately concerned that carrying your checkbook or cash can be a hassle or can be costly if you're mugged.

Debit cards truly offer the best of both worlds. The beauty of the debit card is that it offers you the convenience of making purchases with a piece of plastic without the temptation or ability to run up credit card debt. Debit cards keep you from spending money you don't have and help you live within your means.

A debit card looks just like a credit card with either the VISA or MasterCard logo. The big difference between debit cards and credit cards is that, as with checks, debit card purchase amounts are deducted electronically from your checking account within days. (Bank ATM cards are also debit cards; however, if they lack a VISA or MasterCard logo, bank ATM cards are accepted by far fewer merchants.)

If you switch to a debit card and you keep your checking account balance low and don't ordinarily balance your checkbook, you may need to start balancing it. Otherwise, you may face unnecessary bounced check charges.

Here are some other differences between debit and credit cards:

✔ If you pay your credit card bill in full and on time each month, your credit card gives you free use of the money you owe until it's time to pay the bill; debit cards take the money out of your checking account almost immediately. (Note that some credit cards charge a fee even if you pay your balance in full each month. You didn't think the banks would let you use the float forever, did you?)

✔ Credit cards make it easier for you to dispute charges for problematic merchandise through the issuing bank. Most banks allow you to dispute charges for up to 60 days after purchase and will credit the disputed amount to your account pending resolution. Most debit cards offer a much shorter window, typically less than one week, for making disputes.

Because moving your checking account can be a hassle, see whether your current bank offers VISA or MasterCard debit cards. If your bank doesn't offer one, shop among the major banks in your area, which are likely to offer the cards. Because such cards come with checking accounts, make sure that you do some comparison shopping between the different account features and fees.

What if your debit card is lost or stolen?

Personal credit cards and debit cards have similar so-called "zero liability" should someone illegally use your card. If your debit card is lost or stolen and someone makes fraudulent charges on your debit card, you simply sign statements with your bank that they aren't your charges. You will be reimbursed typically in a matter of days.

However, cards designated and listed as business (commercial) cards may not have the same zero liability as consumer cards. Generally speaking, banks view businesses as riskier and more prone to internal fraud. Suppose, for example, that your business issued debit cards to its employees and one of them gave it to a friend to use and then said the card was lost and those purchases were fraudulent.

Therefore, I recommend getting a separate consumer debit card for your small business (simply keep your name, not the business's on the account) or use a bank that offers the same protections on their business debit cards as on their consumer debit cards. Otherwise, you could get socked with a hefty bill that you didn't deserve.

A number of investment firms offer VISA or MasterCard debit cards with their asset management accounts. Not only can these investment firm "checking accounts" help you break the credit card overspending habit, but they may also get you thinking about saving and investing your money. One drawback of these accounts is that most of them require fairly hefty minimum initial investment amounts — typically $5,000 to $10,000. Among brokerages with competitive investment offerings and prices are TD Waterhouse (800-934-4448; www.tdameritrade.com), Vanguard (800-992-8327; www.vanguard.com), and Muriel Siebert (800-872-0711; www.siebertnet.com).

Turning to Credit Counseling Agencies

Prior to the passage of the 2005 bankruptcy laws discussed later in this chapter, each year hundreds of thousands of debt-burdened consumers sought "counseling" from credit counseling service offices. Now, more than a million people annually are expected to get the required counseling. Unfortunately, many people find that the service doesn't always work the way it's pitched.

Beware biased advice at credit counseling agencies

Leona Davis, whose family racked up significant debt due largely to unexpected medical expenses and a reduction in her income, found herself in trouble with too much debt. So she turned to one of the large, nationally promoted credit counseling services, which she heard about through its advertising and marketing materials.

The credit counseling agency Davis went to markets itself as a "nonprofit community service." Davis, like many others I know, found that the "service" was not objective. After her experience, Davis feels that a more appropriate name for the organization she worked with would be the Credit Card Collection Agency.

Unbeknownst to Davis and most of the other people who use supposed credit counseling agencies is the fact that the vast majority of their funding comes from the fees that creditors pay them. Most credit counseling agencies collect fees on a commission basis — just as collection agencies do! Their strategy is to place those who come in for help on their "debt management program." Under this program, counselees like Davis agree to pay a certain amount per month to the agency, which in turn parcels out the money to the various creditors.

Because of Davis's tremendous outstanding consumer debt (it exceeded her annual income), her repayment plan was doomed to failure. Davis managed to make 10 months' worth of payments, largely because she raided a retirement account for $28,000. Had Davis filed bankruptcy (which she ultimately needed to do), she would've been able to keep her retirement money. But Davis's counselor never discussed the bankruptcy option. "I received no counseling," says Davis. "Real counselors take the time to understand your situation and offer options. I was offered one solution: a forced payment plan."

Others who have consulted various credit counseling agencies, including one of my research assistants who, undercover, visited an office to seek advice, confirm that some agencies use a cookie-cutter approach to dealing with debt. Such agencies typically recommend that debtors go on a repayment plan that has the consumer pay, say, 3 percent of each outstanding loan balance to the agency, which in turn pays the money to creditors.

Unable to keep up with the enormous monthly payments, Davis finally turned to an attorney and filed for bankruptcy — but not before she had unnecessarily lost thousands of dollars because of the biased recommendations.

Although credit counseling agencies' promotional materials and counselors aren't shy about highlighting the drawbacks to bankruptcy, counselors are reluctant to discuss the negative impact of signing up for a debt payment plan. Davis' counselor never told her that restructuring her credit card payments would tarnish her credit reports and scores. The counselor my researcher met with also neglected to mention this important fact. When asked, the counselor was evasive about the debt "management" program's impact on his credit report.

 If you're considering bankruptcy, first be sure to read the rest of this chapter. Second, interview any counseling agency you may be considering working with. Remember that you're the customer and you should do your homework first and be in control. Don't allow anyone or any agency to make you feel that they're in power simply because of your financial troubles.

Ask questions and avoid debt management programs

Probably the most important question to ask a counseling agency is whether they offer debt management programs (DMP) where they put you on a repayment plan with your creditors and get paid a monthly fee for handling the payments. You do _not_ want to work with an agency offering DMPs because of conflicts of interest. An agency can't offer objective advice about all your options for dealing with debt, including bankruptcy, if they have a financial incentive to put you on a DMP.

Two good agencies that don't offer DMPs are the Institute for Financial Literacy (866-662-4932; www.financiallit.org) and Hummingbird Credit Counseling (800-645-4959; www.hummingbirdcreditcounseling.org).

Here are some additional questions that the Federal Trade Commission suggests that you ask prospective counseling agencies you may hire:

- ✔ **What are your fees? Are there setup and/or monthly fees?** Get a specific price quote in writing.

- ✔ **What if I can't afford to pay your fees or make contributions?** If an organization won't help you because you can't afford to pay, look elsewhere for help.

- ✔ **Will I have a formal written agreement or contract with you?** Don't sign anything without reading it first. Make sure all verbal promises are in writing.

- ✔ **Are you licensed to offer your services in my state?**

- ✔ **What are the qualifications of your counselors? Are they accredited or certified by an outside organization? If so, by whom? If not, how are they trained?** Try to use an organization whose counselors are trained by a non-affiliated party.

- ✔ **What assurance do I have that information about me (including my address, phone number, and financial information) will be kept confidential and secure?**

- ✔ **How are your employees compensated? Are they paid more if I sign up for certain services, if I pay a fee, or if I make a contribution to your organization?**

Filing Bankruptcy

For consumers in over their heads, the realization that their monthly income is increasingly exceeded by their bill payments is usually a traumatic one. In many cases, years can pass before people consider drastic measures like filing bankruptcy. Both financial and emotional issues come into play in one of the most difficult and painful, yet potentially beneficial, decisions.

When Helen, a mother of two and a sales representative, contacted a bankruptcy attorney, her total credit card debt equaled her annual gross income. As a result of her crushing debt load, she couldn't meet her minimum monthly credit card payments. Rent and food gobbled up most of her earnings. What little was left over went to the squeakiest wheel.

Creditors were breathing down Helen's back. "I started getting calls from collection departments at home and work — it was embarrassing," relates Helen. Helen's case is typical in that credit card debt was the prime cause of her bankruptcy.

As the debt load grew (partly exacerbated by the high interest rates on the cards), more and more purchases got charged — from the kids' clothing to repairs for the car. Finally, after running out of cash, she had to take a large cash advance on her credit cards to pay for rent and food.

Despite trying to work out lower monthly payments to keep everyone happy, most of the banks to which Helen owed money were inflexible. "When I asked one bank's VISA department if it preferred that I declare bankruptcy because it was unwilling to lower my monthly payment, the representative said 'yes'," Helen says. After running out of options, Helen filed personal bankruptcy.

Understanding bankruptcy benefits

Every year, more than 1.5 million American households (that's about 1 in every 80 households) file personal bankruptcy.

With bankruptcy, certain types of debts can be completely eliminated or *discharged*. Debts that typically can be discharged include credit card, medical, auto, utilities, and rent.

Debts that may *not* be canceled generally include child support, alimony, student loans, taxes, and court-ordered damages (for example, drunk driving settlements). Helen was an ideal candidate for bankruptcy because her debts (credit cards) were dischargeable.

Helen also met another important criterion — her level of high-interest consumer debt relative to her annual income was high (100 percent). When this ratio (discussed in Chapter 2) exceeds more than 25 percent, filing bankruptcy may be your best option.

Eliminating your debt also allows you to start working toward your financial goals. Depending on the amount of debt you have outstanding relative to your income, you may need a decade or more to pay it all off. In Helen's case, at the age of 48, she had no money saved for retirement, and she was increasingly unable to spend money on her children.

What you can keep if you file bankruptcy

In every state, you can retain certain property and assets when you file for bankruptcy. You may be surprised to discover that in some states, you can keep your home regardless of its value! Most states, though, allow you to protect a certain amount of home equity.

Additionally, you're allowed to retain some other types and amounts of personal property and assets. For example, most states allow you to retain household furnishings, clothing, pensions, and money in retirement accounts. So don't empty your retirement accounts or sell off personal possessions to pay debts unless you're absolutely sure that you won't be filing bankruptcy.

Filing bankruptcy offers not only financial benefits but emotional benefits, as well. "I was horrified at filing, but it is good to be rid of the debts and collection calls — I should have filed six months earlier. I was constantly worried. When I saw homeless families come to the soup kitchen where I sometimes volunteer, I thought that someday that could be me and my kids," says Helen.

Coming to terms with bankruptcy drawbacks

Filing bankruptcy, needless to say, has a number of drawbacks. First, bankruptcy appears on your credit report for up to ten years, so you'll have difficulty obtaining credit, especially in the years immediately following your filing. However, if you already have problems on your credit report (because of late payments or a failure to pay previous debts), the damage has already been done. And without savings, you're probably not going to be making major purchases (such as a home) in the next several years anyway.

If you do file bankruptcy, getting credit in the future is still possible. You may be able to obtain a *secured credit card,* which requires you to deposit money in a bank account equal to the credit limit on your credit card. Of course, you'll be better off without the temptation of any credit cards and better served with a debit card. Also, know that if you can hold down a stable job, most creditors will be willing to give you loans within a few years of your filing bankruptcy. Almost all lenders ignore bankruptcy after five to seven years.

Another drawback of bankruptcy is that it costs money, and those expenses have jumped higher due to the new requirements from the 2005 bankruptcy law (more on that in a moment). I know this seems terribly unfair. You're already in financial trouble — that's why you're filing bankruptcy! Court filing and legal fees can easily exceed $1,000, especially in higher cost of living areas.

And finally, most people find that filing bankruptcy causes emotional stress. Admitting that your personal income can't keep pace with your debt obligations is a painful thing to do. Although filing bankruptcy clears the decks of debt and gives you a fresh financial start, feeling a profound sense of failure (and sometimes shame) is common. Despite the increasing incidence of bankruptcy, bankruptcy filers are reluctant to talk about it with others, including family and friends.

Another part of the emotional side of filing bankruptcy is that you must open your personal financial affairs to court scrutiny and court control during the several months it takes to administer a bankruptcy. A court-appointed bankruptcy trustee oversees your case and tries to recover as much of your property as possible to satisfy the *creditors* — those to whom you owe money.

Some people also feel that they're shirking responsibility by filing for bankruptcy. One client I worked with should have filed, but she couldn't bring herself to do it. She said, "I spent that money, and it's my responsibility to pay it back."

Most banks make gobs and gobs of money from their credit card businesses. As a former consultant who worked in the industry, I can tell you that credit cards are one of the most profitable lines of business for banks. If you don't believe me, consider that at a banking conference, CEO John Reed referred to the credit card business for banks as a "high-return, low-risk" business. Now you know why your mailbox is always filled with solicitations for more cards.

So if you file for bankruptcy, don't feel bad about not paying back the bank. The nice merchants from whom you bought the merchandise have already been paid. *Charge-offs* — the banker's term for taking the loss on debt that you discharge through bankruptcy — are the banker's cost, which is another reason why the interest rate is so high on credit cards and why you shouldn't borrow on credit cards.

Deciphering the new bankruptcy laws

In 2005, a new bankruptcy law went into effect — the Bankruptcy Abuse and Prevention Act of 2005. As you may be able to tell from the bill's name, major creditors, such as credit card companies, lobbied heavily for new laws. Although they didn't get everything they wanted, they got a lot, which not surprisingly doesn't benefit those folks in dire financial condition considering bankruptcy. Don't despair, though — help and information can overcome the worst provisions of this new law. Here are the major new elements of the personal bankruptcy laws:

✔ **Required counseling:** Before filing for bankruptcy, individuals are now mandated to complete credit counseling, the purpose of which is to explore your options for dealing with debt, including (but not limited to) bankruptcy and developing a debt repayment plan.

Historically, many supposed "counseling" agencies have provided highly biased advice. Be sure to read the "Turning to Credit Counseling Agencies" section on what conflicts of interest agencies have and for advice on how to pick a top-notch agency.

To actually have debts discharged through bankruptcy, the new law requires a second type of counseling called "Debtor Education." All credit counseling and debtor education must be completed by an approved organization on the U.S. Trustee's Web site (www.usdoj.gov/ust). Click on the link "Credit Counseling & Debtor Education."

✔ **Means testing:** Some high-income earners now may be precluded from filing the form of bankruptcy that actually discharges debts (called Chapter 7) and instead forced to use the form of bankruptcy that involves a repayment plan (called Chapter 13).

Recognizing that folks living in higher cost of living areas tend to have higher incomes, the new law does allow for differences in income by making adjustments based upon your state of residence and family size. The expense side of the equation is considered as well, and allowances are determined by county and metropolitan area. I won't bore you with the details and required calculations here. Studies estimate that only about 5 percent of potential filers are expected to be affected by this new provision. For more information, click on the "Means Testing Information" link on the U.S. Trustee's Web site (www.usdoj.gov/ust).

✔ **Increased requirements placed on filers and attorneys:** The means testing alone has created a good deal of additional work for bankruptcy filers, work generally done by attorneys. Filers including lawyers must also now attest to the accuracy of submitted information, which will have attorneys doing more verification work. Thus, it's no surprise that since the new bankruptcy laws were passed, legal fees increased significantly — jumps of 30 to 40 percent were common.

✔ **New rules for people who recently moved:** Individual states have
their own provisions for how much personal property and home equity
(difference between market value of your home and debt owed on that
home) you could keep. In some cases, soon before filing bankruptcy,
people actually moved to a state that allowed them to keep more. Under
the new law, you must live in the state for at least two years before filing
bankruptcy in that state and using that state's personal property exemptions. To use a given state's *homestead exemption,* which dictates how
much home equity you may protect, you must have lived in that state
for at least 40 months.

Choosing between Chapter 7 and 13

You can file one of two forms of personal bankruptcy, Chapter 7 or Chapter 13.
Chapter 7 allows you to discharge or cancel certain debts. This form of bankruptcy makes the most sense when you have significant debts that you're
legally allowed to cancel. (See "Understanding bankruptcy benefits," earlier
in this chapter, for details on which debts can be canceled, or discharged.)

Chapter 13 comes up with a repayment schedule that requires you to pay
your debts over several years. Chapter 13 stays on your credit record (just
like Chapter 7), *but it doesn't eliminate debt,* so its value is limited — usually
to dealing with debts like taxes that can't be discharged through bankruptcy.
Chapter 13 can keep creditors at bay until a repayment schedule is worked
out in the courts.

Seeking bankruptcy advice

If you want to find out more about the pros, cons, and details of filing for
bankruptcy, pick up a copy of *The New Bankruptcy: Will It Work For You* by
attorney Stephen R. Elias (Nolo Press). If you're comfortable with your decision to file and you think you can complete the paperwork, you may be able
to do it yourself. *How to File for Chapter 7 Bankruptcy,* by attorneys Elias,
Albin Renauer, and Robin Leonard (Nolo Press), comes with all the necessary
filing forms.

Hiring a paralegal typing service to prepare the forms, which can be a cost-
effective way to get help with the process if you don't need heavy-duty legal
advice, is an intermediate approach. To find a paralegal typing service in
your area, check your local yellow pages under "Paralegals."

Stopping the Spend-and-Consumer Debt Cycle

Regardless of how you deal with paying off your debt, you're in real danger of falling back into old habits. Backsliding happens not only to people who file bankruptcy but also to those who use savings or home equity to eliminate their debt. This section speaks to that risk and tells you what to do about it.

Resisting the credit temptation

Getting out of debt can be challenging, but I have confidence that you can do it with this book by your side. In addition to the ideas I discuss earlier in this chapter (such as eliminating all your credit cards and getting a debit card), the following list provides some additional tactics you can use to limit the influence credit cards hold over your life. (If you're concerned about the impact that any of these tactics may have on your credit rating, please see Chapter 2):

- **Reduce your credit limit.** If you're not going to take the advice I give you earlier in this chapter and get rid of all of your credit cards or secure a debit card, be sure to keep a lid on your credit card's credit limit (the maximum balance allowed on your card). You don't have to accept the increase just because your bank keeps raising your credit limit to reward you for being such a profitable customer. Call your credit card service's toll-free phone number and lower your credit limit to a level you're comfortable with.

- **Replace your credit card with a charge card.** A *charge card* (such as the American Express Card) requires you to pay your balance in full each billing period. You have no credit line or interest charges. Of course, spending more than you can afford to pay when the bill comes due is possible. But you'll be much less likely to overspend if you know you have to pay in full monthly.

- **Never buy anything on credit that depreciates in value.** Meals out, cars, clothing, and shoes all depreciate in value. Never buy these things on credit. Borrow money only for sound investments — education, real estate, or your own business, for example.

✔ **Think in terms of total cost.** Everything sounds cheaper in terms of monthly payments — that's how salespeople entice you into buying things you can't afford. Take a calculator along, if necessary, to tally up the sticker price, interest charges, and upkeep. The total cost will scare you. *It should.*

✔ **Stop the junk mail avalanche.** Look at your daily mail — I bet half of it is solicitations and mail-order catalogs. You can save some trees and time sorting junk mail by removing yourself from most mailing lists. To remove your name from mailing lists, write to the Direct Marketing Association, Mail Preference Service, P.O. Box 643, Carmel, NY 10512 (you can register through their Web site at `www.dmaconsumers.org/consumerassistance.html`, but you have to pay a $5 fee to do so; simply print out the form and mail it in to avoid the online fee).

To remove your name from the major credit reporting agency lists that are used by credit card solicitation companies, call 888-567-8688. Also, tell any credit card companies you keep cards with that you want your account marked to indicate that you don't want any of your personal information shared with telemarketing firms.

✔ **Limit what you can spend.** Go shopping with a small amount of cash and no plastic or checks. That way, you can spend only what little cash you have with you!

Identifying and treating a compulsion

No matter how hard they try to break the habit, some people become addicted to spending and accumulating debt. It becomes a chronic problem that starts to interfere with other aspects of their lives and can lead to problems at work and with family and friends.

Debtors Anonymous (DA) is a nonprofit organization that provides support (primarily through group meetings) to people trying to break their debt accumulation and spending habits. DA is modeled after the 12-step Alcoholics Anonymous (AA) program.

Like AA, Debtors Anonymous works with people from all walks of life and socioeconomic backgrounds. You can find people who are financially on the edge, $100,000-plus income earners, and everybody in between at DA meetings. Even former millionaires join the program.

DA has a simple questionnaire that helps determine whether you're a problem debtor. If you answer "yes" to at least 8 of the following 15 questions, you may be developing or already have a compulsive spending and debt accumulation habit:

✔ Are your debts making your home life unhappy?

✔ Does the pressure of your debts distract you from your daily work?

✔ Are your debts affecting your reputation?

✔ Do your debts cause you to think less of yourself?

✔ Have you ever given false information in order to obtain credit?

✔ Have you ever made unrealistic promises to your creditors?

✔ Does the pressure of your debts make you careless when it comes to the welfare of your family?

✔ Do you ever fear that your employer, family, or friends will learn the extent of your total indebtedness?

✔ When faced with a difficult financial situation, does the prospect of borrowing give you an inordinate feeling of relief?

✔ Does the pressure of your debts cause you to have difficulty sleeping?

✔ Has the pressure of your debts ever caused you to consider getting drunk?

✔ Have you ever borrowed money without giving adequate consideration to the rate of interest you're required to pay?

✔ Do you usually expect a negative response when you're subject to a credit investigation?

✔ Have you ever developed a strict regimen for paying off your debts, only to break it under pressure?

✔ Do you justify your debts by telling yourself that you are superior to the "other" people, and when you get your "break," you'll be out of debt?

To find a Debtors Anonymous (DA) support group in your area, check your local phone directory (in the "Business" section) or visit the DA Web site at www.debtorsanonymous.org. You can write to DA's national headquarters for meeting locations in your area and a literature order form at the following address: Debtors Anonymous General Service Office, P.O. Box 920888, Needham, MA 02492-0009. You can also contact the DA's national headquarters by phone at 781-453-2743.

Chapter 6

Reducing Your Spending

· ·

· ·

*T*elling people how and where to spend their money is a risky undertaking, because most people like to spend money and hate to be told what to do. You'll be glad to hear that I don't tell you exactly where you must cut your spending in order to save more and accomplish your personal and financial goals. Instead, I detail numerous strategies that have worked for other people. The final decision for what to cut rests solely on you. Only you can decide what's important to you and what's dispensable (should you cut out your weekly poker games, or cut back on your shoe collection?).

I assume throughout these recommendations that you value your time. Therefore, I don't tell you to scrimp and save by doing things like cutting open a tube of toothpaste so that you can use every last bit of it. And I don't tell you to have your spouse do your ironing to reduce your dry-cleaning bills — no point in having extra money in the bank if your significant other walks out on you!

The fact that you're busy all the time may be part of the reason you spend money as you do. Therefore, the recommendations in this chapter focus on methods that produce significant savings but don't involve a lot of time. In other words, these strategies provide bang for the buck.

Finding the Keys to Successful Spending

For most people, spending money is a whole lot easier and more fun than earning it. Far be it from me to tell you to stop having fun and turn into a penny-pinching, stay-at-home miser. Of course you can spend money. But there's a world of difference between spending money carelessly and spending money *wisely*.

If you spend too much and spend unwisely, you put pressure on your income and your future need to continue working. Savings dwindle, debts may accumulate, and you can't achieve your financial goals.

If you dive into details too quickly, you may miss the big picture. So before I jump into the specific areas where you can trim your budget, I give you my four overall keys to successful spending. These four principles run through my recommendations in this chapter.

Living within your means

Spending too much is a *relative* problem. Two people can each spend $40,000 per year yet still have drastically different financial circumstances. How? Suppose that one of them earns $50,000 annually, while the other makes $35,000. The $50,000 income earner saves $10,000 each year. The $35,000 wage earner, on the other hand, accumulates $5,000 of new debt (or spends that amount from prior savings). Spend within your means.

Don't let the spending habits of others dictate yours. Certain people — and you know who they are — bring out the big spender in you. Do something else with them besides shopping and spending. If you can't find any other activity to share with them, try shopping with limited cash and no credit cards. That way, you can't overspend on impulse.

How much you can safely spend while working toward your financial goals depends on what your goals are and where you are financially. Chapter 4 assists you with figuring how much you should be saving and what you can afford to spend to accomplish your financial goals.

Looking for the best values

You can find high quality and low cost in the same product. Conversely, paying a high price is no guarantee that you're getting high quality. Cars are a good example. Whether you're buying a subcompact, a sports car, or a luxury four-door sedan, some cars are more fuel-efficient and cheaper to maintain than rivals that carry the same sticker price.

When you evaluate the cost of a product or service, think in terms of total, long-term costs. Suppose that you're comparing the purchase of two used cars: the Solid Sedan, which costs $11,995, and the Clunker Convertible, which weighs in at $9,995. On the surface, the convertible appears to be cheaper. However, the price that you pay for a car is but a small portion of what that car ultimately costs you. If the convertible is costly to operate, maintain, and insure over the years, it could end up costing you much more than the sedan would have. Sometimes paying more upfront for a higher-quality product or service ends up saving you money in the long run.

People who sell particular products and services may initially appear to have your best interests at heart when they steer you toward something that isn't costly. However, you may be in for a rude awakening when you discover the ongoing service, maintenance, and other fees you face in the years ahead. Salespeople are generally trained to pitch you a lower-cost product if you indicate that's what you're after.

Don't waste money on brand names

You don't want to compromise on quality, especially in the areas where quality is important to you. But you also don't want to be duped into believing that brand-name products are better or worth a substantially higher price. Be suspicious of companies that spend gobs on image-oriented advertising. Why? Because heavy advertising costs many dollars, and as a consumer of those companies' products and services, you pay for all that advertising.

All successful companies advertise their products. Advertising is cost-effective and good business if it brings in enough new business. But you need to consider the products and services and the claims that companies make.

Does a cola beverage really taste better if "it's the real thing" or "the choice of a new generation"? Consider all the silly labels and fluffy marketing of beers. Blind taste testing demonstrates little if any difference between the more expensive brand name products and the cheaper, less heavily advertised ones.

Now, if you can't live without your Coca-Cola or Pepsi and you think that these products are head and shoulders above the rest, drink them to your heart's content. But question the importance of the name and image of the products you buy. Companies spend a lot of money creating and cultivating an image, which has zero impact on how their products taste or perform.

Branding is used in many fields to sell overpriced, mediocre products and services to consumers. Take the lowly can of paint. Tests show some differences among different brands of paint. However, when you can buy high-quality paints for about $20 a gallon, do you really think that a $100 can of paint blessed with the name of Ralph Lauren or Martha Stewart is that much better?

D/L Laboratories, a testing firm, compared these $100-per-gallon snooty paints to $20-per-gallon high-quality alternatives and found little difference — or at least no difference that was worth paying for. In fact, one of the "gourmet" paints splattered more, had a less uniform sheen, didn't cover the surface as well, was more prone to run when applied, and emitted a high level of volatile organic compounds! Some other snooty brands didn't fare much better. As people in the trade can tell you (thanks to computer-based matching), if you find a particular color of paint you like in a highbrow line, match it in a high-quality but far less costly line.

Consumer Reports is a reputable publication that evaluates products and services based on quality and performance, not brand image. Consult it on major consumer purchases.

Getting your money back

Take a look around your home for items you never use. Odds are you have some (maybe even many). Returning such items to where you bought them can be cathartic; it also reduces your home's clutter and puts more money in your pocket.

Also, think about the last several times you bought a product or service and didn't get what was promised. What did you do about it? Most people do nothing and let the derelict company off the hook. Why? Here are some common explanations for this type of behavior:

- ✔ **Low standards:** We've come to expect shoddy service and merchandise because of the common lousy experiences we've had.

- ✔ **Conflict avoidance:** Most people shun confrontation. It makes us tense and anxious, and it churns our stomachs.

- ✔ **Hassle aversion:** Most companies don't make it easy for complainers to get their money back or obtain satisfaction. To get restitution from some companies, you need the tenacity and determination of a pit bull.

You can increase your odds of getting what you expect for your money by doing business with companies that

- ✔ **Have fair return policies:** Don't purchase any product or service until you understand the company's return policy. Be especially wary of buying from companies that charge hefty "restocking" fees for returned merchandise or simply don't allow returns at all. Reputable companies offer full refunds and don't make you take store credit (although taking credit is fine if you're sure that you'll use it soon and that the company will still be around).

- ✔ **Can provide good references:** Suppose that you're going to install a fence on your property, and as a result, you're going to be speaking with fencing contractors for the first time. You can sift out many inferior firms by asking each contractor that you interview for at least three references from people in your local area who have had a fence installed in the past year or two.

- ✔ **Are committed to the type of product or service they provide:** Suppose that your chosen fencing contractor does a great job, and now that you're in the market for new gutters on your home, the contractor says that he does gutters, too. Although the path of least resistance would be to simply hire the same contractor for your gutters, you should inquire about how many gutters the contractor has installed and also interview some other firms that specialize in such work. Because your fencing contractor may have done only a handful of gutter jobs, he may not know as much about such work.

Following these guidelines can greatly diminish your chances of having unhappy outcomes with products or services you buy. And here's another important tip: Whenever possible, pay with a credit card if your credit's in good standing. Doing so enables you to dispute a charge within 60 days and gives you leverage for getting your money back.

If you find that you're unable to make progress when trying to get compensation for a lousy product or service, here's what I recommend you do:

✔ **Document.** Taking notes whenever you talk to someone at a company can help you validate your case down the road, should problems develop. Obviously, the bigger the purchase and the more you have at stake, the more carefully you should document what you've been promised. In many cases, though, you probably won't start carefully noting each conversation until a conflict develops. Keep copies of companies' marketing literature, because such documents often make promises or claims that companies fail to live up to in practice.

✔ **Escalate.** Some frontline employees either aren't capable of resolving disputes or lack the authority to do so. No matter what the cause, speak with a department supervisor and continue escalating from there. If you're still not making progress, lodge a complaint to whatever state regulatory agency (if any) oversees such companies. Also, be sure to tell your friends and colleagues not to do business with the company (and let the company know that you're doing this until your complaint is resolved to your satisfaction). Also consider contacting a consumer help group — these groups are typically sponsored by broadcast or print media in metropolitan areas. They can be helpful in resolving disputes or shining adverse publicity on disreputable companies or products.

✔ **Litigate.** If all else fails, consider taking the matter to small claims court if the company continues to be unresponsive. (Depending on the amount of money at stake, this tactic may be worth your time.) The maximum dollar limit that you may recover varies by state, but you're usually limited to a few thousand dollars. For larger amounts than those allowed in small claims court in your state, you can, of course, hire an attorney and pursue the traditional legal channels — although you may end up throwing away more of your time and money. Mediation and arbitration are generally a better option than following through on a lawsuit.

Eliminating the fat from your spending

If you want to reduce your overall spending by, say, 10 percent, you can just cut all of your current expenditures by 10 percent. Or you can reach your 10-percent goal by cutting some categories a lot and others not at all. You need to set priorities and make choices about where you want and don't want to spend your money.

Recognizing the Better Business Bureau's conflicts of interest

The Better Business Bureau (BBB) states that its mission is "to promote and foster the highest ethical relationship between businesses and the public." The reality of the typical consumer's experience of dealing with the BBB doesn't live up to the BBB's marketing. BBBs are nonprofits and are not agencies of any governmental body.

"They don't go after local established businesses — they are funded by these same businesses. The BBB certainly has a good public relations image, better than what is warranted. They don't do all that much for consumers," says veteran consumer advocate Ralph Nader.

"It's a business trade organization, and each local BBB is basically independent like a franchise," says John Bear, an author of consumer advocacy books, including *Send This Jerk the Bedbug Letter: How Companies, Politicians, and the Mass Media Deal With Complaints & How to Be a More Effective Complainer* (Ten Speed Press). "By and large, when somebody has a problem with a company and they fill out a complaint form with the BBB, if the company is a member of the BBB, there's ample evidence that consumers often end up not being satisfied. The BBB protects their members."

Particularly problematic among the BBB's pro-business practices are the company reports the BBB keeps on file. The BBB often considers a legitimate complaint satisfactorily resolved even

when you're quite unhappy and the company is clearly not working to satisfy the problems for which it's responsible.

Bear also cites examples of some truly troubling BBB episodes. In one case, he says that a diploma mill (a company that sells degrees but provides little if any education) in Louisiana was a member of the local BBB. "When complaints started coming in," says Bear, "the BBB's response was always that the company met their standards and that the complaints were resolved. The reality was that the complaints weren't satisfactorily resolved and it took about two years until complaints reached into the hundreds for the BBB to finally cancel the diploma mill's membership and give out a bland statement about complaints. Two months later, the FBI raided the company. Millions of consumers' dollars were lost because the BBB didn't do its job."

The president of a South Florida BBB (the fifth largest in the country, according to Bear) was ultimately imprisoned for taking bribes from companies in exchange for maintaining favorable reports on file.

The truth about some BBBs is unfortunate, because as state consumer protection agencies are being cut back and dissatisfied consumers are being shunted to the BBB, more people are in for unsatisfactory experiences with an organization that does not go to bat for them.

What you spend your money on is sometimes a matter of habit rather than a matter of what you really want or value. For example, some people shop at whatever stores are close to them.

Eliminating fat doesn't necessarily mean cutting back on your purchases: You can save money by buying in bulk. Some stores specialize in selling larger packages or quantities of a product at a lower price because they save money on the packaging and handling. If you're single, shop with a friend and split the bulk purchases.

Turning your back on consumer credit

As I discuss in Chapters 3 and 5, buying items that depreciate — such as cars, clothing, and vacations — on credit is hazardous to your long-term financial health. Buy only what you can afford today. If you'll be forced to carry a debt for months or years on end, you can't really afford what you're buying on credit today.

Without a doubt, *renting-to-own* is the most expensive way to buy. Here's how it works: You see a huge ad blaring "$12.95 for a DVD player!" Well, the ad has a big hitch: That's $12.95 per week, for many weeks. When all is said and done (and paid), buying a $100 DVD player through a rent-to-own store costs a typical buyer more than $375!

Welcome to the world of rent-to-own stores, which offer cash-poor consumers the ability to lease consumer items and, at the end of the lease, an option to buy.

If you think that paying an 18-percent interest rate on a credit card is expensive, consider this: The effective interest rate charged on many rent-to-own purchases exceeds 100 percent; in some cases, it may be 200 percent or more! Renting-to-own makes buying on a credit card look like a great deal.

I'm not sharing this information to encourage you to buy on credit cards but to point out what a rip-off renting-to-own is. Such stores prey on cashless consumers who either can't get credit cards or don't understand how expensive renting-to-own really is. Forget the instant gratification, and save a set amount each week until you can afford what you want.

Consumer credit is expensive, and it reinforces a bad financial habit: spending more than you can afford.

Budgeting to Boost Your Savings

When most people hear the word *budgeting,* they usually think unpleasant thoughts — and like *dieting,* rightfully so. But budgeting can help you move from knowing how much you spend on various things to successfully reducing your spending.

The first step in the process of *budgeting,* or planning your future spending, is to analyze where your current spending is going (refer to Chapter 3). After you do that, calculate how much more you'd like to save each month. Then comes the hard part: deciding where to make cuts in your spending.

Suppose that you're currently not saving any of your monthly income and you want to save 10 percent for retirement. If you can save and invest through a tax-sheltered retirement account — for example, a 401(k) or 403(b), or SEP-IRA or Keogh — you don't actually need to cut your spending by 10 percent to reach a savings goal of 10 percent (of your gross income).

When you contribute money to a tax-deductible retirement account, you reduce your federal and state taxes. If you're a moderate-income-earner paying, say, 30 percent in federal and state taxes on your marginal income, you actually need to reduce your spending by only 7 percent to save 10 percent. The "other" 3 percent of the savings comes from the lowering of your taxes. (The higher your tax bracket, the less you need to cut your spending to reach a particular savings goal.)

So to boost your savings rate to 10 percent, go through your current spending category by category until you come up with enough proposed cuts to reduce your spending by 7 percent. Make your cuts in the areas that will be the least painful and where you're getting the least value from your current level of spending. (If you don't have access to a tax-deductible retirement account, budgeting still involves the same process of assessment and making cuts in various spending categories.)

Another method of budgeting involves starting completely from scratch rather than examining your current expenses and making cuts from that starting point. Ask yourself how much you'd like to spend on different categories. The advantage of this approach is that it doesn't allow your current spending levels to constrain your thinking. You'll likely be amazed at the discrepancies between what you think you should be spending and what you actually are spending in certain categories.

Reducing Your Spending: Eric's Strategies

As you read through the following strategies for reducing your spending, please keep in mind that some of these strategies will make sense for you and some of them won't. Start your spending reduction plan with the strategies that come easily. Work your way through them. Keep a list of the options that are more challenging for you — ones that may require more of a sacrifice but be workable if necessary to achieve your spending and savings goals.

No matter which of the ideas in this chapter you choose, rest assured that keeping your budget lean and mean pays enormous dividends. After you implement a spending reduction strategy, you'll reap the benefits for years to come. Take a look at Figure 6-1: For every $1,000 that you shave from your annual spending (that's just $83 per month), check out how much more money you'll have down the road. (This chart assumes that you invest your new-found savings in a tax-favored retirement account, you average 10 percent per year returns on your investments, and you're in a moderate combined federal and state tax bracket of 35 percent — see Chapter 7 for information on tax brackets.)

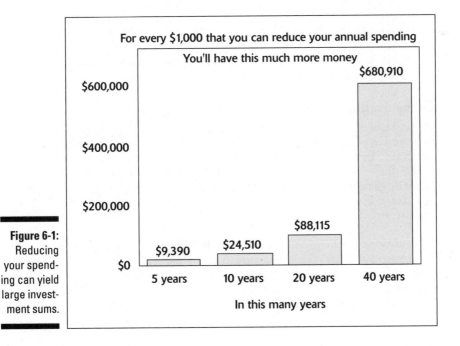

Figure 6-1: Reducing your spending can yield large investment sums.

Managing food costs

Not eating is one way to reduce food expenditures; however, this method tends to make you weak and dizzy, so it's probably not a viable long-term strategy. The following culinary strategies can keep you on your feet — perhaps improve your health — and help you save money.

Eating out frugally

Eating meals out and getting takeout can be time-savers, but they rack up big bills if done too often and too lavishly. Eating out is a luxury — think of it as hiring someone to shop, cook, and clean up for you. Of course, some people either hate to cook or don't have the time, space, or energy to do much in the kitchen. If this sounds like you, choose restaurants carefully and order from the menu selectively.

Here are a couple tips for eating out:

- ✔ **Avoid beverages, especially alcohol.** Most restaurants make big profits on beverages. Drink water instead. (Water is healthy, and it reduces the likelihood that you'll want a nap after a big meal.)

- ✔ **Order vegetarian.** Vegetarian dishes generally cost less than meat-based entrees (and they're generally better for you).

I don't want to be a killjoy. I'm not saying that you should live on bread and water. You can have dessert — heck, have some wine, too, for special occasions! Just try not to eat dessert with every meal. Try eating appetizers and dessert at home, where they're a lot less expensive.

Eating healthy at home without spending a fortune

Obesity and unhealthy eating habits continue to be a big problem. *The Surgeon General's Report on Nutrition and Health* (produced under former U.S. Surgeon General C. Everett Koop, M.D.) states that our reliance on a meat- and dairy-based diet — with its unhealthy fat and cholesterol — is the cause of the majority of premature deaths in the United States. In fact, five out of the top ten causes of death — heart disease, certain types of cancer, stroke, diabetes, and arteriosclerosis — are caused largely by Americans' poor diets.

As evidenced by the preponderance of diet and weight loss books on health book bestseller lists — and the growth of the natural and organic grocery stores like Whole Foods and Trader Joe's — Americans are trying to eat healthier. Concerned about all the pesticides, antibiotics, and hormones that end up in our food supply, organic food purchases are growing at 20 percent annually.

Problem is, financially speaking, better quality food, especially organic foods, can cost more, sometimes much more — but not always. A number of studies I've seen demonstrate that highly processed foods, which are less nutritious and worse for your health, can be as costly or even more expensive than fresh, so-called whole foods. The key to not overspending on fresher, healthier, and organic foods is to be flexible when you're at the grocery store. Buy more of what is currently less expensive, stock up on sale items that aren't perishable, and buy more at stores like Trader Joe's that have competitive pricing. To find the Trader Joe's nearest you, visit their Web site at `www.traderjoes.com` or call 800-SHOPTJS (800-746-7857).

Joining a wholesale superstore

Superstores such as Costco and Sam's Club enable you to buy groceries in bulk at wholesale prices. And contrary to popular perception, you don't have to buy 1,000 rolls of toilet paper at once — just 24.

I performed price comparisons between wholesale superstores and retail grocery stores and found that wholesalers charge about 30 percent less for the exact same stuff — all without the hassle of clipping coupons or hunting for which store has the best price on paper towels this month! (At these discount prices, you only need to buy about $100 per year to recoup Costco and Sam's Club's membership fees, which start at $30 per year.)

Organic food worth spending for

According to a February 2006 study by *Consumer Reports,* spending the money to buy organic makes the most sense when buying the following foods:

✓ **Produce — apples, bell peppers, celery, cherries, imported grapes, nectarines, peaches, pears, potatoes, red raspberries, spinach, and strawberries:** "The U.S. Department of Agriculture's lab testing reveals that even after washing, some fruits and vegetables consistently carry much higher levels of pesticide residue than others."

✓ **Meat, poultry, eggs, and dairy:** "You greatly reduce the risk of exposure to the agent believed to cause mad cow disease and minimize exposure to other potential toxins in nonorganic feed. You also avoid the results of production methods that use daily supplemental hormones and antibiotics, which have been linked to increased antibacterial resistance in humans."

✓ **Baby food:** "Children's developing bodies are especially vulnerable to toxins, and they may be at risk of higher exposure. Baby food is often made up of condensed fruits or vegetables, potentially concentrating pesticide residues."

In addition to saving you lots of money, buying in bulk requires fewer shopping trips. You'll have more supplies around your humble abode — so you'll have less need to eat out (which is costly) or make trips (wasted time and gasoline) to the local grocer, who may be really nice but charges the most.

Perishables run the risk of living up to their name, so don't buy what you can't use. Repackage bulk packs into smaller quantities and store them in the freezer if possible. If you're single, shop with a friend or two and split the order. Also, be careful when you shop at the warehouse clubs — you may be tempted to buy things you don't really need. These stores carry all sorts of items, including the newest TVs, computers, furniture, clothing, complete sets of baseball cards, and giant canisters of biscotti — so wallet and waistline beware! Try not to make impulse purchases, and be especially careful when you have kids in tow.

To find a superstore near you, check your local phone directory. You can also find a Costco store near you by visiting the Costco Web site at www. costco.com or calling 800-774-2678. Sam's Club is on the Internet at www.samsclub.com.

Saving on shelter

Housing and all the costs associated with it (utilities, furniture, appliances, and if you're a homeowner, maintenance and repairs) can gobble a large chunk of your monthly income. I'm not suggesting that you live in an igloo or teepee (though they're probably less costly), but people often overlook opportunities to save money in this category.

Reducing rental costs

Rent can take up a sizable chunk of your monthly take-home pay. Many people consider rent to be a fixed and inflexible part of their expenses, but it's not. Here's what you can do to cut down your rental costs:

- **Move to a lower-cost rental.** Of course, a lower-cost rental may not be as nice — it may be smaller, lack a private parking spot, or be located in a less popular area. Remember that the less you spend renting, the more you can save toward buying your own place. Just be sure to factor in all the costs of a new location, including the possible higher commuting costs.

- **Share a rental.** Living alone has some benefits, but financially speaking, it's a luxury. If you rent a larger place with roommates, your rental costs will go way down, and you'll get more home for your rental dollars. You have to be in a sharing mood, though. Roommates can be a hassle at times, but they can also be a plus — you get to meet all sorts of new people, and you have someone else to blame when the kitchen's a mess.

✔ **Negotiate your rental increases.** Every year, like clockwork, your landlord bumps up your rent by a certain percentage. If your local rental market is soft or your living quarters are deteriorating, stand up for yourself! You have more leverage and power than you probably realize. A smart landlord doesn't want to lose good tenants who pay rent on time. Filling vacancies takes time and money. State your case: You've been a responsible tenant, and your research shows comparable rentals going for less. Crying "poor" may help, too. At the very least, if you can't stave off the rent increase, maybe you can wrangle some improvements to the place.

✔ **Buy rather than rent.** Purchasing your own place can be costly, yes, but in the long run, owning should be cheaper than renting, and you'll have something to show for it in the end. If you purchase real estate with a 30-year fixed-rate mortgage, your mortgage payment (which is your biggest ownership expense) remains constant. Only your property taxes, maintenance, and insurance costs are exposed to the vagaries of inflation.

As a renter, your entire monthly housing cost can rise with increases in the cost of living (unless you're the beneficiary of a rent-controlled apartment). See Chapter 14 to find out how to buy real estate, even if you're short on cash.

Reducing homeowner expenses

As every homeowner knows, houses suck up money. You should be especially careful to watch your money in this area of your budget.

✔ **Know what you can afford.** Don't make the mistake of overspending when buying a home. Whether you're on the verge of buying your first home or trading up to a more costly property, crunch some realistic numbers before you jump. When too little money is left over for your other needs and wants — such as taking trips, eating out, enjoying hobbies, or saving for retirement — your new dream house may become a financial prison.

Calculate how much you can afford to spend monthly on a home by figuring your other needs first. (Doing the exercises in Chapter 3, on where you're spending your money, and Chapter 4, on saving for retirement, can help you calculate the amount you can afford.)

Although real estate can be a good long-term investment, you can end up pouring a large portion of your discretionary dollars into your home. In addition to decorating and remodeling, some people feel the need to trade up to a bigger home every few years. Of course, after they're in their new home, the remodeling and renovation cycle simply begins again, which costs even more money. Appreciate what you have, and remember that homes are for living in, not museums for display. If you have children, why waste a lot of money on expensive furnishings that take up valuable space and require you to constantly nag your kids to tread carefully? And don't covet — the world will always have people with bigger houses and more toys than you.

✔ **Rent out a room.** Because selling your home to buy a less expensive place can be a big hassle, consider taking in a tenant (or charge those adult "children" still living at home!) to reduce your housing expenses. Check out the renter thoroughly: Get references, run a credit report, and talk about ground rules and expectations before sharing your space. Don't forget to check with your insurance company to see whether your homeowner's policy needs adjustments to cover potential liability from renting.

✔ **Refinance your mortgage.** This step may seem like common sense, but surprisingly, many people don't keep up-to-date on mortgage rates. If interest rates are lower than they were when you obtained your current mortgage, you may be able to save money by refinancing (see Chapter 14 for more information).

✔ **Appeal your property-tax assessment.** If you bought your property when housing prices were higher in your area than they are now, you may be able to save money by appealing your assessment. Also, if you live in an area where your assessment is based on how the local assessor valued the property (rather than what you paid for your home), your home may be overassessed.

Check with your local assessor's office for the appeals procedure you need to follow. You generally have to prove that your property is worth less today than it was when you bought it or that the assessor incorrectly valued your property. In the first case, an appraiser's recent evaluation of your property will do — you may already have one if you refinanced your mortgage recently. In the latter case, review how the assessor valued your property compared with similar ones nearby — mistakes happen.

✔ **Reduce utility costs.** Sometimes you have to spend money to save money. Old refrigerators, for example, can waste a lot of electricity. Insulate to save on heating and air-conditioning bills. Install water flow regulators in shower heads and toilet bowls. When planting your yard, don't select water-guzzling plants, and keep your lawn area reasonable. Even if you don't live in an area susceptible to droughts, why waste water (which isn't free) unnecessarily? Recycle — recycling means less garbage, which translates into lower trash bills (because you won't be charged for using larger garbage containers) and benefits the environment by reducing landfill.

Cutting transportation costs

America is a car-driven society. In most other countries, cars are a luxury. More than 90 percent of the people in the rest of the world can't afford a new car. If more people in the United States thought of cars as a luxury,

Americans might have far fewer financial problems (and accidents). Not only do cars pollute the air and clog the highways, but they also cost you a bundle. Purchasing a quality car and using it wisely can save you money. Using other transportation alternatives can also help you save.

Contrary to advertising slogans, cars aren't built to last; manufacturers don't want you to stick with the same car year after year. New models are constantly introduced with new features and styling changes. Getting a new set of wheels every few years is an expensive luxury.

Don't try to keep up with the Joneses as they show off their new cars every year — for all you know, they're running themselves into financial ruin just trying to impress you. Let your neighbors admire you for your thriftiness and wisdom instead.

Research before you buy a car

When you buy a car, you don't just pay the initial sticker price: You also have to pay for gas, insurance, registration fees, maintenance, and repairs. You may also have to pay sales and/or personal property taxes. Don't compare simple sticker prices; think about the total, long-term costs of car ownership.

Speaking of total costs, remember that you're also trusting your life to the car. With about 40,000 Americans killed in auto accidents annually (about half of which are caused by drunk drivers), safety should be an important consideration as well. Air bags, for example, may save your life. The National Highway Traffic Safety Administration Web site (www.nhtsa.gov) has lots of crash test data, as well as information on other car safety issues.

Consumer Reports publishes a number of useful buying guides for new and used cars. You find *Consumer Reports* on the Internet at www.consumer reports.org. For you data jocks, IntelliChoice (www.intellichoice.com) provides information about all categories of ownership costs, warranties, and dealer costs for new cars, which are rated based on total ownership costs. Edmunds (www.edmunds.com) provides more general information about different makes and models of both new and used cars. Please be aware that these latter two sites have advertising and may receive referral fees if you buy a car through a dealer their Web site refers you to.

Don't lease, don't borrow: Buy your car with cash

The main reason people end up spending more than they can afford on a car is that they finance the purchase. As I discuss in Part I, you should avoid borrowing money for consumption purchases, especially for items that depreciate in value (like cars). A car is most definitely *not* an investment.

When buying a car, leasing is generally more expensive than borrowing money. Leasing is like a long-term car rental. We all know how well rental cars get treated — leased cars are treated just as well, which is one of the reasons leasing is so costly.

Unfortunately, the practice of leasing cars or buying them on credit is increasingly becoming the norm in our society. This approach is certainly attributable to a lot of the misinformation that's spread by car dealers and, in some cases, the media. Consider the magazine article entitled "Rewards of Car Leasing." The article claims that leasing is a great deal when compared to buying. Ads for auto dealers advertising auto leasing were placed next to the article. The magazine, by the way, is free to subscribers — which means that 100 percent of its revenue comes from advertisers such as auto dealers. Also be aware that because of the influence of advertising (and ignorance), leasing is widely endorsed on Web sites that purport to provide information on cars.

"But I can't buy a new car with cash," you may be thinking. Some people feel that it's unreasonable of me to expect them to use cash to buy a new car, but I'm trying to look out for your best long-term financial interests. Please consider the following:

- ✔ If you lack sufficient cash to buy a new car, I say, "Don't buy a new car!" Most of the world's population can't even afford a car, let alone a new one! Buy a car that you can afford — which for most people is a used one.

- ✔ Don't fall for the rationale that says buying a used car means lots of maintenance, repair expenses, and problems. Do your homework and buy a good quality used car (see the preceding section, "Research before you buy a car." That way, you can have the best of both worlds. A good used car costs less to buy and, thanks to lower insurance costs (and possibly property taxes), less to operate.

- ✔ A fancy car is not needed to impress people for business purposes. Some people I know say that they absolutely must drive a nice, brand-spanking-new car to set the right impression for business purposes. I'm not going to tell you how to manage your career, but I will ask you to consider that if clients and others see you driving an expensive new car, they may think that you spend money wastefully or you're getting rich off of them!

Replace high-cost cars

Maybe you realize by now that your car is too expensive to operate because of insurance, gas, and maintenance costs. Or maybe you bought too much car — people who lease or borrow money for a car frequently buy a far more expensive car than they can realistically afford.

Dump your expensive car and get something more financially manageable. The sooner you switch, the more money you'll save. Getting rid of a car on a lease is a challenge, but it can be done. I had one client who, when he lost his job and needed to slash expenses, convinced the dealer (by writing a letter to the owner) to take the leased car back.

Keep cars to a minimum

I've seen households that have one car per person — four people, four cars! Some people have a "weekend" car that they use only on days off! For most households, maintaining two or more cars is an expensive extravagance. Try to find ways to make do with fewer cars.

You can move beyond the confines of owning a car by either carpooling or riding buses or trains to work. Some employers give incentives for taking public transit to work, and some cities and counties offer assistance for setting up vanpools or carpools along popular routes. By leaving the driving to someone else, you can catch up on reading or just relax on the way to and from work. You also help reduce pollution.

When you're considering the cost of living in different areas, don't forget to factor in commuting costs. One advantage of living close to work, or at least close to public transit systems, is that you may be able to make do with fewer cars (or no car at all) in your household.

Buy commuter passes

In many areas, you can purchase train, bus, or subway passes to help reduce the cost of commuting. Many toll bridges also have booklets of tickets that you can buy at a discount. Some booths don't advertise that they offer these plans (maybe as a strategy to help keep revenues up). Some areas even allow before-tax dollars to be withheld from your paycheck to buy commuter passes.

Use regular unleaded gas

A number of studies have shown that "super-duper-ultrapremium" gasoline is not worth the extra expense. But make sure that you buy gasoline that has an octane rating recommended for your vehicle. Paying more for the higher octane "premium" gasoline just wastes money. Your car won't run better; you just pay more for gas. Fill up your tank when you're on a shopping trip to the warehouse wholesalers (discussed earlier in this chapter). These superstores are usually located in lower-cost areas, so the gas is often cheaper there, too. Also, don't use credit cards to buy your gas if you have to pay a higher price to do so.

Service your car regularly

Sure, servicing your car (for example, changing the oil every 5,000 miles) costs money, but it saves you dough in the long run by extending the operating life of your car. Servicing your car also reduces the chance that your car will crap out in the middle of nowhere, which requires a humongous towing charge to a service station. Stalling on the freeway during peak rush hour and having thousands of angry commuters stuck behind you is even worse.

Lowering your energy costs

Escalating energy prices remind all of us how much we depend upon and use oil, electricity, and natural gas in our daily lives. There are a number of terrific Web sites packed with suggestions and tips for how to lower your energy costs. Before I present those to you, however, here are the basics:

- **Drive fuel-efficient cars.** If you're safety minded, you know how dangerous driving can be and aren't willing to risk your life driving a pint-size vehicle just to get 50 miles per gallon. That said, you can drive safe cars (see the section, "Research before you buy a car") that are fuel-efficient.

- **Be thrifty at home.** Get all family members on the same page, without driving them crazy, to turn off lights they don't need. Turn down the heat at night, which saves money and helps you sleep better, and turn it down when no one is home. *Hint:* If people are walking around your home during the winter with shorts on instead of wearing sweaters, it's time to turn the heat down!

- **Service and maintain what you have.** Anything that uses energy — from your cars to your furnace — should be regularly serviced. For instance, make sure you clean your filters.

- **Investigate energy efficiency before you buy.** This advice applies not only to appliances but also to an entire home. Some builders are building energy efficiency into their new homes.

The following are my favorite energy information and tip Web sites:

- Alliance to Save Energy (`www.powerisinyourhands.org`)

  This site includes home and business energy saving tips; utility, local, and state incentive programs; and information about federal energy tax credits.

- The Database of State Incentives for Renewable Energy (`www.dsireusa.org`)

- U.S. Department of Energy's Energy Efficiency and Renewable Energy Web site (`www.eere.energy.gov/consumer`)

Controlling clothing costs

Given the amount of money that some people spend on clothing and related accessories, I've come to believe that people in nudist colonies must be great savers! But you probably live among the clothed mainstream of society, so here's a short list of economical ideas:

- ✔ **Avoid clothing that requires dry cleaning.** When you buy clothing, try to stick with cottons and machine-washable synthetics rather than wools or silks that require dry cleaning. Check labels before you buy clothing.

- ✔ **Don't chase the latest fashions.** Fashion designers and retailers are constantly working to tempt you to buy more. Don't do it. Ignore publications that pronounce this season's look. In most cases, you simply don't need to buy racks of new clothes or an entire new wardrobe every year. If your clothes aren't lasting at least ten years, you're probably tossing them before their time or buying clothing that isn't very durable.

  True fashion, as defined by what people wear, changes quite slowly. In fact, the classics never go out of style. If you want the effect of a new wardrobe every year, store last year's purchases away next year and then bring them out the year after. Or rotate your clothing inventory every third year. Set your own fashion standards. Buy basic, and buy classic — if you let fashion gurus be your guide, you'll end up with the biggest wardrobe in the poorhouse!

- ✔ **Minimize accessories.** Shoes, jewelry, handbags, and the like can gobble large amounts of money. Again, how many of these accessory items do you really need? The answer is probably very few, because each one should last many years.

Go to your closet or jewelry box and tally up the loot. What else could you have done with all that cash? Do you see things you regret buying or forgot you even had? Don't make the same mistake again. Have a garage sale if you have a lot of stuff that you don't want. Return recent unused purchases to stores.

Repaying your debt

In Chapter 5, I discuss strategies for reducing the cost of carrying consumer debt. The *best* way to reduce the costs of such debt is to avoid it in the first place when you're making consumption purchases. You can avoid consumer debt by eliminating your access to credit or by limiting your purchase of consumer items to what you can pay off each month. Remember, borrow only for long-term investments (see Chapter 2 for more information).

Don't keep a credit card that charges you an annual fee, especially if you pay your balance in full each month. Many no-fee credit cards exist — and some even offer you a benefit for using them:

- ✔ Discover Card (800-347-2683) rebates up to 1 percent of purchases in cash.
- ✔ GM Card (800-846-2273) gives credits worth 5 percent of your charges that can be used toward the purchase of most GM-manufactured vehicles.
- ✔ AFBA (800-776-2265) offers a basic no-fee card.
- ✔ USAA Federal Savings (800-922-9092) offers a basic no-fee card.

You should consider the cards in the preceding list only if you pay your balance in full each month, because no-fee cards typically levy high interest rates for balances carried month-to-month. The small rewards that you earn really won't do you much good if they're negated by interest charges.

If you have a credit card that charges an annual fee, try calling the company and saying that you want to cancel the card because you can get a competitor's card without an annual fee. Many banks will agree to waive the fee on the spot. Some require you to call back yearly to cancel the fee — a hassle that can be avoided by getting a true no-fee card.

Some cards that charge an annual fee and offer credits toward the purchase of a specific item, such as a car or airline ticket, may be worth your while if you pay your bill in full each month and charge $10,000 or more annually. *Note:* Be careful — you may be tempted to charge more on a card that rewards you for more purchases. Spending more in order to rack up bonuses defeats the purpose of the credits.

Indulging responsibly in fun and recreation

Having fun and taking time out for R and R can be money well spent. But when it comes to fun and recreation, financial extravagance can wreck an otherwise good budget.

Entertainment

If you adjust your expectations, entertainment doesn't have to cost a great deal of money. Many movies, theaters, museums, and restaurants offer discount prices on certain days and times.

Cultivate some interests and hobbies that are free or low-cost. Visiting with friends, hiking, reading, and playing sports can be good for your finances as well as your health.

Vacations

For many people, vacations are a luxury. For others, regular vacations are essential parts of their routine. Regardless of how you recharge your batteries, remember that vacations are not investments, so you shouldn't borrow through credit cards to finance your travels. After all, how relaxed will you feel when you have to pay all those bills?

Try taking shorter vacations that are closer to home. Have you been to a state or national park recently? Take a vacation at home, visiting the sites in your local area. Great places that you've always wanted to see but haven't visited for one reason or another are probably located within 200 miles of you. Or you may want to just block out some time and do what my cats do: Take lots of naps and relax around your home.

If you do travel a long way to a popular destination, travel during the off-season for the best deals on airfares and hotels. Keep an eye out for discounts and "bought-but-unable-to-use" tickets advertised in your local paper. The *Consumer Reports Travel* newsletter and numerous Web sites such as `www.priceline.com`, `www.expedia.com`, and `www.travelocity.com` can help you find low-cost travel options as well. Senior citizens generally qualify for special fares at most airlines — ask the airline what programs it offers.

Also, be sure to shop around, even when working with a travel agent. Travel agents work on commission, so they may not work hard to find you the best deals. Tour packages, when they meet your interests and needs, can also save you money. If you have flexible travel plans, courier services can cut your travel costs significantly (but make sure that the company is reputable).

Using thrift with gifts

Think about how you approach buying gifts throughout the year — especially during the holidays. I know people who spend so much on their credit cards during the December holidays that it takes them until late spring or summer to pay their debts off!

Although I don't want to deny your loved ones gifts from the heart — or deny you the pleasure of giving them — spend wisely. Homemade gifts are less costly to the giver and may be dearer to recipients. Many children actually love durable, classic, basic toys. If the TV commercials dictate your kids' desires, it may be time to toss the TV or set better rules for what the kids are allowed to watch. Use TiVo or similar services to record desired shows so you can zap through the ubiquitous commercials.

Some people forget their thrifty shopping habits when gift buying, perhaps because they don't like to feel cheap when buying a gift. As with other purchases you make, paying careful attention to where and what you buy can save you significant dollars. Don't make the mistake of equating the value of a gift with its dollar cost.

And here's a good suggestion for getting rid of those old, unwanted gifts: One of the most entertaining holiday parties I've ever attended involved a *white elephant* gift exchange: Everyone brought a wrapped, unwanted gift from the past and exchanged it with someone else. After the gifts were opened, trading was allowed. (Just be sure not to bring a gift that was given to you by any of the exchange participants!) Can't be bothered with this? Consider donating unwanted items for a tax write-off if you itemize on Schedule A — see Chapter 7.

Lowering your phone bills

Thanks to increased competition and technology, telephoning costs are falling. If you haven't looked for lower rates recently, you're probably paying more than you need to for quality phone service. Unfortunately, shopping among the many service providers is difficult. Plans come with different restrictions, minimums, and bells and whistles. Here are my recommendations for saving on your phone bills:

- ✔ **Look at your phone company's other calling plans.** You may have to switch companies to reduce your bill, but I find that many people can save significantly with their current phone company simply by getting onto a better calling plan. So before you spend hours shopping around, contact your current local and long distance providers and ask them which of their calling plans offer the lowest cost for you based on the patterns of your calls.

- ✔ **Get help when shopping for other providers.** Two useful sources are Consumer Reports (800-234-1645; www.consumerreports.org) and Telecommunications Research & Action Center, or TRAC (www.trac.org).

The cell phone business is booming. And although being able to make calls from wherever you are can be enormously convenient, you can spend a lot of money for service given the myriad of extra charges. On the other hand, if you're able to take advantage of the free minutes many plans offer (on weekends, for example), a good cell phone service can save you money. Here's how to get your money's worth:

✔ **Question the need for a cell phone.** Okay, I realize that this is a risky point to raise for those cell phone addicts among us. If you enjoy having a cell phone to use during downtime when commuting or for emergency purposes, I won't try to talk you out of your cell phone. However, many people really don't need a cell phone (or one for which they're paying for lots of minutes). And some folks find that always being available raises their stress level.

✔ **Shop around.** Make sure you sign up with the best calling plan and carrier given your typical usage. *Consumer Reports* and TRAC (see previous list) can also help you research wireless phone services. Reputable carriers let you test out their service. They also offer full refunds if you're not satisfied after a week or two of service.

A thoughtful letter is usually cheaper, more appreciated, and longer lasting than a phone call. Just block out an hour, grab a pen and paper, and rediscover the lost art form of letter writing. Formulating your thoughts on paper can be clarifying and therapeutic. Computer users may find that they can also save money by sending e-mail.

Technology: Spending wisely

Today, we've got e-mail, cell phones, voice mail, BlackBerries, satellite TV, the Internet, and too many other ways to stay in touch and entertained 24/7. Visit a store that sells electronics, and you'll find no end to new gadgets.

Although I enjoy choices and convenience as much as the next person, I also see the detrimental impact these technologies have on our families' lives. As it is, most families struggle to find quality time together given their work obligations, long school days, and various other activities. At home, all these technology choices and options compete for attention and often pull families apart. The cost for all these services and gadgets adds up, leading to a continued enslavement to our careers.

Err on the side of keeping your life simple. Doing so costs less, reduces stress, and allows more time for the things that really do matter in life.

Especially when it comes to new technology and gadgets, don't be among the first to get something. HDTV is a good example why — in the early years, these new sets were extremely costly and more prone to problems. Now, prices are coming down and sets are more reliable.

The worst way to shop for electronics and technology-based products is to wander around stores selling lots of these goods and having a salesperson pitch you things. These folks are trained in what buttons to push to get you to whip out your VISA card and be on your way with things you don't know how you ever could've lived without. Educate yourself and determine what you really need instead of going to a store and being seduced by a salesperson.

Read articles — *Consumer Reports* is a very objective publication. CNET (www.cnet.com) is a useful source, and along with Froogle (froogle.google.com), it provides comparison shopping help after you decide to get serious about trying to buy something specific.

Curtailing personal care costs

You have to take care of yourself, but as with anything else, you can find ways to do it that are expensive, and you can find ways that save you money. Try this money-saving advice:

- ✔ **Hair care:** Going bald is one way to save money in this category. I'm working on this one myself. In the meantime, if you have hair to be trimmed, a number of no-frills, low-cost, hair-cutting joints can do the job. Supercuts is one of the larger hair care chains. You may insist that your stylist is the only one who can manage your hair the way you like it. At the prices charged by some of the trendy hair places, you have to really adore what they do to justify the cost. Consider going periodically to a no-frills stylist for maintenance after getting a fabulous cut at a more expensive place. If you're daring, you can try getting your hair cut at a local training school.

   For parents of young children, buying a simple-to-use home haircutting electric shaver (such as Wahl's) can be a great time and money saver — no more agonizing trips with little ones to have their hair cut by a "stranger." The kit pays for itself after just two haircuts!

- ✔ **Other personal-care services:** As long as I'm on the subject of outward beauty, I have to say that, in my personal opinion, the billions spent annually on cosmetics are largely a waste of money (not to mention all the wasted time spent applying and removing it). Women look fine without makeup. (In most cases, they look better.) And having regular facials, pedicures, and manicures can add up quickly.

- ✔ **Health club expenses:** Money spent on exercise is almost always money well spent. But you don't have to belong to a trendy club to receive the benefits of exercise. If you belong to a gym or club for the social scene (whether for dating or business purposes), you have to judge whether it's worth the cost.

Local schools, colleges, and universities often have tennis courts, running tracks, swimming pools, basketball courts, and exercise rooms, and they may provide instruction as well. Community centers offer fitness programs and classes, too. Metropolitan areas that have lots of health clubs undoubtedly have the widest range of options and prices. ***Note:*** When figuring the cost of membership, be sure to factor in the cost of travel to and from the clubs, as well as any parking costs (and the realistic likelihood of going there regularly to work out).

Don't forget that healthy exercise can be done indoors or out, free of charge. Isn't hiking in the park at sunset more fun than pedaling away on a stationary bike, anyway? You may want to buy some basic gym equipment for use at home. Be careful, though: Lots of rowing machines and free weights languish in a closet after their first week at home.

Paring down professional expenses

Accountants, lawyers, and financial advisors can be worth their expense if they're good. But be wary of professionals who create or perpetuate work and have conflicts of interest with their recommendations.

Make sure that you get organized before meeting with a professional for tax, legal, or financial advice. Do some background research to evaluate their strengths and biases. Set goals and estimate fees in advance so you know what you're getting yourself into.

Computer and printed resources (see Chapters 19 and 20) can be useful, low-cost alternatives and supplements to hiring professionals.

Looking for value in publication subscriptions

Everyone has a favorite and not-so-favorite publication. Some people don't realize how much they spend on publications, partly because they never tally up the cost.

Take *The New York Times,* for example. (Actually, consider not taking it.) At $9.70 per week in the New York metro area and $11.90 per week elsewhere, you pay a whopping $504 or $619 per year! Most areas have decent newspapers that cost a fraction of these amounts. You can also keep up with news and events through weekly news magazines such as *Newsweek* — which costs just $40 per year for new subscribers.

If you were to take the money that you're spending on *The New York Times* and invest it in a retirement account that earns a mere 10 percent per year, in 25 years you'd have about $74,000 (New York metro subscribers) or about $93,000 (everyone else in the country)! And this example assumes that the subscription prices won't increase every year, which they always do. After seeing these figures, you'd really have to feel that you're getting good value from *The New York Times* to keep subscribing!

Free publications are often driven by advertisers, so I don't encourage you to load up on them. But take a close look at the total amount you spend on publications and how much each one costs. Keep the ones that you're getting sufficient value from and cancel the rest. You can always read them at your local library.

Managing medical expenses

Health care is a big topic nowadays. The cost of health care is going up fast. Your health insurance — if you have health insurance, that is — probably covers most of your health-care needs. (Chapter 16 explains how to shop for health insurance.) But many plans require you to pay for certain expenses out of your own pocket.

Medical care and supplies are like any other services and products — prices and quality vary. And medicine in the United States, like any other profession, is a business. A conflict of interest exists whenever the person recommending treatment benefits financially from providing that treatment. Many studies have documented some of the unnecessary surgeries and medical procedures that have resulted from this conflict of interest.

Remember to shop around when seeking health insurance. Don't take any one physician's advice as gospel. Always get a second opinion for any major surgery. Most health insurance plans, out of economic self-interest, require a second opinion, anyway.

Therapy can be useful and even lifesaving. Have a frank talk with your therapist about how much total time and money you can expect to spend and what kind of results you can expect to receive. As with any professional service, a competent therapist gives you a straight answer if he or she is looking out for your psychological and financial well-being.

Alternative medicine (holistic, for example) is gaining attention because of its focus on preventive care and the treatment of the whole body or person. Although alternative medicine can be dangerous if you're in critical condition, alternative treatment for many forms of chronic pain or disease may be worth investigating. Alternative medicine may lead to better *and* lower-cost health care.

If you have to take certain drugs on an ongoing basis and pay for them out-of-pocket, ordering through a mail-order company can bring down your costs and help make refilling your prescriptions more convenient. Your health plan should be able to provide more information about this option.

Examine your employer's benefit plans. Take advantage of being able to put away a portion of your income before taxes to pay for out-of-pocket health-care expenses. Make sure that you pay close attention to the "use it or lose it" provisions of each plan.

Eliminating costly addictions

Human beings are creatures of habit. We all have habits we wish we didn't have, and breaking those habits can be very difficult. Costly habits are the worst. The following tidbits may nudge you in the right direction toward breaking your own financially-draining habits.

✔ **Kick the smoking habit.** Despite the decline in smoking over the past few decades, about one in four Americans still smokes. The smokeless tobacco habit, which also causes long-term health problems, is on the increase. Americans spend more than $50 billion annually on tobacco products — that's a staggering $1,000 per year per tobacco user. The increased medical costs and the costs of lost work time are even greater, as they're estimated at more than $50 billion every year. (Of course, if you continue to smoke, you may eliminate the need to save for retirement.)

Check with local hospitals for smoking-cessation programs. The American Lung Association (check your local phone directory) also offers Freedom from Smoking clinics around the country. The National Cancer Institute (800-422-6237, or 800-4CANCER) and the Office on Smoking and Health at the Centers for Disease Control (1600 Clifton Road, Atlanta, GA 30333; 770-488-5703) offer free information guides that contain effective methods for stopping smoking.

✔ **Stop abusing alcohol and other drugs.** Nearly one million Americans seek treatment annually for alcoholism or drug abuse. These addictive behaviors, like spending, transcend all educational and socioeconomic lines in our society. Even so, studies have demonstrated that only one in seven alcohol or drug abusers seek help. Three of the ten leading causes of death — cirrhosis of the liver, accidents, and suicides — are associated with excessive alcohol consumption.

The National Clearinghouse for Alcohol and Drug Information (800-729-6686) can refer you to local treatment programs such as Alcoholics Anonymous. It also provides pamphlets and other literature about the various types of substance abuse. The National Substance Abuse Information and Treatment Hotline (800-662-4357, or 800-662-HELP) can refer you to local drug treatment programs. It provides literature as well.

✔ **Don't gamble.** The house *always* comes out ahead in the long run. Why do you think so many governments run lotteries? Because governments make money on people who gamble, that's why.

Casinos, horse and dog racetracks, and other gambling establishments are sure long-term losers for you. So, too, is the short-term trading of stocks, which isn't investing but gambling. Getting hooked on the dream of winning is easy. And sure, occasionally you win a little bit (just enough to keep you coming back). Every now and then, a few folks win a lot. But your hard-earned capital mostly winds up in the pockets of the casino owners.

If you gamble just for the entertainment, take only what you can afford to lose. Gamblers Anonymous (213-386-8789; www.gamblersanonymous.org) helps those for whom gambling has become an addiction.

Keeping an eye on insurance premiums

Insurance is a vast minefield. In Part IV, I explain the different types of coverage, suggest what to buy and avoid, and detail how to save on policies. The following list explains the most common ways people waste money on insurance:

✔ **Keeping low deductibles.** The *deductible* is the amount of a loss that must come out of your pocket. For example, if you have an auto insurance policy with a $100 collision deductible and you get into an accident, you pay for the first $100 of damage and your insurance company picks up the rest. Low deductibles, however, translate into much higher premiums for you. In the long run, you save money with a higher deductible, even when factoring in the potential for greater out-of-pocket costs to you when you do have a claim. Insurance should protect you from economic disaster. Don't get carried away with a really high deductible, which can cause financial hardship if you have a claim and lack savings.

If you have a lot of claims, you won't come out ahead with lower deductibles, because your insurance premiums will escalate. Plus, low deductibles mean more claim forms to file for small losses (creating more hassle). Filing an insurance claim is usually not an enjoyable or quick experience.

✔ **Covering small potential losses or unnecessary needs.** You shouldn't buy insurance for anything that won't be a financial catastrophe if you have to pay for it out of your own pocket. Although the postal service isn't perfect, insuring inexpensive gifts sent in the mail isn't worth the price. Buying dental or home warranty plans, which also cover relatively small potential expenditures, doesn't make financial sense for the same reason. And if no one's dependent on your income, you don't need life insurance either. (Who'll be around to collect when you're gone?)

✔ **Failing to shop around.** Rates vary *tremendously* from insurer to insurer. In Part IV, I recommend the best companies to call for quotes and other cost-saving strategies.

Trimming your taxes

Taxes are probably one of your largest — if not *the* largest — expenditures. (So why is it last here? Read on to find out.)

Retirement savings plans are one of the best and simplest ways to reduce your tax burden. (I explain more about retirement savings plans in Chapter 11.) Unfortunately, most people can't take full advantage of these plans because they spend everything they make. So not only do they have less savings, but they also pay higher income taxes — a double whammy.

I've attended many presentations where a fast-talking investment guy in an expensive suit lectures about the importance of saving for retirement and explains how to invest your savings. Yet details and tips about finding the money to save (the hard part for most people) are left to the imagination.

In order to take advantage of the tax savings that come through retirement savings plans, you must first spend less than you earn. Only then can you afford to contribute to these plans. That's why the majority of this chapter is about strategies to reduce your spending.

Reduced sales tax is another benefit of spending less and saving more. When you buy most consumer products, you pay sales tax. Therefore, when you spend less money and save more in retirement accounts, you reduce your income and sales taxes. (See Chapter 7 for detailed tax-reduction strategies.)

Chapter 7

Taming Taxes

· ·

· ·

Y ou pay a lot of money in taxes — probably more than you realize. Believe it or not, few people know just how much they pay in taxes each year. Most people remember only whether they received a refund or owed money on their return. But when you file your tax return, all you're doing is settling up with tax authorities over the amount of taxes you paid during the year versus the total tax that you owe based on your income and deductions.

Understanding the Taxes You Pay

Some people feel lucky when they get a refund, but all a refund really indicates is that you overpaid in taxes during the year. You should have had this money in your own account all along. If you're consistently getting big refunds, you need to pay less tax throughout the year. (Fill out a simple tax form, the W-4, to determine how much you should be paying in taxes throughout the year. You can obtain a W-4 through your employer's payroll department. If you're self-employed, you can obtain Form 1040-ES by calling the IRS at 800-TAX-FORM [800-829-3676] or visiting its Web site at www.irs.gov. Also, the IRS Web site has a helpful "withholding calculator" at www.irs.gov/individuals/article/0,,id=96196,00.html.)

Instead of focusing on whether you're going to get a refund when you complete your annual tax return, you should concentrate on the *total* taxes you pay, which I discuss in the following section.

Focusing on the total taxes you pay

To find out the *total* taxes you pay, you need to get out your federal and state tax returns. On each of those returns is a line that shows the *total tax:* This is line 71 on the most recent federal 1040 returns. If you add up the totals from your federal and state tax returns, you'll probably see one of your largest expenses.

The goal of this chapter is to help you legally and permanently reduce the total taxes you pay. Understanding the tax system is the key to reducing your tax burden — if you don't, you'll surely pay more taxes than necessary. Your tax ignorance can lead to mistakes, which can be costly if the IRS and state government catch your underpayment errors. With the proliferation of computerized information and data tracking, discovering mistakes has never been easier.

The tax system, like other public policy, is built around incentives to encourage desirable behavior and activity. Home ownership, for example, is considered desirable because it encourages people to take more responsibility for maintaining buildings and neighborhoods. Clean, orderly neighborhoods are often the result of home ownership. Therefore, the government offers all sorts of tax perks, which I discuss later in this chapter, to encourage people to buy homes.

Not all people follow the path the government encourages — after all, it's a free country. However, the *fewer* desirable activities you engage in, the more you pay in taxes. If you understand the options, you can choose the ones that meet your needs as you approach different stages of your financial life.

Recognizing the importance of your marginal tax rate

When it comes to taxes, *not all income is treated equally.* This fact is far from self-evident. If you work for an employer and earn a constant salary during the course of a year, a steady and equal amount of federal and state taxes is deducted from each paycheck. Thus, it appears as though all that earned income is being taxed equally.

In reality, however, you pay less tax on your first dollars of earnings and more tax on your *last* dollars of earnings. For example, if you're single and your taxable income (see the next section) totals $45,000 during 2006, you pay federal tax at the rate of 10 percent on the first $7,550 of taxable income, 15 percent on income between $7,550 and $30,650, and 25 percent on income from $30,650 up to $45,000.

Table 7-1 gives federal tax rates for singles and married households filing jointly.

Table 7-1	2006 Federal Income Tax Brackets and Rates	
Singles Taxable Income	**Married-Filing-Jointly Taxable Income**	**Federal Tax Rate (Bracket)**
$0–$7,550	$0–$15,100	10%
$7,550–$30,650	$15,100–$61,300	15%
$30,650–$74,200	$61,300–$123,700	25%
$74,200–$154,800	$123,700–$188,450	28%
$154,800–$336,550	$188,450–$336,550	33%
Over $336,550	Over $336,550	35%

Your *marginal tax rate* is the rate of tax you pay on your *last,* or so-called *highest,* dollars of income. In the example of a single person with taxable income of $45,000, that person's federal marginal tax rate is 25 percent. In other words, she effectively pays 25 percent federal tax on her last dollars of income — those dollars in excess of $30,650.

Marginal tax rates are a powerful concept. Your marginal tax rate allows you to quickly calculate the additional taxes you'd have to pay on additional income. Conversely, you can delight in quantifying the amount of taxes you save by reducing your taxable income, either by decreasing your income or by increasing your deductions.

As you're probably already painfully aware, you pay not only federal income taxes but also state income taxes — that is, unless you live in one of the handful of states (Alaska, Florida, Nevada, South Dakota, Texas, Washington, or Wyoming) that have no state income tax. *Note:* Some states, such as New Hampshire, don't tax employment but do tax other income, such as income from investments.

Your *total marginal rate* includes your federal *and* state tax rates (not to mention local income tax rates in the municipalities that have it).

You can look up your state tax rate in your current state income tax preparation booklet.

Defining taxable income

Taxable income is the amount of income on which you actually pay income taxes. (In the sections that follow, I explain strategies for reducing your taxable income.) The following reasons explain why you don't pay taxes on your total income:

- ✔ **Not all income is taxable.** For example, you pay federal tax on the interest you earn on a bank savings account but not on the interest you earn from municipal bonds. As discussed later in this chapter, some income, such as from stock dividends and long-term capital gains, is taxed at lower rates. (For info on how the tax system creates incentives, see "Focusing on the total taxes you pay," earlier in this chapter.)

- ✔ **You get to subtract deductions from your income.** Some deductions are available just for being a living, breathing human being. In 2006, single people get an automatic $5,150 standard deduction, and married couples filing jointly get $10,300. (People over age 65 and those who are blind get a slightly higher deduction.) Other expenses, such as mortgage interest and property taxes, are deductible in the event that these so-called itemized deductions exceed the standard deductions. When you contribute to qualified retirement plans, you also effectively get a deduction.

Being mindful of the second tax system: Alternative minimum tax

You may find this hard to believe, but a second tax system actually exists (as if the first tax system weren't already complicated enough). This second system may raise your taxes even higher than they would normally be. I'll explain while you reach for some aspirin.

Over the years, as the government grew hungry for more revenue, taxpayers who slashed their taxes by claiming lots of deductions or exclusions from taxable income came under greater scrutiny. So the government created a second tax system — the alternative minimum tax (AMT) — to ensure that those with high deductions or exclusions pay at least a certain percentage of taxes on their incomes.

If you have a lot of deductions or exclusions from state income taxes, real estate taxes, certain types of mortgage interest, and passive investments (for example, rental real estate), you may fall prey to AMT. You may also get tripped up by AMT if you exercise certain types of stock options.

AMT restricts you from claiming certain deductions and requires you to add back in income that is normally tax-free (like certain municipal-bond interest). So you have to figure your tax under the AMT system and under the other system and then pay whichever amount is higher. I hope that aspirin is starting to kick in.

Trimming Employment Income Taxes

You're supposed to pay taxes on income you earn from work. Countless illegal ways are available to reduce your employment income — for example, not reporting it — but if you use them, you can very well end up paying a heap of penalties and extra interest charges on top of the taxes you owe. And you may even get tossed in jail. Because I don't want you to serve jail time or lose even more money by paying unnecessary penalties and interest, this section focuses on the *legal* ways to reduce your taxes.

Contributing to retirement plans

A retirement plan is one of the few painless and completely legal ways to reduce your taxable employment income. Besides reducing your taxes, retirement plans help you build up a nest egg so that you don't have to work for the rest of your life.

You can deduct money from your taxable income by tucking it away in employer-based retirement plans, such as 401(k) or 403(b) accounts, or self-employed retirement plans, such as SEP-IRAs or Keoghs. If your combined federal and state marginal tax rate is, say, 33 percent and you contribute $1,000 to one of these plans, you reduce your federal and state taxes by $330. Do you like the sound of that? How about this: Contribute another $1,000, and your taxes drop *another* $330 (as long as you're still in the same marginal tax rate). And when your money is inside a retirement account, it can compound and grow without taxation.

Many people miss this great opportunity for reducing their taxes because they *spend* all (or too much) of their current employment income and, therefore, have nothing (or little) left to put into a retirement account. If you're in this predicament, you need to reduce your spending before you can contribute money to a retirement plan. (Chapter 6 explains how to decrease your spending.)

If your employer doesn't offer the option of saving money through a retirement plan, see whether you can drum up support for it. Lobby the benefits and human resources departments. If they resist, you may want to add this to your list of reasons for considering another employer. Many employers offer this valuable benefit, but some don't. Some company decision-makers either don't understand the value of these accounts or feel that they're too costly to set up and administer.

If your employer doesn't offer a retirement savings plan, individual retirement account (IRA) contributions may or may not be tax-deductible, depending on your circumstances. You should first exhaust contributions to the previously mentioned tax-deductible accounts. Chapter 11 can help you determine whether you should contribute to an IRA, what type you should contribute to, and whether your IRA contributions are tax-deductible.

Married couples filing jointly with adjusted gross incomes (AGIs) of less than $50,000 and single taxpayers with an AGI of less than $25,000 can earn a new tax credit for retirement account contributions. (For info on how the AGI is calculated, see "Deducting miscellaneous expenses.") Unlike a deduction, a *tax credit* directly reduces your tax bill by the amount of the credit. This credit, which is detailed in Table 7-2, is a percentage of the first $2,000 contributed (or $4,000 on a joint return). The credit is not available to those under the age of 18, full-time students, or people who are claimed as dependents on someone else's tax return.

Table 7-2	Special Tax Credit for Retirement Plan Contributions	
Singles Adjusted Gross Income	*Married-Filing-Jointly Adjusted Gross Income*	*Tax Credit for Retirement Account Contributions*
$0–$15,000	$0–$30,000	50%
$15,001–$16,250	$30,001–$32,500	20%
$16,251–$25,000	$32,501–$50,000	10%

Shifting some income

Income shifting, which has nothing to do with money laundering, is a more esoteric tax-reduction technique that's an option only to those who can control *when* they receive their income.

For example, suppose that your employer tells you in late December that you're eligible for a bonus. You're offered the option to receive your bonus in either December or January. If you're pretty certain that you'll be in a higher tax bracket next year, you should choose to receive your bonus in December.

Or suppose that you run your own business and you think that you'll be in a lower tax bracket next year. Perhaps you plan to take time off to be with a newborn or take an extended trip. You can send out some invoices later in the year so that your customers won't pay you until January, which falls in the next tax year.

Increasing Your Deductions

Deductions are amounts you subtract from your income after totaling your taxable income and before calculating the tax you owe. To make things more complicated, the IRS gives you two methods for determining your total deductions. The good news is that you get to pick the method that leads to greater deductions — and hence, lower taxes.

Choosing standard or itemized deductions

The first method for figuring deductions requires no thinking or calculating. If you have a relatively uncomplicated financial life, taking the so-called standard deduction is generally the better option. (Earning a high income; renting your house or apartment; and having unusually large expenses from medical bills, moving, charitable contributions, or loss due to theft or catastrophe are not symptoms of a simple tax life.)

As I mention earlier in this chapter, single folks qualify for a $5,150 standard deduction, and married couples filing jointly get a $10,300 standard deduction in 2006. If you're 65 or older, or blind, you get a slightly higher standard deduction.

Itemizing your deductions on your tax return is the other method for determining your allowable deductions. This method is definitely more of a hassle, but if you can tally up more than the standard amounts noted in the preceding section, itemizing will save you money. Use Schedule A of IRS Form 1040 for summing up your itemized deductions.

Even if you take the standard deduction, take the time to peruse all the line items on Schedule A to familiarize yourself with the many legal itemized deductions. Figure out what's possible to deduct so you can make more-informed financial decisions year-round.

Organize your deductions

Locating Form 1098 and all the other scraps of paper you need when completing your tax return can be a hassle. Setting up a filing system can be a big timesaver:

- ✔ **Folder or shoe box:** If you have a simple financial life (that is, you haven't saved receipts throughout the year), you can confine your filing to January and February. During those months, you receive tax summary statements on wages paid by your employer (Form W-2), investment income (Form 1099), and home mortgage interest (Form 1098) in the mail. Label the shoe box or folder with something easy to remember ("2007 Taxes" is a brilliant choice) and dump these papers and your tax booklet into it. When you're ready to crunch numbers, you'll have everything you need to complete the form.

- ✔ **Accordion type file:** Organizing the bills you pay into individual folders during the entire year is a more thorough approach. This method is essential if you own your own business and need to tabulate your expenditures for office supplies each year. No one is going to send you a form totaling your office expenditures for the year — you're on your own.

- ✔ **Software:** Software programs can help organize your tax information during the year and save you time and accounting fees come tax-preparation time. See Chapter 19 for more information about tax and financial software.

The following sections explain commonly *overlooked* deductions and deduction strategies. Some are listed on Schedule A, and others appear on Form 1040.

Shift or bunch deductions

When you total your itemized deductions on Schedule A and the total is lower than the standard deduction, you should take the standard deduction. This total is worth checking each year, because you may have more deductions in some years, and itemizing may make sense.

Because you can control when you pay particular expenses that are eligible for itemizing, you can *shift* or *bunch* more of them into the select years where you have enough deductions to take advantage of itemizing. Suppose, for example, that you're using the standard deduction this year because you don't have many itemized deductions. Late in the year, though, you become certain that you're going to buy a home next year. With mortgage interest and property taxes to write off, you also know that you can itemize next year. If you typically make more charitable contributions in December because of the barrage of solicitations you receive when you're in the giving mood, you may want to write the checks in January rather than in December.

When you're sure that you're not going to have enough deductions in the current year to itemize, try to shift as many expenses as you can into the next tax year.

Purchasing real estate

When you buy a home, you can claim two big ongoing expenses of home ownership — your property taxes and the interest on your mortgage — as deductions on Schedule A. You're allowed to claim mortgage interest deductions for a primary residence (where you actually live) and on a second home for mortgage debt totaling $1,000,000 (and a home equity loan of up to $100,000). There's no limit on property tax deductions.

In order to buy real estate, you need to first collect a down payment, which requires maintaining a lid on your spending. See Part I for help with prioritizing and achieving important financial goals. Check out Chapter 14 for more on investing in real estate.

Trading consumer debt for mortgage debt

When you own real estate, you haven't borrowed the maximum, and you've run up high-interest consumer debt, you may be able to trade one debt for another. You may be able to save on interest charges by refinancing your mortgage or taking out a home equity loan and pulling out extra cash to pay off your credit card, auto loan, or other costly credit lines. You can usually borrow at a lower interest rate for a mortgage and get a tax deduction as a bonus, which lowers the effective borrowing cost further. Consumer debt, such as that on auto loans and credit cards, is not tax-deductible.

This strategy involves some danger. Borrowing against the equity in your home can be an addictive habit. I've seen cases where people run up significant consumer debt three or four times and then refinance their home the same number of times over the years to bail themselves out.

An appreciating home creates the illusion that excess spending isn't really costing you. But debt is debt, and all borrowed money has to be repaid. In the long run, you wind up with greater mortgage debt, and paying it off takes a bigger bite out of your monthly income. Refinancing and establishing home equity lines cost you more in terms of loan application fees and other charges (points, appraisals, credit reports, and so on).

At a minimum, the continued expansion of your mortgage debt handicaps your ability to work toward other financial goals. In the worst case, easy access to borrowing encourages bad spending habits that can lead to bankruptcy or foreclosure on your debt-ridden home.

Contributing to charities

You can deduct contributions to charities if you itemize your deductions. For example:

- ✔ Most people know that when they write a check for $50 to their favorite church or college, they can deduct it. *Note:* Make sure that you get a receipt for contributions of $250 or more.

- ✔ Many taxpayers overlook the fact that you can also deduct expenses for work you do with charitable organizations. For example, when you go to a soup kitchen to help prepare and serve meals, you can deduct your transportation costs. Keep track of your driving mileage and other commuting expenses.

- ✔ You also can deduct the fair market value (which can be determined by looking at the price of similar merchandise in thrift stores) of donations of clothing, household appliances, furniture, and other goods to charities. (Many charities will even drive to your home to pick up the stuff.) Find out whether organizations such as the Salvation Army, Goodwill, or others are interested in your donation. Just make sure that you keep some documentation — write up an itemized list and get it signed by the charity. Consider taking pictures of your more valuable donations.

- ✔ You can even donate securities and other investments to charity. In fact, donating an appreciated investment gives you a tax deduction for the full market value of the investment and eliminates your need to pay tax on the (unrealized) profit.

Remembering auto registration fees and state insurance

If you don't currently itemize, you may be surprised to discover that your state income taxes can be itemized. When you pay a fee to the state to register and license your car, you can itemize a portion of the expenditure as a deduction (on Schedule A, line 7, "Personal Property Taxes"). The IRS allows you to deduct the part of the fee that relates to the value of your car. The state organization that collects the fee should be able to tell you what portion of the fee is deductible. (Some states detail on the invoice what portion of the fee is tax-deductible.)

Several states have state disability insurance funds. If you pay into these funds (check your W-2), you can deduct your payments as state and local income taxes on line 5 of Schedule A. You may also claim a deduction on this line for payments you make into your state's unemployment compensation fund.

Deducting miscellaneous expenses

A number of so-called *miscellaneous expenses* are deductible on Schedule A. Most of these expenses relate to your job or career and the management of your finances:

- ✔ **Educational expenses:** You may be able to deduct the cost of tuition, books, and travel to and from classes if your education is related to your career. Specifically, you can deduct these expenses if your course work improves your work skills. Courses the law or your employer requires you to take to maintain your position are deductible. Continuing education classes for professionals may also be deductible. **Note:** Educational expenses that lead to your moving into a new field or career are not deductible.

- ✔ **Job searches and career counseling:** After you obtain your first job, you may deduct legitimate costs related to finding another job within your field. For example, suppose that you're a chef in a steakhouse in Chicago and you decide that you want to do stir-fry in Los Angeles. You take a crash course in vegetarian cooking and then fly to L.A. a couple times for interviews. You can deduct the cost of the course and your trips — *even if you don't change jobs.* And if you hire a career counselor to help you, you can deduct that cost as well. On the other hand, if you're burned out on cooking and you decide that you want to become a massage therapist in L.A., that's a new career. You may be rejuvenated, but you won't generate deductions from changing jobs.

- ✔ **Expenses related to your job that aren't reimbursed:** When you pay for your own subscriptions to trade journals to keep up with your field or buy a new desk and chair to ease back pain, you can deduct these costs. If your job requires you to wear special clothes or a uniform (for example, you're an EMT), you can write off the cost of purchasing and cleaning these clothes, as long as they aren't suitable for wearing outside of work. When you buy a computer for use outside the office at your own expense, you may be able to deduct the cost if the computer is for the convenience of your employer, is a condition of your employment, and is used more than half the time for business. Union dues and membership fees for professional organizations are also deductible.

- ✔ **Investment and tax-related expenses:** Investment and tax-advisor fees are deductible, as are subscription costs for investment-related publications. Accounting fees for preparing your tax return or conducting tax planning during the year are deductible; legal fees related to your taxes are also deductible. If you purchase a home computer to track your investments or prepare your taxes, you can deduct that expense, too.

When you deduct miscellaneous expenses, you get to deduct only the amount that exceeds 2 percent of your AGI (adjusted gross income). *AGI* is your total wage, interest, dividend, and all other income minus retirement account contributions, self-employed health insurance, alimony paid, and losses from investments.

Deducting self-employment expenses

When you're self-employed, you can deduct a multitude of expenses from your income before calculating the tax you owe. If you buy a computer or office furniture, you can deduct those expenses. (Sometimes they need to be gradually deducted, or *depreciated,* over time.) Salaries for your employees, office supplies, rent or mortgage interest for your office space, and phone/communications expenses are also generally deductible.

Many self-employed folks don't take all the deductions they're eligible for. In some cases, people simply aren't aware of the wonderful world of deductions. Others are worried that large deductions will increase the risk of an audit. Spend some time finding out more about tax deductions; you'll be convinced that taking full advantage of your eligible deductions makes sense and saves you money.

The following are common mistakes made by people who are their own bosses:

✔ **Being an island unto yourself.** When you're self-employed, going it alone is usually a mistake when it comes to taxes. You must educate yourself to make the tax laws work for rather than against you. Hiring tax help is well worth your while. (See "Professional hired help," later in this chapter, for info on hiring tax advisors.)

✔ **Making administrative tax screw-ups.** As a self-employed individual, you're responsible for the correct and timely filing of all taxes owed on your income and employment taxes on your employees. You need to make estimated tax payments on a quarterly basis. And if you have employees, you also need to withhold taxes from each paycheck they receive and make timely payments to the IRS and the appropriate state authorities. In addition to federal and state income tax, you also need to withhold and send in Social Security and any other state or locally mandated payroll taxes.

To pay taxes on your income, use Form 1040-ES. This form, along with instructions, can be obtained from the IRS (800-829-3676; www.irs.gov). The form comes complete with an estimated tax worksheet and the four payment coupons you need to send in with your quarterly tax payments. If you want to find the rules for withholding and submitting taxes from employees' paychecks, ask the IRS for Form 941 and Form 940, which is for unemployment insurance. And unless you're lucky enough to live in a state with no income taxes, you need to call for your state's estimated income tax package. Another alternative is to hire a payroll firm, such as Paychex, to do all this drudgery for you. Scrutinize and negotiate their expenses.

✔ **Failing to document expenses.** When you pay with cash, following the paper trail for all the money you spent can be hard for you to do (and for the IRS, in the event you're ever audited). At the end of the year, how are you going to remember how much you spent for parking or client meals if you fail to keep a record? How will you survive an IRS audit without proper documentation?

Debit cards are accepted most places and provide a convenient paper trail. (Be careful about getting a debit card in your business's name, because some banks don't offer protection against fraudulent use of business debit cards.) Otherwise, you need a system or written record of your daily petty cash purchases. Most pocket calendars or daily organizers include ledgers that allow you to track these small purchases. If you aren't that organized, at least get a receipt for cash transactions and stash them in a file folder in your desk. Or keep receipts in envelopes labeled with the month and year.

✔ **Failing to fund a retirement plan.** You should be saving money toward retirement anyway, and you can't beat the tax break. People who are self-employed are allowed to save a substantial portion of their net income on an annual basis. To find out more about SEP-IRAs, Keoghs, and other retirement plans, see Chapter 11.

✔ **Failing to use tax numbers to help manage business.** If you're a small-business owner who doesn't track her income, expenses, staff performance, and customer data on a regular basis, your tax return may be the one and only time during the year when you take a financial snapshot of your business. After you go through all the time, trouble, and expense to file your tax return, make sure you reap the rewards of all your work; use those numbers to help analyze and manage your business.

Some bookkeepers and tax preparers can provide you with management information reports on your business from the tax data they compile for you. Just ask! See "Software and Web sites," later in this chapter, for my recommendations.

✔ **Failing to pay family help.** If your children, spouse, or other relatives help with some aspect of your business, consider paying them for the work. Besides showing them that you value their work, this practice may reduce your family's tax liability. For example, children are usually in a lower tax bracket. By shifting some of your income to your child, you cut your tax bill.

Reducing Investment Income Taxes

The distributions and profits on investments that you hold outside of tax-sheltered retirement accounts are exposed to taxation when you receive them. Interest, dividends, and *capital gains* (profits from the sale of an investment at a price that's higher than the purchase price) are all taxed.

Although this section explains some of the best methods for reducing the taxes on investments exposed to taxation, Chapter 12 discusses how and where to invest money held outside of tax-sheltered retirement accounts such as IRAs and 401(k) plans.

Investing in tax-free money market funds and bonds

When you're in a high enough tax bracket, you may find that you come out ahead with tax-free investments. Tax-free investments pay investment income, which is exempt from federal tax, state tax, or both. (See Part III for details.)

Tax-free investments yield less than comparable investments that produce taxable income. But because of the difference in taxes, the earnings from tax-free investments *can* end up being greater than what you're left with from taxable investments.

Tax-free money market funds can be a better alternative to bank savings accounts (where interest is subject to taxation). Likewise, tax-free bonds are intended to be longer-term investments that pay tax-free interest, so they may be a better investment option for you than bank certificates of deposit, Treasury bills and bonds, and other investments that produce taxable income. (See Chapter 12 for specifics on which tax-free investments may be right for your situation.)

Selecting other tax-friendly investments

Too often, when selecting investments, people mistakenly focus on past rates of return. We all know that the past is no guarantee of the future. But choosing an investment with a reportedly high rate of return without considering tax consequences is an even worse mistake. What you get to keep — after taxes — is what matters in the long run.

For example, when comparing two similar funds, most people prefer a fund that averages returns of 14 percent per year to one that earns 12 percent per year. But what if the 14-percent-per-year fund, because of greater taxable distributions, causes you to pay a lot more in taxes? What if, after factoring in taxes, the 14-percent-per-year fund nets just 9 percent, while the 12-percent-per-year fund nets an effective 10 percent return? In such a case, you'd be unwise to choose a fund solely on the basis of the higher (pre-tax) reported rate of return.

I call investments that appreciate in value and don't distribute much in the way of highly taxed income *tax-friendly*. (Some in the investment business use the term *tax-efficient*.) See Chapter 10 for more information on tax-friendly stocks and stock mutual funds.

Real estate is one of the few areas with privileged status in the tax code. In addition to deductions allowed for mortgage interest and property taxes, you can depreciate rental property to reduce your taxable income. *Depreciation* is a special tax deduction allowed for the gradual wear and tear on rental real estate. When you sell investment real estate, you may be eligible to conduct a tax-free exchange when buying a so-called replacement rental property. See Chapter 14 for a crash course in real estate.

Making your profits long-term

As I discuss in Part III, when you buy growth investments such as stocks and real estate, you should do so for the long-term — ideally ten or more years. The tax system rewards your patience with lower tax rates on your profits.

When you're able to hold on to an investment (outside of a retirement account) such as a stock, bond, or mutual fund for more than one year, you get a tax break if you sell that investment at a profit. Specifically, your profit is taxed under the lower capital gains tax rate schedule. If you're in the 25 percent or higher federal income tax bracket, you pay just 15 percent of your long-term capital gains' profit in federal taxes. (The same lower tax rate applies to stock dividends.) If you're in the 10 or 15 percent federal income tax brackets, the long-term capital gains tax rate is just 5 percent (and is actually scheduled to fall to 0 percent in 2008).

Does funding retirement accounts still make sense?

Historically, taking advantage of opportunities to direct money into retirement accounts gives you two possible tax benefits. First, your contributions to the retirement account may be immediately tax-deductible (see Chapter 11 for details). Second, the distributions and growth of the investments in the retirement accounts aren't generally taxed until withdrawal.

In the preceding section, I mention a tax break for long-term capital gains and on stock dividends. This break, unfortunately, applies only to investments held *outside* of retirement accounts. If you realize a long-term capital gain or receive stock dividends *inside* a retirement account, those investment returns are taxed at the relatively ordinary income tax rates. Thus, some have argued you shouldn't fund retirement accounts. In most cases, the people making the argument have a vested interest.

Unless you have a specific goal (such as saving for a home purchase or to start a business) that necessitates having access to your money that you don't have with a retirement account, there are but two atypical situations when not funding a retirement account could make sense:

> ✔ **You're temporarily in a very low tax bracket.** This could happen, for example, if you lose your job for an extended period of time or are in school. In these cases, you're likely not to have lots of spare money to

contribute to a retirement account anyway! If you have some employ-ment income, consider the Roth IRA (see Chapter 11).

✔ **You have too much money socked away already.** If you have a large net worth inside retirement accounts, which could get hit by estate taxes (see Chapter 17), continuing to fund retirement may be counterproductive.

Enlisting Education Tax Breaks

Being so labor intensive, education is often costly. Recognizing that, as well as the overall societal benefits from better-educated people, the government offers plenty of tax reduction opportunities in the tax laws. Knowing that you don't want to read the dreadful tax code, here's a summary of key provisions you should know about for yourself and your kids if you have them:

✔ **Tax deductions for college expenses:** You may take up to a $4,000 tax deduction on IRS Form 1040 for college costs so long as your adjusted gross income (AGI) is less than $65,000 for single taxpayers and less than $130,000 for married couples filing jointly. (***Note:*** You may take up to a $2,000 tax deduction if your AGI is between $65,000 and $80,000 for single taxpayers and between $130,000 and $160,000 for married couples filing jointly.)

✔ **Tax-free investment earnings in special accounts:** Money invested in Education Savings Accounts (ESAs) and in section 529 plans is sheltered from taxation and is not taxed upon withdrawal so long as the money is used to pay for eligible education expenses. Subject to eligibility require-ments, you may contribute up to $2,000 annually to ESAs. 529 plans allow you to sock away over $200,000. Please be aware, however, that funding such accounts may harm your potential financial aid. Please see Chapter 12 for details on these accounts.

✔ **Tax credits:** The Hope Scholarship and Lifetime Learning Credits pro-vide tax relief to low- and moderate-income earners facing education costs. The Hope credit may be up to $1,500 in each of the first two years of college, and the Lifetime Learning credit, up to $2,000 per taxpayer. Each student may take only one of these credits per tax year. And in a year in which a credit is taken, you may neither withdraw money from an ESA or 529 plan nor take a tax deduction for your college expenses.

Please be sure to read Chapter 13 for the best ways and strategies to pay for educational expenses.

Getting Help from Tax Resources

All sorts of ways to prepare your tax return exist. Which approach makes sense for you depends on the complexity of your situation and your knowledge of taxes.

Regardless of which approach you use, you should be taking financial moves during the year to reduce your taxes. By the time you actually file your return in the following year, it's often too late for you to take advantage of many tax-reduction strategies.

IRS assistance

If you have a simple, straightforward tax return, filing it on your own using only the IRS instructions is fine. This approach is as cheap as you can get. The main costs are time, patience, photocopying expenses (you should always keep a copy for your files), and postage for mailing the completed tax return.

IRS publications don't have Tip or Warning icons. And the IRS has been known to give wrong information from time to time. When you call the IRS with a question, be sure to take notes about your conversation to protect yourself in the event of an audit. Date your notes and include the name and identification number of the tax employee you talked to, the questions you asked, and the employee's responses. File your notes in a folder with a copy of your completed return.

In addition to the standard instructions that come with your tax return, the IRS offers some free (actually, paid for with your tax dollars) and sometimes useful booklets. Publication 17, *Your Federal Income Tax,* is designed for individual tax-return preparation. Publication 334, *Tax Guide for Small Businesses,* is for (you guessed it) small-business tax-return preparation. These publications are more comprehensive than the basic IRS instructions. Call 800-829-3676 to request these booklets, or visit the IRS Web site at www.irs.gov.

Preparation and advice guides

Books about tax preparation and tax planning that highlight common problem areas and are written in clear, simple English are invaluable. They supplement the official instructions not only by helping you complete your return correctly but also by showing you how to save as much money as possible.

Consider picking up a copy of the latest edition of *Taxes For Dummies,* which I co-authored (Wiley Publishing).

Software and Web sites

If you have access to a computer, good tax-preparation software can be helpful. TaxCut and TurboTax are programs that I have reviewed and rated as the best. If you go the software route, I highly recommend having a good tax advice book by your side.

For you Web surfers, the Internal Revenue Service Web site (www.irs.gov) is among the better Internet tax sites, believe it or not. The Tax and Accounting Sites Directory at www.taxsites.com is another good Web site with links to many other useful tax sites.

Professional hired help

Competent tax preparers and advisors can save you money — sometimes more than enough to pay their fees — by identifying tax-reduction strategies you may overlook. They can also help reduce the likelihood of an audit, which can be triggered by blunders. Mediocre and lousy tax preparers, on the other hand, may make mistakes and not be aware of sound ways to reduce your tax bill.

Tax practitioners come with varying backgrounds, training, and credentials. The four main types of tax practitioners are preparers, enrolled agents (EAs), Certified Public Accountants (CPAs), and tax attorneys. The more training and specialization a tax practitioner has (and the more affluent his clients), the higher his hourly fee usually is. Fees and competence vary greatly. If you hire a tax advisor and you're not sure of the quality of work performed and the soundness of the advice, try getting a second opinion.

Preparers

Preparers generally have the least amount of training of all the tax practitioners, and a greater proportion of them work part-time. As with financial planners, no national regulations apply to preparers, and no licensing is required.

Preparers are appealing because they're relatively inexpensive — they can do most basic returns for around $100 or so. The drawback of using a preparer is that you may hire someone who doesn't know much more than you do.

Preparers make the most sense for folks who have relatively simple financial lives, who are budget-minded, and who hate doing their own taxes. If you're not good about hanging onto receipts or you don't want to keep your own files with background details about your taxes, you should definitely shop around for a tax preparer who's committed to the business. You may need all that stuff someday for an audit, and many tax preparers keep and organize their clients' documentation rather than return everything each year. Also, going with a firm that's open year-round may be a safer option (some small shops are open only during tax season) in case tax questions or problems arise.

Enrolled agents (EAs)

A person must pass IRS scrutiny in order to be called an *enrolled agent.* This license allows the agent to represent you before the IRS in the event of an audit. Continuing education is also required; the training is generally longer and more sophisticated than it is for a typical preparer.

Enrolled agents' fees tend to fall between those of a preparer and a CPA (see the next section). Returns that require a few of the more common schedules (such as Schedule A for deductions and Schedule D for capital gains and losses) shouldn't cost more than $200 to $300 to prepare.

EAs are best for people who have moderately complex returns and don't necessarily need complicated tax-planning advice throughout the year (although some EAs provide this service as well). You can get names and telephone numbers of EAs in your area by contacting the National Association of Enrolled Agents (NAEA). You can call the NAEA at 202-822-6232 or visit its Web site at www.naea.org.

Certified public accountants (CPAs)

Certified public accountants go through significant training and examination before receiving the CPA credential. In order to maintain this designation, a CPA must also complete a fair number of continuing education classes every year.

CPA fees vary tremendously. Most charge $100+ per hour, but CPAs at large companies and in high-cost-of-living areas tend to charge somewhat more.

If you're self-employed and/or you file lots of other schedules, you may want to hire a CPA. But you don't need to do so year after year. If your situation grows complex one year and then stabilizes, consider getting help for the perplexing year and then using preparation guides, software, or a lower-cost preparer or enrolled agent in the future.

Tax attorneys

Tax attorneys deal with complicated tax problems and issues that usually have some legal angle. Unless you're a super-high-income earner with a complex financial life, hiring a tax attorney to prepare your annual return is prohibitively expensive. In fact, many tax attorneys don't prepare returns as a normal practice.

Because of their level of specialization and training, tax attorneys tend to have the highest hourly billing rates — $200 to $300+ per hour is not unusual.

Dealing with an Audit

On a list of real-life nightmares, most people would rank tax audits right up there with root canals, rectal exams, and court appearances. Many people are traumatized by audits because they feel like they're on trial and being accused of a crime. Take a deep breath and don't panic.

You may be getting audited simply because a business that reports tax information on you, or someone at the IRS, made an error regarding the data on your return. In the vast majority of cases, the IRS conducts its audit by corresponding with you through the mail.

Audits that require you to schlep to the local IRS office are the most feared type of audit. In these cases, about 20 percent of such audited returns are left unchanged by the audit — in other words, the taxpayer didn't end up owing more money. In fact, if you're the lucky sort, you may be one of the 5 percent of folks who actually gets a refund because the audit finds a mistake in your favor!

Unfortunately, you'll most likely be one of the roughly 75 percent of audit survivors who end up owing more tax money. The amount of additional tax that you owe in interest and penalties hinges on how your audit goes.

Getting your act together

Preparing for an audit is sort of like preparing for a test at school. The IRS will let you know which sections of your tax return it wants to examine.

The first decision you face when you get an audit notice is whether to handle it yourself or hire a tax advisor to represent you. Hiring representation may help you save time, stress, and money.

If you normally prepare your own return and you're comfortable with your understanding of the areas being audited, handle the audit yourself. When the amount of tax money in question is small when compared to the fee you'd pay the tax advisor to represent you, self-representation is probably your best option. However, if you're likely to turn into a babbling, intimidated fool and you're unsure of how to present your situation, hire a tax advisor to represent you. (See "Professional hired help," earlier in this chapter, for information about whom to hire.)

If you decide to handle the audit yourself, get your act together sooner rather than later. Don't wait until the night before to start gathering receipts and other documentation. You may need to contact others to get copies of documents you can't find.

You need to document and be ready to speak only about the areas the audit notice says are being investigated. Organize the various documents and receipts into folders. You want to make it as easy as possible for the auditor to review your materials. *Don't* show up, dump shopping bags full of receipts and paperwork on the auditor's desk, and say, "Here it is — *you* figure it out."

Whatever you do, *don't ignore your audit request letter.* The IRS is the ultimate bill-collection agency. And if you end up owing more money (the unhappy result of most audits), the sooner you pay, the less interest and penalties you'll owe.

Surviving the day of reckoning

Two people with identical situations can walk into an audit and come out with very different results. The loser can end up owing much more in taxes and have the audit expanded to include other parts of the return. The winner can end up owing no additional tax or even owing less.

Here's how to be a winner in your tax audit:

- ✔ **Treat the auditor as a human being.** This advice may be obvious, but it isn't practiced by taxpayers very often. You may be resentful or angry about being audited. You may be tempted to gnash your teeth and tell the auditor how unfair it is that an honest taxpayer like you had to spend hours getting ready for this. You may feel like ranting and raving about how the government wastes too much of your tax money, or that the party in power is out to get you. Bite your tongue.

Believe it or not, most auditors are decent people just trying to do their jobs. They're well aware that taxpayers don't like seeing them. Don't suck up, either — just relax and be yourself. Behave as you would around a boss you like — with respect and congeniality.

✔ **Stick to the knitting.** Your audit is for discussing *only* the sections of your tax return that are in question. The more you talk about other areas or things that you're doing, the more likely the auditor will probe into other items. Don't bring documentation for parts of your return that aren't being audited. Besides creating more work for yourself, you may be opening up a can of worms that doesn't need to be opened. Should the auditor inquire about areas that aren't covered by the audit notice, politely say that you're not prepared to discuss those other issues and that another meeting should be scheduled.

✔ **Don't argue when you disagree.** State your case. When the auditor wants to disallow a deduction or otherwise increase the taxes you owe and you disagree, state once why you don't agree with his assessment. If the auditor won't budge, don't get into a knock-down, drag-out confrontation. He or she may not want to lose face and is inclined to find additional tax money — that's the auditor's job.

When necessary, you can plead your case with several people who work above your auditor. If this method fails and you still feel wronged, you can take your case to tax court.

✔ **Don't be intimidated.** Most auditors are not tax geniuses. The work is stressful — being in a job where people dislike seeing you is not easy. Turnover is quite high. Thus, many auditors are fairly young, just-out-of-school types who majored in something like English, history, or sociology. They may know less about tax and financial matters than you do. The basic IRS tax boot camp that auditors go through doesn't come close to covering all the technical details and nuances in the tax code. So you may not be at such a disadvantage in your tax knowledge after all, especially if you work with a tax advisor (most tax advisors know more about the tax system than the average IRS auditor).

Part III

Building Wealth with Wise Investing

The 5th Wave   By Rich Tennant

"Oh, her? That's Ms. Lamont, our Plan
Administrator. She's going to help me determine
your eligibility in our 401(k) Plan."

In this part . . .

1lay out the basics of investing and show you how to choose your investments wisely. Earning and saving are hard work, so you need to be careful where you invest the fruits of your labor. This part is where you find out the real story on such things as stocks, bonds, and mutual funds; the differences between investing in retirement and non-retirement accounts; how to invest for college; and how to buy a home and invest in other real estate.

Chapter 8

Important Investment Concepts

Making wise investments doesn't have to be complicated. However, many investors get bogged down in the morass of the thousands of investment choices out there and the often-conflicting perspectives on how to invest. This chapter helps you grasp the important "bigger picture" issues that can help you ensure that your investment plan meshes with your needs and the realities of the investment marketplace.

Establishing Your Goals

Before you select a specific investment, first determine your investment needs and goals. Why are you saving money — what are you going to use it for? You don't need to earmark every dollar, but you should set some major objectives. Establishing objectives is important because the expected use of the money helps you determine how long to invest it. And that, in turn, helps you determine which investments to choose.

The risk level of your investments should factor in your time frame and your *comfort level.* Investing in high-risk vehicles doesn't make sense if you'll have to spend all your profits on stress-induced medical bills. For example, suppose you've been accumulating money for a down payment on a home you want to buy in a few years. You can't afford much risk with that money. You're going to need that money sooner rather than later. Putting that money in the stock market, then, is probably not a wise move. As I discuss later in this chapter, the stock market can drop a lot in a year or over several consecutive years. So stocks are probably too risky a place to invest money you plan to use soon.

Perhaps you're saving toward a longer-term goal, such as retirement, that's 20 or 30 years away. In this case, you're in a position to make riskier investments, because your holdings have more time to bounce back from temporary losses or setbacks. You may want to consider investing in growth investments, such as stocks, in a retirement account that you leave alone for 20 years or longer. You can tolerate year-to-year volatility in the market — you have time on your side. If you haven't yet done so, take a tour through Chapter 4, which helps you contemplate and set your financial goals.

Understanding the Primary Investments

For a moment, forget all the buzzwords, jargon, and product names you've heard tossed around in the investment world — in many cases, they're only meant to obscure what an investment really is and to hide the hefty fees and commissions. Imagine a world with only two investment flavors — chocolate and vanilla ice cream (or low-fat frozen yogurt for you health-minded folks).

The investment world is really just as simple. You have only two major investment choices: You can be a lender or an owner.

Looking at lending investments

You're a lender when you invest your money in a bank certificate of deposit (CD), a treasury bill, or a bond issued by a company like General Motors, for example. In each case, you lend your money to an organization — a bank, the federal government, or GM. You're paid an agreed-upon rate of interest for lending your money. The organization also promises to have your original investment (the *principal*) returned to you on a specific date.

Getting paid all the interest in addition to your original investment (as promised) is the best that can happen with a lending investment. Given that the investment landscape is littered with carcasses of failed investments, this is not a result to take for granted.

The worst that can happen with a lending investment is that you don't get everything you're promised. Promises can be broken under extenuating circumstances. When a company goes bankrupt, for example, you can lose all or part of your original investment.

Another risk associated with lending investments is that even though you get what you were promised, the ravages of inflation may make your money worth less — it has less purchasing power than you thought it would. Back in the 1960s, for example, high-quality companies issued long-term bonds that paid approximately 4 percent interest. At the time, buying a long-term bond seemed like a good deal, because the cost of living was increasing by only 2 percent per year. When inflation rocketed to 6 percent and higher, those 4 percent bonds didn't seem so attractive. The interest and principal didn't buy nearly the amount they did years earlier when inflation was lower.

Table 8-1 shows the reduction in the purchasing power of your money at varying rates of inflation after just ten years.

Table 8-1	Reduction in Purchasing Power Due to Inflation
Inflation Rate	*Reduction in Purchasing Power after Ten Years*
6 percent	–44 percent
8 percent	–54 percent
10 percent	–61 percent

Some conservative-minded investors make the common mistake of thinking that they're diversifying their long-term investment money by buying several bonds, some CDs, and an annuity. The problem, however, is that all these investments pay a relatively low fixed rate of return that's exposed to the vagaries of inflation.

A final drawback to lending investments is that you don't share in the success of the organization to which you lend your money. If the company doubles or triples in size and profits, your principal and interest rate don't double or triple in size along with it; they stay the same. Of course, such success should ensure that you get your promised interest and principal.

Exploring ownership investments

You're an *owner* when you invest your money in an asset, such as a company or real estate, that has the ability to generate earnings or profits. Suppose that you own 100 shares of Verizon Communications stock. With billions of shares of stock outstanding, Verizon is a mighty big company — your 100 shares represent a tiny piece of it.

What do you get for your small slice of Verizon? As a stockholder, although you don't get free calling, you do share in the profits of a company in the form of annual dividends and an increase (you hope) in the stock price if the company grows and becomes more profitable. Of course, you receive these benefits if things are going well. If Verizon's business declines, your stock may be worth less (or even worthless!).

Real estate is another one of my favorite financially rewarding and time-honored ownership investments. Real estate can produce profits when it's rented out for more than the expense of owning the property or sold at a price higher than what you paid for it. I know numerous successful real estate investors (myself included) who have earned excellent long-term profits.

The value of real estate depends not only on the particulars of the individual property but also on the health and performance of the local economy. When companies in the community are growing and more jobs are being produced at higher wages, real estate often does well. When local employers are laying people off and excess housing is sitting vacant because of previous overbuilding, rent and property values are likely to fall.

Finally, many Americans have also built substantial wealth through small business. According to *Forbes* magazine, more of the United States' (and the world's) wealthiest individuals have built their wealth through their stake in small businesses than through any other vehicle. Small business is the engine that drives much of our economic growth. Although firms with fewer than 20 employees account for about one-quarter of all employees, such small firms were responsible for nearly half of all new jobs created in the past two decades.

You can participate in small business in a variety of ways. You can start your own business, buy and operate an existing business, or simply invest in promising small businesses. In the chapters ahead, I explain each of these major investment types in detail.

Shunning Gambling Instruments and Behaviors

Although investing is often risky, it's not gambling. *Gambling* is putting your money into schemes that are sure to lose you money over time. That's not to say that everyone loses or that you lose every time you gamble. However, the deck is stacked against you. The house wins most of the time.

Horse-racing tracks, gambling casinos, and lotteries are set up to pay out 50 to 60 cents on the dollar. The rest goes to profits and the administration of the system — don't forget that these are businesses. Sure, your chosen horse may win a race or two, but in the long run, you're almost guaranteed to lose about 40 to 50 percent of what you bet. Would you put your money in an "investment" where your expected return was negative 40 percent?

Forsake futures, options, and other derivatives

Futures, options, and commodities are *derivatives,* or financial investments whose value is derived from the performance of another security such as a stock or bond.

You may have heard the radio ad from the firm Fleecem, Cheatem, and Leavem, advocating that you buy heating oil futures because of conflicts in the Middle East and the upcoming rise in heating oil usage due to the cold weather months. You call the firm and are impressed by the smooth-talking vice president who spends so much time with little ol' you. His logic makes sense, and he spent a lot of time with you, so you send him a check for $10,000.

Buying futures isn't much different from blowing $10,000 at the craps tables in Las Vegas. Futures prices depend on short-term, highly volatile price movements. As with gambling, you occasionally win when the market moves the right way at the right time. But in the long run, you're gonna lose. In fact, you can lose it all.

Options are as risky as futures. With options, you're betting on the short-term movements of a specific security. If you have inside information (such as knowing in advance when a major corporate development is going to occur), you can get rich. But insider trading is illegal. You may end up in jail like Martha Stewart did.

Honest brokers who help their clients invest in stocks, bonds, and mutual funds will tell you the truth about commodities, futures, and options. A former broker I know who worked for various major brokerage firms for 12 years told me, "I had one client who made money in options, futures, or commodities, but the only reason he came out ahead was because he was forced to pull money out to close on a home purchase just when he happened to be ahead. The commissions were great for me, but there's no way a customer will make money in them." Remember these words if you're tempted to gamble with futures, options, and the like.

Futures and options are not always used for speculation and gambling. Some sophisticated professional investors use them to hedge, or actually reduce the risk of, their broad investment holdings. When using them in this fashion, things don't often work out the way that the pros hoped. You, the individual investor, should steer clear of futures and options.

Ditch daytrading

Daytrading — which is the rapid buying and selling of securities online — is a newer and equally foolish vehicle for individual investors to pursue. Placing trades via the Internet is far cheaper than the older methods of trading (such as telephoning a broker), but the more you trade, the more trading costs eat into your investment capital.

Frequent trading also increases your tax bill as profits realized over short periods of time are taxed at your highest possible tax rate (see Chapter 7). You can certainly make some profits when daytrading. However, over an extended period of time, you'll inevitably underperform the broad market averages. In those rare instances where you may do a little better than the market averages, it's rarely worth the time and personal sacrifices that you and your family and friends endure.

Understanding Investment Returns

The previous sections describe the difference between ownership and lending investments, and they help you distinguish gambling and speculation from investing. "That's all well and good," you say, "but how do I choose which type of investments to put my money into? How much can I make, and what are the risks?"

Good questions. I'll start with the returns you *might* make. I say "might" because I'm looking at history, and history is a record of the past. Using history to predict the future — especially the near future — is dangerous. History may repeat itself, but not always in exactly the same fashion and not necessarily when you expect it to.

During this past century, ownership investments such as stocks and real estate returned around 10 percent per year, handily beating lending investments such as bonds (around 5 percent) and savings accounts (roughly 4 percent) in the investment performance race. Inflation has averaged 3 percent per year.

If you already know that the stock market can be risky, you may be wondering why investing in stocks is worth the anxiety and potential losses. Why bother for a few extra percent per year? Well, over many years, a few extra percent per year can really magnify the growth of your money (see Table 8-2). The more years you have to invest, the greater the difference a few percent makes in your returns.

Table 8-2	The Difference a Few Percent Makes	
At This Rate of Investment on $10,000	*You'll Have This Much Return in 25 Years*	*You'll Have This Much Return in 40 Years*
4% (savings account)	$26,658	$48,010
5% (bond)	$33,863	$70,400
10% (stocks and real estate)	$108,347	$452,592

Investing is not a spectator sport. You can't earn good returns on stocks and real estate if you keep your money in cash on the sidelines. If you invest in growth investments such as stocks and real estate, don't chase one new investment after another trying to beat the market average returns. *The biggest value is to be in the market, not to beat it.*

Sizing Investment Risks

Many investors have a simplistic understanding of what risk means and how to apply it to their investment decisions. For example, when compared to the yo-yo motions of the stock market, a bank savings account may seem like a less risky place to put your money. Over the long term, however, the stock market usually beats the rate of inflation, while the interest rate on a savings account does not. Thus, if you're saving your money for a long-term goal like retirement, a savings account can be a "riskier" place to put your money.

Before you invest, ask yourself these questions:

- ✔ What am I saving and investing this money for? In other words, what's my goal?
- ✔ What is my timeline for this investment — when will I use this money?
- ✔ What is the historical volatility of the investment I'm considering, and does that suit my comfort level and timeline for this investment?

After you answer these questions, you'll have a better understanding of risk and you'll be able to match your savings goals to their most appropriate investment vehicles. In Chapter 4, I help you consider your savings goals and timeline. I address investment risk and returns in the sections that follow.

Comparing the risks of stocks and bonds

Given the relatively higher historic returns I mention for ownership investments in the previous section, some people think that they should put all their money in stocks and real estate. So what's the catch?

The risk with ownership investments is the short-term fluctuations in their value. During the last century, stocks declined, on average, by more than 10 percent (in one particular year) every five years. Drops in stock prices of more than 20 percent occurred, on average, once every ten years. Real estate prices suffer similar periodic setbacks.

Therefore, in order to earn those generous long-term returns from ownership investments like stocks and real estate, you must be willing to tolerate volatility. You absolutely should not put all your money in the stock or real estate market. You should not invest your emergency money or money you expect to use within the next five years in such volatile investments.

The shorter the time period that you have for holding your money in an investment, the less likely that growth-oriented investments like stocks will beat out lending-type investments like bonds. Table 8-3 illustrates the historical relationship between stock and bond returns based on number of years held.

Table 8-3	Stocks versus Bonds
Number of Years Investment Held	*Likelihood of Stocks Beating Bonds*
1	60%
5	70%
10	80%
20	91%
30	99%

Some types of bonds have higher yields than others, but the risk-reward relationship remains intact (see Chapter 9 for more on bonds). A bond generally pays you a higher rate of interest when it has a

✔ Lower credit rating — to compensate for the higher risk of default and the higher likelihood of losing your investment

✔ Longer-term maturity — to compensate for the risk that you'll be unhappy with the bond's set interest rate if the market level of interest rates moves up

Focusing on the risks you can control

I always asked students in my personal finance class that I used to teach at the University of California to write down what they'd like to learn. Here's what one student had to say: "I want to learn what to invest my money in now, as the stock market is overvalued and interest rates are about to go up, so bonds are dicey and banks give lousy interest — HELP!"

This student recognizes the risk of price fluctuations in her investments, but she also seems to believe, like too many people, that you can predict what's going to happen. How does *she* know that the stock market is overvalued, and why hasn't the rest of the world figured it out? How does she know that interest rates are about to go up, and why hasn't the rest of the world figured that out, either?

When you invest in stocks and other growth-oriented investments, you must accept the volatility of these investments. Invest the money that you have earmarked for the longer-term in these vehicles. Minimize the risk of these investments through diversification. Don't buy just one or two stocks; buy a number of stocks. Later in this chapter, I discuss what you need to know about diversification.

Discovering low-risk, high-return investments

Despite what professors teach in the nation's leading business and finance graduate school programs, low-risk investments that almost certainly lead to high returns are available. I can think of at least four such investments:

✔ **Paying off consumer debt.** If you're paying 10, 14, or 18 percent interest on an outstanding credit card or other consumer loan, pay it off before investing. To get a comparable return through other investment vehicles (after the government takes its share of your profits), you'd have to start a new career as a loan shark. If, between federal and state taxes, you're in a 33 percent tax bracket and you're paying 12 percent interest on consumer debt, you'd need to annually earn a whopping 18 percent on your investments pre-tax to justify not paying off the debt. Good luck!

When your only source of funds for paying off debt is a small emergency reserve equal to a few months' living expenses, paying off your debt may involve some risk. Tap into your emergency reserves only if you have a backup source — for example, the ability to borrow from a willing family member or against a retirement account balance.

✓ **Investing in your health.** Eat healthy, exercise, and relax.

✓ **Investing in friends and family.** Invest time and effort in improving your relationships with loved ones.

✓ **Investing in personal and career development.** Pick up a new hobby, improve your communication skills, or read widely. Take an adult education course or go back to school for a degree. Your investment should lead to greater happiness and perhaps even higher paychecks.

Diversifying Your Investments

Diversification is one of the most powerful investment concepts. It refers to saving your eggs (or investments) in different baskets.

Diversification requires you to place your money in different investments with returns that are not completely correlated. This is a fancy way of saying that when some of your investments are down in value, odds are that others are up in value.

To decrease the chances of all of your investments getting clobbered at the same time, you must put your money in different types of investments, such as bonds, stocks, real estate, and small business. (I cover all these investments and more in Chapter 9.) You can further diversify your investments by investing in domestic as well as international markets.

Within a given class of investments such as stocks, investing in different types of stocks that perform well under various economic conditions is important. For this reason, *mutual funds,* which are diversified portfolios of securities such as stocks or bonds, are a highly useful investment vehicle. When you buy into a mutual fund, your money is pooled with the money of many others and invested in a vast array of stocks or bonds.

You can look at the benefits of diversification in two ways:

✓ Diversification reduces the volatility in the value of your whole portfolio. In other words, your portfolio can achieve the same rate of return that a single investment can provide with less fluctuation in value.

✓ Diversification allows you to obtain a higher rate of return for a given level of risk.

Keep in mind that no one, no matter whom he works for or what credentials he has, can guarantee returns on an investment. You can do good research and get lucky, but no one is free from the risk of losing money. Diversification allows you to hedge the risk of your investments. See Figures 8-1, 8-2, and 8-3 to get an idea of how diversifying can reduce your risk. (The figures in these charts are adjusted for inflation.) Notice that different investments did better during different time periods. Because the future can't be predicted, diversifying your money into different investments is safer. (In the 1990s, stocks appreciated greatly, and bonds did pretty well, too, while gold and silver did poorly. In the early 2000s, stocks did poorly while bonds and precious metals did well. In the mid 2000s, stocks produced the best returns.)

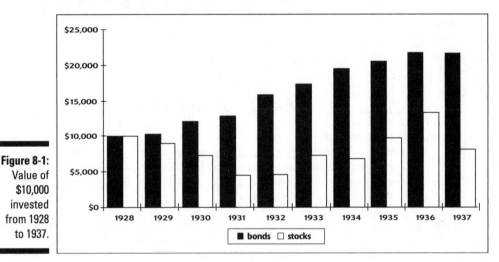

Figure 8-1:
Value of $10,000 invested from 1928 to 1937.

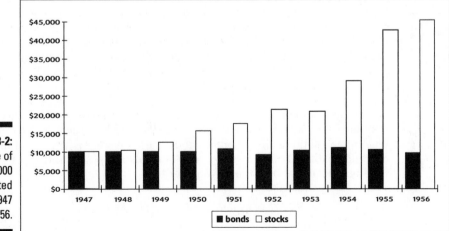

Figure 8-2:
Value of $10,000 invested from 1947 to 1956.

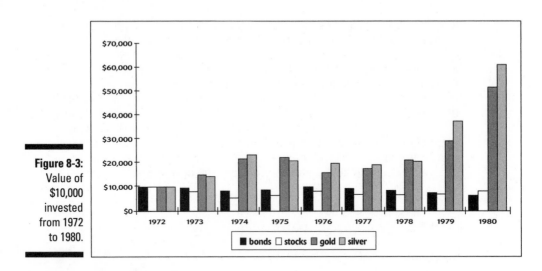

Figure 8-3:
Value of
$10,000
invested
from 1972
to 1980.

Spread the wealth: Asset allocation

Asset allocation refers to how you spread your investing dollars among different investment options (stocks, bonds, money market accounts, and so on).
Before you can intelligently decide how to allocate your assets, you need to
ponder a number of issues, including your present financial situation, your
goals and priorities, and the pros and cons of various investment options.

Although stocks and real estate offer attractive long-term returns, they can
sometimes suffer significant declines. Thus, these investments are not suitable for money that you think you may want or need to use within, say, the
next five years.

Money market and bond investments are good places to keep money that you
expect to use soon. Everyone should have a reserve of money — about three
to six months' worth of living expenses in a money market fund — that they
can access in an emergency. Shorter-term bonds or bond mutual funds can
serve as a higher-yielding, secondary emergency cushion. (Refer to Chapter 4
for more on emergency reserves.)

Bonds can also be useful for some longer-term investing for diversification
purposes. For example, when investing for retirement, placing a portion of
your money in bonds helps buffer stock market declines. The remaining
chapters in Part III detail your various investment options and explain how
to select those that best meet your needs.

Allocating money for the long term

Investing money for retirement is a classic long-term goal that most of us have. Your current age and the number of years until you retire are the biggest factors to consider when allocating money for long-term purposes. The younger you are and the more years you have before retirement, the more comfortable you should be with growth-oriented (and more volatile) investments, such as stocks and investment real estate.

One useful guideline for dividing or allocating your money between longer-term-oriented growth investments such as stocks and more-conservative lending investments such as bonds is to subtract your age from 110 (or 120 if you want to be aggressive; 100 to be more conservative) and invest the resulting percentage in stocks. You then invest the remaining amount in bonds.

For example, if you're 30 years old, you invest from 70 (100 – 30) to 90 (120 – 30) percent in stocks. The portion left over — 10 to 30 percent — is invested in bonds.

Table 8-4 lists some guidelines for allocating long-term money. All you need to figure out is how old you are and the level of risk you're comfortable with.

Table 8-4	Allocating Long-Term Money	
Your Investment Attitude	*Bond Allocation (%)*	*Stock Allocation (%)*
"Play it safe"	= Age	= 100 – age
"Middle-of-the-road"	= Age – 10	= 110 – age
"Aggressive"	= Age – 20	= 120 – age

For example, if you're the conservative sort who doesn't like a lot of risk but recognizes the value of striving for some growth and making your money work harder, you're a *middle-of-the-road* type. Using Table 8-4, if you're 40 years old, you may consider putting 30 percent (40 – 10) in bonds and 70 percent (110 – 40) in stocks.

In most employer retirement plans, mutual funds are the typical investment vehicle. If your employer's retirement plan includes more than one stock mutual fund as an option, you may want to try discerning which options are best by using the criteria I outline in Chapter 10. In the event that all your retirement plan's stock fund options are good, you could simply divide your stock allocation equally among the choices.

When one or more of the choices is an international stock fund, consider allocating a percentage of your stock fund money to overseas investments: at least 20 percent for play-it-safe investors, 25 to 35 percent for middle-of-the-road investors, and as much as 35 to 50 percent for aggressive investors.

If the 40-year-old middle-of-the-roader from the previous example is investing 70 percent in stocks, about 25 to 35 percent of the stock fund investments (which works out to be about 18 to 24 percent of the total) can be invested in international stock funds.

Historically, most employees haven't had to make their own investing decisions with retirement money. Pension plans, in which the company directs the investments, were more common in previous years. It's interesting to note that in a typical pension plan, companies choose to allocate the majority of money to stocks (about 60 percent), with a bit less placed in bonds (about 35 percent) and other investments. For more information on investing in retirement accounts, see Chapter 11.

Sticking with your allocations: Don't trade

The allocation of your investment dollars should be driven by your goals and desire to take risk. As you get older, gradually scaling back on the riskiness (and therefore growth potential) of your portfolio generally makes sense.

Don't tinker with your portfolio daily, weekly, monthly, or even annually. (Every three to five years or so, you may want to rebalance your holdings to get your mix to a desired asset allocation, as discussed in the previous section.) You should not engage in trading with the hopes of buying into a hot investment and selling your losers. Jumping onto a "winner" and dumping a "loser" may provide some short-term psychological comfort, but in the long-term, such an investment strategy can produce below-average returns.

When an investment gets front-page coverage and everyone is talking about its stunning rise, it's definitely time to take a reality check. The higher the value of an investment rises, the greater the danger that it's overpriced. Its next move may be downward. Don't follow the herd.

During the late 1990s, many technology stocks (especially Internet) had spectacular rises, thus attracting a lot of attention. Just because the U.S. economy is increasingly becoming technology-based, it doesn't mean that any price you pay for a technology stock is fine. Some investors who neglected to do basic research and bought into the attention-grabbing, high-flying technology stocks lost 80 percent or more of their investments in the early 2000s — ouch!

Conversely, when things look bleak (as when stocks in general suffered significant losses in the early 2000s), giving up hope is easy — who wants to be associated with a loser? However, investors who forget about their overall asset allocation plan and panic and sell after a major decline miss out on a tremendous buying opportunity.

Many people like buying everything from clothing to cars to ketchup on sale — yet whenever the stock market has a clearance sale, most investors stampede for the exits instead of snatching up great buys. Demonstrate your courage; don't follow the herd.

Investing lump sums via dollar-cost averaging

When you have a large chunk of cash to invest — whether you received it from an accumulation of funds over the years, an inheritance, or a recent windfall from work you've done — you may have a problem deciding what to do with it. Many people, of course, would like to have your problem. (You're not complaining, right?) You want to invest your money, but you're a bit skittish, if not outright terrified, at the prospect of investing the lump of money all at once.

If the money is residing in a savings or money market account, you may feel like it's wasting away. You want to put it to work! My first words of advice are "Don't rush." Nothing is wrong with earning a small return in a money market account. (See Chapter 12 for my recommendations of the best money funds.) Remember that a money market fund beats the heck out of rushing into an investment in which you may lose 20 percent or more. I sometimes get calls from people in a state of near panic. Typically, these folks have CDs coming due, and they feel that they must decide exactly where they want to invest the money in the 48 hours before the CD matures.

Take a deeeep breath. You have absolutely no reason to rush into an important decision. Tell your friendly banker that when the CD matures, you want to put the proceeds into the bank's highest-yielding savings or money market account. That way, your money continues to earn interest while you buy yourself some breathing room.

One approach to investing is called *dollar-cost averaging* (DCA). With DCA, you invest your money in equal chunks on a regular basis — such as once a month — into a diversified group of investments.

For example, if you have $60,000 to invest, you can invest $2,500 per month until it's all invested, which takes a couple years. The money awaiting future investment isn't lying fallow; you keep it in a money market account so it can earn a bit of interest while waiting its turn.

The attraction of DCA is that it allows you to ease into riskier investments instead of jumping in all at once. If the price of the investment drops after some of your initial purchases, you can buy some later at a lower price. If you dump all your money into the "sure win" investment all at once and then it drops like a stone, you'll be kicking yourself for not waiting. (The flip side of DCA is that when your investment of choice appreciates in value, you may wish that you had invested your money faster.)

Keeping your investing wits during uncertain times

During times like the early 2000s, some investors abandon the stock market for good. That's why the rebound from a severe bear market — and the down stock-market cycle that began in 2000 has been the worst in magnitude and duration in decades — takes time to develop. Although some people who have been burned badly learn that they're not cut out for stock investing, the rest of us should take stock of our investing approaches and adjust our practices and expectations.

In the early 2000s, the stock market began falling — with some growth stocks, especially technology stocks, plunging like stocks do in a depression. Layoffs mounted, and September 11 undermined consumer confidence. Then the general public learned that some major companies — Enron, WorldCom, and Global Crossing — pulled the wool over investors' eyes with shady accounting techniques that artificially inflated earnings. Concern about further terrorist attacks, smallpox, and war with Iraq (and perhaps other nations) hung like dark clouds on the horizon.

I see many similarities between the early 2000s and the early 1970s, when a multitude of problems (that could not have been predicted) unfolded. The early '70s saw record trade and budget deficits, inflation was rearing its ugly head, and we had the invasion of Cambodia, the Arab oil embargo, gas lines, and that period's Arab-Israeli conflict — the Yom Kippur War. Vice President Spiro Agnew resigned over the exposure of his personal income tax evasion and acceptance of bribes while working in Maryland's government.

Then news of Watergate broke, and Nixon's impeachment hearings began. After flirting with the 1,000 level since 1966, the Dow Jones Industrial Average plunged below 600 after Nixon resigned in 1974. Many investors soured on stocks and swore off the market forever. That reaction was unfortunate, because even with the recent, severe stock market decline, stocks are still 15-fold higher today than they were back in 1974.

Don't let a poor string of events sour you on stock investing. History has repeatedly proven that continuing to buy stocks during down markets increases your long-term returns. Throwing in the towel is the worst thing you can do in a slumping market. And don't waste time trying to find a way to beat the system. Buy and hold a diversified portfolio of stocks. Remember that the financial markets reward investors for accepting risk and uncertainty.

Another drawback of DCA is that you may get cold feet as you continue to pour money into an investment that's dropping in value. Many people who are attracted to DCA because they fear that they may buy before a price drop end up bailing out of what feels like a sinking ship.

DCA can also cause headaches with your taxes when the time comes to sell investments held outside retirement accounts. When you buy an investment at many different times and prices, the accounting becomes muddied as you sell blocks of the investment.

DCA is most valuable when the money you want to invest represents a large portion of your total assets and you can stick to a schedule. Make DCA automatic so that you're less likely to chicken out should the investment fall after your initial purchases. Most of the investment firms I recommend in the next few chapters provide automatic exchange services.

Acknowledging Differences among Investment Firms

Thousands of firms sell investments and manage money. Banks, mutual fund companies, securities brokerage firms, and even insurance companies all vie for your dollars.

Just to make matters more complicated, each industry plays in the others' backyards. You can find mutual fund companies that offer securities broker-age, insurance firms that are in the mutual fund business, and mutual fund companies that offer banklike accounts and services. You may benefit from this competition and one-stop shopping convenience. On the other hand, some firms are novices at particular businesses and count on some people's shopping by brand-name recognition.

Focusing on the best firms

Make sure that you do business with a firm that

✔ **Offers the best value investments in comparison to their competitors.**
  Value is the combination of performance (including service) and cost.
  Given the level of risk that you're comfortable with, you want investments that offer higher rates of return, but you don't want to have to
  pay a small fortune for them. Commissions, management fees, maintenance fees, and other charges can turn a high-performance investment
  into a mediocre or poor one.

✔ **Employs representatives who do not have an inherent self-interest in steering you into a particular type of investment.** This criterion has nothing to do with whether an investment firm hires polite, well-educated, or well-dressed people. The most important factor is the way the company compensates its employees. If the investment firm's personnel are paid on commission, pass on that firm. Give preference to investing firms that don't tempt their employees to push one investment over another in order to generate more fees.

No-load (commission-free) mutual fund companies

Mutual funds are an ideal investment vehicle for most investors. *No-load mutual fund companies* are firms through which you can invest in mutual funds without paying sales commissions. In other words, every dollar you invest goes to work in the mutual funds you choose — nothing is siphoned off to pay sales commissions. See Chapter 10 for details on investing in mutual funds.

Discount brokers

In one of the most beneficial changes for investors in this century, the Securities and Exchange Commission (SEC) deregulated the retail brokerage industry on May 1, 1975. Prior to this date, investors were charged fixed commissions when they bought or sold stocks, bonds, and other securities. In other words, no matter which brokerage firm an investor did business with, the cost of the firm's services was set (and the level of commissions was high). After the 1975 deregulation, brokerage firms could charge people whatever their little hearts desired.

Competition inevitably resulted in more and better choices. Many new brokerage firms (that didn't do business the old way) opened. They were dubbed *discount brokers* because the fees they charged customers were substantially lower than what brokers charged under the old fixed-fee system.

Even more important than saving customers money, discount brokers established a vastly improved compensation system that greatly reduced conflicts of interest. Discount brokers generally pay the salaries of their brokers. The term *discount broker* is actually not an enlightening one. It's certainly true that this new breed of brokerage firm saves you lots of money when you invest. You can easily save 50 to 80 percent through the major discount brokers. But these firms' investments are not "on sale" or "second-rate." Discount brokers are simply brokers without major conflicts of interest. Of course, like any other for-profit enterprise, they're in business to make money, but they're much less likely to steer you wrong for their own benefit.

Be careful of discount brokers selling load mutual funds. (I discuss the reasons you should shun these brokers in Chapter 10.)

Places to consider avoiding

The worst places to invest are those that charge you a lot, have mediocre- or poor-performing investments, and have major conflicts of interest. The prime conflict of interest arises when investment firms pay their brokers commissions on the basis of what and how much they sell. The result: The investment firms sell lots of stuff that pays fat commissions, and they *churn,* or cause a rapid turnover of, your account. (Because each transaction has a fee, the more you buy and sell, the more money they make.)

Some folks who call themselves *financial planners* or *financial consultants* work on commission. In addition to working at the bigger brokerage firms, many of them belong to so-called *broker-dealer networks,* which provide back-office support and investment products to sell. When a person claiming to be a financial planner or advisor is part of a broker-dealer network, odds are quite high that you're dealing with an investment salesperson. See Chapter 18 for more background on the financial planning industry and questions to ask an advisor you're thinking about hiring.

Commissions and their impact on human behavior

Investment products bring in widely varying commissions. The products that bring in the highest commissions tend to be the ones that money-hungry brokers push the hardest.

Table 8-5 lists the commissions that you pay and that come out of your investment dollars when you work with brokers, financial consultants, and financial planners who work on commission.

Table 8-5	Investment Sales Commissions	
Investment Type	*Average Commission on $20,000 Investment*	*Average Commission on $100,000 Investment*
Annuities	$1,400	$7,000
Initial public offerings (new stock issue)	$1,000	$5,000
Limited partnerships	$1,800	$9,000
Load mutual funds	$1,200	$5,000
Options and futures	$2,000+	$10,000+

What to do when you're fleeced by a broker

You can't sue a broker just because you lose money on that person's investment recommendations. However, if you have been the victim of one of the following cardinal financial sins, you may have some legal recourse:

- **Misrepresentation and omission:** If you were told, for example, that a particular investment guarantees returns of 15 percent per year and then the investment ends up plunging in value by 50 percent, you were misled. Misrepresentation can also be charged if you're sold an investment with hefty commissions after you were originally told that it was commission-free.

- **Unsuitable investments:** Retirees who need access to their capital are often advised to invest in limited partnerships (or LPs, discussed in Chapter 9) for safe, high yields. The yields on most LPs end up being anything but safe. LP investors have also discovered how *illiquid* (or not readily converted into cash) their investments are — some can't be liquidated for up to ten years or more.

- **Churning:** If your broker or financial planner is constantly trading your investments, odds are that his or her weekly commission check is benefiting at your expense.

- **Rogue elephant salespeople:** When your planner or broker buys or sells without your approval or ignores your request to make a change, you may be able to collect for losses caused by these actions.

Two major types of practitioners — securities lawyers and arbitration consultants — stand ready to help you recover your lost money. You can find securities lawyers by looking under "Attorneys — Securities" in the Yellow Pages or calling your local bar association for referrals. Arbitration consultants can be found in the phone book under "Arbitrators." If you come up dry, try contacting business writers at a major newspaper in your area or at your favorite personal finance magazine. These sources may be able to give you names and numbers of folks they know.

Most lawyers and consultants work on a *contingency-fee* basis — they get a percentage of damages (about 20 to 40 percent of the amount collected). They also often ask for an upfront fee, ranging from several hundred to several thousands of dollars, to help them cover their expenses and time. If they take your case and lose, they generally keep the upfront money. Securities lawyers are usually a more expensive option.

You may want to go to *arbitration* — an agreement you made (probably without realizing it) when you set up an account to work with the broker or planner. Arbitration is usually much quicker, cheaper, and easier than going to court. You can even choose to represent yourself. Both sides present their case to a panel of three arbitrators. The arbitrators then make a decision that neither side can squabble over or appeal.

If you decide to prepare for arbitration by yourself, the nonprofit American Arbitration Association can send you a package of background materials to help with your case. Check your phone directory for a local branch, or contact the association's headquarters (335 Madison Avenue, 10th Floor, New York, NY 10017-4605; 800-778-7879; Web site www.adr.org).

Besides the fact that you can never be sure that you're getting an unbiased recommendation from a salesperson working on commission, you're wasting money unnecessarily. All good investments can be bought on a *no-load* (commission-free) basis. For example, you can purchase no-load mutual funds.

When you're unsure about an investment product that's being pitched to you (and even when you *are* sure), ask for a copy of the prospectus. In the first few pages, check out whether the investment includes a commission (also known as a *load*). Although salespeople can hide behind obscure titles such as vice president or financial consultant, a prospectus must detail whether the investment carries a commission.

Investment salespeople's conflicts of interest

Financial consultants (also known as stockbrokers), financial planners, and others who sell investment products can have enormous conflicts of interest when recommending strategies and specific investment products. Commissions and other financial incentives can't help but skew the advice of even the most earnest and otherwise well-intentioned salespeople.

Numerous conflicts of interest can damage your investment portfolio. The following are the most common conflicts to watch out for:

- ✔ **Pushing higher-commission products:** As I discuss earlier in this chapter, commissions on investment products vary tremendously. Products like limited partnerships, commodities, options, and futures are at the worst end of the spectrum for you (and the best end of the spectrum for a salesperson). Investments such as no-load mutual funds and Treasury bills that are 100 percent commission-free are at the best end of the spectrum for you (and therefore, the worst end of the spectrum for a salesperson).

  Surprisingly, commission-based brokers and financial planners don't have to give you the prospectus (where commissions are detailed) before you buy a financial product that carries commissions (as with a load mutual fund). In contrast, commission-free investment companies, such as no-load mutual fund companies, must send a prospectus before taking a mutual fund order. Commission-based investment salespeople should also be required to provide a prospectus and disclose any commissions upfront and in writing before making a sale. I suppose that if they were actually required to follow these guidelines, more people would choose to buy investments elsewhere — and politicians might start telling the truth!

✔ **Recommending active trading:** Investment salespeople often advise you to trade frequently into and out of different securities. They usually base their advice on current news events or an analyst's comments on the security. Sometimes these moves are valid, but more often they're not. In extreme cases, brokers trade on a monthly basis. By the end of the year, they've churned through your entire portfolio. Needless to say, all these transactions cost you big money in trading fees.

Diversified mutual funds (see Chapter 10) make more sense for most people. You can invest in mutual funds free of sales commissions. Besides saving money on commissions, you earn better long-term returns by having an expert money manager work for you.

✔ **Failing to recommend investing through retirement plans:** If you're not taking advantage of retirement savings plans (see Chapter 11), you may be missing out on valuable tax benefits. The initial contributions to most retirement plans are tax-deductible, and your money compounds without taxation over the years. An investment salesperson is not likely to recommend that you contribute to your employer's retirement plan — a 401(k) for example. Such contributions cut into the money you have available to invest with your friendly salesperson.

If you're self-employed, salespeople are somewhat more likely to recommend that you fund a retirement plan because they can set up such plans for you. You're better off setting up a retirement plan through a no-load mutual fund company (see Chapters 10 and 11).

✔ **Pushing high-fee products:** Many of the brokerage firms that used to sell investment products only on commission moved into fee-based investment management. This change is an improvement for investors because it reduces some of the conflicts of interest caused by commissions.

On the other hand, these brokers charge extraordinarily high fees, which are usually quoted as a percentage of assets under management, on their managed-investment (or wrap) accounts. For more information, see the "Wrap (or managed) accounts" sidebar.

Valuing brokerage research

Brokerage firms and the brokers who work for them frequently argue that their research is better. With their insights and recommendations, they say, you'll do better and "beat the market averages."

Wall Street analysts are often overly optimistic when it comes to predicting corporate profits. If analysts were simply inaccurate or bad estimators, you'd expect that they'd sometimes underestimate and, at other times, overestimate companies' earnings. The discrepancy identifies yet another conflict of interest among many of the brokerage firms.

BEWARE

Wrap (or managed) accounts

Wrap accounts (also called managed accounts) are all the rage among commission-based brokerage firms. These accounts go by a variety of names, but they're all similar in that they charge a fixed percentage of the assets under management to invest your money through money managers.

Wrap accounts can be poor investments because their management expenses may be extraordinarily high — up to 3 percent per year (some even higher) of assets under management. Remember that in the long haul, stocks can return about 10 percent per year before taxes. So if you're paying 3 percent per year to have your money managed in stocks, 30 percent of your return (before taxes) is siphoned off. But don't forget — because the government sure won't — that you pay a good chunk of money in taxes on your 10 percent return as well. So the 3 percent wrap actually ends up depleting 40 to 50 percent of your after-tax profits!

The best no-load (commission-free) mutual funds offer investors access to the nation's best investment managers for a fraction of the cost of wrap accounts. You can invest in dozens of top-performing funds for an annual expense of 1 percent per year or less. Some of the best fund companies offer excellent funds for a cost as low as 0.2 to 0.5 percent (see Chapter 10).

You may be told, in the marketing of wrap accounts, that you're getting access to investment managers who don't normally take money from small-fry investors like you. Not a single study shows that the performance of money managers has anything to do with the minimum account they handle. Besides, no-load mutual funds hire many of the same managers who work at other money management firms.

You also may be told that you'll earn a higher rate of return, so the extra cost is worth it. "You could have earned 18 to 25 percent per year," they say, "had you invested with the 'Star of Yesterday' investment management company." The key word here is *had*. History is history. Many of yesterday's winners become tomorrow's losers or mediocre performers.

You also need to remember that, unlike mutual funds, whose performance records are audited by the SEC, wrap account performance records may include marketing hype. Showing only the performance of selected accounts — those that performed the best — is the most common ploy.

Brokerage firm analysts are reluctant to write a negative report about a company because the firms these analysts work for also solicit companies to issue new stock to the public. What better way to show businesses your potential for selling shares to the public at a high price than by showing how much you believe in certain companies and writing glowing reports about their future prospects?

Seeing through Experts Who Predict the Future

Believing that you can increase your investment returns by following the prognostications of certain gurus is a common mistake that some investors make. Many of us may want to believe that some experts can predict the future of the investment world. Believing in gurus makes it easier to accept the risk you know you're taking when trying to make your money grow. The sage predictions that you read in an investment newsletter or hear from an "expert" who is repeatedly quoted in financial publications make you feel protected — sort of like Linus and his security blanket.

Investment newsletter subscribers and guru followers would be better off buying a warm blanket instead — it has a lot more value and costs a whole lot less! No one can predict the future. If they could, they'd be so busy investing their own money and getting rich that they wouldn't have the time and desire to share their secrets with you.

Investment newsletters

Many investment newsletters purport to time the markets, telling you exactly the right time to get into and out of certain stocks or mutual funds (or the financial markets in general). Such an approach is doomed to failure in the long run. By failure, I mean that this approach won't beat the tried-and-true strategy of buy and hold.

I see people paying hundreds of dollars annually to subscribe to all sorts of market-timing and stock-picking newsletters. One client of mine, an attorney, subscribed to several newsletters. When I asked him why, he said that their marketing materials claimed that if you followed their advice, you would make a 20 percent per year return on your money. But in the four years that he'd followed their advice, he actually *lost* money, despite appreciating financial markets overall.

Before you ever consider subscribing to any investment newsletter, examine its historic track record through avenues such as *Hulbert Financial Digest*. The investment newsletter's marketing materials typically hype the supposed returns that the publication's recommendations have produced. Sadly, newsletters seem to be able to make lots of bogus claims without suffering the timely wrath of securities regulators.

Don't get predictive advice from newsletters. If newsletter writers were so smart about the future of financial markets, they'd be making lots more money as money managers. The only types of investment newsletters and periodicals that you should consider subscribing to are those that offer research and information rather than predictions. I discuss the investment newsletters that fit the bill in the subsequent investment chapters.

Investment gurus

Investment gurus come and go. Some of them get their 15 minutes of fame on the basis of one or two successful predictions that someone in the press remembers (and makes famous). A classic example is a former market analyst at Shearson named Elaine Garzarelli.

Garzarelli became famous for predicting the stock market's plummet in the fall of 1987. Her fund, Smith Barney Shearson Sector Analysis, was established just before the crash. Supposedly, Garzarelli's indicators warned her to stay out of stocks, which she did, and in doing so, she saved her fund from the plunge.

Shearson, being a money-minded brokerage, quickly motivated its brokers to sell shares in Garzarelli's fund. In addition to her having avoided the crash, it didn't hurt that Shearson brokers were being rewarded with a hefty 5 percent sales commission for selling her fund. By the end of 1987, investors had poured nearly $700 million into this fund.

In 1988, Garzarelli's fund was the worst-performing fund among funds investing in growth stocks. From 1988 to 1990, Garzarelli's fund underperformed the Standard & Poor 500 average by about 43 percent! In 1987 — the year of the crash — Garzarelli had outperformed the S&P 500 by about 26 percent. So the amount she saved her investors by avoiding the crash was lost — along with more — in the years that followed. In fact, Garzarelli's performance was so dismal in the years following the crash that Shearson eventually fired her.

Despite her poor long-term track record, Garzarelli is still quoted as a market soothsayer. She now manages money privately and hawks investment newsletters. The following marketing hype, promoting her newsletter, recently appeared in a mailed brochure entitled "The Garzarelli Edge":

> "The proven, scientific system that has produced compounded yearly gains of 20.2% since 1982!"

> "Elaine Garzarelli has called every major turn in the Dow since 1982."

Now, if these comments were true, why did Garzarelli's investment fund perform so poorly, and why did Shearson fire her in the mid-1990s following numerous years of inaccurate predictions and the dismal performance of her mutual fund? I also find it humorous that the 20.2 percent return was reportedly "audited by a Big-6 accounting firm." Down in the fine print, however, it says, "Audit Pending." I bet it's still pending — probably with the same folks who audited Enron's financials (and went under)!

New gurus often get exposure and gain popularity through television. Anyone who's done some channel flipping couldn't help but notice Jim Cramer's flailing arms, loud voice, and crazed looking expressions! I've watched portions of his CNBC show on numerous occasions and had followed his career for years prior to his arrival on cable television.

Back in the 1990s, *SmartMoney* magazine did a big article on Cramer, which purported to show what a great stock picker he was with the hedge fund (more on such funds in Chapter 9) that he ran at the time. The article showed Cramer's supposedly high hedge fund returns. However, when I inquired, I learned that all those returns were self-reported by Cramer. I tried on several occasions to contact his company and get more details and documentation and was routinely blown off.

I have long counseled that you should never believe a claimed return unless it's been independently audited (the way that all mutual fund returns are). To date, I've never seen an independent audit of Cramer's claimed hedge fund returns. When I contacted his organization, they simply sent me the same unaudited returns similar to what they provided to *SmartMoney* magazine.

As for the track record of Cramer's online newsletter, the *Hulbert Financial Digest* is the only independent organization that tracks the recommendations of newsletter writers. According to John Kimble, senior analyst with *Hulbert Financial,* "A couple of years ago, they asked us if we wanted to be on the distribution list for their *Action Alerts Plus* online newsletter and they sent us e-mails for about six weeks and then stopped. Mark Hulbert sent them a reminder six months ago and they still haven't sent it."

Commentators and experts who publish predictive newsletters and are interviewed in the media can't predict the future. Ignore the predictions and speculations of self-proclaimed gurus and investment soothsayers. The few people who have a slight leg up on everyone else aren't going to share their investment secrets — they're too busy investing their own money! If you have to believe in something to offset your fears, believe in good information and proven investment managers. And don't forget the value of optimism, faith, and hope — regardless of *what* or *whom* you believe in!

Leaving You with Some Final Advice

I cover a lot of ground in this chapter. In the remaining chapters in this part, I detail different investment choices and accounts and how to build a champion portfolio! Before you move on, here are several other issues to keep in mind as you make important investing choices:

✔ **Don't invest based on sales solicitations.** Companies that advertise and solicit prospective customers aggressively with tactics such as telemarketing offer some of the worst financial products with the highest fees. Companies with great products don't have to reach their potential customers this way. Of course, all companies have to do some promotion. But the companies with the best investment offerings don't have to use the hard-sell approach; they get plenty of new business through the word-of-mouth recommendations of satisfied customers.

✔ **Don't invest in what you don't understand.** The mistake of not understanding the investments you purchase usually follows from the preceding no-no — buying into a sales pitch. When you don't understand an investment, odds are good that it won't be right for you. Slick-tongued brokers (who may call themselves financial consultants, advisors, or planners) who earn commissions based on what they sell can talk you into inappropriate investments. Before you invest in anything, you should know its track record, its true costs, and how liquid (easily convertible to cash) it is.

✔ **Minimize fees.** Avoid investments that carry high sales commissions and management expenses (usually disclosed in a prospectus). Virtually all investments today can be purchased without a salesperson. Besides paying unnecessary commissions, the bigger danger in investing through a salesperson is that you may be directed to a path that's not in your best interests. Management fees create a real drag on investment returns. Not surprisingly, higher-fee investments, on average, perform worse than alternatives with lower fees. High ongoing management fees often go toward lavish offices, glossy brochures, and skyscraper salaries, or toward propping up small, inefficient operations. Do you want your hard-earned dollars to support either of these types of businesses?

✔ **Pay attention to tax consequences.** Even if you never become an investment expert, you're smart enough to know that the more money you pay in taxes, the less you have for investing and playing with. See Chapter 11 for info on how retirement accounts can help boost your investment returns. For investments outside retirement accounts, you need to match the types of investments to your tax situation (see Chapter 12).

Chapter 9

Understanding Your Investment Choices

*W*hich vehicle you choose for your investment journey depends on where you're going, how fast you want to get there, and what risks you're willing to take along the way. If you haven't yet read Chapter 8, please do so now. In it, I cover a number of investment concepts, such as the difference between lending and ownership investments, that will enhance your ability to choose among the common investment vehicles I discuss in this chapter.

Slow and Steady Investments

Everyone should have some money in stable, safe investment vehicles. For example, this would include money that you've earmarked for your short-term bills, both expected and unexpected. Likewise, if you're saving money for a home purchase within the next few years, you certainly don't want to risk that money on the roller coaster of the stock market.

The investment options that follow are appropriate for money you don't want to put at great risk.

Transaction/checking accounts

Transaction/checking accounts are best used for depositing your monthly income and paying for your expenditures. If you want to have unlimited check-writing privileges and access to your money with an ATM card, checking accounts at local banks are often your best bet.

Here's how not to be taken by banks:

- **Use a smaller bank or credit union.** You can generally get a better checking account deal at a credit union or a smaller bank. Because you can easily obtain cash through ATM outlets in supermarkets and other retail stores, you may not need to do business with Big City Bank, which has branch offices at every intersection.

- **Shop around.** Some banks don't require you to maintain a minimum balance to avoid a monthly service charge when you direct deposit your paychecks. Make sure that you shop around for accounts that don't ding you $1.50 here for the use of an ATM and $12 there for a low balance.

- **Limit the amount you keep in checking.** Keep only enough money in the account for your monthly bill payment needs. If you consistently keep more than a few thousand dollars in a checking account, get the excess out. You can earn more in a savings or money market account, which I describe in the following section.

- **Don't do your checking through the bank.** Some folks (myself included) don't have a bank checking account. How do they do that? They have discount brokerage accounts that allow unlimited check-writing within a money market fund. (See Chapter 10 for recommended firms; also see my discussion in Chapter 19 about paying your bills via your computer and through other automatic means.)

Savings accounts and money market funds

Savings accounts are available through banks; money market funds are available through mutual fund companies. Savings accounts and money market funds are nearly identical, except that money market funds generally pay a better rate of interest. The interest rate paid to you, also known as the *yield,* fluctuates over time, depending on the level of interest rates in the overall economy. (Note that some banks offer money market accounts, which are basically like savings accounts and should not be confused with money market mutual *funds.*)

The federal government backs bank savings accounts with Federal Deposit Insurance Corporation (FDIC) insurance. Money market funds are not insured. You shouldn't give preference to a bank account just because your investment (principal) is insured. In fact, your preference should lean toward money market funds, because the better ones are higher yielding than the better bank savings accounts. And money market funds offer check writing and other easy ways to access your money (for more on money funds, please see Chapter 10).

Money market funds have several advantages over bank savings accounts:

- ✔ The best money market funds have higher yields.

- ✔ If you're in a higher tax bracket, you may net more after factoring in taxes using tax-free money market funds. No savings account pays tax-free interest.

- ✔ Most money market funds come with free check-writing privileges. (The only stipulation is that each check must be written for a minimum amount — $250 is common.)

As with money you put into bank savings accounts, money market funds are suitable for money that you can't afford to see dwindle in value.

Bonds

When you invest in a bond, you effectively lend your money to an organization. When a bond is issued, it includes a specified maturity date at which time the principal will be repaid. Bonds are also issued at a particular interest rate, or what's known as a *coupon*. This rate is fixed on most bonds. So, for example, if you buy a five-year, 6 percent bond issued by Home Depot, you're lending your money to Home Depot for five years at an interest rate of 6 percent per year. (Bond interest is usually paid in two equal, semi-annual installments.)

The value of a bond generally fluctuates with changes in interest rates. For example, if you're holding a bond issued at 6 percent and rates increase to 8 percent on comparable, newly issued bonds, your bond decreases in value. (Why would anyone want to buy your bond at the price you paid if it yields just 6 percent and 8 percent can be obtained elsewhere?)

Some bonds are tied to variable interest rates. For example, you can buy bonds that are adjustable-rate mortgages, on which the interest rate can fluctuate. As an investor, you're actually lending your money to a mortgage borrower — indirectly, you're the banker making a loan to someone buying a home.

The overused certificate of deposit

A *certificate of deposit* (CD) is another type of bond that's issued by a bank. With a CD, as with a real bond, you agree to lend your money to an organization (in this case, a bank) for a predetermined number of months or years. Generally, the longer you agree to lock up your money, the higher the interest rate you receive.

With CDs, you pay a penalty for early withdrawal. If you want your money back before the end of the CD's term, you get whacked with the loss of a number of months' worth of interest. CDs also don't tend to pay very competitive interest rates. You can usually beat the interest rate on shorter-term CDs (those that mature within a year or so) with the best money market mutual funds, which offer complete liquidity without any penalty.

Bonds differ from one another in the following major ways:

- ✔ **The type of institution to which you're lending your money:** With municipal bonds, you lend your money to the state government; with Treasuries, you lend your money to the federal government; with GNMAs (Ginnie Maes), you lend your money to a mortgage holder; with corporate bonds, you lend your money to a corporation.

- ✔ **The credit quality of the borrower to whom you lend your money:** This refers to the probability that the borrower will pay you the interest and return your principal as agreed.

- ✔ **The length of maturity of the bond:** Short-term bonds mature within a few years, intermediate bonds within 3 to 10 years, and long-term bonds within 30 years. Longer-term bonds generally pay higher yields but fluctuate more with changes in interest rates.

Bonds are rated by major credit-rating agencies for their safety, usually on a scale where AAA is the highest possible rating. For example, high-grade corporate bonds (AAA or AA) are considered the safest (that is, most likely to pay you back). Next in safety are general bonds (A or BBB), which are still safe but just a little less so. Junk bonds (rated BB or lower), popularized by Michael Milken, are actually not all that junky; they're just lower in quality and have a slight (1 or 2 percent) probability of default.

Some bonds are *callable,* which means that the lender can decide to pay you back earlier than the previously agreed-upon date. This event usually occurs when interest rates fall and the lender wants to issue new, lower-interest-rate bonds to replace the higher-rate bonds outstanding. To compensate you for early repayment, the lender typically gives you a small premium over what the bond is currently valued at.

Building Wealth with Ownership Vehicles

The three best legal ways to build wealth are to invest in stocks, real estate, and small business. I found this to be true from observing many clients and other investors and from my own personal experiences.

Stocks

Stocks, which represent shares of ownership in a company, are the most common ownership investment vehicle. When companies *go public,* they issue shares of stock that people like you and I can purchase on the major stock exchanges, such as the New York Stock Exchange, the American Stock Exchange, and NASDAQ (National Association of Securities Dealers Automated Quotation system), or on the over-the-counter market.

As the economy grows and companies grow with it and earn greater profits, stock prices (and dividend payouts on those stocks) generally follow suit. Stock prices and dividends don't move in lockstep with earnings, but over the years, the relationship is pretty close. In fact, the *price/earnings ratio* — which measures the level of stock prices relative to (or divided by) company earnings — of U.S. stocks has averaged approximately 15 (although it's tended to be higher during periods of low inflation). A price-earnings ratio of 15 simply means that stock prices per share, on average, are selling at about 15 times those companies' earnings per share.

Companies that issue stock (called *publicly held* companies) include automobile manufacturers, computer software producers, fast-food restaurants, hotels, magazine and newspaper publishers, supermarkets, wineries, zipper manufacturers, and everything in between! (You can even invest overseas — see the "International stocks" sidebar.) By contrast, some companies are *privately held,* which means that they've elected to have their stock owned by senior management and a small number of affluent investors. Privately held companies' stocks do not trade on a stock exchange, so folks like you and me can't buy stock in such firms.

Companies differ in what industry or line of business they're in and also in size. In the financial press, you often hear companies referred to by their *market capitalization,* which is the value of their outstanding stock (the number of total shares multiplied by the market price per share). When describing the sizes of companies, Wall Street has done away with such practical adjectives as *big* and *small* and replaced them with expressions like *large cap* and *small cap* (where *cap* stands for *capitalization*). Such is the language of financial geekiness.

Investing in the stock market involves occasional setbacks and difficult moments (just like raising children or going mountain climbing), but the overall journey should be worth the effort. Over the past two centuries, the U.S. stock market has produced an annual average rate of return of about 10 percent. However, the market, as measured by the Dow Jones Industrial Average, fell more than 20 percent during 16 different periods in the 20th century. On average, these periods of decline lasted less than two years. So if you can withstand a temporary setback over a few years, the stock market is a proven place to invest for long-term growth.

International stocks

Not only can you invest in company stocks that trade on the U.S. stock exchanges, but you can also invest in stocks overseas. Aside from folks with business connections abroad, why would the average citizen want to invest in stocks overseas?

I can give you several reasons. First, many investing opportunities exist overseas. If you look at the total value of all stocks outstanding worldwide, the value of U.S. stocks is in the minority.

Another reason for investing in international stocks is that when you confine your investing to U.S. securities, you miss a world of opportunities, not only because of business growth available in other countries but also because you get the opportunity to diversify your portfolio even further. International securities markets don't move in tandem with U.S. markets. During various U.S. stock market drops, some international stock markets drop less, while others actually rise in value.

Some people hesitate to invest in overseas securities for silly reasons. One column I came across in a big city paper was entitled "Plenty of Pitfalls in Foreign Investing: Timing is all in earning a decent return." The piece went on to say, "But as with sex, commuting and baseball, timing is everything in the stock market." Smart stock market investors know better than to try to time their investments. The piece also ominously warned, "Foreign stock markets have been known to evaporate overnight." I wish I could say the same for the jobs of some bone-headed financial journalists!

Others are concerned that overseas investing hurts the U.S. economy and contributes to a loss of American jobs. I have some counterarguments. First, if you don't profit from the growth of economies overseas, someone else will. If there's money to be made, Americans may as well be there to participate. Profits from a foreign company are distributed to all stockholders, no matter where they live. Dividends and stock price appreciation know no national boundaries.

Also, recognize that you already live in a global economy — making a distinction between U.S. and non-U.S. companies is no longer appropriate. Many companies that are headquartered in the United States also have overseas operations. Some U.S. firms derive a large portion of their revenue from their international divisions. Conversely, many firms based overseas also have U.S. operations. An increasing number of companies are worldwide operations. You don't get the full benefit of international investing by buying just large multinational companies headquartered in the United States. The overseas diversification advantage is obtained by investing in companies that trade on foreign exchanges.

You can invest in stocks by making your own selection of individual stocks or by letting a mutual fund manager (discussed in Chapter 10) do it for you.

Discovering the relative advantages of mutual funds

Efficiently managed mutual funds offer investors of both modest and substantial means low-cost access to high-quality money managers. Mutual funds span the spectrum of risk and potential returns, from nonfluctuating money market funds (which are similar to savings accounts) to bond funds (which generally pay higher yields than money market funds but fluctuate with changes in interest rates) to stock funds (which offer the greatest potential for appreciation but also the greatest short-term volatility).

Investing in individual securities should be done only by those who really enjoy doing it. Mutual funds, if properly selected, are a low-cost, quality way to hire professional money managers. Over the long haul, you're not going to beat full-time professional managers who are investing in the securities of the same type and risk level. Chapter 10 is devoted to mutual funds.

Understanding exchange traded and hedge funds and managed accounts

Mutual funds aren't the only game in town when it comes to hiring a professional money manager. In recent years, three somewhat similar options have been increasingly promoted to individual investors:

- **Exchange traded funds (ETFs):** These are the most similar to mutual funds except that they trade on a major stock exchange and, unlike mutual funds, can be bought and sold during the trading day. The best ETFs have very low fees, and like an index fund (see Chapter 10), they invest to track the performance of a stock market index.

- **Hedge funds:** These privately managed funds are for wealthier investors and generally take more risk (some even go bankrupt) than a typical mutual fund. The fees can be steep — typically 20 percent of the hedge fund's annual returns. I do not recommend them.

- **Managed accounts:** The major brokerage firms, which employ brokers on commission, offer access to private money managers. In reality, this option isn't really different from getting access to fund managers via mutual funds, but you'll generally pay a much higher fee, which reduces this option's attractiveness.

Investing in individual stocks

My experience is that plenty of people choose to invest in individual securities because they think that they're smarter or luckier than the rest. I don't know you personally, but it's safe to say that in the long run, your investment choices aren't going to outperform those of a full-time investment professional.

As a financial counselor, I noticed a distinct difference between the sexes on this issue. Perhaps because of the differences in how people are raised, testosterone levels, or whatever, men tend to have more of a problem swallowing their egos and admitting that they're better off not selecting their own individual securities. Maybe the desire to be a stock picker is genetically linked to not wanting to ask for directions!

Investing in individual stocks entails numerous drawbacks and pitfalls:

✔ **You'll have to spend a significant amount of time doing research.** When you're considering the purchase of an individual security, you should know a lot about the company in which you're thinking about investing. Relevant questions to ask about the company include: What products does it sell? What are its prospects for future growth and profitability? How much debt does the company have? You need to do your homework not only before you make your initial investment but also on an ongoing basis for as long as you hold the investment. Research takes your valuable free time and sometimes costs money.

Don't fool yourself or let others fool you into thinking that picking and following individual companies and their stocks is simple, requires little time, or is far more profitable than investing in mutual funds.

✔ **Your emotions will probably get in your way.** Analyzing financial statements, corporate strategy, and competitive position requires great intellect and insight. However, those skills aren't nearly enough. Will you have the stomach to hold on after what you thought was a sure-win stock plunges 50 percent while the overall stock market holds steady or even climbs? Will you have the courage to dump such a stock if your new research suggests that the plummet is the beginning of the end rather than just a big bump in the road? When your money is on the line, emotions often kick in and undermine your ability to make sound long-term decisions. Few people have the psychological constitution to outfox the financial markets.

✔ **You're less likely to diversify.** Unless you have tens of thousands of dollars to invest in different stocks, you probably can't cost-effectively afford to develop a diversified portfolio. For example, when you're investing in stocks, you need to hold companies in different industries, different companies within an industry, and so on. By not diversifying, you unnecessarily add to your risk.

✔ **You'll face accounting and bookkeeping hassles.** When you invest in individual securities outside retirement accounts, you must report that transaction on your tax return every time you sell a specific security. Even if you pay someone else to complete your tax return, you still have the hassle of keeping track of statements and receipts.

Of course, you may find some people (with a vested interest) who try to convince you that picking your own stocks and managing your own portfolio of stocks is easy and more profitable than investing in, say, a mutual fund. In my experience, such stock-picking cheerleaders fall into at least one of the following categories:

✔ **Newsletter writers:** Whether in print, on television, or on a Web site, some pundits pitch the notion that professional money managers are just overpaid buffoons and that you can handily trounce the pros with little investment of your time by simply putting your money into the pundits' stock picks. Of course, what these self-anointed gurus are really selling is either an ongoing newsletter (which can run upwards of several hundred dollars per year) or your required daily visitation of their advertising-stuffed Web sites. How else will you be able to keep up with their announced buy-and-sell recommendations? These supposed experts want you to be dependent on continually following their advice. Of course, you may be wondering, "Hey, if these pundits were such geniuses at picking the best stocks, why aren't they making piles of money just investing rather than selling their supposed brilliant insights on the cheap?" Go to the head of the class and don't waste your time and money following such pundits' picks! (I discuss investment newsletters in Chapter 8 and Web sites in Chapter 19.)

✔ **Book authors:** Go into any bookstore with a decent-sized investing section and you'll find plenty of books claiming that they can teach you a stock-picking strategy for beating the system. Never mind the fact that the author has no independently audited track demonstrating his success! The book publisher of at least one investment group was successfully sued over hyping and distorting the group's actual investment success.

✔ **Stockbrokers:** Some brokers steer you toward individual stocks for several reasons that benefit the broker and not you. First, as I discuss in Chapter 8, the high-commission brokerage firms can make handsome profits for themselves by getting you to buy stocks. Secondly, brokers can use changes in the company's situation to encourage you to then sell and buy different stocks, generating even more commissions. Lastly, as with newsletter writers, this whole process forces you to be dependent on the broker, leaving you broker!

Researching individual stocks can be more than a full-time job, and if you choose to take this path, remember that you'll be competing against the professionals who do so on a full-time basis. If you derive pleasure from picking and following your own stocks, or you want an independent opinion of some stocks you currently own, useful research reports are available from Value Line (800-833-0046) and Morningstar's Web site (www.morningstar.com). I also recommend that you limit your individual stock picking to no more than 20 percent of your overall investments.

Individual stock dividend reinvestment plans

Many corporations allow existing shareholders to reinvest their dividends (their share in company profits) in more shares of stock without paying brokerage commissions. In some cases, companies allow you to make additional cash purchases of more shares of stock, also commission-free.

In order to qualify, you must first generally buy some shares of stock through a broker (although some companies allow the initial purchases to be made directly from them). Ideally, you should purchase these initial shares through a discount broker to keep your commission burden as low as possible.

Some investment associations also have plans that allow you to buy one or just a few shares to get started. I'm not enamored of these plans, because this type of investing is generally available and cost-effective for investments held only outside retirement accounts. You typically need to complete a lot of paperwork to invest in a number of different companies' stock. Life is too short to bother with these plans for this reason alone.

Finally, even with those companies that do sell stock directly without charging an explicit commission like a brokerage firm, you pay plenty of other fees. Many plans charge an upfront enrollment fee, fees for reinvesting dividends, and a fee when you want to sell.

Generating wealth with real estate

Over the generations, real estate owners and investors have enjoyed rates of return comparable to those produced by the stock market, thus making real estate another time-tested method for building wealth. However, like stocks, real estate goes through good and bad performance periods. Most people who make money investing in real estate do so because they invest over many years.

Buying your own home is the best place to start investing in real estate. The *equity* (the difference between the market value of the home and the loan owed on it) in your home that builds over the years can become a significant part of your net worth. Among other things, this equity can be tapped into to help finance other important money and personal goals, such as retirement, college, and starting or buying a business. Moreover, throughout your adult life, owning a home should be less expensive than renting a comparable home. See Chapter 14 for the best ways to buy and finance real estate.

Real estate: Not your ordinary investment

Besides providing solid rates of return, real estate also differs from most other investments in several other respects. Here's what makes real estate unique as an investment:

✔ **Usability:** You can't live in a stock, bond, or mutual fund (although I suppose you could glue together a substantial fortress with all the paper these companies fill your mailbox with each year). Real estate is the only investment you can use (living in or renting out) to produce income.

✔ **Land is in limited supply:** Last time I checked, the percentage of the Earth occupied by land wasn't increasing (actually, land mass is shrinking with the melting of the polar ice caps). And because humans like to reproduce, the demand for land and housing continues to grow. Consider the areas that have the most expensive real estate prices in the world — Hong Kong, Tokyo, Hawaii, San Francisco, and Manhattan. In these densely populated areas, virtually no new land is available for building new housing.

✔ **Zoning shapes potential value:** Local government regulates the zoning of property, and zoning determines what a property can be used for. In most communities these days, local zoning boards are against big growth. This position bodes well for future real estate values. Also know that in some cases, a particular property may not have been developed to its full potential. If you can figure out how to develop the property, you can reap large profits.

✔ **Leverage:** Real estate is also different from other investments because you can borrow a lot of money to buy it — up to 80 to 90 percent or more of the value of the property. This borrowing is known as exercising *leverage:* With only a small investment of 10 to 20 percent down, you're able to purchase and own a much larger investment. When the value of your real estate goes up, you make money on your investment and on all the money you borrowed. (In case you're curious, you can leverage non-retirement-account stock and bond investments through margin borrowing. However, you have to make a much larger "down payment" — about double to triple when compared with buying real estate.)

For example, suppose that you plunk down $20,000 to purchase a property for $100,000. If the property appreciates to $120,000, you make a profit of $20,000 (on paper) on your investment of just $20,000. In other words, you make a 100 percent return on your investment. But leverage cuts both ways. If your $100,000 property decreases in value to $80,000, you actually lose (on paper) 100 percent of your original $20,000 investment, even though the property value drops only 20 percent in value.

✔ **Hidden values:** In an *efficient market,* the price of an investment accurately reflects its true worth. Some investment markets are more efficient than others because of the large number of transactions and easily accessible information. Real estate markets can be inefficient at times. Information is not always easy to come by, and you may find an ultramotivated or uninformed seller. If you're willing to do some homework, you may be able to purchase a property below its fair market value (perhaps by as much as 10 to 20 percent).

Just as with any other investment, real estate has its drawbacks. For starters, buying or selling a property generally takes time and significant cost. When you're renting property, you discover firsthand the occasional headaches of being a landlord. And especially in the early years of rental property ownership, the property's expenses may exceed the rental income, producing a net cash drain.

The best real estate investment options

Although real estate is in some ways unique, it's also like other types of investments in that prices are driven by supply and demand. You can invest in homes or small apartment buildings and then rent them out. In the long run, investment-property buyers hope that their rent income and the value of their properties will increase faster than their expenses.

Comparing real estate and stocks

Real estate and stocks have historically produced comparable returns. Deciding between the two depends less on the performance of the markets than on you and your situation. Consider the following major issues when deciding which investment may be better for you:

✔ The first and most important question to ask yourself is whether you're cut out to handle the responsibilities that come with being a landlord. Real estate is a time-intensive investment (a property manager can help, but their cost takes a sizable chunk of your rental income). Investing in stocks can be time-intensive as well, but it doesn't have to be if you use professionally managed mutual funds (see Chapter 10).

✔ An often-overlooked drawback to investing in real estate is that you earn no tax benefits while you're accumulating your down payment. Retirement accounts such as 401(k)s, SEP-IRAs, Keoghs, and so on (see Chapter 11) give you an immediate tax deduction as you contribute money to them. If you haven't exhausted your contributions to these accounts, consider doing so before chasing after investment real estate.

✔ Ask yourself which investments you have a better understanding of. Some folks feel uncomfortable with stocks and mutual funds because they don't understand them. If you have a better handle on what makes real estate tick, you have a good reason to consider investing in it.

✔ Figure out what will make you happy. Some people enjoy the challenge that comes with managing and improving rental property; it can be a bit like running a small business. If you're good at it and you have some good fortune, you can make money and derive endless hours of enjoyment.

Although few will admit it, some real estate investors get an ego rush from a tangible display of their wealth. Sufferers of this "edifice complex" can't obtain similar pleasure from a stock portfolio detailed on a piece of paper (although others have been known to boast of their stock-picking prowess).

When selecting real estate for investment purposes, remember that local economic growth is the fuel for housing demand. In addition to a vibrant and diverse job base, you want to look for limited supplies of both existing housing and land on which to build. When you identify potential properties in which you may want to invest, run the numbers to understand the cash demands of owning the property and the likely profitability. See Chapter 14 for help determining the costs of real estate ownership.

When you want to invest directly in real estate, residential housing — such as single-family homes or small multi-unit buildings — may be an attractive investment. Buying properties close to "home" offers the advantage of allowing you to more easily monitor and manage what's going on. The downside is that you'll be less diversified — more of your investments will be dependent on the local economy.

If you don't want to be a landlord — one of the biggest drawbacks of investment real estate — consider investing in real estate through real estate investment trusts (REITs). *REITs* are diversified real estate investment companies that purchase and manage rental real estate for investors. A typical REIT invests in different types of property, such as shopping centers, apartments, and other rental buildings. You can invest in REITs either by purchasing them directly on the major stock exchanges or by investing in a real estate mutual fund (see Chapter 10) that invests in numerous REITs.

The worst real estate investments

Not all real estate investments are good; some aren't even real investments. The bad ones are characterized by burdensome costs and problematic economic fundamentals:

- **Limited partnerships:** Avoid limited partnerships (LPs) sold through brokers and financial consultants. LPs are inferior investment vehicles. They're so burdened with high sales commissions and ongoing management fees that deplete your investment that you can do better elsewhere. The investment salesperson who sells you such an investment stands to earn a commission of up to 10 percent or more — so only 90 cents of each dollar gets invested. Each year, LPs typically siphon off another several percent for management and other expenses. Most partnerships have little or no incentive to control costs. In fact, they have a conflict of interest that forces them to charge more to enrich the managing partners.

  Unlike a mutual fund, you can't vote with your dollars. If the partnership is poorly run and expensive, you're stuck. LPs are *illiquid* (not readily convertible into cash without a substantial loss). You can't access your money until the partnership is liquidated, typically seven to ten years after you buy in.

Brokers who sell LPs often tell you that while your investment is growing at 20 percent or more per year, you get handsome dividends of 8 percent or so annually. Many of the yields on LPs have turned out to be bogus. In some cases, partnerships prop up their yields by paying back investors' principals (without telling them, of course). As for returns — well — most LP investors of a decade ago are lucky to have half their original investment left. The only thing limited about a limited partnership is its ability to make you money.

✔ **Time shares:** Time shares are another nearly certain money loser. With a time share, you buy a week or two of ownership, or usage, of a particular unit (usually a condominium in a resort location) per year. If, for example, you pay $8,000 for a week (in addition to ongoing maintenance fees), you're paying the equivalent of more than $400,000 for the whole unit, when a comparable unit nearby may sell for only $150,000. The extra markup pays the salespeople's commissions, administrative expenses, and profits for the time share development company.

People usually get enticed into buying a time share when they're enjoying a vacation someplace. They're easy prey for salespeople who want to sell them a souvenir of the trip. The "cheese in the mousetrap" is an offer of something free (for example, a free night's stay in a unit) for going through the sales presentation.

If you can't live without a time share, consider buying a used one. Many previous buyers, who more than likely have lost a good chunk of money, are trying to dump their shares (which should tell you something). In this case, you may be able to buy a time share at a fair price. But why commit yourself to taking a vacation in the same location and building at the same time each year? Many time shares let you trade your weeks for other times and other places; however, doing so is a hassle — you're charged an extra fee, and your choices are usually limited to time slots that other people don't want (that's why they're trading them!).

✔ **Second homes:** The weekend getaway is a sometimes romantic notion and an extended part of the so-called American dream — a place you can escape to a couple of times a month. When your vacation home is not in use, you may be able to rent it out and earn some income to help defray the expense of keeping it up.

If you can realistically afford the additional costs of a second (or vacation) home, I'm not going to tell you how to spend your extra cash. But please don't make the all-too-common mistake of viewing a second home as an investment. The way most people use them, they're not. Most second-home owners seldom rent out their property — they typically do so 10 percent or less of the time. As a result, second homes are usually money drains.

The supposed tax benefits are part of the attraction of a second home. Even when you qualify for some or all of them, tax benefits only partially reduce the cost of owning a property. In some cases, the second home is such a cash drain that it prevents its owners from contributing to and taking advantage of tax-deductible retirement savings plans.

If you aren't going to rent out a second home most of the time, ask yourself whether you can afford such a luxury. Can you accomplish your other financial goals — saving for retirement, paying for the home in which you live, and so on — with this added expense? Keeping a second home is more of a consumption than investment decision. Few people can afford more than one home.

Investing in small business (and your career)

With what type of investment have people built the greatest wealth? If you said the stock market or real estate, you're wrong. The answer is small business. You can invest in small business by starting one yourself (and thus finding yourself the best boss you've probably ever had), buying an existing business, or investing in someone else's small business. Even if small business doesn't interest you, your own job should, so I present some tips on making the most of your career.

Launching your own enterprise

When you have self-discipline and a product or service you can sell, starting your own business can be both profitable and fulfilling. Consider first what skills and expertise you possess that you can use in your business. You don't need a "eureka"-type idea or invention to start a small business. Millions of people operate successful businesses that are hardly unique, such as dry cleaners, restaurants, tax preparation firms, and so on.

Begin exploring your idea by first developing a written business plan. Such a plan should detail your product or service, how you're going to market it, your potential customers and competitors, and the economics of the business, including the start-up costs.

Of all the small-business investment options, starting your own business involves the most work. Although you can do this work on a part-time basis in the beginning, most people end up running their business full-time — it's your new job, career, or whatever you want to call it.

I've been running my own business for most of my working years, and I wouldn't trade that experience for the corporate life. That's not to say that running my own business doesn't have its drawbacks and down moments. But in my experience counseling small-business owners, I've seen many people of varied backgrounds, interests, and skills succeed and be happy with running their own businesses.

In most people's eyes, starting a new business is the riskiest of all small-business investment options. But if you're going into a business that uses your skills and expertise, the risk isn't nearly as great as you may think. Many businesses can be started with little cash by leveraging your existing skills and expertise. You can build a valuable company and job if you have the time to devote. As long as you check out the competition and offer a valued service at a reasonable cost, the principal risk with your business comes from not doing a good job marketing what you have to offer. If you can market your skills, you're home free.

As long as you're thinking about the risks of starting a business, consider the risks of staying in a job you don't enjoy or that doesn't challenge or fulfill you. If you never take the plunge, you may regret that you didn't pursue your dreams.

Buying an existing business

If you don't have a specific product or service you want to sell but you're skilled at managing and improving the operations of a company, buying a small business may be for you. Finding and buying a good small business takes much time and patience, so be willing to devote at least several months to the search. You may also need to enlist financial and legal advisors to help inspect the company, look over its financial statements, and hammer out a contract.

Although you don't have to go through the riskier start-up period if you buy a small business, you'll likely need more capital to buy an established enterprise. You'll also need to be able to deal with stickier personnel and management issues. The history of the organization and the way things work will predate your ownership of the business. If you don't like making hard decisions, firing people who don't fit with your plans, and coercing people into changing the way they do things, buying an existing business likely isn't for you.

Some people perceive buying an existing business as being safer than starting a new one. Buying someone else's business can actually be riskier. You're likely to shell out far more money upfront, in the form of a down payment, to buy an existing business. If you don't have the ability to run the business and it does poorly, you have more to lose financially. In addition, the business may be for sale for a reason — it may not be very profitable, it may be in decline, or it may generally be a pain in the neck to operate.

Good businesses don't come cheap. If the business is a success, the current owner has already removed the start-up risk from the business, so the price of the business should be at a premium to reflect this lack of risk. When you have the capital to buy an established business and you have the skills to run it, consider going this route.

Investing in someone else's small business

Are you someone who likes the idea of profiting from successful small businesses but doesn't want the day-to-day headaches of being responsible for managing the enterprise? Then investing in someone else's small business may be for you. Although this route may seem easier, few people are actually cut out to be investors in other people's businesses. The reason: Finding and analyzing opportunities isn't easy.

Are you astute at evaluating corporate financial statements and business strategies? Investing in a small, privately held company has much in common with investing in a publicly traded firm (as is the case when you buy stock), but it also has a few differences. One difference is that private firms aren't required to produce comprehensive, audited financial statements that adhere to certain accounting principles. Thus, you have a greater risk of not having sufficient or accurate information when evaluating a small private firm.

Another difference is that unearthing private small-business investing opportunities is harder. The best private companies who are seeking investors generally don't advertise. Instead, they find prospective investors through networking with people such as business advisors. You can increase your chances of finding private companies to invest in by speaking with tax, legal, and financial advisors who work with small businesses. You can also find interesting opportunities through your own contacts or experience within a given industry.

Don't consider investing in someone else's business unless you can afford to lose all of what you're investing. Also, you should have sufficient assets so that what you're investing in small, privately held companies represents only a small portion (20 percent or less) of your total financial assets.

Investing in your career

In my work with financial counseling clients over the years and from observing friends and colleagues, I've witnessed plenty of people succeed working for employers. So I don't want to leave you with the impression that financial success equates with starting, buying, or investing in someone else's small business.

You can and should invest in your career. Some time-tested, proven ways to do that include

- ✔ **Networking:** Some people wait to network until they've been laid off or are really hungry to change jobs. Take an interest in what others do for a living and you'll learn and grow from the experience, even if you choose to stay with your current employer or in your chosen field.

- ✔ **Making sure you keep learning:** Whether it's reading quality books or other publications or taking some night courses, find ways to build on your knowledge base.

- ✔ **Considering the risk in the status quo:** Many folks are resistant to change and get anxious thinking about what could go wrong when taking a new risk. I know when I was ready to walk away from a six-figure consulting job with a prestigious firm and open my own financial counseling firm, a number of my relatives and friends thought I had lost my marbles. I'm glad I didn't listen to their fears and worries!

Off the Beaten Path: Investment Odds and Ends

The investments that I discuss in this section sometimes belong on their own planet (because they're not an ownership or lending vehicle). Here are the basics on these other common, but odd, investments.

Precious metals

Gold and silver have been used by many civilizations as currency or a medium of exchange. One advantage of precious metals as a currency is that they can't be debased by the government. With paper currency, such as U.S. dollars, the government can simply print more. This process can lead to the devaluation of a currency and inflation. It takes a whole lot more work to make more gold. Just ask Rumpelstiltskin.

Holdings of gold and silver can provide a so-called *hedge* against inflation. In the late 1970s and early 1980s, inflation rose dramatically in the United States. This largely unexpected rise in inflation depressed stocks and bonds. Gold and silver, however, rose tremendously in value — in fact, more than 500 percent (even after adjusting for inflation) from 1972 to 1980 (see Chapter 8). Such periods are unusual. Precious metals have produced decent returns in the early and mid 2000s. Over many decades, precious metals tend to be lousy investments. Their rate of return tends to keep up with the rate of inflation but not surpass it.

When you want to invest in precious metals as an inflation hedge, your best option is to do so through mutual funds (see Chapter 10). Don't purchase precious metals futures. They're not investments; they're short-term gambles on which way gold or silver prices may head over a short period of time. You should also stay away from firms and shops that sell coins and *bullion* (not the soup, but bars of gold or silver). Even if you can find a legitimate firm (not an easy task), the cost of storing and insuring gold and silver is quite costly. You won't get good value for your money. I hate to tell you this, but the Gold Rush is over.

Annuities

Annuities are a peculiar type of insurance and investment product. They're a sort of savings-type account with slightly higher yields that are backed by insurance companies.

As with other types of retirement accounts, money placed in an annuity compounds without taxation until it's withdrawn. However, unlike most other types of retirement accounts, such as 401(k)s, SEP-IRAs, and Keoghs, you don't receive upfront tax breaks on contributions you make to an annuity. Ongoing investment expenses also tend to be much higher than in retirement plan accounts. Therefore, consider an annuity only after you fully fund tax-deductible retirement accounts. (For more help on deciding whether to invest in an annuity, read Chapter 12.)

Collectibles

The collectibles category is a catchall for antiques, art, autographs, baseball cards, clocks, coins, comic books, diamonds, dolls, gems, photographs, rare books, rugs, stamps, vintage wine, and writing utensils — in other words, any material object that, through some kind of human manipulation, has become more valuable to certain humans.

Notwithstanding the few people who discover on the *Antiques Roadshow* that they own an antique of significant value, collectibles are generally lousy investment vehicles. Dealer markups are enormous, maintenance and protection costs are draining, research is time-consuming, and people's tastes are quite fickle. All this for returns that, after you factor in the huge markups, rarely keep up with inflation.

Buy collectibles for your love of the object, not for financial gain. Treat collecting as a hobby, not as an investment. When buying a collectible, try to avoid the big markups by cutting out the middlemen. Buy directly from the artist or producer if you can.

Chapter 10

Investing in Mutual Funds

· ·

· ·

*W*hen you invest in a mutual fund, an investment company pools your money with the money of many other like-minded individuals and invests it in stocks, bonds, and other securities. Think of it as a big investment club without the meetings! When you invest through a typical mutual fund, several hundred million to billions of dollars may be invested along with your money.

If you're thinking of joining the club, read on to discover the benefits of investing in mutual funds and the types of funds available. In this chapter, I advise you on analyzing and choosing your funds, explain how to track your investments, and help you decide when to sell.

Understanding the Benefits of Mutual Funds

Mutual funds rank right up there with microwave ovens, sticky notes, and plastic wrap as one of the best modern inventions. To understand their success is to grasp how and why funds can work for you. Here are the benefits you receive when you invest in mutual funds:

✓ **Professional management:** Mutual funds are managed by a portfolio manager and research team whose full-time jobs are to screen the universe of investments for those that best meet the stated objectives of the fund.

These professionals call and visit companies, analyze companies' financial statements, and speak with companies' suppliers and customers. In short, the team does more research and analysis than you could ever hope to do in your free time.

Fund managers are typically graduates of the top business and finance schools in the country, where they learn the principles of portfolio management and securities valuation and selection. The best fund managers typically have a decade of experience or more in analyzing and selecting investments, and many measure their experience in decades rather than years.

✔ **Low cost:** The most-efficiently managed stock mutual funds cost less than 1 percent per year in fees (bonds and money market funds cost much less). Because mutual funds typically buy or sell tens of thousands of shares of a security at a time, the percentage commissions these funds pay are far less than what you pay to buy or sell a few hundred shares on your own. In addition, when you buy a *no-load fund,* you avoid paying sales commissions (known as *loads*) on your transactions. I discuss these types of funds throughout this chapter.

✔ **Diversification:** Mutual fund investing enables you to achieve a level of diversification that is difficult to reach without tens of thousands of dollars and a lot of time to invest. If you go it alone, you should invest money in at least 8 to 12 different securities in different industries to ensure that your portfolio can withstand a downturn in one or more of the investments. Proper diversification allows a mutual fund to receive the highest possible return at the lowest possible risk given its objectives. The most unfortunate investors during major stock market downswings have been individuals who had all their money riding on only a few stocks that plunged in price by 90 percent or more.

✔ **Low cost of entry:** Most mutual funds have low minimum-investment requirements, especially for retirement account investors. Even if you have a lot of money to invest, you should also consider mutual funds. Join the increasing numbers of companies and institutions (who have the biggest bucks of all) that are turning to the low-cost, high-quality, money-management services that mutual funds provide.

✔ **Audited performance records and expenses:** In their prospectuses, all mutual funds are required to disclose historical data on returns, operating expenses, and other fees. The Securities and Exchange Commission (SEC) and accounting firms check these disclosures for accuracy. Also, several firms (such as Morningstar, Inc.) report hundreds of fund statistics, allowing comparisons of performance, risk, and many other factors.

✔ **Flexibility in risk level:** Among the different mutual funds, you can choose a level of risk that you're comfortable with and that meets your personal and financial goals. If you want your money to grow over a long period of time, you may want to select funds that invest more heavily in stocks. If you need current income and don't want investments that fluctuate in value as widely as stocks, you may choose more-conservative bond funds. If you want to be sure that your invested principal doesn't drop in value (perhaps because you may need your money in the short term), you can select a money market fund.

Exploring Various Fund Types

One of the major misconceptions about mutual funds is that they're all invested in stocks. They're not. Figure 10-1 shows how the money currently invested in mutual funds breaks down.

As you can see, much (about 40 percent) of mutual fund money is *not* invested in stocks. When you hear folks talk about the "riskiness" of mutual funds, even in the media, you know that they're overlooking this fact: All mutual funds are not created equal. Some funds, such as money market funds, carry virtually no risk that your investment will decline in value.

When mutual fund companies package and market funds, the names they give their funds aren't always completely accurate or comprehensive. For example, a stock fund may not be *totally* invested in stocks. Twenty percent of it may be invested in bonds. Don't assume that a fund invests exclusively in U.S. companies, either — it may invest in international firms, as well.

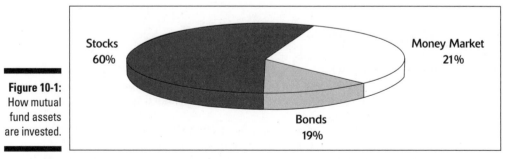

Figure 10-1:
How mutual
fund assets
are invested.

Stocks
60%

Money Market
21%

Bonds
19%

Note: If you haven't yet read Chapters 8 and 9, which provide an overview of investment concepts and vehicles, doing so can enhance your understanding of the rest of this chapter.

Money market funds

Money market funds are the safest type of mutual funds for people concerned about losing their invested dollars. As with bank savings accounts, the value of your original investment does not fluctuate. (For more background on the advantages of money funds, see Chapter 9.)

These funds are closely regulated by the U.S. Securities and Exchange Commission. Hundreds of billions of dollars of individuals' and institutions' money are invested in hundreds of money market funds. The industry has never caused an individual to lose even a penny of principal.

Money market funds are extremely safe. The risk difference versus a bank account is nil. General purpose money market funds invest in safe, short-term bank certificates of deposit, U.S. Treasuries, and *corporate commercial paper* (short-term debt), which is issued by the largest and most creditworthy companies.

Money market fund investments can exist only in the most creditworthy securities and must have an average maturity of less than 120 days. In the unlikely event that an investment in a money market fund's portfolio goes sour, the mutual fund company that stands behind the money market fund will almost certainly cover the loss.

If the lack of insurance on money market funds still spooks you, select a money market fund that invests exclusively in U.S. government securities, which are virtually risk-free because they're backed by the full strength and credit of the federal government (as is the FDIC insurance system). These types of accounts typically pay less interest (usually ¼ percent less), although the interest is free of state income tax.

Bond funds

Bonds are IOUs. When you buy a newly issued bond, you lend your money typically to a corporation or government agency. A *bond mutual fund* is nothing more than a large group (pack, herd, gaggle, whatever) of bonds.

Bond funds typically invest in bonds of similar *maturity* (the number of years that elapse before the borrower must pay back the money you lend). The names of most bond funds include a word or two that provides clues about the average length of maturity of their bonds. For example, a *short-term bond fund* typically concentrates its investments in bonds maturing in the next two to three years. An *intermediate-term fund* generally holds bonds that come due within three to ten years. The bonds in a *long-term fund* usually mature in more than ten years.

In contrast to an individual bond that you buy and hold until it matures, a bond fund is always replacing bonds in its portfolio to maintain its average maturity objective. Therefore, if you know that you absolutely, positively must have a certain principal amount back on a particular date, individual bonds may be more appropriate than a bond fund.

Like money market funds, bond funds can invest in tax-free bonds, which are appropriate for investing money you hold outside retirement accounts if you're in a reasonably high tax bracket.

Bond funds are useful when you want to live off dividend income or you don't want to put all your money in riskier investments such as stocks and real estate (perhaps because you plan to use the money soon).

Stock funds

Stock mutual funds, as their name implies, invest in stocks. These funds are often referred to as *equity funds. Equity* — not to be confused with equity in real estate — is another word for stocks. Stock mutual funds are often categorized by the type of stocks they primarily invest in.

Stock types are first defined by size of company (small, medium, or large). The total market value *(capitalization)* of a company's outstanding stock determines its size. Small-company stocks, for example, are usually defined as companies with total market capitalization of less than $1 billion.

Stocks are further categorized as growth or value. *Growth stocks* represent companies that are experiencing rapidly expanding revenues and profits and typically have high stock prices relative to their current earnings or asset (book) values. These companies tend to reinvest most of their earnings back into their infrastructure to fuel future expansion. Thus, growth stocks typically pay low dividends. (See the later "Dividends" section for more information.)

Value stocks are at the other end of the spectrum. Value stock investors look for good buys. They want to invest in stocks that are cheaply priced in relation to the profits per share and book value (assets less liabilities) of the company. Value stocks are usually less volatile than growth stocks.

These categories are combined in various ways to describe how a mutual fund invests its money. One fund may focus on large-company growth stocks, while another fund may limit itself to small-company value stocks. Funds are further classified by the geographical focus of their investments: U.S., international, worldwide, and so on (see the section "U.S., international, and global funds").

Balancing bonds and stocks: Hybrid funds

Hybrid funds invest in a mixture of different types of securities. Most commonly, they invest in bonds and stocks. These funds are usually less risky and volatile than funds that invest exclusively in stocks. In an economic downturn, bonds usually hold up in value better than stocks do. However, during good economic times when the stock market is booming, the bond portions of these funds tend to drag down their performance a bit.

Hybrid mutual funds are typically known as balanced funds or asset allocation funds. *Balanced funds* generally try to maintain a fairly constant percentage of investments in stocks and bonds. *Asset allocation funds* tend to adjust the mix of different investments according to the portfolio manager's expectations of the market. Of course, exceptions do exist — some balanced funds make major shifts in their allocations, whereas some asset allocation funds maintain a relatively fixed mix. You should note that most funds that shift money around instead of staying put in good investments rarely beat the market averages over a number of years.

Hybrid funds are a way to make fund investing simple. They give you instant diversification across a variety of investing options. They also make it easier for stock-skittish investors to invest in stocks while avoiding the high volatility of pure stock funds.

U.S., international, and global funds

Unless they have words like *international, global, worldwide,* or *world* in their names, most funds focus their investments in the United States. But even funds without one of these terms attached may invest money internationally.

The only way to know for sure where a fund is currently invested (or where the fund may invest in the future) is to ask. You can start by calling the toll-free number of the mutual fund company you're interested in. A fund's annual report (which often can be found on the fund company's Web site) also details where the fund is investing.

When a fund has the term *international* in its name, it typically means that the fund can invest anywhere in the world except the United States. The term *worldwide* or *global* generally implies that a fund invests anywhere in the world, including the United States. I generally recommend avoiding worldwide or global funds for two reasons. First, thoroughly following the financial markets and companies is hard enough for a fund manager to do solely in the United States or a specific international market; following the markets and companies in both is even more difficult. Second, most of these funds charge high operating expenses — often well in excess of 1 percent per year — which puts a drag on returns.

Funds of funds

An increasing number of fund providers are responding to overwhelmed investors by offering a simplified way to construct a portfolio: a mutual fund that diversifies across numerous other mutual funds — or a *fund of funds*. When a fund of funds is done right, it helps focus fund investors on the important big-picture issue of asset allocation — how much of your investment money you put into bonds versus stocks.

Although the best funds of funds appear to deliver a high-quality, diversified portfolio of funds in one fell swoop, funds of funds are not all created equal and not all are worthy of your investment dollars.

The fund of funds idea is not new. In fact, the concept has been around many years. High fees gave the earlier funds of funds, run in the 1950s by the late Bernie Cornfeld, a bad name.

He established a fund of funds outside the United States and tacked on many layers of fees. Although the funds were profitable for his enterprise, duped investors suffered a continual drain of high fees. The Cornfeld episode is an important reason why the Securities and Exchange Commission has been careful in approving new funds of funds.

The "newer" funds of funds developed by the larger fund companies are investor friendly and ones that I recommend. Vanguard's LifeStrategy, Fidelity's Freedom, and T. Rowe Price's Spectrum funds of funds add no extra fees for packaging together the individual funds. Long-term performance of many of these is solid. Annual operating fees on the underlying funds at Vanguard are less than 0.3 percent.

Index funds

Index funds are funds that can be (and are, for the most part) managed by a computer. An index fund's assets are invested to replicate an existing market index such as Standard & Poor's 500, an index of 500 large U.S. company stocks. (***Important note:*** In Chapters 11 and 12, I recommend and prefer, for its better diversification, a total U.S. stock market index fund over the S&P 500 index fund.)

Over long periods (ten years or more), index funds outperform about three-quarters of their peers! How is that possible? How can a computer making mindless, predictable decisions beat an intelligent, creative, MBA-endowed portfolio manager with a crack team of research analysts scouring the market for the best securities? The answer is largely cost. The computer does not demand a high salary or need a big corner office. And index funds don't need a team of research analysts.

Most active fund managers can't overcome the handicap of high operating expenses that pull down their funds' rates of return. As I discuss later in this chapter, operating expenses include all the fees and profit that a mutual fund extracts from a fund's returns before the returns are paid to you. For example, the average U.S. stock fund has an operating expense ratio of 1.4 percent per year. So a U.S. stock index fund with an expense ratio of just 0.2 percent per year has an advantage of 1.2 percent per year.

Another not-so-inconsequential advantage of index funds is that you can't underperform the market. Some funds do just that because of the burden of high fees and/or poor management. For money invested outside retirement accounts, index funds have an added advantage: Lower taxable-capital-gains distributions are made to shareholders because less trading of securities is conducted and a more stable portfolio is maintained.

Yes, index funds may seem downright boring. When you invest in them, you give up the opportunity to brag to others about your shrewd investments that beat the market averages. On the other hand, with a low-cost index fund, you have no chance of doing much worse than the market (which more than a few mutual fund managers do).

Index funds make sense for a portion of your investments, because beating the market is difficult for portfolio managers. The Vanguard Group (800-662-7447, www.vanguard.com), headquartered in Valley Forge, Pennsylvania, is the largest and lowest-cost mutual-fund provider of index funds.

Specialty (sector) funds

Specialty funds don't fit neatly into the previous categories. These funds are often known as *sector funds*, because they tend to invest in securities in specific industries.

Socially responsible funds

Select mutual funds label themselves *socially responsible.* This term means different things to different people. In most cases, though, it implies that the fund avoids investing in companies whose products or services harm people or the world at large — tobacco manufacturers, for example. Because cigarettes and other tobacco products kill hundreds of thousands of people and add billions of dollars to health care costs, most socially responsible funds shun tobacco companies.

Socially responsible investing presents challenges. For example, your definition of social responsibility may not match the definition offered by the investment manager who's running a fund. Another problem is that even if you can agree on what's socially irresponsible (such as selling tobacco products), funds aren't always as clean as you would think or hope. Even though a fund avoids tobacco manufacturers, it may well invest in retailers that sell tobacco products.

If you want to consider a socially responsible fund, review the fund's recent annual report that lists the specific investments the fund owns. Also consider giving directly to charities (and getting a tax deduction) instead.

In most cases, you should avoid investing in specialty funds. Investing in stocks of a single industry defeats one of the major purposes of investing in mutual funds — diversification. Another good reason to avoid specialty funds is that they tend to carry much higher expenses than other mutual funds.

Specialty funds that invest in real estate or precious metals may make sense for a small portion (10 percent or less) of your investment portfolio. These types of funds can help diversify your portfolio, because they can do better during times of higher inflation.

Selecting the Best Mutual Funds

When you go camping in the wilderness, you can do a number of things to maximize your chances for happiness and success. You can take maps to keep you on course, food for nourishment, proper clothing to stay dry and warm, and some first-aid gear to treat minor injuries. But regardless of how much advance preparation you do, you may have a problematic experience. You may take the wrong trail, trip on a rock and break your ankle, or lose your food to a tenacious bear that comes romping through camp one night.

And so it is with mutual funds. Although most mutual fund investors are rewarded for their efforts, you get no guarantees. You can, however, follow some simple, common-sense guidelines to help keep you on the trail and increase your odds of investment success and happiness. The issues in the following sections are the main ones to consider.

Reading prospectuses and annual reports

Mutual fund companies produce information that can help you make decisions about mutual fund investments. Every fund is required to issue a *prospectus*. This legal document is reviewed and audited by the U.S. Securities and Exchange Commission. Most of what's written isn't worth the time it takes to slog through it.

The most valuable information — the fund's investment objectives, costs, and performance history — is summarized in the first few pages of the prospectus. Make sure that you read this part. Skip the rest, which is comprised mostly of tedious legal details.

Funds also produce *annual reports* that discuss how the fund has been doing and provide details on the specific investments a fund holds. If, for example, you want to know which countries an international fund invests in, you can find this information in the fund's annual report.

Keeping costs low

The charges you pay to buy or sell a fund, as well as the ongoing fund operating expenses, can have a big impact on the rate of return you earn on your investments. Many novice investors pay too much attention to a mutual fund's prior performance (in the case of stock funds) or to the fund's current yield (in the case of bond funds). Doing so is dangerous because a fund can inflate its return or yield in many (risky) ways. And what worked yesterday may flop tomorrow.

A study conducted by the Investment Company Institute confirms what I've long observed among fund buyers: Only 43 percent of fund buyers who were surveyed bothered to examine the fees and expenses of the fund they ended up buying. The majority of fund buyers — 57 percent, to be exact — didn't know what the funds were charging them to manage their money!

Fund costs are an important factor in the return you earn from a mutual fund. Fees are deducted from your investment. All other things being equal, high fees and other charges depress your returns. What are a fund's fees, you ask? Good question — read on to find the answers.

Eliminating loads

Loads are upfront commissions paid to brokers who sell mutual funds. Loads typically range from 3 percent to as high as 8.5 percent of your investment. (An astonishing 73 percent of fund buyers surveyed by the Investment Company Institute didn't know whether the fund they bought charged a sales load!) Sales loads have two problems:

✔ **Sales loads are a needless cost that drags down your investment returns.** Because commissions are paid to the salesperson and not to the fund manager, the manager of a load fund doesn't work any harder and isn't any more qualified than a manager of a no-load fund. Common sense suggests, and studies confirm, that load funds perform *worse,* on average, than no-loads when factoring in the load because the load charge is subtracted from your payment before being invested.

✔ **The power of self-interest can bias your broker's advice.** Although this issue is rarely discussed, it's even more problematic than the issue of extra sales costs. Brokers who work for a commission are interested in selling you commission-based investment products; therefore, their best interests often conflict with your best interests.

Although you may be mired in high-interest debt or underfunding your retirement plan, salespeople almost never advise you to pay off your credit cards or put more money into your 401(k). To get you to buy, they tend to exaggerate the potential benefits and obscure the risks and drawbacks of what they sell. They don't take the time to educate investors. I've seen too many people purchase investment products through brokers without understanding what they're buying, how much risk they're taking, and how these investments will affect their overall financial lives.

Invest in no-load (commission-free) funds. The only way to be sure that a fund is truly no-load is to look at the prospectus for the fund. Only there, in black and white and without marketing hype, must the truth be told about sales charges and other fund fees. When you want investing advice, hire a financial advisor on a fee-for-service basis (see Chapter 18), which should cost less and minimize potential conflicts of interest.

Decreasing operating expenses

All mutual funds charge ongoing fees. The fees pay for the operational costs of running the fund — employees' salaries, marketing, servicing the toll-free phone lines, printing and mailing published materials, computers for tracking investments and account balances, accounting fees, and so on. Despite being labeled "expenses," the profit a fund company extracts for running the fund is added to the tab, as well.

The fund's operating expenses are quoted as an annual percentage of your investment and are essentially invisible to you, because they're deducted before you're paid any return. The expenses are charged on a daily basis, so you don't need to worry about trying to get out of a fund before these fees are deducted.

You can find a fund's operating expenses in the fund's prospectus. Look in the expenses section and find a line that says something like "Total Fund Operating Expenses." You can also call the fund's toll-free number and ask a representative.

Within a given sector of mutual funds (for example, money market, short-term bonds, or international stock), funds with low annual operating fees can more easily produce higher total returns for you. Although expenses matter on all funds, some types of funds are more sensitive to high expenses than others. Expenses are critical on money market mutual funds and very important on bond funds. Fund managers already have a hard time beating the averages in these markets; with higher expenses added on, beating the averages is nearly impossible.

With stock funds, expenses are a less important (but still significant) factor in a fund's performance. Don't forget that, over time, stocks average returns of about 10 percent per year. So if one stock fund charges 1 percent more in operating expenses than another fund, you're already giving up an extra 10 percent of your expected returns.

Some people argue that stock funds that charge high expenses may be justified in doing so if they generate higher rates of return. Evidence doesn't show that these stock funds actually generate higher returns. In fact, funds with higher operating expenses tend to produce *lower* rates of return. This trend makes sense, because operating expenses are deducted from the returns a fund generates.

Stick with funds that maintain low total operating expenses and don't charge loads (commissions). Both types of fees come out of your pocket and reduce your rate of return. You have no reason to pay a lot for the best funds. (In Chapters 11 and 12, I provide some specific fund recommendations as well as sample portfolios for investors in different situations.)

Evaluating historic performance

A fund's *performance,* or historic rate of return, is another factor to weigh when selecting a mutual fund. As all mutual funds are supposed to tell you, past performance is no guarantee of future results. An analysis of historic mutual fund performance proves that some of yesterday's stars turn into tomorrow's skid-row bums.

Many former high-return funds achieved their results by taking on high risk. Funds that assume higher risk should produce higher rates of return. But high-risk funds usually decline in price faster during major market declines. Thus, in order for a fund to be considered a *best* fund, it must consistently deliver a favorable rate of return given the degree of risk it takes.

When assessing an individual fund, compare its performance and volatility over an extended period of time (five or ten years will do) to a relevant market index. For example, compare funds that focus on investing in large U.S. companies to the Standard & Poor's 500 Index. Compare funds that invest in U.S. stocks of all sizes to the Wilshire 5000 Index. Indexes also exist for bonds, foreign stock markets, and almost any other type of security you can imagine.

Assessing fund manager and fund family reputations

Much is made of who manages a specific mutual fund. As Peter Lynch, the retired and famous former manager of the Fidelity Magellan fund, said, "The financial press made us Wall Street types into celebrities, a notoriety that was largely undeserved. Stock stars were treated as rock stars. . . ."

Although the individual fund manager is important, no fund manager is an island. The resources and capabilities of the parent company are equally important. Different companies have different capabilities and levels of expertise in relation to the different types of funds. When you're considering a particular fund — for example, the Barnum & Barney High-Flying Foreign Stock fund — examine the performance history and fees not only of that fund but also of similar foreign stock funds at the Barnum & Barney company. If Barnum's other foreign stock funds have done poorly, or Barnum & Barney offers no other such funds because it's focused on its circus business, those are strikes against its High-Flying fund. Also be aware that "star" fund managers tend to be associated with higher-expense funds to help pay their rock-star salaries.

Rating tax friendliness

Investors often overlook tax implications when selecting mutual funds for nonretirement accounts. Numerous mutual funds effectively reduce their shareholders' returns because of their tendency to produce more taxable distributions — that is, capital gains (especially short-term gains, which are taxed at the highest federal income tax rate) and dividends. (See the "Dividends" and "Capital gains" sections later in this chapter.)

Mutual fund capital gains distributions have an impact on an investor's after-tax rate of return. All mutual fund managers buy and sell stocks over the course of a year. Whenever a mutual fund manager sells securities, any gain or loss from those securities must be distributed to fund shareholders. Securities sold at a loss can offset securities sold at a profit.

When a fund manager has a tendency to cash in more winners than losers, investors in the fund receive a high amount of taxable gains. So, even though some funds can lay claim to producing higher total returns, *after* you factor in taxes, they actually may not produce higher total returns.

Choosing mutual funds that minimize capital gains distributions helps you defer taxes on your profits. By allowing your capital to continue compounding as it would in a retirement account, you receive a higher total return. When you're a long-term investor, you benefit most from choosing mutual funds that minimize capital gains distributions. The more years that appreciation can compound without being taxed, the greater the value to you as the investor.

Investors who purchase mutual funds outside tax-sheltered retirement accounts should also consider the time of year they purchase shares in funds. December is the most common month in which mutual funds make capital gains distributions. When making purchases late in the year, ask if and when the fund may make a significant capital gains distribution. Consider delaying purchases in such funds until after the distribution date.

Determining your needs and goals

Selecting the best funds for you requires an understanding of your investment goals and risk tolerance. What may be a good fund for your next-door neighbor may not necessarily be a good fund for you. You have a unique financial profile.

If you've already determined your needs and goals — terrific! If you haven't, refer to Chapter 4. Understanding yourself is a good part of the battle. But don't shortchange yourself by not being educated about the investment you're considering. If you don't understand what you're investing in and how much risk you're taking, stay out of the game.

Deciphering Your Fund's Performance

When you look at a statement for your mutual fund holdings, odds are that you're not going to understand it. Getting a handle on how you're doing is the hardest part. Most people want to know (and have a hard time figuring out) how much they made or lost on their investment.

You can't simply calculate your return by comparing the share price of the fund today to the share price you originally paid. Why not? Because mutual funds make distributions (of dividends and capital gains), which gives you more shares of the fund.

Distributions create an accounting problem, because they reduce the share price of a fund. (Otherwise you could make a profit from the distribution by buying into it just before a distribution is made.) Therefore, over time, following just the share price of your fund doesn't tell you how much money you made or lost.

The only way to figure out exactly how much you made or lost on your investment is to compare the total value of your holdings in the fund today with the total dollar amount you originally invested. If you invested chunks of money at various points in time and you want to factor in the timing of your various investments, this exercise becomes complicated. (Check out my investment software recommendations in Chapter 19 if you want your computer to help you crunch the numbers.)

The *total return* of a fund is the percentage change of your investment over a specified period. For example, a fund may tell you that in 2006, its total return was 15 percent. Therefore, if you invested $10,000 in the fund on the last day of 2005, your investment would be worth $11,500 at the end of 2006. To find out a fund's total return, you can call the fund company's toll-free number, visit the company's Web site, or read the fund's annual report.

The following three components make up your total return on a fund:

- Dividends (includes interest paid by money market or bond funds)
- Capital gains distributions
- Share price changes

Dividends

Dividends are income paid by investments. Both bonds and stocks can pay dividends. Bond fund dividends tend to be higher (as a percentage of the amount you have invested in a fund). When a dividend distribution is made, you can receive it as cash (which is good if you need money to live on) or as more shares in the fund. In either case, the share price of the fund drops to offset the payout. So if you're hoping to strike it rich by buying into a bunch of funds just before their dividends are paid, don't bother. You'll just end up paying more in income taxes.

If you hold your mutual fund outside a retirement account, the dividend distributions are taxable income (unless they come from a tax-free municipal bond fund). Dividends are taxable whether or not you reinvest them as additional shares in the fund. Thanks to the 2003 tax law changes, stock dividends are taxed at a low rate — 5 percent for those in the federal 10 and 15 percent tax brackets and 15 percent for everyone in the higher federal tax brackets.

Capital gains

When a mutual fund manager sells a security in the fund, net gains realized from that sale (the difference from the purchase price) must be distributed to you as a *capital gain*. Typically, funds make one annual capital gains distribution in December, but distributions can be paid multiple times per year.

As with a dividend distribution, you can receive your capital gains distribution as cash or as more shares in the fund. In either case, the share price of the fund drops to offset the distribution.

For funds held outside retirement accounts, your capital gains distribution is taxable. As with dividends, capital gains are taxable whether or not you reinvest them in additional shares in the fund. Capital gains distributions can be partly comprised of short-term and long-term gains. As I discuss in Chapter 7, profits realized on securities sold after more than a one-year holding period are taxed at the lower long-term capital gains rate. Short-term gains are taxed at the ordinary income tax rate.

If you want to avoid making an investment in a fund that is about to make a capital gains distribution, check with the fund to determine when capital gains are distributed. Capital gains distributions increase your current-year tax liability for investments made outside of retirement accounts. (I discuss this concept in more detail in Chapter 12.)

Share price changes

You also make money with a mutual fund when the share price increases. This occurrence is just like investing in a stock or piece of real estate. If the mutual fund is worth more today than it was when you bought it, you made a profit (on paper, at least). In order to realize or lock in this profit, you need to sell your shares in the fund.

There you have it. Here are the components of a mutual fund's total return:

```
Dividends + Capital Gains + Share Price
           Distributions   Changes       = Total Return
```

Evaluating and Selling Your Funds

How closely you follow your funds is up to you, depending on what makes you happy and comfortable. I don't recommend tracking the share prices of your funds (or other investments, for that matter) on a daily basis; it's time-consuming and nerve-racking, and it can make you lose sight of the long-term picture. When you track your investments too closely, you're more likely to panic when times get tough. And with investments held outside of retirement accounts, every time you sell an investment at a profit, you get hit with taxes.

A monthly or quarterly check-in is more than frequent enough for following your funds. Many publications carry total return numbers over varying periods so you can determine the exact rate of return you're earning.

Trying to time and trade the markets so that you buy at lows and sell at highs rarely works. Yet an entire industry of investment newsletters, hotlines, online services, and the like purport to be able to tell you when to buy and sell. Don't waste your time and money on such predictive nonsense. (See Chapter 8 for more info about gurus and newsletters.)

You should consider selling a fund when it no longer meets the criteria mentioned in "Selecting the Best Mutual Funds," earlier in this chapter. If a fund underperforms its peers for at least a two-year period, or if a fund jacks up its management fees, it may be a good time to sell. But if you do your homework and buy good funds from good fund companies, you shouldn't have to do much trading.

Finding and investing in good funds isn't rocket science. Chapters 11 and 12 recommend some specific mutual funds using the criteria discussed earlier in this chapter. If you're still not satiated, pick up a copy of the latest edition of my book *Mutual Funds For Dummies* (Wiley Publishing).

Chapter 11

Investing in Retirement Accounts

* *

* *

This chapter helps you make sense of the various retirement account options and decide how to invest money you currently hold inside — or plan to contribute to — retirement accounts. (To see how much money you should be saving toward retirement, flip to Chapter 4.)

The numerous types of retirement accounts can be confusing; however, when compared to the often overwhelming world of investing outside retirement accounts, investing inside tax-sheltered retirement accounts — IRAs, 401(k)s, SEP-IRAs, and Keoghs — is less complicated for two reasons:

✔ **The range of possible retirement account investments is more limited.** Direct investments, such as real estate and investments in small, privately owned companies, are not generally available or accessible in most retirement accounts.

✔ **When you invest in a retirement account, your returns aren't taxed as you earn them.** Money inside retirement accounts compounds and grows without taxation. You generally pay taxes on these funds only when you withdraw money from the account (except with Roth IRAs, where qualified withdrawals of investment earnings are not taxed). Direct transfers to another investment firm are not withdrawals, so they're not taxed.

Read on. I cover all the bases in this chapter first.

Looking at Types of Retirement Accounts

Retirement accounts offer numerous benefits. In most cases, your contributions to retirement accounts are tax-deductible. The contribution limits increased significantly the earlier part of this decade. And when you place your money inside the retirement account, it compounds without taxation until you withdraw it. (Some accounts, such as the newer Roth IRA, even allow for tax-free withdrawal of investment earnings.) If your adjusted gross income is below $50,000 per year ($25,000 for single taxpayers), you may be eligible for a new, special tax credit for making retirement account contributions — please refer to Table 7-2 in Chapter 7. The following sections detail the types of retirement accounts and explain how to determine whether you're eligible and how to make the best use of them.

Employer-sponsored plans

Your employer sets up this type of retirement plan and usually provides a limited selection of investment options. All you have to do is contribute away and choose how to spread your money among the menu of investment choices.

401(k) plans

For-profit companies offer *401(k) plans*. The silly name comes from the section of the tax code that establishes and regulates these plans. A 401(k) generally allows you to save up to $15,000 per year (for 2006), usually through payroll deductions. If you're age 50 or older, you can stash away even more — $20,000 for 2006. Your employer's plan may have lower limits, though. Your contributions to a 401(k) are excluded from your reported income and thus are generally free from federal and state income taxes (although they are subject to Social Security and Medicare taxes). Future year limits will increase in $500 increments to keep pace with inflation.

Some employers don't allow you to contribute to a 401(k) plan until you work for them for a full year. Others allow you to start contributing right away. Some employers also match a portion of your contributions. They may, for example, match half of your first 6 percent of contributions; so in addition to saving a lot of taxes, you get a bonus from the company.

If you're a high-income earner and you contribute such a significant percentage of each paycheck that you hit the plan maximum before the end of the year, you may lose out on some matching money. You may be better off spreading your contributions over the full calendar year. Check with your company's benefits department for your plan's specifics.

Thanks to technological innovations and the growth of the mutual fund industry, smaller companies (those with fewer than 100 employees) can offer 401(k) plans, too. In the past, it was prohibitively expensive for smaller companies to administer 401(k)s. If your company is interested in this option, contact some of the leading mutual fund organizations and discount brokerage firms that I discuss in Chapter 12 and in the section "Allocating money in plans you design," later in this chapter.

INVESTIGATE

Can your employer steal your retirement plan money?

The short answer, unfortunately, is yes. However, the vast majority of employees, particularly those who work for larger and more established companies, need not worry.

Some companies that administer 401(k) plans have been cited by the U.S. Labor Department for being too slow in putting money that employees had deferred from their paychecks into employee 401(k) investment accounts. In the worst cases, companies diverted employees' 401(k) money to pay corporate bills. Many business owners who engaged in such practices used 401(k) money as a short-term emergency fund.

In cases where companies failed and funds were diverted from employee 401(k) accounts, the funds were lost. In situations where the employer delayed placing the money into the employees' 401(k) accounts, employees simply lost out on earning returns on their investments during the period. When your contributions are in your 401(k) account, they're financially and legally separate from your employer. Thus, your funds are still protected even if your employer goes bankrupt.

After conducting hundreds of investigations, the Labor Department issued rulings requiring employers to contribute employee retirement contributions to their proper accounts within 90 days. In addition to keeping tabs on your employer to ensure that money withheld from your paycheck is contributed into your account within this time frame, you should also periodically check your 401(k) statement to make sure that your contributions are being invested as you instructed.

403(b) plans

Nonprofit organizations offer *403(b) plans* to their employees. As with 401(k)s, your contributions to these plans are excluded from federal and state income taxes. The 403(b) plans are more often known as *tax-sheltered annuities*, the name for insurance company investments that satisfy the requirements for 403(b) plans. For the benefit of 403(b) retirement plan participants, *no-load* (commission-free) mutual funds can be used in 403(b) plans. (See Chapter 10 for more on mutual funds.)

Nonprofit employees are allowed to annually contribute up to 20 percent or $15,000 of their salary ($20,000 if age 50 or older), whichever is less, for tax year 2006. (Future year-limits will increase with the cost of living in $500 increments.) Employees who have 15 or more years of service may be allowed to contribute beyond the standard limits. Ask your employee benefits department or the investment provider for the 403(b) plan about eligibility requirements and the details of your personal contribution limit.

If you work for a nonprofit or public-sector organization that doesn't offer this benefit, make a fuss and insist on it. Nonprofit organizations have no excuse not to offer a 403(b) plan to their employees. Unlike a 401(k), this type of plan requires virtually no out-of-pocket expenses from the employer. The only requirement is that the organization must deduct the appropriate contribution from employees' paychecks and send the money to the investment company handling the 403(b) plan.

Some nonprofits don't offer 403(b)s. Or in addition to 403(b)s, some nonprofits may offer insurance company tax-sheltered annuities. When compared to insurance company annuities, no-load (no sales charges) mutual funds are superior investment vehicles on several fronts:

- ✔ Mutual fund companies have a longer and more successful investment track record than do insurance companies, many of which have only recently entered the mutual fund arena.

- ✔ Insurance annuities charge higher annual operating expenses, often two to three times those of efficiently managed no-load mutual funds. These high expenses reduce your returns.

- ✔ Insurance company *insolvency* (bankruptcy) can risk the safety of your investment in an annuity, whereas the value of a mutual fund depends only on the value of the securities in the fund. Fund companies don't fail.

- ✔ Insurance annuities come with significant charges for early surrender; 403(b) plans with mutual funds don't include these charges.

With some 403(b) plans, you may borrow against your fund balance without penalty. If this capability is important to you, check with your employer to see whether the company plan allows loans. Although many insurance annuities advertise borrowing as an advantage, it can also be a drawback, because it may encourage you to raid your retirement savings.

As long as your employer allows it, you may want to open a 403(b) account at the investment companies I suggest in the section "Allocating money in plans you design," later in this chapter.

457 plans

Some nonprofit organizations offer 457 plans. Like 403(b) or 401(k) plans, 457 plans offer participants the ability to contribute money from their paychecks on a pre-tax basis and thus save on federal and state taxes.

Money that you contribute to a tax-exempt organization's 457 plan is not separate from the organization's finances. Thus, if the nonprofit goes belly up — a rare but not impossible occurrence in the nonprofit world — your retirement funds could be in jeopardy.

Don't consider contributing to a tax-exempt organization's 457 plan until you exhaust contributions to your 403(b). The 2006 tax year contribution limits for a 457 plan are $15,000 per year ($20,000 if age 50 or older). Future year-limits will increase with inflation.

Self-employed plans

When you work for yourself, you don't have an employer to do the legwork necessary for setting up a retirement plan. You need to take the initiative. Although setting up a retirement account on your own requires more work, you can select and design a plan that meets your needs. Self-employment retirement savings plans often allow you to put *more* money away on a tax-deductible basis than do employers' plans.

When you have employees, you're required to provide coverage for them under these plans with contributions comparable to the company owners' (as a percentage of salary). Some part-time (fewer than 1,000 hours per year) and newer employees (less than a few years of service) may be excluded. Many small-business owners either don't know about this requirement or choose to ignore it; they set up plans for themselves but fail to cover their employees. The danger is that the IRS and state tax authorities may discover small-business owners' negligence, sock them with big penalties, and disqualify their prior contributions. Don't muck up this area, because self-employed people and small businesses get their tax returns audited at a relatively high rate.

To get the most from contributions as an employer, consider the following advice:

✔ Educate your employees about the value of retirement savings plans. You want them to understand, but more importantly, you want them to appreciate your investment.

✔ Select a Keogh plan (see "Keoghs," later in this chapter) that requires employees to stay a certain number of years before they vest fully in their contributions. Reward long-term contributors to your company's success.

✔ Consider offering a 401(k) or SIMPLE (Savings Incentive Match Plan for Employees) if you have more than ten employees. (For more information on the SIMPLE, see the Department of Labor's Web site at www.dol.gov/ebsa/publications/simple.html.)

Making retirement contributions doesn't have to increase your personnel costs. In the long run, you build the contributions you make for your employees into their total compensation package — which includes salary and benefits such as health insurance.

SEP-IRAs

SEP-IRA (Simplified Employee Pension Individual Retirement Account) plans require little paperwork to set up. SEP-IRAs allow you to sock away 20 percent of your self-employment income (business revenue minus deductions), up to a maximum of $44,000 (tax year 2006). Future contribution limits will rise with inflation in $1,000 increments.

Each year, you decide the amount you want to contribute — with no minimums. Your contributions to a SEP-IRA are deducted from your taxable income, saving you big-time on federal and state taxes. As with other retirement plans, your money compounds without taxation until you withdraw it.

Keoghs

Setting up and administering Keogh plans requires a bit more paperwork than SEP-IRAs. The historic appeal of certain types of Keoghs was that they allow you to put away a greater amount of your self-employment income (revenue less your deductions). However, Keogh plans now have the same contribution limits (20 percent of net self-employment income up to $44,000 per year) that SEP-IRA plans have. (This is the 2006 tax year limit; future limits will increase with inflation in $1,000 increments.)

Keogh plans still hold some unique appeal for business owners who seek to maximize their own personal retirement plan contributions relative to those made for employees. All types of Keogh plans allow *vesting schedules,* which require employees to remain with the company a number of years before they earn the right to their full retirement account balances.

Don't be hoodwinked into a "private pension plan"

Employers who don't want to make retirement plan contributions on behalf of their employees are bait for insurance salespeople selling so-called "private pension plans." Basically, these plans are cash value life insurance policies that combine life insurance protection with a savings-type account. (See Chapter 16 for more details.)

The selling hook of these plans is that you can save money for yourself, but you don't need to contribute money on your employees' behalf. And your contributions compound without taxation over the years.

Sound too good to be true? Well, life insurance salespeople who earn hefty commissions from selling cash value life policies won't tell you about the big negatives of these plans. Unlike contributions to true retirement savings plans such as SEP-IRAs and Keoghs, you derive *no* upfront tax deduction. Your investment returns will be quite mediocre, especially due to these plans' high and hidden fees.

Also, if you don't need life insurance protection, the cost of such coverage is wasted when you save through these plans.

Keogh plans also allow for Social Security integration. Without going into all the gory tax details, *integration* effectively allows those in the company who are high-income earners (usually the owners) to receive larger-percentage contributions for their accounts than the less-highly compensated employees. The logic behind this idea is that Social Security benefits top out when you earn more than $94,200 (for 2006). Social Security integration allows you to make up for this ceiling.

Keoghs come in several flavors:

- **Profit-sharing plans:** These plans have the same contribution limits as SEP-IRAs. So why would you want the headaches of a more complicated plan when you can't contribute more to it? These plans appeal to owners of small companies who want to minimize the contributions to which their employees are entitled, which is done through the use of vesting schedules and Social Security integration.

- **Money-purchase pension plans:** These plans now have the same contribution limits as SEP-IRA plans. Flexibility is *not* allowed on the percentage contribution you make each year — it's fixed. Thus, these plans make the most sense for employers who are comfortable enough financially to continue making contributions that are a high percentage of their salary.

- **Defined-benefit plans:** These plans are for people who are willing and able to put away more than $44,000 per year — which, as you can imagine, few people can do. If you're a consistently high-income earner who's older than 45 and you want to save more than $44,000 per year in a retirement account, you may want to consider these plans. If you're interested in defined-benefit plans, hire an actuary to crunch the numbers and calculate how much you can contribute to such a plan.

Individual retirement accounts (IRAs)

Anyone with employment income can contribute to an Individual retirement account. You may contribute up to $4,000 each year — $5,000 if you're age 50 or older. (In 2008, the contribution limits increase to $5,000; and if you're 50 and older, then it's $6,000.) If you earn less than these contribution limits, you can contribute up to the amount you earn. This rule has an exception if you're a nonworking spouse: As long as the working spouse earned at least $8,000 in income, the nonworking spouse can put up to $4,000 per year into a so-called *spousal IRA,* and the working spouse, up to $4,000 into his or her own IRA.

Another exception to earning employment income makes you eligible to contribute to an IRA: receiving alimony.

Your contributions to an IRA may or may not be tax-deductible. For tax year 2006, if you're single and your adjusted gross income is $50,000 or less for the year, you can deduct your full IRA contribution. If you're married and file your taxes jointly, you're entitled to a full IRA deduction if your AGI (adjusted gross income) is $75,000 per year or less. (For 2007 and beyond, these thresholds bump up to $50,000 and $80,000, respectively.) If you make more than these amounts, you can take a full IRA deduction if and only if you're *not* an active participant in any other retirement plan. The only way to know for certain whether you're an active participant is to look at your W-2 Form — that small-ish (4-by-8½-inch) document your employer sends you early in the year to file with your tax returns. An X mark in a little box in section 13 on that form indicates whether you're an active participant in an employer retirement plan.

If your adjusted gross income is higher than the previously mentioned amounts by less than $10,000, you're eligible for a partial IRA deduction, even if you're an active participant in another plan. The IRS 1040 instruction booklet comes with a worksheet that allows you to do the calculations for your situation.

If you can't deduct your contribution to a standard IRA, consider making a contribution to a newer type of IRA called the Roth IRA. With the *Roth IRA,* the contribution is not deductible (you're contributing after-tax dollars), but earnings inside the account are shielded from tax; and unlike a standard IRA, qualified withdrawals from the account, including investment earnings, are free from income tax. Single taxpayers with an AGI less than $95,000, and joint filers with an AGI less than $150,000 can contribute up to $4,000 per year to a Roth IRA ($5,000 for those age 50 and older), provided that they have at least that amount in earned income. (As with regular IRAs, Roth IRA contribution limits increase in 2008 to $5,000 for people under 50 and $6,000 for those age 50 and older.)

To make a qualified (tax-free) withdrawal, you must be at least 59½ and have held the account for at least five years. An exception to the age rule is made for first-time home buyers, who can withdraw up to $10,000 toward the down payment on a principal residence.

Annuities: An odd investment

Annuities are peculiar investment products. They're contracts that are backed by an insurance company. If you, the annuity holder (investor), die during the so-called *accumulation phase* (that is, prior to receiving payments from the annuity), your designated beneficiary is guaranteed to receive the amount of your contribution. In this sense, annuities look a bit like life insurance.

WARNING!

Inappropriate retirement account investments

Some investments for retirement accounts simply don't make sense. The basic problem stems from otherwise intelligent folks' forgetting, ignoring, or simply not knowing that retirement accounts are sheltered from taxation; you want to maximize this benefit by selecting investment vehicles that would otherwise be taxed.

Investments that produce income that is tax-free either at the federal or state level don't generally make much sense inside retirement accounts. Tax-free securities always yield less than their taxable counterparts, so you're essentially giving away free yield when you invest in such securities inside retirement accounts.

Investing in municipal bonds inside a retirement account is a big no-no, and the better investment firms don't let you make this mistake. Municipals are free from federal taxation (and state tax, too, if you buy such a bond issued in your state). As such, they yield significantly less than an equivalent bond that pays fully taxable dividends.

Lots of people make the mistake (albeit a smaller one) of investing in Treasuries — that is, U.S. Treasury bills, notes, or bonds — inside retirement accounts. When you buy Treasuries, you get the safety net of a government guarantee, but you also get a bond that produces interest free of state tax. Fully taxable bonds yield more than state-tax-free Treasuries. And the safety of Treasuries can be replicated in other bonds.

Although annuities are retirement vehicles, as noted earlier in this chapter, they have no place inside retirement accounts. Annuities allow your investment dollars to compound without taxation. In comparison to other investments that don't allow such tax deferral, annuities carry much higher annual operating expenses, which depress your returns.

Purchasing an annuity inside an IRA, 401(k), or other type of retirement account is like wearing a belt and suspenders together. Either you have a peculiar sense of style, or you're spending too much time worrying about your pants falling down. In my experience, many people who mistakenly invest in annuities inside retirement accounts have been misled by investment salespeople.

Limited partnerships are treacherous, high-commission, high-cost (and hence low-return) investments sold through investment salespeople. Part of their supposed allure, however, is the tax benefits they generate. But when you buy and hold a limited partnership in a retirement account, you lose the ability to take advantage of many of the tax deductions. The illiquidity of LPs may also mean that you can't make required retirement account withdrawals when needed. These are just some of the many reasons to avoid investing in limited partnerships. (For more reasons, see Chapter 9.)

Annuities, like IRAs, allow your capital to grow and compound without taxation. You defer taxes until withdrawal. Annuities carry the same penalties for withdrawal prior to age 59½ as do other retirement accounts.

Unlike an IRA, which has an annual contribution limit, you can deposit as much as you want into an annuity in any year — even a million dollars or more if you have it! As with a so-called nondeductible IRA, you get no upfront tax deduction for your contributions.

Contributing to an annuity may make sense if

- ✔ **You have exhausted contributions to employer-sponsored and self-employed plans.** Your contributions to these retirement accounts are tax-deductible, while annuity contributions are not.

- ✔ **You have made the maximum contribution possible to an IRA, even if it's not tax-deductible.** Annuities carry higher fees (which reduce your investment returns) because of the insurance that comes with them; IRA investments offer you slightly better returns. Roth IRAs also allow for tax-free withdrawal of investment earnings.

- ✔ **You expect to leave the money compounding in the annuity for at least 15 years.** It typically takes this long for the benefits of tax-deferred compounding to outweigh the higher annuity fees and treatment of all withdrawn annuity earnings at the higher ordinary income tax rates. If you're close to or are actually in retirement, tax-friendly investments made outside of retirement accounts (discussed in Chapter 12) are preferable.

For details about other investment options and the best places to purchase annuities, see Chapter 12, where I discuss investing money outside of retirement accounts.

Allocating Your Money in Retirement Plans

With good reason, people are concerned about placing their retirement account money in investments that can decline in value. You may feel that you're gambling with dollars intended for the security of your golden years.

Most working folks need to make their money work hard in order for it to grow fast enough to provide this security. This involves taking some risk; you have no way around it. Luckily, if you have 15 to 20 years or more before you need to draw on the bulk of your retirement account assets, time is on your side. As long as the value of your investments has time to recover, what's the big deal if some of your investments drop a bit over a year or two? The more years you have before you're going to retire, the greater your ability to take risk.

The section on asset allocation in Chapter 8 can help you decide how to divide your money among different investment options based on your time frame and risk tolerance.

Prioritizing retirement contributions

When you have access to various retirement accounts, prioritize which account you're going to use first by determining how much each gives you in return. Your first contributions should be to employer-based plans that match your contributions. After that, contribute to any other employer or self-employed plans that allow tax-deductible contributions. After you contribute as much as possible to these tax-deductible plans (or if you don't have access to such plans), contribute to an IRA. If you max out on contributions to an IRA or you don't have this choice because you lack employment income, consider an annuity (see "Annuities: An odd investment," earlier in this chapter).

Setting up a retirement account

Investments and account types are different issues. People sometimes get confused when discussing the investments they make in retirement accounts — especially people who have a retirement account, such as an IRA, at a bank. They don't realize that you can have your IRA at a variety of financial institutions (for example, a mutual fund company or brokerage firm). At each financial institution, you can choose among the firm's investment options for putting your IRA money to work.

No-load, or commission-free, mutual fund and discount brokerage firms are your best bet for establishing a retirement account. For more specifics, see my recommendations throughout the remainder of this chapter.

Allocating money when your employer selects the investment options

In some company-sponsored plans, such as 401(k)s, you're limited to the predetermined investment options your employer offers. In the following sections, I discuss typical investment options for 401(k) plans in order of increasing risk and, hence, likely return. Then I follow with examples for how to allocate your money across the different types of common employer retirement plan options.

Money market/savings accounts

For regular contributions that come out of your paycheck, the money market or savings account option makes little sense. Some people who are skittish about the stock and bond markets are attracted to money market and savings accounts because they can't drop in value. However, the returns are low . . . so low that you have a great risk that your investment will not stay ahead of, or even keep up with, inflation and taxes (which are due upon withdrawal of your money from the retirement account).

Don't be tempted to use a money market fund as a parking place until the time that you think stocks and bonds are cheap. In the long run, you won't be doing yourself any favors. As I discuss in Chapter 8, timing your investments to attempt to catch the lows and avoid the peaks is not possible.

You may need to keep money in the money market investment option if you utilize the borrowing feature that some retirement plans allow. Check with your employee benefits department for more details. After you retire, you may also want to use a money market account to hold money you expect to withdraw and spend within a year or so.

Bond mutual funds

Bond mutual funds (which I describe in Chapter 10) invest in a mixture of typically high-quality bonds. Bonds pay a higher rate of interest or dividends than money funds. Depending on whether your plan's option is a short-term, intermediate-term, or long-term fund (maybe you have more than one type), the bond fund's current yield is probably a percent or two higher than the money market fund's yield.

Bond funds carry higher yields than money market funds, but they also carry greater risk, because their value can fall if interest rates increase. However, bonds tend to be more stable in value than stocks.

Aggressive, younger investors should keep a minimum amount of money in bond funds. Older folks who want to invest conservatively can place more money in bonds (see the asset allocation discussion in Chapter 8).

Guaranteed-investment contracts (GICs)

Guaranteed-investment contracts are backed by an insurance company, and they typically quote you a rate of return projected one or a few years forward. The positive return is certain — so you don't have the uncertainty that you normally face with bond or stock investments (unless, of course, the insurance company fails).

The attraction of these investments is that your account value does not fluctuate (at least, not that you can see). Insurers normally invest your money mostly in bonds and maybe a bit in stocks. The difference between what these investments generate for the insurer and what they pay in interest to GIC investors is profit to the insurer. A GIC's yield is usually comparable to that of a bond fund.

For people who hit the eject button the moment that a bond fund slides a bit in value, GICs are soothing to the nerves. And they're certainly higher yielding than a money market or savings account.

Like bonds, however, GICs don't give you the opportunity for long-term growth. Over the long haul, you should earn a better return in a mixture of bond and stock investments. In GICs, you pay for the peace of mind of a guaranteed return with lower long-term returns.

GICs also have another minor drawback: Insurance companies, unlike mutual funds, can and do fail, putting GIC investment dollars at risk. Some employers' retirement plans have been burned by insurance company failures.

Balanced mutual funds

Balanced mutual funds invest primarily in a mixture of stocks and bonds. This one-stop-shopping concept makes investing easier and smoothes out fluctuations in the value of your investments — funds investing exclusively in stocks or in bonds make for a rougher ride. These funds are solid options and, in fact, can be used for a significant portion of your retirement plan contributions. See Chapter 10 to find out more about balanced funds.

Stock mutual funds

Stock mutual funds invest in stocks, which often provide greater long-term growth potential but also wider fluctuations in value from year to year. Some companies offer a number of different stock funds, including funds that invest overseas. Unless you plan to borrow against your funds to purchase a home (if your plan allows), you should have a healthy helping of stock funds. See Chapter 10 for an explanation of the different types of stock funds as well as for details on how to evaluate a stock fund.

Stock in the company you work for

Some companies offer employees the option of investing in the company's stock. I generally advocate avoiding this option for the simple reason that your future income and other employee benefits are already riding on the success of the company. If the company hits the skids, you may lose your job and your benefits. You certainly don't want the value of your retirement account to depend on the same factors.

In the early 2000s, you may have heard all the hubbub about companies such as Enron going under and the employees losing piles of money in their retirement savings plans. Enron's bankruptcy in and of itself shouldn't have caused direct problems in Enron's 401(k) plan. The problem was that Enron required employees to hold substantial amounts of Enron company stock. Thus, when the company tanked, employees lost their jobs *and* their retirement savings balances.

Congress is (belatedly) weighing bills that would greatly limit companies from being able to force employees to hold retirement plan money in company stock. In the meantime, many companies with Enron-like retirement savings plans are redesigning their plans and not requiring employees to hold such large portions in company stock for so many years.

If you think that your company has its act together and the stock is a good buy, investing a portion of your retirement account is fine — but no more than 25 percent. Now, if your company is on the verge of hitting it big and the stock is soon to soar, you'll of course be kicking yourself for not putting more of your money into the company's stock. But when you place a big bet on your company's stock, be prepared to suffer the consequences if the stock tanks. Don't forget that lots of smart investors track companies' prospects, so odds are that the current value of your company's stock is reasonably fair.

Some employers offer employees the option to buy company stock at a discount, sometimes as much as 15 percent, when compared to its current market value. If your company offers a discount on its stock, take advantage of it. When you sell the stock as your employer's plan allows (usually after a certain holding period), you should be able to lock in a decent profit.

Some asset allocation examples

Using the methodology that I outline in Chapter 8 for allocating money, Table 11-1 shows a couple examples of how people in different employer plans may choose to allocate their 401(k) investments among the plan's investment options.

Please note that making allocation decisions is not a science. Use the formulas in Chapter 8 as a guideline.

Table 11-1	Allocating 401(k) Investments		
	25-Year-Old, Aggressive Risk	*45-Year-Old, Moderate Risk*	*60-Year-Old, Moderate Risk*
Bond Fund	0%	35%	50%
Balanced Fund (50% stock/50% bond)	10%	0%	0%
Blue Chip/Larger Company Stock Fund(s)	30–40%	20–25%	25%
Smaller Company Stock Fund(s)	25%	20%	10%
International Stock Fund(s)	25–35%	20–25%	15%

Allocating money in plans you design

With self-employed plans (SEP-IRAs and Keoghs), certain 403(b) plans for nonprofit employees, and IRAs, you may select the investment options as well as the allocation of money among them. In the sections that follow, I give some specific recipes that you may find useful for investing at some of the premier investment companies.

To establish your retirement account at one of these firms, simply pick up your telephone, dial the company's toll-free number, and ask the representative to mail you an account application for the type of account (for example, SEP-IRA, 403(b), and so on) you want to set up. You can also have the company mail you background information on specific mutual funds. If you're enamored with the Internet, many investment firms provide downloadable account applications, and some allow you to complete the application online.

Note: In the examples, I recommend a conservative portfolio and an aggressive portfolio for each firm. I use the terms *conservative* and *aggressive* in a relative sense. Because some of the funds I recommend do not maintain fixed percentages of their different types of investments, the actual percentage of stocks and bonds that you end up with may vary slightly from the targeted percentages. Don't sweat it.

Where you have more than one fund choice, you can pick one or split the suggested percentage among them. If you don't have enough money today to divide your portfolio up as I suggest, you can achieve the desired split over time as you add more money to your retirement accounts.

Vanguard

Vanguard (800-662-7447; www.vanguard.com) is a mutual fund powerhouse. It's the largest no-load fund company, and it consistently has the lowest operating expenses in the business. Historically, Vanguard's funds have excellent performance when compared to those of its peers, especially among conservatively managed bond and stock funds.

A conservative portfolio with 50 percent stocks, 50 percent bonds

If you don't want to risk too much, try this:

- ✔ Vanguard Total Bond Market Index — 25 percent

- ✔ Vanguard Star (fund of funds) — 60 percent

- ✔ Vanguard International Value *and/or* Vanguard Total International Stock Index — 15 percent

An aggressive portfolio with 80 percent stocks, 20 percent bonds

If you can afford to be aggressive, try this:

- ✔ Vanguard Star (fund of funds) — 50 percent
- ✔ Vanguard Total Stock Market Index — 30 percent
- ✔ Vanguard Total International Stock Index — 20 percent

Or you can place 100 percent in Vanguard LifeStrategy Growth (fund of funds). Note that this portfolio places less money overseas than the preceding example.

Fidelity

Fidelity Investments (800-544-8888; www.fidelity.com) is the largest provider of mutual funds in terms of total assets. However, some Fidelity funds assess sales charges (no such funds are recommended in the sections that follow).

A conservative portfolio with 50 percent stocks, 50 percent bonds

If you want to maintain a conservative portfolio, try this:

- ✔ Fidelity Asset Manager — 33⅓ percent
- ✔ Fidelity Puritan — 33⅓ percent
- ✔ Dodge & Cox Balanced — 33⅓ percent

An aggressive portfolio with 80 percent stocks, 20 percent bonds

If you want to maintain an aggressive portfolio, try this:

- ✔ Fidelity Puritan — 35 percent
- ✔ Fidelity Equity-Income — 25 percent
- ✔ Fidelity Low-Priced Stock — 20 percent
- ✔ Vanguard Total International Stock Index *and/or* Masters' Select International — 20 percent

Discount brokers

As I discuss in Chapter 8, a discount brokerage account can allow you centralized, one-stop shopping and the ability to hold mutual funds from a variety of leading fund companies. Some funds are available without transaction fees, although most of the better funds require you to pay a small transaction fee when you buy funds through a discount broker. The reason: The discounter is a middleman between you and the fund companies. You have to weigh the convenience of being able to buy and hold funds from multiple fund companies in a single account versus the lower cost of buying funds directly from their providers. A $25 to $30 transaction fee can gobble a sizeable chunk of what you have to invest, especially if you're investing smaller amounts.

Among brokerage firms or brokerage divisions of mutual fund companies, for breadth of fund offerings and competitive pricing, I like TD Ameritrade (800-934-4448; www.tdwaterhouse.com), T. Rowe Price (800-225-5132; www.troweprice.com), and Vanguard (800-992-8327; www.vanguard.com).

A conservative portfolio with 50 percent stocks, 50 percent bonds

If you want to set up a conservative portfolio, try this:

- ✔ Vanguard Short-Term Investment Grade — 20 percent
- ✔ Harbor Bond *and/or* Dodge & Cox Income — 20 percent
- ✔ Dodge & Cox Balanced — 20 percent
- ✔ T. Rowe Price Spectrum Growth (fund of funds) — 30 percent
- ✔ Master's Select International *and/or* Tweedy Browne Global Value — 10 percent

An aggressive portfolio with 80 percent stocks, 20 percent bonds

If you want to set up an aggressive portfolio, try this:

- ✔ Harbor Bond *and/or* Vanguard Total Bond Market Index — 20 percent
- ✔ Vanguard Total Stock Market Index *and/or* Dodge & Cox Stock *and/or* Masters' Select Equity — 50 percent
- ✔ Masters' Select International *and/or* Vanguard International Growth *and/or* Vanguard Total International Stock — 30 percent

Should I use more than one investment firm?

The firms I recommend in this chapter offer a large-enough variety of investment options, managed by different fund managers, that you can feel comfortable concentrating your money at one firm. Discovering the nuances and choices of just one firm rather than several and having fewer administrative hassles are the advantages of a focused approach.

If you like the idea of spreading your money around, you may want to invest through a number of different firms. With a discount brokerage account (see Chapter 8), you can eat your cake and have it, too. You can diversify across different mutual fund companies through one brokerage firm. However, you'll pay small transaction fees on some of your purchases and sales of funds.

Transferring Retirement Accounts

With the exception of plans maintained by your employer that limit your investment options, such as most 401(k)s, you can move your money held in an SEP-IRA, Keogh, IRA, and many 403(b) plans (also known as *tax-sheltered annuities*) to almost any major investment firm. Moving the money is pretty simple: If you can fill out a couple short forms and send them back in a postage-paid envelope, you can transfer an account. The investment firm to which you're transferring your account does the rest.

Transferring accounts you control

Here's a step-by-step list of what you need to do to transfer a retirement account to another investment firm. Even if you're working with a financial advisor, you should be aware of this process (called a *direct trustee-to-trustee transfer*) to ensure that no hanky-panky takes place on the advisor's part.

1. **Decide where you want to move the account.**

   I recommend several investment companies in this chapter, along with some sample portfolios within those firms. You may also want to consult the latest editions of some of my other books, including *Mutual Funds For Dummies* and *Investing For Dummies* (Wiley Publishing).

2. **Obtain an account application and asset transfer form.**

   Call the toll-free number of the firm you're transferring the money to and ask for an *account application and asset transfer form* for the type of account you're transferring — for example, SEP-IRA, Keogh, IRA, or 403(b). You can also visit the firm's Web site, but for this type of request, I think most people find it easier to speak directly to someone.

   Ask for the form for the *same* type of account you currently have at the company from which you're transferring the money. You can determine the account type by looking at a recent account statement — the account type should appear near the top of the form or in the section with your name and address. If you can't figure out the account type on a cryptic statement, call the firm where the account is currently held and ask a representative to tell you what kind of account you have.

   Never, ever sign over assets such as checks and security certificates to a financial advisor, no matter how trustworthy and honest he or she may seem. The advisor could bolt with them quicker than you can say "Bonnie and Clyde." Transfers should not be completed this way. Besides, you'll find it easier to handle the transfer by following the information in this section.

3. **Complete and mail the account application and asset transfer form.**

   Completing these for your new investment firm opens your new account and authorizes the transfer.

   You shouldn't take possession of the money in your retirement account when moving it over to the new firm. The tax authorities impose huge penalties if you perform a transfer incorrectly. Let the company to which you're transferring the money do the transfer for you. If you have questions or problems, the firm(s) to which you're transferring your account has armies of capable employees waiting to help you. Remember, these firms know that you're transferring your money to them, so they should roll out the red carpet.

4. **Figure out which securities you want to transfer and which need to be liquidated.**

   Transferring existing investments in your account to a new investment firm can sometimes be a little sticky. Transferring such assets as cash (money market funds) or securities that trade on any of the major stock exchanges is not a problem.

   If you own publicly traded securities, transferring them as is (also known as transferring them *in kind*) to your new investment firm is better, especially if the firm offers discount brokerage services. You can then sell your securities through that firm more cheaply.

   If you own mutual funds unique to the institution you're leaving, check with your new firm to see whether it can accept them. If not, you need to contact the firm that currently holds them to sell them.

   Certificates of deposit are tricky to transfer. Ideally, you should send in the transfer forms several weeks or so before the CDs mature — few people do this. If the CD matures soon, call the bank and tell it that when the CD matures, you would like the funds to be invested in a savings or money market account that you can access without penalty when your transfer request lands in the bank's mailbox.

5. **Let the firm from which you're transferring the money know that you're doing so. (This step is optional.)**

   If the place you're transferring the money from doesn't assign a specific person to your account, you can definitely skip this step. When you're moving your investments from a brokerage firm where you dealt with a particular broker, deciding whether to follow this step can be more difficult.

   Most people feel obligated to let their representative know that they're moving their money. In my experience, calling the person with the "bad news" is usually a mistake. Brokers or others who have a direct financial stake in your decision to move your money will try to sell you on staying. Some may try to make you feel guilty for leaving, and some may even try to bully you.

Writing a letter may seem like the coward's way out, but writing usually makes leaving your broker easier for both of you. You can polish what you have to say, and you don't put the broker on the defensive. Although I don't want to encourage lying, not telling the *whole* truth may be an even better idea. Excuses, such as that you have a family member in the investment business who will manage your money for free, may help you avoid an uncomfortable confrontation.

Then again, telling an investment firm that its charges are too high or that it misrepresented and sold you a bunch of lousy investments may help the firm improve in the future. Don't fret too much — do what's best for you and what you're comfortable with. Brokers are not your friends. Even though the broker may know your kids' names, your favorite hobbies, and your birthday, you have a *business* relationship with him.

Transferring your existing assets typically takes a month to complete. If the transfer is not completed within one month, get in touch with your new investment firm to determine the problem. If your old company isn't cooperating, call a manager there to help get the ball rolling.

The unfortunate reality is that an investment firm will cheerfully set up a new account to *accept* your money on a moment's notice, but it will drag its feet, sometimes for months, when the time comes to relinquish your money. To light a fire under the behinds of the folks at the investment firm, tell a manager at the old firm that you're going to send letters to the National Association of Securities Dealers (NASD) and the Securities and Exchange Commission (SEC) if it doesn't complete your transfer within the next week.

Moving money from an employer's plan

When you leave a job, particularly if you're retiring or being laid off after many years of service, money-hungry brokers and financial planners probably will be on you like a pack of bears on a tree leaking sweet honey. If you seek financial help, tread carefully — Chapter 18 helps you avoid the pitfalls of hiring such assistance.

When you leave a job, you're confronted with a slightly different transfer challenge: moving money from an employer plan into one of your own retirement accounts. (As long as your employer allows it, you may be able to leave your money in your old employer's plan. Evaluate the quality of the investment choices using the information I provide in this part of the book.) Typically, employer retirement plan money can be rolled over into your own IRA. Check with your employer's benefits department or a tax advisor for details.

Federal tax law requires employers to withhold, as a tax, 20 percent of any retirement account disbursements to plan participants. So if you're personally taking possession of your retirement account money in order to transfer it to an IRA, you must wait until you file your annual tax return to be reimbursed by the government for this 20 percent withholding. This withholding creates a problem, because if you don't replace the 20 percent withholding into the rollover IRA, the IRS treats the shortfall as an early distribution subject to income tax and penalties.

Never take personal possession of money from your employer's retirement plan. To avoid the 20 percent tax withholding and a lot of other hassles, simply inform your employer of where you want your money to be sent. Prior to doing so, establish an appropriate account (an IRA, for example) at the investment firm you intend to use. Then tell your employer's benefits department where you'd like your retirement money transferred. You can send your employer a copy of your account statement, which contains the investment firm's mailing address and your account number.

Chapter 12

Investing in Taxable Accounts

· ·

· ·

*I*n this chapter, I discuss investment options for money held outside retirement accounts, and I include some sample portfolio recommendations. (Chapter 11 reviews investments for money *inside* retirement accounts.) This distinction may seem somewhat odd — it's not one that's made in most financial books and articles. However, thinking of these two types of investments differently can be useful because

✓ **Investments held outside retirement accounts are subject to taxation.** You have a whole range of different investment options to consider when taxes come into play.

✓ **Money held outside retirement accounts is more likely to be used sooner than funds held inside retirement accounts.** Why? Because you'll generally have to pay far more in income taxes to access money inside rather than outside retirement accounts.

✓ **Funds inside retirement accounts have their own nuances.** For example, when you invest through your employer's retirement plan, your investment options are usually limited to a handful of choices. And special rules govern transfer of your retirement account balances.

Getting Started

Suppose that you have some money sitting around in a bank savings account or money market mutual fund. Your money is earning a small amount of interest, but you want to invest it more profitably. You need to remember two things about investing this type of money:

✔ **Earning a little is better than losing 20 to 50 percent or more.** Just talk to anyone who bought a lousy investment. Be patient. Educate yourself *before* you invest.

✔ **To earn a higher rate of return, you must be willing to take more risk.** In order to earn a better rate of return, you need to consider investments that fluctuate in value — of course, the value can drop as well as rise.

You approach the vast sea of investment options and start stringing up your rod to go fishing. You hear stories of people catching big ones — cashing in big on stocks or real estate that they bought years ago. Even if you don't have delusions of grandeur, you'd at least like your money to grow faster than the cost of living.

But before you cast your investment line, consider the following often overlooked ways to put your money to work and earn higher returns without much risk. These options may not be as exciting as hunting the big fish out there, but they should easily improve your financial health.

Paying off high-interest debt

Many folks have credit card or other consumer debt that costs more than 10 percent per year in interest. Paying off this debt with savings is like putting your money in an investment with a guaranteed return that's equal to the rate you're paying on the debt.

For example, if you have credit card debt outstanding at 14 percent interest, paying off that loan is the same as putting your money to work in an investment with a sure 14 percent annual return. Remember that the interest on consumer debt is not tax-deductible, so you actually need to earn *more* than 14 percent investing your money elsewhere in order to net 14 percent after paying taxes. (See Chapter 5 for more details if you're still not convinced.)

Paying off some of or your entire mortgage may make sense, too. This financial move isn't as clear as erasing consumer debt, because the mortgage interest rate is lower than it is on consumer debt and is usually tax-deductible. (See Chapter 14 for more details on this strategy.)

Taking advantage of tax breaks

Make sure that you take advantage of the tax benefits offered on retirement accounts. If you work for a company that offers a retirement savings plan such as a 401(k), fund it at the highest level you can manage. If you earn self-employment income, look into SEP-IRAs and Keoghs. (I discuss retirement-plan options in Chapter 11.)

If you need to save money outside retirement accounts for shorter-term goals (for example, to buy a car or a home, or to start or buy a small business), then by all means, save money outside retirement accounts. This chapter can assist you with thinking through investing money in taxable accounts (non-retirement accounts exposed to taxation).

Understanding Taxes on Your Investments

When you invest money outside of a retirement account, *investment distributions* — such as interest, dividends, and capital gains — are subject to current taxation. Too many folks (and too many of their financial advisors) ignore the tax impact of their investment strategies. You need to pay attention to the tax implications of your investment decisions *before* you invest your money.

Consider a person in a combined 40 percent tax bracket (federal plus state taxes) who keeps extra cash in a taxable bond paying 5.0 percent interest. If she pays 40 percent of her interest earnings in taxes, she ends up keeping just 3.0 percent. With a similar but tax-free bond, she could easily earn more than this amount, completely free of federal and/or state taxes.

Another mistake some people make is investing in securities that produce tax-free income when they're not in a high enough tax bracket to benefit. Now consider a person in a combined 20 percent tax bracket who is investing in securities that produce tax-free income. Suppose that he invests in a tax-free investment that yields 4.5 percent. A comparable taxable investment is yielding 7 percent. If he had instead invested in the taxable investment at a 7 percent yield, the after-tax yield would have been 5.6 percent. Thus, he is losing out on yield by being in the tax-free investment, even though he may feel happy in it because the yield isn't taxed.

To decide between comparable taxable and tax-free investments, you need to know your *marginal tax bracket* (tax rate you pay on an extra dollar of taxable income) and the rates of interest or yield on each investment. Here are some general guidelines based upon your federal income tax bracket. (Check out Table 7-1 in Chapter 7 to see what tax bracket you're in.)

In the sections that follow, I give specific advice about investing your money while keeping an eye on taxes.

Fortifying Your Emergency Reserves

In Chapter 4, I explain the importance of keeping sufficient money in an emergency reserve account. From such an account, you need two things:

- ✔ **Accessibility:** When you need to get your hands on the money for an emergency, you want to be able to do so quickly and without penalty.

- ✔ **Highest possible return:** You want to get the highest rate of return possible without risking your principal. This doesn't mean that you should simply pick the money market or savings option with the highest yield, because other issues such as taxes are a consideration. What good is earning a slightly higher yield if you pay a lot more in taxes?

The following sections give you info on investments that are suitable for emergency reserves.

Bank and credit union accounts

When you have a few thousand dollars or less, your best and easiest path is to keep this excess savings in a local bank or credit union. Look first to the institution where you keep your checking account.

Keeping this stash of money in your checking account, rather than in a separate savings account, makes financial sense if the extra money helps you avoid monthly service charges when your balance occasionally dips below the minimum. Compare the service charges on your checking account with the interest earnings from a savings account.

For example, suppose that you're keeping $2,000 in a savings account to earn 2 percent interest versus earning no interest on your checking account money. Over the course of a year, you earn $40 interest on that savings account. If you incur a $9 per month service charge on your checking account, you pay $108 per year. So keeping your extra $2,000 in a checking account may be better if it keeps you above a minimum balance and erases that monthly service charge. (However, if you're more likely to spend the extra money in your checking account, keeping it in a separate savings account where you won't be tempted to spend it may be better.)

Money market mutual funds

Money market funds, a type of mutual fund (see Chapter 11), are just like bank savings accounts — but better, in most cases. The best money market funds pay higher yields than bank savings accounts and offer you check-writing privileges. And if you're in a high tax bracket, you can select a tax-free money market fund, which pays interest that's free from federal and/or state tax — a feature you can't get with a bank savings account.

The yield on a money market fund is an important consideration. The operating expenses deducted before payment of dividends is the single biggest determinant of yield. All other things being equal (which they usually are with different money market funds), lower operating expenses translate into higher yields for you. With interest rates as low as they are these days, seeking out money funds with the lowest operating expenses is now more vital than ever.

Doing most or all of your fund shopping (money-market and otherwise) at one good fund company can reduce the clutter in your investing life. Chasing after a slightly higher yield offered by another company is sometimes not worth the extra paperwork and administrative hassle. On the other hand, there's no reason why you can't invest in funds at multiple firms (as long as you don't mind the extra paperwork), using each for its relative strengths.

Most mutual fund companies don't have many local branch offices, so you may have to open and maintain your money market mutual fund through the fund's toll-free phone line, Web site, or the mail. Distance has its advantages. Because you can conduct business by mail, the Internet, and the phone, you don't need to go schlepping into a local branch office to make deposits and withdrawals. I'm *happy* to report that I haven't visited a bank office in years.

Despite the distance between you and your mutual fund company, your money is still accessible via check writing, and you can also have money wired to your local bank on any business day. Don't fret about a deposit being lost in the mail; it rarely happens, and no one can legally cash a check made payable to you, anyway. Just be sure to endorse the check with the notation "for deposit only" under your signature.

(For that matter, driving or walking to your local bank isn't 100 percent safe. Imagine all the things that could happen to you or your money en route to the bank. You could slip on a banana peel, drop your deposit down a sewer grate, get mugged, walk into a bank holdup, get run over by a bakery truck. . . .)

Watch out for "sales"

Beware of money market mutual funds that have a "sale" by temporarily waiving (sometimes called *absorbing*) operating expenses, which lets a fund boost its yield. These sales never last long; the operating expenses come back and deflate that too-good-to-be-true yield like a nail in a bike tire. Some fund companies run sales because they know that a major portion of the fund buyers who are lured in won't bother leaving when they jack up operating expenses.

You're better off sticking with funds that maintain "everyday low operating expenses" to get the highest long-term yield. I recommend such funds in the next section. However, if you want to move your money to companies having specials and then move it back out when the special is over, be my guest. If you have lots of money and don't mind paperwork, it may be worth the bother.

Recommended money market mutual funds

In this section, I recommend good money market mutual funds. As you peruse this list, remember that the money market fund that works best for you depends on your tax situation. Throughout the list, I try to guide you to funds that generally make sense for people in particular tax brackets.

✔ Money market funds that pay taxable dividends are appropriate when you're not in a high tax bracket. Some of my favorites include

  • Fidelity Cash Reserves and Fidelity Money Market (800-544-8888; www.fidelity.com)

  • USAA Money Market (800-382-8722; www.usaa.com)

  • Vanguard Prime Money Market (800-662-7447; www.vanguard.com)

✔ U.S. Treasury money market funds are appropriate if you prefer a money fund that invests in U.S. Treasuries, which have the safety of government backing, or if you're in a high state tax bracket (5 percent or higher) but not in a high federal tax bracket. Vanguard (800-662-7447; www.vanguard.com) offers a couple good options:

  • Vanguard Treasury Money Market

  • Vanguard Admiral Treasury Money Market

✔ The following tax-free money market funds are appropriate when you're in a high federal and state tax bracket:

  • Fidelity Arizona Municipal Money Market (800-544-8888; www.fidelity.com)

  • USAA California Money Market (800-382-8722; www.usaa.com)

  • Vanguard California Tax-Exempt Money Market (800-662-7447; www.vanguard.com)

  • Fidelity Massachusetts AMT Tax-Free Money Market (800-544-8888; www.fidelity.com)

  • Vanguard New Jersey Tax-Exempt Money Market (800-662-7447; www.vanguard.com)

  • USAA New York Money Market (800-382-8722; www.usaa.com)

- Vanguard New York Tax-Exempt Money Market (800-662-7447; www.vanguard.com)

- Vanguard Ohio Tax-Exempt Money Market (800-662-7447; www.vanguard.com)

- Vanguard Pennsylvania Tax-Exempt Money Market (800-662-7447; www.vanguard.com)

- USAA Virginia Money Market (800-382-8722; www.usaa.com)

A number of states don't offer the money market fund options listed in the preceding list (and those that do may have minimums that are too high). In some cases, no options exist. In other cases, the funds available (and not on the recommended list) for that particular state have such high annual operating expenses, and therefore such low yields, that you're better off in one of the more competitively run federal-tax-free-only funds in the following list.

The following federal-tax-free-only money market funds (the dividends on these are state taxable) are appropriate when you're in a high federal but not state bracket, or if you live in a state that doesn't have competitive state- and federal-tax-free funds available:

✔ Vanguard Tax-Exempt Money Market (800-662-7447; www.vanguard.com)

✔ Fidelity AMT Tax-Free Money Market (800-544-8888; www.fidelity.com)

✔ T. Rowe Price Summit Municipal Money Market (800-638-5660; www.troweprice.com)

✔ USAA Tax-Exempt Money Market (800-382-8722; www.usaa.com)

Investing for the Longer Term (A Few Years or More)

Important note: This section (together with its recommended investments) assumes that you have a sufficient emergency reserve stashed away and are taking advantage of tax-deductible retirement account contributions. (Please see Chapter 3 for more on these goals.)

Asset allocation refers to the process of figuring out what portion of your wealth you should invest in different types of investments. You often (and most appropriately) practice asset allocation with retirement accounts, because this money is earmarked for the long-term. Ideally, more of your saving and investing should be conducted through tax-sheltered retirement accounts. These accounts generally offer the best way to lower your long-term tax burden (see Chapter 11 for details).

If you plan to invest outside retirement accounts, asset allocation for these accounts should depend on how comfortable you are with risk. But your choice of investments should also be suited to how much *time* you have until you plan to use the money. That's not because you won't be able to sell these investments on short notice if necessary (most of them you can). Investing money in a more volatile investment is simply riskier if you need to liquidate it in the short term.

For example, suppose that you're saving money for a down payment on a house and are about one to two years away from having enough to make your foray into the real estate market. If you had put this "home" money into the U.S. stock market near the beginning of one of the stock market's 20 to 50 percent corrections (such as what happened in the early 2000s), you'd have been mighty unhappy. You would have seen a substantial portion of your money *vanish* in short order and would've seen your home dreams put on hold.

Defining your time horizons

The different investment options in the remainder of this chapter are organized by time frame. All the recommended investment funds that follow assume that you have *at least* a several-year time frame and are *no-load* (commission-free) mutual funds. Mutual funds can be sold on any business day, usually with a simple phone call. Funds come with all different levels of risk, so you can choose funds that match your time frame and desire to take risk. (Chapter 10 discusses all the basics of mutual funds.)

The recommended investments are also organized by your tax situation. (If you don't know your current tax bracket, be sure to review Chapter 7.) Following are summaries of the different time frames associated with each type of fund:

> ✔ **Short-term investments:** These investments are suitable for a period of a few years — perhaps you're saving money for a home or some other major purchase in the near future. When investing for the short-term, look for liquidity and stability — features that rule out real estate and stocks.
>
> Recommended investments include shorter-term bond funds, which are higher-yielding alternatives to money market funds. If interest rates increase, these funds drop slightly in value — a couple percent or so (unless rates rise tremendously). I also discuss Treasury bonds and certificates of deposit (CDs) later in this chapter.

✔ **Intermediate-term investments:** These investments are appropriate for more than a few years but less than ten years. Investments that fit the bill are intermediate-term bonds and well-diversified hybrid funds (which include some stocks as well as bonds).

✔ **Long-term investments:** If you have a decade or more for investing your money, you can consider potentially higher-return (and therefore riskier) investments. Stocks, real estate, and other growth-oriented investments can earn the most money if you're comfortable with the risk involved. See Chapter 8 for information on investing the portion that you intend to hold for the long term.

Bonds and bond funds

Bond funds that pay taxable dividends are generally appropriate when you're not in a high tax bracket. Here are some of my favorites:

✔ **Short-term:** Vanguard Short-Term Investment-Grade (800-662-7447; www.vanguard.com)

✔ **Intermediate-term:** Dodge & Cox Income (800-621-3979; www.dodge andcox.com); Harbor Bond (800-422-1050; www.harborfunds.com); Vanguard Total Bond Market Index (800-662-7447; www.vanguard.com)

✔ **Long-term:** Vanguard Long-Term Investment-Grade (800-662-7447; www.vanguard.com)

The following sections discuss other bond funds, as well as the individual bonds you can buy through Treasury Direct.

U.S. Treasury bond funds

U.S. Treasury bond funds are appropriate if you prefer a bond fund that invests in U.S. Treasuries (which have the safety of government backing), or when you're in a high state tax bracket (5 percent or higher) but not a high federal tax bracket. For good Treasury bond funds, look no further than the Vanguard Group, which offers short-, intermediate-, and long-term U.S. Treasury funds with a low 0.24 percent operating expense ratio. With a $100,000 minimum, Vanguard's Admiral series of U.S. Treasury funds offers even higher yields thanks to an even lower expense ratio of 0.12 percent.

Buying Treasuries from the Federal Reserve Bank

If you want an even cheaper method of investing in Treasury bonds than you can get through the thrifty Vanguard Treasury funds, try this: Purchase Treasuries directly from the Federal Reserve Bank. To open an account through the Treasury Direct program, call 800-722-2678, or visit their Web site at www.treasurydirect.gov.

Inflation-indexed Treasury bonds

Like a handful of other nations, the U.S. Treasury now offers *inflation-indexed* government bonds. Because a portion of these Treasury bonds' return is pegged to the rate of inflation, the bonds offer investors a safer type of Treasury bond investment option.

To understand the relative advantages of an inflation-indexed bond, take a brief look at the relationship between inflation and a normal bond. When an investor purchases a normal bond, he's committing himself to a fixed yield over a set period of time — for example, a bond that matures in ten years and pays 6 percent interest. However, changes in the cost of living (inflation) are not fixed, so they're difficult to predict.

Suppose that an investor put $10,000 into a regular bond in the 1970s. During the life of his bond, he would've unhappily watched escalating inflation. During the time he held the bond, and by the time his bond matured, he would've witnessed the erosion of the purchasing power of his $600 of annual interest and $10,000 of returned principal.

Enter the inflation-indexed Treasury bond. Say that you have $10,000 to invest and you buy a ten-year, inflation-indexed bond that pays you a real rate of return (this is the return above and beyond the rate of inflation) of, say, 2 percent. This portion of your return is paid out in interest. The other portion of your return is from the inflation adjustment to the principal you invested. The inflation portion of the return gets put back into principal. So if inflation were running at about 2 percent, as it has in recent years, your $10,000 of principal would be indexed upwards after one year to $10,200. In the second year of holding this bond, the 2 percent real return of interest would be paid on the increased ($10,200) principal base.

If inflation skyrocketed and was running at, say, 8 percent rather than 2 percent per year, your principal balance would grow 8 percent per year, and you'd still get your 2 percent real rate of return on top of that. Thus, an inflation-indexed Treasury bond investor would not see the purchasing power of his invested principal or annual interest earnings eroded by unexpected inflation.

The inflation-indexed Treasuries can be a good investment for conservative, inflation-worried bond investors, as well as taxpayers who want to hold the government accountable for increases in inflation. The downside: Inflation-indexed bonds can yield slightly lower returns, because they're less risky compared to regular Treasury bonds.

The Federal Reserve Bank charges $25 annually for accounts with more than $100,000 in Treasury bonds. Smaller accounts are free of any fees. The operating expenses of even the leanest mutual funds can't compete with these rates!

You do sacrifice a bit of liquidity, however, when purchasing Treasury bonds directly from the government. You can sell your bonds, prior to maturity, through the Treasury (for a $45 fee), but it takes some time and hassle. If you want daily access to your money, buy a recommended Vanguard fund and pay the company's low management fee.

State- and federal-tax-free bond funds

State- and federal-tax-free bond funds are appropriate when you're in high federal and state (5 percent or higher) tax brackets. Vanguard (800-662-7447; www.vanguard.com) has the best selection of state-specific tax-free bond funds. USAA (800-382-8722; www.usaa.com) and, to a lesser extent, Fidelity (800-544-8888; www.fidelity.com) — for higher balance ($10,000) customers — offer some of the better state-specific bond funds.

Federal-tax-free-only bond funds

Federal-tax-free-only bond funds (the dividends on them are state-taxable) are appropriate when you're in a high federal bracket but a low state bracket (less than 5 percent) or when you live in a state that doesn't have state- and federal-tax-free funds available. Vanguard (800-662-7447; www.vanguard.com) offers the best selection of federal-tax-free bond funds.

Certificates of deposit (CDs)

For many decades, bank CDs have been a popular investment for folks with some extra cash that isn't needed in the near future. With a CD, you get a higher rate of return than you get on a bank savings account. And unlike with bond funds, your principal does not fluctuate in value.

Compared to bonds, however, CDs have a couple drawbacks:

- ✔ In a CD, your money is not accessible unless you cough up a fairly big penalty — typically six months' interest. With a no-load (commission-free) bond fund, you can access your money without penalty — whether you need some or all of your money next week, next month, or next year.

- ✔ CDs come in only one tax flavor — taxable. Bonds, on the other hand, come in tax-free (federal and/or state) and taxable flavors. So if you're a higher-tax-bracket investor, bonds offer you a tax-friendly option that CDs can't.

In the long run, you should earn more — perhaps 1 to 2 percent more per year — and have better access to your money in bond funds than in CDs. Bond funds make particular sense when you're in a higher tax bracket and you'd benefit from tax-free income on your investments. If you're not in a high tax bracket and you have a bad day whenever your bond fund takes a dip in value, consider CDs. Just make sure that you shop around to get the best interest rate.

One final piece of advice: Don't buy CDs simply for the FDIC (Federal Deposit Insurance Corporation) insurance. Much is made, particularly by bankers, of the FDIC government insurance that comes with bank CDs. The lack of this insurance on high-quality bonds shouldn't be a big concern for you. High-quality bonds rarely default; even if a fund were to hold a bond that defaulted, that bond would probably represent only a tiny fraction (less than 1 percent) of the value of the fund, having little overall impact.

Besides, the FDIC itself is no Rock of Gibraltar. Banks have failed and will continue to fail. Yes, you are insured if you have less than $100,000 in a bank. However, if the bank crashes, you may have to wait a long time and settle for less interest than you thought you were getting. You're not immune from harm, FDIC or no FDIC.

If the government backing you receive through FDIC insurance allows you to sleep better, you can invest in Treasuries (see "Bonds and bond funds," earlier in this chapter), which are government-backed bonds.

Stocks and stock funds

Stocks have stood the test of time for building wealth. (In Chapter 9, I discuss picking individual stocks versus investing through stock mutual funds.) Remember that when you invest in stocks in taxable (non-retirement) accounts, all the distributions on those stocks, such as dividends and capital gains, are taxable. Stock dividends and long-term capital gains do benefit from lower tax rates (maximum of 15 percent).

Some stock picking advocates argue that you should shun stock funds due to tax considerations. I disagree. You can easily avoid stock funds that generate a lot of short-term capital gains, which are taxed at the relatively high ordinary income tax rates. Additionally, increasing numbers of fund companies offer *tax-friendly* stock funds, which are appropriate if you don't want current income or you're in a high federal tax bracket and seek to minimize receiving taxable distributions on your funds. Vanguard (800-662-7447; www.vanguard.com) offers the best menu of tax-managed stock funds. Alternatively, you can invest in a wider variety of diversified stock funds inside an annuity (see the following section). Also consider some of the stock funds I recommend in Chapter 11.

Annuities

As I discuss in Chapter 11, *annuities* are accounts that are partly insurance but mostly investment. Consider contributing to an annuity only after you exhaust contributions to all your available retirement accounts. Because annuities carry higher annual operating expenses than comparable mutual funds, you should consider them only if you plan to leave your money invested, preferably, for 15 years or more. Even if you leave your money invested for that long, the tax-friendly funds discussed in the previous sections of this chapter can allow your money to grow without excessive annual taxation.

The best annuities can be purchased from no-load (commission-free) mutual fund companies — specifically Vanguard (800-662-7447; www.vanguard.com), Fidelity (800-544-4702; www.fidelity.com), and T. Rowe Price (800-638-5660; www.troweprice.com).

Real estate

Real estate can be a financially and psychologically rewarding investment. It can also be a money pit and a real headache if you buy the wrong property or get a "tenant from hell." (I discuss the investment particulars of real estate in Chapter 9 and the nuts and bolts of buying real estate in Chapter 14.)

Small-business investments

Investing in your own business or someone else's established small business can be a high-risk but potentially high-return investment. The best options are those you understand well. See Chapter 9 for more information about small-business investments.

Chapter 13

Investing for Educational Expenses

*I*f you're like most parents (or potential future parents), just turning to this chapter makes you anxious. Such trepidation is understandable. According to much of what you read about educational expenses (particularly college expenses), if costs keep rising at the current rate, you'll have to spend upwards of a million dollars to give your youngster a quality (college and graduate school) education.

Whether you're about to begin a regular college investment plan or you've already started saving, your emotions may lead you astray. The hype about educational costs may scare you into taking a path that's less financially beneficial than others available. However, quality education for your child doesn't have to — and probably won't — cost you as much as those gargantuan projections suggest. In this chapter, I explain the inner workings of the financial aid system, help you gauge how much money you'll need, and discuss educational investment options so that you can keep a cool head (and some money in your pocket) when all is said and done.

Figuring Out How the Financial Aid System Works

Just as your child shouldn't choose a college based solely on whether she thinks she can get in, she shouldn't choose a college on the basis of whether you think you can afford it. Except for the affluent, who have plenty of cash available to pay for the full cost of college, everyone else should apply for financial aid. More than a few parents who don't think that they qualify for financial aid are pleasantly surprised to find that their children have access to loans as well as grants, which don't have to be repaid. (And your ability to pay often isn't a consideration when scholarship committees hand out money — see "Tips for getting loans, grants, and scholarships," later in this chapter, for info on scholarships.)

Completing the Free Application for Federal Student Aid (FAFSA), which is available from any high school or college, is the first step in the financial aid process. (Internet users can fill out the form online at www.fafsa.ed.gov.) As its name implies, you pay nothing for submitting this application other than the time to complete the paperwork. Some private colleges also require that you complete the Financial Aid Form (FAF), which asks for more information than the FAFSA. Some schools also supplement the FAFSA with PROFILE forms; these forms are mainly used by costly private schools to differentiate need among financial aid applicants.

States have their own financial aid programs, so apply to these programs as well if your child plans to attend an in-state college. You and your child can check with your local high school or college financial aid office to get the necessary forms. Some colleges also require submission of supplementary forms directly to them.

The data you supply through student aid forms is run through a *financial needs analysis,* a standard methodology approved by the U.S. Congress. The needs analysis considers a number of factors, such as your income and assets, age and need for retirement income, number of dependents, number of family members in college, and unusual financial circumstances, which you explain on the application.

The financial needs analysis calculates how much money you, as the parent(s), and your child, as the student, are expected to contribute toward educational expenses. Even if the needs analysis determines that you don't qualify for needs-based financial aid, you may still have access to loans that are *not* based on need if you go through the financial aid application process. So make sure that you apply for financial aid!

Treatment of retirement accounts

Under the current financial needs analysis, the value of your retirement plans is *not* considered an asset. By contrast, money that you save *outside* retirement accounts, especially money in the child's name, is counted as an asset and reduces your eligibility for financial aid.

Therefore, forgoing contributions to your retirement savings plans in order to save money in a taxable account for Junior's college fund doesn't make sense. When you do, you pay higher taxes both on your current income and on the interest and growth of the college fund money. In addition to paying higher taxes, you're expected to contribute more to your child's educational expenses.

So while your children are years away from applying to college, make sure that you fully fund your retirement accounts, such as 401(k)s, SEP-IRAs, and Keoghs. In addition to getting an immediate tax deduction in the year you contribute money, future growth on your earnings will grow without taxation while you're maximizing your child's chances of qualifying for aid.

Let me stress the need to get an early start on saving. Most retirement accounts limit how much you can contribute each year. See Chapter 11 for more on saving for your golden years.

Treatment of money in the kids' names

If you plan to apply for financial aid, save money in your name rather than in your children's names (such as via custodial accounts). Colleges expect a much greater percentage of the money in your children's names (35 percent) to be used annually for college costs than the money in your name (about 6 percent).

However, if you're affluent enough to foot your child's college bill without outside help, investing in your kid's name can save you money in taxes. Read on.

Traditional custodial accounts

Parents control a *custodial account* until the child reaches either the age of 18 or 21, depending upon the state in which you reside. Prior to your child's reaching age 14, the first $800 of interest and dividend income is tax free; the next $800 is taxed at 10 percent. Any income above $1,600 is taxed at the parents' marginal tax rate. After age 14, all income generated by investments in your child's name is taxed at your child's rate, presumably a lower tax rate.

Education Savings Accounts

The newer Education Savings Account (ESA) is another option that, like a traditional custodial account, generally makes the most sense for affluent parents who don't expect to apply for or need any type of financial aid. As with regular custodial accounts, parents who have their kids apply for financial aid will be penalized by college financial aid offices for having ESA balances.

Subject to eligibility requirements, you can put up to $2,000 per child per year into an ESA. Single taxpayers with adjusted gross incomes (AGIs) of $110,000 or more and couples with AGIs of $220,000 or more may not contribute to an ESA (although another individual, such as a grandparent, may make the contribution to the child's account). Although the contribution is not tax-deductible, the future investment earnings compound without taxation. Upon withdrawal, the investment earnings are not taxed (unlike with a traditional retirement account) as long as the money is used for qualified education expenses and, in the year of withdrawal, the HOPE or Lifetime Learning tax credit is not claimed for the student. See the latest edition of *Taxes For Dummies,* which I co-wrote (Wiley Publishing), for more details.

Section 529, state-sponsored college savings plans

Section 529 plans (named after Internal Revenue Code Section 529 and also known as *qualified state tuition plans*) are among the newest educational savings plans. A parent or grandparent can generally put more than $200,000 per beneficiary into one of these plans. Up to $55,000 may be placed in a child's college savings account immediately, and this amount counts for the next five years' worth of $11,000 annual tax-free gifts allowed under current gifting laws. (Money contributed to the account is not considered part of the donor's taxable estate. However, if the donor gives $55,000 and then dies before five years are up, a proportionate amount of that gift will be charged back to the donor's estate.)

The attraction of the Section 529 plans is that money inside the plans compounds without tax, and if it's used to pay for college tuition, room and board, and other related higher education expenses, the investment earnings and appreciation can be withdrawn tax-free. You can generally invest in any state plan to pay college expenses in any state, regardless of where you live.

In addition to paying college costs, the money in Section 529 plans may also be used for graduate school expenses. Some states provide additional tax benefits on contributions to their state-sanctioned plan.

Unlike the money in a custodial account, with which a child may do as he pleases when he reaches either the age of 18 or 21 (the age varies by state), these state tuition plans must be used for higher education expenses. However, most state plans do allow you to change the beneficiary. You can also take the money back out of the plan if you change your mind. (You will, however, owe tax on the withdrawn earnings plus a penalty — typically 10 percent.)

A big potential drawback of the Section 529 plans — especially for families hoping for some financial aid — is that college financial aid offices may treat assets in these plans as belonging to the child, which can greatly diminish financial aid eligibility.

Another potential drawback with some plans is that you can't control how the money is invested. Instead, the investment provider(s) may decide how to invest the money. In most plans, the further your child is from college age, the more aggressive the investment mix. As your child approaches college age, the investment mix is tilted to more conservative investments. Some state plans have high investment management fees, and some plans don't allow transfers to other plans.

Please also be aware that a future Congress could change the tax laws affecting these plans, diminishing the tax breaks or increasing the penalties for nonqualified withdrawals.

Clearly, these plans have both pros and cons. They generally make the most sense for affluent parents (or grandparents) to establish for children who don't expect to qualify for financial aid. Do a lot of research and homework before investing in any plan. Check out the investment track record, allocations, and fees in each plan, as well as restrictions on transferring to other plans or changing beneficiaries.

Treatment of home equity and other assets

Your family's assets may also include equity in real estate and businesses that you own. Although the federal financial aid analysis no longer counts equity in your primary residence as an asset, many private (independent) schools continue to ask parents for this information when making their own financial aid determinations. Therefore, paying down your home mortgage more quickly instead of funding retirement accounts can harm you financially: You may end up with less financial aid and a higher tax bill.

Strategizing to Pay for Educational Expenses

Now I get more specific about what college may cost your kids and how you're going to pay for it. I don't have just one solution, because how you help pay for your child's college costs depends on your own unique situation. However, in most cases, you may have to borrow *some* money, even if you have some available cash that can be directed to pay the college bills as you receive them.

Estimating college costs

College can cost a lot. The total costs — including tuition, fees, books, supplies, room, board, and transportation — vary substantially from school to school. The total average annual cost is running around $34,000 per year at private colleges and around $17,000 at public colleges and universities (in-state rate). The more expensive schools can cost up to one-third more. Ouch!

Is all this expense worth it? Although many critics of higher education claim that the cost of a college education shouldn't be rising faster than inflation and that costs can, and should, be contained, denying the value of going to college is hard. Whether you're considering a local community college, your friendly state university, or a selective Ivy League institution, investing in education is usually worth the effort and the cost.

An *investment* is an outlay of money for an expected profit. Unlike a car, which depreciates in value, an investment in education yields monetary, social, and intellectual profits. A car is more tangible in the short term, but an investment in education (even if it means borrowing money) gives you more bang for your buck in the long run.

Colleges are now finding themselves subject to the same types of competition that companies confront. As a result, some colleges are clamping down on rising costs. As with any other product or service purchase, it pays to shop around. You can find good values — colleges that offer competitive pricing *and* provide a quality education. Although you don't want your son or daughter to choose a college simply because it costs the least, you also shouldn't allow a college choice without any consideration or recognition of cost.

Setting realistic savings goals

If you have money left over *after* taking advantage of retirement accounts, by all means, try to save for your children's college costs. You should save in your name unless you know that you aren't going to apply for financial aid, including those loans that are available regardless of your economic situation.

Be realistic about what you can afford for college expenses given your other financial goals, especially saving for retirement (see Chapter 4). Being able to personally pay 100 percent of the cost of a college education, especially at a four-year private college, is a luxury of the affluent. If you're not a high-income earner, consider trying to save enough to pay a third or, at most, half of the cost. You can make up the balance through loans, your child's employment before and during college, and the like.

Use Table 13-1 to help get a handle on how much you should be saving for college.

Table 13-1	How Much to Save for College*
Figure Out This	*Write It Here*
1. **Cost of the school you think your child will attend	$_____
2. Percent of costs you'd like to pay (for example, 20% or 40%)	×_____%
3. Line 1 times line 2 (the amount you'll pay in today's dollars)	= $_____
4. Number of months until your child reaches college age	÷ _____ months
5. *** Line 3 divided by line 4 (amount to save per month today's dollars)	= $_____ / month

Don't worry about correcting the overall analysis for inflation. This worksheet takes care of that through the assumptions made on the returns of your investments as well as the amount that you save over time. This way of doing the calculations works because you assume that the money you're saving will grow at the rate of college inflation. (In the happy event that your investment return exceeds the rate of college inflation, you end up with a little more than you expected.)

**The average cost of a four-year private college education today is about $136,000; the average cost of a four-year public college education is about $68,000. If your child has an expensive taste in schools, you may want to tack 20 to 30 percent onto the average figures.*

*** The amount you need to save (calculated in line 5) needs to be increased once per year to reflect the increase in college inflation — 5 or 6 percent should do.*

Tips for getting loans, grants, and scholarships

A host of financial aid programs, including a number of loan programs, allow you to borrow at fair interest rates. Federal government educational loans have *variable interest rates* — which means that the interest rate you're charged *floats,* or varies, with the overall level of interest rates. Most programs add a few percent to the current interest rates on three-month to one-year Treasury bills. Thus, current rates on educational loans are in the vicinity of rates charged on fixed-rate mortgages. The rates are also capped so that the interest rate on your student loan can never exceed several percent more than the initial rate on the loan.

A number of loan programs, such as unsubsidized Stafford Loans and Parent Loans for Undergraduate Students (PLUS), are available even when your family is not deemed financially needy. Only subsidized Stafford Loans, on which the federal government pays the interest that accumulates while the student is still in school, are limited to students deemed financially needy.

Most loan programs limit the amount that you can borrow per year, as well as the total you can borrow for a student's educational career. If you need more money than your limits allow, PLUS loans can fill the gap: Parents can borrow the full amount needed after other financial aid is factored in. The only obstacle is that you must go through a credit qualification process. Unlike privately funded college loans, you can't qualify for a federal loan if you have negative credit (recent bankruptcy, more than three debts over three months past due, and so on). For more information from the federal government about these student loan programs, call the Federal Student Aid Information Center at 800-433-3243 or visit their Web site at `studentaid.ed.gov`.

If you're a homeowner, you may be able to borrow against the *equity* (market value less the outstanding mortgage loan) in your property. This option is useful because you can borrow against your home at a reasonable interest rate, and the interest is generally tax-deductible. Some company retirement plans — for example, 401(k)s — allow borrowing as well.

Parents are allowed to make penalty-free withdrawals from individual retirement accounts if the funds are used for college expenses. Although you won't be charged an early-withdrawal penalty, the IRS (and most states) will treat the amount withdrawn as income, and your income taxes will increase accordingly. On top of that, the financial aid office will look at your beefed-up income and assume that you don't need as much financial aid.

In addition to loans, a number of grant programs are available through schools, the government, and independent sources. You can apply for federal government grants via the FAFSA (see "Figuring Out How the Financial Aid System Works," earlier in this chapter). Grants available through state government programs may require a separate application. Specific colleges and other private organizations (including employers, banks, credit unions, and community groups) also offer grants and scholarships.

One of the most important aspects of getting financial aid is choosing to apply, even if you're not sure whether you qualify. You may be able to lower your expected contribution by reducing your qualifying assets. (For more information on how those in charge of handing out financial aid evaluate how much of the bill you can foot, see "Figuring Out How the Financial Aid System Works.")

Many scholarships and grants don't require any extra work on your part — simply apply for financial aid through colleges. Other aid programs need seeking out — check directories and databases at your local library, your child's school counseling department, and college financial aid offices. You can also contact local organizations, churches, employers, and so on. You have a better chance of getting scholarship money through these avenues.

Your child can work and save money during high school and college. In fact, if your child qualifies for financial aid, he or she is expected to contribute a certain amount to education costs from savings and employment during the school year or summer breaks. Besides giving Junior a stake in his own future, this training encourages sound personal financial management.

Investing Educational Funds

Financial companies pour billions of dollars into advertising for investment and insurance products that they claim are best for making your money grow for your children. Don't get sucked in by these ads.

What makes for good and bad investments in general applies to investments for educational expenses, too. Stick with basic, proven, lower-cost investments. (Chapter 9 explains what you generally need to look for and beware of.) The following sections focus on considerations specific to college funding.

Good investments: No-load mutual funds

As I discuss in Chapter 10, the professional management and efficiency of the best no-load mutual funds makes them a tough investment to beat. Chapters 11 and 12 provide recommendations for investing money in funds both inside and outside tax-sheltered retirement accounts.

Gearing the investments to the time frame involved until your children will need to use the money is the most important issue with no-load mutual funds. The closer your child gets to attending college and using the money saved, the more conservatively the money should be invested.

Bad investments

Life insurance policies that have cash values are some of the most oversold investments for funding college costs. Here's the usual pitch: "Because you need life insurance to protect your family, why not buy a policy that you can borrow against to pay for college?"

The reason you shouldn't invest in this type of policy to fund college costs is that you're better off contributing to retirement accounts that give you an immediate tax deduction that saving through life insurance doesn't offer. Because life insurance that comes with a cash value is more expensive, parents are more likely to make a second mistake — not buying enough coverage. If you need and want life insurance, you're better off buying lower-cost term life insurance (see Chapter 16).

Another poor investment for college expenses is one that fails to keep you ahead of inflation, such as savings or money market accounts. You need your money to grow so that you can afford educational costs down the road.

Prepaid tuition plans should generally be avoided. A few states have developed plans that allow you to pay college costs at a specific school (calculated for the age of your child). The allure of these plans is that by paying today, you eliminate the worry of not being able to afford rising costs in the future.

This logic doesn't work for several reasons. First, odds are quite high that you don't have the money today to pay in advance. Second, putting money into such plans reduces your eligibility for financial aid dollar for dollar. If you have that kind of extra dough around, you're better off using it for other purposes (and you're not likely to worry about rising costs anyway). You can invest your own money — that's what the school's going to do with it, anyway.

Besides, how do you know which college your child will want to attend and how long it may take him or her to finish? Coercing your child into the school you've already paid for is a sure ticket to long-term problems in your relationship.

Overlooked investments

Too often, I see parents knocking themselves out to make more money so that they can afford to buy a bigger home, purchase more expensive cars, take better vacations, and send their kids to more expensive (and therefore supposedly better) private high schools and colleges. Sometimes families want to send younger children to costly elementary schools, too. Families stretch themselves with outrageous mortgages or complicated living arrangements so that they can get into neighborhoods with top-rated public schools or send their kids to expensive private elementary schools.

The best school in the world for your child is you and your home. The reason many people I know (including my siblings and I) were able to attend some of the top educational institutions in this country is that concerned parents worked hard, not just at their jobs, but at spending time with the kids when they were growing up. Rather than working to make more money (with the best of intentions of buying educational games or trips, or sending the kids to better schools), try focusing more attention on your kids. In my humble opinion, you can do more for your kids by spending more time with them.

I see parents scratching their heads about their child's lack of academic interest and achievement — they blame the school, TV, video games, or society at large. These factors may contribute to the problem, but education begins in the home. Schools can't do it alone.

Living within your means not only allows you to save more of your income but also frees up more of your time for raising and educating your children. Don't underestimate the value of spending more time with your kids and giving them your attention.

Chapter 14

Investing in Real Estate: Your Home and Beyond

*B*uying a home or investing in real estate can be financially and psychologically rewarding. On the other hand, owning real estate can be a real pain in the posterior, because purchasing and maintaining property can be quite costly, time-consuming, and emotionally draining.

Perhaps you're looking to escape your rented apartment and buy your first home. Or maybe you're interested in cornering the local real estate market and making millions in investment property. In either case, you can learn many lessons from real estate buyers who've traveled before you.

Note: Although this chapter focuses primarily on real estate in which you're going to live — otherwise known by those in the trade as *owner-occupied property* — much of what this chapter covers is relevant to real estate investors. (For additional information on buying *investment real estate* — property that you rent out to others — see Chapter 9.)

Deciding Whether to Buy or Rent

You may be tired of moving from rental to rental. Perhaps your landlord doesn't adequately keep up the place, or you have to ask permission to hang a picture on the wall. You may desire the financial security and rewards that seem to come with home ownership. Or maybe you just want a place to call your own.

Any one of these reasons is "good enough" to *want* to buy a home. But you should take stock of your life and your financial health *before* you decide to buy so you can decide whether you still want to buy a home and how much you can really afford to spend. You need to ask yourself some bigger questions.

Assessing your timeline

From a financial standpoint, you really shouldn't buy a place unless you can anticipate being there for at least three years (preferably five or more). Buying and selling a property entails a lot of expenses, including the cost of getting a mortgage (points, application, and appraisal fees), inspection expenses, moving costs, real estate agents' commissions, and title insurance. *To cover these transaction costs plus the additional costs of ownership, a property needs to appreciate about 15 percent.*

If you need or want to move in a couple years, counting on 15 percent appreciation is risky. If you're fortunate and you happen to buy before a sharp upturn in housing prices, you may get it. If you're unlucky, you'll probably lose money on the deal.

Some people are willing to invest in real estate even when they don't expect to live in it for long and would consider turning their home into a rental. Doing so can work well financially in the long haul, but don't underestimate the responsibilities that come with being a landlord. Also, most people need to sell their first home in order to tap all the cash that they have in it so that they can buy the next one.

Determining what you can afford

Although buying and owning your own home can be a wise financial move in the long run, it's a major purchase that can send shock waves through the rest of your personal finances. You'll probably have to take out a 15- to 30-year mortgage to finance your purchase. The home you buy will need maintenance over the years. Owning a home is a bit like running a marathon: Just as you should be in good physical shape to successfully run a marathon, you should be in good financial health when you buy a home.

I have seen too many people fall in love with a home and make a rash decision without taking a hard look at the financial ramifications. Take stock of your overall financial health (especially where you stand in terms of retirement planning), *before* you buy property or agree to a particular mortgage. Don't let the financial burdens of a home control your financial future.

Don't trust a lender when he tells you what you can "afford" according to some formulas the bank uses to figure out what kind of a credit risk you are. To determine how much a potential home buyer can borrow, lenders look primarily at annual income; they pay no attention to some major aspects of a borrower's overall financial situation. Even if you don't have money tucked away into retirement savings, or you have several children to clothe, feed, and help put through college, you still qualify for the same size loan as other people with the same income (assuming equal outstanding debts). Only you can figure out how much you can afford, because only you know what your other financial goals are and how important they are to you.

Here are some important financial questions that no lender will ask or care about but that you should ask yourself before buying a home:

- Are you saving enough money monthly to reach your retirement goals?
- How much do you spend (and want to continue spending) on fun things such as travel and entertainment?
- How willing are you to budget your expenses in order to meet your monthly mortgage payments and other housing expenses?
- How much of your children's expected college educational expenses do you want to be able to pay for?

The other chapters in this book can help you answer these important questions. Chapter 4 in particular will help you think through saving for important financial goals.

Many homeowners run into financial trouble because they don't know their spending needs and priorities or how to budget for them. Some of these owners have trouble curtailing their spending despite the large amount of debt they just incurred; in fact, some spend even more for all sorts of furniture and remodeling. Many people prop up spending habits with credit. For this reason, a surprisingly large percentage — some studies say about half — of people who borrow additional money against their home equity use the funds to pay consumer debts.

Calculating how much you can borrow

Mortgage lenders want to know your ability to repay the money you borrow. So you have to pass a few tests that calculate the maximum amount the lender is willing to lend you. For a home in which you'll reside, lenders total up your monthly housing expenses. They define your housing costs as

```
mortgage payment + property taxes + insurance
```

Lenders typically loan you up to about 35 percent of your monthly gross (before taxes) income for the housing expense. (If you're self-employed, take your net income from the bottom line of your federal tax form Schedule C and divide by 12 to get your monthly gross income.)

Lenders also consider your other debts when deciding how much to lend you. These other debts diminish the funds available to pay your housing expenses. Lenders add the amount you need to pay down your other consumer debts (auto loans, credit cards) to your monthly housing expense. The monthly total costs of these debt payments plus your housing costs typically cannot exceed 40 percent.

One general rule says that you can borrow up to three times (or two and one-half times) your annual income when buying a home. But this rule is a really rough estimate. The maximum that a mortgage lender will loan you depends on interest rates. If rates fall (as they have during much of the past decade), the monthly payment on a mortgage of a given size also drops. Thus, lower interest rates make real estate more affordable.

Table 14-1 gives you a ballpark idea of the maximum amount you may be eligible to borrow. Multiply your gross annual income by the number in the second column to determine the approximate maximum you may be able to borrow. For example, if you're getting a mortgage with a rate around 7 percent and your annual income is $50,000, multiply 3.5 by $50,000 to get $175,000 — the approximate maximum mortgage allowed.

Comparing the costs of owning versus renting

The cost of owning a home is an important financial consideration for many renters. Some people assume that owning costs more. In fact, owning a home doesn't have to cost a truckload of money; it may even cost less than renting.

Table 14-1	The Approximate Maximum You Can Borrow
When Mortgage Rates Are	*Multiply Your Gross Annual Income* by This Figure*
4%	4.6
5%	4.2
6%	3.8
7%	3.5
8%	3.2
9%	2.9
10%	2.7
11%	2.5

*If you're self-employed, this is your net income (after expenses but before taxes).

On the surface, buying a place seems a lot more expensive than renting. You're probably comparing your monthly rent (measured in hundreds of dollars to more than $1,000, depending on where you live) to the purchase price of a property, which is usually a much larger number — perhaps $150,000 to $500,000 or more. When you consider a home purchase, you're forced to think about your housing expenses in one huge chunk rather than in small monthly installments (like a rent check).

Tallying up the costs of owning a place can be a useful and not-too-complicated exercise. To make a fair comparison between ownership and rental costs, you need to figure what it will cost on a *monthly basis* to buy a place you desire versus what it will cost to rent a *comparable* place. The worksheet in Table 14-2 enables you to do such a comparison. *Note:* In the interest of reducing the number of variables, all this "figuring" assumes a fixed-rate mortgage, *not* an adjustable-rate mortgage. (For more info on mortgages, see "Financing Your Home," later in this chapter.)

Also, I ignore what economists call the *opportunity cost of owning*. In other words, when you buy, the money you put into your home can't be invested elsewhere, and the foregone investment return on that money, say some economists, should be considered a cost of owning a home. I choose to ignore this concept for two reasons. First, and most importantly, I don't agree with this line of thinking. When you buy a home, you're investing your money in real estate, which historically has offered solid long-term returns (see Chapter 8). And secondly, I have you ignore opportunity cost because it greatly complicates the analysis.

Table 14-2	Monthly Expenses: Renting versus Owning
Figure Out This ($ per Month)	*Write It Here*
1. Monthly mortgage payment (see "Mortgage")	$_____
2. Plus monthly property taxes (see "Property taxes")	+ $_____
3. Equals total monthly mortgage plus property taxes	= $_____
4. Your income tax rate (refer to Table 6-1 in Chapter 6)	%_____
5. Minus tax benefits (line 3 multiplied by line 4)	– $_____
6. Equals after-tax cost of mortgage and property taxes (subtract line 5 from line 3)	= $_____
7. Plus insurance ($30 to $150/mo., depending on property value)	+ $_____
8. Plus maintenance (1% of property cost divided by 12 months)	+ $_____
9. Equals total costs of owning (add lines 6, 7, and 8)	= $_____

Now compare line 8 in Table 14-2 with the monthly rent on a comparable place to see which costs more — owning or renting.

Mortgage

To determine the monthly payment on your mortgage, simply multiply the relevant number (or multiplier) from Table 14-3 by the size of your mortgage expressed in thousands of dollars (divided by 1,000). For example, if you're taking out a $100,000, 30-year mortgage at 6.5 percent, you multiply 100 by 6.32 for a $632 monthly payment.

Property taxes

You can ask a real estate person, mortgage lender, or your local assessor's office what your annual property tax bill would be for a house of similar value to the one you're considering buying (the average is 1.5 percent of your property's value). Divide this amount by 12 to arrive at your monthly property tax bill.

Tax savings in home ownership

Generally speaking, mortgage interest and property tax payments for your home are tax-deductible on Schedule A of IRS Form 1040 (see Chapter 7). Here's a shortcut that works quite well in determining your tax savings in home ownership: Multiply your federal tax rate (see Table 7-1 in Chapter 7) by the total amount of your property taxes and mortgage payment. Technically speaking, not all of your mortgage payment is tax-deductible — only the portion of the mortgage payment that goes toward interest. In the early years

Table 14-3	Your Monthly Mortgage Payment Multiplier	
Interest Rate	*15-Year Mortgage Multipliers*	*30-Year Mortgage Multipliers*
4.0%	7.40	4.77
4.5%	7.65	5.07
5.0%	7.91	5.37
5.5%	8.17	5.68
6.0%	8.44	6.00
6.5%	8.71	6.32
7.0%	8.99	6.65
7.5%	9.27	6.99
8.0%	9.56	7.34
8.5%	9.85	7.69
9.0%	10.14	8.05
9.5%	10.44	8.41
10.0%	10.75	8.78

of your mortgage, nearly all of your payment goes toward interest. On the other hand, your property taxes will probably rise over time. You may earn state tax benefits from your deductible mortgage interest and property taxes, as well.

If you want to more accurately determine how home ownership may affect your tax situation, get out your tax return and try plugging in some reasonable numbers to estimate how your taxes will change. You can also speak with a tax advisor or pick up a copy of the latest edition of *Taxes For Dummies,* which I co-authored (Wiley Publishing).

Considering the long-term costs of renting

When you crunch the numbers to find out what owning rather than renting a comparable place may cost you on a monthly basis, you may discover that owning isn't as expensive as you thought. Or you may find that owning costs more than renting. This discovery may tempt you to think that, financially speaking, renting is cheaper than owning.

Be careful not to jump to conclusions. Remember that you're looking at the cost of owning versus renting *today*. What about 5, 10, 20, or 30 years from now? As an owner, your biggest monthly expense — the mortgage payment — does not increase (assuming that you buy your home with a fixed-rate mortgage). Your property taxes, homeowner's insurance, and maintenance expenses — which are generally far less than your mortgage payment — increase with the cost of living.

When you rent, however, your entire monthly rent is subject to the vagaries of inflation. Living in a rent-controlled unit, where the annual increase allowed in your rent is capped, is the exception to this rule. Rent control does not eliminate price hikes; it just limits them.

Suppose that you're comparing the costs of owning a home that costs $240,000 to renting that same home for $1,200 a month. Table 14-4 compares the cost per month of owning the home (after factoring in tax benefits) to your rental costs over 30 years. This comparison assumes that you take out a mortgage loan equal to 80 percent of the cost of the property at a fixed rate of 7 percent and that the rate of inflation of your homeowner's insurance, property taxes, maintenance, and rent is 4 percent per year. I further assume that you're in a moderate combined 35 percent federal and state tax bracket.

Table 14-4	Cost of Owning versus Renting over 30 Years	
Year	*Ownership Cost per Month*	*Rental Cost per Month*
1	$1,380	$1,200
5	$1,470	$1,410
10	$1,620	$1,710
20	$2,040	$2,535
30	$2,700	$3,750

As you can see in Table 14-4, in the first few years, owning a home costs a little more than renting it. In the long run, however, owning is less expensive, because more of your rental expenses increase with inflation. And don't forget that you're building equity in your property as a homeowner; that equity will be quite substantial by the time that you have your mortgage paid off.

You may be thinking that if inflation doesn't rise 4 percent per year, renting could end up being cheaper. This is not necessarily so. Suppose that inflation didn't exist. Your rent wouldn't escalate, but home ownership expenses wouldn't either. And with no inflation, you could probably refinance your mortgage at a rate lower than 7 percent. If you do the math, owning would still cost less in the long run with lower inflation, but the advantage of owning is less than during periods of higher inflation. Also, in case you're wondering what happens in this analysis if you're in a different tax bracket, owning would still cost less in the long run — the cost savings widen a bit for people in higher tax brackets and lessen a bit for those in lower tax brackets.

Recognizing advantages to renting

Although owning a home and investing in real estate generally pay off handsomely over the long-term, to be fair and balanced, I must say that renting has its advantages. Some of the financially successful renters I've seen include people who pay low rent, either because they made housing sacrifices or they live in a rent-controlled building. If you're consistently able to save 10 percent or more of your earnings, you're probably well on your way to achieving your future financial goals.

As a renter, you can avoid worrying about or being responsible for fixing up the property — that's your landlord's responsibility. You also have more financial and psychological flexibility as a renter. If you want to move, you can generally do so a lot easier as a renter than you can as a homeowner.

Having a lot of your money tied up in your home is another challenge that you don't face when renting over the long haul. Some people enter their retirement years with a substantial portion of their wealth in their homes. As a renter, you can have all your money in financial assets that you can tap into more easily. Homeowners who have a major chunk of equity tied up in a home at retirement can downsize to a less costly property to free up cash and/or take out a reverse mortgage (discussed later in this chapter) on their home equity.

Financing Your Home

After you look at your financial health, figure out your timeline, and compare renting costs to owning costs, you need to confront the tough task of obtaining a hunk of debt to buy a home (unless you're independently wealthy). A mortgage loan from a bank or other source makes up the difference between the cash you intend to put into the purchase and the agreed-upon selling price of the real estate.

Understanding the two major types of mortgages

Like many other financial products, you have zillions of mortgages to choose from. The differences can be important or trivial, expensive or not. Two major types of mortgages exist — those with a fixed interest rate and those with a variable or adjustable rate.

Fixed-rate mortgages, which are usually issued for a 15- or 30-year period, have interest rates that never, ever change. The interest rate you pay the first month is the same rate you pay the last month (and every month in between). Because the interest rate stays the same, your monthly mortgage payment amount doesn't change. With a fixed-rate mortgage, you have no uncertainty or interest rate worries.

Fixed-rate loans are not risk-free, however. If interest rates fall significantly after you obtain your mortgage, you face the danger of being stuck with your higher-cost mortgage if you're unable to refinance (see "Refinancing your mortgage," later in this chapter). You can be turned down for a refinance because of deterioration in your financial situation or a decline in the value of your property. Even if you're eligible to refinance, you may have to spend significant time and money to complete the process.

In contrast to a fixed-rate mortgage, an *adjustable-rate mortgage* (ARM) carries an interest rate that varies over time. With an adjustable-rate mortgage, you can start with one interest rate and then have different rates for every year (or possibly every month) during a 30-year mortgage. Thus, the size of your monthly payment fluctuates. Because a mortgage payment makes an unusually large dent in most homeowners' checkbooks anyway, signing up for an ARM without understanding its risks is dangerous.

The attraction of ARMs is the potential interest savings. For the first few years of an adjustable loan, the interest rate is typically lower than it is on a comparable fixed-rate loan. After that, the cost depends on the overall trends in interest rates. When interest rates drop, stay level, or rise just a little, you probably continue to pay less for your adjustable. On the other hand, when rates rise more than a percent or two and then stay elevated, the adjustable can cost you more than a fixed-rate loan.

Choosing between fixed- and adjustable-rate mortgages

You should weigh the pros and cons of each mortgage type and decide what's best for your situation *before* you go out to purchase a piece of real estate or refinance a loan. In the real world, most people ignore this advice. The excitement of purchasing a home tends to cloud one's judgment. My experience has been that few people look at their entire financial picture before making major real estate decisions. You may end up with a mortgage that could someday seriously overshadow the delight you have for your little English herb garden out back.

Consider the issues I discuss in this section before you decide which kind of mortgage — fixed or adjustable — is right for you.

How willing and able are you to take on financial risk?

Take stock of how much risk you can take with the size of your monthly mortgage payment. You can't afford much risk, for example, if your job and income are unstable and you need to borrow a lot. I define *a lot* as "close to the maximum a bank is willing to lend you." *A lot* can also mean that you have no slack in your monthly budget — in other words, you're not regularly saving money. If you're in this situation, stick with a fixed-rate loan.

Don't take an adjustable simply because the initially lower interest rates allow you to afford the property you want to buy (unless you're absolutely certain that your income will rise to meet future payment increases). Try setting your sights on a property that you can afford — with a fixed-rate mortgage.

If interest rates rise, a mushrooming adjustable mortgage payment may test the lower limits of your checking account balance. When you don't have emergency savings you can tap to make the higher payments, how can you afford the monthly payments — much less all the other expenses of home ownership?

And don't forget to factor in reasonably predictable future expenses that may affect your ability to make payments. For example, are you planning to start a family soon? If so, your income may fall while your expenses rise (as they surely will).

If you can't afford the highest allowed payment on an adjustable-rate mortgage, *don't take it.* You shouldn't accept the chance that the interest rate may not rise that high — it might, and then you could lose your home! Ask your lender to calculate the highest possible *maximum monthly payment* on your loan. That's the payment you'd face if the interest rate on your loan were to go to the highest level allowed (the *lifetime cap*).

You need to also consider your stress level. If you have to start following interest rate movements, it's probably not worth gambling on rates. Life is too short!

On the other hand, maybe you're in a position to take the financial risks that come with an adjustable-rate mortgage. An adjustable places much of the risk of fluctuating rates on you (most adjustables, however, limit, or *cap,* the rise in the interest rate allowed on your loan). In return for your accepting some interest-rate risk, lenders cut you a deal — an adjustable's interest rate starts lower and stays lower if the overall level of interest rates doesn't rise substantially. Even if rates go up, they'll probably come back down over the life of your loan. So if you can stick with your adjustable for better and for worse, you may still come out ahead over the long term. Typical caps are 2 percent per year and 6 percent over the life of the loan.

You may feel financially secure in choosing an adjustable loan if you have a hefty financial cushion accessible in the event that rates go up, you take out a smaller loan than you're qualified for, or you're saving more than 10 percent of your income.

How long do you plan to keep the mortgage?

A mortgage lender takes extra risk when committing to a constant interest rate for 15 to 30 years. Lenders don't know what may happen in the intervening years, so they charge you a premium for their risk.

The savings on most adjustables is usually guaranteed in the first two or three years, because an adjustable-rate mortgage starts at a lower interest rate than a fixed one. If rates rise, you can end up giving back or losing the savings you achieve in the early years of the mortgage. In most cases, if you aren't going to keep your mortgage more than five to seven years, you're probably paying unnecessary interest costs to carry a fixed-rate mortgage.

Another mortgage option is a *hybrid loan,* which combines features of both the fixed- and adjustable-rate mortgages. For example, the initial rate may hold constant for a number of years — three to five years is common — and then adjust once a year or every six months thereafter. These hybrid loans may make sense for you if you foresee a high probability of keeping your loan seven to ten years or less but want some stability in your monthly payments. The longer the initial rate stays locked in, the higher the rate.

Shopping for fixed-rate mortgages

Of the two major types of mortgages I discuss earlier in this chapter, fixed-rate loans are generally easier to shop for and compare. The following sections cover what you need to know when shopping for fixed-rate mortgages.

Trading off interest rates and points

The *interest rate* is the annual amount a lender charges you for borrowing its money. The interest rate on a fixed-rate loan must always be quoted with the points on the loan.

Points are upfront fees paid to your lender when you close on your loan. Points are actually percentages: One point is equal to 1 percent of the loan amount. So when a lender tells you that 1.5 points are on a quoted loan, you pay 1.5 percent of the amount you borrow as points. On a $100,000 loan, for example, 1.5 points cost you $1,500.

If one lender offers 30-year mortgages at 6.75 percent and another lender offers them at 7 percent, the 7 percent loan isn't necessarily worse. You also need to consider how many points each lender charges.

The interest rate and points on a fixed-rate loan go together and move in opposite directions. If you're willing to pay more points on a given loan, the lender will often reduce the interest rate. Paying more in upfront points can save you a lot of money in interest, because the interest rate on your loan determines your payments over a long, long time — 15 to 30 years. If you pay fewer points, your interest rate increases. Paying less in points may appeal to you if you don't have much cash for closing on your loan.

Suppose Lender X quotes you 6.75 percent on a 30-year fixed-rate loan and charges one point (1 percent). Lender Y, who quotes 7 percent, doesn't charge any points. Which is better? The answer depends mostly on how long you plan to keep the loan.

The 6.75-percent loan is 0.25 percent less than the 7 percent loan. Year in and year out, the 6.75 percent loan saves you 0.25 percent. But because you have to pay 1 percent (one point) upfront on the 6.75 percent loan, it takes about four years to earn back the savings to cover the cost of that point. So if you expect to keep the loan less than four years, go with the 7 percent option.

To perform an apples-to-apples comparison of mortgages from different lenders, get interest rate quotes at the same point level for each mortgage. For example, ask each lender for the interest rate on a loan for which you pay one point.

Be wary of lenders who advertise no-point loans as though they're offering something for nothing. Remember, if a loan has no points, it's *guaranteed* to have a higher interest rate. That's not to say that the loan is better or worse than comparable loans from other lenders. But don't get sucked in by a no-points sales pitch. Most lenders who spend big bucks advertising these types of loans rarely have the best deals.

Understanding other lender fees

In addition to charging you points and the ongoing interest rate, lenders tack on all sorts of other upfront fees when processing your loan. You need to know the total of all lender fees so that you can compare different mortgages and determine how much completing your home purchase is going to cost you.

Lenders can nickel and dime you with a number of fees other than points. Actually, you pay more than nickels and dimes — $300 here and $50 there adds up in a hurry! Here are the main culprits:

✔ **Application and processing fees:** Most lenders charge several hundred dollars to complete your paperwork and process it through their *underwriting* (loan evaluation) department. The justification for this fee is that if your loan is rejected or you decide not to take it, the lender needs to cover the costs. Some lenders return this fee to you upon closing if you go with their loan (after you're approved).

✔ **Credit report:** Many lenders charge a modest fee (about $50) for obtaining a copy of your credit report. This report tells the lender whether you've been naughty or nice to other lenders in the past. If you have problems on your credit report, clean them up before you apply (see "Increasing your approval chances," later in this chapter; also check out Chapter 2 for info on checking your credit report).

✔ **Appraisal:** The property for which you're borrowing money needs to be valued. If you default on your mortgage, your lender doesn't want to get stuck with a property worth less than you owe. For most residential properties, the appraisal cost is typically several hundred dollars.

✔ **Title and escrow charges:** These not-so-inconsequential costs are discussed in the section, "Remembering title insurance and escrow fees," later in this chapter.

Get a written itemization of charges from all lenders you are seriously considering so that you can more readily compare different lenders' mortgages and so you have no surprises when you close on your loan. And to minimize your chances of throwing money away on a loan for which you may not qualify, ask the lender whether you may not be approved for some reason. Be sure to disclose any problems you're aware of that are on your credit report or with the property.

Some lenders offer loans without points or other lender charges. ***Note:*** Lenders aren't charities. If they don't charge points or other fees, they have to make up the difference by charging a higher interest rate on your loan. Consider such loans only if you lack cash for closing or if you're planning to use the loan for just a few years.

Shunning balloon loans

Be wary of balloon loans. They look like fixed-rate loans, but they really aren't. With a *balloon loan,* the large remaining loan balance becomes fully due at a predetermined time — typically within three to ten years. Balloon loans are dangerous because you may not be able to refinance into a new loan to pay off the balloon loan when it comes due. What if you lose your job or your income drops? What if the value of your property drops and the appraisal comes in too low to qualify you for a new loan? What if interest rates rise and you can't qualify for the higher rate on a new loan? Taking a balloon loan is a high-risk maneuver that can backfire.

Don't take a balloon loan unless the following three conditions are true:

✔ You really, really want a certain property.

✔ The balloon loan is your only financing option.

✔ You're positive that you're going to be able to refinance when the balloon loan comes due.

If you take a balloon loan, get one that takes as much time as possible before it comes due.

Inspecting adjustable-rate mortgages (ARMs)

Although sorting through myriad fixed-rate mortgage options is enough to give most people a headache, comparing the bells and whistles of ARMs can give you a mortgage migraine. Caps, indexes, margins, and adjustment periods — you can spend weeks figuring it all out. If you're clueless about personal finances — or just think that you are — shopping for adjustables scores a 9.9 degree of difficulty on the financial frustration scale.

Unfortunately, you have to wade through a number of details to understand and compare one adjustable to another. Bear with me. And remember throughout this discussion that calculating exactly which ARM is going to cost you the least is impossible, because the cost depends on so many variables. Selecting an ARM has a lot in common with selecting a home: You have to make trade-offs and compromises based on what's important to you.

Understanding the start rate

Just as the name implies, the *start rate* is the interest rate your ARM starts with. Don't judge a loan by this rate. You won't be paying this attractively low rate for long. The interest rate will rise as soon as the terms of the mortgage allow.

Start rates are probably one of the least important items to focus on when comparing adjustables. (You'd never know this from the way some lenders advertise adjustables — you see ads with the start rate in 3-inch bold type and everything else in microscopic footnotes!)

Beware of prepayment penalties

Avoid loans with prepayment penalties. You pay this charge, usually 2 to 3 percent of the loan amount, when you pay off your loan before you're supposed to.

Prepayment penalties don't typically apply when you pay off a loan because you sell the property. But if you refinance such a loan in order to take advantage of lower interest rates, you almost always get hit by the prepayment penalties if the loan calls for such penalties.

The only way to know whether a loan has a prepayment penalty is to ask. If the answer is yes, find yourself another mortgage.

The formula (which includes index and margin) and rate caps are far more important for determining what a mortgage will cost you in the long run. Some people have labeled the start rate a *teaser rate,* because the initial rate on your loan is set artificially low to entice you. In other words, even if the market level of interest rates doesn't change, your adjustable is destined to increase — 1 to 2 percent is not uncommon.

Determining the future interest rate

You'd never (I hope) agree to a loan if your lender's whim and fancy determined your future interest rate. You need to know exactly how a lender figures out how much your interest rate is going to increase. All adjustables are based on the following formula, which specifies how the future interest rate on your loan is set:

```
index + margin = interest rate
```

Indexes are often (but not always) widely quoted in the financial press, and the specific one used on a given adjustable loan is chosen by the lender. The six-month Treasury bill rate is an example of an index that's used on some mortgages.

The *margin* is the amount added to the index to determine the interest rate you pay on your mortgage. Most loans have margins of around 2.5 percent.

So, for example, the interest rate of a mortgage could be driven by the following formula:

```
six-month Treasury bill rate + 2.5 percent = interest rate
```

In this situation, if six-month Treasuries are yielding 4.5 percent, the interest rate on your loan should be 7.0 percent. This figure is known as the *fully indexed rate.* If this loan starts at 5.0 percent and the rate on six-month Treasuries stays the same, your loan should eventually increase to 7.0 percent.

The margin on a loan is hugely important. When you're comparing two loans that are tied to the same index and are otherwise equivalent, the loan with the lower margin is better. The margin determines the interest rate for every year you hold the mortgage.

Indexes differ mainly in how rapidly they respond to changes in interest rates. Following are the more common indexes:

✔ **Treasury bills (T-bills):** These indexes are based on government IOUs (Treasury bills), and there are a whole lot of them out there. Most adjustables are tied to the interest rate on 6-month or 12-month T-bills.

- ✔ **Certificates of deposit (CDs):** Certificates of deposit are interest-bearing bank investments that lock you in for a specific period of time. ARMs are usually tied to the average interest rate banks are paying on six-month CDs. Like T-bills, CDs tend to respond quickly to changes in the market level of interest rates. Unlike T-bills, CD rates tend to move up a bit more slowly when rates rise and come down faster when rates decline.

- ✔ **11th District Cost of Funds:** This index tends to be among the slower-moving indexes. ARMs tied to 11th District Cost of Funds tend to start out at a higher interest rate. A slower-moving index has the advantage of moving up less quickly when rates are on the rise. On the other hand, you need to be patient to realize the benefit of falling interest rates.

Avoid negative amortization and interest-only loans if you're stretching

As you make mortgage payments over time, the loan balance you still owe is gradually reduced — this process is known as *amortizing* the loan. The reverse of this process — increasing your loan balance — is called *negative amortization.*

Negative amortization is allowed by some ARMs. Your outstanding loan balance can grow even though you're continuing to make mortgage payments when your mortgage payment is less than it really should be.

Some loans cap the increase of your monthly payment but not of the interest rate. The size of your mortgage payment may not reflect all the interest you owe on your loan. So rather than paying off the interest and some of your loan balance (or principal) every month, you're paying off some but not all of the interest you owe. Thus, the extra unpaid interest you still owe is added to your outstanding debt.

Taking on negative amortization is like paying only the minimum payment required on a credit card bill. You keep racking up greater interest charges on the balance as long as you make only the artificially low payment. Doing so defeats the whole purpose of borrowing an amount that fits your overall financial goals. And you may never get your mortgage paid off!

Another type of potentially concerning loan, the interest-only mortgage, is being promoted heavily in higher cost housing markets that stretch buyers' budgets. In the early years of an interest-only loan, the monthly payment is kept lower because only interest is being paid; no payment is going to reduce the loan balance. What many folks don't realize is that at a set number of years into the mortgage (for instance, three, five, or seven), principal payments kick in as well, which dramatically increases the monthly payment.

Avoid negative-amortization mortgages. The only way to know for certain whether a loan includes negative amortization is to ask. Some lenders aren't forthcoming about telling you. You'll find it more frequently on loans that lenders consider risky. If you're having trouble finding lenders who are willing to deal with your financial situation, be especially careful.

Tread carefully with interest-only mortgages. Do not consider interest-only loans if you're stretching to be able to afford a home, and consider one only if you understand how they work and can afford the inevitable jump in payments.

Adjustment period or frequency

Every so many months, the mortgage-rate formula is applied to recalculate the interest rate on an adjustable-rate loan. Some loans adjust monthly. Others adjust every 6 or 12 months.

In advance of each rate change, the lender should send you a notice telling you what your new rate is. All things being equal, the less frequently your loan adjusts, the less financial uncertainty you have in your life. Less-frequent adjustments usually coincide with a loan starting at a higher interest rate.

Understanding rate caps

When the initial interest rate expires, the interest rate fluctuates based on the formula of the loan. Almost all adjustables come with rate caps. The *adjustment cap* limits the maximum rate change (up or down) allowed at each adjustment. On most loans that adjust every six months, the adjustment cap is 1 percent.

Loans that adjust more than once per year often limit the maximum rate change allowed over the entire year as well. On most such loans, the *annual rate cap* is 2 percent.

Almost all adjustables come with *lifetime caps,* which limit the highest rate allowed over the entire life of the loan. ARMs often have lifetime caps that are 5 to 6 percent higher than the start rate (though higher lifetime caps are increasingly common during the current low-interest-rate period). Before taking an adjustable, figure out the maximum possible payment at the lifetime cap to be sure that you can handle it.

Other ARM fees

Just as with fixed-rate mortgages, ARMs can carry all sorts of additional lender-levied charges. See the section "Understanding other lender fees," earlier in this chapter, for details.

Avoiding the down-payment blues

You can generally qualify for the most favorable mortgage terms by making a down payment of at least 20 percent of the purchase price of the property. In addition to saving money on interest, you can avoid the added cost of private mortgage insurance (PMI) by putting down this much. (To protect against losing money in the event you default on your loan, lenders usually require PMI, which costs several hundred dollars per year on a typical mortgage.)

Many people don't have the equivalent of 20 percent or more of the purchase price of a home so that they can avoid paying private mortgage insurance. Here are a number of solutions for coming up with that 20 percent faster or buying with less money down:

- ✔ **Go on a spending diet.** One sure way to come up with a down payment is to raise your savings rate by slashing your spending. Take a tour through Chapter 6 to find strategies for cutting back on your spending.

- ✔ **Consider lower-priced properties.** Some first-time home buyers have expectations that are too grand. Smaller properties and ones that need some work can help keep down the purchase price and, therefore, the required down payment.

- ✔ **Find partners.** You can often get more home for your money when you buy a building in partnership with one, two, or a few people. Make sure you write up a legal contract to specify what's going to happen if a partner wants out, divorces, or passes away.

- ✔ **Seek reduced down-payment financing.** Some lenders will offer you a mortgage even though you may be able to put down only 3 to 10 percent of the purchase price. You must have solid credit to qualify for such loans, and you generally have to obtain and pay for the extra expense of private mortgage insurance (PMI), which protects the lender if you default on the loan. When the property value rises enough or you pay down the mortgage enough to have 20 percent equity in the property, you can drop the PMI.

  Some property owners or developers may be willing to finance your purchase with 10 percent or less down. You can't be as picky about properties, because not as many are available under these terms — many need work or haven't been sold yet for other reasons.

- ✔ **Get assistance from family.** If your parents, grandparents, or other relatives have money dozing away in a savings or CD account, they may be willing to lend (or even give) you the down payment. You can pay them an interest rate higher than the rate they're currently earning but lower than what you'd pay to borrow from a bank — a win/win situation for both of you. Lenders generally ask whether any portion of the down payment is borrowed and will reduce the maximum amount they're willing to loan you accordingly.

For more home-buying strategies, get a copy of the latest edition of *Home Buying For Dummies* (Wiley Publishing), which I co-authored with real estate guru Ray Brown.

Comparing 15-year and 30-year mortgages

Many people don't have a choice between 15- and 30-year mortgages. To afford the monthly payments on their desired home, they need to spread the loan payments over a longer period of time, and a 30-year mortgage is the only answer. A 15-year mortgage has higher monthly payments because you pay it off faster. With fixed-rate mortgages hovering around 6 percent, a 15-year mortgage comes with payments that are about 35 to 40 percent higher than those for a 30-year mortgage.

Even if you can afford these higher payments, taking the 15-year option isn't necessarily better. The money for making extra payments doesn't come out of thin air. You may have better uses (which I discuss later in this section) for your excess funds.

And if you opt for a 30-year mortgage, you maintain the flexibility to pay it off faster (except in those rare cases where you have to pay a prepayment penalty). By making additional payments on a 30-year mortgage, you can create your own 15-year mortgage. But if the need arises, you can fall back to making only the payments required on your 30-year schedule.

Locking yourself into higher monthly payments with a 15-year mortgage comes with a risk. If money gets too tight in the future, you can fall behind in your mortgage payments. You may be able to refinance your way out of the predicament, but you can't count on it. If your finances worsen or your property declines in value, you may have trouble qualifying for a refinance.

Suppose that you qualify for a 15-year mortgage and you're financially comfortable with the higher payments; the appeal of paying off your mortgage 15 years sooner is enticing. Besides, the interest rate is lower — generally up to ½ percent lower — on a 15-year mortgage. So if you can afford the higher payments on the 15-year mortgage, you'd be silly not to take it, right? Not so fast. You're really asking whether you should pay off your mortgage slowly or more quickly. And the answer isn't simple — it depends.

If you have the time and inclination (and a good financial calculator), you can calculate how much interest you can save or avoid through a faster payback. I have a friendly word of advice about spending hours crunching numbers: *don't.* You can make this decision by considering some qualitative issues.

First, think about *alternative uses* for the extra money you'd be throwing into paying down the mortgage. What's best for you depends on your overall financial situation and what else you can do with the money. If you would end up blowing the extra money at the racetrack or on an expensive car, pay down the mortgage. That's a no-brainer.

But suppose that you take the extra $100 or $200 per month that you were planning to add to your mortgage payment and contribute it to a retirement account instead. This step may make financial sense. Why? Because contributions to 401(k)s, SEP-IRAs, Keoghs, and other types of retirement accounts (discussed in Chapter 11) are tax-deductible.

When you add an extra $200 to your mortgage payment to pay off your mortgage faster, you receive *no* tax benefits. When you dump that $200 into a retirement account, you get to subtract that $200 from the income on which you pay taxes. If you're paying 35 percent in federal and state income taxes, you shave $70 (that's $200 multiplied by 35 percent) off your tax bill.

In most cases, you get to deduct your mortgage interest on your tax return. So if you're paying 6 percent interest, your mortgage may really cost you only around 4 percent after you factor in the tax benefits. If you think you can do better (remember to consider the taxes on investment returns) by investing elsewhere (stocks, investment real estate, and so on), go for it. Investments such as stocks and real estate have generated better returns over the long haul. These investments carry risk, though, and they're not guaranteed to produce any return.

If you're uncomfortable investing and you'd otherwise leave the extra money sitting in a money market fund or savings account, you're better off paying down the mortgage. When you pay down the mortgage, you invest your money in a sure thing with a modest return.

If you have pre-college-age kids, you have an even better reason to fund retirement accounts before you consider paying down your mortgage quickly. Retirement account balances are generally not counted as an asset when determining financial aid for college expenses. By contrast, many schools still count equity in your home (the difference between its market value and your loan balance) as an asset. Your reward for paying down your mortgage balance may be less financial aid! (See Chapter 13 for more details about financing educational expenses.)

Paying down your mortgage faster, especially when you have children, is rarely a good financial decision if you haven't exhausted contributions to your retirement accounts. Save in your retirement accounts first and get the tax benefits.

Finding the best lender

As with other financial purchases, you can save a lot of money by shopping around. It doesn't matter whether you shop around on your own or hire someone to help you. Just do it!

On a 30-year, $180,000 mortgage, for example, getting a mortgage that costs 0.5 percent less per year saves you about $20,000 in interest over the life of the loan (given current interest rate levels). That's enough to buy a decent car! On second thought, save it!

Shopping for a lender on your own

In most areas, you can find many mortgage lenders. Although having a large number of lenders to choose from is good for competition, it also makes shopping a chore.

Large banks whose names you recognize from their advertising usually don't offer the best rates. Make sure that you check out some of the smaller lending institutions in your area. Also, check out mortgage bankers, who, unlike banks, only do mortgages. The better mortgage bankers offer some of the most competitive rates.

Real estate agents can also refer you to lenders with whom they've previously done business. These lenders may not necessarily offer the most competitive rates — the agent simply may have done business with them in the past.

You can also look in the real estate section of one of the larger Sunday newspapers in your area for charts of selected lender interest rates. These tables are by no means comprehensive or reflective of the best rates available. In fact, many of them are sent to newspapers for free by firms that distribute mortgage information to mortgage brokers. Use the tables as a starting point by calling the lenders who list the best rates.

HSH Associates (800-873-2837; www.hsh.com) publishes mortgage information for each of the 50 states. For $23, the company will send you a list of dozens of lenders' rate quotes. You need to be a real data junkie to wade through these multipage reports full of numbers and abbreviations, though.

Hiring a mortgage broker

Insurance agents peddle insurance, real estate agents sell real estate, and mortgage brokers deal in mortgages. They buy mortgages at wholesale from lenders and then mark them up to retail before selling them to you. The mortgage brokers get their income from the difference, or *spread*. The terms of the loan obtained through a broker are generally the same as the terms you obtain from the lender directly.

Mortgage brokers get paid a percentage of the loan amount — typically 0.5 to 1 percent. This commission is negotiable, especially on larger loans that are more lucrative. Ask a mortgage broker what his cut is. Many people don't ask for this information, so some brokers may act taken aback when you inquire. Remember, it's your money!

The chief advantage of using a mortgage broker is that the broker can shop among lenders to get you a good deal. If you're too busy or disinterested to shop around for a good deal on a mortgage, a competent mortgage broker can probably save you money. A broker can also help you through the tedious process of filling out all those horrible documents lenders demand before giving you a loan. And if you have credit problems or an unusual property, a broker may be able to match you up with a hard-to-find lender who's willing to offer you a mortgage.

When evaluating a mortgage broker, be on guard for those who are lazy and don't continually shop the market looking for the best mortgage lenders. Some brokers place their business with the same lenders all the time, and those lenders don't necessarily offer the best rates. Also watch out for salespeople who earn big commissions pushing certain loan programs that aren't in your best interests. These brokers aren't interested in taking the time to understand your needs and discuss your options. Thoroughly check a broker's references before doing business.

Even if you plan to shop on your own, talking to a mortgage broker may still be worthwhile. At the very least, you can compare what you find with what brokers say they can get for you. Just be careful. Some brokers tell you what you want to hear and then aren't able to deliver when the time comes.

When a loan broker quotes you a really good deal, ask who the lender is. (Most brokers refuse to reveal this information until you pay the few hundred dollars to cover the appraisal and credit report.) You can check with the actual lender to verify the interest rate and points the broker quotes you and make sure that you're eligible for the loan.

Increasing your approval chances

A lender can take several weeks to complete your property appraisal and an evaluation of your loan package. When you're under contract to buy a property, having your loan denied after waiting several weeks can mean that you lose the property as well as the money you spent applying for the loan and having the property inspected. Some property sellers may be willing to give you an extension, but others won't.

Here's how to increase your chances of having your mortgage approved:

✔ **Get your finances in shape before you shop.** You won't have a good handle on what you can afford to spend on a home until you whip your personal finances into shape. Do so before you begin to make offers on properties. This book can help you. If you have consumer debt, eliminate it — the more credit card, auto loan, and other consumer debt you rack up, the less mortgage you qualify for. In addition to the high inter-est rate and the fact that it encourages you to live beyond your means, you now have a third reason to get rid of consumer debt. Hang onto the dream of owning a home, and plug away at paying off consumer debts.

✔ **Clear up credit report problems.** If you think you may have errors on your credit report, get a copy before you apply for a mortgage. Chapter 2 provides contact information for the major credit bureaus and explains how to obtain a free copy of your credit report, as well as correct any mistakes or clear up blemishes.

✔ **Get preapproved or prequalified.** When you get *prequalified,* a lender speaks with you about your financial situation and then calculates the maximum amount they're willing to lend you based on what you tell them. *Preapproval* is much more in-depth and includes a lender's review of your financial statements. Just be sure not to waste your time and money getting preapproved if you're not really ready to get serious about buying.

✔ **Be upfront about problems.** Late payments, missed payments, or debts that you never bothered to pay can come back to haunt you. The best defense against loan rejection is to avoid it in the first place. You can sometimes head off potential rejection by disclosing to your lender any-thing that may cause a problem before you apply for the loan. That way, you have more time to correct problems and find alternate solutions. Mortgage brokers (see the preceding section) can also help you shop for lenders who are willing to offer you a loan despite credit problems.

✔ **Work around low/unstable income.** When you've been changing jobs or you're self-employed, your recent economic history may be as unstable as a country undergoing a regime change. Making a larger down pay-ment is one way around this problem. If you put down 25 percent or more, you may be able to get a no-income verification loan. You may try getting a co-signer, such as a relative or good friend. As long as they aren't borrowed up to their eyeballs, they can help you qualify for a larger loan than you can get on your own. Be sure that all parties understand the terms of the agreement, including who's responsible for monthly payments!

✔ **Consider a backup loan.** You certainly should shop among different lenders, and you may want to apply to more than one for a mortgage. Although applying for a second loan means additional fees and work, it can increase your chances of getting a mortgage if you're attempting to buy a difficult-to-finance property or if your financial situation makes some lenders leery. Be sure to disclose to each lender what you're doing — the second lender to pull your credit report will see that another lender has already done so.

Finding the Right Property

Shopping for a home can be fun. You get to peek inside other people's cupboards and closets. But for most people, finding the right house at the right price can take a lot of time. When you're buying with partners or a spouse (or children, if you choose to share the decision-making with them), finding the right place can also entail a lot of compromise. A good agent (or several who specialize in different areas) can help with the legwork. The following sections cover the main things you need to consider when shopping for a home to call your own.

Condo, town house, co-op, or detached home?

Some people's image of a home is a single-family dwelling — a stand-alone house with a lawn and white picket fence. In some areas, however — particularly in higher-cost neighborhoods — you find *condominiums* (you own the unit and a share of everything else), *town homes* (attached or row houses), and *cooperatives* (you own a share of the entire building).

The allure of such higher-density housing is that it's generally less expensive. In some cases, you don't have to worry about some of the general maintenance, because the owner's association (which you pay for, directly or indirectly) takes care of it.

If you don't have the time, energy, or desire to keep up a property, shared housing may make sense for you. You generally get more living space for your dollar and it may also provide you with more security than a stand-alone home.

As investments, however, single-family homes generally do better in the long run. Shared housing is easier to build and hence easier to overbuild; on the other hand, single-family houses are harder to put up because more land is required. But most people, when they can afford it, still prefer a stand-alone home.

With that being said, you should remember that a rising tide raises all boats. In a good real estate market, all types of housing appreciate, although single-family homes tend to do better. Shared housing values tend to increase the most in densely populated urban areas with little available land for new building.

From an investment return perspective, if you can afford a smaller single-family home instead of a larger shared-housing unit, buy the single-family home. Be especially wary of buying shared housing in suburban areas with lots of developable land.

Casting a broad net

You may have an idea about the type of property and location you're interested in or think you can afford before you start your search. You may think, for example, that you can afford only a condominium in the neighborhood you're interested in. But if you take the time to check out other communities, you may be surprised to find one that meets most of your needs and also has affordable single-family homes. You'd never know about this community if you narrowed your search too quickly.

Even if you've lived in an area for a while and you think you know it well, look at different types of properties in a number of communities before you narrow your search. Be open-minded, and figure out which of your many criteria for a home you *really* care about.

Finding out actual sale prices

Don't look at just a few of the homes listed at a particular price and then get depressed because they're all dogs or you can't afford what you really want. Before you decide to renew your apartment lease, remember that properties often sell for less than the price at which they're listed.

Find out what the places you look at eventually sell for. Doing so gives you a better sense of what you can really afford as well as what places are really worth. Ask the agent or owner who sold the property what the sale price was, or contact the town's assessors' office for information on how to obtain property sale price information.

Researching the area

Even (and especially) if you fall in love with a house at first sight, go back to the neighborhood at various times of the day and on different days of the week. Travel to and from your prospective new home during commute hours to see how long your commute will really take. Knock on a few doors and meet your potential neighbors. You may discover, for example, that a flock of chickens lives in the backyard next door or that the street and basement frequently flood.

What are the schools like? Go visit them. Don't rely on statistics about test scores. Talk to parents and teachers. What's really going on at the school? Even if you don't have kids, the quality of the local school has direct bearing on the value of your property. Is crime a problem? Call the local police department. Will future development be allowed? If so, what type? Talk to the planning department. What are your property taxes going to be? Is the property located in an area susceptible to major risks, such as floods, mudslides, fires, or earthquakes? Consider these issues even if they're not important to you, because they can affect the resale value of your property. Make sure that you know what you're getting yourself into *before* you buy.

Working with Real Estate Agents

When you buy (or sell) a home, you'll probably work with a real estate agent. Real estate agents earn their living on commission. As such, their incentives can be at odds with what's best for you.

Real estate agents usually don't hide the fact that they get a cut of the deal. Property buyers and sellers generally understand the real estate commission system. I credit the real estate profession for calling its practitioners "agents" instead of coming up with some silly obfuscating title such as "housing consultants."

A top-notch real estate agent can be a significant help when you purchase or sell a property. On the other hand, a mediocre, incompetent, or greedy agent can be a real liability. The following sections help you sort the good from the bad.

Recognizing conflicts of interest

Real estate agents, because they work on commission, face numerous conflicts of interest. Some agents may not even recognize the conflicts in what they're doing. The following list presents the most common conflicts of interest that you need to watch out for:

✔ Because agents work on commission, it costs them when they spend time with you and you don't buy or sell. They want you to complete a deal, and they want that deal as soon as possible — otherwise, they don't get paid. Don't expect an agent to give you objective advice about what you should do given your overall financial situation. Examine your overall financial situation *before* you decide to begin working with an agent.

✔ Because real estate agents get a percentage of the sales price of a property, they have a built-in incentive to encourage you to spend more. Adjustable-rate mortgages (see "Financing Your Home," earlier in this chapter) allow you to spend more, because the interest rate starts at a lower level than that of a fixed-rate mortgage. Thus, real estate agents are far more likely to encourage you to take an adjustable. But adjustables are a lot riskier — you need to understand these drawbacks before signing up for one.

✔ Agents often receive a higher commission when they sell listings that belong to other agents in their office. Beware. Sometimes the same agent represents both the property seller and the property buyer in the transaction — a real problem. Agents who are holding open houses for sale may try to sell to an unrepresented buyer they meet at the open house. There's no way one person can represent the best interests of both sides.

✔ Because agents work on commission and get paid a percentage of the sales price of the property, many are not interested in working with you if you can't or simply don't want to spend a lot. Some agents may reluctantly take you on as a customer and then give you little attention and time. Before you hire an agent, check references to make sure that he works well with buyers like you.

✔ Real estate agents typically work a specific territory. As a result, they usually can't objectively tell you the pros and cons of the surrounding region. Most won't admit that you may be better able to meet your needs by looking in another area where they don't normally work. Before you settle on an agent (or an area), spend time figuring out the pros and cons of different territories on your own. If you want to seriously look in more than one area, find agents who specialize in each area.

✔ If you don't get approved for a mortgage loan, your entire real estate deal may unravel. So some agents may refer you to a more expensive lender who has the virtue of high approval rates. Be sure to shop around — you can probably get a loan more cheaply. Be especially wary of agents who refer you to mortgage lenders and mortgage brokers who pay agents referral fees. Such payments clearly bias a real estate agent's "advice."

✔ Home inspectors are supposed to be objective third parties who are hired by prospective buyers to evaluate the condition of a property. Some agents may encourage you to use a particular inspector with a reputation of being "easy" — meaning he may not "find" all the house's defects. Remember, it's in the agent's best interest to seal the deal, and the discovery of problems may sidetrack those efforts.

✔ Some agents, under pressure to get a house listed for sale, agree to be accomplices and avoid disclosing known defects or problems with the property. In most cover-up cases, it seems, the seller doesn't explicitly ask an agent to help cover up a problem; the agent just looks the other way or avoids telling the whole truth. Never buy a home without having a home inspector look it over from top to bottom.

Buyer's agents/brokers

An increasing number of agents are marketing themselves as buyer's agents/brokers. Supposedly, these folks represent your interests as a property buyer exclusively.

Legally speaking, buyer's agents may sign a contract saying that they represent your — and only your — interests. Before this enlightened era, all agents contractually worked for the property seller.

The title "buyer's agent" is one of those things that sounds better than it really is. Agents who represent you as buyer's brokers still get paid only when you buy. And they still get a commission as a percentage of the purchase price. So they still have an incentive to sell you a piece of real estate; and the more expensive it is, the more commission they make.

Looking for the right qualities in real estate agents

When you hire a real estate agent, you want to find someone who's competent and with whom you can get along. Working with an agent costs a lot of money — so make sure that you get your money's worth.

Interview several agents. Check references. Ask agents for the names and phone numbers of at least three clients they worked with in the past six months (in the geographical area in which you're looking). You should look for the following traits in any agent you work with:

- ✔ **Full-time employment:** Some agents work in real estate as a second or even third job. Information in this field changes constantly. The best agents work at it full-time so that they can stay on top of the market.

- ✔ **Experience:** Hiring someone with experience doesn't necessarily mean looking for an agent who's been kicking around for decades. Many of the best agents come into the field from other occupations, such as business or teaching. Some sales, marketing, negotiation, and communication skills can certainly be picked up in other fields, but experience in buying and selling real estate does count.

- ✔ **Honesty and integrity:** You trust your agent with a lot. If your agent doesn't level with you about what a neighborhood or particular property is really like, you suffer the consequences.

- ✔ **Interpersonal skills:** An agent has to be able to get along not only with you but also with a whole host of other people who are typically involved in a real estate deal: other agents, property sellers, inspectors, mortgage lenders, and so on. An agent doesn't have to be Mr. or Ms. Congeniality, but he or she should be able to put your interests first without upsetting others.

✔ **Negotiation skills:** Putting a real estate deal together involves negotiation. Is your agent going to exhaust all avenues to get you the best deal possible? Be sure to ask the agent's references how well the agent negotiated for them.

✔ **High quality standards:** Sloppy work can lead to big legal or logistical problems down the road. If an agent neglects to recommend thorough and complete inspections, for example, you may be stuck with undiscovered problems after the deal is done.

Agents sometimes market themselves as *top producers,* which means that they sell a relatively large volume of real estate. This title doesn't count for much for you, the buyer. It may be a red flag for an agent who focuses on completing as many deals as possible. When you're buying a home, you need an agent who has the following additional traits:

✔ **Patience:** When you're buying a home, the last thing you want is an agent who tries to push you into making a deal. You need an agent who's patient and willing to allow you the necessary time it takes to get educated and make the best decision for yourself.

✔ **Local market and community knowledge:** When you're looking to buy a home in an area in which you're not currently living, an informed agent can have a big impact on your decision.

✔ **Financing knowledge:** As a buyer (especially a first-time buyer or someone with credit problems), you should look for an agent who knows which lenders can best handle your type of situation.

Buying real estate requires somewhat different skills than selling real estate. Few agents can do both equally well. No law or rule says that you must use the same agent when you sell a property as you do when you buy a property.

Putting Your Deal Together

After you do your homework on your personal finances, discover how to choose a mortgage, and research neighborhoods and home prices, you'll hopefully be ready to close in on your goal. Eventually you'll find a home you want to buy. Before you make that first offer, though, you need to understand the importance of negotiations, inspections, and the other elements of a real estate deal.

Negotiating 101

When you work with an agent, the agent usually handles the negotiation process. But you need to have a plan and strategy in mind; otherwise, you may end up overpaying for your home. Here are some recommendations for getting a good deal:

- ✔ **Never fall in love with a property.** If you have money to burn and can't imagine life without the home you just discovered, pay what you will. Otherwise, remind yourself that other good properties are out there. Having a backup property in mind can help.

- ✔ **Find out about the property and owner before you make your offer.** How long has the property been on the market? What are its flaws? Why is the owner selling? For example, if the seller is moving because she got a job in another town and is about to close on a home purchase, she may be willing to reduce the price to get her money out of the home. The more you understand about the property and the seller's motivations, the better able you'll be to draft an offer that meets both parties' needs.

- ✔ **Get comparable sales data to support your price.** Too often, home buyers and their agents pick a number out of the air when making an offer. But if the offer has no substance behind it, the seller will hardly be persuaded to lower his asking price. Pointing to recent and comparable home sales to justify your offer price strengthens your case.

- ✔ **Remember that price is only one of several negotiable items.** Sometimes sellers get fixated on selling their homes for a certain amount. Perhaps they want to get at least what they paid for it years ago. You may be able to get a seller to pay for certain repairs or improvements, to pay some of your closing costs, or to offer you an attractive loan without the extra loan fees that a bank would charge. Likewise, the real estate agent's commission is negotiable.

Games agents play to get a deal done

The thirst for commission brings out the worst in some real estate agents. They tell you fibs to motivate you to buy on the seller's terms. Saying that other offers are coming in on the property you're interested in is one common fib. Or they say that the seller already turned down an offer for X dollars because he's holding out for a higher offer.

The car dealer trick — blaming the office manager for not allowing them to reduce their commission — is another tactic. Be sure to spend the time needed to find a good agent and to understand an agent's potential conflicts of interest (see the section on agents earlier in the chapter).

Inspecting before you buy

When you buy a home, you may be making one of the biggest (if not *the* biggest) purchases of your life. Unless you build homes and do contracting work, you probably have no idea what you're getting yourself into when it comes to furnaces and termites.

Spend the time and money to locate and hire good inspectors and other experts to evaluate the major systems and potential problem areas of the home. Areas that you want to check include

- ✔ Overall condition of the property
- ✔ Electrical, heating, and plumbing systems
- ✔ Foundation
- ✔ Roof
- ✔ Pest control and dry rot
- ✔ Seismic/slide/flood risk

Inspection fees often pay for themselves. When problems that you weren't aware of are uncovered, the inspection reports give you the information you need to go back and ask the property seller to fix the problems or reduce the purchase price of the property to compensate you for correcting the deficiencies yourself.

As with other professionals whose services you retain, you need to make sure that you interview at least a few inspection companies. Ask which systems they inspect and how detailed a report they're going to prepare for you (ask for a sample copy). Ask them for names and phone numbers of three people who used their service within the past six months.

Never accept a seller's inspection report as your only source of information. When a seller hires an inspector, he may hire someone who won't be as diligent and critical of the property. What if the inspector is a buddy of the seller or his agent? By all means, review the seller's inspection reports if available, but get your own as well.

And here's one more inspection for you to do: The day before you close on the purchase, do a brief walk-through of the property. Make sure that everything is still in good order and that all the fixtures, appliances, curtains, and other items that were to be left per the contract are still there. Sometimes sellers (and their movers) "forget" what they're supposed to leave or try to test your powers of observation.

Remembering title insurance and escrow fees

Mortgage lenders require *title insurance* to protect against someone else claiming legal title to your property. This claim can happen, for example, when a husband and wife split up and the one who remains in the home decides to sell and take off with the money. If both spouses are listed as owners on the title, the spouse who sells the property (possibly by forging the other's signature) has no legal right to do so.

Both you and the lender can get stuck holding the bag if you buy the home that the one spouse of this divided couple is selling. But title insurance acts as the salvation for you and your lender. Title insurance protects you against the risk that the spouse whose name was forged will come back and reclaim rights to the home after it's sold.

If you're in the enviable position of paying cash for a property, you should still buy title insurance, even though a mortgage lender won't prod you to do so. You need to protect your investment.

Escrow charges pay for neutral third-party services to ensure that the instructions of the purchase contract or refinance are fulfilled and that everyone gets paid.

Many people don't seem to understand that title insurance and escrow fees vary from company to company. As a result, they don't bother to comparison shop; they simply use the company that their real estate agent or mortgage lender suggests.

When you call around for title insurance and escrow fee quotes, make sure that you understand all the fees. Many companies tack on all sorts of charges for things such as courier fees and express mail. If you find a company with lower prices and want to use it, ask for an itemization in writing so that you don't have any surprises.

Real estate agents and mortgage lenders can be a good starting point for referrals because they usually have a broader perspective on the cost and service quality of different companies. Call other companies as well. Agents and lenders may be biased toward a company simply because they're in the habit of using it or they referred clients to it before.

After You Buy

After you buy a home, you'll make a number of important decisions over the months and years ahead. This section discusses the key issues you need to deal with as a homeowner and tells what you need to know to make the best decision for each of them.

Refinancing your mortgage

Three reasons motivate people to *refinance,* or obtain a new mortgage to replace an old one. One is obvious: to save money because interest rates have dropped. Refinancing can also be a way to raise capital for some other purpose. You can use refinancing to get out of one type of loan and into another. The following sections can help you to decide on the best option in each case.

Spending money to save money

If your current loan has a higher rate of interest than comparable new loans, you may be able to save money by refinancing. Because refinancing costs money, whether you can save enough to justify the cost is open to question. If you can recover the expenses of the refinance within a few years, go for it. If recovering the costs will take longer, refinancing may still make sense if you anticipate keeping the property and mortgage that long.

Be wary of mortgage lenders or brokers who tout how soon your refinance will pay for itself; they usually oversimplify their calculations. For example, if the refinance costs you $2,000 to complete (accounting for appraisals, loan fees and points, title insurance, and so on) and reduces your monthly payment by $100, lenders or brokers typically say that it's going to take 20 months for you to recoup the refinance costs. This estimate isn't accurate, however, because you lose some tax write-offs if your mortgage interest rate and payment are reduced. You can't simply look at the reduced amount of your monthly payment. (Mortgage lenders like to look at it, however, because it makes refinancing more attractive.) And your new mortgage will be reset to a different term than the number of years remaining on your old one.

If you want a better estimate of your likely cost savings but don't want to spend hours crunching numbers, take your tax rate — for example, 27 percent — and reduce your monthly payment savings on the refinance by this amount (see Chapter 7). Continuing with the example in the preceding paragraph, if your monthly payment drops by $100, you're really saving only about $73 a month after factoring in the lost tax benefits. So it takes about 28 months ($2,000 divided by $73) — not 20 — to recoup the refinance costs.

Note that not all refinances cost tons of money. So-called no-cost refinances or no-point loans minimize your out-of-pocket expenses, but as I discuss earlier in this chapter, they may not be your best long-term options. Such loans usually come with higher interest rates.

Using money for another purpose

Refinancing to pull out cash from your home for some other purpose can make good financial sense because under most circumstances, mortgage interest is tax-deductible. Paying off other higher-interest consumer debt — such as on credit cards or on an auto loan — is a common reason for borrowing against a home. The interest on consumer debt is not tax-deductible and is generally at a much higher interest rate than what mortgages charge you.

If you're starting a business, consider borrowing against your home to finance the launch of your business. You can usually do so at a lower cost than on a business loan.

You need to find out whether a lender is willing to lend you more money against the equity in your home (which is the difference between the market value of your house and the loan balance). You can use Table 14-1, earlier in this chapter, to estimate the maximum loan for which you may qualify.

Changing loans

You may want to refinance even though you aren't forced to raise cash or you're able to save money. Perhaps you're not comfortable with your current loan — holders of adjustable-rate mortgages often face this problem. You may find out that a fluctuating mortgage payment makes you anxious and wreaks havoc on your budget. The certainty of a fixed-rate mortgage may be your salvation.

Paying money to go from an adjustable to a fixed rate is a lot like buying insurance. The cost of the refinance is "insuring" you a level mortgage payment. Consider this option only if you want peace of mind and you plan to stay with the property for a number of years.

Sometimes jumping from one adjustable to another makes sense. Suppose that you can lower the maximum lifetime interest rate cap and the refinance won't cost much. Your new loan should have a lower initial interest rate than the one you're paying on your current loan. Even if you don't save megabucks, the peace of mind of a lower ceiling can make refinancing worth your while.

Mortgage life insurance

Shortly after you buy a home or close on a mortgage, you start getting mail from all kinds of organizations who keep track of publicly available information about mortgages. Most of these organizations want to sell you something, and they don't tend to beat around the bush. "What will your dependents do if you meet with an untimely demise and they're left with a gargantuan mortgage?" these organizations ask. In fact, this is a good financial-planning question. If your family is dependent on your income, can they survive financially if you pass away?

Don't waste your money on mortgage life insurance. You may need life insurance to provide for your family and help meet large obligations such as mortgage payments or educational expenses for your children, but mortgage life insurance is typically grossly overpriced. (Check out the life insurance section in Chapter 16 for advice about term life insurance.) You should consider mortgage life insurance only if you have a health problem and the mortgage life insurer does not require a physical examination. Be sure to compare it with term life options.

Is a reverse mortgage a good idea?

An increasing number of homeowners are finding, particularly in their later years of retirement, that they lack cash. The home in which they live is usually their largest asset. Unlike other investments, such as bank accounts, bonds, or stocks, a home does not provide any income to the owner unless he or she decides to rent out a room or two.

A *reverse mortgage* allows a homeowner who's low on cash to tap into home equity. For an elderly homeowner, tapping into home equity can be a difficult thing to do psychologically. Most people work hard to feed a mortgage month after month, year after year, until it's finally all paid off. What a feat and what a relief after all those years!

Taking out a reverse mortgage reverses this process. Each month, the reverse mortgage lender sends you a check that you can spend on food, clothing, travel, or whatever suits your fancy. The money you receive each month is really a loan from the bank against the value of your home, which makes the monthly check free from taxation. A reverse mortgage also allows you to stay in your home and use its equity to supplement your monthly income.

The main drawback of a reverse mortgage is that it can diminish the estate that you may want to pass on to your heirs or use for some other purpose. Also, some loans require repayment within a certain number of years. The fees and the effective interest rate you're charged to borrow the money can be quite high.

Because some loans require the lender to make monthly payments to you as long as you live in the home, lenders assume that you'll live many years in your home so that they won't lose money when making these loans. If you end up keeping the loan for only a few years because you move, for example, the cost of the loan is extremely high.

You may be able to create a reverse mortgage within your own family network. This technique can work if you have family members who are financially able to provide you with monthly income in exchange for ownership of the home when you pass away.

You have other alternatives to tapping the equity in your home. Simply selling your home and buying a less expensive property (or renting) is one option. Under current tax laws, qualifying house sellers can exclude a sizable portion of their profits from capital gains tax: up to $250,000 for single taxpayers and $500,000 for married couples.

Selling your house

The day will someday come when you want to sell your house. If you're going to sell, make sure you can afford to buy the next home you desire. Be especially careful if you're a trade-up buyer — that is, if you're going to buy an even more expensive home. All the affordability issues discussed at the beginning of this chapter apply. You also need to consider the following issues.

Selling through an agent

When you're selling a property, you want an agent who can get the job done efficiently and for as high a price as possible. As a seller, you need to seek an agent who has marketing and sales expertise and is willing to put in the time and money necessary to sell your house. Don't necessarily be impressed by an agent who works for a large company. What matters more is what the agent will do to market your property.

When you list your house for sale, the contract you sign with the listing agent includes specification of the commission to be paid if the agent is successful in selling your house. In most areas of the country, agents usually ask for a 6 percent commission. In an area that has lower-cost housing, they may ask for 7 percent.

Regardless of what an agent says is "typical," "standard," or "what my manager requires," *always* remember that commissions are negotiable. Because the commission is a percentage, you have a much greater possibility of getting a lower commission on a higher-priced house. If an agent makes 6 percent selling both a $200,000 house and a $100,000 house, the agent makes twice as much on the $200,000 house. Yet selling the higher-priced house does not take twice as much work. (Selling a $400,000 house certainly doesn't take four times the effort of selling a $100,000 house.)

If you're selling a higher-priced home (above $250,000), you have no reason to pay more than a 5 percent commission. For expensive properties ($500,000 and up), a 4 percent commission may be reasonable. You may find, however, that your ability to negotiate a lower commission is greatest when an offer is on the table. Because you don't want to give other agents (working with buyers) a reason not to sell your house, have your listing agent cut his take rather than reduce the commission that you advertise you're willing to pay to an agent who brings you a buyer.

In terms of the length of the listing sales agreement you make with an agent, three months is reasonable. When you give an agent a listing that's too long (6 to 12 months) in duration, the agent may simply toss your listing into the multiple listing book and expend little effort to sell your property. Practically speaking, if your home hasn't sold, you can fire your agent whenever you want, regardless of the length of the listing agreement. However, a shorter listing may be more motivating for your agent.

Selling without a real estate agent

You may be tempted to sell without an agent so that you can save the commission that's deducted from your house's sale price. If you have the time, energy, and marketing experience and you can take the time to properly value your home, you can sell your house without an agent and possibly save some money.

The major problem with attempting to sell your house on your own is that agents who are working with buyers don't generally look for or show their clients properties that are for sale by owner.

Besides saving you time, a good agent can help ensure that you're not sued for failing to disclose the known defects of your property. If you decide to sell your house on your own, make sure you have access to a legal advisor who can review the contracts. Whether you sell through an agent or not, be sure to read the latest edition of *House Selling For Dummies,* which I co-wrote with real estate expert Ray Brown (Wiley).

Should you keep your home until prices go up?

Many homeowners are tempted to hold onto their properties (when they need to move) if the property is worth less than when they bought it or if the real estate market is soft. Renting out your property is probably not worth the hassle, and holding onto it is probably not worth the financial gamble. If you need to move, you're better off, in most cases, selling your house.

You may reason that, in a few years (during which you'd rent the property), the real estate storm clouds will clear and you'll be able to sell your property at a much higher price. Here are three risks associated with this line of thinking:

> ✔ You can't know whether property prices in the next few years are going to rebound, stay the same, or drop even further. A property generally needs to appreciate at least a few percent per year just to make up for all the costs of holding and maintaining it.

✔ You may be unprepared for legal issues and dealings with your tenants. If you've never been a landlord, don't underestimate the hassle and headaches associated with this job.

✔ If you convert your home into a rental property in the meantime and it appreciates in value, you're going to pay capital gains tax on your profit when you sell it. This tax wipes out much of the advantage of having held onto the property until prices recovered. (If you want to be a long-term rental property owner, you can do a *tax-free exchange* into another rental property when you sell.)

However, if you would realize little cash from selling *and* you lack other money for the down payment to purchase your next property, you have good reason for holding onto a home that has dropped in value.

Should you keep your home as investment property after you move?

Converting your home into rental property is worth considering if you need or want to move. Don't consider doing so unless it really is a long-term proposition (ten years or more). As discussed in the preceding section, selling rental property has tax consequences.

If you want to convert your home into an investment property, you have an advantage over someone who's looking to buy an investment property, because you already own your home. Locating and buying investment property takes time and money. You also know what you have with your current home. If you go out and purchase a property to rent, you're starting from scratch.

If your property is in good condition, consider what damage renters may do to it; few renters will take care of your home the way that you would. Also consider whether you're cut out to be a landlord. For more information, see the section on real estate as an investment in Chapter 9.

Part IV

Insurance: Protecting What You've Got

The 5th Wave   By Rich Tennant

"We can't insure your happiness, however we do offer an extended warranty on joie de vivre."

In this part . . .

*J*ust because insurance is boring doesn't mean you can ignore it! I show you how to obtain the right kind of insurance to shield you from the brunt of unexpected major expenses and protect your assets and future earnings. I also reveal which types of insurance you do and do not need, explain what to include and what not to include in your policies, and tell you how much of which things you should insure. Plus, I help you face other creepy but important stuff such as wills, probate, and estate planning.

Chapter 15

Insurance: Getting What You Need at the Best Price

In This Chapter

▶ Understanding my three laws of buying insurance

▶ What to do if you're denied coverage

▶ Getting your claim money

*U*nless you work in the industry, you may find insurance to be a dreadfully boring topic. Most people associate insurance with disease, death, and disaster and would rather do just about anything other than review or spend money on insurance. But because you won't want to deal with money hassles when you're coping with catastrophes — illness, disability, death, fires, floods, earthquakes, and so on — you have to secure insurance well before you need it.

Insurance is probably the most misunderstood and least monitored area of personal finance. Studies show that more than ninety percent of Americans purchase and carry the wrong types and amounts of insurance coverage. My own experience as a financial counselor confirms this statistic. Most people are overwhelmed by all the jargon in sales and policy statements. Thus, they pay more than necessary for their policies and fail to get coverage through the best companies.

In this chapter, I tell you how to determine what kinds of insurance you need, explain what you can do if you're denied coverage, and give you advice on getting your claims filled. Later chapters discuss types of insurance in detail, including insurance on people (Chapter 16) and on possessions (Chapter 17).

Discovering My Three Laws of Buying Insurance

I know your patience and interest in finding out about insurance may be limited, so I boil the subject down to three fairly simple but powerful concepts that can easily save you thousands of dollars over the rest of your insurance-buying years. And while you're saving money, you can still get the coverage you need in order to avoid a financial catastrophe.

Law 1: Insure for the big stuff; don't sweat the small stuff

Imagine, for a moment, that you're offered a chance to buy insurance that reimburses you for the cost of a magazine subscription in the event that the magazine folds and you don't get all the issues you paid for. Because a magazine subscription doesn't cost much, I don't think you'd buy that insurance.

What if you could buy insurance that pays for the cost of a restaurant meal if you get food poisoning? Even if you're splurging at a fancy restaurant, you don't have a lot of money at stake, so you'd probably decline that coverage as well.

The point of insurance is to protect against losses that would be financially catastrophic to you, not to smooth out the bumps of everyday life. The preceding examples are silly, but some people buy equally foolish policies without knowing it. In the following sections, I tell you how to get the most appropriate insurance coverage for your money. I start off with the "biggies" that are worth your money, and then I work down to some of insurance options that are less worthy of your dollars.

Buy insurance to cover financial catastrophes

You should insure against what could be a huge financial loss for you or your dependents. The price of insurance isn't cheap, but it is relatively small in comparison to the potential total loss from a financial catastrophe.

The beauty of insurance is that it spreads risks over millions of other people. Should your home burn to the ground, paying the rebuilding cost out of your own pocket probably would be a financial catastrophe. If you have insurance, the premiums paid by you and all the other homeowners collectively can easily pay the bills.

Think for a moment about what your most valuable assets are. (No, I don't mean your dry wit and your charming personality.) Also consider potential large expenses. Perhaps they include the following:

✔ **Future income:** During your working years, your most valuable asset is probably your future earnings. If you were disabled and unable to work, what would you live on? Long-term disability insurance exists to help you handle this type of situation. If you have a family that's financially dependent on your earnings, how would your family manage if you died? Life insurance can fill the monetary void left by your death.

✔ **Business:** If you're a business owner, what would happen if you were sued for hundreds of thousands of dollars or a million dollars or more for negligence in some work that you messed up? Liability insurance can bail you out.

✔ **Health:** In this age of soaring medical costs, you can easily rack up a $100,000 hospital bill in short order. Major medical health insurance coverage helps you handle such expenses. And yet, a surprising number of people don't carry any health insurance — particularly those who work in small businesses. (See Chapter 16 for more on health insurance.)

Psychologically, buying insurance coverage for the little things that are more likely to occur is tempting. You don't want to feel like you're wasting your insurance dollars. You want to get some of your money back, darn it! You're more *likely* to get into a fender bender with your car or have a package lost in the mail than you are to lose your home to fire or suffer a long-term disability. But if the fender bender costs $500 (which you end up paying out of your pocket because you took my advice to take a high deductible) or the Postal Service loses a package worth $50 or $100, you won't be facing a financial disaster.

On the other hand, if you lose your ability to earn an income because of a disability, or if you're sued for $1,000,000 and you're not insured against such catastrophes, not only will you be extremely unhappy, but you'll also face financial ruin. "Yes, but what are the odds," I hear people rationalize, "that I'll suffer a long-term disability or that I'll be sued for $1,000,000?" I agree that the odds are quite low, but the risk is there. The problem is that you just don't know what, or when, bad luck may befall you.

And don't make the mistake of thinking that you can figure the odds better than the insurance companies can. The insurance companies predict the probability of your making a claim, large or small, with a great deal of accuracy. They employ armies of number-crunching actuaries to calculate the odds that bad things will happen and the frequency of current policyholders' making particular types of claims. The companies then price their policies accordingly.

So buying (or not buying) insurance based on your perception of the likelihood of needing the coverage is foolish. Insurance companies aren't stupid; in fact, they're ruthlessly smart! When insurance companies price policies, they look at a number of factors to determine the likelihood of your filing a claim. Take the example of auto insurance. Who do you think will pay more for auto insurance — a single male who's age 20, lives the fast life in a high-crime city, drives a macho, turbo sports car, and has received two speeding tickets in the past year? Or a couple in their 40s, living in a low-crime area, driving a four-door sedan, and having a clean driving record?

Take the highest deductible you can afford

Most insurance policies have *deductibles* — the maximum amount you must pay, in the event of a loss, before your insurance coverage kicks in. On many policies, such as auto and homeowner's/renter's coverage, most folks opt for a $100 to $250 deductible.

Here are two benefits to taking a higher deductible:

- ✔ **You save premium dollars.** Year in and year out, you can enjoy the lower cost of an insurance policy with a high deductible. You may be able to shave 15 to 20 percent off the cost of your policy. Suppose, for example, that you can reduce the cost of your policy by $150 per year by raising your deductible from $250 to $1,000. That $750 worth of coverage is costing you $150 per year. Thus, you'd need to have a claim of $1,000 or more every five years — highly unlikely — to come out ahead. If you are that accident-prone — guess what — the insurance company will raise your premiums.

- ✔ **You don't have the hassles of filing small claims.** If you have a $300 loss on a policy with a $100 deductible, you need to file a claim to get your $200 (the amount you're covered for after your deductible). Filing an insurance claim can be an aggravating experience that takes hours of time. In some cases, you may even have your claim denied after jumping through all the necessary hoops. Getting your due may require prolonged haggling.

When you have low deductibles, you may file more claims (although this doesn't necessarily mean that you'll get more money). After filing more claims, you may be "rewarded" with higher premiums — in addition to the headache you get from preparing all those blasted forms! Filing more claims may even cause cancellation of your coverage!

Avoid small-potato policies

A good insurance policy can seem expensive. A policy that doesn't cost much, on the other hand, can fool you into thinking that you're getting something for next to nothing. Policies that cost little also cover little — they're priced low because they don't cover large potential losses.

Following are examples of common "small-potato" insurance policies that are generally a waste of your hard-earned dollars. As you read through this list, you may find examples of policies that you bought and that you feel paid for themselves. I can hear you saying, "But I collected on that policy you're telling me not to buy!" Sure, getting "reimbursed" for the hassle of having something go wrong is comforting. But consider all such policies that you bought or may buy over the course of your life. You're not going to come out ahead in the aggregate — if you did, insurance companies would lose money! These policies aren't worth the cost relative to the small potential benefit. On average, insurance companies pay out just 60 cents in benefits on every dollar collected. Many of the following policies pay back even less — around 20 cents in benefits (claims) for every insurance premium dollar spent:

- **Extended warranty and repair plans:** Isn't it ironic that right after the salesperson persuades you to buy a television, computer, or car — in part by saying how reliable the product is — he tries to convince you to spend more money to insure against the failure of the item? If the product is so good, why do you need such insurance?

  Extended warranty and repair plans are expensive and unnecessary insurance policies. Product manufacturers' warranties typically cover any problems that occur in the first three months to a year. After that, paying for a repair out of your own pocket won't be a financial catastrophe. Reputable manufacturers often fix problems or replace the product without charge after a warranty has expired (within a reasonable time period).

- **Home warranty plans:** If your real estate agent or the seller of a home wants to pay the cost of a home warranty plan for you, turning down the offer would be ungracious. (As Grandma would say, you shouldn't look a gift horse in the mouth.) But don't buy this type of plan for yourself. In addition to requiring some sort of fee (around $50) if you need a contractor to come out and look at a problem, home warranty plans limit how much they'll pay for problems.

  Your money is best spent hiring a competent inspector to uncover problems and fix them *before* you purchase the home. If you're buying a house, you should expect to spend money on repairs and maintenance; don't waste money purchasing insurance for such expenses.

- **Dental insurance:** If your employer pays for dental insurance, take advantage of it. But you shouldn't pay for this coverage on your own. Dental insurance generally covers a couple teeth cleanings each year and limits payments for more expensive work.

- **Credit life and credit disability policies:** *Credit life policies* pay a small benefit if you die with an outstanding loan. *Credit disability policies* pay a small monthly income in the event of a disability. Banks and their credit card divisions usually sell these policies. Some companies sell insurance to pay off your credit card bill in the event of your death or disability.

The cost of such insurance seems low, but that's because the potential benefits are relatively small. In fact, given what little insurance you're buying, these policies are usually extraordinarily expensive. If you need life or disability insurance, purchase it. But get enough coverage, and buy it in a separate, cost-effective policy (see Chapter 16 for more details).

If you're in poor health and you can buy these insurance policies without a medical evaluation, you represent an exception to the "don't buy it" rule. In this case, these policies may be the only ones to which you have access — another reason these policies are expensive. If you're in good health, you're paying for the people with poor health who can enroll without a medical examination and who undoubtedly file more claims.

✔ **Daily hospitalization insurance:** Hospitalization insurance policies that pay a certain amount per day, such as $100, prey on people's fears of running up big hospital bills. Health care is expensive — there's no doubt about that.

But what you really need is a comprehensive (major medical) health insurance policy. One day in the hospital can lead to thousands, even tens of thousands, of dollars in charges, so that $100-per-day policy may pay for less than an hour of your 24-hour day! Daily hospitalization policies don't cover the big-ticket expenses. If you lack a comprehensive health insurance policy, make sure you get one (see Chapter 16)!

✔ **Insuring packages in the mail:** You buy a $40 gift for a friend, and when you go to the post office to ship it, the friendly postal clerk asks if you want to insure it. For a few bucks, you think, "Why not?" The U.S. Postal Service may have a bad reputation for many reasons, but it rarely loses or damages things. Go spend your money on something else — or better yet, invest it.

✔ **Contact lens insurance:** The things that people in this country come up with to waste money on just astound me. Contact lens insurance really does exist! The money goes to replace your contacts if you lose or tear them. Lenses are cheap. Don't waste your money on this kind of insurance.

✔ **Little stuff riders:** Many policies that are worth buying, such as auto and disability insurance, can have all sorts of riders added on. These *riders* are extra bells and whistles that insurance agents and companies like to sell because of the high profit margin they provide (for *them*). On auto insurance policies, for example, you can buy a rider for a few bucks per year that pays you $25 each time your car needs to be towed. Having your vehicle towed isn't going to bankrupt you, so it isn't worth insuring against.

Likewise, small insurance policies that are sold as add-ons to bigger insurance policies are usually unnecessary and overpriced. For example, you can buy some disability insurance policies with a small amount of life insurance added on. If you need life insurance, purchasing a sufficient amount in a separate policy is less costly.

Law 11: Buy broad coverage

Purchasing coverage that's too narrow is another major mistake people make when buying insurance. Such policies often seem like cheap ways to put your fears to rest. For example, instead of buying life insurance, some folks buy flight insurance at an airport self-service kiosk. They seem to worry more about their mortality when getting on an airplane than they do when getting into a car. If they die on the flight, their beneficiaries collect. But should they die the next day in an auto accident or get some dreaded disease — which is statistically far more likely than going down in a jumbo jet — the beneficiaries don't collect anything from flight insurance. Buy life insurance (broad coverage to protect your loved ones financially in the event of your death no matter how you die), not flight insurance (narrow coverage).

The medical equivalent of flight insurance is cancer insurance. Older people, who are fearful of having their life savings depleted by a long battle with this dreaded disease, are easy prey for this narrow insurance. If you get cancer, cancer insurance pays the bills. But what if you get heart disease, diabetes, or some other disease? Cancer insurance won't pay these costs. Purchase major medical coverage, not cancer insurance.

Recognizing fears

Our fears, such as getting cancer, are natural and inescapable. Although we may not have control over the emotions that our fears invoke, we must often ignore those emotions in order to make rational insurance decisions. In other words, getting shaky in the knees and sweaty in the palms when boarding an airplane is okay, but letting your fear of flying cause you to make poor insurance decisions is not okay, especially when those decisions affect the financial security of your loved ones.

Preparing for natural disasters — insurance and otherwise

In the chapters following this one, in which I discuss specific types of insurance such as disability insurance and homeowner's insurance, I highlight the fact that you'll find it nearly impossible to buy broad coverage. For example, when purchasing homeowner's coverage, you find that losses from floods and earthquakes are excluded. You can secure such coverage in separate policies, which you should do if you live in an area subject to such risks (more on this particular risk in Chapter 17). Many people don't understand these risks, and it's annoying and troubling that the insurance industry doesn't do more to educate customers about such gaping holes in their policies.

Examining misperceptions of risks

How high do you think your risks are for expiring prematurely if you're exposed to toxic wastes or pesticides, or if you live in a dangerous area that has a high murder rate? Well, actually, these risks are quite small when compared to the risks you're subjecting yourself to when you get behind the wheel of a car or light up yet another cigarette.

ABC reporter John Stossel was kind enough to share with me the results of a study done for him by physicist Bernard Cohen. In the study, Cohen compared different risks. Cohen's study showed that our riskiest behaviors are smoking and driving. Smoking whacks an average of seven years off a person's life, whereas driving a car results in a bit more than half a year of life lost, on average. Toxic waste shaves an average of one week off an American's life span.

Unfortunately, you can't buy a formal insurance policy to protect yourself against all of life's great dangers and risks. But that doesn't mean that you must face these dangers as a helpless victim; simple changes in behavior can help you improve your security.

Personal health habits are a good example of the types of behavior you can change. If you're overweight and you eat unhealthy, highly processed foods, drink alcohol excessively, and don't exercise, you're asking for trouble, especially during post-middle age. Engage in these habits, and you dramatically increase your risk of heart disease and cancer.

So does this mean that we should all eat carrots, tofu, and free range eggs; stay out of cars; and cease being concerned about toxic waste? No. But you should understand the consequences of your behaviors before you engage in them and minimize your risks accordingly.

You can buy all the types of traditional insurance that I recommend in this book and still not be well protected for the simple reason that you're overlooking uninsurable risks. However, not being able to buy formal insurance to protect against some dangers doesn't mean that you can't drastically reduce your exposure to such risks by modifying your behavior. For example, you can't buy an auto insurance policy that protects your personal safety against drunk drivers, who are responsible for about 17,000 American deaths annually. However, you can choose to drive a safe car, practice safe driving habits, and minimize driving on the roads during the late evening hours and on major holidays when drinking is prevalent (such as New Year's Eve, July 4th, and so on).

In addition to filling those voids, you should also think and plan for the nonfinancial issues that inevitably arise in a catastrophe. For example, make sure you have

- A meeting place for you and your loved ones if you're separated during a disaster
- An escape plan should your area by hit with flooding or some other natural disaster (tornado, hurricane, earthquake, fire, or mudslide)

✔ Steps you can take to make your home safer in the event of an earthquake or fire (for instance, securing shelving and heavy objects from falling and tipping, and installing smoke detectors and fire extinguishers)

✔ A plan for what you'll do for food, clothing, and shelter should your home become uninhabitable

You get the idea. Although you can't possibly predict what's going to happen and when, you can find out about the risks of your area. In addition to buying the broadest possible coverage, you should also make contingency plans for disasters.

Law 111: Shop around and buy direct

Whether you're looking at auto, home, life, disability, or other types of coverage, some companies may charge double or triple the rates that other companies charge for the same coverage. Insurers that charge the higher rates may not be better about paying claims, however. You may even end up with the worst of both possible worlds — high prices *and* lousy service.

Most insurance is sold through agents and brokers who earn commissions based on what they sell. The commissions, of course, can bias what they recommend you buy.

Not surprisingly, policies that pay agents the biggest commissions also tend to be more costly. In fact, insurance companies compete for the attention of agents by offering bigger commissions. When I browse through magazines and other publications targeted to insurance agents, I often see ads in which the largest text is the commission percentage offered to agents who sell the advertiser's products.

Besides the attraction of policies that pay higher commissions, agents also get hooked, financially speaking, to companies whose policies they sell frequently. After an agent sells a certain amount of a company's insurance policies, he or she is rewarded with higher commission percentages (and other perks) on any future sales. Just as airlines bribe frequent fliers with mileage bonuses, insurers bribe agents with fatter commissions and awards such as trips and costly goods.

Shopping around is a challenge not only because most insurance is sold by agents working on commission but also because insurers set their rates in mysterious ways. Every company has a different way of analyzing how much of a risk you are; one company may offer low rates to me but not to you, and vice versa.

Despite the obstacles, several strategies exist for obtaining low-cost, high-quality policies. The following sections offer smart ways to shop for insurance. (Chapters 16 and 17 recommend how and where to get the best deals on specific types of policies.)

Employer and other group plans

When you buy insurance as part of a larger group, you generally get a lower price because of the purchasing power of the group. Most of the health and disability policies that you can access through your employer are less costly than equivalent coverage you can buy on your own.

Likewise, many occupations have professional associations through which you may be able to obtain lower-cost policies. Not all associations offer better deals on insurance — compare their policy features and costs with other options.

Life insurance is the one exception to the rule that states that group policies offer better value than individual policies. Group life insurance plans usually aren't cheaper than the best life insurance policies that you can buy individually. However, group policies may have the attraction of convenience (ease of enrollment and avoidance of lengthy sales pitches from life insurance salespeople). Group life insurance policies that allow you to enroll without a medical evaluation are probably going to be more expensive, because such plans attract more people with health problems who can't get coverage on their own. If you're in good health, you should definitely shop around for life insurance (see Chapter 16 to find out how).

Insurance agents who want to sell you an individual policy can come up with 101 reasons why buying from them is preferable to buying through your employer or some other group. In most cases, agents' arguments for buying an individual policy from them include a lot of self-serving hype. In some cases, agents tell outright lies (which are hard to detect if you're not insurance-savvy).

One valid issue that agents raise is that if you leave your job, you'll lose your group coverage. Sometimes that may be true. For example, if you know that you're going to be leaving your job to become self-employed, securing an individual disability policy before you leave your job makes sense. However, your employer's health insurer may allow you to buy an individual policy when you leave.

In the chapter that follows, I explain what you need in the policies you're looking for so that you can determine whether a group plan meets your needs. In most cases, group plans, especially through an employer, offer good benefits. So as long as the group policy is cheaper than a comparable individual policy, you'll save money overall buying through the group plan.

Insurance without sales commissions

Buying policies from the increasing number of companies that are selling their policies directly to the public without the insurance agent and the agent's commission is your best bet for getting a good insurance value. Just as you can purchase no-load mutual funds directly from an investment company without paying any sales commission (see Chapter 10), you also can buy no-load insurance. Be sure to read Chapters 16 and 17 for more specifics on how to buy insurance directly from insurance companies.

Choosing financially stable insurers

In addition to the price of the policy and the insurer's reputation and track record for paying claims, an insurer's financial health is important to consider when choosing a company. If you faithfully pay your premium dollars year after year, you're going to be upset if the insurer goes bankrupt right before you have a major claim.

Insurance companies can fail just like any other company, and dozens do in a typical year. A number of organizations evaluate and rate, with some sort of letter grade, the financial viability and stability of insurance companies. The major rating agencies include A. M. Best, Fitch, Moody's, Standard & Poor's, and Weiss.

The rating agencies' letter-grade system works just the way it does in high school: A is better than B or C. Each company uses a different scale. Some companies have AAA as their highest rating, and then AA, A, BBB, BB, and so on. Others use A+, A, A–, B+, B, B–, and so on. Just as some teachers grade more easily, some firms, such as A. M. Best, have a reputation for giving out a greater number of high grades. Other firms, such as Weiss, are tough graders. Unlike in school, however, you want the tough critics when researching where to put your money and future security.

Just as getting more than one medical opinion is a good idea, getting two or three financial ratings can give you a better sense of the safety of an insurance company. Stick with companies that are in the top two — or, at worst, three — levels on the different rating scales.

You can obtain current rating information about insurance companies, free of charge, by asking your agent for a listing of the current ratings. If you're interested in a policy sold without the involvement of an agent, you can request the current ratings from the insurer itself.

Although the financial health of an insurance company is important, it's not as big a deal as some insurers (usually those with the highest ratings) and agents make it out to be. Just as financially unhealthy banks are taken over and merged into viable ones, sickly insurers usually follow a similar path under the direction of state insurance regulators.

With most insurance company failures, claims still get paid. The people who had money invested in life insurance or annuities with the failed insurer are the ones who usually lose out. Even then, you typically get back 80 cents to 90 cents on the dollar of your account value with the insurer, but you may have to wait years to get it.

The straight scoop on commissions

The commission paid to an insurance agent is never disclosed through any of the documents or materials that you receive when buying insurance. The only way you can know what the commission is and how it compares with other policies is to ask the agent. Nothing is wrong or impolite about asking. After all, your money pays the commission. You need to know whether a particular policy is being pitched harder because of its higher commission.

Commissions are typically paid as a percentage of the first year's premium on the insurance policy. (Many policies pay smaller commissions on subsequent years' premiums.) With life and disability insurance policies, for example, a 50 percent commission on the first year's premium is not unusual. With life insurance policies that have a cash value, commissions of 80 to 100 percent of your first year's premium are possible. Commissions on health insurance are lower but generally not as low as commissions on auto and homeowner's insurance.

Annuities, investment/insurance products traditionally sold through insurance agents, are also now available directly to the customer, without commission. Simply contact some of the leading no-load mutual fund companies such as Vanguard or T. Rowe Price (see Chapter 11).

Dealing with Insurance Problems

When you seek out insurance or have insurance policies, sooner or later you're bound to hit a roadblock. Although insurance problems can be among the more frustrating in life, in the following sections, I explain how to successfully deal with the more common obstacles.

Knowing what to do if you're denied coverage

Just as you can be turned down when you apply for a loan, you can also be turned down when applying for insurance. With medical, life, or disability insurance, a company may reject you if you have an existing medical problem (a preexisting condition) and are therefore more likely to file a claim. When it comes to insuring assets such as a home, you may have difficulty getting coverage if the property is deemed to be in a high-risk area.

Here are some strategies to employ if you're denied coverage:

✔ **Ask the insurer why you were denied.** Perhaps the company made a mistake or misinterpreted some information that you provided in your application. If you're denied coverage because of a medical condition, find out what information the company has on you and determine whether it's accurate.

✔ **Request a copy of your medical information file.** Just as you have a credit report file that details your use (and misuse) of credit, you also have a medical information report. Once per year, you can request a free copy of your medical information file (which typically highlights only the more significant problems over the past seven years, not your entire medical file or history) by calling 866-692-6901 or visiting its Web site at www.mib.com (click on the link on the homepage for the consumer site). If you find a mistake on your report, you have the right to request that it be fixed. However, the burden is on you to prove that the information in your file is incorrect. Proving that your file is incorrect can be a major hassle — you may even need to contact physicians you saw in the past, because their medical records may be the source of the incorrect information.

✔ **Shop other companies.** Just because one company denies you coverage, that doesn't mean all insurance companies will deny you coverage. Some insurers better understand certain medical conditions and are more comfortable accepting applicants with those conditions. Most insurers, however, charge higher rates to people with blemished medical histories than they do to people with perfect health records, but some companies penalize you less than others. An agent who sells policies from multiple insurers, called an *independent agent,* can be helpful, because he or she can shop among a number of different companies.

✔ **Find out about state high-risk pools.** A number of states act as the insurer of last resort and provide insurance for those who can't get it from insurance companies. State high-risk pool coverage is usually bare bones, but it beats going without any coverage. The Health Insurance Resource Center Web site provides links to all (30+) state health coverage high-risk pool Web sites at www.healthinsurance.org/riskpoolinfo. Alternatively, you can check with your state department of insurance (see the "Government" section of your local white pages) for high-risk pools for other types of insurance, such as property coverage.

✔ **Check for coverage availability before you buy.** If you're considering buying a home, for example, and you can't get coverage, the insurance companies are trying to tell you something. What they're effectively saying is "We think that property is so high-risk, we're not willing to insure it even if you pay a high premium."

Getting your due on claims

In the event that you suffer a loss and file an insurance claim, you may hope that your insurance company is going to cheerfully and expeditiously pay your claims. Given all the money that you shelled out for coverage and all the hoops you jumped through to get approved for coverage in the first place, that's a reasonable expectation.

Insurance companies may refuse to pay you what you think they owe you for many reasons, however. In some cases, your claim may not be covered under the terms of the policy. At a minimum, the insurer wants documentation and proof of your loss. Other people who have come before you have been known to cheat, so insurers won't simply take your word, no matter how honest and ethical you are.

Some insurers view paying claims as an adversarial situation and take a "negotiate tough" stance. Thinking that all insurance companies are going to pay you a fair and reasonable amount even if you don't make your voice heard is a mistake.

The tips that I discuss in this section can help you ensure that you get paid what your policy entitles you to.

Documenting your assets and case

When you're insuring assets, such as your home and its contents, having a record of what you own can be helpful if you need to file a claim. The best defense is a good offense. If you keep records of valuables and can document their cost, you should be in good shape.

A videotape is the most efficient record for documenting your assets, but a handwritten list detailing your possessions works, too. Just remember to keep this record someplace away from your home — if your home burns to the ground, you'll lose your documentation, too!

If you're robbed or are the victim of an accident, get the names, addresses, and phone numbers of witnesses. Take pictures of property damage and solicit estimates for the cost of repairing or replacing whatever has been lost or damaged. File police reports when appropriate, if for no other reason than to bolster your documentation for the insurance claim.

Preparing your case

Filing a claim should be viewed the same way as preparing for a court trial or an IRS audit. Any information you provide verbally or in writing can and will be used against you to deny your claim. First, you should understand whether your policy covers your claim (this is why getting the broadest possible coverage helps). Unfortunately, the only way to find out whether the policy covers your claim is to read it. Policies are hard to read because they use legal language in non-user-friendly ways.

A possible alternative to reading your policy is to call the claims department and, *without* providing your name (and using caller ID blocking on your phone if you're calling from home), ask a representative whether a particular loss (such as the one that you just suffered) is covered under its policy. You have no need to lie to the company, but you don't have to tell the representative who you are and that you're about to file a claim, either. Your call is so you can understand what your policy covers. However, some companies aren't willing to provide detailed information unless a specific case is cited.

After you initiate the claims process, keep records of all conversations and copies of all the documents you gave to the insurer's claims department. If you have problems down the road, this "evidence" may bail you out.

For property damage, you should get at least a couple of reputable contractors' estimates. Demonstrate to the insurance company that you're trying to shop for a low price, but don't agree to use a low-cost contractor without knowing that he or she can do quality work.

Approaching your claim as a negotiation

To get what you're owed on an insurance claim, you must approach most claims' filings for what they are — a negotiation that is often not cooperative. And the bigger the claim, the more your insurer will play the part of adversary.

A number of years ago, when I filed a homeowner's insurance claim after a major rain and wind storm significantly damaged my backyard fence, I was greeted on a weekday by a perky, smiley adjuster. When the adjuster entered my yard and started to peruse the damage, her demeanor changed dramatically. She had a combative, hard-bargainer type attitude that I last witnessed when I worked on some labor-management negotiations during my days as a consultant.

The adjuster stood on my back porch, a good distance away from the fences that had been blown over by wind and crushed by two large trees, and said that my insurer preferred to repair damaged fences rather than replace them. "With your deductible of $1,000, I doubt this will be worth filing a claim for," she said.

The fence that had blown over, she reasoned, could have new posts set in concrete. Because we had already begun to clean up some of the damage for safety reasons, I presented to her some pictures of what the yard looked like right after the storm; she refused to take them. She took some measurements and said that she'd have her settlement check to us in a couple of days. The settlement she faxed was for $1,119 — nowhere near what it would cost me to fix the damage that was done.

Practicing persistency

When you take an insurance company's first offer and don't fight for what you're due, you may be leaving a lot of money on the table. To make my long fence-repair story somewhat shorter, after *five* rounds of haggling with the adjusters, supervisors, and finally managers, I was awarded payment to replace the fences and clean up most of the damage. Even though all the contractors I contacted recommended that the work be done this way, the insurance adjuster discredited their recommendations by saying, "Contractors try to jack up the price and recommended work once they know an insurer is involved."

My final total settlement came to $4,888, more than $3,700 higher than the insurer's first offer. Interestingly, my insurer backed off its preference for repairing the fence when the contractor's estimates for doing that work exceeded the cost of a new fence.

I was disappointed with the behavior of that insurance company. I know from conversations with others that my homeowner's insurance company is not unusual in its adversarial strategy, especially with larger claims. And to think that this insurer at the time had one of the better track records for paying claims!

Enlisting support

If you're doing your homework and you're not making progress with the insurer's adjuster, ask to speak with supervisors and managers. This is the strategy I used to get the additional $3,700 needed to get things back to where they were before the storm.

The agent who sold you the policy may be helpful in preparing and filing the claim. A good agent can help increase your chances of getting paid — and getting paid sooner. If you're having difficulty with a claim for a policy obtained through your employer or other group, speak with the benefits department or a person responsible for interacting with the insurer. These folks have a lot of clout, because the agent and/or insurer doesn't want to lose the entire account.

If you're having problems getting a fair settlement from the insurer of a policy you bought on your own, try contacting the state department of insurance. You can find the phone number in the "Government" section of the white pages of your phone book or possibly in your insurance policy, or you can peruse the list at the National Association of Insurance Commissioners Web site at www.naic.org (you can find the "Link to Department of Insurance Web sites" on their homepage).

Hiring a public adjuster who, for a percentage of the payment (typically 5 to 10 percent), can negotiate with insurers on your behalf is another option.

When insurers (and government) move slowly

In 2005, when two hurricanes caused unprecedented damage and loss along the Gulf Coast, I received many complaints from folks in that region. Typical is the following note I received from a New Orleans family in December of 2005, more than three months after hurricane Katrina:

"We had substantial damage to our home in New Orleans due to hurricane Katrina. We had roof damage on August 29th and three feet of water August 31st. Our flood insurance is through an insurance company acting as an agent for FEMA's program. Our adjuster has still not turned in the necessary paperwork for our claim. Our home insurer made no allowance for proper removal and disposal of asbestos shingles and we have gotten just $2,000 for living expenses out of the $21,000 we're now owed. We have just gotten a first partial payment ($40,000 out of $160,000) on the flood insurance, but it was made out to the wrong mortgage company so we had to send the check back. We only know people with State Farm insurance have received any checks.

"It is shocking that it has gone on this long. It has been all over the papers about the delay of some flood insurance payments being due to FEMA not having adequate money in the till. There's no doubt the insurers are overwhelmed, but why is this taking so long? I called the Louisiana Department of Insurance and was told that insurers normally have 30 days for claims according to the insurance department (who has said they can have 45 days in this case). It's been over 60 days since the adjuster came out to our home."

Stories like this make me disappointed and mad. There's simply no excuse for large insurance companies who are in the business of insuring for such events not to bring the proper resources to bear to make timely payments. The fact that they did not do so for Gulf Coast victims is even more reprehensible given the widespread problems in that area. In addition to home losses, many people also had job losses to deal with and could ill afford to be without money. Large insurers that have written flood policies for which FEMA temporarily lacked money should pay their policyholders. Although the Federal government and FEMA officials should be taken to task for allowing FEMA's accounts to run dry, customer-service oriented insurers can step up and advance money that they know will soon be coming from FEMA.

In situations like this, if you do your homework and you're not making progress with the insurer's adjuster, ask to speak with supervisors and managers. If you're having problems getting a fair and timely settlement from the insurer, try contacting your state's department of insurance. This person who wrote me was from Louisiana, where the state department of insurance had more than 1,600 hurricane-related complaints in the first three months after hurricane Katrina. To my surprise, the department's Director of Public Information told me that no insurance companies have yet been fined and penalized for delaying payments. It's no wonder these companies weren't getting on the stick!

When all else fails and you have a major claim at stake, try contacting an attorney who specializes in insurance matters. You can find these specialists in the yellow pages under "Attorneys — Insurance Law." Expect to pay $100+ per hour. Look for a lawyer who's willing to negotiate on your behalf, help draft letters, and perform other necessary tasks on an hourly basis without filing a lawsuit. Your state department of insurance, the local bar association, or other legal, accounting, or financial practitioners also may be able to refer you to someone.

Chapter 16

Insurance on You: Life, Disability, and Health

. . . .

In This Chapter

▶ Checking out life insurance

▶ Looking into disability insurance

▶ Selecting the best health insurance

▶ Considering an overlooked form of personal insurance

. . . .

During your working years, multiplying your typical annual income by the number of years you plan to continue working produces a pretty big number. That dollar amount equals what is probably your most valuable asset — your ability to earn an income. You need to protect this asset by purchasing some insurance on *you*.

This chapter explains the ins and outs of buying insurance to protect your income: life insurance in case of death and disability insurance in case of an accident or severe medical condition that prevents you from working. I tell you what coverage you should have, where to look for it, and what to avoid.

In addition to protecting your income, you also need to insure against financially catastrophic expenses. I'm not talking about December's credit card bill — you're on your own with that one. I'm talking about the type of bills that are racked up from a major surgery and a multi-week stay in the hospital. Medical expenses today can make even the most indulgent shopping sprees look dirt-cheap. To protect yourself from potentially astronomical medical bills, you also need to have comprehensive health insurance.

Providing for Your Loved Ones: Life Insurance

You generally need life insurance only when other people depend on your income. The following types of people don't need life insurance to protect their incomes:

- Single people with no children
- Working couples who could maintain an acceptable lifestyle if one of the incomes were to disappear
- Independently wealthy people who don't need to work
- Retired people who are living off their retirement nest egg
- Minor children (are you financially dependent upon your children?)

If others are either fully or partly dependent on your paycheck (usually a spouse and/or child), you should buy life insurance, especially if you have major financial commitments such as a mortgage or years of child rearing ahead. You may also want to consider life insurance if an extended family member is currently or is likely to be dependent on your future income.

Determining how much life insurance to buy

Determining how much life insurance to buy is as much a subjective decision as it is a quantitative decision. I've seen some worksheets that are incredibly long and tedious (some are worse than your tax returns). There's no need to get fancy. If you're like me, your eyes start to glaze over if you have to complete 20-plus lines of calculations. Figuring out how much life insurance you need doesn't have to be that complicated.

The main purpose of life insurance is to provide a lump sum payment to replace the deceased person's income. You need to ask yourself how many years of income you want to replace. Table 16-1 provides a simple way to figure how much life insurance you need to consider purchasing. To replace a certain number of years' worth of income, simply multiply the appropriate number in the table by your annual after-tax income.

Table 16-1	Life Insurance Calculation
Years of Income to Replace	*Multiply Annual After-Tax Income* By*
5	4.5
10	8.5
20	15
30	20

*You can roughly determine your annual after-tax income in one of two ways: You can calculate it by getting out last year's tax return (and Form W-2) and subtracting the federal, state, and Social Security taxes you paid from your gross employment income; or you can estimate it by multiplying your gross income by 80 percent if you're a low-income earner, 70 percent if you're a moderate-income earner, or 60 percent if you're a high-income earner. (Because life insurance policy payouts are not taxed, you need to replace only after-tax income and not pre-tax income.)

Another way to determine the amount of life insurance to buy is to think about how much you'll need to pay for major debts or expenditures, such as your mortgage, other loans, and college for your children. For example, suppose that you want your spouse to have enough of a life insurance death benefit to pay off your mortgage and half of your children's college education. Simply add your mortgage amount to half of your children's estimated college costs (see Chapter 13 for approximate numbers) and then buy that amount of life insurance.

Social Security, if you're covered, can provide survivors' benefits to your spouse and children. However, if your surviving spouse is working and earning even a modest amount of money, he or she is going to get little if any survivor's benefits. Prior to reaching "full retirement age," which is between the ages of 65 and 67, depending on when you were born (see Chapter 4), your survivor's benefits get reduced by $1 for every $2 you earn above $12,480 (in 2006).

If either you or your spouse anticipates earning such a low income, however, you may want to factor your Social Security survivor's benefits into how much life insurance to buy. Contact the Social Security Administration by phone at 800-772-1213 or visit its Web site at www.ssa.gov to request Form 7004, which gives you an estimate of your Social Security benefits.

The Social Security Administration can tell you how much your survivors will receive per month in the event of your death. You should factor this benefit into the amount of life insurance that you calculate in Table 16-1. For example, suppose that your annual after-tax income is $25,000 and that Social Security provides a survivor's benefit of $10,000 annually. Therefore, for the purposes of Table 16-1, you should determine the amount of life insurance needed to replace $15,000 annually ($25,000 − $10,000), not $25,000.

"Other" life insurance

Contemplating the possibility of your untimely demise is surely depressing. You'll likely feel some peace of mind when purchasing a life insurance policy to provide for your dependents. However, let's take things a step further. Suppose that you (or your spouse) pass away. Do you think that simply buying a life insurance policy will be sufficient "help" for the loved ones you leave behind? Surely your contribution to your household involves far more than being a breadwinner.

For starters, you should make sure that all your important financial documents — investment account statements, insurance policies, employee benefits materials, small-business accounting records, and so on — are kept in one place (such as a file drawer) that your loved ones know about.

Do you have a will? See Chapter 17 for more details on wills and other estate-planning documents.

You may also want to consider providing a list of key contacts — such as who you recommend calling (or what you recommend reading) in the event of legal, financial, or tax quandaries.

So, in addition to trying to provide financially for your dependents, you also need to take some time to reflect on what else you can do to help point them in the right direction on matters you normally handle. With most couples, it's natural for one spouse to take more responsibility, say, for money management. That's fine; just make sure to talk about what's being done so that in the event that the responsible spouse dies, the surviving person knows how to jump into the driver's seat.

If you have kids (and even if you don't), you may want to give some thought to sentimental leave-behinds for your loved ones. These leave-behinds can be something like a short note telling them how much they meant to you and what you'd like them to remember about you.

Comparing term life insurance to cash value life insurance

I'm going to tell you how you can save hours of time and thousands of dollars. Ready? *Buy term life insurance.* (The only exception is if you have a high net worth — several million bucks or more — in which case you may want to consider other options. See the estate-planning section in Chapter 17.) If you already figured out how much life insurance to purchase and this is all the advice you need to go ahead, you can skip the rest of this section and the next and jump to the "Buying term insurance" section that follows.

If you want the details behind my recommendation for term insurance, the following information is for you. Or maybe you heard (and have already fallen prey to) the sales pitches from life insurance agents, most of whom love selling cash value life insurance because of its huge commissions.

Despite the variety of names that life insurance marketing departments have cooked up for policies, life insurance comes in two basic flavors:

- ✔ **Term insurance:** This insurance is pure life insurance. You pay an annual premium for which you receive a predetermined amount of life insurance protection. If you, the insured person, pass away, your beneficiaries collect; otherwise, the premium is gone but you're grateful to be alive!

- ✔ **Cash value insurance:** All other life insurance policies (whole, universal, variable, and so on) combine life insurance with a supposed savings feature. Not only do your premiums pay for life insurance, but some of your dollars are also credited to an account that grows in value over time, assuming you keep paying your premiums. On the surface, this sounds potentially attractive. People don't like to feel that all their premium dollars are getting tossed away.

  But cash value insurance has a big catch. For the same amount of coverage (for example, for $100,000 of life insurance benefits), cash value policies cost you about eight times (800 percent) more than comparable term policies.

Insurance salespeople know the buttons to push to get you interested in buying the wrong kind of life insurance. In the following sections, I give you some of the typical arguments they make for purchasing cash value polices, followed by my perspective on each one.

"Cash value policies are all paid up after X years. You don't want to be paying life insurance premiums for the rest of your life, do you?"

Agents who pitch cash value life insurance present projections that imply that after the first ten or so years of paying your premiums, you don't need to pay more premiums to keep the life insurance in force. The only reason you may be able to stop paying premiums is if you pour a lot of extra money into the policy in the early years of payment. Remember that cash value life insurance costs about eight times as much as term insurance.

Imagine that you're currently paying $500 a year for auto insurance and that an insurance company comes along and offers you a policy for $4,000 per year. The representative tells you that after ten years, you can stop paying and still keep your same coverage. I'm sure that you wouldn't fall for this sales tactic, but many people do when they buy cash value life insurance.

You also need to be wary of the projections, because they often include unrealistic and lofty assumptions about the investment return that your cash balance can earn. When you stop paying into a cash value policy, the cost of each year's life insurance is deducted from the remaining cash value. If the rate of return on the cash balance is not sufficient to pay the insurance cost, the cash balance declines, and eventually you receive notices saying that your policy needs more funding to keep the life insurance in force.

"You won't be able to afford term insurance when you're older."

As you get older, the cost of term insurance increases because the risk of dying rises. But life insurance is not something you need all your life! It's typically bought in a person's younger years when financial commitments and obligations outweigh financial assets. Twenty or thirty years later, the reverse should be true — if you use the principles in this book!

When you retire, you don't need life insurance to protect your employment income, because there isn't any to protect! You may need life insurance when you're raising a family and/or you have a substantial mortgage to pay off, but by the time you retire, the kids should be out on their own (you hope!), and the mortgage should be paid down.

In the meantime, term insurance saves you a tremendous amount of money. For most people, it takes 20 to 30 years for the premium they're paying on a term insurance policy to finally catch up to (equal) the premium they've been paying all along on a comparable amount of cash value life insurance.

"You can borrow against the cash value at a low interest rate."

Such a deal! It's your money in the policy, remember? If you deposited money in a savings or money market account, how would you like to pay for the privilege of borrowing your own money back? Borrowing on your cash value policy is potentially dangerous: You increase the chances that the policy will lapse — leaving you with nothing to show for your premiums.

"Your cash value grows tax-deferred."

Ah, a glimmer of truth at last. The cash value portion of your policy grows without taxation until you withdraw it, but if you want tax-deferral of your investment balances, you should first take advantage of funding 401(k)s, 403(b)s, SEP-IRAs, and Keoghs. Such accounts give you an immediate tax deduction for your current contributions in addition to growth without taxation until withdrawal.

The money you pay into a cash value life policy gives you no upfront tax deductions. If you exhaust the tax-deductible plans, consider a Roth IRA and then variable annuities, which provide access to better investment options and tax-deferred compounding of your investment dollars. Roth IRAs have the added bonus of tax-free withdrawal of your investment earnings. (See Chapter 11 for details on retirement accounts.)

Life insurance tends to be a mediocre investment. The insurance company generally quotes you an interest rate for the first year; after that, the company pays you what it wants. If you don't like the future interest rates, you can be penalized for quitting the policy. Would you ever invest your money in a bank account that quoted an interest rate for the first year and then penalized you for moving your money within the next seven to ten years?

"Cash value policies are forced savings."

Many agents argue that a cash value plan is better than nothing — at least it's forcing you to save. This line of thinking is silly because so many people drop cash value life insurance policies after just a few years of paying into them.

You can accomplish "forced savings" without using life insurance. Any of the retirement savings accounts mentioned in Chapter 11 can be set up for automatic monthly transfers. Employers offering such a plan can deduct contributions from your paycheck — and it doesn't take a commission! You can also set up monthly electronic transfers from your bank checking account to contribute to mutual funds (see Chapter 10).

"Life insurance is not part of your taxable estate."

If the ownership of a life insurance policy is properly structured, the death benefit is free of estate taxes. This part of the sales pitch is about the only sound reasoning that exists for buying cash value life insurance. Under current federal laws, you can pass on $2,000,000 free of federal estate taxes for tax years 2006–2008 ($3,500,000 in 2009). But even if you've got that large of a nest egg, you have numerous other ways to reduce your taxable estate (see Chapter 17).

Making your decision

Insurance salespeople aggressively push cash value policies because of the high commissions that insurance companies pay them. Commissions on cash value life insurance range from 50 to 100 percent of your first year's premium. An insurance salesperson, therefore, can make *eight to ten times more money* (yes, you read that right) selling you a cash value policy than he can selling you term insurance.

Ultimately, when you purchase cash value life insurance, you pay the high commissions that are built into these policies. As you can see in the policy's cash value table, you don't get back any of the money that you dump into the policy if you quit the policy in the first few years. The insurance company can't afford to give you any of your money back in those early years because so much of it has been paid to the selling agent as commission. That's why these policies explicitly penalize you for withdrawing your cash balance within the first seven to ten years.

Because of the high cost of cash value policies relative to the cost of term, you're more likely to buy less life insurance coverage than you need — that's the sad part of the insurance industry's pushing of this stuff. *The vast majority of life insurance buyers need more protection than they can afford to buy with cash value coverage.*

Cash value life insurance is the most oversold insurance and financial product in the history of the financial services industry. Cash value life insurance makes sense for a small percentage of people, such as small-business owners who own a business worth at least several million dollars and don't want their heirs to be forced to sell their business to pay estate taxes in the event of their death. (See "Considering the purchase of cash value life insurance," later in this chapter.)

Purchase low-cost term insurance and do your investing separately. Life insurance is rarely a permanent need; over time, you can reduce the amount of term insurance you carry as your financial obligations lessen and you accumulate more assets.

Buying term insurance

Term insurance policies have several features to choose from. I cover the important elements of term insurance in this section so you can make an informed decision about purchasing it.

Choosing how often your premium adjusts

As you get older, the risk of dying increases, so the cost of your insurance goes up. Term insurance can be purchased so that your premium adjusts (increases) annually or after 5, 10, 15, or 20 years. The less frequently your premium adjusts, the higher the initial premium and its incremental increases will be.

The advantage of a premium that locks in for, say, 15 years is that you have the security of knowing how much you'll be paying each year for the next 15 years. You also don't need to go through medical evaluations as frequently to qualify for the lowest rate possible.

The disadvantage of a policy with a long-term rate lock is that you pay more in the early years than you do on a policy that adjusts more frequently. In addition, you may want to change the amount of insurance you carry as your circumstances change. You may throw money away when you dump a policy with a long-term premium guarantee before its rate is set to change.

Policies that adjust the premium every five to ten years offer a happy medium between price and predictability.

Ensuring guaranteed renewability

Guaranteed renewability, which is standard practice on the better policies, assures that the policy can't be canceled because of poor health. Don't buy a life insurance policy without this feature unless you expect that your life insurance needs will disappear when the policy is up for renewal.

Deciding where to buy term insurance

A number of sound ways to obtain high-quality, low-cost term insurance are available. You may choose to buy through a local agent because you know her or prefer to buy from someone close to home. However, you should invest a few minutes of your time getting quotes from one or two of the following sources to get a sense of what's available in the insurance market. Gaining familiarity with the market can prevent an agent from selling you an overpriced, high-commission policy.

Here are some sources for high-quality, low-cost term insurance:

- ✔ **USAA:** This company sells low-cost term insurance directly to the public. You can contact USAA by phone at 800-531-8000.

- ✔ **Insurance agency quotation services:** These services provide proposals from the highest-rated, lowest-cost companies available. Like other agencies, the services receive a commission if you buy a policy from them, which you're under no obligation to do. They ask questions such as your date of birth, whether you smoke, some basic health questions, and how much coverage you want. Services that are worth considering include

    - **ReliaQuote:** www.reliaquote.com; 888-847-8683

    - **SelectQuote:** www.selectquote.com; 800-963-8688

    - **Term4Sale:** www.term4sale.com

See Chapter 19 for information on how to use your computer when making life insurance decisions.

Getting rid of cash value life insurance

If you were snookered into buying a cash value life insurance policy and you want to part ways with it, go ahead and do so. *But don't cancel the coverage until you first secure new term coverage.* When you need life insurance, you don't want to have a period when you're not covered (Murphy's Law says *that's* when disaster will strike).

Ending a cash value life insurance policy has tax consequences. For most of these policies, you must pay tax on the amount you receive in excess of the premiums you paid over the life of the policy. Because some life insurance policies feature tax-deferred retirement savings, you may incur a 10 percent federal income tax penalty on earnings withdrawn before age 59½, just as you would with an IRA. If you want to withdraw the cash balance in your life insurance policy, consider checking with the insurer or a tax advisor to clarify what the tax consequences may be.

You can avoid federal income tax early withdrawal penalties and sidestep taxation on accumulated interest in a life insurance policy by doing a tax-free exchange into a no-load (commission-free) variable annuity. The no-load mutual fund company through which you buy the annuity takes care of transferring your existing balance. (See Chapter 12 for more information about annuities.)

Considering the purchase of cash value life insurance

Don't expect to get objective information from anyone who sells cash value life insurance. Beware of insurance salespeople masquerading under the guise of self-anointed titles, such as estate-planning specialists or financial planners.

As I discuss earlier in the chapter, purchasing cash value life insurance may make sense if you expect to have an estate-tax "problem." However, cash value life insurance is just one of many ways to reduce your estate taxes (see the section on estate planning in Chapter 17).

Among the best places to shop for cash value life insurance policies are

- ✔ **USAA:** 800-531-8000
- ✔ **Ameritas Direct:** 800-552-3553

If you want to obtain some cash value life insurance, make sure you avoid local insurance agents, especially while you're in the learning stage. Agents aren't as interested in educating as they are in selling (big surprise). Besides, the best cash value policies can be obtained free of most (or all) sales commissions when you buy them from the sources I provide in the preceding list. The money saved on commissions (which can easily be thousands of dollars) is reflected in a much higher cash value for you.

Preparing for the Unpredictable: Disability Insurance

As with life insurance, the purpose of disability insurance is to protect your income. The only difference is that with disability insurance, you're protecting the income for yourself (and perhaps also your dependents). If you're completely disabled, you still have living expenses, but you probably can't earn employment income.

I'm referring to long-term disabilities. If you throw out your back while reliving your athletic glory days and you wind up in bed for a couple weeks, it won't be as much of a financial disaster as if you were disabled in such a way that you couldn't work for several years. This section helps you figure out whether you need disability insurance, how much to get, and where to find it.

Deciding whether you need coverage

Most large employers offer disability insurance to their employees. Many small-company employees and all self-employed people are left to fend for themselves without disability coverage. Being without disability insurance is a risky proposition, especially if, like most working people, you need your employment income to live on.

If you're married and your spouse earns a large enough income that you can make do without yours, you may want to consider skipping disability coverage. The same is true if you've already accumulated enough money for your future years (in other words, you're financially independent). Keep in mind, though, that your expenses may go up if you become disabled and require specialized care.

For most people, dismissing the need for disability coverage is easy. The odds of suffering a long-term disability seem so remote — and they are. But if you meet up with bad luck, disability coverage can relieve you (and possibly your family) of a major financial burden.

Most disabilities are caused by medical problems, such as arthritis, heart conditions, hypertension, and back/spine or hip/leg impairments. Some of these ailments occur with advancing age, but more than one-third of all disabilities are suffered by people under the age of 45. The vast majority of these medical problems cannot be predicted in advance, particularly those caused by random accidents.

If you think you have good disability coverage through government programs, you'd better think again:

- **Social Security disability:** Social Security pays long-term benefits only if you're not able to perform any substantial, gainful activity for more than a year or if your disability is expected to result in death. Furthermore, Social Security disability payments are quite low because they're intended to provide only for basic, subsistence-level living expenses.

- **Workers' compensation:** Workers' compensation (if you have such coverage through your employer) pays you benefits if you're injured on the job, but it doesn't pay any benefits if you get disabled away from your job. You need coverage that pays regardless of where and how you're disabled.

- **State disability programs:** A few states have disability insurance programs, but the coverage is typically bare bones. State programs are also generally not a good value because of the cost for the small amount of coverage they provide. Benefits are paid over a short period of time (rarely more than a year).

Determining how much disability insurance you need

You need enough disability coverage to provide you with sufficient income to live on until other financial resources become available. If you don't have much saved in the way of financial assets and you want to continue with the lifestyle supported by your current income if you suffer a disability, get enough disability coverage to replace your entire monthly take-home (after-tax) pay.

The benefits you purchase on a disability policy are quoted as the dollars per month you receive if disabled. So if your job provides you with a $3,000-per-month income after payment of taxes, seek a policy that provides a $3,000-per-month benefit.

If you pay for your disability insurance, the benefits are tax-free (but hopefully you won't ever have to collect them). If your employer picks up the tab, your benefits are taxable, so you need a greater amount of benefits.

In addition to the monthly coverage amount, you also need to select the duration for which you want a policy to pay you benefits. You need a policy that pays benefits until you reach an age at which you become financially self-sufficient. For most people, that's around age 65, when their Social Security benefits kick in. If you anticipate needing your employment income past your mid-60s, you may want to obtain disability coverage that pays you until a later age.

On the other hand, if you crunched some numbers (see Chapter 3) and you expect to be financially independent by age 55, shop for a policy that pays benefits up to that age — it'll cost you less than one that pays benefits to you until age 65. If you're within five years of being financially independent or able to retire, five-year disability policies are available, too. You may also consider such short-term policies when you're sure that someone (for example, a family member) can support you financially over the long-term.

Identifying other features you need in disability insurance

Disability insurance policies have many confusing features. Here's what to look for — and look out for — when purchasing disability insurance:

- **Definition of disability:** An *own-occupation* disability policy provides benefit payments if you can't perform the work you normally do. Some policies pay you only if you're unable to perform a job for which you are *reasonably trained.* Other policies revert to this definition after a few years of being own-occupation.

  Own-occupation policies are the most expensive because there's a greater chance that the insurer will have to pay you. The extra cost may not be worth it unless you're in a high-income or specialized occupation and you'd have to take a significant pay cut to do something else (and you wouldn't be happy about a reduced income and the required lifestyle changes).

- **Noncancelable and guaranteed renewable:** These features ensure that your policy can't be canceled because of your falling into poor health. With policies that require periodic physical exams, you can lose your coverage just when you're most likely to need it.

- **Waiting period:** This is the "deductible" on disability insurance — the lag time between the onset of your disability and the time you begin collecting benefits. As with other types of insurance, you should take the highest deductible (longest waiting period) that your financial circumstances allow. The waiting period significantly reduces the cost of the insurance and eliminates the hassle of filing a claim for a short-term disability. The minimum waiting period on most policies is 30 days. The maximum waiting period can be up to one to two years. Try a waiting period of three to six months if you have sufficient emergency reserves.

- **Residual benefits:** This option pays you a partial benefit if you have a disability that prevents you from working full-time.

- **Cost-of-living adjustments (COLAs):** This feature automatically increases your benefit payment by a set percentage annually or in accordance with changes in inflation. The advantage of a COLA is that it retains the purchasing power of your benefits. A modest COLA, such as 4 percent, is worth having.

✔ **Future insurability:** A clause that many agents encourage you to buy, future insurability allows you, regardless of health, to buy additional coverage. For most people, paying for the privilege of buying more coverage later is not worth it if the income you earn today fairly reflects your likely long-term earnings (except for cost-of-living increases). Disability insurance is sold only as a proportion of your income. You may benefit from the future insurability option if your income is artificially low now and you're confident that it will rise significantly in the future. (For example, you just got out of medical school and you're earning a low salary while being enslaved as a resident.)

✔ **Insurer's financial stability:** As I discuss in Chapter 15, you should choose insurers that'll be here tomorrow to pay your claim. But don't get too hung up on the stability of the company; benefits are paid even if the insurer fails, because the state or another insurer will almost always bail the unstable insurer out.

Deciding where to buy disability insurance

The place to buy disability insurance with the best value is through your employer or professional association. Unless these groups have done a lousy job shopping for coverage, group plans offer a better value than disability insurance you can purchase on your own. Just make sure that the group plan meets the specifications discussed in the preceding section.

Don't trust an insurance agent to be enthusiastic about the quality of a disability policy your employer or other group is offering. Agents have a conflict of interest when they criticize these options, because they won't make a commission if you buy through a group.

If you don't have access to a group policy, check with your agent or a company you already do business with. You can also contact USAA, which offers competitively priced disability policies, by calling 800-531-8000.

Tread carefully when purchasing disability insurance through an agent. Some agents try to load down your policy with all sorts of extra bells and whistles to pump up the premium along with their commission.

If you buy disability insurance through an agent, use a process called list billing. With *list billing,* you sign up with several other people for coverage at the same time and are invoiced together for your coverage. It can knock up to 15 percent off an insurer's standard prices. Ask your insurance agent how list billing works.

Other types of "insurance" for protecting your income

Life insurance and disability insurance replace your income if you die or suffer a disability. But you may also see your income reduced or completely eliminated if you lose your job. Although no formal insurance exists to protect you against the forces that can cause you to lose your job, you can do some things to reduce your exposure to such risk:

✔ Make sure that you have an emergency reserve of money that you can tap into if you lose your job. (Chapter 4 offers specific guidelines for deciding how much money is right for you.)

✔ Attend to your skills and professional development on a continual basis. Not only does upgrading your education and skills ensure that you'll be employable if you have to look for a new job, but it may also help you keep your old job and earn a higher income.

Getting the Care You Need: Health Insurance

Almost everyone (except the super-wealthy) needs health insurance, but not everyone has it. Some people who can afford health insurance choose not to buy it because they believe that they're healthy and they're not going to need it. Others who opt not to buy health insurance figure that if they ever really need health care, they'll get it even if they can't pay. To a large extent, they're right. People without health insurance generally put off getting routine care, which can lead to small problems' turning into big ones (which cost more due to advanced illness, emergency room visits, and so on).

Choosing the best health plan

Before Medicare (the government-run insurance program for the elderly) kicks in at age 65+, odds are that you'll obtain your health insurance through your employer. Be thankful if you do. Employer-provided coverage eliminates the headache of having to shop for coverage, and it's usually cheaper than coverage you buy on your own.

Whether you have options through your employer or you have to hunt for a plan on your own, the following sections cover the major issues to consider when selecting among the health insurance offerings in the marketplace.

Major medical coverage

You need a plan that covers the *big* potential expenses: hospitalization, physician, and ancillary charges, such as X-rays and laboratory work. If you're a woman and you think that you may want to have children, make sure that your plan has maternity benefits.

Choice of health care providers

Plans that allow you to use any health care provider you want are becoming less common and more expensive in most areas. Health maintenance organizations (HMOs) and preferred provider organizations (PPOs) are the main plans that restrict your choices. They keep costs down because they negotiate lower rates with selected providers.

HMOs and PPOs are more similar than they are different. The main difference is that PPOs still pay the majority of your expenses if you use a provider outside their approved list. If you use a provider outside the approved list with an HMO, you typically aren't covered at all.

If you have your heart set on particular physicians or hospitals, find out which health insurance plans they accept as payment. Ask yourself whether the extra cost of an open-choice plan is worth being able to use their services if they're not part of a restricted-choice plan. Also be aware that some plans allow you to go outside their network of providers as long as you pay a portion of the incurred medical costs. If you're interested in being able to use alternative types of providers, such as acupuncturists, find out whether the plans you're considering cover these services.

Don't let stories of how hard it is to get an appointment with a doctor or other logistical hassles deter you from going with an HMO or PPO plan. These things can happen in plans with open choice, too — some doctors are always running late or are overbooked. The idea that doctors who can't get patients on their own are the only ones who sign up with restricted-choice plans is a myth. Although HMO and PPO plans do offer fewer choices when it comes to providers, objective surveys show that customer satisfaction with these plans is as high as it is for plans that offer more choices.

Lifetime maximum benefits

Health insurance plans specify the maximum total benefits they'll pay over the course of time you're insured by their plan. Although a million dollars may be more money than you could ever imagine being spent on your health care, it's the minimum acceptable level of total benefits. With the cost of health care today, you can quickly blow through that if you develop major health problems. Ideally, choose a plan that has no maximum or that has a maximum of at least 5 million dollars.

Deductibles and co-payments

To reduce your health insurance premiums, choose a plan with the highest deductible and co-payment you can afford. As with other insurance policies, the more you're willing to share in the payment of your claims, the less you'll have to pay in premiums. Most policies have annual deductible options (such as $250, $500, $1,000, and so on), as well as co-payment options, which are typically 20 percent or so.

When choosing a co-payment percentage, don't let your imagination run wild and unnecessarily scare you. A 20 percent co-payment does not mean that you have to come up with $20,000 for a $100,000 claim. Insurance plans generally set a maximum out-of-pocket limit on your annual co-payments (such as $1,000, $2,000, and so on); the insurer covers 100 percent of any medical expenses that go over that cap.

Saving on taxes when spending on health care

If you expect to have out-of-pocket medical expenses, find out whether your employer offers a flexible spending or health care reimbursement account. These accounts enable you to pay for uncovered medical expenses with pre-tax dollars. If, for example, you're in a combined 35 percent federal and state income tax bracket, these accounts allow you to pay for necessary health care at a 35 percent discount. These accounts can also be used to pay for vision and dental care.

Be forewarned of the major stumbling blocks you face when saving through medical reimbursement accounts. First, you need to elect to save money from your paycheck prior to the beginning of each plan year. The only exception is at the time of a "life change," such as a family member's death, marriage, spouse's job change, divorce, or the birth of a child. You also need to use the money within the year you save it, because these accounts contain a "use or lose it" feature.

Health Savings Accounts (HSAs) are for the self-employed and people who work for small firms. To qualify, you must have a high-deductible (at least $1,000 for individuals; $2,000 for families) health insurance policy; then you can put money earmarked for medical expenses into an investment account that offers the tax benefits — deductible contributions and tax-deferred compounding — of a retirement account (see Chapter 4). And unlike in a flexible spending account, you don't have to deplete the HSA by the end of the year: Money can compound tax-deferred inside the HSA for years. Begin to investigate an HSA through insurers offering health plans you're interested in or with the company you currently have coverage through.

You may also be able to save on taxes if you have a substantial amount of health care expenditures in a year. You can deduct medical and dental expenses as an itemized deduction on Schedule A to the extent that they exceed 7.5 percent of your adjusted gross income (refer to Chapter 7). Unless you're a low income earner, you need to have substantial expenses, usually caused by an accident or major illness, to take advantage of this tax break.

For insurance provided by your employer, consider plans with low out-of-pocket expenses if you know that you have health problems. Because you're part of a group, the insurer won't increase your individual rates just because you're filing more claims.

Most HMO plans don't have deductible and co-payment options. Most just charge a set amount — such as $25 — for a physician's office visit.

Guaranteed renewable

You want a health insurance plan that keeps renewing your coverage without your having to prove continued good health.

Buying health insurance

You can buy many health plans through agents, and you can also buy some directly from the insurer. When health insurance is sold both ways, buying through an agent usually doesn't cost more.

If you're self-employed or you work for a small employer that doesn't offer health insurance as a benefit, get proposals from the larger and older health insurers in your area. Larger plans can negotiate better rates from providers, and older plans are more likely to be here tomorrow.

Many insurers operate in a bunch of different insurance businesses. You want those that are the biggest in the health insurance arena and are committed to that business. If your coverage is canceled, you may have to search for coverage that allows an existing medical problem. Other health insurers won't want to insure you. (Find out whether your state department of insurance offers a plan for people unable to get coverage.)

Nationally, Blue Cross, Blue Shield, Kaiser Permanente, Aetna, UnitedHealth Group, CIGNA, Assurant, Golden Rule, Health Net, WellPoint, and Anthem are among the older and bigger health insurers.

Also check with professional or other associations that you belong to, as such plans sometimes offer decent benefits at a competitive price due to the purchasing power clout that they possess. A competent independent insurance agent who specializes in health insurance can help you find insurers who are willing to offer you coverage.

Health insurance agents have a conflict of interest that's common to all financial salespeople working on commission: The higher the premium plan they sell you, the bigger the commission they earn. So an agent may try to steer you into higher-cost plans and avoid suggesting some of the strategies I discuss in the previous section for reducing your cost of coverage.

Dealing with insurance denial

When you try to enroll in a particular health insurance plan, you may be turned down because of current or previous health problems. Your *medical information file* (the medical equivalent of a credit report) may contain information explaining why you were turned down. (See Chapter 15 for more about medical information files.)

If you have a so-called *preexisting condition* (current or prior medical problems), you have several options to pursue when trying to secure health insurance:

- ✓ **Try health insurance plans that don't discriminate.** A few plans — typically Blue Cross, Blue Shield, and some HMO plans, such as Kaiser Permanente — will sometimes take you regardless of your condition.

- ✓ **Find a job with an employer whose health insurer doesn't require a medical exam.** Of course, this shouldn't be your only reason for seeking new employment, but it can be an important factor. If you're married, you may also be able to get into an employer group plan if your spouse takes a new job.

- ✓ **Find out whether your state offers a plan.** A number of states maintain "high-risk" pools that insure people who have preexisting conditions and are unable to find coverage elsewhere (see Chapter 15 for how to find out which states offer such plans). If your state doesn't offer one of these plans, I suppose that, in a drastic situation, you could move to a nearby state that does.

Looking at retiree medical care insurance

Medicare, the government-run health insurance plan for the elderly, is a multi-part major medical plan. Enrollment in Part A (hospital expenses) is automatic. Part B, which covers physician expenses and other charges, including home health care coverage; Part C, supplemental Medicare coverage (sold through private insurers); and Part D, for prescription drugs (provided through private insurers), are optional. Supplemental insurance policies may be of interest to you if you want help paying for the costs that Medicare doesn't pay.

Closing Medicare's gaps

Medigap coverage generally pays the deductibles and co-payments that Medicare charges. For the first 60 days of hospitalization, you pay $952 total out of your own pocket. If you have an unusually long hospital stay, you pay $238 per day for the 61st through 90th day, $476 per day for the 91st through 150th day, and all costs beyond 150 days. Clearly, if you stay in a hospital for many months, your out-of-pocket expenses can escalate; however, the longest hospitalizations tend not to last for many months. Also note that Medicare's hospitalization benefits refresh when you're out of the hospital for 60 consecutive days.

If the costs from a long hospital stay would be a financial catastrophe for you and if you're unable to pay for the deductibles and co-payments because your income is low, *Medicaid* (the state-run medical insurance program for low-income people) may help pay your bills. Alternatively, Medigap insurance can help close the gap.

Dealing with medical claims headaches

If you sign up for a health plan that has deductibles and co-payments, make sure that you review the benefits statements your insurer sends you. Errors often pop up on these statements and during the claims filing process. Not surprisingly, the errors are usually at your expense.

Make sure that your insurer has kept accurate track of your contributions toward meeting your plan's annual deductible and maximum out-of-pocket charges. Also, don't pay any health care providers who send you bills until you receive proper notification from the insurance company detailing what you are obligated to pay those providers according to the terms of your plan. Because most insurance companies have negotiated discounted fee schedules with health care providers, the amount that a provider bills you is often higher than the amount they're legally due as per the terms of their contract with your insurer. Your insurer's benefits statement should detail the approved and negotiated rate once the claim is processed.

And don't let providers try to bully you into paying them the difference between what they billed you for and what the insurer says they are due. Providers are due only the discounted fees they agreed to with your insurer.

Haggling with your health insurer is a real pain, and it usually happens after you rack up significant medical expenses and may still not be feeling well. But if you don't stay on top of your insurer, you can end up paying thousands of dollars in overpayments.

If you're overwhelmed with an avalanche of claims and benefits statements, you may want to consider using a health insurance claims processing service. You can get a referral to firms that engage in this line of work by visiting the Alliance of Claims Assistance Professionals Web site at www.claims.org.

Check with your physician(s) to see that he or she does not charge a fee higher than the one listed on Medicare's fee schedule. If your physician does charge a higher fee, you may want to consider going to another physician if you can't afford the fee or if you want to save some money. Medicare often pays only 80 percent of the physician charges that the program allows on its fee schedule. Some physicians charge higher fees than those allowed by Medicare.

The biggest reason that elderly people consider extra health insurance is that Medicare pays only for the first 100 days in a skilled nursing facility. Anything over that is your responsibility. Unfortunately, Medigap policies don't address this issue, either.

Long-term care insurance

Insurance agents who are eager to earn a hefty commission will often tell you that long-term care (LTC) insurance is the solution to your concerns about an extended stay in a nursing home. Don't get your hopes up. Policies are complicated and filled with all sorts of exclusions and limitations. On top of all that, they're expensive, too.

The decision to purchase LTC insurance is a trade-off. Do you want to pay thousands of dollars annually, beginning at age 60, to guard against the possibility of a long-term stay in a nursing home? If you live into or past your mid-80s, you can end up paying $100,000 or more on an LTC policy (not to mention the lost investment earnings on these insurance premiums).

People who end up in a nursing home for years on end may come out ahead financially when buying LTC insurance. The majority of people who stay in a nursing home are there for less than a year, though, because they either pass away or move out.

Medicare pays for the bulk of the cost of the first 100 days in a nursing home as long as certain conditions are satisfied. Medicare pays for all basic services (telephone, television, and private room charges excluded) for the first 20 days and then requires a co-payment of $119 per day for the next 80 days. First, the nursing-home stay must follow hospitalization within 30 days, and the nursing-home stay must be for the same medical condition that caused the hospitalization. When you're discharged from the nursing home, you can qualify for an additional 100-day benefit period as long as you haven't been hospitalized or in a nursing home in the 60 days prior to your readmission.

If you have relatives or a spouse who will likely care for you in the event of a major illness, you should definitely *not* waste your money on nursing-home insurance. You can also bypass this coverage if you have and don't mind using retirement assets to help pay nursing-home costs.

Even if you do deplete your assets, remember that you have a backup: Medicaid (state-provided medical insurance) can pick up the cost if you can't. However, be aware of a number of potential drawbacks to getting coverage for nursing-home stays under Medicaid:

✔ **Medicaid patients are at the bottom of the priority list.** Most nursing homes are interested in the bottom line, so the patients who bring in the least revenue — namely Medicaid patients — get the lowest priority on nursing-home waiting lists.

✔ **Some nursing homes don't take Medicaid patients.** Check with your preferred nursing homes in your area to see whether they accept Medicaid.

✔ **The states may squeeze Medicaid further.** Deciding which medical conditions warrant coverage is up to your state. With the budget noose tightening, some states are disallowing certain types of coverage (for example, mental problems for elderly people who are otherwise in good physical health).

If you're concerned about having your stash of money wiped out by an extended nursing-home stay and you have a strong desire to pass money to your family or a favorite charity, you can start giving your money away while you're still healthy. (If you're already in poor health, legal experts can strategize to preserve your assets and keep them from being used to pay nursing-home costs.)

Discovering the most overlooked form of insurance

You buy health insurance to cover large medical expenses, disability insurance to replace your income in the event of a long-term disability, and perhaps life insurance to provide money to those dependent on your income in the event of your death. Many people buy all the right kinds of personal insurance, spending a small fortune over the course of their lives. Yet they overlook the obvious, virtually free protection: taking care of themselves.

If you work at a desk all day and use many of life's modern conveniences, you may end up being the Great American Couch Potato. Odds are that you've heard of most of these methods of enhancing longevity and quality of life, but if you're still on the couch, the advice apparently didn't sink in. So, for you sofa spuds, here are seven health tips:

✔ Don't smoke.

✔ Drink alcohol in moderation if you drink at all.

✔ Get plenty of rest.

✔ Exercise regularly.

✔ Eat a healthful diet (see Chapter 6 for diet tips that can save you money and improve your health).

✔ Get regular health care checkups to detect medical, dental, and vision problems.

✔ Take time to smell the roses.

Consider buying nursing-home insurance if you want to retain and protect your assets and if it gives you peace of mind to know that a long-term nursing-home stay is covered. But do your homework. Do some comparison shopping, and make sure that you buy a policy that pays benefits for the long term. A year's worth (or even a few years' worth) of benefits won't protect your assets if your stay lasts longer. Also be sure to get a policy that adjusts the daily benefit amount for increases in the cost of living. Watch out for policies that restrict benefits to limited types of facilities and settings. Get a policy that covers care in your home or other settings if you don't need to be in a high-cost nursing home, and make sure that it doesn't require prior hospitalization for benefits to kick in. To keep premiums down, also consider a longer exclusion or waiting period — three to six months or a year before coverage starts.

You may also want to consider retirement communities if you're willing to live as a younger retiree in such a setting. After paying an entrance fee, you pay a monthly fee, which usually covers your rent, care, and meals. Make sure that any such facility you're considering guarantees care for life and accepts Medicaid in case you deplete your assets.

Making sense of Medicare's prescription drug program

As if there weren't enough confusing government programs, Uncle Sam had to create yet another that began in 2006 — the Medicare (Part D) prescription drug plan. Here are some key facts you need to know about these relatively complicated plans, which are offered through private insurers:

- ✔ Plans make the most sense for those who expect to spend more than $5,000 on prescription drugs. You will pay for $3,600 out of pocket of the first $5,100 in expenses before "catastrophic coverage" kicks in. Medicare pays 95 percent of additional drug costs above $5,100 during the calendar year.

- ✔ If you choose not to enroll when you're first eligible and then later enroll, you'll be charged a penalty equal to 1 percent of the national average Part D premium for each month that has elapsed since you were first eligible to participate. You will pay this penalty for as long as you're in the plan.

- ✔ If you're on the fence about enrolling, consider starting with a low premium plan that then gives you the right to transfer into a higher cost and better coverage plan without paying the late enrollment penalty.

- ✔ Visit www.medicare.gov for helpful information on drug plans and how to select one. For example, click on the Formulary (drug) Finder to identify specific insurer plans that cover your current medications or your anticipated future medications. AARP's Web site, www.aarp.org, also has plenty of information and resources to find out more about these confusing plans.

Chapter 17

Covering Your Assets

· ·

In This Chapter

▶ Checking out homeowner's/renter's insurance

▶ Considering automobile insurance

▶ Looking at umbrella insurance

▶ Planning your estate

· ·

*I*n Chapter 16, I discuss the importance of protecting your future income from the possibilities of disability, death, or large, unexpected medical expenses. But you also have to insure major assets that you acquired in the past: your home, your car, and your personal property. You need to protect these assets for two reasons:

✔ **Your assets are valuable.** If you were to suffer a loss, replacing the assets with money out of your own pocket could be a financial catastrophe.

✔ **A lawsuit could drain your finances.** Should someone be injured or killed in your home or because of your car, a lawsuit could be financially devastating.

In this chapter, I explain why, how, and for how much to insure your home, personal property, and vehicle. I also discuss excess liability insurance and how to determine where your money will go in the event of your death.

Insuring Where You Live

When you buy a home, most lenders require that you purchase homeowner's insurance. But even if they don't, you're wise to do so, because your home and the personal property within it are worth a great deal and would cost a bundle to replace.

As a renter, damage to the building in which you live is not your immediate financial concern, but you still have personal property you may want to insure. You also have the possibility (albeit remote) that you'll be sued by someone who's injured in your rental.

When shopping for a homeowner's or renter's policy, consider the important features that I cover in the following sections.

Dwelling coverage: The cost to rebuild

How much would you have to spend to rebuild your home if it were completely destroyed in a fire, an attack of locusts, or whatever? The cost to rebuild should be based on the size (square footage) of your home. Neither the purchase price nor the size of your mortgage should determine how much *dwelling coverage* you need.

If you're a renter, rejoice that you don't need dwelling coverage. If you're a condominium owner, find out whether the coverage the condo association bought for the entire building is sufficient.

Be sure that your homeowner's policy includes a *guaranteed replacement cost* provision. This useful feature ensures that the insurance company will rebuild the home even if the cost of construction is more than the policy coverage. If the insurance company underestimates your dwelling coverage, it has to make up the difference.

Unfortunately, insurers define guaranteed replacement cost differently. Some companies pay for the full replacement cost of the home, no matter how much it ends up costing. Other insurers set limits. For example, some insurers may pay up to only 25 percent more than the dwelling coverage on your policy. Ask your insurer how it defines guaranteed replacement cost.

If you have an older property that doesn't meet current building standards, consider buying a rider (supplemental coverage to your main insurance policy) that pays for code upgrades. This rider covers the cost of rebuilding your home, in the event of a loss, to comply with current building codes that may be more stringent than the ones in place when your home was built. Ask your insurance company what your basic policy does and doesn't cover. Some companies include a certain amount (for example, 10 percent of your dwelling coverage) for code upgrades in the base policy.

Personal property coverage: For your things

On your homeowner's policy, the amount of personal property coverage is typically derived from the amount of dwelling coverage you carry. Generally, you get personal property coverage that's equal to 50 to 75 percent of the dwelling coverage. This amount is usually more than enough.

Regarding riders to cover jewelry, computers, furs, and other somewhat costly items that may not be fully covered by typical homeowner's policies, ask yourself whether the out-of-pocket expense from the loss of such items would constitute a financial catastrophe. Unless you have tens of thousands of dollars worth of jewelry or computer equipment, skip such riders.

Some policies come with *replacement cost guarantees* that pay you the cost to replace an item. This payment can be considerably more than what the used item was worth before it was damaged or stolen. When this feature is not part of the standard policy sold by your insurer, you may want to purchase it as a rider, if available.

As a renter or condominium owner, you need to choose a dollar amount for the personal property you want covered. Tally it up instead of guessing — the total cost of replacing all your personal property may surprise you.

Make a list of your belongings — or even better, take pictures or make a video — with an estimate of what they're worth. Keep this list updated; you'll need it if you have to file a claim. Retaining receipts for major purchases may also help your case. No matter how you document your belongings, don't forget to keep the documentation somewhere besides your home — otherwise, it could be destroyed along with the rest of your house in a fire or other disaster.

Liability insurance: Coverage for when others are harmed

Liability insurance protects you financially against lawsuits that may arise if someone gets injured on your property, including wounds inflicted by the family pit bull or terrible tabby. (Of course, you should keep Bruno restrained when guests visit — even your cranky in-laws.) At a minimum, get enough liability insurance to cover your financial assets — covering two times your assets is better. Buying extra coverage is inexpensive and well worth the cost.

The probability of being sued is low, but if you are sued and you lose, you could end up owing big bucks. If you have substantial assets to protect, you may want to consider an umbrella, or excess liability, policy. (See "Protecting against Mega-Liability: Umbrella Insurance," later in this chapter.)

Liability protection is one of the side benefits of purchasing a renter's policy — you protect your personal property as well as insure against lawsuits. (But don't be reckless with your banana peels if you get liability insurance!)

Flood and earthquake insurance: Protection from Mother Nature

You should purchase the broadest possible coverage when buying any type of insurance (see Chapter 15). The problem with homeowner's insurance is that it's not comprehensive enough — it doesn't typically cover losses due to earthquakes and floods. You must buy such disaster coverage piecemeal.

If an earthquake or flood were to strike your area and destroy your home, you'd be out tens (if not hundreds) of thousands of dollars without proper coverage. Yet many people don't carry these important coverages, often as a result of some common misconceptions:

✔ **"Not in my neighborhood."** Many people mistakenly believe that earthquakes occur only in California. I wish this were true for those of you who live in the other 49 states, but it's not. In fact, one of the strongest earthquakes in the United States occurred in the Midwest, and known (though less active) fault lines lie along the East Coast. The cost of earthquake coverage is based on insurance companies' assessment of the risk of your area and property type, so you shouldn't decide whether to buy insurance based on how small you think the risk is. The risk is already built into the price.

An estimated 20,000 communities around the country face potential flood damage. Like earthquakes, floods are not a covered risk in standard homeowner's policies, so you need to purchase a flood insurance rider. Check with your current homeowner's insurer or with the insurers recommended in this chapter. The federal government flood insurance program (phone 888-379-9531; Web site www.floodsmart.gov) provides background information on flood insurance policies.

✔ **"The government will bail me out."** The vast majority of government financial assistance is obtained through low-interest loans. Loans, unfortunately, need to be repaid, and the money comes out of your pocket.

✔ **"In a major disaster, insurers would go bankrupt anyway."** This is highly unlikely given the reserves insurers are required to keep and the fact that the insurance companies *reinsure* — that is, they buy insurance to back up the policies they write.

People who have little equity in their property and are willing to walk away from their property and mortgage in the event of a major quake or flood may consider not buying earthquake or flood coverage. Keep in mind that walking away damages your credit report, because you're essentially defaulting on your loan.

You may be able to pay for much of the cost of earthquake or flood insurance by raising the deductibles (discussed in the next section) on the main part of your homeowner's/renter's insurance and other insurance policies (such as auto insurance). You can more easily afford the smaller claims, not the big ones. If you think flood or earthquake insurance is too costly, compare those costs with the costs you may have to incur to completely replace your home and personal property. Buy this insurance if you live in an area that has a chance of being affected by these catastrophes. To help keep the cost of earthquake insurance down, consider taking a 10 percent deductible. Most insurers offer deductibles of 5 or 10 percent of the cost to rebuild your home. Ten percent of the rebuilding cost is a good chunk of money. But losing the other 90 percent is what you want to insure against.

Deductibles: Your cost with a claim

As I discuss in Chapter 15, the point of insurance is to protect against cata-strophic losses, not the little losses. By taking the highest deductibles you're comfortable with, you save on insurance premiums year after year, and you don't have to go through the hassle of filing small claims.

Special discounts

You may qualify for special discounts. Companies and agents that sell home-owner's and renter's insurance don't always check to see whether you're eli-gible for discounts. After all, the more you spend on policy premiums, the more money they make! If your property has a security system, you're older, or you have other policies with the same insurer, you may qualify for a lower rate. Remember to ask.

Buying homeowner's or renter's insurance

Each insurance company prices its homeowner's and renter's policies based on its own criteria. So the lowest-cost company for your friend's property may not be the lowest-cost company for you. You have to shop around at sev-eral companies to find the best rates. The following list features companies that historically offer lower-cost policies for most people and have decent track records regarding customer satisfaction and the payment of claims:

✔ **Amica:** Although Amica does have good customer satisfaction, its prices are high in some areas. You can contact the company by calling 800-242-6422.

  - ✔ **Erie Insurance:** This company does business primarily in the Midwest and Mid-Atlantic. Check your local phone directory for agents, or call 800-458-0811 for a referral to a local agent.
  - ✔ **GEICO:** You can contact the company by calling 800-841-3000.
  - ✔ **Liberty Mutual:** Check your local phone directory for agents.
  - ✔ **Nationwide Mutual:** Check your local phone directory for agents.
  - ✔ **State Farm:** Check your local phone directory for agents.
  - ✔ **USAA:** This company provides insurance for members of the military and their families. Call the company at 800-531-8080 (or visit their Web site at www.usaa.com) to see whether you qualify.

Don't worry that some of these companies require you to call a toll-free number for a price quote. This process saves you money, because these insurers don't have to pay commissions to local agents hawking their policies. These companies have local claims representatives to help you if and when you have a claim.

A number of the companies mentioned in the preceding list sell other types of insurance (for example, life insurance) that aren't as competitively priced. Be sure to check out the relevant sections in this part of the book for the best places to buy these other types of coverage if you need them.

Some state insurance departments conduct surveys to determine the insurers' prices and tabulate complaints received. Look up your state's department of insurance phone number in the government section of your local phone directory or visit the National Association of Insurance Commissioners' Web site at www.naic.org/state_web_map.htm to find links to each state's department of insurance site.

Auto Insurance 101

Over the course of your life, you may spend tens of thousands of dollars on auto insurance. Much of the money people spend on auto insurance is not spent where it's needed most. In other cases, the money is simply wasted. Look for the following important features when searching for an auto insurance policy.

Bodily injury/property damage liability

As with homeowner's liability insurance, auto liability insurance provides insurance against lawsuits. Accidents happen, especially with a car. Make sure that you have enough bodily injury liability insurance, which pays for harm done to others, to cover your assets. (Coverage of double your assets is preferable.)

If you're just beginning to accumulate assets, don't mistakenly assume that you don't need liability protection. Many states require a minimum amount — insurers should be able to fill you in on the details for your state. Also, don't forget that your future earnings, which are an asset, can be garnished in a lawsuit.

Property damage liability insurance covers damage done by your car to other people's cars or property. The amount of property damage liability coverage in an auto insurance policy is usually determined as a consequence of the bodily injury liability amount selected. Coverage of $50,000 is a good minimum to start with.

Uninsured or underinsured motorist liability

When you're in an accident with another motorist and he doesn't carry his own liability protection (or doesn't carry enough), *uninsured or underinsured motorist liability coverage* allows you to collect for lost wages, medical expenses, and pain and suffering incurred in the accident.

Coping with teen drivers

If you have a teenage driver in your household, you're going to be spending a lot more on auto insurance (in addition to worrying a lot more). Try to keep your teenager out of your car as long as possible — this is the best advice I can offer.

If you allow your teenager to drive, you can take a number of steps to avoid spending all your take-home pay on auto insurance bills:

✔ Make sure that your teen does well in school. Some insurers offer discounts if your child is a strong academic achiever and has successfully completed a driver's education class (which is not required).

✔ Get price quotes from several insurers to see how adding your teen driver to your policy affects the cost.

✔ Have your teenager share in the costs of using the car. If you pay all the insurance, gas, and maintenance bills, your teenager won't value the privilege of using your "free" car.

Of course, not letting your teen drive shouldn't just be about keeping your insurance bills to a minimum. Auto accidents are the number one cause of death for teens. For more on driving responsibly, see the upcoming sidebar titled "Driving safely: Overlooked auto insurance."

If you already have comprehensive health and long-term disability insurance, uninsured or underinsured motorist liability coverage is largely redundant. However, if you drop this coverage, you do give up the ability to sue for general pain and suffering and to insure passengers in your car who may lack adequate medical and disability coverage.

To provide a death benefit to those financially dependent on you in the event of a fatal auto accident, buy term life insurance (see Chapter 16).

Deductibles

To minimize your auto insurance premiums and eliminate the need to file small claims, take the highest deductibles you're comfortable with. (Most people should consider a $500 to $1,000 deductible.) On an auto policy, two deductibles exist: collision and comprehensive. *Collision* applies to claims arising from collisions. (Note that if you have collision coverage on your own policy, you can generally bypass collision coverage when you rent a car.) *Comprehensive* applies to other claims for damages not caused by collision (for example, a window broken by vandals).

As your car ages and loses its value, you can eventually eliminate your comprehensive and collision coverages altogether. The point at which you do this is up to you. Insurers won't pay more than the book value of your car, regardless of what it costs to repair or replace it. Remember that the purpose of insurance is to compensate you for losses that are financially catastrophic to you. For some people, this amount may be as high as $5,000 or more — others may choose $1,000 as their threshold point.

Special discounts

You may be eligible for special discounts on auto insurance. Don't forget to tell your agent or insurer if your car has a security alarm, air bags, or anti-lock brakes. If you're older or you have other policies or cars insured with the same insurer, you may also qualify for discounts. And make sure that you're given appropriate "good driver" discounts if you've been accident- and ticket-free in recent years.

And here's another idea: *Before* you buy your next car, call insurers and ask for insurance quotes for the different models you're considering. The cost of insuring a car should factor into your decision of which car you buy, because the insurance costs represent a major portion of your car's ongoing operating expenses.

Driving safely: Overlooked auto insurance

Tragic events (murders, fires, hurricanes, plane crashes, and so on) are well-covered by the media, but the number of deaths that make the front pages of our newspapers pales in comparison to the approximately 40,000 people who die on America's roads every year.

I'm not suggesting that our national media should start reporting every automobile fatality. Even 24 hours of daily CNN coverage probably couldn't keep up with all the accidents on our roads. But the real story with auto fatalities lies not in the *who, what,* and *where* of specific accidents but in the *why*. When we ask the *why* question, we see how many of them are preventable.

No matter what kind of car you drive, you can and should drive safely. Stay within the speed limits and don't drive while intoxicated or tired or in adverse weather conditions. Wear your seat belt — a U.S. Department of Transportation study found that 60 percent of auto passengers killed were not wearing their seat belts. And don't try to talk on your cell phone and write notes on a pad of paper attached to your dashboard while balancing your coffee cup between your legs!

You can also greatly reduce your risk of dying in an accident by driving a safe car. You don't need to spend buckets of money to get a car with desirable safety features. The *Consumer Reports* annual auto-buying guide has lots of good information on individual car model safety.

Little-stuff coverage to skip

Auto insurers have dreamed up all sorts of riders, such as towing and rental car reimbursement. On the surface, these riders appear to be inexpensive. But they're expensive given the little amount you'd collect from a claim and the hassle of filing.

Riders that waive the deductible under certain circumstances make no sense, either. The point of the deductible is to reduce your policy cost and eliminate the hassle of filing small claims.

Medical payments coverage typically pays a few thousand dollars for medical expenses. If you and your passengers carry major medical insurance coverage, this rider isn't really necessary. Besides, a few thousand dollars of medical coverage doesn't protect you against catastrophic expenses.

Roadside assistance, towing, and rental car reimbursement coverage pay only small dollar amounts, and they aren't worth buying. In fact, if you belong to an automobile club, you may already have some of these coverages.

Buying auto insurance

You can use the homeowner's insurers list I present earlier in this chapter to obtain quotes for auto insurance. In addition, you can contact Progressive by calling 800-288-6776 or visiting their Web site at www.progressive.com.

Protecting against Mega-Liability: Umbrella Insurance

Umbrella insurance (which is also referred to as *excess liability insurance*) is additional liability insurance that's added on top of the liability protection on your home and car(s). If, for example, you have $700,000 in assets, you can buy a $1,000,000 umbrella liability policy to add to the $300,000 liability insurance that you have on your home and car. Expect to pay a couple hundred dollars — a small cost for big protection. Each year, thousands of people suffer lawsuits of more than $1,000,000 related to their cars and homes.

Umbrella insurance is generally sold in increments of $1,000,000. So how do you decide how much you need if you have a lot of assets? As with other insurance coverages, you should have at least enough liability insurance to protect your assets and preferably enough to cover twice the value of those assets.

To purchase umbrella insurance, start by contacting your existing homeowner's or auto insurance company.

Diversification: Investment insurance

Insurance companies don't sell policies that protect the value of your investments, but you can shield your portfolio from many of the dangers of a fickle market through diversification.

If all your money is invested in bank accounts or bonds, you're exposed to the risks of inflation, which can erode your money's purchasing power. Conversely, if the bulk of your money is invested in one high-risk stock, your financial future could go up in smoke if that stock explodes.

Chapter 9 discusses the benefits of diversification and tells you how to choose investments that do well under different conditions. Chapter 10 discusses why mutual funds are powerful investment vehicles that make diversification easy and cost-effective.

You Can't Take It with You: Planning Your Estate

Estate planning is the process of determining what will happen to your assets after you die. Thinking about your mortality in the context of insurance may seem a bit odd. But the time and cost of various estate-planning maneuvers is really nothing more than buying insurance: You're ensuring that, after you die, everything will be taken care of as you wish and taxes will be minimized. Thinking about estate planning in this way can help you better evaluate whether certain options make sense at particular points in your life.

Depending upon your circumstances, you may eventually want to contact an attorney who specializes in estate-planning matters. However, educating yourself first about the different options is worth your time. More than a few attorneys have their own agendas about what you should do, so be careful. And most of the estate-planning strategies that you're likely to benefit from don't require hiring an attorney.

Wills, living wills, and medical powers of attorney

When you have children who are minors (dependents), a will is a necessity. The will names the guardian to whom you entrust your children if both you and your spouse die. Should you and your spouse both die without a will (called *intestate*), the state (courts and social-service agencies) decides who will raise your children. Therefore, even if you can't decide at this time who you want to raise your children, you should *at least* appoint a trusted guardian who can decide for you.

Having a will makes good sense even if you don't have kids, because it gives instructions on how to handle and distribute all your worldly possessions. If you die without a will, your state decides how to distribute your money and other property, according to state law. Therefore, your friends, distant relatives, and favorite charities will probably receive nothing. Without any living relatives, your money may go to the state government!

Without a will, your heirs are legally powerless, and the state may appoint an administrator to supervise the distribution of your assets at a fee of around 5 percent of your estate. A bond typically must also be posted at a cost of several hundred dollars.

A living will and a medical power of attorney are useful additions to a standard will. A *living will* tells your doctor what, if any, life-support measures you prefer. A *medical* (or *health care*) *power of attorney* grants authority to someone you trust to make decisions regarding your medical care options.

The simplest and least costly way to prepare a will, a living will, and a medical power of attorney is to use the high-quality, user-friendly software packages that I recommend in Chapter 19. Be sure to give copies of these documents to the guardians and executors named in the documents.

You don't need an attorney to make a legal will. Most attorneys, in fact, prepare wills and living trusts using software packages! What makes a will valid is that three people witness your signing it.

If preparing the will all by yourself seems overwhelming, you can (instead of hiring an attorney) use a paralegal typing service to help you prepare the documents. These services generally charge 50 percent or less of what an attorney charges.

Avoiding probate through living trusts

Because of our quirky legal system, even if you have a will, some or all of your assets must go through a court process known as probate. *Probate* is the legal process for administering and implementing the directions in a will. Property and assets that are owned in joint tenancy or inside retirement accounts, such as IRAs or 401(k)s, generally pass to heirs without having to go through probate. However, passing through probate is necessary for most other assets.

A *living trust* effectively transfers assets into a trust. As the trustee, you control those assets, and you can revoke the trust whenever you desire. The advantage of a living trust is that upon your death, assets can pass directly to your beneficiaries without going through probate. Probate can be a lengthy, expensive hassle for your heirs — with legal fees tallying 5+ percent of the value of the estate. In addition, your assets become a matter of public record as a result of probate.

Living trusts are likely to be of greatest value to people who meet the following criteria:

- Age 60 or older
- Single
- Assets worth more than $100,000 that must pass through probate (including real estate, nonretirement accounts, and small businesses)
- Real property held in other states

As with a will, you do *not* need an attorney to establish a legal and valid living trust. (See my software recommendations in Chapter 19 and consider the paralegal services that I mention in the preceding section on wills.) Attorney fees for establishing a living trust can range from hundreds to thousands of dollars. Hiring an attorney is of greatest value to people with large estates (see the next section) who do not have the time, desire, and expertise to maximize the value derived from estate planning.

Note: Living trusts keep assets out of probate but have nothing to do with minimizing estate or inheritance taxes.

Reducing estate taxes

Thanks to the tax law changes passed in the early 2000s, fewer and fewer people will have an estate tax "problem" in the years ahead. An individual can pass $2,000,000 to beneficiaries without having to pay federal estate taxes. (This exclusion increases to $3,500,000 in 2008.)

Whether you should be concerned about possible estate taxes depends on several issues. How much of your assets you're going to use up during your life is the first and most important issue you need to consider. This amount depends on how much your assets grow over time, as well as how rapidly you spend money. During retirement, you'll (hopefully) be utilizing at least some of your money.

I've seen too many affluent individuals worry about estate taxes on their money throughout their retirements. If your intention is to leave your money to your children, grandchildren, or a charity, why not start giving while you're still alive so you can enjoy the act? You can give $12,000 annually to each of your beneficiaries, *tax-free.* By giving away money, you reduce your estate and, therefore, the estate taxes owed on it. Any appreciation on the value of the gift between the date of the gift and your date of death is also out of your estate and not subject to estate taxes.

In addition to gifting, a number of trusts allow you to minimize estate taxes. For example, if you're married, both you and your spouse can each pass up to $2,000,000 to your heirs (for a total of $4,000,000), free of federal estate taxes. You can accomplish this by establishing a *bypass trust.* Upon the death of the first spouse, assets held in his or her name go into the bypass trust, effectively removing those assets from the remaining spouse's taxable estate. Because the amount that can be passed free of estate taxes escalates to $3,500,000 by 2008, a bypass trust will allow for the estate-tax-free passage of up to $7,000,000.

Cash value life insurance is another estate planning tool. Unfortunately, it's a tool that's overused. People who sell cash value insurance — that is, insurance salespeople and others masquerading as financial planners — too often advocate life insurance as the one and only way to reduce estate taxes. Other methods for reducing estate taxes are usually superior, because they don't require wasting money on life insurance.

Small-business owners whose businesses are worth several million dollars or more may want to consider cash value life insurance under specialized circumstances. If you lack the necessary additional assets to pay expected estate taxes and you don't want your beneficiaries to be forced to sell the business, you can buy cash value life insurance to pay expected estate taxes.

To find out more about how to reduce your estate (and other) taxes, pick up a copy of the latest edition of *Taxes For Dummies,* co-written by Margaret Munro, David J. Silverman, and me (Wiley Publishing).

Part V

Where to Go for More Help

The 5th Wave   By Rich Tennant

"The first thing we should do is get you two into a good mutual fund. Let me get out the 'Magic 8-Ball' and we'll run some options."

In this part . . .

1 help you sift through the morass of financial resources competing for your attention and dollars. Many people who call themselves financial planners claim to be able to make you rich, but I show you how you may end up poorer if you don't choose an advisor wisely. I also cover software and Internet resources and name the best of the bunch. Finally, I discuss how to benefit from the financial coverage in print and on the air, as well as how to side-step the sometimes problematic advice in these media.

Chapter 18

Working with Financial Planners

*H*iring a competent, ethical, and unbiased financial planner or advisor to help you make and implement financial decisions can be money well spent. But if you pick a poor advisor or someone who really isn't a financial planner but a salesperson in disguise, your financial situation can get worse instead of better. So before I talk about the different types of help to hire, I discuss the options you have for directing the management of your personal finances.

Surveying Your Financial Management Options

Everyone has three basic choices for managing money: You can do nothing, you can do it yourself, or you can hire someone to help you.

Doing nothing

The do-nothing approach has a large following (and you thought you were alone!). People who fall into this category may be leading exciting, interesting lives and are therefore too busy to attend to something as mundane as dealing with their personal finances. Or they may be leading mundane existences but are too busy fantasizing about more-appealing ways to spend their time. For both types, everything from a major UFO sighting to taking out the garbage captures their imagination more than thinking about financial management.

 But the dangers of doing nothing are many. Problem areas, when left to themselves, get worse. Putting off saving for retirement or ignoring your buildup of debt eventually comes back to haunt you. If you don't carry adequate insurance, accidents can be devastating. Fires and earthquakes in California, flooding in the Midwest, and hurricanes in the South show how precarious living in paradise actually is.

If you've been following the do-nothing approach all your life, you're now officially promoted out of it! You bought this book to find out more about personal finance and make changes in your money matters, right? So take control and keep reading!

Doing it yourself

The do-it-yourselfers learn enough about financial topics to make informed decisions on their own. Doing anything yourself, of course, requires you to invest some time in learning the basic concepts and keeping up with changes. For some, personal financial management becomes a challenging and absorbing interest. Others focus on what they need to do to get the job done efficiently.

The idea that you're going to spend endless hours on your finances if you direct them yourself is a myth. The hardest part of managing money for most people is catching up on things that they should have done previously. After you get things in order, which you can easily do with this book as your companion, you shouldn't have to spend more than an hour or two working on your personal finances every few months (unless a major issue, like a real estate purchase, comes up).

 Some people in the financial advisory business like to make what they do seem so complicated, comparing it to brain surgery! Their argument goes, "You wouldn't perform brain surgery on yourself, so why would you manage your money yourself?" Well, to this I say, "Personal financial management ain't brain surgery — not even close." You can manage on your own. In fact, you can do a better job than most advisors. Why? Because you're not subject to their conflicts of interest, and you care the most about your money.

Hiring financial help

Realizing that you need to hire someone to help you make and implement financial decisions can be a valuable insight. Spending a few hours and several hundred dollars to hire a competent professional can be money well spent, even if you have a modest income or assets. But you need to know what your money is buying.

Financial planners or advisors make money in one of three ways:

✔ They earn commissions based on the sales of financial products.

✔ They can charge a percentage of your assets they're investing.

✔ They can charge by the hour.

The following sections help you differentiate among the three main types of financial planners.

Commission-based "planners"

Commission-based planners aren't really planners, advisors, or counselors at all — they're salespeople. Many stockbrokers and insurance brokers are now called *financial consultants* or *financial service representatives* in order to glamorize the profession and obscure how they're compensated. Ditto for insurance salespeople calling themselves *estate planning specialists*.

A stockbroker referring to himself as a financial consultant is like a Honda dealer calling himself a transportation consultant. A Honda dealer is a salesperson who makes a living selling Hondas — period. He's definitely not going to tell you nice things about Ford, Chrysler, or Toyota cars — unless, of course, he happens to sell those, too. He also has no interest in educating you about money-saving public-transit possibilities!

Salespeople and brokers masquerading as planners can have an enormous self-interest when they push certain products, particularly those products that pay generous commissions. Getting paid on commission tends to skew their recommendations toward certain strategies (such as buying investment or life-insurance products) and to cause them to ignore or downplay other aspects of your finances. For example, they'll gladly sell you an investment rather than persuade you to pay off your high-interest debts or save and invest through your employer's retirement plan, thereby reducing your taxes.

Table 18-1 gives you an idea of the commissions that a financial planner/ salesperson can earn by selling particular financial products.

Table 18-1	Financial Product Commissions
Product	**Commission**
Life Insurance ($250,000, age 45):	
Term Life	$125 to $500
Universal/Whole Life	$1,000 to $2,500
Disability Insurance:	
$4,000/month benefit, age 35	$400 to $1,500
Investments ($20,000):	
Mutual Funds	$800 to $1,700
Limited Partnerships	$1,400 to $2,000
Annuities	$1,000 to $2,000

Percentage-of-assets-under-management advisors

A financial advisor who charges a percentage of the assets that are being managed or invested is generally a better choice than a commission-based planner. This compensation system removes the incentive to sell you products with high commissions and initiate lots of transactions (to generate more of those commissions).

The fee-based system is an improvement over product-pushers working on commission, but it has flaws, too. Suppose that you're trying to decide whether to invest in stocks, bonds, or real estate. A planner who earns her living managing your money likely won't recommend real estate, because that will deplete your investment capital. The planner also won't recommend paying down your mortgage for the same reason — she'll claim that you can earn more investing your money (with her help, of course) than it'll cost you to borrow.

Fee-based planners are also only interested in managing the money of those who have already accumulated a fair amount of it — which rules out most people. Many have minimums of $250,000, $500,000, or more.

Hourly-based advisors

Your best bet for professional help with your personal finances is an advisor who charges for his time. Because he doesn't sell any financial products, his objectivity is maintained. He doesn't perform money management, so he can help you make comprehensive financial decisions with loans, retirement planning, and the selection of good investments, including real estate, mutual funds, and small business.

Hiring someone incompetent is the primary risk you face when selecting an hourly-based planner. So be sure to check references and find out enough about finances on your own to discern between good and bad financial advice. Another risk comes from not clearly defining the work to be done and the approximate total cost (consider getting this all in writing) of the planner's service before you begin. You should also review some of the other key questions that I outline in "Interviewing Financial Advisors: Asking the Right Questions," later in this chapter.

An entirely different kind of drawback occurs when you don't follow through on your advisor's recommendations. You paid for his work but didn't act on it, so you didn't capture its value. If part of the reason you hired the planner in the first place was that you're too busy or not interested enough to make changes to your financial situation, look for this type of support in the services you buy from the planner.

If you just need someone to act as a sounding board for ideas or to recommend a specific strategy or product, you can hire an hourly-based planner for one or two sessions of advice. You save money doing the legwork and implementation on your own. Just make sure that the planner is willing to give you specific advice so that you can properly implement the strategy.

Deciding Whether to Hire a Financial Planner

If you're like most people, you don't need to hire a financial planner, but you may benefit from hiring some help at certain times in your life. Good reasons for hiring a financial planner can be similar to the reasons you have for hiring someone to clean your home or do your taxes. If you're too busy, you don't enjoy doing it, or you're terribly uncomfortable making decisions on your own, using a planner for a second opinion makes good sense. And if you shy away from numbers and bristle at the thought of long division, a good planner can help you.

How a good financial advisor can help

The following list gives you a rundown of some of the important things a competent financial planner can assist you with:

   ✔ **Identifying problems and goals:** Many otherwise intelligent people have a hard time being objective about their financial problems. They may ignore their debts or have unrealistic goals and expectations given their financial situations and behaviors. And many are so busy with other aspects of their lives that they never take the time to think about what their financial goals are. A good financial planner can give you the objective perspective you need.

Surprisingly, some people are in a better financial position than they thought they were in relation to their goals. Good counselors really enjoy this aspect of their jobs — good news is easier and much more fun to deliver.

✔ **Identifying strategies for reaching your financial goals:** Your mind may be a jumble of various plans, ideas, and concerns, along with a cobweb or two. A good planner can help you sort out your thoughts and propose alternative strategies for you to consider as you work to accomplish your financial goals.

✔ **Setting priorities:** You may be doing dozens of things to improve your financial situation, but making just a few key changes will likely have the greatest value. Identifying the changes that fit your overall situation and that won't keep you awake at night is equally important. Good planners help you prioritize.

✔ **Saving research time and hassle:** Even if you know what major financial decisions are most important to you, doing the research can be time-consuming and frustrating if you don't know where to turn for good information and advice. A good planner does research to match your needs to the best available strategies and products. So much lousy information on various financial topics is out there that you can easily get lost, discouraged, sidetracked, or swindled. A good advisor can prevent you from making a bad decision based on poor or insufficient information.

✔ **Purchasing commission-free financial products:** When you hire a planner who charges for her time, you can easily save hundreds or thousands of dollars by avoiding the cost of commissions in the financial products you buy. Purchasing commission-free is especially valuable when you purchase investments and insurance.

✔ **Providing an objective voice for major decisions:** When you're trying to figure out when to retire, how much to spend on a home purchase, and where to invest your money, you're faced with some big decisions. Getting swept up in the emotions of these issues can cloud your perspective. A competent and sensitive advisor can help you cut through the cloud and provide you with sound counsel.

✔ **Helping you to just do it:** Deciding what you need to do is not enough — you have to actually do it. And although you can use a planner for advice and then make all the changes on your own, a good counselor can help you follow through with your plan. After all, part of the reason you hired the advisor in the first place may be that you're too busy or uninterested to manage your finances.

✔ **Mediating:** If you have a spouse or partner, financial decisions can produce real fireworks — particularly financial decisions involving the extended family. Although a counselor can't be a therapist, a good one can be sensitive to the different needs and concerns of each party and can try to find middle ground on the financial issues you're grappling with.

✔ **Making you money and allowing you peace of mind:** The whole point of professional financial planning is to help you make the most of your money and plan for and attain your financial and personal goals. In the process, the financial planner should show you how to enhance your investment returns; reduce your spending, taxes, and insurance costs; increase your savings; improve your catastrophic-insurance coverage; and achieve your financial-independence goals. Putting your financial house in order should take some weight off your mind — like that clean, lightheaded feeling after a haircut.

Why advisors aren't for everyone

Finding a good financial planner isn't easy, so make sure that you want to hire an advisor before you venture out in search of a competent one.

You should also consider your personality type before you decide to hire help. My experience has been that some people (believe it or not) enjoy the research and number-crunching. If this sounds like you, or if you're not really comfortable taking advice, you may be better off doing your own homework and creating your own plan.

If you have a specific tax or legal matter, you may be better off hiring a good professional who specializes in that specific field rather than hiring a financial planner.

The Frustrations of Finding Good Financial Planners

Overwhelmed consumers, especially those in low- and middle-income brackets, have few attractive options when hiring financial help. The vast majority of the people who call themselves *financial planners* and *financial consultants* sell products and work on commission, which creates enormous conflicts of interest. The conflicts of interest stem from the fact that the broker has an incentive to recommend strategies and sell products that pay generous commissions and to ignore strategies and products that pay no or low commissions.

The few financial advisors who are fee-only make most of their fees from money-management services. (*Fee-only* or *fee-based* means that the advisors' fees are paid by their clients, not by companies whose products they recommend.) Thus, fee-based advisors tend to focus on clients who have already accumulated significant wealth. Fee-based advisors may also have conflicts of interest in that they gravitate toward strategies and recommendations that involve their ongoing management of your money, and they may ignore or dismiss tactics that diminish the pool of investment money they can manage for you for an ongoing fee.

The following sections describe some of the problems associated with finding a good planner.

Recognizing conflicts of interest

All professions have conflicts of interest. Some fields have more than others, and the financial-planning field is one of those fields. Knowing where some of the land mines are located can certainly help. Here, then, are the most common reasons that planners may not have 20/20 vision when giving financial directions.

Selling and pushing products that pay commissions

If a financial planner isn't charging you a fee for her time, you can rest assured that she's earning commissions on the products she tries to sell you. To sell financial products, this planner needs a broker's license. A person who sells financial products and then earns commissions from those products is a salesperson, *not* a financial planner. Financial planning done well involves taking an objective, holistic look at your financial puzzle to determine which pieces fit it well — something brokers are neither trained nor financially motivated to do.

To make discerning a planner's agenda even harder, you can't assume that planners who charge fees for their time don't also earn commissions selling products. This compensation double dipping is common.

Selling products that provide a commission tends to skew a planner's recommendations. Products that carry commissions result in fewer of your dollars going to the investments and insurance you buy. Because a commission is earned only when a product is sold, such a product or service is inevitably more attractive in the planner's eyes than other options. For example, consider the case of a planner who sells disability insurance that you can obtain at a lower cost through your employer or a group trade association (see Chapter 16). She may overlook or criticize your most attractive option (buying through your employer) and focus on *her* most attractive option — selling you a higher-cost disability policy on which she derives a commission.

Another danger of trusting the recommendation of a commission-based planner is that she may steer you toward the products that have the biggest payback for her. These products are among the *worst* for you because they siphon off even more of your money upfront to pay the commission. They also tend to be among the costliest and riskiest financial products available.

"Financial planning" in banks

Over recent decades, banks have witnessed an erosion of the money in their coffers and vaults because increasing numbers of investors realized that banks are generally lousy places to build wealth. The highest-yielding bank savings accounts and certificates of deposit barely keep an investor ahead of inflation. If you factor in both inflation and taxes, these bank "investments" provide no real growth on your investment dollars.

Increasingly, banks have "financial representatives" and "investment specialists" sitting in their branches, waiting to pounce on bank customers with big balances. In many banks, these "financial planners" are simply brokers who are out to sell investments that pay them (and the bank) hefty sales commissions.

Although you may expect your bank account balances to be confidential and off-limits to the eager eyes of investment salespeople in banks, numerous studies have demonstrated that banks are betraying customer trust.

Customers often have no idea that these bank reps are earning commissions and that those commissions are being siphoned out of customers' investment dollars. Many customers are mistaken (partly due to the banks' and salespeople's poor disclosure) in believing that these investments, like bank savings accounts, are FDIC-insured and cannot lose value.

Planners who are commission-greedy may also try to *churn* your investments. They encourage you to buy and sell at the drop of a hat, attributing the need to changes in the economy or the companies you invested in. More trading means more commissions for the broker.

Taking a narrow view

Because of the way they earn their money, many planners are biased in favor of certain strategies and products. As a result, they typically don't keep your overall financial needs in mind. For example, if you have a problem with accumulated consumer debts, some planners may never know (or care) because they're focused on selling you an investment product. Likewise, a planner who sells a lot of life insurance tends to develop recommendations that require you to purchase it.

Not recommending saving through your employer's retirement plan

Taking advantage of saving through your employer's retirement savings plan(s) is one of your best financial options. Although this method of saving may not be as exciting as risking your money in cattle futures, it's not as dull as watching paint dry — and most importantly, it's tax-deductible. Some planners are reluctant to recommend taking full advantage of this option: It doesn't leave much money for the purchase of their commission-laden investment products.

Ignoring debts

Sometimes paying off outstanding loans — such as credit card, auto, or even mortgage debts — is your best investment option. But most financial planners don't recommend this strategy because paying down debts depletes the capital with which you could otherwise buy investments — the investments that the broker may be trying to sell you to earn a commission or that the advisor would like to manage for an ongoing fee.

Not recommending real estate and small business investments

Investing in real estate and small business, like paying off debts, takes money away from your investing elsewhere. Most planners won't help with these choices. They may even tell you tales of real-estate- and small-business-investing disasters to try to give you cold feet.

The value of real estate can go down just like any other investment. But over the long haul, owning real estate makes good financial sense for most people. With small business, the risks are higher, but so are the potential returns. Don't let a financial planner convince you that these options are foolish — in fact, if you do your homework and know what you're doing, you can make higher rates of return investing in real estate and small business than you can in traditional securities such as stocks and bonds. See Part III to read more about your options.

Selling ongoing money-management services

The vast majority of financial planners who don't work on commission make their money by managing your money for an ongoing fee percentage (typically 1 to 2 percent of your investment annually). Although this fee removes the incentive to *churn* your account (frequently trade your investments) to run up more commissions, the service is something that you're unlikely to need. (As I explain in Part III, you can hire professional money managers for less.)

An ongoing fee percentage still creates a conflict of interest; the financial planner will tend to steer you away from beneficial financial strategies that reduce the asset pool from which he derives his percentage. Financial strategies such as maximizing contributions to your employer's retirement savings plan, paying off debts like your mortgage, investing in real estate or small business, and so on may make the most sense for you. Advisors who work on a percentage-of-assets-under-management basis may be biased against such strategies.

Selling legal services

Some planners are in the business of drawing up *trusts* and providing other estate-planning services for their clients. Although these and other legal documents may be right for you, legal matters are complex enough that the competence of someone who isn't a full-time legal specialist should be carefully scrutinized. And lower-cost options may be available if your situation is not complicated.

If you need help determining whether you need these legal documents, do a little investigating: Do some additional reading or consult an advisor who won't actually perform the work. If you do ultimately hire someone to perform estate-planning services for you, make sure that you hire someone who specializes and works at it full time. See Chapter 17 to find out more about estate planning.

Scaring you unnecessarily

Some planners put together nifty computer-generated projections that show you that you're going to need millions of dollars by the time you retire to maintain your standard of living or that show that tuition will cost hundreds of thousands of dollars by the time your 2-year-old is ready for college.

Waking up a client to the realities of his or her financial situation is an important and difficult job for good financial planners. But some planners take this task to an extreme, deliberately scaring you into buying what they're selling. They paint a bleak picture and imply that you can fix your problems only if you do what they say. Don't let them scare you; read this book and get your financial life in order.

Creating dependency

Many financial planners create dependency by making things seem so complicated that their clients feel as though they could never manage their finances on their own. If your advisor is reluctant to tell you how you can educate yourself about personal money management, you probably have a self-perpetuating consultant. Financial planning is hardly the only occupation guilty of this. As author George Bernard Shaw put it, "All professions are conspiracies against the laity."

Regulatory problems

The financial-planning field has a problem when it comes to oversight. Oversight is minimal *at best.* In many states, anyone can hang out a shingle and call him- or herself a financial planner. The U.S. Securities and Exchange Commission (SEC) polices only those financial planners who provide investment advice/management on a regular basis and oversee more than $25 million; these advisors must register with the SEC as registered investment advisors (RIAs). The SEC provides no oversight of planners who don't provide investment advice/management.

States police the hundreds of thousands of people who call themselves financial planners. But most states have done little to monitor planners and protect consumers. Thus, as the nonprofit Consumer Federation of America said in its assessment of the industry, "Today's investors go up against a deadly combination of abusive securities industry practices and regulatory inattentiveness when investing their money."

Finding a Good Financial Planner

Locating a good financial planner who is willing to work with the not-yet-rich-and-famous and who doesn't have conflicts of interest can be like trying to find a needle in a haystack. Personal referrals and associations are two methods that can serve as good starting points.

Soliciting personal referrals

Getting a personal referral from a satisfied customer you trust is one of the best ways to find a good financial planner. Obtaining a referral from an accountant or attorney whose judgment you tested can help as well. (Beware that such professionals in other fields may also do some financial planning and recommend themselves.)

The best financial planners continue to build their practices through word of mouth. Satisfied customers are a professional's best and least costly marketers. However, you should *never* take a recommendation from anyone as gospel. I don't care *who* is making the referral — even if it's your mother or the pope. You must do your homework. Ask the planner the questions I list in the upcoming section "Interviewing Financial Advisors: Asking the Right Questions." I've seen people get into real trouble because of blindly accepting someone else's recommendation. Remember that the person making the recommendation is (probably) not a financial expert. He or she may be just as bewildered as you are.

You may get referred to a planner or broker who returns the favor by sending business to the tax, legal, or real estate person who referred you. On more than a few occasions, professionals in other fields have made it clear that they would refer business to me if I referred business to them. I refused, of course. Good professionals don't agree to scratch each others' backs. Hire professionals who make referrals to others based on their competence and ethics.

Seeking advisors through associations

Associations of financial planners are more than happy to refer you to planners in your area. But as I discuss earlier in this chapter, the major trade associations are composed of planners who sell products and work on commission.

BEWARE

Warning signs in planners' cultivation techniques

The channel through which you hear of a planner may provide clues to the planner's integrity and way of doing business. Beware of planners you find (or who find you) through these avenues:

✓ **Cold calling:** You've just come home after a hard day. No sooner has your posterior hit the recliner to settle in for the night when the phone rings. It's Joe the financial planner, and he wants to help you achieve all your financial dreams. *Cold calling* (the salesperson calls you, without an appointment) is the most inefficient way for a planner to get new clients. Cold calling is intrusive, and it's typically used by aggressive salespeople who work on commission.

Keep a log beside your telephone. Record the date, time, name of the organization, and name of the caller every time you receive a cold call. Politely but firmly tell cold callers to never call you again. Then, if they do call you again, you can sue them for $500 in small claims court!

✓ **Adult education classes:** Here's what often happens at the adult education classes that are offered at local universities: You pay a reasonable fee for the course. You go to class giddy at the prospect of learning how to manage your finances. And then the instructor ends up being a broker or financial planner hungry for clients. He confuses more than he conveys. He's short on specifics. But he's more than happy to show you the way if you contact (and hire) him outside of class.

The instructors for these courses are paid to teach. They don't need to solicit clients in class, and, in fact, it's unethical for them to do so. I should note, however, that part of the problem is that some universities take advantage of the fact that such "teachers" want to solicit business, setting the pay at a low level. So *never* assume that someone who is teaching a financial-planning course at a local college is ethical, competent, or looking out for your best interests. Although I may sound cynical, assume that these people are none of the above until they clearly prove otherwise.

Ethical instructors who are there to teach do *not* solicit clients. In fact, they may actively discourage students from hiring them. Smart universities pay their instructors well and weed out the instructors who are more interested in building up their client base than they are in teaching.

✓ **"Free" seminars:** This is a case of "you get what you pay for." Because you don't pay a fee to attend "free seminars" and the "teachers" don't get paid either, these events tend to be clear-cut sales pitches. The "instructor" may share some information, but smart seminar leaders know that the goal of a successful seminar is to establish himself or herself as an expert and to whet the prospects' appetites.

Note: Be wary of seminars targeted at select groups, such as special seminars for people who have received retirement-plan distributions or seminars touting "Financial Planning for Women." Financial planning is not specific to gender, ethnicity, or marital status.

Don't assume that the financial planner giving a presentation at your employer's office is the right planner for you, either. You may be surprised at how little some corporate benefits departments investigate the people they let in. In most cases, planners are accepted simply because they don't charge. One organization I'm familiar with gave preference to planners who, in addition to doing free presentations, also brought in a catered lunch! Guess what — this preference attracted a lot of brokers who sell high-commission products.

Here are three solid places to start searching for good financial planners:

- ✔ **The National Association of Personal Financial Advisors:** The NAPFA (800-366-2732; www.napfa.org) is made up of fee-only planners. Its members are not supposed to earn commissions from products they sell or recommend. However, most planners in this association earn their living by providing money-management services and charging a fee that is a percentage of assets under management. And most have minimums, which can put them out of reach of the majority of people.

- ✔ **The American Institute of Certified Public Accountants:** The AICPA (888-999-9256; www.cpapfs.org) is the professional association of CPAs that can provide names of members who have completed the Institute's Personal Financial Specialist (PFS) program. Many of the CPAs who have completed the PFS program provide financial advice on a fee basis. Competent CPAs have the advantage of understanding the tax consequences of different choices, which are important components of any financial plan. On the other hand, it can be hard for a professional to keep current in two broad fields.

- ✔ **Garrett Planning Network:** This for-profit company (www.garrett planningnetwork.com) has developed a system for screening planners who focus on providing advice on an hourly, as needed basis with clients. Established in 2000, they have about 250 member planners throughout the U.S. Member planners have a variety of credentials and training including CFPs, Ph.D.s, MBAs, and CFAs. To join, planners must pay a $7,500 initiation fee and $1,200 annually thereafter.

Interviewing Financial Advisors: Asking the Right Questions

Don't consider hiring a financial advisor until you read the rest of this book. If you're not educated about personal finance, how can you possibly evaluate the competence of someone you may hire to help you make important financial decisions?

I firmly believe that you are your own best financial advisor. However, I know that some people don't want to make financial decisions without getting assistance. Perhaps you're busy or simply can't stand making money decisions.

You need to recognize that you have a lot at stake when you hire a financial advisor. Besides the cost of his services, which generally don't come cheap, you're placing a lot of trust in his recommendations. The more you know, the better the advisor you end up working with, and the fewer services you need to buy.

The following questions will help you get to the core of an advisor's competence and professional integrity. Get answers to these questions *before* you decide to hire a financial advisor.

What percentage of your income comes from clients' fees versus commissions?

Asking this question first may save you the trouble and time of asking the next nine questions. The right answer is "100 percent of my income comes from fees paid by clients." Anything less than 100 percent means that the person you're speaking to is a salesperson with a vested interest in recommending certain strategies and products.

Sadly, more than a few financial advisors don't tell the truth. In an undercover investigation done by *Money* magazine, nearly one-third of advisors who claimed that they were fee-only turned out to be brokers who also sold investment and insurance products on a commission basis.

How can you ferret these people out? Advisors who provide investment advice and oversee at least $25 million must register with the U.S. Securities and Exchange Commission (SEC); otherwise, they generally must register with the state that they make their principal place of business. They must file Form ADV, otherwise known as the Uniform Application for Investment Adviser Registration. This lengthy document asks for the following specific information from investment advisors:

- ✔ A breakdown of where their income comes from

- ✔ Relationships and affiliations with other companies

- ✔ Education and employment history

- ✔ The types of securities the advisory firm recommends

- ✔ The advisor's fee schedule

In short, Form ADV provides — in black and white — answers to all the essential questions. With a sales pitch over the phone or marketing materials sent in the mail, a planner is much more likely to gloss over or avoid certain issues. Although some advisors fib on Form ADV, most advisors are more truthful on this form than they are in their own marketing.

You can ask the advisor to send you a copy of Form ADV. You can also find out whether the advisor is registered and whether he or she has a track record of problems by calling the U.S. Securities and Exchange Commission (SEC) at 800-732-0330 or by visiting its Web site at www.sec.gov. You can also contact the department that oversees investment advisors in your state.

What percentage of fees paid by clients is for ongoing money management versus hourly financial planning?

The answer to how the advisor is paid provides clues to whether he has an agenda to convince you to hire him to manage your money. If you want objective and specific financial planning recommendations, give preference to advisors who derive their income from hourly fees. Many counselors and advisors call themselves "fee-based," which usually means that they make their living managing money for a percentage.

If you want a money manager, you can hire the best quite inexpensively through a mutual fund. Or if you have substantial assets, you can hire an established money manager (refer to Chapter 10).

What is your hourly fee?

The rates for financial advisors range from as low as $75 per hour all the way up to several hundred dollars per hour. If you shop around, you can find terrific planners who charge around $100 to $150 per hour.

As you compare planners, remember that what matters is the total cost that you can expect to pay for the services you're seeking.

Do you also perform tax or legal services?

Be wary of someone who claims to be an expert beyond one area. The tax, legal, and financial fields are vast in and of themselves, and they're difficult for even the best and brightest advisor to cover simultaneously.

One exception is the accountant who also performs some basic financial planning by the hour. Likewise, a good financial advisor should have a solid grounding in the basic tax and legal issues that relate to your personal finances. Large firms may have specialists available in different areas.

What work and educational experience qualifies you to be a financial planner?

This question doesn't have one right answer. Ideally, a planner should have experience in the business or financial services field. Some say to look for planners with at least five or ten years of experience. I've always wondered how planners earn a living their first five or ten years if folks won't hire them until they reach these benchmarks! A good planner should also be good with numbers, speak in plain English, and have good interpersonal skills.

Education is sort of like food. Too little leaves you hungry. Too much can leave you feeling stuffed and uncomfortable. And a small amount of high quality is better than a lot of low quality.

Because investment decisions are a critical part of financial planning, take note of the fact that the most-common designations of educational training among professional money managers are MBA (master of business administration) and CFA (chartered financial analyst). And some tax advisors who work on an hourly basis have the PFS (personal financial specialist) credential.

Have you ever sold limited partnerships? Options? Futures? Commodities?

The correct answers here are *no, no, no,* and *no.* If you don't know what these disasters are, refer to Chapter 9. You also need to be wary of any financial advisor who used to deal in these areas but now claims to have seen the light and reformed his ways.

Professionals with poor judgment may not repeat the same mistakes, but they're more likely to make some new ones at your expense. My experience is that even advisors who have been "reformed" are unlikely to be working by the hour. Most of them either work on commission or want to manage your money for a hefty fee.

Do you carry liability (errors and omissions) insurance?

Some counselors may be surprised by this question or think that you're a problem customer looking for a lawsuit. On the other hand, accidents happen; that's why insurance exists. So if the planner doesn't have liability insurance, she missed one of the fundamental concepts of planning: Insure against risk. Don't make the mistake of hiring her.

You wouldn't (and shouldn't) let contractors into your home to do work without knowing that they have insurance to cover any mistakes they make. Likewise, you should insist on hiring a planner who carries protection in case she makes a major mistake for which she is liable. Make sure that she carries enough coverage given what she is helping you with.

Can you provide references from clients with needs similar to mine?

Take the time to talk to other people who have used the planner. Ask what the planner did for them, and find out what the advisor's greatest strengths and weaknesses are. You can learn a bit about the planner's track record and style. And because you want to have as productive a relationship as possible with your planner, the more you find out about him, the easier it'll be for you to hit the ground running if you hire him.

Some financial advisors offer a "complimentary" introductory consultation. If an advisor offers a free consultation to allow you to check him out and it makes you feel more comfortable about hiring him, fair enough. But be careful: Most free consultations end up being a big sales pitch for certain products or services the advisor offers.

The fact that a planner doesn't offer a free consultation may be a good sign. Counselors who are busy and who work strictly by the hour can't afford to burn an hour of their time for an in-person free session. They also need to be careful of folks seeking free advice. Such advisors usually are willing to spend some time on the phone answering background questions. They should also be able to send background materials by mail and provide references.

Will you provide specific strategies and product recommendations that I can implement on my own if I choose?

This is an important question. Some advisors may indicate that you can hire them by the hour. But then they provide only generic advice without specifics. Some planners even *double dip* — they charge an hourly fee initially to make you feel like you're not working with a salesperson, and then they try selling commission-based products. Also be aware of advisors who say that you can choose to implement their recommendations on your own and then recommend financial products that carry commissions.

How is implementation handled?

Ideally, you should find an advisor who lets you choose whether you want to hire him to help with implementation after the recommendations have been presented to you. If you know that you're going to follow through on the advice and you can do so without further discussions and questions, don't hire the planner to help you implement his recommendations.

On the other hand, if you hire the counselor because you lack the time, desire, and/or expertise to manage your financial life in the first place, building implementation into the planning work makes good sense.

Learning from Others' Mistakes

Over the many years that I've worked as a financial counselor and now fielding questions from readers, I hear too many problems that people encounter from hiring incompetent and unethical financial advisors. To avoid repeating others' mistakes, please remember the following:

- ✔ You absolutely *must* do your homework before hiring any financial advisor. Despite recommendations from others about a particular advisor, you can end up with bad advice from biased advisors.

- ✔ The financial planning and brokerage fields are minefields for consumers. The fundamental problem is the enormous conflict of interest that is created when "advisors" sell products that earn them sales commissions. Selling ongoing money management services creates a conflict of interest as well.

  Imagine that you have flu symptoms. Would you be comfortable seeing a physician who didn't charge for office visits but instead made money only by selling you drugs? Maybe you don't *need* the drugs — or at least not so many expensive ones. Maybe what you really need is Mom's chicken soup and ten hours of sleep.

- ✔ The more you know, and the more you understand that investing and other financial decisions needn't be complicated, the more you realize that you don't need to spend gobs of money (or any money at all) on financial planners and advisors. When you look in the mirror, you see the person who has your best interests at heart and is your best financial advisor.

Chapter 19

Computer Money Management

• •

In This Chapter

▶ Evaluating the different types of software and Web sites

▶ Performing financial tasks with your computer

• •

A lthough a computer may be able to assist you with your personal finances, it simply represents one of many tools. Computers are best for performing routine tasks (such as processing lots of bills or performing many calculations) more quickly and for aiding you with research.

This chapter gives you an overview of how to use software and cyberspace as you work with your finances. I tell you how to use this technology to pay your bills, prepare taxes, research investments, plan for retirement, trade securities, buy insurance, and plan your estate, and I direct you to the best software and Web sites.

Surveying Software and Web Sites

You can access two major repositories of personal finance information through your computer. Although the lines are sometimes a bit blurry between these two categories, they're roughly defined as software and the Internet:

✔ *Software* refers to computer programs that are either packaged in a box or DVD case or are available to be downloaded online. Most of the mass-marketed financial software packages sell for under $100. If you've ever used a word-processing program such as Word or WordPerfect or a spreadsheet program such as Excel, then you've used software.

✔ *The Internet* is a vast ocean of information that you can generally access via a modem, cable modem, or DSL (digital subscriber line). These devices allow your computer to talk with other computers. To access the Internet, you need a Web browser, which you can obtain through your Internet service provider (ISP). Most of the financial stuff on the Internet is supplied by companies marketing their wares and, hence, is available for free. Some sites sell their content for a fee.

Adding up financial software benefits

Although the number of personal-finance software packages and Web sites is large and growing, quality is having a hard time keeping up, especially among the free Internet sites. The best software can

- ✔ Guide you to better organization and management of your personal finances
- ✔ Help you complete mundane tasks or complex calculations more quickly and easily and provide basic advice in unfamiliar territory
- ✔ Make you feel in control of your financial life

Mediocre and bad software, on the other hand, can make you feel stupid or, at the very least, make you want to tear your hair out. Lousy packages usually end up in the software graveyard.

Having reviewed many of the packages available, I can assure you that if you're having a hard time with some of the programs out there (and sometimes even with the more useful programs), you're not at fault. Too many packages assume that you already know things such as your tax rate, your mortgage options, and the difference between stock and bond mutual funds. Much of what's out there is too technically oriented and isn't user-friendly. Some of it is even flawed in its financial accuracy.

A good software package, like a good tax or financial advisor, should help you better manage your finances. It should simply and concisely explain financial terminology, and it should help you make decisions by offering choices and recommendations, allowing you to "play" with alternatives before following a particular course of action.

With increasing regularity, financial software packages are being designed to perform more than one task or to address more than one area of personal finances. But remember that no software package covers the whole range of issues in your financial life. Later in this chapter, I recommend some of my favorite financial software.

Treading carefully on the Web

Like the information you receive from any medium, you have to sift out the good from the bad when you surf the Internet. If you blindly navigate the Internet and you naively think that everything out there is useful "information," "research," or "objective advice," you're going to be in for a rude awakening.

Most personal-finance sites on the Internet are free, which — guess what — means that these sites are basically advertising or are dominated and driven by advertising. If you're looking for written material by unbiased experts or writers — well — you can find some on the Web, but you'll find far more biased and uninformed stuff.

Consider the source so you can recognize bias

A report on the Internet published by a leading investment-banking firm provides a list of the "coolest finance" sites. On the list is the Web site of a major bank. Because it's been a long time since I was in junior high school, I'm not quite sure what "cool" means anymore. If cool can be used to describe a well-organized and graphically pleasing Web site, then I guess I can say that the bank's site is cool.

However, if you're looking for sound information and advice, then the bank's site is decidedly "uncool." It steers you in a financial direction that benefits (not surprisingly) the bank and not you. For example, in the real-estate section, users are asked to plug in their gross monthly income and down payment. The information is then used to spit out the supposed amount that users can "afford" to spend on a home. No mention is given to the other financial goals and concerns — such as saving for retirement — that affect one's ability to spend a particular amount of money on a home.

Consider this advice in the lending area of the site: "When you don't have the cash on hand for important purchases, we can help you borrow what you need. From a new car, to that vacation you've been longing for, to new kitchen appliances, you can make these dreams real now." Click on a button at the bottom of this screen — and presto, you're on your way to racking up credit card and auto debt. Why bother practicing delayed gratification, living within your means, or buying something used if getting a loan is "easy" and comes with "special privileges"?

Watch out for "sponsored" content

"Sponsored" content, a euphemism for advertising under the guise of editorial content, is another problem to watch out for on Web sites. You may find a disclaimer or note, which is often buried in small print in an obscure part of the Web site, saying that an article is sponsored by (in other words, paid advertising by) the "author."

For example, one mutual-fund site states that its "primary purpose is to provide viewers with an independent guide that contains information and articles they can't get anywhere else." The "content" of the site suggests otherwise. In the "Expert's Corner" section of the site, material is reprinted from a newsletter that advocates frequent trading in and out of mutual funds to time market moves. Turns out that the article is "sponsored by the featured expert": In other words, it's a paid advertisement. (The track record of the newsletter's past recommendations, which isn't discussed on the site, is poor.)

Steer clear of biased financial-planning advice

I also suggest skipping the financial-planning advice offered by financial service companies that are out to sell you something. Such companies can't take the necessary objective, holistic view required to render useful advice.

For example, on one major mutual-fund company's Web site, you find a good deal of material on the company's mutual funds. The site's college-planning advice is off the mark because it urges parents to put money in a custodial account in the child's name. Ignored is the fact that this will undermine your child's ability to qualify for financial aid (see Chapter 13), that your child will have control of the money at either age 18 or 21 depending upon your state, and that you're likely better off funding your employer's retirement plan. If you did that, though, you couldn't set up a college savings-plan account at the fund company, which this area of the site prods you to do.

Shun short-term thinking

Many financial Web sites provide real-time stock quotes as a hook to a site that is cluttered with advertising. My experience working with individual investors is that the more short-term they think, the worse they do. And checking your portfolio during the trading day certainly promotes short-term thinking.

Also, beware of tips offered around the electronic water cooler — message boards. As in the real world, chatting with strangers and exchanging ideas is sometimes fine. However, if you don't know the identity and competence of message-board posters or chat-room participants, why would you follow their financial advice or stock tips? Getting ideas from various sources is okay, but educate yourself and do your homework before making personal financial decisions.

If you want to best manage your personal finances and find out more, remember that the old expression "You get what you pay for" contains a grain of truth. Free information on the Internet, especially information provided by companies in the financial-services industry, is largely self-serving. Stick with information providers who have proven themselves offline or who don't have anything to sell except objective information and advice.

Accomplishing Computer Money Tasks

In the remainder of this chapter, I detail important personal financial tasks that your computer can assist you with. I also provide my recommendations for the best software and Web sites to help you accomplish these chores.

Paying your bills and tracking your money

Checkbook software automates the process of paying your bills, and it can track your check writing and prepare reports that detail your spending by category so you can get a handle on where the fat in your budget is. One drawback of using these programs to track your spending is that it captures only what you enter. Thus, the amount and spending category of your individual credit card and cash purchases, which for most people are substantial, are omitted unless you enter such data (or get a credit card from the software company, which allows you to download your credit card transactions via your computer). For a complete discussion on how to track your spending, see Chapter 3.

Quicken and Microsoft Money are good programs that I've reviewed in this category. In addition to offering the printed checks and electronic bill-payment features, both of these packages are financial organizers. The programs allow you to list your investments and other assets, along with your loans and other financial liabilities.

In addition to the significant investment of time necessary to figure out how to use the software program, another drawback is cost — computer checks are pricey. If you order checks directly from the software manufacturers (order forms come with your software), expect to pay about $95 plus shipping costs for 500 checks. You can chop these costs in half by ordering from other companies. Checks Tomorrow (`www.checkstomorrow.com`), for example, sells 500 checks for $40 plus shipping costs.

You can avoid dealing with paper checks — written or printed — by signing up for *online bill payment.* With such services, you save on stamps and envelopes, and the cost of the service may be comparable to what you're spending on those supplies. Such services are available to anyone with a checking account through an increasing number of banks, credit unions, and brokerage firms, as well as through the checkbook programs. An intermediary company that receives your electronic instructions and pays the bill for you enacts the service. No more stamp sticking and envelope stuffing. You can even set up regularly recurring bills to be paid automatically.

You don't need a checkbook program to pay your bills online. Simply sign up through a financial institution offering the service. CheckFree's Web site (`www.checkfree.com`) can direct you to firms that offer its bill-paying service. Because most online bill-payment services charge a minimum monthly fee, you can find cheaper ways to avoid check writing and stamp sticking. For example, some businesses that you must pay monthly allow you to establish a monthly electronic payment service directly with them.

Planning for retirement

Good retirement-planning software and online tools can help you plan for retirement by crunching the numbers for you. But they can also teach you how particular changes — such as your investment returns, rate of inflation, or your savings rate — can affect when and in what style you can retire. The biggest time-saving aspect of retirement-planning software and Web sites is that they let you more quickly play with and see the consequences of changing the assumptions.

Some of the major investment companies I profile in Part III of this book are sources for some high-quality, low-cost retirement-planning tools. Here are some good ones to consider:

- ✔ T. Rowe Price's Web site (www.troweprice.com) has several tools that can help you determine where you stand in terms of reaching a given retirement goal. T. Rowe Price (800-638-5660) also offers some excellent workbooklets for helping you plan for retirement. The company's Retirement Planning Guide is for those who are more than five years from retirement, and the Retirement Readiness Guide is intended for people who are already retired or are within five years of retirement. Expect some marketing of T. Rowe Price's mutual funds in these booklets and software.

- ✔ Vanguard's Web site (www.vanguard.com) can help with figuring savings goals to reach retirement goals as well as with managing your budget and assets in retirement.

Preparing your taxes

Good, properly used tax-preparation software can save you time and money. The best programs "interview" you to gather the necessary information and select the appropriate forms based on your responses. Of course, you're still the one responsible for locating all the information needed to complete your return. More-experienced taxpayers can bypass the interview and jump directly to the forms they know they need to complete. These programs also help flag overlooked deductions and identify other tax-reducing strategies.

TurboTax and TaxCut are among the better tax-preparation programs I've reviewed.

In addition to the federal tax packages, tax-preparation programs are available for state income taxes, too. Many state tax forms are fairly easy to complete because they're based on information from your federal form. If your state tax forms are based on your federal form, you may want to just skip buying the state income-tax preparation packages and prepare your state return by hand.

If you're mainly looking for tax forms, you can get them at no charge in tax-preparation books or through the IRS Web site (www.irs.gov).

Researching investments

Instead of schlepping off to the library and fighting over the favorite investing reference manuals, ponying up hundreds of dollars to buy print versions for your own use, or slogging through voice-mail hell when you call government agencies, you can access a variety of materials on your computer. You can also often pay for just what you need:

- ✔ **Sec.gov:** This site allows unlimited free access to Securities and Exchange Commission documents. All public corporations, as well as mutual funds, file their reports with the agency. Be aware, however, that navigating this site takes patience.

- ✔ **Morningstar.com:** This site provides access to Morningstar's individual stock and mutual fund reports. The reports are free, but they're watered-down versions of the company's comprehensive software and paper products. If you want to buy Morningstar's unabridged fund reports online, you can do so for a fee.

- ✔ **Vanguard.com:** Although I'm leery of financial service company "educational" materials because of bias and self-serving advice, some companies do a worthy job on these materials. The investor-friendly, penny-pinching Vanguard Group of mutual funds has an online university on its Web site, where investors can learn the basics of fund investing. Additionally, investors in Vanguard's funds can access up-to-date personal account information through the site.

Trading online

If you do your investing homework, trading securities online may save you money and perhaps some time. For years, discount brokers (which I discuss in Chapter 8) were heralded as the low-cost source for trading. Now, online brokers such as E*TRADE Financial (800-822-2021; www.etrade.com) and Scottrade (800-619-7283; www.scottrade.com) have set a new lower-cost standard. The major mutual fund companies, such as T. Rowe Price and Vanguard, also offer competitive online services.

A number of the newer discount brokers have built their securities brokerage business around online trading. By eliminating the overhead of branch offices and by accepting and processing trades by computer, online brokers keep their costs and brokerage charges to a minimum. Cut-rate electronic brokerage firms are for people who want to direct their own financial affairs and don't want or need to work with a personal broker. However, some of these brokers have limited products and services. For example, some don't offer many of the best mutual funds. And my own experience with reaching live people at some online brokers has been trying — I've had to wait on hold for more than ten minutes before a customer service representative answered the call.

Although online trading may save you on transaction costs, it can also encourage you to trade more than you should, resulting in higher total trading costs, lower investment returns, and higher income tax bills. Following investments on a daily basis encourages you to think short term. Remember that the best investments are bought and held for the long haul (see Part III for more information).

Reading and searching periodicals

Many business and financial publications are online offering investors news and financial market data. *The Wall Street Journal* provides an online personalized edition of the paper (`online.wsj.com`). You can tailor the content to meet your specific needs. The cost is $99 per year ($49 if you're already a *Journal* subscriber).

Leading business publications such as *Forbes* (`www.forbes.com`) and *BusinessWeek* (`www.businessweek.com`) put their current magazines' content on the Internet. However, increasing numbers of publications are charging for archived articles and for some current content for nonsubscribers to their print magazine. Be careful to take what you read and hear in the mass media with many grains of salt (see Chapter 20 for more on mass media). Much of the content revolves around tweaking people's anxieties and dwelling on the latest crises and fads.

Buying life insurance

If loved ones are financially dependent on you, you probably know that you need some life insurance. But add together the dread of life-insurance salespeople and a fear of death, and you have a recipe for procrastination. Although your computer can't stave off the Grim Reaper, it can help you find a quality, low-cost policy that can be more than 80 percent less costly than the most expensive options, all without having you deal with high-pressure sales tactics.

The best way to shop for term life insurance online is through one of the quotation services that I discuss in Chapter 16. At each of these sites, you fill in your date of birth, whether you smoke, how much coverage you'd like, and for how long you'd like to lock in the initial premium. When you're done filling in this information, a new Web page pops up with a list of low-cost quotes (based on assumed good health) from highly rated (for financial stability) insurance companies.

Invariably, the quotes are ranked by how cheap they are. Although cost is certainly an important factor, many of these services don't do as good of a job explaining other important factors to consider when doing your comparison shopping. For example, the services sometimes don't cover the projected and maximum rates after the initial term has expired. Be sure to ask about these other future rates before you agree to a specific policy.

If you decide to buy a policy from one of the online agencies, you can fill out an online application form. The quotation agency will then mail you a detailed description of the policy and insurer, along with your completed application. In addition to having to deal with snail mail, you'll also have to deal with a *medical technician,* who will drop by your home to check on your health status . . . at least until some computer genius figures out a way for you to give a blood and urine sample online!

Preparing legal documents

Just as you can prepare a tax return with the advice of a software program, you can also prepare common legal documents. This type of software may save you from the often difficult task of finding a competent and affordable attorney.

Using legal software is generally preferable to using fill-in-the-blank documents. Software has the built-in virtues of directing and limiting your choices and preventing you from making common mistakes. Quality software also incorporates the knowledge and insights of the legal eagles who developed the software. And it can save you money.

If your situation isn't unusual, legal software may work well for you. As to the legality of documents that you create with legal software, remember that a will, for example, is made legal and valid by your witnesses; the fact that an attorney prepares the document is *not* what makes it legal.

An excellent package for preparing your own will is Quicken WillMaker Plus, which is published by Nolo, a name synonymous with high quality and user-friendliness in the legal publishing world. In addition to allowing you to prepare wills, WillMaker can also help you prepare a living will and medical power of attorney document. The software also allows you to create a living trust that serves to keep property out of probate in the event of your death (see Chapter 17). Like wills, living trusts are fairly standard legal documents that you can properly create with the guidance of a top-notch software package. The package advises you to seek professional guidance for your situation, if necessary.

Chapter 20

On Air and in Print

You don't lack options when it comes to finding radio and television news, Web sites, newspapers, magazines, and books that talk about money and purport to help you get rich. Tuning out poor resources and focusing on the best ones is the real challenge.

Because you probably don't consider yourself a financial expert, more often than not you won't know who to believe and listen to. I help you solve that problem in this chapter.

Observing the Mass Media

For better and for worse, America's mass media has a profound influence on our culture. On the good side, news is widely disseminated these days. So if a product is recalled or a dangerous virus breaks out in your area, you'll probably hear about it, perhaps more than you want to, through the media — or perhaps from tuned-in family members!

The downsides of the mass media are plenty, though.

Alarming or informing us?

Imagine sitting down to watch the evening news and hearing the following stock market report:

"On Wall Street today, stock prices dropped a bit less than 1 percent, extending the market's decline of the past week. The reason: More people wanted to sell than buy. For the year, the U.S. market is still up 15 percent, which is well above the historic average annual return of 10 percent."

Now contrast that report with the following report for the same day:

"Stocks plunged sharply today as the Dow Jones Industrial Average plummeted more than 100 points to close at its lowest level in the past 168 hours. Dell Computer saw its shares get creamed 10 percent, as the company issued a profit warning that third-quarter revenues would take a big hit due to the Taiwan earthquake. Banking stocks got hammered again, and the sector has been off more than 20 percent for the past three months."

Although the second news report goes into more detail, it's meant to be more provocative and anxiety producing. Most of the daily stock market reports I hear in the media sound more like the second report than they do the mundane, calming first report. News producers, in their quest for ratings and advertising dollars, try to be alarming. The more you watch, the more unnerved you get over short-term, especially negative, events.

Teaching what kind of values?

Daily doses of American mass media, including all the advertising that comes with it, essentially communicate the following messages to us:

- ✔ Your worth as a person is directly related to your physical appearance (including the quality of clothing and jewelry you wear) and your material possessions — cars, homes, electronics, and other gadgets.

- ✔ The more money you make, the more "successful" you clearly are.

- ✔ The more famous you are (especially as a movie or sports star), the more you're worth listening to and admiring.

- ✔ Don't bother concerning yourself with the consequences before engaging in negative behavior.

- ✔ Delaying gratification and making sacrifices is for boring losers.

Continually inundating yourself with poor messages can cause you to behave in a way that undermines your long-term happiness and financial success. Don't support (by watching, listening, or reading) forms of media that don't reflect your values and morals.

Worshipping prognosticating pundits

Quoting and interviewing experts is perhaps the only thing that the media loves more than hyping short-term news events. What's the economy going to do next quarter? What's stock XYZ going to do next month? What's the stock market going to do in the next hour? No, I'm not kidding about that last one — the stock market cable channel CNBC regularly interviews floor traders from the New York Stock Exchange late in the trading day to get their opinions about what the market will do in the last hour before closing!

Prognosticating pundits keep many people tuned in because their advice is constantly changing (and is therefore entertaining and anxiety producing), and they lead investors to believe that investments can be maneuvered in advance to outfox future financial market moves. Common sense suggests, though, that no one has a working crystal ball, and if she did, she certainly wouldn't share such insights with the mass media for free. (For more on experts who purport to predict the future, see Chapter 8.)

Rating Radio and Television Financial Programs

Over the years, money issues have received increased coverage through the major media of television and radio. Some topics gain more coverage in radio and television because they help draw more advertising dollars (which follow what people are watching). When you click on the radio or television, you don't pay a fee to tune in to a particular channel (with pay cable channels being an exception). Advertising doesn't necessarily prevent a medium from delivering coverage that is objective and in your best interests, but it sure doesn't help foster this type of coverage either.

For example, can you imagine a financial radio or television correspondent saying:

> "We've decided to stop providing financial market updates every five min-utes because we've found it causes some investors to become addicted to tracking the short-term movements in the markets and to lose sight of the bigger picture. We don't want to encourage people to make knee-jerk reactions to short-term events."

Sound-bite-itis is another problem with both of these media. Producers and network executives believe that if you go into too much detail, viewers and listeners will change the channel.

Now, radio and television are hardly the only types of media that offer poor advice and cause investor myopia. The Internet can be even worse. And I've read plenty of lousy money books over the years.

Finding the Best Web Sites

Yes, the Internet is changing the world, but certainly not always for the better and not always in such a big way. Consider the way we shop. Okay, you can buy things online that you couldn't in the past. Big deal — what's the difference between buying something by calling a toll-free number or doing mail order (which many of us did for years before the Internet got commercialized) and buying something by clicking your computer mouse? Purchasing things online simply broadens the avenues through which you can spend money. I see a big downside here: Overspending is easier to do when you surf the Internet a lot.

Some of the best Web sites allow you to more efficiently access information that may help you make important investing decisions. However, this doesn't mean that your computer allows you to compete at the same level as professional money managers. No, the playing field isn't level. The best pros work at their craft full time and have far more expertise and experience than the rest of us. Some nonprofessionals have been fooled into believing that investing online makes them better investors. My experience has been that people who spend time online every day dealing with investments tend to trade and react more to short-term events and have a harder time keeping the bigger picture and their long-term goals and needs in focus.

If you know where to look, you can more easily access some types of information. However, you often find a lot of garbage online — just as you do on other advertiser-dominated media like television and radio. In Chapter 19, I explain how to safely navigate online to find the best of what's out there.

Navigating Newspapers and Magazines

Compared with radio and television, print publications generally offer lengthier discussions of topics. And in the more financially focused publications, the editors who work on articles generally have more background in the topics they write about.

Even within the better publications, I find a wide variety of quality. So don't instantly believe what you read, even if you read a piece in a publication you like. Here's how to get the most from financial periodicals:

- ✔ **Read some back issues.** Go to your local library (or perhaps visit the publication's Web site) and read some issues that are at least one to two years old. Although reading old issues may seem silly and pointless, it can actually be enlightening. By reviewing a number of past issues in one sitting, you can begin to get a flavor for a publication's style, priorities, and philosophies.

- ✔ **Look for solid information and perspective.** Headlines reveal a lot about how a publication perceives its role. Publications with cover stories such as "10 hot stocks to buy now!" and "Funds that will double your money in the next three years!" are probably best avoided. Look for articles that seek to educate with accuracy, not predict.

- ✔ **Note bylines.** As you read a given publication over time, you should begin to make note of the different writers. After you get to know who the better writers are, you can skip over the ones you don't care for and spend your limited free time reading the best.

- ✔ **Don't react without planning.** Here's a common example of how not to use information and advice you glean from publications: I had a client who had some cash he wanted to invest. He would read an article about investing in real estate investment trusts and then go out the next week and buy several of them. Then he'd see a mention of some technology stock funds and invest in some of those. Eventually his portfolio was a mess of investments that reflected the history of what he had read rather than an orchestrated, well-thought-out investment portfolio.

Betting on Books

Reading a good book is one of my favorite ways to get a crash course on a given financial topic. Good books can go into depth on a topic in a way that simply isn't possible with other resources. Books also aren't cluttered with advertising and the conflicts inherent therein.

As with the other types of resources I discuss in this chapter, you definitely have to choose carefully — there's plenty of mediocrity and garbage out there.

Understanding the book publishing business

Book publishers are businesses first. And like most businesses, their business practices vary. Some have a reputation for care and quality; others just want to push a product out the door with maximum hype and minimum effort.

For instance, you may think that book publishers check out an author before they sign him or her to write an entire book. Well, you may be surprised to find out that some publishers don't do their homework.

What most publishers care about first is how marketable a book and an author are. Some authors are marketable because of their well-earned reputation for sound advice. Others are marketable because of stellar promotional campaigns built on smoke and mirrors.

Even more troubling is that few publishers require advice guides to be technically reviewed for accuracy by an expert in the field other than the author, who sometimes is not an expert. You, the reader, are expected to be your own technical reviewer. But do you have the expertise to do that? (Don't worry; this book has been checked for accuracy.)

As an author and financial counselor, I know that financial ideas and strategies can differ considerably. Different is not necessarily wrong. When a technical reviewer looks at my text and tells me that a better way is out there, I take a second look. I may even see things in a new way. If I were the only expert to see my book before publication, I wouldn't get this second expert opinion. How do you know whether a book's been technically reviewed? Check the credits page or the author's acknowledgments.

Authors write books for many reasons other than to teach and educate. The most common reason financial book authors write books is to further their own business interests. Taking care of business interests may not always be a bad thing, but it's not the best thing for you when you're trying to educate yourself and better manage your own finances. For example, some investment newsletter sellers write investment books. Rather than teach you how to make good investments, the authors make the investment world sound complicated so that you feel the need to subscribe to their ongoing newsletters.

Books at the head of their class

ERIC'S PICKS

In addition to books that I've recommended at various places throughout this book, here's a list of some of my other favorite financial titles:

- ✔ *The Ultimate Credit Handbook: How to Cut Your Debt and Have a Lifetime of Great Credit* by Gerri Detweiler (Plume)

- ✔ *A Random Walk Down Wall Street* by Burton G. Malkiel (Norton)

- ✔ *Built to Last: Successful Habits of Visionary Companies* by Jim Collins and Jerry I. Porras (HarperCollins)

- ✔ *Good to Great: Why Some Companies Make the Leap . . . and Others Don't* by Jim Collins (HarperCollins)

- ✔ *Paying for College without Going Broke* by Kalman A. Chany (Princeton Review)

- ✔ *Don't Miss Out: The Ambitious Student's Guide to Financial Aid* by Anna and Robert Leider (Octameron Associates)

- ✔ Nolo's legal titles

- ✔ *Mind Over Money: Your Path to Wealth and Happiness* (CDS Books) — my most recent book, which helps readers identify and overcome problematic financial habits

- ✔ And, not surprisingly, my *For Dummies* books on *Investing, Mutual Funds, Taxes, Home Buying, House Selling, Mortgages, Real Estate Investing,* and *Small Business* (Wiley Publishing)

Part VI
The Part of Tens

The 5th Wave   By Rich Tennant

"Coming out of bankruptcy, I can say I learned my lesson – don't spend what your relatives don't have."

In this part . . .

You find some fun and useful chapters that can help you with financial strategies for ten life changes and guide you with ten tips for avoiding identity theft and fraud. Why "tens"? Why not?

Chapter 21

Survival Guide for Ten Life Changes

. . . .

In This Chapter
▶ Handling the financial challenges that arise during life changes
▶ Minimizing financial worries so you can focus on what matters most

. . . .

Some of life's changes come unexpectedly, like earthquakes. Others you can see coming when they're still far off, like a big storm moving in off the horizon. Whether a life change is predictable or not, your ability to navigate successfully through its challenges and adjust quickly to new circumstances depends largely on your degree of preparedness.

Perhaps you find my comparison of life changes to natural disasters to be a bit negative. After all, some of the changes I discuss in this chapter should be occasions for joy. But understand that what one defines as a "disaster" has everything to do with preparedness. To the person who has stored no emergency rations in his basement, the big snowstorm that traps him in his home can lead to problems. But to the prepared person with plenty of food and water, that same storm may mean a vacation from work and some relaxing days in the midst of a winter wonderland.

First, here are some general tips that apply to all types of life changes:

✔ **Stay in financial shape.** An athlete is best able to withstand physical adversities during competition by training and eating well in advance. Likewise, the sounder your finances are to begin with, the better you'll be able to deal with life changes.

✔ **Changes require change.** Even if your financial house is in order, a major life change — starting a family, buying a home, starting a business, divorcing, retiring — should prompt you to review your personal financial strategies. Life changes affect your income, spending, insurance needs, and ability to take financial risk.

✔ **Don't procrastinate.** With a major life change on the horizon, procrastination can be costly. You (and your family) may overspend and accumulate high-cost debts, lack proper insurance coverage, or take other unnecessary risks. Early preparation can save you from these pitfalls.

✔ **Manage stress and your emotions.** Life changes often are accompanied by stress and other emotional upheavals. Don't make knee-jerk decisions during these changes. Take the time to become fully informed and recognize and acknowledge your feelings. Educating yourself is key. You may want to hire experts to help (see Chapter 18). Don't abdicate decisions and responsibilities to advisors — the advisors may not have your best interests at heart or fully appreciate your needs.

Here, then, are the major changes you may have to deal with at some point in your life. I wish you more of the good changes than the bad.

Starting Out: Your First Job

If you just graduated from college or some other program, or you're otherwise entering the workforce, your increased income and reduction in educational expenses are probably a welcome relief. You'd think, then, that more young adults would be able to avoid financial trouble and challenges. But they face these challenges largely because of poor financial habits picked up at home or from the world at large. Here's how to get on the path to financial success:

✔ **Don't use consumer credit.** The use and abuse of consumer credit can cause long-term financial pain and hardship. To get off on the right financial foot, young workers need to shun the habit of making purchases on credit cards that they can't pay for in full when the bill arrives in the mail. Here's the simple solution for running up outstanding credit card balances: Don't carry a credit card. If you need the convenience of making purchases with a piece of plastic, get a debit card (see Chapter 5).

✔ **Get in the habit of saving and investing.** Ideally, your savings should be directed into retirement accounts that offer tax benefits unless you want to accumulate down-payment money for a home or small-business purchase (see Chapter 4). Thinking about a home purchase or retirement is usually not in the active thought patterns of first-time job seekers. I'm often asked, "At what age should a person start saving?" To me, that's similar to asking at what age you should start brushing your teeth. Well, when you have teeth to brush! So I say you should start saving and investing money from your first paycheck. Try saving 5 percent of every paycheck and then eventually increase your saving to 10 percent. If you're having trouble saving money, track your spending and make cutbacks as needed (refer to Chapters 3 and 6).

✔ **Get insured.** When you're young and healthy, imagining yourself feeling otherwise is hard. Many twentysomethings give little thought to the potential for health care expenses. But because accidents and unexpected illnesses can strike at any age, forgoing coverage can be financially devastating. Buying disability coverage, which replaces income lost to a long-term disability, in your first full-time job with more-limited benefits is also wise. And as you begin to build your assets, consider making out a will so that your assets go where you want in the event of your death.

✔ **Continue your education.** After you get out in the work force, you (like many other people) may realize how little you learned in formal schooling that can actually be used in the real world and, conversely, how much you need to learn (like personal financial management) that school never taught you. Read, learn, and continue to grow. Continuing education can help you advance in your career and enjoy the world around you.

Changing Jobs or Careers

During your adult life, you'll almost surely change jobs — perhaps several times a decade. I hope that most of the time you'll be changing by your own choice. But let's face it: Job security is not what it used to be. Downsizing has made victims of even the most talented workers.

Always be prepared for a job change. No matter how happy you are in your current job, knowing that your world won't fall apart if you're not working tomorrow can give you an added sense of security and encourage openness to possibility. Whether you're changing your job by choice or necessity, the following financial maneuvers can help ease the transition:

✔ **Structure your finances to afford an income dip.** Spending less than you earn always makes good financial sense, but if you're coming up to a possible job change, spending less is even more important, particularly if you're entering a new field or starting your own company and you expect a short-term income dip. Many people view a lifestyle of thriftiness as restrictive, but ultimately those thrifty habits can give you more freedom to do what you want to do. Be sure to keep an emergency reserve fund (see Chapter 8).

If you lose your job, batten down the hatches. You normally get little advance warning when you lose your job through no choice of your own. It doesn't mean, however, that you can't do anything financially. Evaluating and slashing your current level of spending may be necessary. Everything should be fair game, from how much you spend on housing to how often you eat out to where you do your grocery shopping. Avoid at all costs the temptation to maintain your level of spending by accumulating consumer debt.

✔ **Evaluate the total financial picture when relocating.** At some point in your career, you may have the option of relocating. But don't call the moving company until you understand the financial consequences of such a move. You can't simply compare salaries and benefits between the two jobs. You also need to compare the cost of living between the two areas: That includes housing, commuting, state income and property taxes, food, utilities, and all the other major expenditure categories that I cover in Chapter 3.

✔ **Track your job search expenses for tax purposes.** If you're seeking a new job in your current (or recently current) field of work, your job search expenses may be tax-deductible, even if you don't get a specific job you desire. Remember, however, that if you're moving into a new career, your job search expenses are not tax-deductible.

Getting Married

Ready to tie the knot with the one you love? Congratulations — I hope that you'll have a long, healthy, and happy life together. In addition to the emotional and moral commitments that you and your spouse will make to one another, you're probably going to be merging many of your financial decisions and resources. Even if you're largely in agreement about your financial goals and strategies, managing as two is different from managing as one. Here's how to prepare:

✔ **Take a compatibility test.** Many couples never talk about their goals and plans before marriage, and failing to do so breaks up way too many marriages. Finances are just one of the many issues you need to discuss. Ensuring that you know what you're getting yourself into is a good way to minimize your chances for heartache. Ministers, priests, and rabbis sometimes offer premarital counseling to help bring issues and differences to the surface.

✔ **Discuss and set joint goals.** After you're married, you and your spouse should set aside time once a year, or every few years, to discuss personal and financial goals for the years ahead. When you talk about where you want to go, you help ensure that you're both rowing your financial boat in unison.

✔ **Decide whether to keep finances separate or jointly managed.** Philosophically, I like the idea of pooling your finances better. After all, marriage is a partnership, and it shouldn't be a his-versus-hers affair. In some marriages, however, spouses may choose to keep some money separate so they don't feel the scrutiny of a spouse with different spending preferences. Spouses who have been through divorce may choose to keep the assets they bring into the new marriage separate in order to protect their money in the event of another divorce. As long as you're jointly accomplishing what you need to financially, some separation of money is okay. But for the health of your marriage, don't hide money from one another, and if you're the higher-income spouse, don't assume power and control over your joint income.

✔ **Coordinate and maximize employer benefits.** If one or both of you have access to a package of employee benefits through an employer, understand how best to make use of those benefits. Coordinating and using the best that each package has to offer is like getting a pay raise. If you both have access to health insurance, compare which of you has better benefits. Likewise, one of you may have a better retirement savings plan — one that matches and offers superior investment options. Unless you can afford to save the maximum through both your plans, saving more in the better plan will increase your combined assets. (*Note:* If you're concerned about what will happen if you save more in one of your retirement plans and then you divorce, in most states, the money is considered part of your joint assets to be divided equally.)

✔ **Discuss life and disability insurance needs.** If you and your spouse can make do without each other's income, you may not need any income-protecting insurance. However, if, like many husbands and wives, you both depend on each other's incomes, or if one of you depends fully or partly on the other's income, you may each need long-term disability and term life insurance policies (refer to Chapter 16).

✔ **Update your wills.** When you marry, you should make or update your wills. Having a will is potentially more valuable when you're married, especially if you want to leave money to others in addition to your spouse, or if you have children for whom you need to name a guardian. See Chapter 17 for more on wills.

✔ **Reconsider beneficiaries on investment and life insurance.** With retirement accounts and life insurance policies, you name beneficiaries to whom the money or value in those accounts will go in the event of your passing. When you marry, you'll probably want to rethink your beneficiaries.

Buying a Home

Most Americans eventually buy a home. You don't need to own a home to be a financial success, but home ownership certainly offers financial rewards. Over the course of your adult life, the real estate you own is likely going to appreciate in value. Additionally, you're going to pay off your mortgage someday, which will greatly reduce your housing costs. If you're thinking about buying a home:

✔ **Get your overall finances in order.** Before buying, analyze your current budget, your ability to afford debt, and your future financial goals. Make sure your expected housing expenses allow you to save properly for retirement and other long- or short-term objectives. Don't buy a home based on what lenders are willing to lend.

✔ **Determine whether now's the time.** Buying a house when you don't see yourself staying put three to five years rarely makes financial sense, especially if you're a first-time home buyer. Buying and selling a home gobbles up a good deal of money in transaction costs — you'll be lucky to recoup all those costs even within a five-year period. Also, if your income is likely to drop or you have other pressing goals, such as starting a business, you may want to wait to buy.

For more about buying a home, be sure to read Chapter 14.

Having Children

If you think that being a responsible adult, holding down a job, paying your bills on time, and preparing for your financial future are tough, wait 'til you add kids to the equation. Most parents find that with kids in the family, the already precious commodities of free time and money become even more precious. The sooner you discover how to manage your time and money, the better able you'll be to have a sane, happy, and financially successful life as a parent. Here are some key things to recognize and do both before and after you begin your family:

✔ **Set your priorities.** As with many other financial decisions, starting or expanding a family requires that you plan ahead. Set your priorities and structure your finances and living situation accordingly. Is having a bigger home in a particular community important, or would you rather feel less pressure to work hard, giving you more time to spend with your family? Keep in mind that a less hectic work life not only gives you more free time but also often reduces your cost of living by decreasing meals out, dry-cleaning costs, day care expenses, and so on.

✔ **Take a hard look at your budget.** Having children requires you to increase your spending. At a minimum, expenditures for food and clothing will increase. But you're also likely to spend more on housing, insurance, day care, and education. On top of that, if you want to play an active role in raising your children, working at a full-time job won't be possible. So while you consider the added expenses, you may also need to factor in a decrease in income.

No simple rules exist for estimating how children will affect your household's income and expenses. On the income side, figure out how much you want to cut back on work. On the expense side, government statistics show that the average household with school-age children spends about 20 percent more than those without children. Going through your budget category by category and estimating how kids will change your spending is a more scientific approach. (You can use the worksheets in Chapter 3).

✔ **Boost insurance coverage *before* getting pregnant.** Make sure your health insurance plan offers maternity benefits. (Ask about waiting periods that may exclude coverage for a pregnancy within the first year or so of the insurance.) With disability insurance, pregnancy is considered a preexisting condition, so women should secure this coverage before getting pregnant. And most families-to-be should buy life insurance. Buying life insurance *after* the bundle of joy comes home from the hospital is a risky proposition — if one of the parents develops a health problem, he or she may be denied coverage. You should also consider buying life insurance for a stay-at-home parent. Even though the stay-at-home parent is not bringing in income, if he or she were to pass away, hiring assistance could cripple the family budget.

✔ **Check maternity leave with your employers.** Many of the larger employers offer some maternity leave for women and, in rare but thankfully increasing cases, for men. Some employers offer paid leaves, while others may offer unpaid leaves. Understand the options and the financial ramifications before you consider the leave and, ideally, before you get pregnant.

✔ **Update your will.** If you have a will, you'll need to update it; if you don't have a will, make one now. With children in the picture, you need to name a guardian who will be responsible for raising your children should you and your spouse both pass away.

✔ **Enroll the baby in your health plan.** After your baby is welcomed into this world, enroll him or her in your health insurance plan. Most insurers give you about a month or so to enroll.

✔ **Understand child-care tax benefits.** For every one of your children with an official Social Security number, you get a $3,300 deduction on your income taxes (tax year 2006). So if you're in the 25 percent federal tax bracket, each child saves you $825 in federal taxes. On top of that, you may be eligible for a $1,000 tax credit for each child under the age of 17. That should certainly motivate you to apply for your kid's Social Security number!

If you and your spouse both work and you have children under the age of 13, you can also claim a tax credit for child-care expenses. Or you may work for an employer who offers a flexible benefit or spending plan. These plans allow you to put away up to $5,000 per year on a pre-tax basis for child-care expenses. For many parents, especially those in higher income tax brackets, these plans can save a lot in taxes. Keep in mind, however, that if you use one of these plans, you can't claim the child-care tax credit. Also, if you don't deplete the account every tax year, you forfeit any money left over.

✔ **Skip saving in custodial accounts.** One common concern is how to sock away enough money to pay for the ever-rising cost of a college education. If you start saving money in your child's name in a so-called custodial account, however, you may harm your child's future ability to qualify for financial aid and miss out on the tax benefits that come with investing elsewhere (see Chapter 13).

✔ **Don't indulge the children.** Toys, art classes, sports, field trips, and the like can rack up big bills, especially if you don't control your spending. Some parents fail to set guidelines or limits when spending on children's programs. Others mindlessly follow the examples set by the families of their children's peers. Introspective parents have told me that they feel some insecurity about providing the best for their children. The parents (and kids) who seem the happiest and most financially successful are the ones who clearly distinguish between material luxuries and family necessities.

As children get older and become indoctrinated into the world of shopping, all sorts of other purchases come into play. Consider giving your kids a weekly allowance and letting them discover how to spend and manage it. And when they're old enough, having your kids get a part-time job can help teach financial responsibility.

Starting a Small Business

Many people aspire to be their own bosses, but far fewer people actually leave their jobs in order to achieve that dream. Giving up the apparent security of a job with benefits and a built-in network of co-workers is difficult for most people, both psychologically and financially. Starting a small business is not for everyone, but don't let inertia stand in your way. Here are some tips to help get you started and increase your chances for long-term success:

✔ **Prepare to ditch your job.** To maximize your ability to save money, live as Spartan a lifestyle as you can while you're employed; you'll develop thrifty habits that'll help you weather the reduced income and increased expenditure period that come with most small-business start-ups. You may also want to consider easing into your small business by working at it part-time in the beginning, with or without cutting back on your normal job.

✔ **Develop a business plan.** If you research and think through your business idea, not only will you reduce the likelihood of your business's failing and increase its success if it thrives, but you'll also feel more comfortable taking the entrepreneurial plunge. A good business plan should describe in detail the business idea, the marketplace you'll compete in, your marketing plans, and expected revenue and expenses.

✔ **Replace your insurance coverage.** Before you finally leave your job, get proper insurance. With health insurance, employers allow you to continue your existing coverage (at your own expense) for 18 months. Individuals with existing health problems are legally entitled to purchase an individual policy at the same price that a healthy individual pays. With disability insurance, secure coverage before you leave your job so you have income to qualify for coverage. If you have life insurance through your employer, obtain new individual coverage as soon as you know you're going to leave your job. (See Chapter 16 for details.)

✔ **Establish a retirement savings plan.** After your business starts making a profit, consider establishing a retirement savings plan such as a SEP-IRA or Keogh. As I explain in Chapter 11, such plans allow you to shelter up to 20 percent of your business income from federal and state taxation.

Caring for Aging Parents

For many of us, there comes a time when we reverse roles with our parents and become the caregivers. As your parents age, they may need help with a variety of issues and living tasks. Although you probably won't have the time or ability to perform all these functions yourself, you may end up coordinating the service providers who will. Here are some things to consider when caring for aging parents:

✔ **Get help where possible.** In most communities, a variety of nonprofit organizations offer information and sometimes even counseling to families who are caring for elderly parents. You may be able to find your way to such resources through your state's department of insurance, as well as through recommendations from local hospitals and doctors. You'll especially want to get assistance and information if your parents need some sort of home care, nursing home care, or assisted living arrangement.

✔ **Get involved in their health care.** Your aging parents may already have a lot on their minds, or they simply may not be able to coordinate and manage all the health care providers that are giving them medications and advice. Try, as best as you can, to be their advocate. Speak with their doctors so you can understand their current medical condition, the need for various medications, and how to help coordinate caregivers. Visit home care providers and nursing homes, and speak with prospective care providers.

✔ **Understand tax breaks.** If you're financially supporting your parents, you may be eligible for a number of tax credits and deductions for elder care. Some employers' flexible benefit plans allow you to put away money on a pre-tax basis to pay for the care of your parents. Also explore the dependent care tax credit, which you can take on your federal income tax Form 1040. And if you provide half or more of the support costs for your parents, you may be able to claim them as dependents on your tax return.

✔ **Discuss getting the estate in order.** Parents don't like thinking about their demise, and they may feel awkward discussing this issue with their children. But opening a dialogue between you and your folks about such issues can be healthy in many ways. Not only does discussing wills, living wills, living trusts, and estate planning strategies (see Chapter 17) make you aware of your folks' situation, but it can also improve their plans to both their benefit and yours.

✔ **Take some time off.** Caring for an aging parent, particularly one who is having health problems, can be time-consuming and emotionally draining. Do your parents and yourself a favor by using some vacation time to help get things in order. Although this time off may not be the kind of vacation you were envisioning, it should help you reduce your stress and get more on top of things.

Divorcing

In most marriages that are destined to split up, there are usually early warning signs that both parties recognize. Sometimes, however, one spouse may surprise the other with an unexpected request for divorce. Whether the divorce is planned or unexpected, here are some key things to consider when getting a divorce:

✔ **Question the divorce.** Some say that divorcing in America is too easy, and I tend to agree. Although some couples are indeed better off parting ways, others give up too easily, thinking that the grass is greener elsewhere, only to later discover that all lawns have weeds and crabgrass. Just as with lawns that aren't watered and fertilized, relationships can wither without nurturing.

Money and disagreements over money are certainly contributing factors in marital unhappiness. Unfortunately, in many relationships, money is wielded as power by the spouse who earns more of it. Try talking things over, perhaps with a marital counselor. If you invest in making your relationship stronger, you'll reap the dividends for years to come.

✔ **Separate your emotions from the financial issues.** Feelings of revenge may be common in some divorces, but they'll probably only help ensure that the attorneys get rich as you and your spouse butt heads. If you really want a divorce, work at doing it efficiently and harmoniously so that you can get on with your lives and have more of your money to work with.

✔ **Detail resources and priorities.** Draw up a list of all the assets and liabilities that you and your spouse have. Make sure you list all the financial facts, including investment account records and statements. After you know the whole picture, begin to think about what is and is not important to you financially and otherwise.

✔ **Educate yourself about personal finance and legal issues.** Divorce sometimes forces nonfinancially oriented spouses to get a crash course in personal finance at a difficult emotional time. This book can help educate you financially. Visit a bookstore and pick up a good legal guide or two about divorce.

✔ **Choose advisors carefully.** Odds are that you'll retain the services of one or more specialists to assist you with the myriad issues, negotiations, and concerns of your divorce. Legal, tax, and financial advisors can help, but make sure you recognize their limitations and conflicts of interest. The more complicated things become and the more you haggle with your spouse, the more attorneys, unfortunately, benefit financially. Don't use your divorce attorney for financial or tax advice — your lawyer probably knows no more than you do in these areas. Also, realize that you don't need an attorney to get divorced. As for choosing tax and financial advisors, if you think you need that type of help, see Chapters 7 and 18 for advice on how to find good advisors.

✔ **Analyze your spending.** Although your household expenses will surely be less when you go back to being single, you'll probably have to make do with less income. Some divorcees find themselves financially squeezed in the early years following a divorce. Analyzing your spending needs pre-divorce can help you adjust to a new budget and negotiate a fairer settlement with your spouse.

✔ **Review needed changes to your insurance.** If you're covered under your spouse's employer's insurance plan, make sure you get this coverage replaced (see Chapter 16). If you or your children will still be financially dependent upon your spouse post-divorce, make sure that the divorce agreement mandates life insurance coverage. You should also revise your will (see Chapter 17).

✔ **Revamp your retirement plan.** With changes to your income, expenses, assets, liabilities, and future needs, your retirement plan will surely need a post-divorce overhaul. Refer to Chapter 4 for a reorientation.

Receiving a Windfall

Whether through inheritance, stock options, small-business success, or lottery winnings, you may receive a financial windfall at some point in your life. Like many people who are totally unprepared psychologically and organizationally for their sudden good fortune, you may find that a flood of money can create more problems than it solves. Here are a few tips to help you make the most of your financial windfall:

✔ **Educate yourself.** If you never had to deal with significant wealth, I don't expect you to know how to handle it. Don't pressure yourself to invest it as soon as possible. Leaving the money where it is or stashing it in one of the higher-yielding money market funds I recommend in Chapter 12 is far better than jumping into investments that you don't understand and haven't researched.

✔ **Beware of the sharks.** You may begin to wonder whether someone has posted your net worth, address, and home telephone number in the local newspaper and on the Internet. Brokers and financial advisors may flood you with marketing materials, telephone solicitations, and lunch date requests. These folks pursue you for a reason: They want to convert your money into their income either by selling you investments and other financial products or by managing your money. Stay away from the sharks, educate yourself, and take charge of your own financial moves. Decide on your own terms whom to hire, and then seek them out. Most of the best advisors that I know don't have the time or philosophical orientation to chase after prospective clients.

✔ **Recognize the emotional side of coming into a lot of money.** One of the side effects of accumulating wealth quickly is that you may have feelings of guilt or otherwise be unhappy, especially if you expected money to solve your problems. If you didn't invest in your relationship with your parents and after their passing, you regret how you interacted with them, getting a big inheritance from your folks may make you feel guilty. If you poured endless hours into a business venture that finally paid off, all that money in your investment accounts may leave you with a hollow feeling if you're divorced and you lost friends by neglecting your relationships.

✔ **Pay down debts.** People generally borrow money to buy things that they otherwise can't buy in one fell swoop. Paying off your debts is one of the simplest and best investments you can make when you come into wealth.

✔ **Diversify.** If you want to protect your wealth, don't keep it all in one pot. Mutual funds (see Chapter 10) are an ideally diversified, professionally managed investment vehicle to consider. And if you want your money to continue growing, consider the wealth-building investments — stocks, real estate, and small-business options — that I discuss in Part III of this book.

✔ **Make use of the opportunity.** Most people work for a paycheck their whole lives so they can pay a never-ending stream of monthly bills. Although I'm not advocating a hedonistic lifestyle, why not take some extra time to travel, spend time with your family, and enjoy the hobbies you've long been putting off? And how about trying a new career that you may find more fulfilling and that may make the world a better place?

Retiring

If you spent the bulk of your adult life working, retiring can be a challenging transition. Most Americans have an idealized vision of how wonderful retirement will be — no more irritating bosses and pressure of work deadlines; unlimited time to travel, play, and lead the good life. Sounds good, huh? Well, the reality for most Americans is far different, especially for those who don't plan ahead (financially and otherwise). Here are some tips to help you through retirement:

- ✔ **Plan both financially and personally.** Leaving behind a full-time career creates big challenges, such as what to do with all your free time. Planning your activities is even more important than planning financially. If the focus during your working years is solely on your career and saving money, you may lack interests, friends, and the ability to know how to spend money when you retire.

- ✔ **Take stock of your resources.** Many people worry and wonder whether they have sufficient assets for cutting back on work or retiring completely, yet they don't crunch any numbers to see where they stand. Ignorance may cause you to misunderstand how little or how much you really have for retirement when compared to what you need. See Chapter 4 for help with retirement planning.

- ✔ **Reevaluate your insurance needs.** When you have sufficient assets to retire, you don't need to retain insurance to protect your employment income any longer. On the other hand, as your assets grow over the years, you may be underinsured with regards to liability insurance (refer to Chapter 17).

- ✔ **Decide on health care/living options.** Medical expenses in your retirement years (particularly the cost of nursing home care) can be daunting. Which course of action you take — supplemental insurance, buying into a retirement community, or not doing anything — depends on your financial and personal situation. Early preparation increases your options; if you wait until you have major health problems, it may be too late to choose specific paths. (See Chapter 16 for more details on health care options.)

- ✔ **Decide what to do with your retirement plan money.** If you have money in a retirement savings plan, many employers offer the option of leaving the money in the plan rather than rolling it over into your own retirement account. Brokers and financial advisors clearly prefer that you do the latter because it means more money for them, but it could also give you many more (and perhaps better) investment choices to consider. Read Part III of this book to find out about investing and evaluating the quality of your employer's retirement plan investment options.

✔ **Pick a pension option.** Selecting a *pension option* (a plan that pays a monthly benefit during retirement) is similar to choosing a good investment — each pension option carries different risks, benefits, and tax consequences. Pensions are structured by actuaries, who base pension options on reasonable life expectancies. The younger you are when you start collecting your pension, the less you get per month. Check to see whether the amount of your monthly pension stops increasing past a certain starting age. You obviously don't want to delay access to your pension benefits past that age, because you won't receive a reward for waiting any longer and you'll collect the benefit for fewer months.

If you know that you have a health problem that shortens your life expectancy, you may benefit from drawing your pension sooner. If you plan to continue working in some capacity and earning a decent income after retiring, waiting for higher pension benefits when you're in a lower tax bracket is probably wise.

At one end of the spectrum, you have the risky single life option, which pays benefits until you pass away and then provides no benefits for your spouse thereafter. This option maximizes your monthly take while you're alive. Consider this option only if your spouse can do without this income. The least risky option, and thus least financially rewarding while the pensioner is still living, is the *100 percent joint and survivor option,* which pays your survivor the same amount that you received while still alive. The other joint and survivor options fall somewhere between these two extremes and generally make sense for most couples who desire decent pensions early in retirement but want a reasonable amount to continue should the pensioner die first.

✔ **Get your estate in order.** Confronting your mortality is never a joy, but when you're considering retirement or you're already retired, getting your estate in order makes all the more sense. Find out about wills and trusts that may benefit you and your heirs. You may also want to consider giving monetary gifts now if you have more than you need.

Chapter 22

Ten Tactics to Thwart Identity Theft and Fraud

In This Chapter

▶ Protecting your personal information

▶ Paying attention to activity in your accounts and credit history

*H*ucksters and thieves are often several steps ahead of law enforcement officials. Eventually, some of the bad guys get caught, but many don't, and those who do get nabbed often get back to their unsavory ways after penalties and some jail time. They may even be in your neighborhood or on your local Little League Board. (For an enlightening read, check out Dr. Martha Stout's book *The Sociopath Next Door* [Broadway Books].)

Years ago when I lived on the West Coast, I got a call from my bank informing me that they had just discovered "concerning activity" on the joint checking account I held with my wife. Specifically, what had happened was that a man with a bogus ID in my name had gone into five different Bank of America branches on the same day and withdrawn $80 from our checking account at each one. After some detective work on my part, I discovered that someone had pilfered our personal banking information at my wife's employer's payroll offices. Fortunately, the bank made good on the money that they'd allowed to be withdrawn by the Eric Tyson impostor.

I had been the victim of identity theft. In my situation, the crook had accessed one of my accounts; in other cases, the criminal activity may develop with someone opening an account (such as a credit card) using someone's stolen personal information. Victims of identity theft can suffer trashed credit reports, reduced ability to qualify for loans and even jobs (with employers who check credit reports), out-of-pocket costs and losses, and dozens of hours of time to clean up the mess and clear one's credit records and name.

Unfortunately, identity theft is hardly the only way to be taken to the cleaners by crooks. All sorts of scamsters hatch schemes to separate you from your money. Please follow the ten tips in this chapter to keep yourself from falling prey and unnecessarily losing money.

Save Phone Discussions for Friends Only

Never, ever give out personal information over the phone, especially when you aren't the one who initiated the call. Suppose you get a call and the person on the other end of the line claims to be with a company you conduct business with (such as your credit card company or bank). Ask for the caller's name and number and call back to be sure he or she is indeed with that company and has a legitimate business reason for contacting you.

With caller ID on your phone line, you may be able to see what number a call is originating from, but more often than not, calls from business-registered phone numbers come up as "unavailable." A major red flag: if you try calling back the number that comes through on caller ID and discover that the number is bogus (a nonworking number).

Never Respond to E-mails Soliciting Information

If you're an e-mail user, you may have seen or heard about official looking e-mails sent from companies you know of and may do business with asking you to promptly visit their Web site to correct some sort of billing or account problem. Hackers have become very clever and can generate a return/sender e-mail address that looks like it comes from a known institution but really does not. This unscrupulous practice is known as phishing, and if you bite at the bait, visit the site, and provide the requested personal information, your reward is likely to be some sort of future identity theft problem.

To find out more about how to protect yourself from phishing scams, visit the Anti-Phishing Working Group's Web site at www.antiphishing.org.

Review Your Monthly Financial Statements

Although financial institutions such as banks may call you if they notice unusual activity on one of your accounts, some people discover problematic account activity by simply reviewing their monthly credit card, checking-account, and other statements.

Do you need to balance bank account statements to the penny? No, you don't. I haven't for years (decades actually), and I don't have the time or patience for such minutiae. The key is to review the line items on your state-ment to be sure that all the transactions were yours.

Secure All Receipts

When you make a purchase, be sure to keep track of and secure receipts, especially those that contain your personal financial or account information. You could keep these in an envelope in your home and then cross check them against your monthly statement.

If you don't need to retain your receipts, be sure to dispose of them in a way that would prevent a thief from being able to decipher the information on them should someone get into your garbage. Rip up the receipts, or if you feel so inclined, buy a small paper shredder for your home and/or small business.

Close Unnecessary Credit Accounts

Open your wallet and remove all the pieces of plastic within it that enable you to charge purchases. The more credit cards and credit lines that you have, the more likely you are to have problems with identity theft and fraud and the more likely you are to overspend and carry debt balances. Also, reduce preapproved credit offers by contacting 888-5OPTOUT (888-567-8688) or visiting www.optoutprescreen.com.

Unless you maintain a card for small business transactions, you really "need" only one piece of plastic with a VISA or MasterCard logo. Give preference to a debit card if you've had a history with accumulating credit card debt balances.

Regularly Review Your Credit Reports

You may also be tipped off to shenanigans going on in your name when you review your credit report. Some identity theft victims have learned about credit accounts opened in their name from reviewing their credit reports.

Because you're entitled to a free credit report from each of the three major credit agencies every year, I recommend reviewing your reports at least that often. The reports generally contain the same information, so you could request and review one agency report every four months, which would enable you to keep a closer eye on your reports and still obtain them without cost.

I don't recommend spending the $100 or so annually for a so-called credit monitoring service that will update you when something happens on your credit reports. If you're concerned about someone illegally applying for credit in your name, know that another option for you (in some states) to stay on top of things is to "freeze" your personal credit reports and scores (see the next tip).

Freeze Your Credit Reports

To address the growing problem of identity theft, increasing numbers of states are passing credit freeze laws, which enable consumers to prevent access to their reports. At the time of this writing, the following states enable consumers, typically for a nominal fee, to freeze their credit information: CA, CO, CT, IL, KS, KY, LA, ME, NV, NJ, NC, SD, TX, UT, VT, WA, and WI. (In some of these states — IL, KS, SD, TX, VT, and WA — only identity theft victims may freeze their reports.)

The individual whose credit report is frozen is the only person who may grant access to the frozen credit report.

For an up-to-date listing of state freeze laws, visit the Web site www.pirg. org/consumer/credit/statelaws.htm.

Keep Personal Information off Your Checks

Don't place personal information on checks. Information that would be useful to identity thieves and that you should not put on your checks includes your credit card number, driver's license number, Social Security number, and so on. I also encourage you to leave your home address off of your preprinted checks when you order them. Otherwise, every Tom, Dick, and Jane whose hands your check passes through knows exactly where you live.

When writing a check to a merchant, question the need for adding personal information to the check (in fact, in numerous states, it's against the law to request and place credit card numbers on checks). Use a debit card instead for such transactions and remember that your debit card doesn't advertise your home address and other financial account data, so there's no need to publicize it to the world on your checks.

Protect Your Computer and Files

Especially if you keep personal and financial data on your computer, consider the following safeguards to protect your computer and the confidential information on it:

- Install a firewall.
- Use virus protection software.
- Password-protect access to your programs and files.

Protect Your Mail

Some identity thieves have collected personal information by simply helping themselves to mail in home mailboxes. Especially if your mail is delivered to a curbside box, stealing mail is pretty easy.

Consider using a locked mailbox or a post office box to protect your incoming mail from theft. Be careful with your outgoing mail as well, such as bills with checks attached. Minimize your outgoing mail and save yourself hassles by signing up for automatic bill payment for as many bills as you are able. Drop the rest of your outgoing mail in a secure U.S. postal box such as you find at the post office.

Glossary

· ·

adjustable-rate mortgage (ARM): A mortgage whose interest rate and monthly payments vary throughout its life. ARMs typically start with an artificially low interest rate that gradually rises over time. The interest rate is determined by a formula: margin (which is a fixed number) plus index (which varies). Generally speaking, if the overall level of interest rates drops, as measured by a variety of different indexes, the interest rate of your ARM generally follows suit. Similarly, if interest rates rise, so does your mortgage's interest rate and monthly payment. Caps limit the amount that the interest rate can fluctuate. Before you agree to an ARM, be certain that you can afford its highest possible payments.

adjusted cost basis: For capital gains tax purposes, the adjusted cost basis is how the IRS determines your profit or loss when you sell an asset such as a home or a security. For an investment such as a mutual fund or stock, your cost basis is what you originally invested plus any reinvested money. For a home, you arrive at the adjusted cost basis by adding the original purchase price to the cost of any capital improvements (expenditures that increase your property's value and life expectancy).

adjusted gross income (AGI): The sum of your taxable income (such as wages, salaries, and tips) and taxable interest less allowable adjustments (such as retirement account contributions and moving expenses). AGI is calculated before subtracting your personal exemptions and itemized deductions, which are used to derive your taxable income.

after-tax contributions: Some retirement plans allow you to contribute money that has already been taxed. Such contributions are known as after-tax contributions.

alternative minimum tax (AMT): The name given to a sort of shadow tax system that may cause you to pay a higher amount in federal income taxes than you otherwise would. The AMT was designed to prevent higher income earners from lowering their tax bills too much through large deductions.

American Stock Exchange (AMEX): The second largest stock exchange in the United States; it typically lists mid-sized firms and many of the new exchange-traded stock funds.

annual percentage rate (APR): The figure that states the total yearly cost of a loan as expressed by the actual rate of interest paid. The APR includes the base interest rate and any other add-on loan fees and costs. The APR is thus inevitably higher than the rate of interest that the lender quotes.

annuity: An investment that is a contract backed by an insurance company. An annuity is frequently purchased for retirement purposes. Its main benefit is that it allows your money to compound and grow without taxation until withdrawal. Selling annuities is a lucrative source of income for insurance agents and financial planners who work on commission, so don't buy an annuity until you're sure that it makes sense for your situation.

asset allocation: When you invest your money, you need to decide how to proportion it (allocate) between risky, growth-oriented investments (such as stocks), whose values fluctuate, and more stable, income-producing investments (like bonds). How soon you'll need the money and how tolerant you are of risk are two important determinants when deciding how to allocate your money.

audit: An IRS examination of your financial records, generally at the IRS offices, to substantiate your tax return. IRS audits are among life's worst experiences.

bank prime rate: See *prime rate.*

bankruptcy: Legal action that puts a halt to creditors' attempts to collect unpaid debts from you. If you have a high proportion of consumer debt to annual income (25 percent or greater), filing for bankruptcy may be your best option.

bear market: A period (such as the early 2000s) when the stock market experiences a strong downward swing. It is often accompanied by (and sometimes precedes) an economic recession. Imagine a bear in hibernation, because this is what happens in a bear market: Investors hibernate and the market falters. During a bear market, the value of stocks can decrease significantly. The market usually has to drop at least 20 percent before it is considered a bear market.

beneficiaries: The people to whom you want to leave your assets (or in the case of life insurance or a pension plan, benefits) in the event of your death. You denote beneficiaries for each of your retirement accounts.

blue chip stock: The stock of the largest and most consistently profitable corporations. This term comes from poker, where the most valuable chips are blue. The list of these stocks is unofficial and changes.

bond: A loan investors make to a corporation or government. Bonds generally pay a set amount of interest on a regular basis. They're an appropriate investment vehicle for conservative investors who don't feel comfortable with the risk involved in investing in stocks and who want to receive a steady income. All bonds have a maturity date when the bond issuer must pay back the bond at *par* (full) value to the bondholders (lenders). Bonds should not be your primary long-term investment vehicle, because they produce little real growth on your original investment after inflation is factored in.

bond rating: See *Standard & Poor's ratings* and *Moody's ratings.*

bond yield: A yield is quoted as an annual percentage rate of return that a bond will produce based on its current value if it makes its promised interest payments. How much a bond will yield to an investor depends on three important factors: the stated interest rate paid by the bond, changes in the creditworthiness of the bond's issuer, and the maturity date of the bond. The better the rating a bond receives, the less risk involved and, thus, the lower the yield. As far as the maturity date is concerned, the longer you loan your money, the higher the risk (because it is more likely that rates will fluctuate) and the higher your yield generally will be.

broker: A person who acts as an intermediary for the purchase or sale of investments. When you buy a house, insurance, or stock, you most likely do so through a broker. Most brokers are paid on commission, which creates a conflict of interest with their clients: The more the broker sells, the more he or she makes. Some insurance companies let you buy their policies directly, and many mutual fund families bypass stockbrokers. If you're going to work with a broker, a discount broker can help you save on commissions.

bull market: A period (such as most of the 1990s in the United States) when the stock market moves higher, usually accompanied and driven by a growing economy and increasing corporate profits.

callable bond: A bond for which the lender can decide to pay the holder earlier than the previously agreed-upon maturity date. If interest rates are relatively high when a bond is issued, lenders may prefer to issue callable bonds because they have the flexibility to call back these bonds and issue new, lower-interest rate bonds if interest rates decline. Callable bonds are risky for investors, because if interest rates decrease, the bond holder will get his investment money returned early and may have to reinvest his money at a lower interest rate.

capital gain: The profit from selling your stock at a higher price than the price for which it was purchased. For example, if you buy 50 shares of Rocky and Bullwinkle stock at $20 per share and two years later you sell your shares when the price rises to $25 per share, your profit or capital gain is $5 per share, or $250. If you hold this stock outside of a tax-sheltered retirement account, you'll owe federal tax on this profit when you sell the stock. Many states also levy such a tax.

capital gains distribution: Taxable distribution by a mutual fund or real estate investment trust (REIT) created by securities that are sold within the fund or REIT at a profit. These distributions may be either short-term (assets held a year or less) or long-term (assets held for more than one year).

cash value insurance: A type of life insurance that is extremely popular with insurance salespeople because it commands a high commission. In a cash value policy, you buy life insurance coverage but also get a savings-type account. Unless you're looking for ways to limit your taxable estate (if you're extremely wealthy, for example), avoid cash value insurance. The investment returns tend to be mediocre, and your contributions are not tax-deductible.

certificate of deposit (CD): A specific-term loan that you make to your banker. The maturity date for CDs ranges from a month up to several years. The interest paid on CDs is fully taxable, thus making CDs inappropriate for higher tax-bracket investors investing outside tax-sheltered retirement accounts.

closed-end mutual fund: A mutual fund that decides upfront exactly how many shares it is going to issue to investors. After all the shares are sold, an investor seeking to invest in the closed-end fund can only do so by purchasing shares from an existing investor. Shares of closed-end funds trade on the major stock exchanges and therefore sell at either a discount if the sellers exceed the buyers or at a premium if demand exceeds supply.

COBRA (Consolidated Omnibus Budget Reconciliation Act): Name of the federal legislation that requires health insurers and larger employers to continue to offer health insurance, at the employee's expense, for 18 months after coverage would otherwise end — for example, when an employee is laid off.

commercial paper: A short-term debt or IOU issued by larger, stable companies to help make their businesses grow and prosper. Credit-worthy companies can sell this debt security directly to large investors and thus bypass borrowing money from bankers. Money market funds invest in soon-to-mature commercial paper.

commission: The percentage of the selling price of a house, stock, bond, or other investment that's paid to agents and brokers. Because most agents and brokers are paid by commission, understanding how the commission can influence their behavior and recommendations is important for investors and home buyers. Agents and brokers make money only when you make a purchase, and they make more money when you make a bigger purchase. Choose an agent carefully, and take your agent's advice with a grain of salt, because this conflict of interest can often set an agent's visions and goals at odds with your own.

commodity: Raw materials (gold, wheat, sugar, and gasoline, for example) traded on the futures market.

common stock: Shares in a company that don't offer a guaranteed amount of dividend to investors; the amount of dividend distributions, if any, is at the discretion of company management. Although common-stock investors may or may not make money through dividends, they hope that the stock price will appreciate as the company expands its operations and increases its profits. Common stock tends to offer you a better return (profit) than other investments, such as bonds or preferred stock. However, if the company falters, you may lose some or all of your original investment.

comparable market analysis (CMA): A written analysis of similar houses currently being offered for sale and those that have recently sold. CMAs are usually completed by real estate agents.

consumer debt: Debt on consumer items that depreciate in value over time. Credit card balances and auto loans are examples of consumer debt. This type of debt is bad for your financial health because it's high-interest and it encourages you to live beyond your means.

Consumer Price Index (CPI): The Consumer Price Index reports price changes, on a monthly basis, in the cost of living for such items as food, housing, transportation, health care, entertainment, clothing, and other miscellaneous expenses. The CPI is used to adjust government benefits, such as Social Security, and is used by many employers to determine cost-of-living increases in wages and pensions. An increase in prices is also known as inflation.

co-payment: The percentage of your medical bill that your health plan requires you to pay out of your own pocket after you satisfy your annual deductible. A typical co-payment is 20 percent.

credit report: A report that details your credit history. It's the main report that a lender uses to determine whether to give you a loan. You may now obtain a free copy of your credit reports annually.

debit card: Although they may look like credit cards, debit cards are different in one important way: When you use a debit card, the cost of the purchase is deducted from your checking account. Thus, a debit card gives you the convenience of a credit card without the danger of building up a mountain of consumer debt.

deductible: You may be thinking that this is a new product from the Keebler elves. Unfortunately, a deductible is actually much more mundane. With insurance, the deductible is the amount you pay when you file a claim. For example, say that your car sustains $800 of damage. If your deductible is $500, the insurance covers $300 and you pay $500 out of your own pocket for the repairs. The higher the deductible, the lower your insurance premiums and the less paperwork you expose yourself to when filing claims (because small losses that are less than the deductible don't require filing a claim). Take the highest deductibles that you can afford when selecting insurance.

deduction: An expense you may subtract from your income to lower your taxable income. Examples include mortgage interest, property taxes (itemized deductions), and most retirement account contributions.

derivative: An investment instrument whose value is derived from other securities. For example, an option to buy IBM stock does not have value in itself; the value is derived from the price of IBM's stock.

disability insurance: Disability insurance replaces a portion of your employment income in the unlikely event that you suffer a disability that keeps you from working.

discount broker: Unlike a full-service broker, a discount broker generally offers no investment advice and has employees who work on salary rather than on commission. In addition to trading individual securities, most discount brokerage firms also offer no-load (commission-free) mutual funds.

diversification: If you put all your money into one type of investment, you're potentially setting yourself up for a big shock. If that investment collapses, so does your investment world. By spreading (diversifying) your money among different investments — bonds, U.S. stocks, international stocks, real estate, and so on — you ensure yourself a better chance of investing success and fewer sleepless nights.

dividend: The dividend is the income paid to investors holding an investment. With stock, the dividend is a portion of a company's profits paid to its shareholders. For example, if a company has an annual dividend of $2 per share and you own 100 shares, your total dividend is $200. Usually, established and slower-growing companies pay dividends, while smaller and faster growing companies reinvest their profits for growth. For assets held outside retirement accounts, dividends (except from tax-free money market and tax-free bond funds) are taxable.

Dow Jones Industrial Average (DJIA): A widely followed stock market index comprised of 30 large, actively traded U.S. company stocks. Senior editors at the *Wall Street Journal* select the stocks in the DJIA.

down payment: The part of the purchase price for a house that the buyer pays in cash upfront and does not finance with a mortgage. Generally, the larger the down payment, the better the deal you can get on a mortgage. You can usually get access to the best mortgage programs with a down payment of at least 20 percent of the home's purchase price.

earthquake insurance: Although the West Coast is often associated with earthquakes, other areas are also quake prone. An earthquake insurance rider (which usually comes with a deductible of 5 to 10 percent of the cost to rebuild the home) on a homeowner's policy pays to repair or rebuild your home if it is damaged in an earthquake. If you live in an area with earthquake risk, get earthquake insurance coverage!

Emerging Markets Index: The Emerging Markets Index, which is published by Morgan Stanley, tracks stock markets in developing countries. The main reason for investing in emerging markets is that these economies typically experience a higher rate of economic growth than developed markets. However, the potential for higher returns is coupled with greater risk.

equity: In the real estate world, this term refers to the difference between the market value of your home and what you owe on it. For example, if your home is worth $250,000, and you have an outstanding mortgage of $190,000, your equity is $60,000. Equity is also a synonym for stock.

estate: The value, at the time of your death, of your assets minus your loans and liabilities.

estate planning: The process of deciding where and how your assets will be transferred when you die and structuring your assets during your lifetime so as to minimize likely estate taxes.

Federal National Mortgage Association (FNMA): The FNMA (or Fannie Mae) is one of the best-known institutions in the secondary mortgage market. Fannie Mae buys mortgages from banks and other mortgage-lending institutions and, in turn, sells them to investors. These loan investments are considered safe because Fannie Mae buys mortgages only from companies that conform to its stringent mortgage regulations, and Fannie Mae guarantees the repayment of principal and interest on the loans that it sells.

financial assets: A property or investment (such as real estate or a stock, mutual fund, or bond) that has value that can be realized if sold.

financial liabilities: Your outstanding loans and debts. To determine your net worth, subtract your financial liabilities from your financial assets.

financial planners (or advisors): A motley crew that professes an ability to direct your financial future. Financial planners come with varying backgrounds and degrees: MBAs, Certified Financial Planners, and Certified Public Accountants, to name a few. A useful way to distinguish among this mixed bag of nuts is to determine whether the planners are commission-, fee-, or hourly-based.

fixed-rate mortgage: The granddaddy of all mortgages. You lock into an interest rate (for example, 7 percent), and it never changes during the life (term) of your 15- or 30-year mortgage. Your mortgage payment will be the same amount each and every month. If you become a cursing, frothing maniac when you miss your morning coffee or someone is five minutes late, then this mortgage may be for you!

flood insurance: If there's even a remote chance that your area may flood, having flood insurance, which reimburses rebuilding your home and replacing its contents in the event of a flood, is prudent.

401(k) plan: A type of retirement savings plan offered by many for-profit companies to their employees. Your contributions compound without taxation over time and are usually exempt (yes!) from federal and state income taxes until withdrawal.

403(b) plan: Similar to a 401(k) plan but for employees of nonprofit organizations.

full-service broker: A broker who gives advice and charges a high commission relative to discount brokers. Because the brokers work on commission, they have a significant conflict of interest: namely, to advocate strategies that will benefit them financially.

futures: An obligation to buy or sell a commodity or security on a specific day for a preset price. When used by most individual investors, futures represent a short-term gamble on the short-term direction of the price of a commodity. Companies and farmers use futures contracts to hedge their risks of changing prices.

guaranteed-investment contracts (GICs): Insurance company investments that appeal to skittish investors. GICs generally tell you one year in advance what your interest rate will be for the coming year. Thus, you don't have to worry about fluctuations and losses in your investment value. On the other hand, GICs offer you little upside, because the interest rate is comparable to what you may get on a short-term bank certificate of deposit.

home equity: See *equity.*

home-equity loan: Technical jargon for what used to be called a second mortgage. With this type of loan, you borrow against the equity in your house. If used wisely, a home-equity loan can help pay off high-interest consumer debt or be tapped for other short-term needs (such as a remodeling project). In contrast with consumer debt, mortgage debt usually has a lower interest rate and is tax-deductible.

homeowner's insurance: Dwelling coverage that covers the cost of rebuilding your house in the event of fire or other calamity. The liability insurance portion of this policy protects you against lawsuits associated with your property. Another essential element of homeowner's insurance is the personal property coverage, which pays to replace your damaged or stolen worldly possessions.

index: (1) A security market index, such as the Standard & Poor's 500 Index, is a statistical composite that measures the performance of a particular type of security. Indexes exist for various stock and bond markets and are typically set at a round number such as 100 at a particular point in time. See also *Dow Jones Industrial Average* and *Russell 2000.* (2) The index can also refer to the measure of the overall level of interest rates that a lender uses as a reference to calculate the specific interest rate on an adjustable-rate loan. The index plus the margin is the formula for determining the interest rate on an adjustable-rate mortgage.

individual retirement account (IRA): A retirement account into which anyone with sufficient employment income or alimony may contribute up to $4,000 per year ($5,000 if age 50 or older). Based on your eligibility for other employer-based retirement programs and which type of IRA you select (regular or Roth), your contributions may be tax-deductible.

inflation: The technical term for a rise in prices. Inflation usually occurs when too much money is in circulation and not enough goods and services are available to spend it on. As a result of this excess demand, prices rise. A link is present between inflation and interest rates: If interest rates do not keep up with inflation, no one will invest in bonds issued by the government or corporations. When the interest rates on bonds are high, it usually reflects a high rate of inflation that will eat away at your return.

initial public offering (IPO): The first time a company offers stock to the investing public. An IPO typically occurs when a company wants to expand more rapidly and seeks additional money to support its growth. A number of studies have demonstrated that buying into IPOs in which the general public can participate produces subpar investment returns. A high level of IPO activity may indicate a cresting stock market, as companies and their investment bankers rush to cash in on a "pricey" marketplace. (IPO could stand for *It's Probably Overpriced.*)

interest rate: The rate lenders charge you to use their money. The higher the interest rate, the higher the risk entailed in the loan. With bonds of a given maturity, a higher rate of interest means a lower quality of bond — one that's less likely to return your money.

international stock markets: Stock markets outside of the United States account for a significant portion of the world stock market capitalization (value). Some specific stock indices track international markets (see ***Morgan Stanley EAFE index*** and ***Emerging Markets Index***). International investing offers one way for you to diversify your portfolio and reduce your risk. Some of the foreign countries with major stock exchanges outside the United States include Japan, Britain, France, Germany, and Canada.

junk bond: A bond rated Ba (Moody's) or BB (Standard & Poor) and lower. Historically, these bonds have had a 1 to 2 percent chance of default, which is not exactly "junky." Of course, the higher risk is accompanied by a higher interest rate.

Keogh plan: A tax-deductible retirement savings plan available to self-employed individuals. Certain Keoghs allow you to put up to 25 percent of your self-employment income into the account.

leverage: Financial leverage affords its users a disproportionate amount of financial power relative to the amount of their own cash invested. In some circumstances, you can borrow up to 50 percent of a stock price and use all funds (both yours and those that you borrow) to make a purchase. You repay this so-called margin loan when you sell the stock. If the stock price rises, you make money on what you invested plus what you borrowed. Although this money sounds attractive, remember that leverage cuts both ways — when prices decline, you lose money not only on your investment but also on the money you borrowed.

limited partnership (LP): These partnerships, which are often promoted in a way that promises high returns, generally limit one thing: your investment return. Why? Because they're burdened with high commissions and management fees. Another problem is that they're typically not liquid for many years.

load mutual fund: A mutual fund that includes a sales load, which is the commission paid to brokers who sell commission-based mutual funds. The commission typically ranges from 4 to 8.5 percent. This commission is deducted from your investment money, so it reduces your returns.

marginal tax rate: The rate of income tax you pay on the last dollars you earn over the course of a year. Why the complicated distinction? Because not all income is treated equally: You pay less tax on your first dollars of your annual earnings and more tax on the last dollars of your annual income. Knowing your marginal tax rate is helpful because it can help you analyze the tax implications of important personal financial decisions.

market capitalization: The value of all the outstanding stock of a company. Market capitalization is the quoted price per share of a stock multiplied by the number of shares outstanding. Thus, if Rocky and Bullwinkle Corporation has 100 million shares of outstanding stock and the quoted price per share is $20, the company has a market capitalization of $2 billion (100 million × $20).

Moody's ratings: Moody's rating service measures and rates the credit (default) risks of various bonds. Moody's investigates the financial condition of a bond issuer. Its ratings use the following grading system, which is expressed from highest to lowest: Aaa, Aa, A, Baa, Ba, B, Caa, Ca, C. Higher ratings imply a lower risk but also mean that the interest rate will be lower.

Morgan Stanley EAFE (Europe, Australia, Far East) index: The Morgan Stanley EAFE index tracks the performance of the more established countries' stock markets in Europe and Asia. This index is important for international-minded investors who want to follow the performance of overseas stock investments.

mortgage-backed bond (GNMAs and FNMAs): The Government National Mortgage Association (GNMA, or Ginnie Mae) specializes in mortgage-backed securities. It passes the interest and principal payment of borrowers to investors. When a homeowner makes a mortgage payment, GNMA deducts a small service charge and forwards the mortgage payments to its investors. The payments are guaranteed in case a borrower fails to pay his or her mortgage. The Federal National Mortgage Association (FNMA or Fannie Mae) is a publicly owned, government-sponsored corporation that purchases mortgages from lenders and resells them to investors. FNMA mainly deals with mortgages backed by the Federal Housing Administration.

mortgage broker: Mortgage brokers buy mortgages wholesale from lenders and then mark the mortgages up (typically from 0.5 to 1 percent) and sell them to borrowers. A good mortgage broker is most helpful for people who don't want to shop around on their own for a mortgage or people who have blemishes on their credit reports.

mortgage life insurance: Mortgage life insurance guarantees that the lender will receive its money in the event that you meet an untimely demise. Many people may try to convince you that you need this insurance to protect your dependents and loved ones. Mortgage life insurance is relatively expensive given the cost of the coverage provided. If you need life insurance, buy low-cost, high-quality term life insurance instead.

municipal bond: A loan for public projects, such as highways, parks, or cultural centers, that an investor makes to cities, towns, and states. The tax-exempt status of their interest is what makes municipal bonds special:

They're exempt from federal taxes and, if you reside in the state where the bond is issued, state taxes. Municipal bonds are most appropriate for people in high tax brackets who invest money outside of tax-sheltered retirement accounts.

mutual fund: A portfolio of stocks, bonds, or other securities that is owned by numerous investors and managed by an investment company. See also ***no-load mutual fund.***

National Association of Securities Dealers Automated Quotation (NASDAQ) system: An electronic network that allows brokers to trade from their offices all over the country. With NASDAQ, brokers buy and sell shares using constantly updated prices that appear on their computer screens.

negative amortization: Negative amortization occurs when your outstanding mortgage balance increases despite the fact that you're making the required monthly payments. Negative amortization occurs with adjustable-rate mortgages that cap the increase in your monthly payment but do not cap the interest rate. Therefore, your monthly payments don't cover all the interest that you actually owe. Avoid loans with this "feature."

net asset value (NAV): The dollar value of one share of a mutual fund. For a no-load fund, the market price is its NAV. For a load fund, the NAV is the "buy" price minus the commission.

New York Stock Exchange (NYSE): The largest stock exchange in the world in terms of total volume and value of shares traded. It lists companies that tend to be among the oldest, largest, and best-known companies.

no-load mutual fund: A mutual fund that doesn't come with a commission payment attached to it. Some funds claim to be no-load but simply hide their sales commissions as an ongoing sales charge; you can avoid these funds by educating yourself and reading the prospectuses carefully.

open-end mutual fund: A mutual fund that issues as many shares as investors demand. These open-end funds do not generally limit the number of investors or amount of money in the fund. Some open-end funds have been known to close to new investors, but investors with existing shares can often still buy more shares from the company.

option: The right to buy or sell a specific security (such as a stock) for a preset price during a specified period of time. Options differ from futures in that with an option, you pay a premium fee upfront and you can either exercise the option or let it expire. If the option expires worthless, you lose 100 percent of your original investment. The use of options is best left to companies as hedging tools. Investment managers may use options to reduce the risk in their investment portfolio. As with futures, when most individual investors buy an option, they're doing so as a short-term gamble, not as an investment. For example: You have an option to buy 100 shares of Rocky and Bullwinkle Co. stock at $20 per share in the next six months. You pay $3 per share upfront as the premium. During this time period, R&B's share price rises to $30, and you exercise your right to buy at $20. You then sell your shares at the market price of $30; you make a $10 profit per share, which is a return more than three times larger than your original investment.

pension: Pensions (also known as defined benefit plans) are a benefit offered by some employers. These plans generally pay you a monthly retirement income based on your years of service and former pay with the employer.

performance: You traditionally judge an investment's performance by looking at the historic rate of return. The longer the period over which these numbers are tallied, the more useful they are. Considered alone, these numbers are practically meaningless. You must also note how well a fund has performed in comparison to competitors with the same investment objectives. Beware of advertisements that tout the high returns of a mutual fund, because they may not be looking at risk-adjusted performance, or they may be promoting performance over a short time period. Keep in mind that high return statistics are usually coupled with high risk and that this year's star may turn out to be next year's crashing meteor.

pre-certification: A condition for health insurance benefit coverage that requires a patient to get approval before being admitted to a hospital for nonemergency care.

preferred stock: Preferred stock dividends must be paid before any dividends are paid to the common stock shareholders. Although preferred stock reduces your risk as an investor (because of the more secure dividend and greater likelihood of getting your money back if the company fails), it also often limits your reward if the company expands and increases its profits.

price/earnings (P/E) ratio: The current price of a stock divided by the current (or sometimes the projected) earnings per share of the issuing company. This ratio is a widely used stock analysis statistic that helps an investor get an idea of how cheap or expensive a stock price is. In general, a relatively high P/E ratio indicates that investors feel that the company's earnings are likely to grow quickly.

prime rate: The rate of interest that major banks charge their most creditworthy corporate customers. Why should you care? Well, because the interest rates on various loans you may be interested in are often based on the prime rate. And, guess what — you pay a higher interest rate than those big corporations!

principal: No, I'm not talking about the big boss from elementary school who struck fear into the hearts of most 8-year-olds. The principal is the amount you borrow for a loan. If you borrow $100,000, your principal is $100,000. Principal can also refer to the amount you originally placed in an investment.

prospectus: Individual companies and mutual funds are required by the Securities and Exchange Commission to issue a prospectus. For a company, the prospectus is a legal document presenting a detailed analysis of that company's financial history, its products and services, its management's background and experience, and the risks of investing in the company. A mutual fund prospectus tells you about the fund's investment objectives, costs, risk, and performance history.

real estate investment trust (REIT): Real estate investment trusts are like a mutual fund of real estate investments. Such trusts invest in a collection of properties (from shopping centers to apartment buildings). REITs trade on the major stock exchanges. If you want to invest in real estate while avoiding the hassles inherent in owning property, real estate investment trusts may be right for you.

refinance: Refinance, or refi, is a fancy word for taking out a new mortgage loan (usually at a lower interest rate) to pay off an existing mortgage (generally at a higher interest rate). Refinancing is not automatic, nor is it guaranteed. Refinancing can also be a hassle and expensive. Weigh the costs and benefits of refinancing carefully before proceeding.

return on investment: The percentage of profit you make on an investment. If you put $1,000 into an investment and then one year later it's worth $1,100, you make a profit of $100. Your return on investment is the profit ($100) divided by the initial investment ($1,000) — in this case, 10 percent.

reverse mortgage: A reverse mortgage enables elderly homeowners, typically those who are low on cash, to tap into their home's equity without selling their home or moving from it. Specifically, a lending institution makes a check out to you each month, and you can use the check as you want. This money is really a loan against the value of your home, so it's tax-free when you receive it. The downside of these loans is that they deplete your equity in your estate, the fees and interest rates tend to be on the high side, and some require repayment within a certain number of years.

Russell 2000: An index that tracks the returns of 2,000 small-company U.S. stocks. Small-company stocks tend to be more volatile than large-company stocks. If you invest in small-company stocks or stock funds, this is an appropriate benchmark to compare your performance to.

Securities and Exchange Commission (SEC): The federal agency that administers U.S. securities laws and regulates and monitors investment companies, brokers, and financial advisors.

simplified employee pension individual retirement account (SEP-IRA): Like other retirement plans, a SEP-IRA allows your money to compound over the years without the parasitic effect of taxes. SEP-IRAs are relatively easy to set up, and they allow self-employed people to make annual contributions on a pre-tax basis.

Social Security: If you're retired or disabled, Social Security is a government safety net that can provide you with some income. The program is based on the idea that government is responsible for the social welfare of its citizens. Whether you agree with this notion or not, part of your paycheck goes to Social Security, and when you retire, you receive money from the program.

Standard & Poor's 500 Index: An index that measures the performance of 500 large-company U.S. stocks that account for about 80 percent of the total market value of all stocks traded in the United States. If you invest in larger-company stocks or stock funds, the S&P 500 Index is an appropriate benchmark to compare the performance of your investments to.

Standard & Poor's (S&P) ratings: Standard & Poor's rating service is one of two services that measure and rate the risks in buying a bond. The S&P ratings use the following grading system, listed from highest to lowest: AAA, AA, A, BBB, BB, B, CCC, CC, C. See also *Moody's ratings.*

stock: Shares of ownership in a company. When a company goes public, it issues shares of stock to the public (see also *initial public offering*). Many, but not all, stocks pay dividends — a distribution of a portion of company profits. In addition to dividends, you make money investing in stock via appreciation in the price of the stock, which normally results from growth in revenues and corporate profits. You can invest in stock by purchasing individual shares or by investing in a stock mutual fund that offers a diversified package of stocks.

term life insurance: If people are dependent on your income for their living expenses, you may need this insurance. Term life insurance functions simply: You determine how much protection you would like and then pay an annual premium based on that amount. Although much less touted by insurance salespeople than cash value insurance, it's the best life insurance out there for the vast majority of people.

Treasury bill: IOUs from the federal government that mature within a year. The other types of loans that investors can make to the federal government are Treasury notes, which mature within one to ten years, and Treasury bonds, which mature in more than ten years. The interest that these federal government bonds pay is free of state taxes, but it's federally taxable.

underwriting: The process an insurance company uses to evaluate a person's likelihood of filing a claim on a particular type of insurance policy. If significant problems are discovered, an insurer will often propose much higher rates or refuse to sell the insurance coverage.

will: A legal document that ensures that your wishes regarding your assets and the care of your minor children are heeded when you die.

zero-coupon bond: A bond that doesn't pay explicit interest during the term of the loan. Zero-coupon bonds are purchased at a discounted price relative to the principal value paid at maturity. Thus, the interest is implicit in the discount. These bonds do not offer a tax break, because the investor must pay taxes on the interest he would have received.

Index

• I •

• U •

umbrella (excess liability) insurance, 358
underwriting, 440
U.S. Securities and Exchange Commission (SEC), 375, 379, 391, 438
U.S. Treasuries
  bond funds, 247–248
  described, 439
  as indexes for ARMs, 280
  inside retirement accounts, 225
  as lending investments, 154–155
  money market funds, 244
USAA
  bond funds, 249
  disability insurance, 338
  homeowner's/renter's insurance, 354
  life insurance, 333, 334
  money market funds, 244–245
  Web site, 354

• V •

vacations, 34, 117, 194, 414
Value Line research reports, 189
value stocks, 205
Vanguard funds
  aggressive retirement accounts, 232, 233
  annuities, 251
  bond funds, 247, 249
  checking accounts, 86
  for conservative retirement accounts, 231
  discount brokers, 233
  fund of funds, 207
  index funds, 208
  money market funds, 244–245
  retirement planning tools, 390
  stock mutual funds, 250
  Web site, 390, 391
vesting schedules, 222
Veverka, Mark (journalist), 15

• W •

warranties, extended, 311
wealth, 55–59, 415–416

Wealth Without Risk (Givens), 16, 17
Web sites
  annuities, 251
  auto insurance, 358
  biased financial advice on, 388
  bond funds, 247
  brokers, 391–392
  car buying guides, 111
  Consumer Reports, 111
  credit bureaus, 282
  discount brokers, 233
  energy information and tips, 114
  financial planners associations, 378
  Internet, defined, 385
  investment firm "checking accounts," 86
  IRS, 127, 136, 144
  Medicare, 347
  money market funds, 244–245
  mortgage information, 286
  periodicals, 392
  "sponsored" content, 387
  tax preparation help, 145
  telephone service shopping, 118
  tips for using, 386–388, 398
  trading online, 391–392
Weston, Liz (*Your Credit Score*), 30
wholesale superstores, 107–108
wills, 359–360, 393, 409, 440
Wilshire 5000 Index, 212
windfalls, receiving, 415–416
worker's compensation, 336
wrap or managed accounts, 175, 187

• Y •

Your Credit Score (Weston), 30
Your Federal Income Tax (IRS Publication 17), 144

• Z •

zero-coupon bond, 440
zoning, real estate value, 191

BUSINESS, CAREERS & PERSONAL FINANCE

0-7645-5307-0

0-7645-5331-3 *†

Also available:

- Accounting For Dummies †
  0-7645-5314-3
- Business Plans Kit For Dummies †
  0-7645-5365-8
- Cover Letters For Dummies
  0-7645-5224-4
- Frugal Living For Dummies
  0-7645-5403-4
- Leadership For Dummies
  0-7645-5176-0
- Managing For Dummies
  0-7645-1771-6

- Marketing For Dummies
  0-7645-5600-2
- Personal Finance For Dummies *
  0-7645-2590-5
- Project Management For Dummies
  0-7645-5283-X
- Resumes For Dummies †
  0-7645-5471-9
- Selling For Dummies
  0-7645-5363-1
- Small Business Kit For Dummies *†
  0-7645-5093-4

HOME & BUSINESS COMPUTER BASICS

0-7645-4074-2

0-7645-3758-X

Also available:

- ACT! 6 For Dummies
  0-7645-2645-6
- iLife '04 All-in-One Desk Reference
  For Dummies
  0-7645-7347-0
- iPAQ For Dummies
  0-7645-6769-1
- Mac OS X Panther Timesaving
  Techniques For Dummies
  0-7645-5812-9
- Macs For Dummies
  0-7645-5656-8

- Microsoft Money 2004 For Dummies
  0-7645-4195-1
- Office 2003 All-in-One Desk Reference
  For Dummies
  0-7645-3883-7
- Outlook 2003 For Dummies
  0-7645-3759-8
- PCs For Dummies
  0-7645-4074-2
- TiVo For Dummies
  0-7645-6923-6
- Upgrading and Fixing PCs For Dummies
  0-7645-1665-5
- Windows XP Timesaving Techniques
  For Dummies
  0-7645-3748-2

FOOD, HOME, GARDEN, HOBBIES, MUSIC & PETS

0-7645-5295-3

0-7645-5232-5

Also available:

- Bass Guitar For Dummies
  0-7645-2487-9
- Diabetes Cookbook For Dummies
  0-7645-5230-9
- Gardening For Dummies *
  0-7645-5130-2
- Guitar For Dummies
  0-7645-5106-X
- Holiday Decorating For Dummies
  0-7645-2570-0
- Home Improvement All-in-One
  For Dummies
  0-7645-5680-0

- Knitting For Dummies
  0-7645-5395-X
- Piano For Dummies
  0-7645-5105-1
- Puppies For Dummies
  0-7645-5255-4
- Scrapbooking For Dummies
  0-7645-7208-3
- Senior Dogs For Dummies
  0-7645-5818-8
- Singing For Dummies
  0-7645-2475-5
- 30-Minute Meals For Dummies
  0-7645-2589-1

INTERNET & DIGITAL MEDIA

0-7645-1664-7

0-7645-6924-4

Also available:

- 2005 Online Shopping Directory
  For Dummies
  0-7645-7495-7
- CD & DVD Recording For Dummies
  0-7645-5956-7
- eBay For Dummies
  0-7645-5654-1
- Fighting Spam For Dummies
  0-7645-5965-6
- Genealogy Online For Dummies
  0-7645-5964-8
- Google For Dummies
  0-7645-4420-9

- Home Recording For Musicians
  For Dummies
  0-7645-1634-5
- The Internet For Dummies
  0-7645-4173-0
- iPod & iTunes For Dummies
  0-7645-7772-7
- Preventing Identity Theft For Dummies
  0-7645-7336-5
- Pro Tools All-in-One Desk Reference
  For Dummies
  0-7645-5714-9
- Roxio Easy Media Creator For Dummies
  0-7645-7131-1

* Separate Canadian edition also available
† Separate U.K. edition also available

Available wherever books are sold. For more information or to order direct: U.S. customers visit www.dummies.com or call 1-877-762-2974.
U.K. customers visit www.wileyeurope.com or call 0800 243407. Canadian customers visit www.wiley.ca or call 1-800-567-4797.

SPORTS, FITNESS, PARENTING, RELIGION & SPIRITUALITY

0-7645-5146-9

0-7645-5418-2

Also available:
- Adoption For Dummies
  0-7645-5488-3
- Basketball For Dummies
  0-7645-5248-1
- The Bible For Dummies
  0-7645-5296-1
- Buddhism For Dummies
  0-7645-5359-3
- Catholicism For Dummies
  0-7645-5391-7
- Hockey For Dummies
  0-7645-5228-7

- Judaism For Dummies
  0-7645-5299-6
- Martial Arts For Dummies
  0-7645-5358-5
- Pilates For Dummies
  0-7645-5397-6
- Religion For Dummies
  0-7645-5264-3
- Teaching Kids to Read For Dummies
  0-7645-4043-2
- Weight Training For Dummies
  0-7645-5168-X
- Yoga For Dummies
  0-7645-5117-5

TRAVEL

0-7645-5438-7

0-7645-5453-0

Also available:
- Alaska For Dummies
  0-7645-1761-9
- Arizona For Dummies
  0-7645-6938-4
- Cancún and the Yucatán For Dummies
  0-7645-2437-2
- Cruise Vacations For Dummies
  0-7645-6941-4
- Europe For Dummies
  0-7645-5456-5
- Ireland For Dummies
  0-7645-5455-7

- Las Vegas For Dummies
  0-7645-5448-4
- London For Dummies
  0-7645-4277-X
- New York City For Dummies
  0-7645-6945-7
- Paris For Dummies
  0-7645-5494-8
- RV Vacations For Dummies
  0-7645-5443-3
- Walt Disney World & Orlando For Dummies
  0-7645-6943-0

GRAPHICS, DESIGN & WEB DEVELOPMENT

0-7645-4345-8

0-7645-5589-8

Also available:
- Adobe Acrobat 6 PDF For Dummies
  0-7645-3760-1
- Building a Web Site For Dummies
  0-7645-7144-3
- Dreamweaver MX 2004 For Dummies
  0-7645-4342-3
- FrontPage 2003 For Dummies
  0-7645-3882-9
- HTML 4 For Dummies
  0-7645-1995-6
- Illustrator CS For Dummies
  0-7645-4084-X

- Macromedia Flash MX 2004 For Dummies
  0-7645-4358-X
- Photoshop 7 All-in-One Desk Reference For Dummies
  0-7645-1667-1
- Photoshop CS Timesaving Techniques For Dummies
  0-7645-6782-9
- PHP 5 For Dummies
  0-7645-4166-8
- PowerPoint 2003 For Dummies
  0-7645-3908-6
- QuarkXPress 6 For Dummies
  0-7645-2593-X

NETWORKING, SECURITY, PROGRAMMING & DATABASES

0-7645-6852-3

0-7645-5784-X

Also available:
- A+ Certification For Dummies
  0-7645-4187-0
- Access 2003 All-in-One Desk Reference For Dummies
  0-7645-3988-4
- Beginning Programming For Dummies
  0-7645-4997-9
- C For Dummies
  0-7645-7068-4
- Firewalls For Dummies
  0-7645-4048-3
- Home Networking For Dummies
  0-7645-42796

- Network Security For Dummies
  0-7645-1679-5
- Networking For Dummies
  0-7645-1677-9
- TCP/IP For Dummies
  0-7645-1760-0
- VBA For Dummies
  0-7645-3989-2
- Wireless All In-One Desk Reference For Dummies
  0-7645-7496-5
- Wireless Home Networking For Dummies
  0-7645-3910-8